China's Ambition in Space

CHINA'S AMBITION IN SPACE

PROGRAMS, POLICY AND LAW

XIAODAN WU

Published, sold and distributed by Eleven
P.O. Box 85576
2508 CG The Hague
The Netherlands
Tel.: +31 70 33 070 33
Fax: +31 70 33 070 30
e-mail: sales@elevenpub.nl
www.elevenpub.com

Sold and distributed in USA and Canada
Independent Publishers Group
814 N. Franklin Street
Chicago, IL 60610
USA
Order Placement: (800) 888-4741
Fax: (312) 337-5985
orders@ipgbook.com
www.ipgbook.com

Eleven is an imprint of Boom uitgevers Den Haag.

ISBN 978-94-6236-277-2
ISBN 978-90-5189-466-0 (E-book)

© 2022 Xiaodan Wu | Eleven

This publication is protected by international copyright law.
All rights reserved. No part of this publication may be reproduced, stored in a retrieval system, or transmitted in any form or by any means, electronic, mechanical, photocopying, recording or otherwise, without the prior permission of the publisher.

Preface

No other country has, in the past two decades, developed its space capabilities and capacities in such an expansive way as China. Today it is mastering practically all space activities and applications and, furthermore, can set 'firsts' as landing on the far side of the moon. These impressive achievements make China not only an ever-important actor in outer space but also an object of research and analysis. This book, by Xiaodan Wu, responds to this growing academic interest and approaches the task within three perspectives: the programmatic, the policy and the legal areas. This multifaceted study allows for analysis of the separate key areas but also connects them in an enlightening way, providing a comprehensive analysis of China's space activities. Documents, specifically translated for this study, add considerably to the value of this book, providing not only information and analysis but also food for thought to its readers.

The title of the book refers to China's space ambitions, which can be better understood in its historical perspective and its current elaboration in programmes, policies and regulations. Such a deeper understanding will be necessary to deal with China as an actor on the civilian, military, economic and diplomatic levels related to space. Since China is growing increasingly assertive in the international arena, such a deeper understanding is a precondition for fruitful cooperation. We will inevitably see in the near future policy and regulatory initiatives by China in international forums for issues as exploration, the global space economy, space traffic management or space security. Assessing them with a solid foundation of knowledge about China's approach to programmes, policies and the rule of law will prove essential for a constructive dialogue. This book will certainly be of support in this endeavour.

Kai-Uwe Schrogl

President
International Institute of Space Law (IISL)

Table of Contents

Preface	v
Introduction	xiii
1. China's Space Programmes	1
1.1. A Brief Historical Review of China's Space Programmes	1
1.2. China's Major Space Programmes and Its Achievements	3
1.2.1. Satellite Capabilities	3
1.2.2. Launch Capabilities	4
1.2.3. The Manned Space Programme	7
1.2.4. Lunar and Deep Space Exploration	10
1.3. China's Space Actors	14
1.3.1. The Governmental Institutions	14
1.3.2. Military Sectors	17
1.3.3. Space Programme Organs	19
1.3.4. Two Major State-Owned Space Companies: CASTC and CASIC	21
1.3.5. The Science and Education Community	24
1.3.6. The Emergence of New Space Actors	27
1.4. The Comparative and Future Perspective of China's Space Programmes	29
2. China's Space Policy	33
2.1. The Space Policy Documents and Diplomatic Statements	33
2.1.1. Comprehensive Development Plans and Policy Papers	33
2.1.2. The White Papers on Space Activities	35
2.1.3. Other Policy Documents of Implementing Nature	36
2.1.4. Relevant Diplomatic Policy Documents and Positions	37
2.2. The Fundamental Constituent Elements of National Strategy for Space Programme	39
2.2.1. The Development of Space Capabilities Conforms to China's Vital Interests	39
2.2.2. China Adheres to the International Legal Framework for Space Activities	41
2.2.3. Civil and Military Integration	44
2.2.4. An Emphasis on the Effects and Influence of Space Science and Technology	47
2.3. The Basic Principles for the Development of Space Activities	48

- 2.3.1. Space Industry as an Indispensable Part of National Development — 49
- 2.3.2. Self-Reliant and Innovative Development — 50
- 2.3.3. Peaceful Development — 52
- 2.3.4. Coordinated Development — 59
- 2.3.5. Cooperative Development — 61
- 2.4. The Evaluation of China's International Space Cooperation — 64
  - 2.4.1. The Overall Situation of China's International Space Cooperation — 65
  - 2.4.2. Some Cooperative Partners and Their Joint Space Activities — 66
  - 2.4.3. The Achievement and Limitation of China's Space Cooperation — 70
- 2.5. Concluding Remarks — 74

3. China's Space Law — 77
- 3.1. The Trend Towards Strengthening National Space Legislation — 77
- 3.2. The Status Quo of China's Space Regulatory Framework — 79
  - 3.2.1. Major Documents Relevant for the Space Regulatory Framework — 79
  - 3.2.2. Evaluation of the Current Regulatory Framework — 85
- 3.3. Why Has No Space Law Been Adopted for Six Decades? — 93
  - 3.3.1. The Starting-Late Development of the Rule of Law — 93
  - 3.3.2. The Initial Lack of Need for Space Legislation Owing to China's Model Development — 97
  - 3.3.3. The Bureaucratic Setbacks and Conundrum About Space Legislation — 99
- 3.4. The Emerging and Increasing Indigenous Need to Improve Space Legislation — 101
  - 3.4.1. The Space Activities Have Outgrown the Traditional Regulatory Framework — 101
  - 3.4.2. The New Height of Administrative Reforms Requires Upgrading the Space Governance — 103
  - 3.4.3. To Better Concretize and Implement the Obligations Assumed by China and Be Considered as a Responsible Space Power — 107
  - 3.4.4. To Regulate and Encourage Commercial Space Activities and Foster A Sustainable Space Economy — 114
  - 3.4.5. To Break Down Political Obstacles and Unlock the Potential of Space Cooperation — 118
- 3.5. The Prospects of Space Legislation — 121
  - 3.5.1. The Legislation Path and Major Content of Future Outer Space Law — 121

	3.5.2. The Core Controversy Over the Space Legislation	124
3.6.	Concluding Remarks	127

Annexes Policy Documents, Regulatory Rules and Diplomatic Statements — 129

1. White Papers on Space Activities — 131
   1.1. China's Space Activities of 2000 — 131
   1.2. China's Space Activities of 2006 — 143
   1.3. China's Space Activities of 2011 — 158
   1.4. China's Space Activities of 2016 — 174
   1.5. China's Beidou Navigation Satellite System of 2016 — 193
   1.6. China's Space Program: A 2021 Perspective — 203

2. Other Policy Documents on Space Activities — 225
   2.1. Notice on Promoting the Development of Satellite Application Industry — 225
   2.2. Medium and Long-Term Development Plan for China's Satellite Navigation Industry — 231
   2.3. Medium and Long-Term Development Plan for National Civil Space Infrastructure (2015-2025) — 245
   2.4. The Guiding Opinions on Accelerating the Construction and Application of the "One Belt One Road" Space Information Corridor — 263

3. Policy Documents Applicable to Space Activities — 275
   3.1. White Paper on China's National Defense — 275
   3.2. White Paper on China's Military Strategy — 276
   3.3. Made in China 2025 — 276
   3.4. National 13th Five-Year Plan for the Scientific and Technological Innovation — 277
   3.5. National 13th Five-Year Plan for the Development of Strategic Emerging Industries — 281
   3.6. National 13th Five-Year Plan for Satellite Surveying and Mapping — 282
   3.7. Guidelines on Deepening Civil-Military Integration in Science and Technology and Industry for National Defense — 285
   3.8. White Papers on China's National Defense — 286
   3.9. White Paper on China's International Development Cooperation in the New Era — 287

4. Regulatory Rules on Space Activities — 291
   4.1. Law on National Security — 291
   4.2. Law on National Defense — 291

4.3. Measures for the Administration of Registration of Objects Launched into Outer Space ... 292
4.4. Interim Measures on the Administration of Licensing the Projects of Launching Civil Space Objects ... 295
4.5. Regulation on the Licensing Administration of the Scientific Research and Production of Arms and Equipment ... 301
4.6. Measures for the Implementation of Scientific Research and Production Licensing of Arms and Equipment ... 311
4.7. Interim Measures for the Recordation Administration of the Scientific Research and Production of Arms and Equipment ... 326
4.8. Regulation on the Export Control of Military Items ... 334
4.9. Regulation on the Export Control of Missiles and Related Items and Technologies ... 339
4.10. Interim Measures for the Management of Civil Satellite Projects ... 344
4.11. Interim Measures for the Management of Remote Sensing Satellites Data in the National Major Specialized Project of High-Resolution Earth Observation System ... 353
4.12. Interim Measures for the Management of Remote Sensing Satellites Data from China's Civilian Satellites ... 362
4.13. Measures for the Management of Scientific Data of Lunar and Deep Space Exploration Project ... 370
4.14. Measures for the Management of Lunar Samples ... 375

5. **China's Space-Related Statements and Proposals in the UN** ... 383
   5.1. China's Statements, Proposals and Other Information Submitted to UNCOPUOS ... 383
       5.1.1. China's Activities on International Cooperation in the Peaceful Uses of Outer Space ... 383
       5.1.2. China's Submissions Regarding the UNCOPUOS Discussion on the Safety of Space Nuclear Power Sources ... 389
       5.1.3. China's Activities in the Field of International Cooperation in the Peaceful Uses of Outer Space ... 394
       5.1.4. Statement by Ma Xinmin ... 400
       5.1.5. Keynote Speech of Shi Zhongjun ... 402
       5.1.6. Safety Practice of Space Nuclear Power Sources in China ... 405
       5.1.7. Position Paper on the Issue of Long-Term Sustainability of Outer Space Activities ... 409
       5.1.8. China's Activities in the Field of International Cooperation in the Peaceful Uses of Outer Space ... 415

	5.1.9.	China's Replies on Transparency and Confidence-Building Measures in Outer Space Activities	418
	5.1.10.	China's Views on Transparency and Confidence-Building Measures in Outer Space Activities	419
	5.1.11.	Note Verbale on the Re-entry of Tiangong-1	424
	5.1.12.	Note Verbale on the Re-entry of Tiangong-1	425
	5.1.13.	Note Verbale on the Re-entry of Tiangong-1	425
	5.1.14.	Note Verbale on the Re-entry of Tiangong-1	426
	5.1.15.	Note Verbale on the Planned Re-entry of Tiangong-2	426
5.2.	China's Statements and Proposals Submitted to the Conference on Disarmament		427
	5.2.1.	Position on and Suggestions for Ways to Address the Issue of Prevention of An Arms Race in Outer Space	427
	5.2.2.	Working Paper on Possible Elements of the Future International Legal Instrument on the Prevention of the Weaponization of Outer Space	432
	5.2.3.	Working Paper on Possible Elements of a Future International Legal Agreement on the Prevention of the Deployment of Weapons in Outer Space, the Threat or Use of Force against Outer Space Objects	436
	5.2.4.	Draft Treaty on Prevention of the Placement of Weapons in Outer Space and of the Threat of Use of Force against Outer Space Objects (PPWT)	439
	5.2.5.	Answers to the Principal Questions and Comments on the Draft PPWT	443
	5.2.6.	The Updated Draft Treaty on Prevention of the Placement of Weapons in Outer Space and of the Threat of Use of Force against Outer Space Objects (PPWT)	449
	5.2.7.	Comments Regarding the USA Analysis of the 2014 Updated Draft PPWT	454
	5.2.8.	Joint Statement from XI Jinping, President of China, and Vladimir V. Putin, President of the Russian Federation, to the Conference on Disarmament on Strengthening Contemporary Global Strategic Stability	460
5.3.	Xi's Speeches Regarding a Community of Shared Future for Mankind		462
	5.3.1.	Working Together to Create a New Mutually Beneficial Partnership and Community of Shared Future for Mankind	462
	5.3.2.	Working Together to Build a Community of Shared Future for Mankind	467

TABLE OF CONTENTS

6. Agreements on International Space Cooperation — 477
    6.1. Memorandum on Agreement on Liability for Satellite Launches between China and the United States — 477
    6.2. Memorandum of Agreement on Satellite Technology Safeguard — 479
    6.3. Memorandum of Agreement Regarding International Trade in Commercial Launch Services — 484
    6.4. Memorandum of Agreement on Satellite Technology Safeguards — 490
    6.5. Memorandum of Agreement Regarding International Trade in Commercial Launches Services — 496
    6.6. Agreement on Cooperation in the Exploration and Use of Outer Space for Peaceful Purposes — 503

7. The Judicial Cases Applying and Interpreting the Outer Space Treaties — 507
    7.1. The CEO of Moon Village of China Lost His Case against Beijing Administration for Industry and Commerce — 507
    7.2. The Moon Village Sued Beijing Administration for Industry and Commerce and Lost the Final Trial — 508

Bibliography — 511
  Books and Chapters — 511
  Articles — 514
  Documents, Evaluations and Reports — 517
  News Articles and Websites — 518
  China's Law and Regulatory Rules — 519
  China's Policy Documents — 520
  China's Diplomatic Statements — 522
  China's Space Cooperation Agreements and Other Documents — 523

About the Author — 525
  Acknowledgements — 525

Introduction

China's space activities have undergone extensive and far-reaching developments in exploratory as well as experimental technologies and have thereby accomplished a host of major missions during the past 60 years. China has been recognized worldwide as the third global actor in this respect with a wide array of space capabilities. Consequently, the international community has become increasingly interested in and sensitive to China's space programmes, policy and law. However, owing to the original characteristics of China's space programmes and the lack of internal transparency as well as because of external misunderstanding and misinterpretations, its organizational, bureaucratic, strategic and regulatory structure have been most difficult to understand. This introduction provides the basic background information and the fundamental clues to help properly comprehend the annexed documents – which currently form the 'cornerstones' and the general framework for China's space programmes, policy and law.

Useful documents have been added in the annex to the book. Annexes 2, 3 and 7 are unofficial translations.

1. China's Space Programmes

This part provides an introductory overview of China's space programmes with a history of more than 60 years, involving a complex network of actors, as well as organizational and bureaucratic structures. Despite China's traditional attitude of acting with care and circumspection, it is evident that it is entering a new, fast trajectory with accumulating capacities and national strength.

1.1. A Brief Historical Review of China's Space Programmes

In March 1956, a draft document of the State Council, entitled 'The Long-Term Program for the Development of Science and Technology (1956-1967)', listed the development of missile technology among national priorities. A month later, the National Aviation Industry Commission (NAIC) was established with the competence of supervising the missile technology research. On 15 October 1956, the NAIC president, the then vice Prime Minister, NIE Rongzhen, presented a report to the Communist Party's Central Committee on the know-how for the development of missiles, which laid down the basic principles for the development of a self-reliant national industry, striving for possible foreign aid.[1]

With the approval of the 'Long-Term Program for the Development of Science and Technology', this document became the first plan for China's space programmes. This was exactly a year before the Soviet Union succeeded in launching its first satellite, the Sputnik 1, on 4 October 1957. The firm intention to develop indigenous satellite launching capabilities was announced in 1958 by Chairman Mao Zedong during the 8th Chinese Communist Party's Second Plenary Session.[2] Another climax was reached in March 1986: following the advice of four leading scientists, all of whom were members of the China Academy of Science (CAS), a strategic, state-sponsored project, called 'Project 863', was initiated in November 1986.[3] It aimed at accelerating high-tech R&D in seven key S&T areas, including the space sector. Its long-term goal was defined as the development of a heavy-lift space transportation system and the launch of a space

---

1   Chronicle of Events of China's Space Activities (中国航天事业大事记), www.xinhuanet.com//mil/2016-06/25/c_129089772_2.htm. Last accessed August 2021.
2   J. Zhang, *Contemporary China: Establishment of Space Cause*, Beijing: Present Day China Press, 2009, pp. 7-9.
3   The projects in China are usually named after the year and month or month and date of their approval. In this case, Project 863 stands for March 1986.

station.[4] The rapid rhythm and the high-level involvement of the decision-making process demonstrated China's responses to international pressure and its strong desire not to lag behind in the international competition relating to space technology.

Over the years, China's space programmes have evolved, achieving significant milestones. Some of them are listed in what follows. As to the achievement of manned space flight and lunar exploration, see Sections 1.2.3 and 1.2.4.

Table 1.1   List of the Events of China's Major Space Capabilities[5]

Date	Event	Space Capabilities Obtained
19 February 1960	Launch of Rocket T-7M	First liquid meteorological rocket
24 April 1970*	Launch of Dongfanghong-1	First satellite: China thereby becoming the fifth country worldwide with respect to such an achievement
26 November 1975	Launch of a returnable remote sensing satellite	First recovered satellite: China becoming the third country in this respect
20 September 1981	Launch of three satellites	Fourth country to launch multiple satellites
08 April 1984	Launch of Dongfanghong-2	First geostationary orbit satellite and fifth country in this respect
08 April 1990	Launch of AsiaSat-1	Beginning of China's commercial launch service
30 October 2000	Launch of experimental satellite, Beidou 1A	First navigation satellite
15 October 2003	Launch of Shenzhou V	Third country to launch man into space
24 October 2007	Launch of Chang'e 1	Fourth country to orbit the moon
27 December 2012	Initiation of Beidou satellites network	Providing GPS services to the customers in the Asia-Pacific region
20 September 2015	Launch of Long March 6	20 microsatellites were carried on one space vehicle
16 August 2016	Launch of Long March 2D	World's first quantum science satellite
05 May 2020	Launch of Long March 5B	The new-generation spacecraft
23 July 2020	Launch of Long March 5	China's first Mars mission, Tianwen-1

* This marked the start of China's space era. The launch date, 24 April, was nominated as China Space Day in 2016 to honour the advancement ever since, according to No. 50 Approval Letter by the State Council (国务院关于同意设立"中国航天日"的批复), of 8 March 2016, www.gov.cn/zhengce/content/2016-03/21/content_5055835.htm. Last accessed August 2021.

4   Actual Events Record of China's Manned Space Program (载人航天工程纪实), People's Daily, 26 July 2013, http://politics.people.com.cn/n/2013/0726/c1001-22331926.html. Last accessed August 2021.
5   Chronicle of Events of China's Space Activities (中国航天事业大事记), www.xinhuanet.com//mil/2016-06/25/c_129089772_2.htm, and www.sastind.gov.cn/n152/n6706318/index.html. Last accessed August 2021.

1.2. CHINA'S MAJOR SPACE PROGRAMMES AND ITS ACHIEVEMENTS

1.2.1. Satellite Capabilities

China's satellite capabilities have gone from rudimentary to advanced in certain areas. Prior to 1988, China's satellites in orbit were either experimental satellites or low-capacity communication satellites, while its satellite capabilities today have been substantially developed, providing a wide range of applications.

The major satellite series are the following: (1) communication and broadcasting satellites, including the satellite series of Dongfanghong-1 to 5, Tiantong-1 and Tianlian-1, (2) the Earth observation satellites, including the series Fengyun, Haiyang, Ziyuan, Gaofen, Yaogan and Tianhui for weather forecasting, environmental protection, resources exploitation and disaster monitoring, (3) the Beidou navigation and positioning satellite series and (4) the scientific exploration and technological test satellite series, concentrating on micro-gravity experiments, space astronomical observation and space environment research.[6] Among the scientific exploration and technological test satellite series, the Shijian satellite series was the earliest born with the biggest 'family members'.[7] Shijian-1, China's second satellite, was launched on 3 March 1971, less than a year later than Dongfanghong-1, and was in orbit for eight years. In 1981, China's first launch of multiple satellites occurred with Shijian-2, Shijian-2-A and Shijian-2-B. All the other Shijian satellites, namely 4, 5, 6, 7, 8, 9, 10, 11, 12, 13, 15 and 16, have brought about breakthrough developments, including launches into sun-synchronous orbit, producing high-resolution remote images, carrying mutation breeding and other micro-gravity experiments and providing communication, covering almost the entire territory of China. The aim of the 13th Five-Year Plan (from 2016 to 2020) is the construction of an entire satellite system, consisting of remote sensing, communication and navigation satellites in the framework of a civil space infrastructure as well as the establishment of a data-sharing mechanism.[8]

China began to develop navigation satellite systems in the 1990s. It seemed to be open to a joint undertaking in the development of such a sensitive, dual-use technology. However, its participation in the Galileo satellite project with the EU was aborted, possibly because of security and military concerns and pressure from the US. Meanwhile, China has formulated a three-step development plan for the Beidou

---

6   The 2016 White Paper on China's Space Activities, Section II.
7   History of the Shijian Satellites Family, http://news.sciencenet.cn/htmlnews/2016/4/343104.shtm. Last accessed August 2021.
8   Medium and Long Term Development Strategy of China's Civil Space Infrastructure, Section IV (2), www.sastind.gov.cn/n4235/c6182809/content.html. The 13th Five-Year Plan for National Strategic Emerging Industries, Section 3.3, The State Council, No. 67 [2016], www.gov.cn/zhengce/content/2016-12/19/content_5150090.htm. Last accessed February 2021.

Navigation Satellite System (henceforth 'Beidou system' abbreviated to BDS), a limited test system, BDS-1, designed to serve the whole country; a regional system, BDS-2, providing services to the Asia-Pacific region; and, finally, a full-scale global system of BDS.[9]

BDS-1, composed of three satellites, has been operating since 2000 in China and its neighbouring regions. BDS-2 became operational in China in 2011. On completion, the BDS-2 network, composed of 10 satellites, has been providing service to customers in the Asia-Pacific region since 2012. The Beidou-3 system is a constellation of 30 satellites, providing global coverage for timing, location and navigation.[10] It was officially announced to be completed and commissioned in 2020, marking the end of the 'three step' BDS development strategy.[11] The International Maritime Organization approved the use of this system for operations at sea in 2014, whereby it became the third system worldwide, after Global Positioning System (GPS) and Global Navigation Satellite Navigation System (GLONASS), in this respect.[12]

1.2.2. Launch Capabilities

Launch capabilities are a key element in the determination of the range and impact of space activities among spacefaring nations. China's work in the field of rocketry has been successful, resulting in the creation of advanced launch vehicles. The mainstay of Chinese space lift operations has been the Long March rocket family, i.e., an expendable launch system, containing multiple launch vehicles, capable of sending satellites into near-Earth orbit, geosynchronous orbit and sun-synchronous orbit. Till the end of 2018, 297 Long March missions were undertaken and a rather high success rate was reached: only 10 failures occurred in total, i.e., less than 3%.[13] From 2014 to April 2019, the Long March

---

9   The 2016 White Paper on China's Beidou Navigation Satellite System, Section 2 (1).
10 Medium and Long Term Development Strategy of the National Satellite Navigation Industry, Section III (1). The State Council General Office, No. 97 [2013], www.sastind.gov.cn/n4235/c61188/content.html. China successfully launched the 54th DBS satellite, 19 March 2020, http://en.beidou.gov.cn/WHATSNEWS/202004/t20200401_20279.html. Last access January 2022.
11 Completion and Commissioning of the Beidou Navigation Satellite System (BDS-3), 3 August 2020, http://en.beidou.gov.cn/WHATSNEWS/202008/t20200803_21013.html. Last accessed January 2022.
12 Briefing, 94th Session of the Maritime Safety Committee of the International Maritime Organization, 26 November 2014.
13 These 10 failed launches are Long March 5B, on 2 July 2017; Long March 4D, on 9 December 2013; Long March 2D, on 18 August 2011; Long March 3, on 18 August 1996; Long March 3B, on 15 February 1996; Long March 2E, on 26 January 1995; Long March 2E, on 12 December 1992; Long March 3 on 28 December 1991; Long March 3, on 8 April 1984; and Long March 2, on 5 November 1974. See the Launch Record of Long March Rockets, (长征火箭发射纪录), http://cn.cgwic.com/Launchservice/LaunchRecord.html. Last accessed August 2021.

rocket series completed 113 launch missions, sending over 150 spacecraft into target orbit with a success rate of more than 97%.[14]

The Long March rockets are categorized into different series: Long March (or Chang Zheng in Pinyin) rocket family of 1, 2, 3, 4, 5, 6, 7, 8, 9 and 11 (there is no Long March 10). Besides Long March 1 and 9, all other series are still active, although some rocket types are no more in use or have been cancelled. Long March 1 rocket launched China's first satellite, Dongfanghong-1, into low Earth Orbit. Long March 2F and 3 have been China's launch vehicles for the Shenzhou spacecraft and the Chang'e lunar orbiter. Initially, the Chang Zheng-4 served as a backup vehicle for Chang Zheng-3, and over the years, this series has been developed to launch different kinds of satellites into different orbits and to launch multiple satellites. The series of CZ-6 consists of liquid-propellant vehicles designed for small-load launch missions, and the first CZ-6 was successfully launched in 2015. The 2016 and 2021 White Paper on Space Activities identified the implementation of 'new-generation launch vehicles' as a major task for the next five years.[15] The heavy-lift launch vehicles are the most important launch vehicle projects for the future plans, more than doubling the maximum payload mass of previous launches. Following a successful first launch in 2016, the second Long March-5 launch failed in 2017. A Long March-5 rocket launched Tianwen-1, China's first Mars Mission in July 2020 at the Wenchang Space Launch Center.[16] This lift-off marked the new generation rocket's operational debut. Long March series of 9 is currently being developed for high-orbit launch and heavy-lift carriers as part of the lunar and Mars exploration programmes. Series of 7 aims at the medium lift. CZ-7 made its inaugural flight in 2016, and CZ-7A succeeded in 2021 after one failure in 2020. The CZ-8 rockets family is the newest two-stage launch vehicle with reusable components and intends to meet the growing demand for commercial launch service. CZ-8 has one successful launch record, being launched from Wenchang in December 2020. Series of 11 was designed to meet the need for launching satellites rapidly in case of emergencies or disasters with the record of one successful launch in 2015.[17]

The early launchers focused on the launching of Chinese satellites only. But then, AsiaSat 1 was launched by Long March 3 in 1990 as the first foreign payload on a Chinese rocket, and thereby Long March rockets entered the international commercial

---

14 China's Space Activities in 2016, Section II (1) and the Launch Record of Long March Rockets (长征火箭发射纪录), *Ibid*.
15 The 2016 White Paper on China's Space Activities, Section 3 (1). The 2021 White Paper on China's Space Activities, Section 2 (1).
16 Tianwen means 'quest for heavenly truth' and is taken from the title of a poem by Qu Yuan (340-278 BC). The Tianwen-1 probe has a mass of about 5 tons. It is expected to reach Mars around August 2021, and the scientific observation phase will start in August 2021. The lander/rover will perform a soft landing on the Martian surface two to three months after arrival of the spacecraft, with a candidate landing site in Utopia Planitia.
17 A Comprehensive Introduction to China's Long March Rocket Series (中国长征系列火箭家族全解析), www.cnsa.gov.cn/n6758968/n6758973/c6771604/content.html. Last accessed August 2021.

launch market. Over the years, despite embargoes of the US, Long March rockets have carried satellites for foreign states and companies, including Australia, Algeria, Belarus, Bolivia, Brazil, France, Indonesia, Laos, Nigeria, Turkey, Pakistan and Venezuela.

As for the Kuaizhou carrier rocket series, a family of small, solid-fuelled and quick reaction orbital launch vehicles, it is manufactured and operated by CASIC Launch Vehicle Technology Ltd. Co. (Expace), a subsidiary of China Aerospace Science and Industry Corporation (CASIC), with the aim of providing commercial launch services. The rocket's low requirements for launch are saving cost and reducing the launch preparation time span from months and weeks to days and even hours, at a launch price of $5000 per kilogram of payload, which is very competitive in comparison with the general level in the international commercial launch market. The basic variant of the Kuaizhou launchers, which was developed by Harbin Institute of Technology, made two successful flights in 2013-2014 with two small remote sensing satellites. Its first commercial launch in 2017 placed three small satellites into orbit. In 2018, at least five launches were scheduled for this rocket series, but four of them were postponed to 2019.[18] There were five launch attempts in 2020, but two of them failed.[19] Kuaizhou is the world's first integrated launcher-satellite system, similar in concept to those, used by the US, for the operationally increasing responsiveness and flexibility in launch activities. This is an addition to China's development in the field of launch capabilities and service possibilities available to domestic and foreign clients.

There are four launch sites in China – Jiuquan (province of Gansu), Xichang (province of Sichuan), Taiyuan (province of Shanxi) and Wenchang (province of Hainan). Various launch vehicles, satellites and spacecraft have been successfully launched from these sites. As the most geographically proximate to the geostationary orbit, the addition of the fourth site, Wenchang, with its first launch in June 2016, could significantly enhance China's launching capabilities.[20] Most of the commercial launches had been conducted from Xichang, and Wenchang would also be the main location for future commercial launches. While all four launch sites are owned and operated by the People's Liberation Army (PLA), there are some policy signals and indications already of welcoming the participation and capital from non-military and non-governmental investors (see Section 3.4.4).

The road map for the long-term development of the space transportation system refers to: (1) first-class level rockets, providing diversified commercial launch services

---

18 www.chinanews.com/gn/2018/01-03/8415594.shtml; http://scitech.people.com.cn/n1/2019/0901/c1007-31329685.html; and http://scitech.people.com.cn/n1/2019/1114/c1007-31454873.html. Last accessed August 2021.
19 China's Kuaizhou-11 carrier rocket fails in maiden flight on 7 July 2020, resulting in the loss of two satellites, www.xinhuanet.com/english/2020-07/10/c_139202652.htm; another launch failed to enter the orbit in September 2021 and cost a remote-sensing satellite, Jinlin-1 Gaofen 02C, www.xinhuanet.com/english/2020-09/12/c_139363535.htm. Last accessed August 2021.
20 The 2011 White Paper on China's Space Activities, Section 2 (5).

globally by 2020, (2) heavy launch vehicles with a 100-ton capacity by 2030, (3) fully reusable launch vehicles by 2035, (4) the development of a nuclear-powered launch shuttle by 2040, (5) a combined-power reusable launch vehicle by 2045.[21] Thereby, China is clearly demonstrating its determination to obtain world leadership in the field of space flight and technology.

1.2.3. The Manned Space Programme

China has developed its own system for manned spaceflight technology, which is an indicator of having entered the elite club of space powers. The first proposal to send astronauts into space was in the early 1960s, inspired by the human space flights of the Soviet Union and the US. This proposal was approved as 'Project 714' in April 1971 after the launch of Dongfanghong-1 but was terminated two years later, owing to financial, technical and political reasons.[22] The human space flight programme was refuelled in the mid-1980s during the debate over the role of S&T in China's national development, which led to 'Project 863'. The manned space programme was eventually approved by the politburo of the Communist Party on 21 September 1992, under the name of 'Project 921' with the ultimate goal of building a permanently manned Earth-orbiting space station.[23] Remarkably, while during the whole period between Project 714 and Project 921, consensus prevailed over the final aim of the undertaking, namely the construction of a space station, there were still questions among the scientific community and the political leadership over the need for manned space flights. This discrepancy has been persistent in the crucial decisions all through the construction of the space station as well as during the current discussion of a moon station programme. Previously, the opposition had focused on the appropriateness of this ambitious endeavour since China lacked the necessary resources. Currently, however, the objections are based on the advantages of artificial intelligence, whereby risks and cost could be deceased substantially and the available resources could rather be used for the improvement of people's livelihood.

---

21 Roadmap for the Development of the Space Transportation System (2017-2045), released by the China Aerospace Science and Technology Corporation on 17 November 2017, China Space News, 17 November 2017, p. 1.

22 Project 741 stands for 14 July of that year. Project 714, or Project Shuguang, originally planned the first flight in 1973. A squad of astronauts, 20 military airplane pilots, were selected and trained. However, the space flight race was inappropriately extravagant when the Cultural Revolution almost bankrupted the whole country. Prime Minister Zhou Enlai declared that earthly need must come first and that China shall not be involved in the US-Soviet competition. Accordingly, investments in space activities were limited to the building of application satellites and the development of Long March Rockets. See the Background of the Establishment of Chinas Manned Flights Program: the Four-Decade Debate and the Decision-Making Process (中国载人工程立项的背后: 40年的争论与决策), *China Youth Daily*, of 16 October 2003, p. 5.

23 The project name stands for 21 September of that year.

Project 921 is divided into the following three stages, relating to: (1) unmanned versions of manned spacecraft as well as manned missions into low Earth orbit, (2) development of a space lab, development and testing of technologies required for the construction of a space station, including extravehicular activity (EVA) as well as orbital rendezvous and docking, (3) construction of a space station capable of supporting a crew of three astronauts living and working in orbit continuously.[24] Barring adjustments and delays in the implementation timetable, the plan has remained broadly the same. The unmanned launch was original scheduled for 1998, the manned launch for 2002, the completion of a space lab for 2007 and that of a space station for 2010. The implementation plan for a manned space station programme was approved by the politburo of the Communist Party on 25 September 2010. And it rescheduled the finalization of the 8-tonne space lab and of the 20-tonne space station for 2016 and 2020.[25] The achievement of an unmanned and a manned launch as well as the construction of a space lab was effected in 1999, 2003 and 2016, respectively. The completion of the space station, however, has been postponed until 2022.[26] The core module of the space station was launched and followed by two manned flights in 2021 and the experimental modules will be docked in 2022.

Once operational, it is planned that the crews will be shuttled by Shenzhou spacecraft between the space station and the Earth every couple of months and that the station will be refuelled and resupplied by Tianzhou cargo vehicles. The willingness to open the station to international partners for cooperation has been reiterated with a variety of options: joint experiments onboard, joint manned missions, docking of foreign visiting vehicles with the option of adding a module, to be built and launched either by China or by foreign partners.[27] The collaboration between the China Manned Space Agency (CMSA) and the United Nations Office for Outer Space Affairs (UNOOSA)-led Human Space Technology Initiative (HSTI) has contributed to the elaboration of a framework agreement as well as to a funding agreement in 2016, providing UN

24　Brief introduction to China's manned space flights (中国载人航天工程简介), www.cmse.gov.cn/art/2011/4/23/art_24_1054.html. Last accessed August 2021.

25　*Ibid.*

26　The Comprehensive Carrying out of the Third Stage of Manned Space Program (我国载人航天工程第三步任务已全面展开), 6 March 2018, www.cmse.gov.cn/art/2018/3/6/art_18_32303.html, March 2018. China will complete the construction of the space station by 2022 (中国将于2022年完成空间站建设), first released by news press of 2016 China's Space Day. Last accessed August 2021.

27　L. Chen, B. Carey, T. Pirard, Welcome to Beijing for Space, Report from the 64h International Astronautical Congress, in L. Chen, J. Myrrhe (Eds.). *Go Taikonauts: All About China's Space Program*, Issue 10, 2013, p. 16. China offered the utilization of the facilities on its planned manned station to the world during the 56th session of COPOUS in 2013. Human Space Technology Initiative (HSTI) Activities in 2011-2013 and Plans for 2014 and Beyond, A/AC.105/2013/CRP.16, 5 June 2013, para. 40. X. Zhang, China Manned Space Agency, Presentation of China Manned Space Program to 58th Session of UNCOPUOS, June 2015.

member states and developing countries, in particular, with the opportunities for experiments onboard and the participation in manned flights.[28]

Table 1.2 List of China's Manned Space Programme Missions[29]

Mission	Date	Objective	Crew
Shenzhou 1	20 November 1999	Experimental prototype flight test	Unmanned
Shenzhou 2	10 January 2001	Prototype flight test	Unmanned
Shenzhou 3	25 March 2002	Flight test	Unmanned
Shenzhou 4	30 December 2002	Flight test	Unmanned
Shenzhou 5	15 October 2003	First manned flight	YANG Liwei
Shenzhou 6	12 October 2005	Two-man crew, multiday	FEI Junlong; NIE Haisheng
Shenzhou 7	25 September 2008	Three-man crew, First EVA	ZHAI Zhigang; LIU Boming; JING Haipeng
Tiangong 1	29 September 2011	Prototype space lab	Unmanned
Shenzhou 8	01 November 2011	First unmanned docking with Tiangong 1	Unmanned
Shenzhou 9	16 June 2012	First crewed visit to Tiangong	JING Haipeng; LIU Wang; LIU Yang
Shenzhou 10	11 June 2013	Second crewed visit to Tiangong	NIE Haisheng; ZHANG Xiaoguang; WANG Yaping
Tiangong 2	15 September 2016	First space lab	Unmanned
Shenzhou 11	17 October 2016	First Manned Docking with Tiangong 2	JING Haipeng; CHEN Dong
Tianzhou 1	20 April 2017	First cargo spaceship docking with Tiangong 2	Unmanned

---

28 United Nations and China agree to increased space cooperation, www.unoosa.org/oosa/en/informationfor/media/2016-unis-os-468.html. Last accessed August 2021.

29 Missions of China Manned Space (中国载人航天飞行任务), http://en.cmse.gov.cn/missions/. Last accessed August 2021.

1.2.4. Lunar and Deep Space Exploration

China's lunar exploration programme once surfaced in the 1970s and began to be seriously discussed in 1991.[30] Stimulated by the renewed interest in the moon by other countries, the scientific community pleaded and pressed the government for a commitment. In April 1997, three top-ranking scientists submitted to the State Council a document entitled 'Recommendations for the development of China's Lunar Exploration Program' within Project 863. As a result, in 1999, the Commission of Science, Technology and Industry for National Defence (COSTIND) appointed a group of experts to initiate a preliminary study on a lunar exploration programme. In the same year, some experts, under the PLA General Armaments Department (GAD), evaluated the lunar rover project application as submitted by Tsinghua University, China Aerospace Science and Technology Corporation (CASTC), National University of Defence Technology and China University of Science and Technology.[31] On 5 October 2000, during the first International Space Week, LUAN Enjie, the then director of China National Space Administration (CNSA), revealed, for the first time, that China was planning to explore the moon. A month later, China's first White Paper on space activities identified the exploration of deep space among the medium-term priorities.[32] After a comprehensive argumentation organized by the COSTIND, regarding the scientific and technological objectives and their feasible execution solutions, the lunar exploration programme was eventually approved by Prime Minister Wen Jiabao on 23 January 2004 as Project Chang'e, named after the Chinese moon goddess.[33] Lunar exploration was defined as China's first step in its deep space exploration effort.[34] In January 2016, a robotic probe mission to Mars was officially approved.[35] A Mars probe was scheduled to be launched around 2020, carrying 13 types of payloads (seven orbiters and six rovers) in order to achieve three goals

---

30 Chinese scientists have been following the progress of lunar exploration by the Soviet Union and by the United States since the 1960s. One interesting event is that the United States gave China one gram of lunar soil as a gift in 1978 and China's scientists not only conducted a series of researches with this gift but also proposed a robotic mission along this research process. See Mission to bring back lunar soil, www.chinadaily.com.cn/china/2012-03/16/content_14845410.htm. Last accessed August 2021.
31 The Layout Plan of China's Lunar Exploration, 1 March 2004, http://clep.cnsa.gov.cn/n487137/index.html. Last accessed August 2021.
32 The White Paper on China's Space Activities, Section 3.2.
33 Brief Introduction to China's Lunar Exploration Program (中国探月工程简介), www.clep.org.cn/n487137/index.html. Last accessed August 2021.
34 The White Paper on China's Space Activities of 2006, 2011 and 2016, Section 2.1.6, Section 2.4 and Section 2.4.
35 The official Approval of the Mars Exploration Program, http://scitech.people.com.cn/n1/2016/0422/c1007-28297858.html. Last accessed August 2021.

– orbiting, landing and roving exploration – at the same time.[36] Tianwen 1, China's first interplanetary mission, consists of an orbiter and a rover named Zhurong. It arrived in Mars orbit in February 2021 and Zhurong landed in May 2021.[37]

The lunar exploration programme is a three-phase plan relating to orbiting, landing and sample returning. The aims of each phase are, specifically, launch and orbit of a probe with the main tasks of testing lunar orbiting technology, the deep space telemetry and tracking network, surveying the topography and geological structure of the moon, analysing the content and distribution of its mineral and chemical elements, surveying the space environment between the moon, the Earth and the sun and carrying out optical astronomy observations from the moon, spacecraft soft landing on the lunar surface, collecting samples with sampling and drilling machines and robotics and returning the samples to the Earth.[38]

The first phase ended with the successful launch of the lunar probe, Chang'e 1. This mission succeeded in making a map of the lunar surface, analysing its chemistry and thickness and characterizing the lunar environment. A capsule was carried aboard Chang'e 2 to lunar orbit, where it circled the moon before returning to Earth and conducting an atmospheric re-entry at a speed much higher than that of an Earth-orbiting spacecraft. The successful recovery of this capsule, on 31 October 2014, marked a new historic achievement for the Chinese space programme, becoming the third country, after the USSR and the US, to accomplish a round-trip mission to the moon.[39] The robotic rover, Yutu (Jade Rabbit), landed on the moon's surface on 14 December 2013. Caused by mechanical abnormality, Yutu entered into hibernation mode. Despite its non-accomplished scientific tasks, its soft landing marked the achievement of the second phase. Chang'e 4 was built as a backup to Chang'e 3, and after the success of the Chang'e 3 mission, Chang'e 4 was adjusted to meet new scientific objectives, and it marked a historic breakthrough in lunar exploration, becoming the world's first landing rover on the far side of the moon. The first part of Chang'e 4 was launched on 21 May 2018, carrying a relaying satellite, stationed some 60,000 km behind the moon, and the second part sent a lander and rover guided by that

---

36 Revealed by ZHANG Rongqiao, the chief architect of China's Mars mission, at the 3rd Beijing International Forum on Lunar and Deep-space Exploration, 20 September 2017, China's Lunar and Deep Space Exploration, 21 September 2017, www.clep.org.cn/n5982341/c6794911/content.html. Last accessed August 2021.
37 The Successful landing of Mars rover of Tianwen 1, www.gov.cn/xinwen/2021-05/15/content_5606647.htm, last accessed January 2022.
38 The Overall Plan of Chang'e Program, www.clep.org.cn/n487137/index.html. Last accessed August 2021.
39 L. David, China's First Round-Trip Moon Shot Sets Stage for Bigger Lunar Feats, www.space.com/27661-china-moon-mission-sample-return.html. Last accessed August 2021.

satellite to the far side of the moon on 3 January 2019.[40] This successful deployment demonstrated China's ability and desire to accomplish increasingly sophisticated missions in space. In a third phase, a robotic mission will collect and return samples to the Earth. Chang'e 5, however, which had once been scheduled for November 2017, was suspended because of the failure of Long March 5 in July 2017. On 23 November 2020, Chang'e 5 spacecraft was launched from Wenchang and flew directly into a lunar orbit, where a small module carrying the sample return capsule was released, landed on the moon, collected 1731g of lunar samples and returned to Inner Mongolia on 16 December 2020.

Table 1.3   List of China's Lunar Exploration Programme Missions[41]

Date	Mission	Capabilities Obtained
24 October 2007	Launch of Chang'e 1 and reached its moon orbit in two weeks	Its first lunar probe
1 October 2010	Launch of Chang'e 2 and reached the moon orbit in four days	Third nation to accomplish a round-trip mission to the moon
02 December 2013	Launch of Chang'e 3, consisting of a service module and a landing vehicle, Yutu	Third nation to soft land on the moon surface
23 November 2020	Launch of Chang'e 5 spacecraft	Third nation to deliver lunar samples to Earth

There have been speculations over a plan to land astronauts on the moon since the early 2000s and some explicit policy signals in this respect during the last decade as well. The document entitled 'Science and Technology in China – A Roadmap to 2050', issued by the Chinese Academy of Science (CAS) in 2009, identified a manned lunar landing as a medium-term target to be reached by 2030.[42] China's Space Activities in 2011 and 2016 stated that China would conduct studies on the preliminary plan for a human lunar landing and strive to acquire key technologies to lay a foundation for exploring and developing a lunar manned station.[43] Despite the differing opinions regarding the

---

40 The Space Mission of Chang'e 4 is the world's first landing on the far side of the moon, China's Lunar and Deep Space Exploration, 3 January 2019, www.clep.org.cn/n5982341/c6805036/content.html. The successful launch of the Queqiao relay satellite, www.clep.org.cn/n5982341/c6801552/content.html. The landing of Yutu 2 rover, www.clep.org.cn/n5982341/c6805058/content.html. Last accessed August 2021.
41 Chronicle of Events of Chang'e Program, www.clep.org.cn/n487137/n5989576/index.html. Last accessed August 2021.
42 Moon Base Camp Possible by 2030, http://english.cas.cn/resources/archive/china_archive/cn2009/200909/t20090923_43409.shtml. Last accessed August 2021.
43 The 2011 White Paper on China's Space Activities, Section 3.3. The 2016 White Paper on China's Space Activities, Section 3.3.

benefit of the enormous expense and the various elements influencing this ambitious plan, the possibility of a human lunar landing cannot be ruled out.[44]

China has developed a vision for an International Lunar Research Station (ILRS) since 2016 to seek international involvement at a more extensive and intensive level.[45] China National Space Agency (CNSA) formally announced the ILRS initiative in 2019, extending cooperation on an open, inclusive, cooperative and win-win basis to promote the international cause of deep space exploration.[46] The ILRS will be developed throughout a number of missions from the 2020s to 2040s, including robotic missions and human presence, supporting scientific experiments and utilizing lunar resources.[47] The essential goal is to establish a research platform and infrastructure on the moon through the participation of multiple countries following the principles of sufficient discussion, joint construction and international sharing.[48] In 2021, the CNSA and the Russian State Space Corporation, ROSCOMOS, signed an MoU on cooperation for the construction of the ILRS and a joint statement in which they declared its nature as a comprehensive scientific experiment base and their determination to be open to all interested countries and international partners.[49]

Tianwen-1 is ambitious and aims to complete a comprehensive mission of orbiting, landing and roving to obtain scientific exploration data on Mars. China developed one Mars probe before, an orbiter called Yinghuo-1, which was launched with Russian Phobos-Grunt mission in 2011 but suffered a launch failure. The success of the Tianwen-1 mission could possibly succeed in returning samples from Mars beginning around 2030, an achievement that would mark dramatic progress for China's space programme and put China among space leaders.

---

44 M. Aliberti, *When China Goes to the Moon*, New York: Springer, 2015, pp. 129-182.
45 China to Build scientific research station on Moon's south pole, www.xinhuanet.com/english/2019-04/24/c_138004666.htm. Last accessed August 2021.
46 By CNSA spokesman PEI Zhaoyu at the 4th International Conference on Lunar and Deep Space Exploration, China Emphasizes International Cooperation in Future Lunar and Deep Space Exploration, InFocus, *Bulletin of the Chinese Academy of Science*, Vol. 33(2), 2019, p. 74.
47 The Introduction of Chang'e 4 mission and the vision of future Chinese lunar exploration activities, CNSA's Technical Presentation at the 57th Session of Scientific and Technical Subcommittee of UN Committee of Peaceful Use of Outer Space, 2019.
48 The Speech of WU Yanhua, Vice Director of CNSA at the 4th International Conference on Lunar and Deep Space Exploration, China Emphasizes International Cooperation in Future Lunar and Deep Space Exploration, InFocus, *Bulletin of the Chinese Academy of Science*, Vol. 33(2), 2019, p. 74.
49 China and Russia signed a Memorandum of Understanding regarding Cooperation for the Construction of the International Lunar Research Station, 9 March 2021, www.cnsa.gov.cn/english/n6465652/n6465653/c6811380/content.html. Joint Statement between CNSA and ROSCOSMOS regarding Cooperation for Cooperation for the Construction of the International Lunar Research Station, 29 April 2021, www.cnsa.gov.cn/english/n6465652/n6465653/c6811967/content.html. Last accessed August 2021.

1.3. China's Space Actors

China's space industry extends from government and military organs to different sectors and involves research and production units from enterprises, universities and research institutions. Traditionally, these actors are all within the power structures of the People's Republic of China, and none of them are autonomous or independent players. They have formed a complex structure and relationship in strategy formulation, policy adoption, decision-making and activities organization and implementation, although occasionally without clear external borders and efficient coordination mechanisms. The emergence of new actors, including local governments, universities, research institutions and commercial companies, further complicates this diversity and necessitates its reformation and update.

1.3.1. The Governmental Institutions

Governmental institutions play a prominent role in the organizational, strategic and regulatory aspects of China's space activities. Thereby, China's space programmes have been government-dominated right from their inception. The governmental institutions play a prominent role in the organizational, strategic and regulatory aspects of China's space activities. The State Council, as the highest-ranking governmental organ, exercises its authority over space affairs through its ministries, particularly by drafting, implementing or supervising the implementation of space-related national strategy, policy and regulatory documents, approving space programmes and allocating financial resources, representing China in international forums and promoting and executing cooperative space activities.

The governmental institutions have gone through numerous organizational reforms and name changes since the beginning of China's space activities in 1956. Already during the reform and opening up era since 1978, there have been eight rounds of State Council reorganizations in 1982, 1988, 1993, 2003, 2008, 2013 and 2018. The frequency revealed the rapid rhythm of development in China, transiting from planned economy to market economy. As to the governmental structure in the space realm, however, it has been relatively stable and immune from several rounds of reformation.

The initial primary missile developer was the Fifth Academy established by the Ministry of National Defence on 8 October 1956. In 1964, the Seventh Ministry of Machine Building Industry was set up, based on the Fifth Academy, to provide a unified administrative regime for the research, design, tracking, production and basic construction of missiles and launch vehicles.[50] The Seventh Ministry of Machine Building Industry was renamed the Ministry of Space Industry in 1982. The structural reform of the government, i.e., downsizing the government, led to the merging of the Ministry of Space Industry with the Ministry of Aviation Industry into one single ministry, namely the Ministry of Aerospace Industry in 1988. In 1992, during a trip to southern China, Deng Xiaoping put forward a firm proposal to move China's economic reform in the direction of a 'socialist market economy', which was proclaimed as the ultimate objective of the economic reform by the 14th Chinese Communist Party Congress later that year. 1992 marked the turning point for China toward the creation of a market economy and introducing modern corporate systems to the state-owned enterprises: the State Council was institutionally reformed to adapt to the needs of constructing a socialist market economy in 1993.[51] Accordingly, the governmental organ, Ministry of Aerospace Industry, was split up into China Aviation Industry Corporation and China Aerospace Industry Corporation, approved by the 8th National People's Congress in 1993.[52]

The COSTIND, as a civilian ministry within the State Council, was formed in 1982 to centralize defence procurement technology, which was previously distributed among several agencies. In the late 1990s, during the massive reorganization of the defence industry, the COSTIND was authorized to determine the development policy for the defence industry. Ever since, it has acted as the administrative and regulatory hub for questions relating to the general aspects of China's defence and aerospace industry. Concretely, the COSTIND drafted and promulgated defence industry policy as well as regulations and supervised their implementation. In addition, it allocated R&D funds through research programmes. The majority of the regulatory and policy space documents in China were drafted, issued and monitored by the COSTIND, in coordination with other ministries within the State Council and with the PLA, thereby becoming the primary governmental organ in China's space realm. In 2008, the State Council was reformed to consolidate and rearrange a number of existing government bodies into large 'super-ministries', and the COSTIND was integrated into the newly established Ministry of Industry and Information Technology (MIIT) and was renamed the State Administration of Science and Technology and Industry for National Defence (SASTIND).[53] The SASTIND inherited its statutory authority from the COSTIND and is mainly in charge of enacting and supervising the implementation of plans, policies,

---

50   The historic evolution of China Aerospace Science and Technology Corporation, China Aerospace Science and Technology Corporation, www.spacechina.com/n25/n142/n152/n174/index.html. Last accessed August 2021.
51   The 1993 Institutional Reformation of the State Council (1993年国务院机构改革), 16 January 2009, www.gov.cn/test/2009-01/16/content_1206993.htm. Last accessed August 2021.
52   The historic evolution of China Aerospace Science and Technology Corporation, *Ibid.*
53   The 2008 Institutional Reform of State Council, 16 January 2009, www.gov.cn/test/2009-01/16/content_1207014.htm. Last accessed January 2021.

standards and rules for science, technology and industry for national defence.[54] However, as a subordinate agency but not under the direct authority of the State Council, the SASTIND no longer had the independent power of formulating administrative regulations, and this stalled the space legislation process for some years. After the incorporation of space law into the National People's Congress work plan in 2013, SASTIND regained its enthusiasm in space legislation and has made substantial progress. As for the latest, eighth round of State Council institutional reform in 2018, similar to the previous round, it aimed at an operational, rules-based and highly effective governance functioning system. Despite the discussion of how to reform the SASTIND, it remained intact as an agency of MIIT.[55]

CNSA was established in 1993 within China Aerospace Industry Corporation and was assigned in 1998 as an internal division of the COSTIND. It assumes the following responsibilities: signing governmental cooperation agreements, representing the country in international organizations and events and working with foreign national space agencies as well as releasing relevant information and documents.[56] In spite of its name, the CNSA is not an all-encompassing national space agency but acts as a publicly recognized face of China's space programmes.[57]

Some other ministries and ministerial-level institutions exercise authority over certain space activities. The Ministry of Science and Technology coordinates science and technology activities in the country, including the administration of Project 863. Its approval of national research programmes has an impact on the establishment and development of space programmes and has even some say in decisions on their funding.[58] The National Remote Sensing Center is affiliated to the Ministry of Science and Technology, dealing with the application of remote sensing data and relevant materials. The space enterprises are state-owned or state-controlled companies. The National Development and Reform Commission and State-owned Assets Supervision and Administration Commission are the two major organs overseeing their

---

54 Specifically, the functions of SASTIND are drafting policy and plans in defence-related industries, including in the fields of nuclear, aerospace, aviation, research on policies, laws and regulations for the defence industry and dual-use conversions as well as formulating rules for the defence industry and for industry management, www.sastind.gov.cn. Last accessed January 2021.
55 2018 State Council Institutional Reform Plan, approved by the National People's Congress, www.gov.cn, 17 March 2018, www.gov.cn/xinwen/2018-03/17/content_5275116.htm. The State Council Notice on the Establishment and Hierarchy of State-Level Administrations within Ministries, No. 08 [2018], www.gov.cn/zhengce/content/2018-03/24/content_5277123.htm. Last accessed January 2021.
56 The website of the China National Space Administration has an English version, www.cnsa.gov.cn. Last accessed January 2021.
57 CNSA is the country's governmental organization that is responsible for the management of space activities for civilian use and international space cooperation with other countries and responsible for implementing corresponding governmental functions. See Section IV, Development Policies and Measures, China's Space Activities, 2006.
58 The website of the Ministry of Science and Technology has an English version, www.most.gov.cn, Last accessed January 2021.

management and operations. The National Development and Reform Commission participated in drafting certain space-related national strategies and policies, for instance, those for space infrastructure and civil-military integration. The Ministry of Foreign Affairs is in charge of organizing the participation in international events and the negotiation of space cooperation.

1.3.2. *Military Sectors*

The military participation in space programmes originated in the historical context of China's space activities. Similarly to the US and the USSR, China's space programmes began with military missions, and a crucial part was initially institutionalized under the People's Liberation Army (PLA). The PLA has been instrumental in the evolution of China's overall space activities, managing both civilian and military efforts. Important functions in the space programmes have been and – even after several rounds of reformation – are still performed by or together with the military.

Until the recent military reformation, one of the four general departments under the PLA Central Military Commission, namely the General Armaments Department (GAD), was founded in 1998 and primarily oversaw the procurement and acquisition of weapon systems for the PLA and ensured defence industry core capabilities. GAD was also engaged in the defence industry as a regulator. Thereby, it issued regulations and monitored their implementation in collaboration with SASTIND. GAD was also a major player in space activities, including the training of astronauts, the provision of a support system and the spacecraft and astronaut recovery system for the manned space programme. In addition, it also administered space-related infrastructure, especially the launch and tracking facilities.

The recent round of military reformation unfolded in late 2015. Its overall goal has been adjusting to the developments of modern warfare towards joint operations, the optimization of military structure and the enhancement of civilian-military integration.[59] This round of reformation effects the most wide-ranging restructuring since 1949 and is a key milestone in PLA's modernization efforts. Most of the key organizations have undergone major changes to strengthen joint operational capabilities.[60] The four general departments were disbanded, and a new branch, the Strategic Support Force (SSF), was established in 2015.[61] The role of the SSF is to improve the integration of the PLA's support system and the links between the civilian

---

59 China's Military in 2015: Towards Historic Reformation, 23 December 2015, www.gov.cn/xinwen/2015-12/23/content_5027047.htm. Last accessed August 2021.
60 T. Ren, Comprehensive Deepening Reform: The Road of Building a Strong Army with Chinese Characteristics (全面深化改革: 中国特色强军之路), *Guangming Daily*, 23 December 2015.
61 China Inaugurates PLA Rocket Force as Military Reform Deepens, *Xinhua News*, 1 January 2016, www.xinhuanet.com/politics/2016-01/01/c_1117646667.htm. Last accessed August 2021.

and the defence sector in the information domain, to provide full-range support to commanders and to oversee warfare activities.[62] A major function of the SSF will be to provide battlefield support to combat forces in areas ranging from reconnaissance to navigation and communication.[63] The Equipment Development Department (EDD) replaces the former GAD and plays an important role in organizing and overseeing space activities. It is responsible for the research and development of satellites, launch vehicles, spacecraft and counter-space weapons. The EDD has retained control over the special entities for space programmes, such as CMSA, and the R&D entities which had previously been overseen by the GAD, while the SFF took over the launch facilities, control centres and their associated research entities.

This goal of civil-military integration is not alien to the PLA, as it had already embarked on a series of institutional reforms before. Since the 2000s there have been reformative efforts to connect the defence and commercial industrial bases more tightly in order to give the PLA greater access to civilian scientific and technological advances and to enable the civilian economy to incorporate dual-use technology that had initially been developed for military purposes. Civil-military integration was uplifted as a national-level strategy, and a specialized central commission was established in 2017 to deal with this issue.[64] The space sector was prioritized as part of this strategy in order to strengthen military-civil coordination, resource and data sharing in space programmes and opening up to non-governmental capital, which could be a milestone for reconstructing China's space industry.[65] This is an ongoing process, and the specific arrangement is still uncertain. A reasonable speculation is that certain parts of space programmes, such as the Beidou navigation satellites and manned space programme, will be reorganized and demilitarized to a substantial degree – if not entirely – with PLA retaining the primary control and access rights within the military (probably within the SSF).

---

62 Three New Military Branches Created in Key PLA Reform, *China Daily*, 2 February 2016, www.chinadaily.com.cn/kindle/2016-01/02/content_22904989.htm. Last accessed August 2021.

63 What Kind of Military Force is the PLA Strategic Support Force? (我军战略支援部队是一支什么样的军事力量?), 24 January 2016, www.gov.cn/xinwen/2016-01/24/content_5035622.htm. Last accessed August 2021.

64 The civil-military integration as a national strategy relates to national security as a whole as well as to its development, http://cpc.people.com.cn/xuexi/n1/2017/0123/c385474-29043923.html. The meeting of the Political Bureau of the Communist Party Central Committee decided the establishment of the Central Committee of Developing Civil-military Integration, www.gov.cn/xinwen/2017-01/22/content_5162263.htm. Last accessed August 2021.

65 Guideline on deepening military-civilian integration in science, technology and industry for national defence, State Council General Office, No. 91 [2017], preamble and para. 19, www.gov.cn/zhengce/content/2017-12/04/content_5244373.htm. Last accessed August 2021.

1.3.3.   Space Programme Organs

A salient feature for the organization of space activities in China is programmes and missions designed to centralize all available resources for achieving breakthrough developments in certain areas. The establishment of specific organs is necessary to strengthen the overall and systematic management, such as the Manned Space Agency, the Center of Lunar Exploration Program and the National Administration Office of Satellite Navigation System (Satellite Navigation Office or Beidou Office).

The manned space programme relates to a variety of constituent systems: the Long March launch vehicles; the Shenzhou space capsules; the Tiangong space labs and modules; the space application systems, including payloads development and onboard scientific experiments packages; the selection of astronauts; the training and supporting system, including spacesuits and life support; the mission launch sites; the spacecraft tracking and communications network as well as spacecraft and astronaut recovery systems.[66] The mission for the development of this system was assigned to different sectors, including the PLA GAD, the China Academy of Space Technology (CAST), the CAS, CASIC and the CASTC, the Jiuquan and Wenchang launch centres as well as satellite tracking and control centres. In order to coordinate all these efforts (similar to contractors), the Manned Space Agency was established in 1992.[67] The lunar exploration programme has five constituent systems: the lunar exploration spacecraft, launch vehicle, telemetry, tracking and control system, launch site and ground application system. Similarly to the functioning of the Manned Space Agency, the Lunar Exploration Office was established by and within COSTIND in 2004.[68] Based on previous experience, the Beidou office was established with the approval of the Beidou Navigation Satellite programme. The multisystem composition, satellite system, ground and space-based augmentation system and application system determine which of the military, governmental or research organs or enterprises are involved in their development.

Based on the activities conducted, these organs are responsible for overall planning, designing, developing, managing and implementing the programme activities; they represent the government, sign international agreements and carry out international cooperation and release news and information.[69] News release and information sharing through their websites and verbal note submitted to the UNOOSA has become an important channel for improving the transparency of China's space activities over the years, particularly the Manned Space Agency. Since Tiangong-1 ceased to function, on

---

66   The Constitutes of China Manned Space, www.cmse.gov.cn/gygc/xtzc/htyxt. Last accessed August 2021.
67   Organization and Management of the China Manned Space Program (中国载人航天工程组织管理), www.cmse.gov.cn/gygc/zzgl/gcld. Last accessed August 2021.
68   Organizational Structure of the Lunar Exploration Program, www.clep.org.cn/n487137/n6000894/c6001099/content.html. Last accessed August 2021.
69   *See* www.cmse.gov.cn, www.clep.org.cn and www.beidou.gov.cn. The website of the Manned Space Agency has an English version. Last accessed August 2021.

16 March 2016, the orbital status and other information regarding its re-entry (both in Chinese and English) were posted and updated weekly on the basis of new monitoring data through the website of the Manned Space Agency from 21 March 2017 to 11 March 2018 and daily from 14 March 2018 to 1 April 2018 as well as three times a day on 2 April 2018, twice before and once after the re-entry.[70] In July 2019, the Manned Space Agency announced the controlled re-entry of Tiangong-2 ex-ante and ex-post.[71]

To rally all resources and to guarantee efficient and effective management, these project organs are a mixture of being military and civilian, being affiliated to the PLA and/or to COSTIND/SASTIND with no accurate definition of their nature and authority. In accordance with the Law on Legislation, only ministerial-level government organs, which are subordinate to the State Council, are authorized to issue administrative rules for the sake of implementing laws promulgated by the National People's Congress and the State Council's administrative regulations within the scope of their functions.[72] Although not officially entrusted with the authority of drafting and issuing regulation documents, but probably empowered by special order from the State Council or the PLA Central Committee, the Beidou office did draft and issue some documents with regulatory elements, such as the standard system of the Beidou Navigation Satellite in 2015 and regulatory rules on strengthening the service performance of the Beidou ground infrastructure in 2017.[73]

Only the State Council and its departments, but not the military, can represent the People's Republic of China and negotiate and sign a treaty with foreign nations.[74] However, the uncertainty about the Manned Space Agency – whether being a governmental or military department – has not prevented it from signing cooperative documents with other states, foreign governmental organs and international organizations. For instance, the Manned Space Agency signed cooperation agreements with the Italian Space Agency, the ESA and the United Nations, either with the explicit authorization from the Ministry of Foreign Affairs or by neglecting the provisions of the Law on the Procedures of Treaty Conclusion.[75] However, this possible violation of

---

70 Note Verbal from the Permanent Mission of China to the United Nations Secretary-General on the Re-entry of Tiangong-1, 4 May 2017, 8 December 2017, 26 March 2018, and 11 April 2018, A/AC.105/1150, A/AC.105/1150/Add.1, A/AC.105/1150/Add.2, A/AC.105/1150/Add.3. Notice and Announcement of China's Manned Space Agency on Tiangong I Orbital Status, http://en.cmse.gov.cn. Last accessed August 2021.
71 Note Verbal from the Permanent Mission of China to the United Nations Secretary-General on the Planned Re-entry of Tiangong-2 space lab, 16 July 2019, A/AC.105/1201. See http://en.cmse.gov.cn/news/201907/t20190713_44588.html, and http://en.cmse.gov.cn/news/201907/t20190719_44589.html. Last accessed August 2021.
72 Art. 71 of the Law on Legislation, adopted by the 3rd Session of the 9th National People's Congress on 15 March 2000, entered into force on 1 July 2000.
73 Official Announcement of the Beidou Office, www.beidou.gov.cn/yw/gfgg/index.html. Last accessed August 2021.
74 Arts. 4 and 5, China's Law on the Procedures of Treaty Conclusion.
75 For exchange and international cooperation activities of the Manned Space Agency, see www.cmse.gov.cn/col/col22/index.html. Last accessed August 2021.

domestic law relating to competences has no impact on the legitimacy and implementation of these agreements but undermines the authority of the Law on Procedures of Treaty Conclusion and confuses China's national legal order.[76]

1.3.4. *Two Major State-Owned Space Companies: CASTC and CASIC*

China Aerospace Science and Industry Corporation (CASIC) and China Aerospace Science and Technology Corporation (CASTC), two state-owned companies under the supervision of the COSTIND/SASTIND, are the backbone of China's space capacities and are actively involved in the execution and administration of China's space programmes.[77] They have a similar history: originally, they had both been governmental entities and were transformed into corporations. As previously mentioned, the Ministry of Aerospace Industry was split up into the China Aviation Industry Corporation and the China Aerospace Industry Corporation in 1993. In 1999, the China Aerospace Corporation was restructured and split up into the China Aerospace Science and Technology Corporation (CASTC) and the China Aerospace Machinery and Electronic Corporation, as approved by the 9th National People's Congress. The China Aerospace Machinery and Electronic Corporation were renamed the China Aerospace Science and Industry Corporation (CASIC) in 2001.[78] The CASTC and CASIC have taken on different names since 1956, namely, Fifth Academy of the Ministry of Defence, the Ministry of the Seventh Machinery Industry, the Ministry of Aerospace Industry, the Ministry of Aviation and Aerospace Industry, the China Aerospace Corporation and the China Aerospace Machinery and Electronics Corporation.

The CASTC is a large state-owned enterprise with outstanding innovative capabilities and strong core competitiveness, engaged mainly in the research, design, manufacture and launch of space systems, including launch vehicles, satellites and manned spaceship and missiles, such as Long March and Shenzhou. The CASTC operates 8 research, development and production complexes, 12 specialized companies and 5 directly affiliated units in Beijing, Shanghai, Xi'an, Chengdu and Hainan. Some of them have

---

76 A state may not invoke the fact that its consent to be bound by a treaty has been expressed in violation of a provision of its internal law regarding the competence to conclude treaties, as invalidating its consent, unless that violation was manifest and concerned a rule of its internal law of fundamental importance. *See* Art. 46 (1), Vienna Convention on the Law of Treaties. M. N. Shaw, *International Law*, 6th ed., Cambridge: Cambridge University Press, 2008, p. 940.

77 At www.spacechina.com and www.casic.com.cn, both of which have an English version. Last accessed August 2021.

78 The historic evolution of the China Aerospace Science and Industry Corporation and the historic evolution of the China Aerospace Science and Technology Corporation, *Ibid.*

holding rights over 12 publicly listed companies.[79] Among the eight complexes, the China Academy of Launch Vehicle Technology (CALT), founded in 1957 and subordinated to the CASTC, is China's largest entity for the research, design, testing and manufacturing of launch vehicles, including the Long March rocket series;[80] the CAST, established in 1968, was to facilitate the research and design of China's first satellite and is currently estimated as a world-class spacecraft designer and manufacturer, covering telecommunication, remote sensing, navigation and human space flights.[81] By virtue of space technology, CASTC pays close attention to product development in areas such as satellite applications, information technology, space technology applications, space vehicles and space biology. It has been promoting exchanges and cooperation and has dedicated itself to innovation and building itself into a leading international space enterprise group, thus making new contributions to the national economic and social development and scientific and technical progress.

The China Great Wall Industry Corporation (CGWIC) was established in 1980 to conduct satellite trade, commercial launch services and other cooperation activities and was later incorporated into CASTC before entering into the space market in 1985. It is now able to offer a full package of satellite trade, including commercial launch services,

---

79 Company file and organization structure of the China Aerospace Science and Technology Corporation, www.spacechina.com/n25/n142/n152/n164/index.html and www.spacechina.com/n25/n142/n152/n12989/index.html. Last accessed August 2021. The eight complexes are: China Academy of Launch Vehicle Technology, Academy of Aerospace Solid Propulsion Technology, China Academy of Space Technology, Academy of Aerospace Propulsion Technology, Sichuan Academy of Aerospace Technology, Shanghai Academy of Space Flight Technology, China Academy of Aerospace Electronics Technology, China Academy of Aerospace Aerodynamics. The 12 specialized companies are: China Satellite Communication Co. Ltd., China Lucky Group Corporation, China Great Wall Industry Corporation, China Center for Resources Satellite Data and Application, Aerospace Science and Technology Finance Co. Ltd., China Aerospace Investment Holdings Co. Ltd., China Aerospace International Holdings Ltd., Beijing Shenzhou Aerospace Software Technology Co. Ltd., Zhenzhen Academy of Aerospace Technology, Aerospace Times Properties Development Co. Ltd., Aerospace Long-March International Trade Co. Ltd., and China Siwi Surveying and Mapping Technology Co. Ltd. The 12 publicly listed companies are: China Spacesat Co. Ltd; Shanghai Aerospace Automobile Electromechanical Co. Ltd., Shaanxi Aerospace Power Energy Saving Technology Co. Ltd., China Aerospace Times Electronics Co. Ltd., China Energize International Holdings Co. Ltd., China Aerospace International Holdings Co. Ltd., APT Satellite Holdings Ltd., Navinfo Co. Ltd., Lucky Film Co. Ltd., Changzheng Engineering Co. Ltd., Baoding Lucky Innovative Materials Co. Ltd., Beijing Ctrowell Technology Co. Ltd.

80 CALT is the birthplace of China's space activities and famous scientist, Qian Xuesen, was its founding president. Over the last decades, CALT has undergone remarkable development with the hard work of generations of space researches. It has gradually formed a scientific research and production structure with the capabilities of multi-model development and batch production. CALT plays an important role in the three milestones of China's space activities: LM-1 launch vehicle launched successfully the first satellite of China, the opening of China's space industry; LM-2F launch vehicle made a success of launching manned spaceship, the start of China's manned missions; LM-3A launch vehicle launched 'Chang'e' lunar exploration satellite, the beginning of deep-space exploration. See www.calt.com, with an English version. Last accessed August 2021.

81 Since the establishment in 1968, CAST has become one of the world-class spacecraft designers and manufacturers, providing the full range of integrated space-ground system solutions for global customers. www.cast.cn, with an English version. Last accessed August 2021.

satellite export, ground tracking and related training.[82] All the satellite and launch service trade provided by China has been organized by CGWIC as the contractor with support from the CALT and the CAST. The CGWIC has provided launch services for more than 50 times to foreign clients, including payloads and in-orbit delivery of satellites. In recent years, the CGWIC has begun to provide one-stop launch services to domestic operators.

The CASIC is China's largest developing and manufacturing company for missile weapon systems and has a complete infrastructure for the development, research and manufacturing of air defence missile systems and cruise missile systems, solid propellant rockets and other high-tech products, especially for space technology. It has 6 academies, 17 affiliated units, wholly-owned subsidiaries and holding companies as well as over 500 other companies and institutes all over the country.[83] CASIC has developed a series of high-tech products in space defence, information technology, equipment manufacture and intelligence industry fields by means of its technology superiority. It boasts a comprehensive system for developing, researching and manufacturing air defence missile systems, cruise missile systems, solid rockets and space products. Up to now, CASIC has successively developed dozens of advanced missile systems, which contributes greatly to the modernization of China's national defence weaponry and equipment. As the main force of China's space industry, CASIC has devoted itself to building a space-ground integrated security and support system in manned space flights, lunar exploration and other major national space projects. Advancing towards the future, CASIC will stick to the national strategies of civilian-military integration, innovation-driven development, self-building with talents and winning out of quality. It will build itself into a global first-class space and defence corporation with missiles as its leading industry, with information technology and equipment manufacture as its major supporting industries, and its persistent efforts in the innovation in technology, business mode and management.

The dual-use nature of space technology and several rounds of governmental and enterprise reformation during the transition from planned economy to market economy entail the CASIC's and CASTC's multiple nature. The overall principle of reformation was loosening the state's control over the running of the enterprises, thereby spurring innovation and injecting competition into the aerospace and defence industry. A notable result of this transformation is that some professional companies under the CASTC and CASIC, namely the non-space-related ones and those providing telecommunications, remote sensing and broadcasting services, have been partly privatized through public listing on the stock exchange or through receiving direct investment from private entities.[84] Although labelled as corporations, they are more

---

82 *See* www.cgwic.com, with an English version. Last accessed August 2021.
83 Introduction to CASIC, www.casic.com/n189298/n189314/index.html. Last accessed August 2021.
84 Y. Zhao, *National Space Law in China: An Overview of the Current Situation and Outlook for the Future*, Leiden: Brill Nijhoff, 2014, p. 32.

than that. First, they (at least the directly space-related units) do not operate strictly on a cost-benefit basis. Their R&D units have greater resemblance to state-financed research organs, and their primary concern is not guided by an input-output ratio while implementing national space programmes. Second, they are not competitors in the strict sense. Over the years, they managed to diminish their competition to the minimum by focusing on different scientific and technical sections within space programmes, and they are rather complementing each other in developing space technologies and conducting space activities. Third, they had been governmental entities and retained their (original) administrative responsibilities and functions to some extent. The China Aerospace Industry Corporation had been named CNSA from 1993 to 1998, before it was assigned as an internal division of COSTIND. CASTC and CASIC are capable of wielding power in shaping the related strategy, policy and regulation as well as the administration of space activities. Besides, being full-fledged players, their executives are representatives in the national or provincial People's Congress or the Political Consultative Conference and on the career track to official positions. Some of their documents are treated as quasi-official policy, such as the long-term development road map for space transportation system, issued by CASTC in 2017.

1.3.5. The Science and Education Community

The science and education community in China has played an active and important role in the space programmes. They exert influence on the decision-making process, particularly through the scientists' agenda setting and idea proposing efforts, participate in R&D and implement certain parts of space programmes as well as cultivate and educate younger generations.

China's space science and education community is composed of universities, research units and institutes, including those within the CAS, CASIC and CASTC. The universities with notable research and educational abilities in space science and technology are Tsinghua University, Beihang University, Beijing Institute of Technology, Harbin Institute of Technology and the National University of Defence Technology.[85]

In this community, the CAS, as the primary academic organ in natural sciences and the largest comprehensive R&D organization, is the linchpin of China's drive to explore and harness high technology and science and has been acting as the 'think tank' of China's space programmes.[86] Since its foundation in 1949, CAS has fulfilled multiple

---

85 Tsinghua University ranks at the top of academic institutions in China and Asia and belongs to the top 20 worldwide. *See* www.tsinghua.edu.cn, with an English version. Last accessed August 2021.
86 Introduction to the Chinese Academy of Science, 1 May 2016, http://english.cas.cn/about_us/introduction/201501/t20150114_135284.shtml. The English version of other universities websites are: http://ev.buaa.edu.cn; http://english.bit.edu.cn; http://en.hit.edu.cn and https://english.nudt.edu.cn. Last accessed August 2021.

roles, functioning as a national team and a locomotive, driving national technology innovation, being a pioneer in supporting nationwide S&T development and a think tank for S&T advice as well as a community for training young talent. CAS comprises three major parts: a comprehensive R&D network of over 100 research institutes, a merit-based academic society and a system of higher education based on two universities. There are nearly 60,000 professional researchers and over 50,000 students, mostly postgraduate students, in the CAS all over the country, undertaking over 10% of the 863 Project.[87]

The merit-based academic society of CAS is represented by its membership in academic divisions, also known by the title of Academician, which is the highest academic title in China. This is a lifetime honour awarded to Chinese and foreign scientists for significant achievements in science research.[88] Currently, there are 797 national and 92 foreign members.[89] The CAS academic divisions and its members hold an important position in the Chinese advisory system, providing scientific advice to the government, especially on complicated and comprehensive issues involving science and technology.[90] From 2000 to 2015, CAS has submitted 160 study reports and proposals to the State Council and other government agencies through its members.[91] Since 1950s, the CAS members have been space programme entrepreneurs, and their advocating and planning reports have been an important source as well as the origin and crucial element leading up to the materialization of space programmes. As to the process leading to the eventual approval of Project 863, project 921 and the lunar exploration programme, their common feature is to be seen in the role and the influence of the Academicians and their advocacy in actively presenting and promoting their proposals to the decision makers, the high levels of government and the party. In recent years, the CAS has been advocating several science platforms to be installed on China's space station.[92]

The implementation of space programmes has seen the active involvement of multiple CAS research institutes, such as the Technology and Engineering Center for Space

---

87   The institutes of the Chinese Academy of Science, http://english.cas.cn/institutes. Last accessed August 2021.
88   Bylaw on the Academician of the Chinese Academy of Science, adopted in 1992 and amended in 2014, english.casad.cas.cn/au/re/. Last accessed August 2021.
89   The recent round of nomination took place in November 2021, and 65 Chinese and 25 foreign scholars were nominated, casad.cas.cn/yszx2017/yszx2021/tzgg_2021zx/202111/t20211118_4814539.html. The List of Chinese CAS Members, www.casad.cas.cn/chnl/371/index.html. The List of Foreign CAS Members, english.casad.cas.cn/mem/fm/. Last accessed August 2021.
90   X. Li, K. Yang, X. Xiao, Scientific Advice in China: The Changing Role of the Chinese Academy of Sciences, *Palgrave Communications*, Vol. 2, 2016, p. 45.
91   The CAS members can forward suggestions and thereby influence the state's S&T related policy. Obligations and Rights of A CAS Member, http://english.casad.cas.cn/Me/OR/200905/t20090515_3152.html. Sixty years growth and accomplishments of CAS Academic Divisions, https://link.springer.com/content/pdf/10.1007/s11434-015-0779-y.pdf. Last accessed August 2021.
92   H. Guo, J. Wu (eds.), *Space Science and Technology in China: A Roadmap to 2050*, Beijing: Science Press and New York: Springer, 2010, pp. 87-89.

Utilization (CSU), the Institute of Remote Sensing and Digital Earth, the National Space Science Center, the Lunar Exploration and Engineering Center, China Remote Sensing Satellite Ground Station (RSGS), the National Astronomical Observatories (NAO) and Space Debris Observation and Data Application Center (SDODAC). Established in 1986, RSGS is a major national infrastructure and a member of the international ground stations group on Earth Observation, with five ground stations in Miyun, Kashi, Sanya, Kunming, and North Pole.[93] The lunar exploration programme ground application system within the NAO is associated with the Lunar Exploration Program as a supporting entity of SASTIND in lunar exploration data management. Its main function is to develop and manage the capabilities for receiving data from lunar exploration satellites, to coordinate the operation of these satellites and to process and manage the data thus obtained.[94] The SDODAC was established in 2015 and co-supervised by CAS and SASTIND. Some of them are key actors in China's space programmes. For instance, the predecessor of CSU is the General Establishment of Space Science and Application (GESSA), founded in 1993 and upgraded to CSU in 2011. As an overall management of the application system of China's manned space programme, CSU is responsible for the planning, implementation, international cooperation and promotion of the results of the relevant space science and its utilization, so as to serve the national strategic demands.[95]

In 2014, the Regional Center for Space Science and Technology Education in Asia and the Pacific (RCSSTEAP-China) was inaugurated at Beihang University in Beijing, affiliated to the UN through a memorandum of understanding with the UN Office for Outer Space Affairs.[96] This is the sixth in a series of regional centres for space science and technology education, established worldwide within existing institutions in developing countries, assisting UN member states in enhancing indigenous capabilities in different areas of space science and technology in order to advance social and economic development.[97] Like the other regional centres in India, Jordan, Morocco, Nigeria, Brazil and Mexico, RCSSTEAP-China provides in-depth education, research and application programmes for university educators and scientists on the following four

---

93 China Remote Sensing Satellite Ground Station (RSGS), english.radi.cas.cn/RD/crssgs. Last accessed August 2021.
94 Measures for the Management of Scientific Data of Lunar and Deep Space Exploration Projects, Arts. 5 and 7. See http://english.nao.cas.cn/research/researchdivisions/lunardeepspaceexploration/. Last accessed August 2021.
95 Technology and Engineering Center for Space Utilization, http://english.csu.cas.cn/About_CSU/General_Information. Last accessed August 2021.
96 Beihang University is China's first university focusing on astronautics and is a leading university in China. The enrolment of international postgraduates at Beihang University started in 1993, among the earliest in China. In response to the UN Space Application Program, Beihang International Space Education Center was founded in 2004 and began to offer master's and doctoral programmes on space technology application in 2006 and 2013, respectively.
97 The regional centres initiatives are recommended by General Assembly resolutions 45/72 of 1990, 50/27 of 1995, 54/58 of 1999, and 60/99 of 2005.

1. China's Space Programmes

core disciplines: remote sensing and geographic information system, meteorological satellite applications, satellite communications and geo-positioning system and space and atmospheric sciences. Currently, RCSSTEAP-China has ten member states: Algeria, Argentina, Bangladesh, Bolivia, Brazil, China, Indonesia, Peru and Venezuela.[98] RCSSTEAP-China offers a doctoral programme on space technology applications and a master's programme on global navigation satellite systems, micro-satellite technology, remote sensing and geo-information system as well as space law and policy.[99] The centre has organized a couple of short-training programmes with CGWIC, the CNSA, United Nations Platform for Space-based Information for Disaster Management and Emergency Response (UN-SPIDER), the National Disaster Reduction Center of China and the Asia-Pacific Space Cooperation Organization.

1.3.6.   The Emergence of New Space Actors

In China, an initial evolution of commercial space activities has taken place with the participation and growing interest of quite a number of various actors. Local governments, universities, research institutions and commercial entities are seeking to expand their participation in space activities. Encouraged by the policy direction and space commerce achievement in other nations, untraditional space actors, particularly commercial entities outside the space industry, are watching closely, researching and considering how far they could also join this burgeoning economic sector. It is more accurate to describe this diversification of space actors as commercialization, rather than privatization, as financing and investment come from both government and private entities, including foreign commercial participation.[100] This will strengthen the industrial base of space economy and help to forge new development modes for space activities and thereby achieve the long-term sustainable development of China's economy.

---

98 Introduction of RCSSTEAP-China, hrcssteap.buaa.edu.cn/kjkjjyev/About_us/Introduction.htm. Last accessed August 2021.
99 Education Programmes of RCSSTEAP-China, http://rcssteap.buaa.edu.cn/kjkjjyev/Education.htm Last accessed August 2021.
100 Over the last few decades, the growth of commercialization and privatization of space-related activities entails financing and investing from government and private entities and an increase in the development and use of innovative space technologies. But the fact that the space domain has become increasingly driven by the private sector does not amount to privatization of space activities, although the primary sources of capital will always significantly influence the incentive and the operations of a space enterprise. R. Ronci, et al., Communicating Value: Investigating Terminology Challenges in "New Space" and "Commercial Space", *New Space*, Vol. 8(3), www.liebertpub.com/doi/10.1089/space.2020.0023. Last accessed August 2021.

Some 100 companies have been registered over the last years, focusing on the production and launch of satellites and rockets.[101] For instance, the 21st Century Aerospace Technology Company, founded in 2001, aims to become a remote sensing satellite operator and data and service provider. It is the owner of several microsatellites, including a DMC3/TripleSat Constellation.[102] China RS Geo-informatics C., Ltd, established in 2007, is funded by the CAS Institute of Remote Sensing and Digital Earth (RADI) with the aim of accelerating the transformation and industrialization of technological achievements of the RADI and of becoming a remote sensing information industry chain group, providing services of data collection and processing as well as for generating and providing information products.[103] Changguang Satellite Technology was founded in 2014 with shareholders, including the Jilin provincial government. Its satellite, Jijin-1, is China's first R&D high-resolution commercial video integral satellite.[104] Siwei Worldview, with a mixed investment from China and from the US companies, provides remote sensing data.[105] The LinkSpace Aerospace Technology Group was established in 2014 with the main business of spacecraft design, liquid and solid engine production, and its self-developed satellite was launched in 2018.[106] The CASIC Launch Vehicle Technology Ltd. Co. (Expace) was registered in Wuhan (Hubei Province) in 2016, serving as the commercial front of corporations to offer commercial satellite launch services using the Kuaizhou rockets and responding thereby to the national strategy of civil-military integration.[107] OneSpace Technologies, jointly invested by governmental and private organs and established in 2015, focuses on developing low-cost, small-scale launch vehicles for microsatellites.[108] Its solid-fuel rocket conducted China's first private launch in May 2018. i-Space, founded in 2016, is committed to developing launch vehicles and is providing cost-effective launch services to commercial space customers. Its first rocket, Hyperbola-1s, conducted a successful test launch from Wenchang up to an altitude of 108 km on 4 April 2018,

---

101 According to a report, there are 78 commercial space companies in China involved in satellite manufacturing, launch, remote-sensing operation, communication and downstream analytics. Among them, 49 were established after 2014. 71% are privately owned, start-ups or subsidiaries of private companies, while the rest are CAS or university spin-offs or the subsidiaries of state-owned enterprises. I. Liu et al., Evaluation of China's Commercial Space Sector, Institute for Defence Analysis, Science and Technology Policy Institute, September 2019, pp. 28-40. This report did not take into account the investment from local governments and human resource connection with the traditional space actors. Also, the statistics are incomplete, since there are still more commercial space companies according to governmental data on company registration. Although some of them are not actively operational, the number of commercial space companies might increase every year. Therefore, 100 is just an estimate.
102 See www.21at.com.cn. Last accessed August 2021.
103 See www.chinarsgeo.com, with an English version. Last accessed August 2021.
104 See www.charmingglobe.com, with an English version. Last accessed August 2021.
105 See www.webmap.cn. Last accessed August 2021.
106 See www.linkspace.com.cn, with an English version. Last accessed August 2021.
107 See www.casic.com.cn/n12377419/n12378166/c13784113/content.html. Last accessed August 2021.
108 See www.onespacechina.com. Last accessed August 2021.

and Hyperbola-1 rocket put satellites into orbit for the first time on 25 July 2019, a step forward for China's nascent space start-ups.[109] Most of these companies have been newly established since 2014, being in certain connection with the traditional space actors through investment, technology support or human resources.[110]

Their interest in space commerce, so far, focuses on the production and sale of launchers and satellites. Their ambitions are rather limited in comparison with the US space commercial ecosystem, led by SpaceX and Blue Origin, the former aiming at the conquest of Mars and the latter at the exploitation of space resources. Their capitalization is significantly lower than that of the American counterparts.[111] Also, the entrance of many start-ups in recent years on the upstream segment of launchers and satellites is hardly in competition with the giant state-owned conglomerates in financial and technological terms. Their business model is to rely on market demand, and some of them might collapse in the years to come for not being profitable.

1.4. THE COMPARATIVE AND FUTURE PERSPECTIVE OF CHINA'S SPACE PROGRAMMES

China's space programme started comparatively late, with its first launch in 1970, and only in the 1980s did China begin to emerge as a fledgling space power. Its heavy investment in the development of space manufacturing infrastructure and personnel in the 1980s and 1990s, although making only small advances in near-term capability, set the foundation for later growth and began to bear fruit in the early 2000s, particularly its first astronaut successfully launched by Shenzhou V in 2003.

China's achievements and innovations are gaining momentum on its way to becoming a space power. Its greatest strength and most marketable advantage in the field of space technology lies in its launch capability, and space vehicles have been working with a remarkable record of success.[112] In recent years, China has made extraordinary progress in terms of the frequency of its launches into outer space, reflecting its growth and demonstrating its technological advances in comparison with the United States and Russia. Globally, a total of 81, 92, 87, 85 and 90 space launches, respectively, were made in 2013, 2014, 2015, 2016 and 2017, of which China performed 16, 16, 19, 22 and 18, thereby being stably responsible for 20% of the global launch activity. There were 39 launches in 2018, twice the number of China's launches in 2017,

---

109 See www.i-space.com.cn, with an English version. Last accessed August 2021.
110 This is motivated by The Guidance on Encouraging Social Investment in the Key Innovation Domains (国务院关于创新重点领域投融资机制鼓励社会投资的指导意见), the State Council, No. 60 [2014], para. 24. For more information, see the next part of this introduction.
111 M. Julienne, *China's Ambitions in Space: The Sky is the Limit*, Paris: French Institute of International Relations, January 2021, pp. 22-26.
112 R. Cliff, *Ready for Takeoff: China's Advancing Aerospace Industry*, Santa Monica, CA: Rand Corporation, 2011, p. 112.

which made 60% more launches than in 2016. This launch rate accounted for one-third of the total number of launches worldwide and the biggest launch number by country. The year 2019 witnessed 34 launches in China, which, once again, was one-third of the total number of launches worldwide and again the biggest launch number by country. The number for 2020 was 39 (fewer than the United States) after being number one around the world for two years. Among the 44 launches of the US for the year 2020, the Space X Falcon accounted for 26 missions. However, till the end of 2021, the total launch number of China just exceeds 400, much less than the corresponding number of the US. China still lags behind in important areas in comparison with other space powers. US space technology remains by far the best in the world, while China is still passing milestones that had already been established by the US and Russia decades or years ago. For example, China's satellite capabilities fall quite short of those of the United States with respect to the resolution of optical satellites. Neither are China's space vehicles as powerful as those of the US, the European Space Agency (ESA) or Russia. However, this gap tends to be narrowing. China has been the world's fastest growing major economy for the last four decades and has strong motivation and aspiration to move forward in space programmes that conform to the principles of its goals in scientific, technological, economic and social terms. Its achievement in this century, including the success of manned flights, the completion of a global navigation satellite system and the landing on the moon's far side, demonstrated its willingness to undertake high-risk, high-reward missions. While in the US, in the ESA member states as well as in the Russian Federation, there is a lack of political will to fund ambitious space programmes, such as manned spaceflights and Mars exploration, in China, these goals are considered as the pride of the nation and a symbol of national strength, although there is an ongoing debate about their general benefit and spillover effect.

Contrary to the assumption of working with undue haste, as well as of being competitive and even aggressive, China has been developing space programmes at a slow and steady pace, taking substantial steps forward in each programme, with the aim of continuously advancing towards certain capabilities in space. This conservative attitude has been rewarded by a relatively low rate of incidents.[113] The development of a manned programme was characterized by considerable caution and was slower than in the US and the former Soviet Union in the 1950s and 1960s. There were four unmanned missions (1999, 2001 and two in 2002) before a single astronaut was put on board for a short mission (2003). Two years passed before the next multiday mission of two astronauts (2005) was affected, another three before the spacewalk mission (2008) was undertaken and a further four before the first flight to the space station (2012) took place. China was the third nation, after the Soviet Union and the US, to put a man into orbit. The Shenzhou V manned spacecraft was launched and retrieved with the first taikonaut,

---

113 B. Harvey, *China in Space: The Great Leap Forward*, New York: Springer, 2013, p. 307.

Yang Liwei, on 15 October 2003, followed by 12 other taikonauts (10 men and 2 women) – two of them participating three times, while three participated twice. Until now, their duration in space has gradually extended from 21 hours to 6 months.

Notably, with its accumulating space capacity, growing economic size and governmental support, China's space sector growth has accelerated in the 21st century, as demonstrated by the number of space launches per year, strides in space stations and deep space exploration, more transparent policy documents and regulatory framework as well as confident efforts in promoting and expanding space cooperation. On China's first Space Day, 24 April 2016, President Xi called on the country to open a new chapter in space programme development in order to become a major space power, "seizing the strategic opportunity and to keep innovating with the aim of making a greater contribution to the country's overall growth and to the welfare of mankind".[114] As an indispensable part of China's new concept for development and its modernized economy, the aim of becoming a major space power, first emerging in 2013, was highlighted in Xi Jinping's report to the 19th National Congress of the Communist Party in 2017.[115] As a powerful pillar for China's infrastructure system and its scientific and technological advancement as well as a source of national pride, the consistently high level of political support and funding ensures progress towards establishing China as a major space power. To achieve this goal, soft power capacity is as important as hard power. Correspondingly, there is a greater need and requirement for China to upgrade its development model, improve its space legislation and governance mechanism, streamline civil and military relations, expand cooperation, ensure greater compliance with international law and assume a more active role in maintaining space order.

---

114 XI Jinping's remarks in 2016 on Space Day and those on scientific innovation in 2017, www.xinhuanet.com/politics/2016-04/24/c_1118719221.htm and www.chinadaily.com.cn/china/xismoments/2017-06/01/content_29575750.htm. Last accessed August 2021.

115 Secure a Decisive Victory in Building a Moderately Prosperous Society in All Respects and Strive for the Great Success of Socialism with Chinese Characteristics for a New Era, 18 October 2017. Official bilingual version, at http://language.chinadaily.com.cn/19thcpcnationalcongress/2017-11/06/content_34188086.htm. Last accessed August 2021.

2. China's Space Policy

National space policy provides an original source of information about a state's space efforts, strategic focus and direction. It is of paramount importance not only for providing the necessary basis for achieving a state's developmental goals but also for addressing challenges with respect to the sustainable development of space activities. This part outlines and analyses Chinese space policy, focusing on its structural framework as laid out in the relevant documents, the fundamental constituent elements of its national strategy, the basic principles of development and the approaches with respect to future improvement.

2.1. The Space Policy Documents and Diplomatic Statements

Space policies are usually a subset of overall strategic, scientific and technical as well as industrial policies and diplomatic positions. Four document categories constitute the policy framework of China's space activities:

2.1.1. Comprehensive Development Plans and Policy Papers

China's space industry is facing important strategic opportunities owing to the importance of innovation and science during the transitional period of the country's development. Its priority status is outlined in primary national development plans. The Five-Year Plans (5YP) provide an overall coordinating and planning framework for economic and social development. They have been issued since 1953.[1] In this context space programmes have been set out and implemented, and the policy tone and content over the decades have demonstrated the increasing importance of the space sector for economic and social development. The 11th 5YP stressed the importance of proceeding further with the industrialization of satellites as well as with space activities

---

1 The 5YP was based on the Soviet model since planning was a key characteristic of a planned economy. It is drafted and discussed under the leadership of the politburo of the Chinese Communist Party and ratified by the National People's Congress. China is in transition from a planned to a market economy, and the more accurate definition and role of the 5YP is guidelines instead of plan. The earlier ones were intended for economic and industrial expansion, but currently they provide the grand blueprint of the overall objectives and goals related to economic and social growth and industrial planning in key sectors and regions, among which much attention is given to environmental protection and social problems, such as health insurance and the rule of law construction.

for the national economy.[2] In the 13th 5YP, the space industry was listed among the priorities for innovation in science and technology (S&T) as well as emerging industries bolstering the economy. Deep space exploration, in-orbit spacecraft servicing and the development of maintenance systems, together with the construction of heavy-lift launch vehicles and new types of satellites as well as the acceleration of the development of civil space infrastructure, were specified as programmes to be carried out.[3] This priority status of the space industry remains in the 14th 5YP and in the vision for 2035.[4]

The National Outlines of Medium and Long-Term Plans for Science and Technology (2006-2020) underline the necessity and significance of promoting the development of space activities whereby the manned space programme and the lunar exploration programme are listed among the 16 national key S&T programmes.[5] In 2015, the State Council unveiled its first 10-year national plan for transforming China's manufacturing, entitled 'Made in China 2025'.[6] This plan is designed to put China on a new path to industrialization, realizing the transformation of this 'manufacturing giant' from focusing on quantity to qualification with greater emphasis on innovation, expanded use of information and intelligence technology. Aeronautical equipment is listed among the ten key sectors for breakthrough development.

Space activities are integrated into the national defence policy documents. There are ten of them, including the White Papers[7] on China's National Defence of 1998, 2000, 2002, 2004, 2006, 2008, 2010 and 2019, on the Diversified Employment of China's Arms Forces of 2013 and on China's Military Strategy of 2015. These White Papers provide a detailed picture of China's public statements, the logic and drivers behind its military modernization programme and China's strategic view of the world. They are a series of policy documents, demonstrating the evolution of Chinese 'thinking', efforts and changes

---

2   The National 11th Five-Year Guidelines For Economic and Social Development, promulgated by the 4th meeting of the 10th National People's Congress on 14 March 2006, Chapter 10(3), 15(3) and 27(1).
3   The 13th Five-Year Plan for Economic and Social Development, Chapter 6, 22, 23, translated by Central Compilation & Translation Bureau.
4   The 14th Five-Year Plan for Economic and Social Development and Vision Goals Outline for 2035, Chapter 8 and 9, www.gov.cn/xinwen/2021-03/13/content_5592681.htm. Last accessed August 2021.
5   National Outlines of Medium and Long-Term Plans for Science and Technology (2006-2020), State Council, 2006, Section 2(2), 5 and 6(9).
6   Made in China 2025, the State Council, No. 28 [2015], www.gov.cn/zhengce/content/2015-05/19/content_9784.htm. Last accessed August 2021.
7   From the first one, in 1991, until the end of 2022, the Chinese government has issued 148 White Papers on various topics, providing information about its relevant positions, principles, development plans and achievement. The primary aims are increasing transparency, resolving doubts abroad, improving mutual understanding and building confidence between China and the international community. Usually, the topics are carefully chosen to respond to some politically sensitive issues, such as human rights; intellectual property protection; national defence, arms control and disarmament; international trade and WTO; space activities; and regional issues in Tibet and Xinjiang. All these policy documents can be found at the website of the State Council Information Office, www.scio.gov.cn/zfbps/index.htm, and some English versions can be found at www.china.org.cn/e-white. Last accessed August 2021.

2. China's Space Policy

in regard to national defence over the years. The major information regarding outer space in these Defence White Papers is consistent: they emphasize space programmes as an important constituent of the national defence industry, stressing the dangers of the potential weaponization of outer space and articulating China's position and efforts in advocating the peaceful uses of outer space.[8]

2.1.2. The White Papers on Space Activities

Till now, all the specific policy documents for space activities include the White Papers on Space Activities of 2000, 2006, 2011, 2016 and 2021 and on the Beidou Navigation Satellite System of 2016. They are the most detailed policy documents with respect to China's space activities. The 2000 Space White Papers, as the first in this policy series, are of particular significance since their publication indicated that Beijing had realized that transparency is the key to building mutual confidence, whereas secrecy might give rise to and deepen suspicion and lead to misunderstanding and misjudgment. It described China's achievement in space since 1956 and filled an information gap regarding the development of China's space programmes during 45 years.

The five Space White Papers serve as a comprehensive policy documentation on China's space activities, summarizing and enunciating China's policy, position and views on space activities and setting guidelines for the development of the medium-term national strategy relating to space undertakings with an emphasis on the civilian aspects of the space programmes. They are all similarly structured and cover the following aspects: aims and principles of development, progress during the past years, development targets and major tasks for the next five years, development policies and measures and international exchanges and cooperation. Although covering the same aspects, the 2021 White Paper is structured differently. The major difference is that the development measures are expressed as the modernization of governance, demonstrating that the diverse roles of the government are being emphasized, a governor as well as an actor. They are consistent and stable with respect to their statements and perspectives and serve as the (FYP) for the space sector.

The Beidou White Paper, however, differs from the three other documents in that it focuses on the policy of one particular space activity. Besides the generic repetition of the aims and principles of development and international exchanges and cooperation, it deals with the sustainable development of the Beidou system and the question of how to guarantee reliable and safe services and to promote its application.

---

[8] Among them, 2010 and 2019 China's National Defence and 2015 China's Military Strategy have English versions, www.scio.gov.cn/zfbps/index.htm. Last accessed August 2021.

2.1.3. Other Policy Documents of Implementing Nature

There are numerous policy documents implementing the aforementioned development plans or policy papers while targeting certain aspects of the space industry, such as those contained in the 11th, 12th and 13th 5YP for space activities development; the 12th and 13th 5YP for strategic emerging industries;[9] the space debris action (2006-2010); the development strategies for the satellite navigation industry and the civil space infrastructure;[10] and other documents promoting the development of the satellite application industry and of commercial or cooperative space activities. They were drafted within the State Council, the executive branch of China's government, and, in most cases, by the Commission of Science, Technology and Industry for National Defence (COSTIND)/State Administration of Science and Technology and Industry for National Defence (SASTIND) in coordination with other ministerial-level organs. For example, a notice that had been released by the National Development and Reform Commission (NDRC) and the COSTIND in 2007 specified the general principle, methods and objectives for the development of the satellite application industry.[11] In 2013, according to the 12th 5YP, the State Council approved and issued the medium- and long-term development plan of the national satellite navigation industry, which had been drafted by the SASTIND, to promote the development of Beidou navigation satellites and its application system. The NDRC, the Ministry of Finance and the SASTIND then released the development strategy of civil space infrastructure in 2015, aiming at the promotion of a fast and healthy development of space infrastructure and space technology application.[12] Corresponding to the 'One Belt One Road' initiative, the SASTIND and the NDRC issued guiding opinions on the construction of the One Belt One Road space information corridor.[13] In 2019, SASTIND was concerned about the rapid development of commercial space activities and the inadequacy of current

---

9   The National 12th and 13th Five-Year Plans for Strategic Emerging Industries, the State Council, No. 28 [2012] and No. 67 [2016], www.gov.cn/zwgk/2012-07/20/content_2187770.htm and www.gov.cn/zhengce/content/2016-12/19/content_5150090.htm. Last accessed August 2021.

10 Medium and Long Term Development Strategy of National Satellite Navigation Industry, the State Council General Office, No. 97 [2013], www.sastind.gov.cn/n4235/c61188/content.html. Medium and Long Term Development Strategy of China's Civil Space Infrastructure, Section IV (2), www.sastind.gov.cn/n4235/c6182809/content.html. Last accessed August 2021. The 13th Five-Year Plan for National Strategic Emerging Industries, the State Council, No. 67 [2016].

11 Notice on Promoting the Development of Satellite Application Industry, on 16 November 2007, www.gov.cn/gzdt/2007-11/18/content_808611.htm. Last accessed August 2021. The NDRC is a macroeconomic management agency that formulates policies for economic and social development, maintaining the balance of economic development and guiding the restructuring of the economic system.

12 Medium and Long Term Development Strategy of China's Civil Space Infrastructure, www.sastind.gov.cn/n4235/c6182809/content.html. Last accessed August 2021.

13 The Guiding Opinions of the SASTIND and NDRC on Accelerating the Construction and Application of the "One Belt One Road" Space Information Corridor, the SASTIND and the NDRC, www.scio.gov.cn/31773/35507/35519/Document/1534094/1534094.htm. Last accessed August 2021.

regulations and issued a notice on the regulation of the commercial carrier rockets with the aim of promoting orderly development.[14]

There are also policy documents issued by local governments implementing the national development plans and policy documents. For instance, the 2013 development plan of navigation industry encouraged local governments to adopt their counterpart policies for supporting the industrial development of Beidou system application, and, consequently, the vast majority of the provincial governments have their own plans relating to the Beidou navigation industry.[15]

2.1.4. Relevant Diplomatic Policy Documents and Positions

China's delegation attended the 23rd session of the UN Committee on the Peaceful Uses of Outer Space (COPUOS) as an observer in June 1980, which was the beginning of China's contact with UN space organs and became a member of COPUOS on 3 November 1980, the 53rd member state of this Committee. China has ever since participated in all meetings, including the sessions of the UNCOPUOS scientific and technical committee as well as its legal subcommittee.[16] China sent delegations to the second and third UN conferences on the Exploration and Peaceful Uses of Outer Space in 1982 and 1999. At the Conference on Disarmament (CD) China has strongly argued in favour of a treaty prohibiting the deployment of weapons in outer space since the 1980s and has submitted a number of relevant working papers and treaty proposals. In June 1995, the Chinese National Space Agency joined the Inter-Agency Space Debris Mitigation Committee (IADC) and has actively participated in its work, in particular by presenting a status report on space debris mitigation research and activities at its annual meeting.

China's position on certain aspects of space activities, such as the role of international law, the peaceful uses of outer space as well as the prevention of an arms race in outer space, international cooperation, transparency and confidence-building measures (TCBMs) and the long-term sustainability of outer space activities as reflected in the statements, proposals and speeches at various multilateral forums, within or outside the United Nations, including the UN General Assembly, the COPUOS, the CD and the IADC. As for an overall and systematic analysis of China's attitude, position and participation in the international legal order, it is helpful to understand China's status and involvement in the international arena as well as its policies concerning space activities.

---

14 www.sastind.gov.cn/n157/c6806483/content.html, SASTIND, No. 647 [2019]. Last accessed August 2021.
15 The 2016 White Paper on China's Beidou Navigation Satellite System, Section 4 (1).
16 Enlargement of the Committee on the Peaceful Uses of Outer Space, A/Res/35/16, 3 November 1980.

In recent years, the notion of space cooperation has been specified with more specific information, and its growing importance has been emphasized in policy documents released by the Ministry of Foreign Affairs in relation to a number of countries, regions and international organizations such as the European Union, Italy, Latin America and the Caribbean, the Association of Southeast Asian Nations (ASEAN), Arabic countries and Africa.[17] These documents demonstrated the increasing incorporation of space cooperation into China's international relations and diplomatic policy and its confidence in using space capacity as an incentive for expanding cooperation. This can be witnessed as follows: on the EU level, cooperation was extended from the negotiation of basic elements relating to the prevention of space weaponization and an arms race in outer space in 2003 to a range of cooperation fields in 2018, including Earth observation, deep space exploration and manned space flight as well as the establishment of a space policy dialogue mechanism. In Africa, cooperation developed from the mere mentioning of efforts towards the strengthening of technology cooperation and the sharing of knowledge in 2015 to specific cooperative activities with respect to communication and remote sensing satellites and their application in 2018.[18] In Latin American and the Caribbean, cooperation developed from merely listing space as one field in scientific and educational cooperation in 2008 to a separate section about space cooperation with a broad 'wish list' in 2016.[19] In the ASEAN, development can be noted from the mere mentioning of a possibility for building a platform for sharing recourse satellite data as a joint project under a 'science and technology partnership' in 2012 to a separate section on

---

17 Policy Paper on European Union of 2018 and 2003; China-Italy Action Plan on Strengthening Economic, Trade, Cultural and Scientific and Technological Cooperation (2017-2020) of 2017; Action Plan to Implement the Joint Declaration on ASEAN-China Strategic Partnership for Peace and Prosperity (2016-2020) of 2016 and Cooperation between China and ASEAN of 2012; Beijing Action Plan (2019-2021) of Form on China-Africa Cooperation of 2018 and Policy Paper on Africa of 2015; Policy Paper on Latin America and the Caribbean of 2016 and 2008; Policy Paper on Arab Countries of 2016; China's Participation in Greater Mekong Sub-Regional Cooperation of 2008. For all these policy documents, see www.fmprc.gov.cn/web/ziliao_674904/tytj_674911/zcwj_674915. Last accessed August 2021.

18 To support Africa in developing the single African air transport market, China and Africa will continue to cooperate in communication, remote sensing satellites and their application. China will continue to provide support in implementing the satellite TV project, provide Fengyun meteorological satellite data, products and necessary technical support and provide meteorological and remote-sensing application equipment and training support for African countries, in order to contribute to the implementation of the integrated African Strategy on Meteorology and to better equip African countries for disaster prevention and mitigation as well as climate change response. In times of disaster emergency, China will provide quick mapping service using space technology on the request of African countries. See Beijing Action Plan (2019-2021) of Form on China-Africa Cooperation of 2018, para. 3.3.4, 4.3.1 and 4.6.12.

19 China will actively explore potential for cooperation between the two sides in such fields as communication and remote sensing satellites, satellite data application, aerospace infrastructure and space education and training and promote space technology application in disaster prevention and mitigation, agricultural and forestry monitoring, climate change and other fields. China will pay full attention to the role of space technology as a driving force for the scientific, technological and industrial development of Latin American and the Caribbean countries and promote sustainable development in the fields of S&T and the economy. See Section 9 in Policy Paper on Latin America and the Caribbean of 2016.

space cooperation in 2015.[20] The importance of space cooperation between China and Italy has improved from 'space' merely being listed among the priority areas of cooperation in 2014 to specifying space cooperation sectors in 2017.[21] Also, there is a section on space cooperation in the policy paper of 2016 regarding Arab countries.[22] This indicates that space cooperation might become a routine part of content with suitable issues in such documents.

2.2. THE FUNDAMENTAL CONSTITUENT ELEMENTS OF NATIONAL STRATEGY FOR SPACE PROGRAMME

Usually, the basic elements of a state's space strategy include its attitude and emphasis on the relevance of space activities for national security, the development of S&T and the consideration of its relationship with other states and international organization. None of the aforementioned policy documents explicitly and specifically use the term 'national strategies for space activities' except for some general principles. Nonetheless, some basic elements of China's strategic stances regarding its space activities can be derived from a careful analysis of the relevant documents and activities.

2.2.1. The Development of Space Capabilities Conforms to China's Vital Interests

Outer space is humankind's fourth frontier, after land, sea and air. The important value of this region cannot be estimated, for example, on behalf of successful launchings alone but also has to be assessed on the basis of strategic, political, scientific, technological, social and economic implications. Space activities have never been about exploration alone but have also been linked to other goals.[23] Since the beginning of the space era, the Chinese government has encouraged and supported the development of space

---

20 Encourage the peaceful uses of outer space and cooperation in areas such as the transfer of technologies, joint technological research and development, capacity building efforts in space technology and its applications in accordance with international law, national law and regulations of the participating states. Action Plan to Implement the Joint Declaration on China-ASEAN Strategic Partnership for Peace and Prosperity of 2016, Section 2.7.

21 China-Italy Action Plan on Strengthening Cooperation from 2014 to 2016 of 2014, Section 1.5, http://world.people.com.cn/n/2014/0612/c1002-25138422.html. The China-Italy Action Plan on Strengthening Economic, Trade, Cultural and Scientific and Technological Cooperation (2017-2020) of 2017, para. 3.4.

22 Satellites are listed as one of the three breakthroughs in new tech cooperation fields under the "One Belt One Road Initiative". China will further develop space cooperation with Arab countries and actively explore joint projects in space technology, satellite and their application, space education and training, accelerate the application of the Beidou navigation satellites system in Arab countries and promote exchange and cooperation on manned space flights, so as to enhance the level of cooperation. China's Arab Policy Paper of 2016, para. 2.7.

23 R. Handberg, Z. Li, *Chinese Space Policy: A Study in Domestic and International Politics*, New York: Routledge, 2007, p. 5.

undertaking and has integrated the space programmes into its overall development strategy and plan. In different historic phases, space programmes have also made their unique contribution to the strengthening of national pride and self-confidence, ensuring national security and advancing defence modernization, maintaining internationally competitive advantages, promoting scientific and technological progress, stimulating economic growth and supporting social development.

Outer space activities started in the military sense.[24] China's earlier research and exploration activities focused on the military potential of outer space and used space deterrence as a major strategy for safeguarding national security. This focus is still valid, as evidenced by all the National Defence White Papers. The vital importance of outer space for national security was emphasized by China through codification into the National Security Law, which was the first time that the issue of safeguarding the security of space activities and of space assets was specifically laid down by law. The National Security Law, as endorsed by the NPC in 2015, adopted a 'holistic security concept', which is defined as being a condition under which the sovereignty, unification, territorial integrity, people's well-being, sustainable and healthy development of economy and society and other major interests are relatively secure from internal and external threats. This concept applies to outer space as an indispensable part of strategic security.

The development of space activities and the ever-increasing dependence of mankind on space-based services revolutionized the strategic importance of outer space.[25] Space technologies have become an intrinsic component of modern economies, and the space sector is beginning to play a pivotal role in economic development. Satellite infrastructure and satellites enabled services that have been incorporated into every aspect of modern life and are thereby becoming an important source of economic growth, social well-being and sustainable development.[26] Since 2010, the central government has announced two plan versions for the development of emerging strategic industries as part of an effort to upgrade China's industry structure as the backbone of its next phase of industrial modernization and technological development. As for communication, navigation and

---

24 H. E. McCurdy, *Space and the American Imagination*, Washington, DC: Smithsonian Institution Press, 1997, pp. 9-28. F. E. Morgan, *Deterrence and First-Strike Stability in Space: A Preliminary Assessment*, Santa Monica: Rand Corporation, 2010, pp. 21-22.
25 The Impact of Space Activities upon Society, Co-Sponsored by the International Academy of Astronautics and the European Space Agency, EAS BR-237, February 2005, www.esa.int/esapub/br/br237/br237.pdf. Last accessed August 2021.
26 The Space Economy at a Glance, second edition, 2011, p. 3 and third edition, 2014, p. 16. Organization for Economic Cooperation and Development.

remote sensing satellites, their related ground systems and applications as well as other satellites and launch vehicles, they have also been an important part of these plans.[27] Investments in space systems are providing support to the economic and social development through various means such as the modernization of China's high-technology industries, contribution to natural disaster warning and responses and the development of commercial applications based on space technology.

Space capacity is a significant metric of national power. The initiation of China's space programmes is rooted in the systematic competition of the superpowers during the Cold War. Space capabilities had then been viewed as an element of a broader international competition in comprehensive strength as well as S&T. One of China's motives in the pursuit of a space programme was to gain national prestige and to improve international competitiveness, similarly to those that drove other spacefaring nations to undertake space missions. The remarkable achievements in its space programmes, undertaken with limited resources in a span of only a few decades, helped to raise China's international stature. Now, China is about to solidify its reputation in the coming years as a space power.

2.2.2. *China Adheres to the International Legal Framework for Space Activities*

People's Republic of China gained membership in the United Nations in 1971, and significant changes have occurred both in the world and in China thereafter. China has evolved from a largely isolated state to one fully involved in global affairs by accepting, following and internalizing international legal rules. China has become a firm advocate and proactive supporter of the international legal order and international rule of law. It repeatedly stressed its conviction that the United Nations is the bedrock for maintaining international order, whereby the UN Charter establishes the multilateralism order and forms the basic principles of international law and code of conduct governing international relationships.[28]

Since the 1970s, Beijing has grown more willing to address many of its most important external concerns in international legal terms and through international legal means. Its entry into the World Trade Organization (WTO) in 2001 signified a historic moment of China becoming an indispensable part of the globalized economy.[29] China's

---

27 The Decision on Accelerating the Development of Strategic Emerging Industries, the State Council, No. 32 [2010], www.gov.cn/zwgk/2010-10/18/content_1724848.htm; The First Five-Year Plan for Strategic Emerging Industries, the State Council, No. 28 [2012], www.gov.cn/zhengce/content/2012-07/20/content_3623.htm; the 13th Five-Year Plan for Strategic Emerging Industries, the State Council, No. 67 [2016], www.gov.cn/zhengce/content/2016-12/19/content_5150090.htm. Last accessed August 2021.
28 China's Position Paper on the Issues of Long-Term Sustainability of Outer Space Activities, A/AC.105/C.1/2016/CRP.13, para. 15.
29 J. DeLisle, China's Approach to International Law: A Historical Perspective, in 94 *Annual Proceedings of American Meeting of American Society of International Law*, 2000, p. 267.

growing participation in the international legal regime reflects its increasing prominence as an emerging international player as well as its willingness to engage with other states according to established rules. In recent years, there has been a steady growth of multilateral treaties ratified or acceded to by China: 5 in 2013; 6 in 2014; 13 in 2015; 15 in 2016; 7 in 2017; 2 in 2018; 2 in 2019; 3 in 2020 and more than usual to be expected in the coming years. There has been a remarkable increase in the bilateral agreements, namely 80 in 2012 and 73 in 2013, up to 267 in 2017 and 280 in 2018 and over 200 in 2019 and 2020, which means that China's conclusion of bilaterals even tripled and stabilized in several years.[30]

The development of China benefits from the existing international legal order, and its space capacity could not have been achieved without the rule-based order in space activities. It is most unwise to fundamentally change or systematically challenge this order. However, there are still views that China does not play by the rules or that it is even a lawbreaker in international matters. Partly owing to the lack of mutual confidence and the differences caused by long-existing ideological considerations, there is an unusually huge gap between China's stated position and role and the perception of other states.[31] In view of its size and actual development, China's occasional ignorance or violation of its international legal obligations (whether purposefully or inadvertently) attracts excessive attention. Therefore, it will be able to cope with this situation and dispel suspicion only if it complies with international law even to a higher degree than Western states.[32]

China acceded to the Outer Space Treaty in 1983, and the Rescue Agreement, the Liability Convention and the Registration Convention in 1988. China insists that the exploration and use of outer space should be carried out in accordance with international law and upholds the international space governance regime of the COPUOS through dialogue and cooperation.[33] The Chinese government declares its commitment to the peaceful use of outer space in various documents and forums.[34] Multilateral measures to prevent the weaponization of outer space have been a cornerstone of China's diplomatic policy since the 1980s. In recent years, China is beginning to attach greater importance to the international space order by intentionally assuming new roles in international space law development. It actively participates in the relevant international negotiation to ensure its views presented within and beyond the

---

30 Ministry of Foreign Affairs, Annual Statistics of Multilateral Treaties Concluded and Acceded by China, www.fmprc.gov.cn/web/ziliao_674904/tytj_674911/tyfg_674913. Last accessed August 2021.
31 X. Wu, China and Space Security: How to Bridge the Gap between Its Stated and Perceived Intentions, *Space Policy*, Vol. 33, 2015, pp. 20-28.
32 B. Saul, China, National Resources, Sovereignty and International Law, *Asian Studies Review*, Vol. 37(2), 2013, pp. 196-214.
33 Statement by Ambassador Shi Zhongjun at the UNISPACE+50 High-Level Segment, 22 June 2018, www.fmprc.gov.cn/ce/cgvienna/eng/hyyfy/t1570762.htm. Last accessed August 2021.
34 The first sections of the 2000, 2006, 2011, 2016 and 2021 White Papers on China's Space Activities.

UN framework, such as the long-term sustainability of space activities at the COPUOS, the PAROS at the CD, and EU's initiative for space activities code of conduct. China is trying to be a shaping force for, more than a follower of, international law.

China seems to be ready to bring up a new concept and provide a new perspective to the future development of international law. The concept of a 'community of common destiny' or 'a community of shared future for mankind' was proposed to the 18th Congress of the Communist Party in 2012 by former president Hu Jintao and was elaborated and advocated by President Xi Jinping thereafter in the international arena, including the UN General Assembly and United Nations in Geneva.[35] In President Xi's work report during the 19th National Congress in 2017, this concept was elevated to a strategic level for China's future diplomacy.[36] A few months later, a phase of "promoting the building of a community of common destiny while developing diplomatic relations and economic and cultural exchanges with outer countries" was incorporated into the constitutional amendment adopted by the National People's Congress.[37]

The core of a community of common destiny for mankind is the ultimate goal of building a new type of international relations, featuring win-win cooperation to create a community of shared future through the recognition of common values and the interdependence of all countries. This is particularly suitable to the nature of outer space, which is a public domain for all countries and is also consistent with the objectives and purposes as laid down in the Outer Space Treaty, which stipulates that the exploration and use of outer space shall be carried out for the benefit and in the interest of all countries. This concept could be helpful for the negotiation of new rules and regimes or could also serve as a revolutionary interpretation of current treaties to handle the challenges posed by the growing size and importance of space activities, the continued emergence of new participants and the uneven development of space capabilities.[38] Since 2017, several UN General Assembly resolutions on the prevention

---

35 XI Jinping, Towards a Community of Common Destiny and a New Future for Asia, Keynote Speech at the Boao Forum for 2015 Asia Annual Conference, 18 March 2015, www.china.org.cn/chinese/2015-03/31/content_35201394.htm. Xi's speech at the General Debate of the 70th Session of the UN General Assembly, www.china.org.cn/chinese/2015-11/06/content_36999256.htm. Xi's speech at the UN Geneva Office, www.china.org.cn/chinese/2017-01/25/content_40175608.htm. Last accessed August 2021.
36 XI Jinping, Secure a Decisive Victory in Building a Moderately Prosperous Society in All Respects and Strive for the Great Success of Socialism with Chinese Characteristics for a New Era, the 19th National Congress of the Community Party, 18 October 2017, www.xinhuanet.com/english/download/Xi_Jinping's_report_at_19th_CPC_National_Congress.pdf. Last accessed August 2021.
37 Preamble Paragraph 12 of Constitution, amended in March 2018.
38 Statement by Ambassador Shi Zhongjun at the UNISPACE+50 High-Level Segment, 22 June 2018, www.fmprc.gov.cn/ce/cgvienna/eng/hyyfy/t1570762.htm. Last accessed August 2021.

of an arms race in outer space have been referring to the idea of shaping a common future for mankind.[39]

2.2.3. Civil and Military Integration

The inherent dual-use nature of technology and activities warrants the necessity of civil and military integration (CMI). Space systems are capable of supporting both civilian and military users. This is even truer in China because of the pragmatic method of pooling resources and a very complex governing regime, a result of multiple bureaucratic restructuring in the past, which caused the lack of compatibility, complementariness and mutual accessibility between the military and civilian space sector.

The guiding principle of integrating military with civilian purposes and combining military efforts with civilian support can be traced back to the 1950s. The importance of integration has never been entirely neglected ever since. Both Mao Zedong and Deng Xiao deliberately sought to leverage the residual benefit of integrating military and civilian R&D and production system as a means of advancing defence modernization and for providing support for economic development. After the Cold War, the US's practice of cultivating commercial-military ties, particularly furthering the role of the private sector in their space programme, was inspirational.[40] The pooling of commercial and military resources is thus viewed as imperative for technological innovation and sustainable development. In China, there have been intense reformative efforts to integrate the defence and commercial industrial bases more tightly since the 2000s, for the People's Liberation Army (PLA) to have greater access to civilian scientific and technological advances and for the civilian economy to incorporate dual-use technology initially developed for military purposes. However, these efforts have been frustrated by limited information sharing, bureaucratic resistance and poor coordination between the military and the civilian community.

---

39 The Resolutions of "No First Placement of Weapons in Outer Space" reaffirmed that "practical measures should be examined and taken in the search for agreements to prevent an arms race in outer space in a common effort towards a community of shared future for mankind", UNGA Res. 72/28, 2 November 2017; UNGA Res. 73/31, 11 December 2018; UNGA Res. 74/22, 18 December 2019; UNGA Res. 75/37, 16 December 2020. The Resolutions of "Further Practical Measures for the Prevention of an Arms Race in Outer Space" encouraged all states to promote and strengthen international cooperation with the objective of shaping a community of shared future for mankind. UNGA Res. 72/250, 24 December 2017; UNGA Res. 74/34, 18 December 2019.

40 In the US, civil-military integration (CMI) is defined as the process of uniting the defence technology and industrial base and the larger commercial technology and industrial bases into a unified national technology and industrial base that can be used to meet both defence and commercial needs. In the early 1990s, CMI was advocated as a means to preserve the US defence capability in the face of budget reductions and the industrial and commercial isolation problem as a result of the four-decade-long Cold War. U.S. Congress, Office of Technology Assessment, *Assessing the Potential for Civil-Military Integration: Technologies, Process and Practice*, 1991, pp. iii and 5.

During the 17th Party Congress in 2007, Hu Jintao declared that China was embarking on the road to civil-military integration with Chinese characteristics. In 2015, the Party Central Committee decided on a strategy of building an extensive and efficient multisectoral structure for integrating civilian and military resources. A strategy for national civilian-military integration was identified in President Xi's report to the 19th Party Congress as one of the seven strategies for realizing the goal of building a moderately prosperous society and a major step towards strengthened coordination between economic development and a strong military. CMI's elevation to a national-level strategy resulted in a specialized central commission in 2017, the establishment of unified leadership and coordination.[41] This strategy is aimed at fusing the country's military and civilian-industrial and S&T resources and ensuring their mutually beneficial coordination so as to achieve an optimal configuration of resources in market economy and achieve a more balanced development. The space sector was prioritized in this strategy with specified means of joint building and utilization of infrastructure, opening up to non-governmental capital and shared use of resources such as surveying and mapping, navigation and meteorology.[42]

In order to boost private sector participation, the SASTIND issued several policy and legal directives focusing on streamlining the licensing processes, military and civil product standards and constructing more transparent procurement platforms. The SASTIND published a new weaponry research and production licence directory to reduce the number of projects requiring licences. National standards are critical for detailed cooperation and provide a common language for domestic and international exchange and cooperation. In accordance with the State Council's Directive for Deepening Standardization Work Form, the efforts of SASTIND and Standardization Administration to internationalize national defence standards led to the publication of the first version of the China Space Standards in 2015.[43] Approved by the MIIT, the SASTIND and the Ministry of Finance in 2014, the civil-military integration public

---

41 President Xi Jinping's speech on the civil-military integration: It is national strategy in close relation with national security and whole development (习近平谈军民融合：是国家战略 关乎国家安全和发展全局), http://cpc.people.com.cn/xuexi/n1/2017/0123/c385474-29043923.html. The Political Bureau of the Communist Party Central Committee decided the establishment of Civil-military Integration Development Central Commission (中共中央政治局召开会议决定设立中央军民融合发展委员会), www.gov.cn/xinwen/2017-01/22/content_5162263.htm. Last accessed August 2021.
42 China's 2015 Military Strategy, Section 4.3. The Guidelines on Deepening Military-Civilian Integration in Science and Technology and Industry for National Defence (国务院办公厅关于推动国防科技工业军民融合深度发展的意见), Section 5, para. 19, the State Council General Office, No. 91 [2017], preamble and para. 19, www.gov.cn/zhengce/content/2017-12/04/content_5244373.htm. Last accessed August 2021.
43 China issued guidelines to deepen reforms of standardization system, 26 March 2015, http://english.www.gov.cn/policies/latest_releases/2015/03/26/content_281475078008940.htm; The publication of China Space Standards System and first version of China Space Standards, 22 September 2015, www.cnsa.gov.cn/n6758823/n6758839/c6796167/content.html. Last accessed August 2021.

service platform was established as an online hub to streamline procurement processes and promote commercial spin-offs of military technologies.[44]

Two state-owned space companies, the China Aerospace Science and Technology Corporation (CASTC) and the China Aerospace Science and Industry Corporation (CASIC), have signed some agreements and contracts with research organs, state-owned enterprises and local governments with the express purposes of extending forms and approaches of CMI, combining the technological advantages of CASTC and CASIC and international trade experiences of other state-owned enterprises and promoting the marketization of satellite applications in products and services.[45]

CMI is at the nexus of technological innovation, national security and economic development. Potentially, it could change the outdated military-industrial-separation development model, foster the sustainable growth of the national defence sector and inject new momentum into the private sector.[46] This strategy could be a milestone on the way to reconstructing China's space industry and its impact has already emerged. CMI, together with other liberalizing policy signals, was instrumental in the emergence of dozens of new registered space companies in recent years. But the successful implementation of the CMI strategy requires a long-term commitment because of the sheer complexity and extensive reformation involved. This includes issues such as removing long-standing institutional barriers by separating civilian and defence S&T system and avoiding the frustration of previous attempts to invigorate the defence industrial base through market forces, determining the demarcation between military and civilian and the depth of private enterprises' participation in the national defence sector and guaranteeing the beneficial effect for the economy and livelihood. Deliberations on these issues could lead to a systematic overhaul of China's national defence industry.

---

44 *See* http://jmjh.miit.gov.cn/loadWebMessage.action. Last accessed August 2021.
45 As reported in the newspaper *China Space News*, under the guidance of CMI strategy, for six months, from November 2017 to April 2018, CASIC signed strategic cooperation agreements with one research organ, Chinese Academy of Military Sciences, several governments, including Zhejiang province, Ningbo city and Rizhao economic development zone, and several big state-owned companies, such as Dongfang Electric Corporation and China Resources Group.
46 L. Zhao, Civil-Military Integration Will Deepen, *China Daily*, 3 March 2018, www.chinadaily.com.cn/a/201803/03/WS5a99d67ca3106e7dcc13f437.html. Last accessed August 2021.

2.2.4.   An Emphasis on the Effects and Influence of Space Science and Technology

Innovation in S&T is a source of strength for the continuous development of human society, impetus for a country's progress and an important scale for measuring a country's contribution to the world.[47] There is a long-standing craving for scientific and technical self-sufficiency in China. Since its defeat in the First Opium War (1839-1842), successive generations of Chinese intellectual, reformers and revolutionaries tied the survival of Chinese civilization to their ability to understand science and apply technology. Space S&T not only serves to expand the realm of our understanding of the universe but also represent the most powerful source of support for a country's economic and social development. Space technologies have exerted the most profound influence on modern society, and their development and use have become an important element of the modernization drive of countries worldwide.

The evolution of China's strategy regarding scientific and technological innovation can be divided into three broad phases: national overall planning (1949-1977), marketization reformation (1978-2011) and the national strategy of innovation-driven development and the hallmark strategy attributable to the Xi Jinping leadership (2012 to the present).[48] Innovation-driven development strategy was listed among the seven strategies for completing the building of a moderately prosperous society by the 18th Congress of the Communist Party in 2012.[49] Extensive implementation measures were incorporated into the 13th FYP, a crucial period to build a well-off society. China joined the world's top 25 most innovative countries for the first time in 2016.[50] A three-step road map was proposed in 2016, namely, building an innovative nation by 2020; moving to the forefront of innovation countries by 2030 and becoming a world-class innovative power by 2050.[51]

---

47   Among the five development concepts proposed by China in 2015, innovation, coordination, green, openness and sharing, innovation ranks first and is the prerequisite and guarantee for other development concepts. These concepts are the guiding principles of the 13th FYP, from 2016 to 2020. R. L. Kuhn, The Five Major Development Concepts, 23 September 2016, www.chinadaily.com.cn/opinion/2016-09/23/content_26872399.htm. Last accessed August 2021.
48   Scientific and technological innovation is the supporting pillar of the effort to improve productive forces and comprehensive strengthen, and must be regarded as the core issue for national development. China will implement the innovation-driven development strategy. *See* Resolution of the 18th Congress of the Communist Party, 14 November 2012, www.chinatoday.com.cn/english/zhuanti/2012-11/14/content_500755.htm. Last accessed August 2021.
49   XI Jinping report delivered to the 19th Party Congress, Secure a Decisive Victory in Building a Moderately Prosperous Society in All Respects and Strive for the Great Success of Socialism with Chinese Characteristics for a New Era, 18 October 2017, www.xinhuanet.com/english/download/Xi_Jinping's_report_at_19th_CPC_National_Congress.pdf. Last accessed August 2021.
50   The Global innovation index survey conducted by the World Intellectual Property Organization.
51   National Innovation-Driven Development Strategy Outline, Section 2.3, the State Council, 2016, www.gov.cn/zhengce/2016-05/19/content_5074812.htm. Last accessed August 2021.

The concept of scientific and technical self-sufficiency played a decisive role in the key decisions for the start and major component of China's space programmes, which were developed on the basis of weak infrastructure industries and a relatively backward scientific and technological level under special national and historical conditions. Project 863 was drafted to ensure that China had not fallen too far behind in the international scientific and technological contest. Today, space programmes are viewed as being a means of enhancing a climate of scientific innovation and as a crucial element in revitalizing the country with S&T development. A consistent driving force behind the constant pursuit of space capabilities is to seize the strategic high ground in space development and to fully utilize the supporting role of space S&T in China's national development and national security. The technological achievement in space programmes and China's ranking among the most advanced countries in some fields accorded with this concept, also explaining the popular support for and national pride originating from space programmes, particularly the expensive ones of manned flights and lunar and Mars exploration. The central role played by the CAS in the satellite programme verified that China's space programmes were infused with a broader, non-military version of the role of space technology in its national development.[52]

While parts are rapidly industrializing and developing, the nation as a whole remains relatively poor. Consequently, the developing approach is to select a limited number of targets to make breakthroughs in key areas and to thereby accelerate the industrialization and marketization of the available technologies and applications to meet the wide range of demands for economic and social progress, S&T development and national security. The programmes that are of vital significance to the national economy and social development are selected to concentrate strength and to tackle major difficulties and challenges. In the mid-1980s, China began to develop telecommunication satellites technologies to meet the increasing demands of communications, broadcasting and education. The satellites for TV broadcasting were started in 1985 and soon formed a satellite transmission network with dozens of satellites, solving the problem of communication in remote areas. After the establishment of infrastructure satellite constellations for communication, navigation and remote sensing, the emphasis has been shifting to advanced satellite capabilities and scientific aims.

2.3. The Basic Principles for the Development of Space Activities

The five Space White Papers and other space-related policy documents provide a basic consistent elaboration of principles for the development of China's space activities.

---

52 G. Kulacki, Strategic Options for Chinese Space Science and Technology: A Translation and Analysis of the 2013 Report from Chinese Academy of Sciences, 2013, p. 2, www.ucsusa.org/assets/documents/nwgs/strategic-options-for-chinese-space-science-and-technology-11-13.pdf. Last accessed August 2021.

2.3.1. *Space Industry as an Indispensable Part of National Development*

The development of space activities must serve the state's comprehensive development strategy by vigorously contributing to national economy and modernization.

The development principles of China's space activities are determined by their status and their purpose of implementing the development goals of revitalizing the country with science and education as well as safeguarding sustainable development, social progress and national security. Driven by the deeper involvement of the market economy, the space undertakings are being more responsive to the needs of the market by enhancing the social and economic returns of space activities and by optimizing products and services in view of potential markets and client demands.

The countries with space programmes are increasingly investing in down-to-earth space applications for economic reasons,[53] and so is China. There is a specific linkage between space exploration and long-term economic developmental goals, and the industrial system and capacity of space activities have been increasingly strengthened for the spin-on effect and the scientific, economic and social benefits.[54] Its efforts to develop space technologies are seen as enabling and furthering the development of other essential foundations of its economy. China's space programmes are in the process of transitioning from a technological testing stage to technological application as well as to a business and service-oriented stage.[55] Telecommunications, navigation and remote sensing satellite account for nearly 70% of the total number of satellites developed and launched by China over recent decades, and the related application systems have grown into a new industry that is beginning to yield intangible economic and social benefits. The satellite navigation and positioning service industry is booming, with an annual growth rate of 15% to 20%, and the annual output value has increased from 0.18 billion RMB in 2006 to about 300 billion RMB in 2018, 345 billion RMB in 2019 and 400 billion RMB in 2020, of which about 70% to 80% was contributed by the Beidou system.[56]

Extending the gains from space S&T into other domains and industries is imperative for China to tackle new issues and challenges in the course of developments. The policy

---

53 The Space Economy at a Glance, Organization for Economic Cooperation and Development, second edition, 2011, p. 74.
54 The 2016 White Paper on Space Activities, Section 1. The 2021 White Paper on Space Activities, Section 1 and Section 5 (2).
55 Y. Zhao, *National Space Law in China: An Overview of the Current Situation and Outlook for the Future*, Leiden: Brill Nijhoff, 2014, p. 10.
56 The White Papers on the development of satellite navigation and positioning service industry of 2013, 2014, 2015, 2016, 2018, 2019 and 2020, drafted and released by China GNSS and LBS Association. This is an NGO in global navigation satellite system application and location-based service, affiliated with the National Administration of Surveying, Mapping and GeoInformation of China, with more than 1000 members, including universities, research institutes, enterprises and manufactures and geospatial data providers, www.glac.org.cn/index.php?m=content&c=index&a=lists&catid=18. Last accessed August 2021.

documents, such as the 15-year plan for S&T and Made in China 2025, reflects China's determination to overcome growing domestic social and environmental problems through scientific and technological development.[57] With hundreds of satellites functioning in orbit, satellite applications have become an indispensable means of protecting resources and environment and predicting, preventing and mitigating natural disaster, environmental deterioration and extreme weather incidents.

2.3.2. *Self-Reliant and Innovative Development*

National independence, or self-reliance, started as a 'had-to' choice because of the foreign legal and policy constraints based on political considerations. From the outset of the People's Republic of China in 1949, the ability to be self-reliant has been viewed as essential to reducing its vulnerability to external aggression and pressure. Adherence to the principle of independence and the belief in taking the initiative in its own hands finally helped forge the country emerge as a space power. Self-reliance does not exclude international cooperation but could combine organically. China's space industry is willing to be and capable of being self-reliant and internationally relevant.

In the endeavour to acquire basic space capabilities, the pursuit of independent innovation and creativity has been a guiding principle.[58] As mentioned previously, the advancement and expansion of space programmes is driven by China's longing for scientific and technological advancement. At least since Deng Xiaoping, every national leader emphasized that innovation is the key force in propelling development and that independent innovative strength is crucial to realizing sustainable and healthy development. To achieve the strategic goal of self-transformation into a well-off society in an all-round way, one criterion and approach is to rank among the countries with the best innovative capabilities. Renovation is supported and encouraged to improve self-reliant capability and industrialization of space activities. Since the 1980s, China has gone to great lengths to strengthen intellectual property rights legislation, not only to

---

57   National 13th Five-year Plans for the Development of Strategic Emerging Industries, Sections 3.3 and 7.1, the State Council, No. 67[2016], www.gov.cn/zhengce/content/2016-12/19/content_5150090.htm. Made in China 2025, Section 3.6.3, No. 28 [2015], the State Council, No. 28 [2015], www.gov.cn/zhengce/content/2015-05/19/content_9784.htm. Last accessed August 2021.
58   The common Sections 1 (3) of the 2000, 2006, 2011, 2016 and 2021 White Papers on China's Space Activities.

attract foreign capital, companies and their technological know-how but also to enhance its own innovative capacity.[59]

China fields a range of indigenously space products and capabilities. It is the third country in the world to have mastered the technology of satellite recovery, launched an astronaut into Earth's orbit, created a large and modular space station, developed its own space-based navigation and positioning system and the fifth country to have acquired the capability to develop and launching geostationary telecommunications satellites independently. All the key components of the Beidou system, such as travelling-wave tub amplifiers, microwave switches and high-power current source controllers, are made in China, i.e., its construction is equal to the process of mastering all the core technologies without importation.[60] China is the first country to have sent a quantum satellite, a new type of encrypted communications technology, into orbit in 2016. Its first X-ray space telescope developed by the CAS, named Huiyan (the Chinese name for insight), was sent into orbit in 2017.[61] Launched in 2017 and operationalized in 2018, its first high-flux communication satellite, ChinaSat No.16, created many firsts. It has a larger capacity, exceeding the combined capacity of all the communication satellites developed and launched by China, and the two-way laser communication experiment conducted onboard made China the first country to master the high-speed space information transmission technology.[62]

Besides S&T advancement, innovative development also refers to the application of new methods and approaches to development, such as the implementation of the CMI strategy, sustainable development in space industry, promotion of commercial space activities and expansion of space cooperation.

---

59 The Law on Trademark was adopted by National People's Congress in 1982 and was amended in 1993, 2001, 2013 and 2019. Similarly, the Law on Patent was adopted in 1984 and amended in 1992, 2000, 2008 and 2020. The Law on Copyright was adopted in 1990 and amended in 1990, 2001, 2010 and 2020. The updating of simple, first versions of these laws in the 1990s was intended to keep up with rapid economic and social development, and the amendments in 2000 or 2001 aimed at implementing China's obligations under the WTO agreements. The reasons for the recent two rounds of amendments were the fundamental changes of ideas for development, requiring a better protection for intellectual property, i.e., changing the economic development pattern, becoming an innovative economy and improving the core competitiveness.
60 All key parts of Beidou satellites make in China, www.xinhuanet.com/english/2018-01/02/c_136867598.htm. Last accessed August 2021.
61 China's first space observatory turns on X-ray detectors, http://english.cas.cn/newsroom/news/201709/t20170908_182911.shtml. Last accessed August 2021.
62 China's first high-flux communications satellite is put into practice, www.chinasatcom.com/n782724/n782804/c1635703/content.html. Last accessed August 2021.

2.3.3. Peaceful Development

China's military strategy is based on the principle of "active defence", which means that "we will not attack unless we are attacked; if we are attacked, we will certainly counter-attack."[63] China does not seek world dominance and values multilateral cooperation in the international security arena. It will not, however, shrink from defending its core national security interests by developing its ability to react effectively to an attack. The dual-track approach of seeking peace and common ground while emphasizing defence is the reflection of a principle of harmony rooted in its traditional military tactics.[64]

The goal of China's nuclear strategy is to maintain national strategic security by deterring other countries from using or threatening to use nuclear weapons against China. China's declaration not to be the first to use nuclear weapons has been a staple of Beijing's foreign policy, constantly being reiterated since its first nuclear explosion in October 1964, protecting its own interest and exerting pressure on other nuclear-weapons states.[65] Half a century later, this policy has not been altered, adjusted or amended.[66]

China repeatedly declares that the primary goal of its space activities is not to gain asymmetric military advantages and continuously maintains it has not the least intention to start an arms race but every interest to avoid triggering a confrontation in outer space. Maintaining a peaceful outer space is the cardinal principle that all space activities must abide by.[67] As a strong proponent of an arms control regime, China's diplomatic space policy has long included a strong focus on multilateral measures to prevent militarization and weaponization of an arms race in outer space. It has strongly advocated for a treaty

---

63   China's National Defence in 2010, Section 2, www.scio.gov.cn/zfbps/ndhf/2011/Document/883534/883534. htm. Last accessed August 2021.
64   The Art of War, by Sun Tzu, written more than 2000 years ago, has three basic principles: war is a matter of vital importance to the state; military forces are to be used only for the maintenance of peace and order in a cautious manner; and the supreme art of war is to subdue the enemy without fighting.
65   In the first speech of PRC to the United Nations, Qiao Guanhua, the leader of Beijing's delegation, solemnly declared the no-first-use nuclear policy and called on the United States and the Soviet Union to make the same commitment for disarmament ends. R. H. Ullman, No First Use of Nuclear Weapons, *Foreign Affairs*, Vol. 50(4), 1972, pp. 669-683.
66   China is always committed to a policy of no first use of nuclear weapons at any time and under any circumstances and of not using or threatening to use nuclear weapons against non-nuclear-weapons states or nuclear-weapon-free zones unconditionally. China advocates the ultimate complete prohibition and thorough destruction of nuclear weapons. It does not engage in any nuclear arms race with other countries and keeps its nuclear capabilities at the minimum level required for national security. See China's Nation Defence in the New Era, Section 2.3, 2019, www.scio.gov.cn/zfbps/32832/Document/1660325/1660325.htm. Last accessed August 2021.
67   See the statement given by the Chinese ambassador in the UN framework regarding arms control in outer space, 10 May 2014. The common Sections 1 (3), Guiding Principles for Development, of the 2000, 2006, 2011, 2016 and 2021 White Papers on China's Space Activities.

prohibiting the deployment of weapons in outer space and the re-establishment of an ad hoc committee on the prevention of arms race in outer space ever since the 1980s in the CD.[68] Together with the Russian Federation, China argued for a new treaty as a simple, direct way to plug the existing loopholes in the international outer space law and urged the negotiation of an international treaty on the prevention of an arms race in outer space (PAROS).

It seems, however, that the international negotiations and national space policy have not always been coordinated with China's space activities; when on 11 January 2007 China launched a ballistic missile and successfully destroyed its own non-functional weather satellite, Fengyun-1C, strong objections and criticisms resounded worldwide, particularly from the United States, Australia, Canada, United Kingdom, the European Union, Japan and South Korea. However, the destruction of a non-functional satellite by a ground-based missile without hostile intention does not violate the principles governing the exploration and use of outer space for peaceful purposes according to the Outer Space Treaty or any treaty on arms control.[69]

The widespread diplomatic reactions against China were founded on two main reasons: they criticized the corresponding increase in space debris caused in near-Earth orbit at an altitude of 836 km and the lack of information on the part of the Chinese government.[70] In this connection, however, it should be taken into account that throughout the Cold War, both the US and the USSR had conducted similar tests in 53 cases. Nonetheless, the situation and the assessment of such activities have changed fundamentally, and all countries now have a compelling common interest in avoiding the massive increase in space debris. China might have miscalculated the potential impact of the debris created and underestimated the intensity of the international reaction it would trigger.[71]

As for transparency of the Fengyun-1C experiment, no advance warning or information was provided to the scientific community or to the general public on behalf of China. Only 12 days after the completion of the case, a brief official statement was issued by the Ministry of Foreign Affairs, declaring that: "it was an *experiment* that did not target or threaten any country and China opposed the weaponization of space or

---

68 China's draft decision on the re-establishment of an ad hoc committee on the prevention of an arms race in outer space and its mandate, CD/1576, 18 March 1999 and CD/1682, 30 August 2002.
69 State parties undertake not to place in orbit around the Earth any objects carrying nuclear weapons or any other kind of weapons of mass destruction, install such weapons on celestial bodies or station such weapons in outer space in any other manner. The moon and other celestial bodies shall be used by all states parties exclusively for peaceful purposes, and the conduct of military manoeuvres on celestial bodies shall be forbidden. Art. IV of Outer Space Treaty.
70 S. Marchisio, Art. IX, S. Hobe, B. Schmidt-Tedd, K. Schrogl (eds.), *Cologne Commentary on Space Law on Outer Space Treaty*, Vol. I, Cologne: Carl Heymanns Verlag, 2009, p. 180.
71 Statement of Mr. William B. Scott, Former Bureau Chief, Aviation Week & Space Technology, in *China's Proliferation Practices, and the Development of Its Cyber and Space Warfare Capabilities*, U.S. – China Economic and Security Review Commission, 20 May 2008, p. 23.

an arms race in space." Prime Minister Wen Jiabao also reiterated this during a press conference in March 2007. Such information is insufficient – raising more questions than answers – and, in fact, even years later, there has been opacity with respect to the details of this test, such as the question of who took the final decision for the realization of the Fengyun-1C test and what was its purpose, motivation and implications with respect to the choice of its timing?[72]

It might also be considered that hardly a year later, China's test was answered by the United States by targeting and successfully shooting down its re-entering satellite on 20 February 2008. The US government made a significant public case for its legitimate and responsible behaviour in conducting that interception. Before the interception, a note was sent to the United Nations as well as to several states, justifying this intentional action in order to avoid the extremely serious consequences of a potential crash on Earth of the satellite's tank, which was carrying toxic hydrazine fuel.[73] After the interception, a US government press release informed that "nearly all of the debris will burn up on reentry with 24-48 hours and the remaining debris should re-enter within 40 days".[74] This procedure is in contrast to the 2007 Chinese attitude and provided an example of how to perform space activities with due regard to the corresponding interests of other states and how to conduct consultations when national action might interfere with others states' space operation.[75] Further anti-satellite (ASAT) tests by India and Russia from 2019 to 2021 raised a new round of concern with respect to environment protection and militarization and weaponization of outer space.[76]

A further event to be mentioned is the launch of a sounding rocket on 13 May 2013, carrying several detecting instruments, including the Langmuir probe and a high-energy

---

72 Without an official explanation, broad speculation filled the void of reasons: a deterrence to the US and Taiwan; an effort to bring the US to the negotiating table over space weapons; a reaction to the emerging trend of space weaponization and the unilateral US approach to space security adopted in its 2006 space policy; assurance of space security stability, etc. E. Hagt, China's ASAT Test: Strategic Response, *China Security*, Vol. 3, 2007, pp. 14-15; M. Krepon, China's Military Space Strategy: An Exchange, *Survival*, Vol. 50(1), 2008, pp. 171-176.
73 Statement made by Ambassador C. Rocca, Permanent Representative of the United States of America to the Conference on Disarmament, Geneva, 15 February 2008.
74 At www.defense.gov/releases/release.aspx?releaseid=11704. Last assessed August 2021.
75 In the exploration and use of outer space, states parties shall conduct all their activities in outer space with due regard for the corresponding interest of all other states parties. If a state party has reason to believe that an activity or experiment planned by it or its nationals in outer space would cause potentially harmful interference with activities of other states parties in the peaceful exploration and use of outer space, it shall undertake appropriate international consultations before proceeding with any such activity or experiment. Art. IX of Outer Space Treaty.
76 Further ASAT tests are the destructive test performed by India in 2019 and the nondestructive and the destructive ones conducted by the Russian Federation, respectively, in 2020 in 2021. A kinetic kill vehicle intercepted an Indian satellite at an altitude of 282 kilometres, making India the fourth country to demonstrate such capability after the United States, Russia and China. The 2020 test is claimed to be part of the Russian direct-assent missile system, and the 2021 test destroyed a defunct satellite, weighing about 2000 kilograms, and created a certain amount of debris.

particle detector. The Chinese Academy of Sciences informed the general public the very next day about the purpose of this mission, which was serving scientific research.[77] The clear avoidance of intentionally generating debris by destructing space objects of any kind since the Fengyun-1C experiment in 2007 as well as the prompt official news release after launch in 2013 demonstrated some improvement in terms of due regard for the corresponding interests of other states and transparency. However, prior information or warning as well as a clear admission of the mission's military significance due to its dual-use nature would have been helpful in building confidence and disarm suspicion. However, China has learned a valuable lesson from the Fengyun-1C-experience, and transparency was significantly improved with respect to the re-entry of Tiangong-1 and Tiangong-2 in 2018 and 2019. (See part I).

The Fengyun-1C experiment and the unanswered questions in this respect have been undercutting China's long-established reputation, on which Chinese leadership had been steadily building in the international space community to forestall reckless actions from being initiated with respect to space activities, raising worldwide concern about China's space capabilities to attack other countries' satellites and affecting the credibility of its long-standing efforts for a PAROS treaty.[78]

This ill-proportioned price that China had to pay for a one-time miscalculation of the situation also reflected the lack of trust, the negative perception and deeply hidden apprehensions of some countries in respect of China's growing space capacity over the years.

In February 2008, the Russian Federation and China submitted to the CD a draft 'Treaty on the Prevention of the Placement of Weapons in Outer Space, the Threat or Use of Force against Outer Space Objects' (PPWT) based on the two rounds of compiling comments and suggestions on the Working Paper on PAROS in 2002 and 2007.[79] The PPWT forbids the placement of any kinds of weapons in outer space, including the Earth's orbit and celestial bodies. Both the US and the EU expressed the need for furthering address the issue of the ASAT test.[80] In response, China recognized a provision banning ground-based, anti-satellite weapons as a possible amendment,

---

77 See www.xinhuanet.com/science/2017-05/13/c_136334002.htm. Last accessed August 2021.
78 T. Hitchens, U.S. – Sino Relations in Space: From "War of Words" to Cold War in Space?, *China Security*, Vol. 3, 2007, pp. 13-14.
79 In 2002, China and Russia submitted a joint working paper on "Possible Elements for A Future International Legal Agreement on the Prevention of the Deployment of Weapons in Outer Space, the Threat or Use of Force against Outer Space Objects". In 2007, the two countries informally distributed a draft "Treaty on the Prevention of the Placement of Weapons in Outer Space, the Threat or Use of Force Against Outer Space Objects" to a number of delegations for consultation. For the PPWT draft, *see* Letter from Permanent Representative of the Russian Federation and the Permanent Representative of China Addressed to the Secretary-General of the Conference on Disarmament, *See* CD/1839, 29 February 2008.
80 Letter dated 19 August 2008 from the Permanent Representative of the USA Addressed to the CD Secretary-General Transmitting Comments on the Draft PPWT, CD/1847, 26 August 2008 and Statement of the European Union on "Prevention of Arms Race in Outer Space", 5 June 2012.

proving its sincerity in the negotiation of an international PAROS treaty.[81] In 2014, Russia and China submitted an update version of the draft PPWT with amendments in terms of definition, use of collective defence, institutional arrangements and dispute settlement mechanism.[82] Despite the absence of specifications regarding verification of compliance, it contemplates the future negotiation of an additional protocol to deal with this crucial element. At the UN General Assembly in 2014, Mr Buck, the representative of the US, declared, "the updated draft PPWT distracts attention from the ASAT systems".[83] This attitude towards China, a rising space power, has gained more attention than the specific content of the PPWT and the fact that the US consistently abstained from and occasionally voted against the United Nations General Assembly (UNGA) PAROS resolutions and its apparent reluctance to accept a legally binding arms control agreement.[84] The PPWT failed to gain sufficient support from some states, particularly the US, India and Israel. The US criticized the shortcomings of the PPWT vigorously and in detail as not being an equitable, effectively verifiable means that could enhance space security.[85] The absence of a climate for dialogue indicates that this can hardly serve as the basis for productive negotiations to break the decade-long deadlock on PAROS negotiation in the CD.[86] Taking the initiative on PAROS and proposing PPWT as the

---

81 Letter from the Permanent Representative of the Russian Federation and the Permanent Representative of China to the Conference on Disarmament, CD/1818, 7 March 2007, p. 23, para. 158. Zero-weapons Outer Space: Foundation for a Safer Space Environment, presentation by Chinese Delegation at the UNIDIR Conference on Space Security 2009, www.fmprc.gov.cn/mfa_eng/wjb_663304/zzjg_663340/jks_665232/kjfywj_665252/t575050.shtml. Last accessed August 2021.

82 The main amendments are as follows: one additional paragraph of the Preamble on the importance of compliance with the existing outer space treaties; removal of the disputable definition of the term 'outer space' in Art. I; the addition of the obligations of not engaging in, assisting or participating in activities in consistence with the purpose of PPWT in Art. II; the recognition of a possibility to use the right of collective defence in Art. IV; the recognition of the need to elaborate compliance control measures and the establishment of an organization to facilitate PPWT implementation in Arts. V and VI; the elements of a dispute resolution mechanism in Art. VII; the participation of intergovernmental organization in Art. VIII; the entry into force of amendments; and withdrawal from PPWT in Arts. X, XI and XII. *See* Updated draft Treaty on Prevention of the Placement of Weapons in Outer space and of the Threat, Use of Force Against Outer Space Objects, and Comments Regarding the US Analysis of the 2014 Updated PPWT, CD/1985, 12 June 2014, CD/2042, 14 September 2015.

83 C. L. Buck, Statement by the Delegation of the United States of America at the Sixty-Ninth UNGA First Committee, Thematic Discussion on Disarmament Aspects of Outer Space, 27 October 2014, https://unoda-web.s3-accelerate.amazonaws.com/wp-content/uploads/assets/special/meetings/firstcommittee/69/pdfs/TD_OS_27_Oct_USA.pdf. Last accessed August 2021.

84 For instance, an article wrongfully claimed that the PPWT draft did not address anti-satellite systems and overlooked the dangerous aspect of ground-based assets targeting outer space assets. M. Listner, R. P. Rajagopalan, The 2014 PPWT: A New Draft with the Same and Different Problems, 11 August 2014, www.thespacereview.com/article/2575/1. Last accessed August 2021.

85 F. A. Rose, Continuing Progress on Ensuring the Long-Term Sustainability and Security of the Space Environment Conference on Disarmament Plenary, 10 June 2014, https://2009-2017.state.gov/t/avc/rls/2014/227370.htm. Last accessed August 2021.

86 D. A. Koplow, The Fault Is Not in Our Stars: Avoiding an Arms Race in Outer Space, *Harvard International Law Journal*, Vol. 59, 2018, p. 352.

first legally binding treaty outlawing the weaponization of space has brought Beijing political and propaganda dividends: it is considered as playing a decisive role in the prevention of an arms race in outer space, although its efforts were eroded by the clear lack of coordination between the domestic space activities and the diplomatic negotiations.

Despite the assertions of peaceful aims and diplomatic efforts on the Chinese side,[87] there is concern and criticism about the purposes and motives for advancing its space capabilities and suspicion as to whether China is acting responsibly by expanding and deepening its development of space activities. Besides ideological prejudice and military considerations from other countries, this discrepancy between China's stated intention and others' perception is caused by its ambiguous position on military space activities and the PLA's involvement in the management and execution of space programmes. Although safeguarding China's security interests in outer space has been listed as one of the aims of national defence,[88] China never admits the existence of military space activities and military satellites, which is not outlawed by the international law but conforms to the non-aggressive interpretation of 'peaceful purposes' in Article IV of Outer Space Treaty and the relevant state practice.[89] The difference between 'non-aggressive' and 'non-military' lies in the two exceptional circumstances, namely self-defence and Security Council authorization, according to the UN Charter principle on the prohibition of the use or threat of use of force in international relations. In keeping with its 'active defence' military strategy, China's space activities are non-aggressive in nature.[90] The military participation was a pragmatic approach of rallying all the available

---

87 China advocates the peaceful use of outer space, opposes the weaponization of outer space and the space arms race in outer space, and actively participates in international space cooperation. *White Paper on China's Military Strategy*, 2015, www.scio.gov.cn/zfbps/ndhf/2015/document/1435161/1435161.htm. The Chinese government considers the space industry as an important part of the overall national development strategy and adheres to the principle of exploration and utilization of outer space for peaceful purposes. The 2016 *White Paper on China's Space Activities*, Preamble. With a view to ensuring the peaceful use of outer space, China has actively participated in international space cooperation and improved the ability of safe access and open use of outer space. Safeguard Interests in Major Security Fields, Part III, *White Paper on National Defence in the New Era*, 2019, www.gov.cn/zhengce/2019-07/24/content_5414325.htm. Last accessed in August 2021. China adheres to the peaceful exploration and use of outer space, enhances its capacity for safe access, scientific investigation, development and utilization, and strengthens international cooperation to ensure the security of China's activities, assets and other interests in outer space. Art. 32 of *China's National Security Law*.
88 Outer space is a critical domain in international strategic competition, and space security provides strategic assurance for national and social development, and China will strengthen space situational awareness and safeguards space assets. Section II of National Defence Policy, *White Papers on China's National Defence* of 2008, 2010 and 2019.
89 Art. 4 of the Outer Space Treaty establishes the dual-track system of peaceful use of celestial bodies and other parts of outer space and the use of force and weapons in outer space, and military use of outer space is not completely prohibited.
90 H. Guo, J. Wu, *Space Science and Technology in China: A Road Map to 2050*, Beijing: Science Press and Berlin, Heidelberg: Springer-Verlag, 2010; S. Hobe, B. Schmidt-Tedd, K. Schrogl (eds.), *Cologne Commentary on Space Law*, Vol. 1, Cologne: Carl Heymanns Verlag, 2009, pp. 70-93.

resources and spurring civil-military integration in the defence, science, technology and industry system, rather than a priority given to the military component of the space programmes.[91] China's reservations on TCBMs cast doubt on its cooperativeness and readiness to develop and implement these measures and made its PPWT proposal more like a diplomatic show.[92] The Chinese government repeatedly emphasized the non-binding nature and complementary conducive role of TCBMs in maintaining space security. China has expressed its support for the UN Resolutions on no first placement of weapons in outer space but has not made such a commitment.[93] The long overdue silence or denial of military space activities and the inflexible position in the negotiation and interpretation of international rules is a reflection of lack of expertise and confidence in interpreting international rules and the lack of coordination between the Ministry of Foreign Affairs and the PLA, or the low level of influential power of the former over the latter.[94]

A 180-degree shift of a critical position would not be easy and would also need a top-level decision and prudent handling. Interpreting CMI strategy as implying the existence of military space activities might be overstretched since there is a difference between military activities and military participation, which is explicitly allowed by the Outer Space Treaty.[95] A new provision, Article 30 of the Law on National Defence, as revised in 2020, stipulates that necessary measures shall be taken to preserve the safety of China's activities, assets and other interests in outer space. This article explicitly incorporates outer space into the traditional concept of national defence and implies the possibility of taking measures for China's safety in outer space. This is a cautious start for the admission of military space activities.

---

91 W. Rathgeber, *China's Posture in Space: Implications for Europe,* Vienna: European Space Policy Institute, 2007, p. 32; M. Aliberti, *When China's Goes to the Moon,* Berlin: Springer, 2015, p. 15.
92 Working Paper of China and the Russian Federation on TCBMs in outer space activities and the prevention of placement of weapons in outer space, CD/1778, 22 May 2006. China's Replies and Views on Transparency and Confidence-Building Measures in Outer Space Activities, A/72/65, A/AC.105/1145, 2017.
93 The unilateral pledge was introduced by the Russian Federation in 2004. Till the end of 2020, 23 states made a political statement that they would not be the first to place weapons in outer space. Since 2014, the related UN Resolutions were approved by a recorded vote of more than 100 in favour. UNGA Res. 69/32, 2 December 2014; UNGA Res. 70/27, 7 December 2015; UNGA Res. 71/32, 5 December 2016; UNGA Res. 72/27, 4 December 2017; UNGA Res. 73/31, 5 December 2018; UNGA Res. 74/22, 18 December 2019; UNGA Res. 75/37, 16 December 2020.
94 X. Wu, China and Space Security: How to Bridge the Gap between Its Stated and Perceived Intentions, *Space Policy,* Vol. 33, 2015, p. 24.
95 Among others, Art. 6.2 of Outer Space Treaty provides for the exclusive peaceful purposes of all activities on the moon and other celestial bodies, forbidding the establishment of military bases, installations and fortifications, weapons test and military manoeuvers but allowing the use of military personnel, equipment and facilities for peaceful purposes.

2.3.4. Coordinated Development

The Chinese government develops space science, technology and application through overall planning and rational arrangement with the aim of promoting China's space capabilities as a pathway to development that can achieve the integration of technological advance and economic rationality as well as the combination of long-term and short-term development.

The expansion of private sector investment in space-related activities has been an overall worldwide trend since the 1990s, and promotion of the commercial use of space has become an inevitable way to ensure coordinated development. China's entire space industry chain, from components to system assembly, remains government directed. The lack of competitiveness and a low degree of marketization would reduce the enthusiasm for innovation and would be insufficient for its sustainable development. In recent years, the commercial use of space has been transiting from long-term, strategic goals to a series of concrete and more open policy signals. The 2011 and 2016 Space White Papers designated a diversified investment system as part of the development measures, the latter White Paper using the term 'space commerce' for the very first time in this policy documents series and specified that the access mechanism would be established by a list of allowing for non-governmental investment.[96] It is further stressed in the 2021 Space White Paper by a separate subsection of encouraging the development of space commerce.[97] In 2014, the State Council encouraged and directed social capital into the construction of civil space infrastructure through government procurement. Thereby, remote sensing satellites and navigation ground systems were listed as priority sectors.[98] Accordingly, the NDRC and the MIIT encouraged 'commercial use-oriented aerospace products' and declared the goal of completing the construction of satellite system for remote sensing, communication and navigation before 2020 with the pledge of loan and taxation support.[99] The 2021 Space White Paper promises to optimize the participation of commercial companies in space industry and expand the scope of government procurement to foster the commercial market for space product and services.[100] Under the guidance of civil-military integration strategy, multiple

---

96 The common Sections 4, Policies and Measures for Development, of the 2011 and 2016 White Papers on China's Space Activities.
97 The 2021 White Paper on China's Space Activities, Section 5 (4).
98 The Guidance on Encouraging Social Investment in the Key Innovation Domains (国务院关于创新重点领域投融资机制鼓励社会投资的指导意见), the State Council, No. 60 [2014], para. 24, www.gov.cn/zhengce/content/2014-11/26/content_9260.htm. Last accessed August 2021.
99 Notice on implementing the major projects of industrial transformation and upgrade (关于实施制造业升级改造重大工程包的通知), www.gov.cn/xinwen/2016-05/18/content_5074373.htm. Medium and Long Term Planning for National Civil Space Infrastructure (2015-2025) (国家民用空间基础设施中长期发展规划), www.ndrc.gov.cn/xxgk/zcfb/ghwb/201510/W020190905497791202653.pdf. Last accessed August 2021.
100 The 2021 White Paper on China's Space Activities, Section 5 (4).

documents have called for increasing the joint construction and shared use of space infrastructure between military and civil organizations, including opening the launch sites and track and control system to commercial use.[101] A new launch pad has been installed at Jiuquan launch site for commercial use.[102]

China embraced the 'negative list' system to facilitate overseas investment, which is being shortened almost on a yearly basis.[103] Space industry never appears on the prohibition list, and foreign investment is therefore permitted, although the access mechanism in the space industry is not entirely clear. Meanwhile, foreign investment is encouraged to invest in developing and manufacturing environment-friendly new material for the space industry, and a ground testing facility for launch vehicles and the production of space equipment is encouraged in Hainan province owing to the operation of the new launch site, Wenchang. With the further development of the rule of law, the meanings of 'the absence of legal prohibition means freedom' with respect to private rights and 'the absence of legal authorization means prohibition' with respect to public power are beginning to be widely recognized. Consequently, there is no need to establish an access list for non-governmental capital in the space industry, as pledged by the 2021 Space White Paper.[104] However, the access threshold is not quite clear or might even be unreasonably high – owing to the lack of space legislation and the fragmented rules in other regulatory documents of relevance.

The open signal and supportive guidance in the policy documents offers ample opportunities for the evolvement of unconventional space actors. After four decades of rapid economic development, Chinese national-owned or even private-owned enterprises are financially capable of pursuing space programmes in a non-monopolistic, competitive manner. China is starting to witness purely commercial companies showing a keen interest in investing in outer space. The CASIC and the CASTC are eager to be adaptive to the more industrial-like context and to promote the virtuous cycle of 'faster, better, cheaper' for launching vehicles, satellite constellations and related services, as evidenced by the development of Long March 11 and Kuaizhou rockets series.

Although the opening and encouraging signals are generous, the policy promoting commercial space development is mostly at the ministerial level, scarcely coordinated and just vaguely covering certain aspects. It is therefore necessary to integrate these fragmented signals into a special, coherent, practical and comprehensive strategy that

---

101 Guidelines on Deepening Civil-Military Integration in Science and Technology and Industry for National Defence, State Council, No. 91 [2017], para. 19. The 14th Five-Year Plan for Economic and Social Development and Vision Goals Outline for 2035, Chapter 11, www.gov.cn/xinwen/2021-03/13/content_5592681.htm. Last accessed August 2021.
102 The 2021 White Paper on China's Space Activities, Section 5 (4).
103 The Industry Guidance Catalogue for Foreign Investment, first issued in 1995, was realigned to conform to the 'negative list' system in 2015, which is divided into three categories: encouraged, restricted and prohibited. The 2015, 2017, 2018, 2019 and 2020 Industry Guidance Catalogue for Foreign Investment are at www.gov.cn. Last accessed August 2021.
104 The 2021 White Paper on China's Space Activities, Section 5 (4).

should be developed into a national-level policy in order to establish an open market environment and a healthy, dynamic and sustainable space industry. Also, the policy signals of opening the space industry to stimulate innovation and to create new financing channels are not enough to infuse new energy into the space sector. In response to the emergence of commercial space companies over the last years, the 2021 Space White Paper sees the necessity of formulating the guidelines for space commerce.[105] This might lead to something, but will probably be insufficient. There is also an indigenous need for the improvement of the space legislation, and close and effective interaction between law and policy is required.

2.3.5. Cooperative Development

The complexity of technologies involved, the heavy expenses involved in space activities and the international nature of outer space entail international cooperation. The importance of international cooperation in accruing benefit for the human being has been acknowledged by the international community since the inception of the space era.[106] The principle of international cooperation was laid down in the UN General Assembly Resolution in 1961, adopted formally in the 1967 Outer Space Treaty and further elaborated in the 1996 UN Resolution on Cooperation.[107] For the international community, cooperation is at the nexus of implementing the basic principles listed in space treaties, advancing the common interests, improving transparency and building confidence to ensure peaceful purpose, building capacity to guarantee the freedom of exploration and outer space being the province of all mankind, and interfering with the dangerous trend of competition or race prevailing over cooperation.[108] For one state, space cooperative endeavours can be catered to pool financial and technical resources with added value and synergies, such as accumulating experience of multinational projects and forging allies and diplomatic partners. In this century, space programmes are becoming increasingly economically and scientifically oriented, further increasing the necessity, significance and feasibility of international cooperation.

---

105 The 2021 White Paper on China's Space Activities, Section 5 (4).
106 S. N. Hosenball, The United Nations Committee on the Peaceful Uses of Outer Space: Past Accomplishments and Future Challenges, *Journal of Space Law*, Vol. 7, 1979, pp. 95-106.
107 International Cooperation in the Peaceful Uses of Outer Space, UNGA Res. 1721(XVI), 20 December 1961. Arts. 1(3), 3 and 9 of the Outer Space Treaty. Declaration on International Cooperation in the Exploration and Use of Outer Space for the Benefit and in the Interest of All States, Taking into Particular Account the Needs of Developing Countries, UNGA Res. 51/122, 13 December 1996.
108 S. Gorove, Freedom of Exploration and Uses in the Outer Space Treaty: A Textual Analysis and Interpretation, *Denver International Journal of Law and Policy*, Vol. 1, 1971, pp. 96-101. A. Voronina, The How's and Why's of International Cooperation in Outer Space: International Legal Norms of Cooperation of States in Exploration and Uses of Outer Space, 2016, pp. 35-53, https://digitalcommons.unl.edu/spacelawthesis/1. Last accessed August 2021.

Since the beginning of its space programmes, the Chinese government has realized the importance of international space-related interactions to further the political, scientific, technological and economic goals, as evidenced by the separate sections on international exchange and cooperation in the six White Papers on Space Activities, although for almost two decades there was minimum space cooperation until the mid-1970s. The basic principles underlying China's international cooperation are equality, openness, inclusiveness, mutual benefit and common development, particular attention being paid to capacity building needs in the developing countries.[109] The policy tone regarding international cooperation is carrying out active and pragmatic cooperation in an overall, multilevel and multiform modality with other countries, governmental and non-governmental organizations and enterprises. The Chinese government encourages and endorses the efforts of domestic scientific research institutes, industrial enterprises, institutions of higher learning, as well as social organizations to conduct international exchange and cooperation in different forms and at different levels under the guidance of relevant policies, laws and regulations. As the world's largest developing country, China is willing to provide technical and financial assistance to other developing countries within the framework of South-South cooperation through various channels to achieve common development.

The purposes and motivations are practicality and participatory. Sharing the international market for space products, technologies and services and improving the space capacity of other countries can serve as a demonstration of transparency, cooperativeness and responsibility. It improves transparency and mutual trust and understanding, enhances influence over space activities and policy at the international level, helps to meet the needs of the national modernized construction by rational utilization of domestic and international markets and resources, trying to cope with the non-conventional challenges in safeguarding space security. The idea of South-South solidarity or solidarity among the Third World has been a special bond and motivates space relations between China and Asian, African and Latin American countries.

In recent years, the more assertive tone of foreign policy under President Xi Jinping is injecting new motivation to strive for achievement in cooperative undertaking.[110] China is forging its new role as a responsible power, particularly by upgrading its international cooperation model and by contributing to the resolution of global development issues, one of which would be the most frequently discussed new initiative, the Belt and Road

---

109 Part IV of International Exchange and Cooperation, 2001, 2006, 2011 and 2016 White Papers on China's Space Activities, and Part VI of International Cooperation, 2021 White Paper on China's Space Activities.

110 China's diplomatic strategy was put forward by Deng Xiaoping at the end of the 1980s as "hide our capabilities, bide our time and strive for achievement". The notion of 'keeping a low profile' has been the keystone of China's diplomacy for decades, but Deng Xiaoping had never been weak in preserving core national interests, such as protecting the territorial integrity as verified by the returning of Hong Kong and Macau. The fundamental tone of this strategy might remain, but, in recent years, the paradigm has shifted towards 'striving for achievement'.

Initiative (BRI),[111] supported by the Asian Infrastructure Investment Bank.[112] China is becoming increasingly open to space collaboration, which is part of the country's proactive institution establishment and agenda-setting efforts.[113] South-south cooperation remains its focus, and outer space capacity, including satellite application, is a listed area for promoting technological progress.[114]

In 2013, China announced its intention to revitalize the ancient trade routes of Silk Road from China to Europe.[115] This venture was further developed into two major components: one of them is overland and known as the Silk Road Economic Belt, while the other, the maritime component, is termed the Maritime Silk Road. The BRI proposes the creation of new economic corridors, spanning countries that contain almost two-thirds of the world's population and account for one-third of the world's wealth. The Vision and Actions on the BRI was drafted and issued by NDRC, MFA and Ministry of Commerce in 2015.[116] In this document, the BRI was defined as an overall proposal for promoting socio-economic cooperation with three targets: building a community of shared interest, destiny and responsibility featuring economic integration and cultural inclusiveness; four core themes of peace, cooperation, development and win-win; as well as five priorities of cooperation, namely policy coordination, facilities connectivity, free trade connection, financial cooperation and people-to-people bond.[117] In 2017, the 19th Party National Congress listed the BRI as the first priority in the pursuit of opening up strategy and major country diplomacy.[118] BRI is defined as the major platform for

---

111 It is also labelled as Belt and Road (B&R) or the One Belt One Road Initiative (OBOR).
112 White Paper on China's International Development Cooperation in the New Era, the State Council Information Office, 2021, www.scio.gov.cn/zfbps/ndhf/44691/Document/1696698/1696698.htm. Last accessed August 2021.
113 The Asian Infrastructure Investment Bank is a multilateral development bank with a mission to improve social and economic outcomes in Asia. Headquartered in Beijing, its operations began in 2016 and it has 103 members till now, www.aiib.org. Last accessed August 2021.
114 White Paper on China's International Development Cooperation in the New Era, the State Council Information Office, 2021, Section 6.2.
115 President Xi Jinping originally announced One Belt One Road during his visits to Indonesia and Kazakhstan in 2013 and was thereafter promoted by Prime Minister Li Keqiang during visits to Asia and Europe.
116 Vision and Actions on Jointly Building Silk Road Economic Belt and 21st Century Maritime Silk Road (推动共建丝绸之路经济带和21世纪海上丝绸之路的愿景与行动), the NRDC, the MFA and the MOC, 28 March 2015, www.gov.cn/xinwen/2015-03/28/content_2839723.htm. Last accessed August 2021.
117 W. Liu, An Introduction to China's Belt and Road Initiative, Oxford International Infrastructure Consortium, Global Infrastructure Conference 2016, www.oxiic.org/wp-content/uploads/2016/09/Session-1_Weidong-Liu_Oxford_Belt-and-Road-Initiative.pdf. Last accessed August 2021.
118 XI Jinping, Secure a Decisive Victory in Building a Moderately Prosperous Society in All Respects and Strive for the Great Success of Socialism with Chinese Characteristics for a New Era, the 19th National Congress of the Community Party, 18 October 2017. In 2012, China embarked on a road of major-country diplomacy, not only upholding national sovereignty and interest and facilitating domestic reform and development but also fostering a new type of international relations, Foreign Minister Wang Yi Meets the Press, 9th March 2018, www.fmprc.gov.cn/mfa_eng/wjb_663304/wjbz_663308/2461_663310/t1540928.shtml. Last accessed August 2021.

international development cooperation in 2021.[119] Corresponding to the concept of space-based infrastructure, cooperative undertakings in satellites and related application are included in the BRI. China is willing to strengthen cooperation in the application of the Beidou Navigation Satellite System and remote sensing system to provide satellite positioning and information services.[120] To promote regional cooperation, China proposed a spatial information corridor whose services will focus on South-East, South, West and Middle Asia and North Africa and could potentially extend to Oceania, East and Middle Europe and other African regions.[121]

The initial objectives of the BRI are to establish a connection among China, Asia, Europe and Africa largely through the infrastructural and transportation projects, satisfying the insatiable Asian and African thirst for quality infrastructure. The BRI, in many ways, is emblematic of the shift in China's 'going out' strategy by the effort to transform China's economic development model, to integrate its chronically underperforming regions into a holistic, externally oriented development programme and to absorb its massive excess industrial capacity. This initiative could enable closer connections among nations and enhance development by creating new opportunities for trade, investment, economic activities, technological innovation and the movement of people. This ambitious venture comes at the dawn of changing global dynamics and is interpreted as the clearest manifestation of the Chinese policy shift in international relations. The BRI has been portrayed as a mostly geopolitical project with potentially far-reaching ramifications. However, for the time being, the BRI is still at the very initial phase of realization, and its success depends essentially on the formation of an efficient institutional and regulatory environment along the trade routes.[122]

2.4. The Evaluation of China's International Space Cooperation

For a better understanding of China's space programme and policy, this part focuses on the evaluation of its space cooperation. In recent decades, at the bilateral, multilateral, regional and international levels, the intention to expand international cooperation in different forms has been more obvious, as evidenced by the growing number of

---

119 White Paper on China's International Development Cooperation in the New Era, the State Council Information Office, 2021, Section 1.2.
120 Section 4.3, Maritime Security, Vision for Maritime Cooperation under the Belt and Road Initiative, the NDRC and the State Oceanic Administration, 19 June 2017, www.china.org.cn/world/2017-06/20/content_41063286.htm. Last accessed August 2021.
121 Guiding Opinions on Accelerating the Construction and Application of the "One Belt One Road" Space Information Corridor, the SASTIND and NDRC, www.scio.gov.cn/31773/35507/35519/Document/1534094/1534094.htm. Last accessed August 2021.
122 Editorial, Transnational Dispute Management, One Belt One Road Initiative, 2017, p. 1. L. Wei, *China's One Belt One Road Initiative*, London: Imperial College Press, 2016.

agreements on space cooperation. However, in concrete terms such cooperative activities are still limited in many ways, although bearing fruit in certain areas.

2.4.1. The Overall Situation of China's International Space Cooperation

At the global level, China actively participates in almost all the space-related cooperation within and outside the UN framework, for example advocating the establishment of the UN Platform for Space-based Information for Disaster Management and Emergency Response (UN-SPIDER). Since 2014, the UN Regional Center for Space Science and Technology Education in Asia and the Pacific (RCSSTEAP-China) has provided education on space science to students from more than ten countries. The framework agreement between CMSA and the UNOOSA, signed in 2016, aims at inviting other countries to do experiments onboard China's space station or extravehicular experiments. CNSA is a member of International Charter of Space and Major Disasters, International Deep Space Exploration Strategy and Coordination mechanism as well as International Committee on Global Navigation Satellite systems. The satellites of the Fengyun series are listed by the World Meteorological Organization in the international satellite series for meteorological services. Relying on the mechanism of the International Charter on Space and Major Disaster, China has provided emergency satellite services for disasters such as floods in Sri Lanka and Bangladesh and earthquakes in Mexico, India and Ecuador.

At the regional level, after the Convention of the Asia-Pacific Space Cooperation Organization (ASPCO) came into force, in 2006, the organization inaugurated in Beijing in 2008 with a focus on promoting the peaceful uses of outer space and contributing to the prosperity of Asia-Pacific region through education and cooperative research on space science, technology and its applications.[123] Currently, there are eight member states, Bangladesh, China, Iran, Mongolia, Pakistan, Peru, Thailand and Turkey.[124] As for the Forum on China-Africa Cooperation (FOCAC), China helped the African countries improve their ability to cope with climate change through meteorological satellites monitoring and by building meteorological stations and providing personnel training and exchanges. China has participated in the promotion of China-ASEAN Information Application Center and implemented the Lancang-

---

123 The Convention of the Asia-Pacific Space Cooperation Organization, Para. 1 of the Preamble, www.apsco.int/upload/file/20180525/2018052510341620388.pdf. Last accessed August 2021.
124 The foundation of APSCO is a further institutionalization of a continued process of regional exchange in space technologies and know-how, which began more than 10 years earlier on a smaller and more ad hoc scale by a number of countries in that region, the Asia-Pacific Multilateral Cooperation in Space Technology and Applications, www.apsco.int/html/comp1/content/historytrace/2018-06-26/21-153-1.shtml. Last accessed August 2021.

Mekong Spatial Information Exchange and Cooperation Center Project with Thailand, Laos, Myanmar and Cambodia.

Since 1984, China has signed intergovernmental or inter-agency cooperative agreements, protocols and memorandums with dozens of countries, including the United States, Italy, Germany, Britain, France, Japan, Sweden, Argentina, Brazil, Chile, Ecuador, Mexico, Peru, Venezuela, Nigeria, Russian, Bolivia, Ukraine and Chile. Between 2011 and 2016, China concluded more than 40 agreements and memorandums with governments, space agencies or other entities of 29 countries.[125] Between 2017 and 2021, 46 agreements and memorandums were concluded with 19 countries and 4 intergovernmental organizations.[126] China intends to provide services to other nations relating to their satellite needs, cooperate with developed countries in the West on space research, as well as support and aid other less developed countries by offering low-cost space-related services. In 1985, the Chinese government declared the entrance of Long March rockets to the international market. Sinosat-1, which was successfully launched in 1998, was the first cooperative project on satellite development between the Chinese and European aerospace industries. Over the years, China has launched satellites for Brazil, Nigeria, Venezuela, Pakistan, Indonesia, Bolivia, Belarus, Laos, Venezuela, Algeria, Uruguay and Denmark, either in the form of payload launches or in-orbit deliveries. The Fengyun series meteorological satellites are providing highly and timely data to users in more than 80 countries and regions for the purpose of weather forecasting, disaster prevention and mitigation and scientific research.[127]

2.4.2.　　*Some Cooperative Partners and Their Joint Space Activities*

Cooperation between the Soviet Union and China started in the 1950s, and Russia is one of the key partners in China's space programmes. Under the guidance of the 2001 Sino-Russian Treaty of Good Neighborliness, Friendship and Cooperation and within their strategic partnership, close cooperation has been undertaken between China and the Russian Federation to achieve technical and resource complementarity.[128] The two countries have set up a space cooperation committee within the mechanism of regular

---

125 Section 5.2, 2016 White Paper of China's Space Activities.
126 Section 6.2, 2021 White Paper of China's Space Activities.
127 Statement by Chinese Delegation on General Exchange and Introduction to National Activities at the 55th Session of Scientific and Technical Subcommittee, COPUOS, 14 February 2018, www.fmprc.gov.cn/ce/cgvienna/eng/hyyfy/t1535268.htm. Last accessed August 2021.
128 The following are some of the space cooperation agreements: Agreement between Chinese government and Russian Federation Government regarding the Peaceful Utilization and Research of Outer Space, 1992; Protocol between China National Space Agency and Russian COSMOS regarding the Peaceful Utilization and Research of Outer Space, 1994; MoU between CNSA and COSMOS regarding Earth Observation Data Exchange, 2015; Agreement and MoU between CNSA and ROSCOSMOS on Lunar and Deep Space Exploration, 2018.

meetings between their mutual heads of governments.[129] Russia has provided assistance in China's manned space programme. In the Shenzhou 7 manned space mission, two astronauts, respectively, were dressed in the 'Flying' extravehicular spacesuit developed by China and the 'Hawk' extravehicular spacesuit imported from Russia, signalling an important event of Sino-Russian cooperation. The two states pledged to cooperate in exploring the moon and Mars and in Earth observation, satellite communication and space debris. China and Russia share a common position on the non-weaponization of space and jointly drafted the PPWT.

The space cooperation between China and the US is tortuous and minimal. They had their 'space honeymoon' period in the 1980s and 1990s, albeit occasionally interrupted for political reasons. A China Remote Sensing Satellite Ground Station (RSGS) was founded in 1986 and the first batch of data that RSGS received and processed was from the U.S. LANDSAT-5, according to the Sino-American Scientific-Technical Cooperation Memorandum.[130] China and the US signed memorandums of agreement on Satellite Technology Safeguards, Liability for Satellites Launches and International Trade in Commercial Launch Service in 1988 and 1989.[131] From 1990 to 1999, these memorandums, conducted by the Great Wall Industry Corporation, eventually allowed 26 American commercial satellites to be launched on Long March rockets by the end of the next decade. Despite the newly signed Memoranda of Agreement on Satellite Technology Safeguards and International Trade in Commercial Launch Service in 1993 and 1995,[132] this cooperation came to a halt in 1999 because of the alleged transfer of sensitive information.[133] The US 1999 National Defence Authorization Act stipulated that any items related to the missile technology control regime must be authorized by the president before its exportation to China. The US perceives China's space activities as

---

129 China open to international cooperation in future space missions, www.xinhuanet.com/english/2019-01/15/c_137743685.htm. Last accessed August 2021.
130 RSGS is one of the world's busiest ground stations and has received, processed and archived more than 40 satellites and 3.6 million scenes of satellite imagery from 1986 to 2018, http://english.radi.cas.cn/RD/crssgs/201806/t20180613_194153.html. Last accessed August 2021.
131 Memorandum on Agreement on Liability for Satellite Launches between China and the U.S., 1988, see www.unoosa.org. Last accessed August 2021. Memorandum of Agreement on Satellite Technology Safeguard between China and the U.S., 1988 and Memorandum of Agreement Regarding International Trade in Commercial Launch Service between China and the U.S., 1989, *International Legal Materials*, Vol. 28(3), 1989, pp. 595-609.
132 Memorandum of Agreement on Satellite Technology Safeguard between China and the U.S., 1993; Memorandum of Agreement Regarding International Trade in Commercial Launch Service between China and the U.S., 1995, see https://aerospace.org and www.jaxa.jp. Last accessed August 2021.
133 House Report of the Select Committee on U.S. National Security and Military/Commercial Concerns with the People's Republic of China, 105th Congress, 1st Session, 1999, www.congress.gov/congressional-report/105th-congress/house-report/851/1. Last accessed August 2021.

a possible or imminent threat to space security.[134] Some American governmental and military officers progressively advocate that China is aggressively pursuing a space programme that has military applications and that its advances would pose a greater challenge to the US military assets, thereby increasing its cost of any future conflict with China and changing the balance of power in the Asia Pacific and the world. Since 2002, in accordance with the 2000 National Defense Authorization Act, the US Secretary of Defense has submitted annual reports on military and security development involving the People's Republic of China, of which space capabilities form an important section. A consistent finding is that there is uncertainty about certain aspects of China's space strategies, policies and activities with military potential and how to use its growing capabilities.[135] Occasionally, there are positive signs. The negotiation towards Sino-US space agency cooperation on space technology started in 2006 but ceased in 2007. In January 2011, the Sino-US Joint Communiqué, following the official talks between President Hu Jintao and President Obama, revealed that the two leaders agreed to take specific actions to deepen the common dialogue and exchanges in the field of space, and reciprocal visiting arrangements for the China National Space Administration (CNSA) and the National Aeronautics and Space Administration (NASA) were initiated.[136] All these efforts were completely ended by a bill passed by the U.S. Congress in April 2011 stipulating that no appropriated funds shall be used by the NASA or the White House Office of Science and Technology Policy

> to develop, design, plan, promulgate, implement, or execute a bilateral policy, program, order or contract of any kind to participate, collaborate, or coordinate bilaterally in any way with China.

The National Defence Authorization Act (2013), which was the result of American export control system reformation since 2009, continued the prohibition on satellite sales or launches by China. Thereafter, Sino-US space cooperation has hit its lowest point, namely zero, even lower than that between the US and the Soviet Union during the Cold War.

Cooperation between China and France started in 1997 with the signing of an agreement that emphasized the scientific aspect of space activities. An MoU on the development of the China France Oceanography Satellite (CFOSAT) was signed in 2007, to study ocean surface wind and waves, and CFOSAT, the first satellite jointly

---

134 J. C. Moltz (ed.), *New Challenges in Missile Proliferation, Missile Defense and Space Security*, Special Joint Series on Missile/Space Issues, Monterey, CA: Monterey Institute of International Studies, 2003. L. M. Wortzel, *The Chinese People's Liberation Army and Space Warfare: Emerging United States – China Military Competition*, Washington, DC: American Enterprise Institute, 2007, pp. 7-8.

135 *See* www.defense.gov. Last accessed August 2021.

136 Sino-US Joint Statement, 19 January 2011, https://obamawhitehouse.archives.gov/the-press-office/2011/01/19/us-china-joint-statement. Last accessed August 2021.

developed by China and France, was launched in 2018. Space cooperation has been one of the highlights between them since the two countries entered a new 'global strategic partnership' in 2014.[137] In the same year, there was an agreement between the CNSA and the French National Center for Space Studies (FCNES) that aimed at achieving closer cooperation in oceanography and astrophysics, and they have worked on a satellite of Space Variable Objects Monitor (SVOM) to study gamma-ray bursts, which is expected to be launched in 2021. In 2016, a French device, Cardiospace, was installed on the Tiangong II module to monitor the crew's cardiovascular systems. In 2017, another MoU was concluded between the CNSA and the FCNES on the joint application on space technology for climate change research and space exploration, including near-Earth orbit, lunar and Mars exploration and manned flights.

The three-decade-long cooperation between China and Brazil in the space sector exemplifies the importance of financial and non-financial assistance efforts in the realization of sustainable cooperation.[138] On the basis of an agreement in 1984, there was a Protocol on Research and Production of the Earth Resource Satellite between Chinese Academy of Space Technology and Brazilian National Institute for Space Research in 1988 to establish a complete remote sensing system composed of space and ground segments to supply both countries with multispectral remote sensed images.[139] Afterwards, the first satellite, CBERS-1, was launched in 1999, and the signature of three more protocols led to the launches of four satellites: CBERS-2, CBERS-3, CBERS-4 and CBERS-4A in 2003, 2007, 2014 and 2019, respectively.[140] This remote sensing satellites programme not only gave Brazil a powerful tool to monitor its vast territory, but also brought significant scientific advances to Brazil. China bore 70% of the cost of the first satellite to initiate the programme and an equal sharing of investment thereafter. The Brazilian launch capability developed with the implementation of this programme. So far, all the launches have been conducted from the Taiyuan Satellite Launch Center in China, but there was a proposal to launch CBERS-4 from Brazil, demonstrating Brazilian indigenous launch capability and its viability as a future commercial launch site.[141] The impact of this bilateral cooperation has gone beyond these two countries and benefited

---

137 Sino-France Space projects put nations on right trajectory, China Daily Global, www.chinadaily.com.cn/a/201903/26/WS5c9a153fa3104842260b2b12.html. Last accessed August 2021.

138 Y. Zhao, Emerging Approaches in Development Efforts: Chinese Perspective on Space and Sustainable Development, C. Al-Ekabi, S. Berretti, *Yearbook on Space Policy* 2016, Dordrecht: Springer, 2018, pp. 265-280. Y. Zhao, The 2002 Space Cooperation Protocol between China and Brazil: An Excellent Example of South-South Cooperation, *Space Policy*, Vol. 21, 2005, pp. 213-219.

139 J. M. Filho, A. F. dos Santos, Chinese-Brazilian Protocol on Distribution of CBERS Products, *Journal of Space Law*, Vol. 31, 2005, p. 271.

140 China-Brazil Earth Resources Satellite Program, www.cbers.inpe.br/sobre/index.php. Last accessed August 2021.

141 Y. Zhao, Emerging Approaches in Development Efforts: Chinese Perspective on Space and Sustainable Development, C. Al-Ekabi, S. Berretti, *Yearbook on Space Policy* 2016, Dordrecht: Springer, 2018, pp. 265-280.

other countries also by gradually granting free access to data. After the launch of CBERS-2, China and Brazil reached a consensus on the use of CBERS data outside both territories in 2004: the downlink data were accessible to all countries and international organization through the payment of an annual fee determined by ground stations.[142] Four years later, another agreement was reached, according to which all Latin American countries and some African countries could obtain images for free, and further, in 2010, all developing countries have open and free access to the CBERS data.[143]

The space industry is identified as one of the priority cooperation areas between China and Italy.[144] CNSA signed a framework agreement with the Italian Space Agency (ASI) in 2011. Another one was concluded between CMSA and ASI in 2017 for Italian participation in the Chinese space station programme through the production of habitable modules and the performance of scientific experiments, providing also the flight opportunities for Italian astronauts.[145] A Chinese satellite, China Seismo-Electromagnetic Satellite (CSES), launched in February 2018, carried an Italian particle detector. Under the Action Plan for Cooperation of the partners, the joint intergovernmental meetings attached considerable importance to the strategic value of long-term sustainable space cooperation with increasingly specific information in the sector of space science, satellite application, deep space exploration (payloads on Chang'e 6) and manned space missions.[146]

China and Argentina signed agreements in 2004 and 2015, the latter authorizing the construction of China's satellite tracking and control centre in southern Argentina. This centre opened in 2017 and was designed to track China's robotic missions to the moon and Mars.

2.4.3.   *The Achievement and Limitation of China's Space Cooperation*

The advancement of China's space programmes and its willingness to cooperate has improved in related international negotiations and has also opened the way to potentially available platforms for international cooperation. The active involvement in multilateral cooperation mechanisms and in bilateral cooperation by providing assistance

---

142 CBERS Data Policy, June 2004, APPL-07-2004, Arts. 2, 3 and 6(b), http://mtc-m16c.sid.inpe.br/col/dpi.inpe.br/banon/2006/08.03.19.25/doc/appl_07_2004.pdf. Last accessed August 2021.
143 *See* www.inpe.br/dados_abertos. Last accessed August 2021.
144 China-Italy Three-Year Action Plan for Technologic Cooperation from 2016 to 2018; Strengthening Economic, Trade, Cultural and Scientific and Technological Cooperation between China and Italy (2017-2020) of 2017.
145 Joint Statement on the 9th Meeting of the China-Italy Joint Government Committee, January 2019, www.esteri.it/mae/en/sala_stampa/archivionotizie/comunicati/2019/01/comunicato-congiunto.html. Last accessed August 2021.
146 The Common Declaration of the 7th, 8th, 9th and 10th the joint inter-governmental meetings between China and Italy of 2016, 2017, 2019 and 2020, www.fmprc.gov.cn/web/ziliao_674904/tytj_674911/zcwj_674915/default.shtml. Last accessed August 2021.

in space capacity building and the initiative of establishing APSCO cemented China's sincerity by complying with the commitments and principles as laid down in the 1996 Cooperation Resolution and its White Papers, i.e., aiming at common development and taking into particular account the needs of developing countries. However, China collaborates with only a limited number of countries in finite fields of space exploration and utilization. China's space cooperation is more non-reciprocal and aid providing in nature rather than of mutual benefit, as its basic principles indicate. Its space partners are more on paper in the form of cooperation agreements and willingness statements than in actual cooperative and joint actions. Joint space undertakings are based more on political than economic considerations.

At the multilateral level, most cooperation is restricted to the forms of plans and proposals declarations. APSCO has merely begun to fulfil its potential of giving developing countries a collective and competitive edge into space. As the world's second intergovernmental space organization, ASPCO was inspired by its predecessor, the European Space Organization (ESA). Its aims and ambitions resemble those of ESA, and the text and provisions of the APSCO Convention borrow heavily from its European counterpart, such as cooperation patterns and dispute settlement mechanism. While ESA gears itself towards the pursuit of an integrated regional space policy, APSCO aims to promote and strengthen the development of collaborative space programmes.[147] Its member states have not traditionally been at the forefront of space activities, but at least six of its member states, China, Iran, Mongolia, Pakistan, Thailand and Bangladesh, have undertaken a compatible general socio-economic development object and space industry development as part of their national strategy. However, this theoretically high cooperative potential surrendered to impediments, primarily of a political nature.[148] The lack of strong forces towards regional integration in the Asia-Pacific region weakens APSCO's ability to become as integrated and successful as its European model. Although the Asia-Pacific region has emerged as one of the fastest growing markets for space-based services, its accomplishment, after 10 years of the water-testing phase, still remains at the rudimentary level of training courses and conferences, limited data sharing and joint development of small satellites among the universities for educational purposes, instead of establishing satellite and remote sensing capabilities covering the Asia-Pacific region, as envisaged by the original plan.[149]

There are hundreds of cooperative agreements, protocols and memorandums between China and dozens of countries, but only a few of them are steady partners, and there is rarely special treatment or priority status on the Chinese side. The volume of Sino-

---

147 Art. 2.1 of ESA Convention and Art. 4.1 of APSCO Convention.
148 C. Beischl, APSCO after Its First Decade: A Critical Assessment of Its Current Political and Legal Cooperative Potential and Related Impediments, 29th Symposium on Space Policy, Regulations and Economics, International Academy of Astronautics, 2016, IAC-16-E3.1.8.
149 For information on international cooperation of APSCO, see www.apsco.int/html/comp1/channel/International_Cooperation/28.shtml. Last accessed August 2021.

Russian cooperation is smaller than that of Russia's cooperation with the US, Europe and India. Their relations in this field have mainly been of a buyer-seller nature. The Chinese astronauts received training from Russia, but none of them ever flew with the Russian spaceships. Future cooperation would continue on a similar approach because of the Russian need for and concern of maintaining its technological lead with respect to China. The Brazilian Space Agency was a bilateral partner of NASA in the International Space Station (ISS),[150] but this cooperation was terminated owing to cost issues, and no Brazilian astronaut had been on board the ISS. NASA, however, did fund and install small Brazilian-made components in 2009.[151] There is no such cooperation between China and Brazil on the Tiangong stations. To some Latin American countries, China's space enterprises are often just one of the several international parties bidding for satellite construction and launching contracts. China Great Wall Industries Corporation (CGWIC) placed bids to build satellites for Bolivia and Venezuela and, after winning the open international bidding process, provided the majority of the financing for the development and launch of these satellites. CGWIC won the subsequent bids of Venezuela but lost Bolivia to the ESA. The relationship of Bolivia's and Venezuela's space programmes with international partners remains open and competitive.[152]

Joint efforts for actual space activities are undertaken mostly at a bilateral level in the forms of small projects, such as launches services, satellite development, import of components, construction of ground segment, space-related training as well as education and scientific experimentation onboard space station and lunar exploration. The available options for cooperation are varied. Between China and Brazil, for instance, there are several multilateral platforms for coordination and cooperation, such as the UN, the APSCO, the BRI and the BRICS.[153] Besides sharing common positions on the issue of ensuring peaceful use of outer space,[154] their cooperation activities have been merely at the bilateral levels, such as in constructing a remote sensing system over Brazil's territory,

---

150 The agreement between Brazilian Space Agency and NASA was signed in 1997 for the design, development, operation and use of Brazilian developed flight equipment and payloads for the ISS. www.nasa.gov/mission_pages/station/structure/elements/partners.html. Last accessed August 2021.
151 Space Station Assembly: the Element of EXPRESS Pallet, www.nasa.gov/mission_pages/station/structure/elements/ep.html. Last accessed August 2021.
152 J. M. Klinger, A Brief History of Outer Space Cooperation between Latin America and China, *Journal of Latin American Geography*, Vol. 17(2), 2018, p. 58.
153 Brazil signed the APSCO Convention in 2017. During the 9th BRICS Summit, Brazil, Russia, India, China, and South Africa announced the Xiamen Declaration, stressing the need to strengthen international cooperation in space activities, and the space agencies in BRICS decided to work closely to expand satellite capabilities across the global South, particularly by the programme of remote sensing satellite constellation. BRICS Leaders Xiaman Declaration, 4 September 2017, www.xinhuanet.com//english/2017-09/04/c_136583396.htm. Last accessed August 2021.
154 For example, both Brazil and China support the Russian 'No First Placement Initiative'. But the Brazilian response seems more active. It became the first country to officially heed this call outside the Commonwealth of Independent States by signing a bilateral statement at the presidential level in 2012 and prepared a draft UN resolution together in 2014.

whose data are freely available to all Latin American countries, and some African countries on the basis of their bilateral consensus without resort to any multilateral framework.

Joint space undertakings are based more on political than on economic considerations. Some bilateral cooperation was carried out within the framework of South-South cooperation through China's development assistance scheme, with benefits that are more of a unilateral than mutual nature, such as highly subsidized nature of the sales of on-orbit satellites and low-cost launches.[155] After 1999, China gradually gained a small part of the commercial market owing to the European efforts in developing satellites without US components. But this market remained modest. China's development pattern of space activities and capacity originated from the Cold War period, when the United States and the Soviet Union created space programmes focusing on military and civil programmes relying on state-controlled innovation and development. This highly state-focused strategy is becoming anachronistic for domestic transition from the planned to the market economy as well as for the development towards commercialization of space activities.

Despite its sufficient capabilities, China is not being considered as a key member of the international space club. Its scope for space cooperation is constrained by political and legal obstacles based on ideological considerations and national security concern. The major space powers strictly control the export of space-related technologies and products to China, attempting to thwart the latter's space development. Some countries, mainly the Western ones, adopt a series of technical blockades, isolation and suppression measures against China and also use international mechanisms. China currently does not have membership of any major international export control mechanisms, including the missile technology control regime and the Wassenaar Arrangement.[156] The US export control reforms, namely the International Traffic in Arms Regulations (ITAR), in recent

---

155 The budget for China's foreign aid, titled Official Development Assistance, was under the management of the Ministry of Finance, and the Ministry of Foreign Affairs and Ministry of Commerce are in charge of the actual implementation of foreign aid. According to the institutional restructuring plan of the State Council in 2018, the newly established International Development Cooperation Agency has taken over the foreign aid duties of the Ministries of Commerce and Foreign Affairs and the duties of drafting strategic guidelines, planning and foreign air policies, supervising, coordinating and evaluating the implementation of foreign aid programmes.

156 The aim of the missile technology control regime is to restrict the proliferation of missiles, complete rocket systems, unmanned air vehicle and related technology for those systems capable of carrying a 500-kilogram payload at least 300 kilometres, as well as systems intended for the delivery of weapons of mass destruction, https://mtcr.info. The Wassenaar Arrangement was established to contribute to regional and international security and stability by promoting transparency and greater responsibility in transfer of conventional arms and dual-use good and technologies, thus preventing destabilizing accumulations. The aim is also to prevent the acquisition of these items by terrorists, www.wassenaar.org. Last accessed August 2021.

years, largely aim at tightening technology trade with China and addressing the concerns aroused by national policies such as Made in China 2025 and civil-military integration.[157] The silver lining of the international and national export controls shadow is that China has built up its domestic space capabilities to the point where its satellites and launchers are becoming competitive in the global market. But these rules are a barrier to China space cooperation, at least when sponsoring large-scale cooperation programmes, such as the ILRS.

China should make efforts to change the unsatisfying situation of space cooperation and be proactive towards external sanctions and heightened export controls, particularly with the US, mainly owing to whose objections, China is excluded from major international space projects, especially the ISS, which is the most important international cooperation project in manned space activities.[158] Initially, American rejection of Chinese overtures to the ISS could be attributed to its lack of either money or technology. When China's technologies matured to the point where they could have made a useful contribution, exclusion was due to political considerations.[159] Almost all satellites, even non-US satellites, tend to include at least some American components, but tougher enforcement of US export control laws have hamstrung China's global ambitions since the late 1990s. Since 2012, no international launches have been serviced by Long March rockets owing to the US cooperation ban and export controls. The need to improve national legislation in this regard is dealt with in the next section.

2.5. Concluding Remarks

China's progress in outer space evidences the effectiveness of its policy documents. But these documents still follow the traditional top-down administrative management model. There have been attempts to replace this outdated model with a more competitive and less policy-oriented regulatory regime, such as the modern concept of civil-military integration, the transformation from independent and self-reliant development to innovative and coordinated development and the welcome policy and already signalled possibility for involving non-conventional space actors. However, more political reforms of the space activities development model and of the governance mechanism are necessary in order to stimulate a truly 'bottom-up' innovation. Relevant response and

---

157 I. F. Fergusson, K. M. Sutter, U. S. Export Control Reforms and China: Issues for Congress, IF11627, 15 January 2021; K. M. Sutter, "Made in China 2025" Industrial Policies: Issues for Congress, IF10964, 11 August 2020. See https://crsreports.congress.gov. Last accessed August 2021.
158 H. Zhao, X. Wu, Legal Aspects of International Cooperation in China's Manned Space Flights, *Proceedings of the 53rd (2010) IISL Colloquium on Law of Outer Space*, AIAA, 2012, pp. 454-465.
159 Contrary to what the name indicates, the United States assumes a dominant role and became the choice partner for space-related activities not only for its expertise but also for its willingness to share information. See K. O'Brien, China and the International Space Station: China's Distance from this Project, *The Newsletter of International Institute for Asian Studies*, Vol. 63, 2013, p. 10.

deliberations in China have only begun to take shape towards this new approach as well as to a commercially led space innovation that promises faster, cheaper and more timely technological developments.[160]

The most obvious inadequacy shows in the low level of transparency. Incremental improvements have been made in regard to the transparency of China's military and security apparatuses, and its space programmes are not as secretive as before. The release of policy and planning documents on space activities, in general, and national defence, in particular, has lifted the veil, yet certain aspects of China's space policies, strategies and activities are ambiguous, ranging from the lack of public access to some documents, such as the Space Debris Action Plan (2006-2010), the five-year plans for space activities development and the space cooperation agreements,[161] to the inconsistency and inadequacy of information on the related websites of major space actors and the uncertainty of the military significance of outer space to China.

The opaqueness in China's space policy causes and increases misperceptions and mistrust and endangers its ability to achieve long-term sustainable development. Mere information release is not sufficient, and institutional reform is required in the following aspects: first, in the unveiling and clarification of China's long-term plans and intentions relating to outer space; second, in reducing military involvement in space programmes and drawing a clearer line between civil and military programmes; third, in resorting to diplomatic instruments of dialogue in order to increase clarity on a range of defence and security issues at the bilateral, regional and multilateral levels; and, finally, in unlocking its potential in space cooperation with the aim of advancing common interests and promoting mutual trust and respect. For this reform, legislative improvement, i.e., the elaboration of a well-structured and comprehensive legal system consisting of a basic law and a set of lower-level regulation documents, is critical.

---

160 J. C. Moltz, The Changing Dynamics of Twenty-First-Century Space Power, *Journal of Strategic Security*, Vol. 12(1), 2019, p. 15.

161 13 space-related cooperation agreements with 13 countries can be found at the treaty database of Ministry of Foreign Affairs, but only one of them has the official English version, the one between CNSA and Peru National Aerospace Research and Development Commission. The five agreements between China and USA are found at www.oosa.org, https://aerospace.org and *International Legal Materials*. See the annex 6.1, 6.2, 6.3, 6.4, and 6.5.

3. China's Space Law

Within the highly political realm of space activities, space law and policy, although different in form and effect, are not always clearly distinguishable; ties between them are often short, direct and bidirectional.[1] Such interaction defines the basic tone and long-term potential of many nations' space programmes, while policies, but also capacities, give impetus to the adoption of their legal regulations and influence the content of the law.[2]

This assessment, however, does not apply in the case of China. The prerequisite for this interaction between law and policy is the existence of a comprehensive body of law and policy. Neither policy nor law has been systematically developed in China, so dynamic influence or visible institutional interaction between them is hardly distinguishable. There exists no law with special regard to regulating and governing space activities – only two ministerial regulations and a series of regulatory documents. Thereby, China's regulatory framework is disproportionally underdeveloped in comparison with its space activities and also in comparison with space legislation of other leading space nations. This is due to a variety of historical, political, legal and bureaucratic factors but certainly also to Chinese characteristics.

Outer Space Law has already been listed twice in the legislation plan of the National People's Congress (NPC) since 2013 but without indication of a definite timeline for its adoption. However, general consensus on the necessity and importance of its enactment is evolving, based on the need for a comprehensive regulation and the new emphasis on the rule of law, taking into account China's role as an important global power.

3.1. The Trend Towards Strengthening National Space Legislation

The term 'outer space law' refers to two legal branches: international and national law.[3] The foundation for the law of outer space was established at the dawn of the space era

---

1 F. von der Dunk, Current and Future Development of National Space Law and Policy, Proceedings of UN/Brazil Workshop on Space Law, Disseminating and Developing International and National Space Law: The Latin American and Caribbean Perspective, 2005.
2 V. S. Vereshchetin, The Law of Outer Space in the General Legal Field (Commonality and Particularities), *Proceedings of the 52nd Colloquium on the Law of Outer Space (2009)*, AIAA, 2010, p. 11.
3 Space law is considered as the cumulative body of national and international legislation, regulation, treaties, agreements and conventions created to enable, manage and regulate worldwide, regional and national commercial, civil government and national or regional activities in or related to outer space. Nandarisi Jasentuliyana Keynote Address on Space Law, A Concise History of Space Law, *Proceedings of the 55th Colloquium on the Law of Outer Space (2010)*, AIAA, 2011, p. 3.

when only states and international organizations were active in this regard. Therefore, space law in its beginning inevitably emerged as part of public international law.[4]

The relatively late development of national space law closely relates to the need for the further development of the existing international regime in order to attract national and foreign non-governmental investment, taking into account the increasing interests of states and non-governmental entities in commercial space activities. After all, the commercial value of space activities and the greater involvement of non-governmental entities have altered the paradigms of traditional space activities which had been taken at the time when the space treaties were drafted. Therefore, technological advancement and political development have outstripped the existing framework for international governance in many ways.[5]

In this situation, national space legislation not only plays an important role in transforming international obligations into a domestic context – for example, by ensuring that national space activities are carried out in conformity with Article VI of the Outer Space Treaty by authorization and continuing supervision of the non-governmental entities, but also[6] serve to complement international norms with regard to internal matters under the jurisdiction of individual states.[7] Thereby, national space legislation takes care of domestic needs and considerations – be it with respect to commercial interests but also with respect, e.g., to national security, export control and foreign policy interests.[8] This procedure has the great advantage of easier enactment and more flexibility, in contrast to the adoption of international treaties, thereby providing a practicable approach to fill in the gaps in international regulations.

---

4 International space law includes mainly the Treaty on Principles Governing the Activities of States in the Exploration and Use of Outer Space, Including the Moon and Other Celestial Bodies (Outer Space Treaty); the Agreement on the Rescue of Astronauts, the Return of Astronauts and the Return of Objects Launched into Outer Space; the Convention on International Liability for Damage Caused by Space Objects; the Convention on Registration of Objects Launched into Outer Space; the Agreement Governing the Activities of States on the Moon and other Celestial Bodies. V. S. Vereshchetin, The Law of Outer Space in the General Legal Field (Commonality and Particularities), *Proceedings of the 52nd Colloquium on the Law of Outer Space*, AIAA, 2010, p. 3.
5 B. Zheng, The Commercial Development of Space: The Need for New Treaties, *Journal of Space Law*, Vol. 19(1), 1991, pp. 17-44.
6 Arts. VI and VII of the Outer Space Treaty. A. G. Koroma, Foreword, National Regulation of Space Activities, in R. S. Jakhu (ed.), *National Regulations of Space Activities*, Dordrecht: Springer, 2010, p. v. I. Marboe, National Space Legislation, in C. Brünner, A. Soucek (eds.), *Outer Space in Society, Politics and Law, Studies in Space Policy*, Vol. 8, Vienna: European Space Policy Institute, 2011, p. 439. I. Marboe, Introduction and Context of 2013 National Legislation Resolution, in S. Hobe, B. Schmidt-Tedd, K. Schrogl (eds.), *Cologne Commentary on Space Law*, Volume III, Cologne: Carl Heymanns, 2015, p. 492.
7 V. Kopal, Origins of Space Law and the Role of United Nations, in C. Brünner, A. Soucek (eds.), *Outer Space in Society, Politics and Law, Studies in Space Policy*, Vol. 8, Vienna: European Space Policy Institute, 2011, p. 232.
8 M. Gerhard, Kai-Uwe Schrogl, Report of the "Project 2001" Working Group on National Space Legislation – Legal Framework for the Commercial Use of Outer Space, Cologne: Heymanns, 2002, p. 530.

The 'Act on Launching Objects from Norwegian Territory into Outer Space' was adopted in 1969 as the first national space legislation in the world, and after the late 1990s, a burgeoning of space legislation was witnessed. So far, over 40 states have enacted national laws directly related to space activities, and several others are in the legislation process.[9] Some states, e.g., the United States of America, the United Kingdom, the Russian Federation, France, Australia, Japan, Ukraine, Kazakhstan and Indonesia, have adopted special laws and established extensive legal regimes governing the important facets of space activities carried out under their jurisdiction. Others, such as Spain, Austria and Canada, have adopted laws or regulatory rules for certain aspects of space activities, including the establishment of space agencies, the licensing of launches, the registration of space objects and the management of remote sensing activities. Germany is in the process of formulating a comprehensive law, and India and Brazil are considering the adoption of a basic law.

The content of national space laws, with regard to their structure, completeness and complexity as well as to their legislative approach, are different. However, their overall objective for enacting national space law is basically the same, i.e., the implementation of international obligations and the establishment of a safe and favourable regulatory framework for space activities conducted by non-governmental entities.

3.2. The Status Quo of China's Space Regulatory Framework

Since the beginning of the space industry in the 1950s, China has accumulated a wealth of experience in space technologies and programmes enablement, management and regulation, but this is rarely mirrored in binding legislation. In spite of the importance of space capability on the government's agenda, there are no high-level laws in the national legal system for regulating, governing and promoting space activities. In sharp contrast with the other space powers, China is the only state lacking structured space legislation.

3.2.1. Major Documents Relevant for the Space Regulatory Framework

Essentially, the current regulatory framework for space activities is policy oriented with regulations and low-level regulations in the legislative hierarchy, serving as

---

9   National Space Law Database of UN Office for Outer Space Affairs, at www.unoosa.org/oosa/en/ourwork/spacelaw/nationalspacelaw/index.html. Last accessed August 2021. Among others, the essential air and space series of Eleven International Publishing provides a valuable study on national space law and policy from an academic insider and practitioner perspective. N. R. Malysheva, *Space Law and Policy in the Post-Soviet States*, The Hague: Eleven, 2018. P. Clerc, *Space Law in the European Context: National Architectures, Legislation and Policy in France*, The Hague: Eleven, 2018. M. Ogasawara, J. Greer, *Japan in Space: National Architecture, Policy, Legislation and Business in the 21st Century*, The Hague: Eleven, 2021.

supplementary support without an integrated space law.[10] The primary instruments for the administration of space activities are policy, ministerial regulations, governmental decisions and a multitude of regulatory documents and internal management rules and standards.

Outer space was mentioned for the first time in two recent laws: Article 32 of National Security Law of 2015 provides that

> the State persists in the peaceful exploration and use of outer space, increasing capacity for safe access, scientific investigation, development and exploitation, strengthening international cooperation and preserving the safety of our nation's activities and assets in outer space.

A newly added provision, Article 30 of the Law on National Defence as revised in 2020, stipulates that,

> necessary measures shall be taken to preserve the safety of China's activities, assets and other interests in outer space.

The wording of these two laws is policy tone prone, i.e., position declaration.[11] The former emphasizes the role of space capacity in ensuring national security and space security as an element of the holistic national security concept,[12] while the latter

---

10 National Legislation Relevant to the Peaceful Exploration and Use of Outer Space, UN. Doc. A/AC.105/932, 2 February 2009. The Law on Legislation divides the law in into five broad categories: constitution or basic law, law enacted by the NPC and its Standing Committee, the national legislative organ, administrative regulations formulated by the State Council, the national administrative organ, ministerial regulations formulated by the ministries and commissions endowed with administrative functions within the State Council and locally regulatory rules enacted by provincial and sub-provincial legislative and administrative organs. Besides, military regulations and rules belong to a special series of regulations. The Central Military Commission formulates military regulations in accordance with the Constitution and laws. The organs under the Central Military Commission may formulate military rules within the limits of their competence in accordance with laws and the Central Military Commission's military regulations, decrees and orders. Arts. 2 and 93 of the Law on Legislation.

11 Although the era has now passed when the policy was considered as law, the policy continues to emerge in legislation, as it did in the past. Policy expression is evident occasionally, in phrases like 'the State encourages, or supports or grants'.

12 Since 2014, the 'holistic national security concept' has started to serve as the guiding principle of China's national security strategy. In 2014, President Xi Jinping chaired the first meeting of the newly established National Security Commission and delivered a speech about China's national security. In his speech, he pledged a path with Chinese characteristics to ensure the country's overall security and specified a national security system that covers security and safety in 11 fields: politics, territory, military, economy, culture, society, science and technology, information, ecology, nuclear and natural resources. This concept expanded China's previous definition of national security, covering all the international and domestic, traditional and non-traditional security issues.

incorporates the safety of space activities, assets and interests into the traditional concept of national defence.

Furthermore, there are two ministerial regulations directly related to space activities, with registration rules for space objects and the licensing regimes for civil launches. On 8 February 2001, the Commission of Science, Technology and Industry for National Defence (COSTIND) and the Ministry of Foreign Affairs (MFA) promulgated the Measures for the Administration of Registration of Space Objects (the Registration Measures), which entered into force on the date of promulgation.[13] This is the first ministerial regulation devoted to space activities. Its main elements comprise the definition of the terms 'space objects' and 'launching state', the enumeration of the space objects to be registered, the parties obliged to register, as well as the procedures, time limits and contents of national and international registration.[14]

Space objects for the purpose of registration are defined as artificial satellites, manned spacecraft, space probes, space stations, launch vehicles and parts thereof and other man-made objects launched into outer space with the exception of sounding rockets and ballistic missiles.[15] This definition follows the Registration Convention, which defines the term 'space object' in Article Ib, including its components parts as well as its space vehicle and parts thereof, whereby according to Article II.1 objects launched into Earth orbit or beyond (which means that objects that only temporarily pass through outer space) are exempted from the registration obligation.[16]

As for the term "launching state", the Registration Measures also follow the definition of the Registration Convention, namely "a State which launches or procures the launching of a space object and a State from whose territory or facility a space object is launched",[17] by stipulating that all space objects launched from Chinese territory as well as space objects jointly launched abroad by China and other states shall be registered.[18]

The registration regime consists of two stages: national and international. The COSTIND takes charge of the administrative management of national registration and maintains the national registry, whereas international obligations shall be carried out via the MFA.[19] In the case of joint launching, the COSTIND and the MFA shall jointly identify the party obliged.[20]

---

13 The Measures for the Administration of Registration of Space Objects, the COSTIND, 2001, www.sastind. gov.cn/n4235/c16215/content.html. Last accessed August 2021.
14 X. Liu, X. Wang, The First Administrative Regulation on Space Activities in China, in Proceedings of United Nations/International Institute of Air and Space Law Workshop on Capacity Building in Space Law, ST/SPACE/14, United Nations Office for Outer Space Affairs, 2003, p. 107.
15 Art. 2 of the Registration Measures.
16 Art. 1(2) of the Registration Convention.
17 Art. 3(1) of the Registration Measures. Art. 1(1) of the Registration Convention.
18 Art. 3(2) of the Registration Measures.
19 Arts. 5, 11 and 12 of the Registration Measures.
20 Art. 5 of the Registration Measures.

The COSTIND promulgated the Interim Measures on the Administration of Licensing for Civil Space Launching Projects (the Licensing Measures) on 21 November 2002, which came into force a month later.[21] These 28 articles formulate a basic administrative structure of the launch-licensing regime and lay down a legal basis applicable to commercial launching activities. The main body of the Licensing Measures provides for the application, examination and authorization procedures for civil launch licences, supervision and administrative authority for launch licences.[22] The COSTIND is in charge of administering civil launching projects, including the examination, approval and supervision of their launch permits.[23] It must be clarified that, although the name 'interim' suggests that the Licensing Measures are temporary and will be replaced by a more permanent regulation on the same subject matter, this is not always the case. Also, other numerous interim regulations, owing to legislative delay, are not only governing but also permanently applicable regulations in nature, despite their provisional terminology.[24] But the development of rule of law and the legal restraints imposed by the 2003 Law on Administrative Licensing underline the inadequacy and inappropriateness of the Licensing Measures and clearly demonstrate that a temporary ministerial regulation, which has a lesser effect in comparison with laws and administrative regulations, is unsuitable to establish a proper licensing regime for launching activities.

In addition to these legal instruments, there are some ministerial regulations applicable to space activities. As to export control, the Regulation on the Administration of Arms Export was jointly adopted by the State Council and the People's Liberation Army (PLA) Central Military Commission in 1997. It entered into force on 1 January 1998 and was amended in 2002. The main content is that arms export should be licensed and conducted by government-designated arms trading companies in order to strengthen the unified management of the export of military products.[25] Accordingly, the COSTIND and the PLA General Arms Department published the Military Product Export Control List in 2002. In order to further strengthen the export control system and to prevent the proliferation of missiles and other delivery systems that can be used for delivering weapons of mass destruction, the State Council promulgated the Regulations on Export Control of Missiles and Missile-Related Items and

---

21 The Interim Measures on the Administration of Licensing for Civil Space Launching Projects, the COSTIND, 2002, www.sastind.gov.cn/n4235/c16064/content.html. Last accessed August 2021.
22 Arts. 5 to 23 of the Licensing Measures.
23 Art. 4 of the Licensing Measures.
24 C. Yang, G. Gao, Overview of the Current Situation and Improvement of Chinese Space Legislation, *Annals of Air and Space Law*, 2013, p. 411.
25 Several guarantees must be satisfied before allowing the export of military products: the product must be useful to the self-defence capability of the recipient country, not being harmful to the peace, security and stability of the relevant region of the world and not interfering in the recipient country's internal affairs. The Regulation on Administration of Arms Export, www.sastind.gov.cn/n4235/c61756/content.html. Last accessed August 2021.

Technologies together with the corresponding list in 2002.[26] These two regulations and the corresponding lists apply to satellites, rockets, missiles (ballistic and cruise missiles) and other missile-related items and technologies.

Fourth, the vast majority of rules regulating space activities are contained in the so-called 'regulatory documents' or 'administrative normative documents', which are non-legislative in nature.[27] There are a multitude of them covering the major aspects of space activities under the traditional development model. The CONSTIND/SASTIND and other governmental organs have accelerated the adoption process of regulatory documents and promulgated a series of them since the millennium, owing to the lack of an integrated space law and the need for ensuring the orderly performance of space programmes and to implement international obligations.

In order to quote an example, there is a systematic quasi-regulatory mechanism for space debris mitigation.[28] China's first comprehensive national action plans on space debris research and monitoring were initiated in 2001. The Space Debris Mitigation Guidelines (the Mitigation Guidelines), adopted in 2005 and amended in 2010, furnish the primary principles for space debris control. They are based on the relevant Inter-Agency Space Debris Mitigation Committee (IADC) and UN Committee on the Peaceful Uses of Outer Space (COPUOS) guidelines and specify the authority of the COSTIND for the mitigation of space debris and the protection of space objects in orbits. In 2005, the COSTIND adopted the Standard QJ3221 for Space Debris Mitigation.[29] It is currently formulating standards for the design and planning phase, as well as for launch, operational and post-mission disposal phases of spacecraft and launch vehicles to be injected into the Earth's orbit and beyond. Its basic requirements include refraining from the intentional production of debris during normal operation as well as intentional break-ups in orbit or removal of spacecraft from the protection zone into a disposal phase and call for the implementation of a debris mitigation action plan for each

---

26 The Regulations on Export Control of Missiles and Missile-related Items and Technologies, the State Council, No. 361 of 2002, www.sastind.gov.cn/n4235/c61771/content.html. Last accessed August 2021.

27 The regulatory documents are frequently called 'red-headed' documents owing to the official letterhead on which they are issued. Usually, they are presented in the decisions, orders and other official documents issued by the government agencies. They are not subject to the Law on Legislation, even though they might be considered generally binding, and not required to go through the increasingly transparent rulemaking procedures that apply to legally binding regulations and rules adopted at all levels of the Chinese governments. They have been long complained about, at least by the business community since China entered the WTO in 2001. The State Council has adopted several rounds of corresponding reformation measures and, in 2018, imposed a detailed set of requirements to govern the content and management of regulatory documents, including mandatory assessment of their legality prior to adoption. After the latest revision of the Administration Litigation Law in 2014, the regulatory documents can be the basis for contested government actions, and the courts formally began to have authority to review regulatory documents in administrative litigations. *See* Art. 53 of the Administration Litigation Law.

28 S. Li, The Role of International Law in Chinese Space Law and Its Relevance to Pacific Rim Space Law and Activities, *Journal of Space Law*, Vol. 35, 2009, pp. 546-547.

29 According to Art. 4 of the Law on Standardization, the industrial standards shall be formulated by the competent administrative authorities within the State Council.

launch activity and covering the whole course of each space object. Based on the Mitigation Guidelines, the Registration Measures and the Licensing Measures, the Interim Measures for the Mitigation of Space Debris and Protection of Space Objects (the Debris Mitigation Measures) were adopted by the State Administration of Science and Technology and Industry for National Defence (SASTIND) in 2009. They entered into force on 1 January 2010 and were amended in 2015. The Debris Mitigation Measures establish the coordination, the emergency management and the surveillance mechanisms for the control of space debris and regulate the general requirements, responsibilities and liabilities to be observed by space actors.[30] The purpose is to effectively control the generation of space debris, to prevent damage and to adhere to the requirements of international guidelines. This is viewed as China's commitment to the international community as a competent and responsible space nation.[31]

There is also another example in this respect relating to the management of remote sensing data, where the gradual growth of regulatory documents has become a relatively complete body along with the national project on high-resolution Earth observation. These regulatory documents, mostly formulated by a division within the SASTIND, include the following: the 2012 Measures on the Implementation and Management Method of National Major Specialized Project of High-Resolution Earth Observation Systems, the 2012 Notice on the Management of Civil Remote Sensing Satellite Data for Scientific Research (annulled in 2019), the 2014 Interim Provisions of Secrecy Management in Implementing the National Major Specialized Project of High-Resolution Earth Observation Systems, the 2015 Interim Measures for the Management of Remote Sensing Satellite Data in the National Major Specialized Project of High-Resolution Earth Observation Systems,[32] the 2016 Notice on Promoting the Application of Remote Sensing Satellite Data in the National Major Specialized Project of High-Resolution Earth Observation Systems[33] and the 2017 Interim Measures for the Earth System Operation Management of the National Major Specialized Project of High-Resolution Earth Observation Systems. Additional rules and standards have been formulated to promote the application of remote sensing data in some provinces, as, for instance, in Jiangxi and Hubei, and in certain industries, as, for instance, in the construction of railway and highway, aviation, forestry and mining. Based on these documents and their implementation, the Interim Measures for the Management of

---

30 Y. Li, L. Shen, An Analysis on the Interim Measures for the Mitigation of Space Debris and Protection of Space Objects, *Space Debris Research (China's Journal in Chinese)*, Vol. 17, 2017, p. 42.
31 X. Wu, China and Space Environment Protection: An Evaluation from an International Perspective, Proceedings of the 56th IISL Colloquium on the Law of Outer space, Eleven, 2014, pp. 425-430. Z. Gong, China Practices on Satellites Post Mission Disposals towards Space Long Term Sustainability, the 53rd session of the COPUOS Scientific and Technical Subcommittee, February 2016, www.unoosa.org/documents/pdf/copuos/stsc/2016/tech-21E.pdf. Last accessed August 2021.
32 http://gaofenplatform.com/contents/153/1019.html. Last accessed August 2021.
33 www.hbeos.org.cn/xwzx/3/2017-03-20/71.html. Last accessed August 2021.

Remote Sensing Data from China's Civilian Satellites have been promulgated by the SASTIND, the NDRC and the Ministry of Finance in 2018.

This pattern might also be followed by the lunar exploration project, i.e., with respect to the rules and standards concerning different aspects of the project that are expanding and materializing into a relatively complete regulatory body. The Measures for the Management of Scientific Data from Lunar and Deep Space Exploration Projects were jointly issued by the SASTIND and the China's National Space Administration (CNSA) in 2016, prescribing the administration structure and competence, the categorization of the administration method, the procedure for data release and the promotion of international exchange and data application. The Measures for the Management of Lunar Samples were issued by the CNSA in 2021 and also cover the storage and use of lunar samples on which has been collected during China's moon probe missions.[34] The singling out of CNSA for the administration of lunar samples as well as the publication of this document in an official English version – which is the very first one of this kind – emphasizes the international nature of the lunar exploration and demonstrates an improvement in international openness and transparency in the lunar programme.

3.2.2.   *Evaluation of the Current Regulatory Framework*

The existing regulatory framework has proved to be useful and effective, as evidenced by the achievement of China's space programmes. But with the increasing scale of space activities and the development in the context of the rule of law, its weaknesses and shortcomings are becoming apparent with regard to insufficient transparency, fragmentation of regimes by general rules with obvious loopholes at the low levels of legislative hierarchy.

As a first point to be considered in this regard, China's space governance is much less developed in comparison with its proficiency in space activities. There is no governing authority designated by law or by a publicly known mechanism for official decision-making and coordination. China's space bureaucracy consisted of confusing lines of authority, with a mix of different overlapping military and governmental organs, research institutions and state-owned enterprises, accompanied by complicated cooperative and collaborative relations, finance allotments and chain-of-order connections and responsibility distribution among them. This complex and unclear, multi-departmental decentralized approach of administration is one of the causes of the low degree of transparency and consistency in terms of policy and regulatory documents as well as of the absence of a transparent, coherent and compelling national strategy and a

---

34   www.clep.org.cn/n487142/n6006876/c6811125/content.html, with an English version. X. Deng, China Rolls Out Management Regulation on Chang'e-5 Lunar Samples to Boost Global Cooperation, www.globaltimes.cn/page/202101/1213156.shtml. Last accessed August 2021.

comprehensive policy guiding the long-term pursuit of space activities, including the ambiguity of the military space activities.[35] Considering the enormous size, the dynamic and acute development in China's space industry as well as the civilized and commercialized trend of space activities in recent years, such a reactive and responsive style of policy and regulatory actions are no more suitable for the country.[36]

The involvement of policymakers and approving entities and their working procedures are not entirely clear.[37] Important decisions are made 'behind the curtain', and little is known about which officials or bodies are the final decision makers – or at least the major ones, such as those responsible for lunar exploration or the 2007 antisatellite (ASAT) test. There is also secrecy about which entity has the final say in space programmes, for instance, for the lunar exploration (whether it will be manned or unmanned) and according to which priorities or elements decisions will be taken: national prestige, military relevance, technological advancement or livelihood economy? Very limited information can be found about the small groups leading the space domain. Their establishment reflects the importance ascribed to space programmes, but how these groups are selected and organized is not publicly known. According to the scarce official information, the state council formed a leading group in 1989, comprising the high-level, key stakeholders of science, industry and foreign affairs officials in order to coordinate space planning.[38] In 2004, the State Council and the Central Military Commission formed a joint small leading group for the lunar exploration programme, and a similar arrangement is reported to be contemplated for human space flight, Earth observation satellites and heavy-lift launch vehicles.

---

35 The content of White Papers on China's Aerospace released in 2000, 2006, 2011 and 2016 has followed the same pattern: purpose, vision and principles for development, programmes under way and assessment of progress during the last five years, development priorities and measures for the next five years and international exchange and cooperation. They are more like a five-year plan than a policy statement. D. M. Houpt, Does China Have a Comprehensive, Coordinated, and Consistent Space Policy? Implications for U.S. Policymakers, UMI Number: 1491425, Washington, DC, 2011, pp. 1-64.
36 Within the State Council, more and more organs are involved in the space industry with a certain power of regulating or granting critical support, including the Ministry of Industry and Information Technology, the Ministry of Foreign Affairs, the Ministry of Commerce, the Ministry of Finance, the National Development and Reform Commission, and the Commission of State-owned Assets Supervision and Administration. This created either no or reduplicative regulations in certain areas, lowering the quality and efficiency of space governance.
37 It seems that there are broadly two kinds of approval procedures for space programmes. First, a space programme is approved at the policy level after the identification of technological components required for the programme and completing a feasibility study. Second, a programme is planned in relevant policy but withholding formal approval until the researchers have proven the requisite technologies. The conventional space actors carry out the feasibility studies and act as the researchers and contractors.
38 The Notice on the Establishment of National Leading Group for Space Activities, the State Council and the Central Military Commission, see the State Council, No. 27, 1989, www.gov.cn/zhengce/content/2012-01/29/content_3295.htm. Last accessed August 2021. Y. Chen, China's Space Commercialization Effort: Organization, Policy and Strategies, Space Policy, Vol. 9, 1993, p. 48.

There is no state organ in charge of the administration of space activities designated by law. The role of CONSTIND/SASTIND relates to practical development based on its role in space industry. All governmental, military and specific space programme organs have certain power to draft and promulgate regulatory rules and are also responsible for their elaboration, interpretation, implementation, and monitoring. According to the practice, the COSTIND/SASTIND is individually or collectively responsible for the civil administration of space programmes, and the administration of military participation in space programmes is entrusted mainly to the PLA General Armament Department/ Equipment Development Department (GAD/EDD). The COSTIND/SASTIND collaborates and consults with other governmental and military departments when drafting, adopting and promulgating rules within their competence. This could relate, e.g., to the fulfilment of obligations resulting from international treaties. Then collaboration and consultation would take place with the MFA. In the case of the export control of space products, technologies and services, its partners would be the Ministry of Commerce, General Administration of Customs and the PLA. However, this overgeneralized line between the relevant actors cannot solve the complicated administrative and regulatory puzzle of space activities, which is further complicated by the nature of civil and military activities, which in many cases cannot be clearly separated from each other.

A second point is that there is no unified law codifying the fundamental and comprehensive regimes and principles governing space activities, and the current rules are scattered across various documents, with obvious loopholes. The patch-up model of legislation partially responds to some aspects of the reality needs, yet without comprehensive and visionary consideration. This has proved to be insufficient, since it does not provide a systematic and complete regulation and is not ready for the actually existing and fast-involving new conditions.

The adoption of Registration Measures was a responsive action to China's unsatisfactory practice in submitting registration information to the UN and the peer pressure from other states. However, the institutional arrangement in respect of Registration Measures is incomplete. There is no regulatory provision concerning the consequences for non-registration or late or incomplete action in this respect.[39] In view of the lack of a visionary perspective, there are no provisions either concerning the ownership transfer of a space object in orbit, taking into account the growing frequency of ownership changes in space commerce. Article 9 stipulates that registration information should be amended in the case of major changes in the conditions of a space object registered, regardless of whether it has ceased to be functional or has re-

---

39 J. Li, Progressing Towards New National Space Law: Current Legal Status and Recent Developments in Chinese Space Law and Its Relevant to Pacific Rim Space Law and Activities, *Journal of Space Law*, Vol. 35, 2009, p. 450. H. Zhao, The Status Quo and the Future of Chinese Space Legislation, *Zeitschrift für Luft- und Weltraumrecht (German Journal of Air and Space Law)*, Vol. 58(1), 2009, pp. 107-108.

entered the Earth's atmosphere. But the date of ownership change and the identification of the new owner, operator and controller is not included in the major changes, contrary to the UNGA Resolution on Recommendation for Registration of Space Objects.[40]

'Unconventional space actors', such as Tsinghua University and Harbin Institute of Technology, for example, developed their own microsatellites around the millennium and their inquiries for legal rules and procedures even embarrassed the government.[41] The adoption of the Licensing Measures was based on the practice gained from issuing licences in these cases. Twenty years later, the substantive contents of Licensing Measures are still being applied, being almost parallel to the regime design in other countries. Now, however, the Licensing Measures are outdated. They are still adhering, e.g., to the notion of launching activities sponsored by governmental capital, defined as launch projects that were common in former times – without consideration of private participation.[42]

Among the authorization conditions, it is obligatory to obtain third-party liability insurance, albeit with no indication of the amount to be purchased or the criteria to be determined. It is uncertain whether such an obligation is relevant only for the launch itself or whether it also covers damages in orbit. There is no state recourse arrangement towards private actors after compensation for damages caused by their space activities to a third party.[43] After years of practice, the SASTIND seemed to realize the inadequacy of the insurance clause, and the documents on purchasing third-party liability insurance were listed as a precondition for launch authorization in a 2018 regulatory document.[44]

---

40 *See* the Resolution on Recommendations on Enhancing the Practice of States and International Governmental Organizations in Registering Space Objects, 17 December 2007, UNGA Res. 62/101.
41 The microsatellite, Tsinghua-1, was jointly developed by Tsinghua University and UK Surrey Satellite Technology Limited. In December 1999, the Ministry of Education, on behalf of Tsinghua University, submitted an application to the COSTIND for its launch, and the Commission of Science, Technology, and Industry for National Defence (CONSTIND) issued the licence within that month. Tsinghua-1 was launched in Russia on 28 June 2000. Soon after the launch of Tsinghua-1, Space Tsinghua Satellite Technology Company was established. In China, this is the first time that a first-class university collaborates with a foreign enterprise to fund and share resources in a joint space business venture. H. Zhao, The Status Quo and the Future of Chinese Space Legislation, *Zeitschrift für Luft- und Weltraumrecht (German Journal of Air and Space Law)*, Vol. 58(1), 2009, p. 112.
42 The COSTIND shall generally plan and administrate a project and shall be responsible for examining, approving and supervising the project, which means that a project could not acquire the launch licence if the project has not been listed in the plan of the COSTIND. *See* Art. 4 of the Licensing Measures.
43 A permit holder must comply with the relevant national regulations to insure himself against liability incurred in respect to damage or loss suffered by third parties and against other liability incurred by launching a space object. *See* Art. 19 of the Licensing Measures. This article constitutes the legal framework for space insurance. But it is the 'permit holder' who must purchase insurance before the relevant launch activity rather than the applicant of the permit. This means that the conditions for applying for a permit as regulated by the Licensing Measures do not include the necessity of purchasing insurance.
44 In 2018, the SASTIND released the Application Guidance for the civil space launch projects, www.sastind.gov.cn/n6195634/n6195706/n6195716/n6427833/c6428394/content.html. Last accessed August 2021. H. Yu, Studies on National Space Legislation for the Purpose of Drafting China's Space Law, Doctoral Dissertation, Leuphana University Lueneburg, pp. 153-155.

However, this can hardly qualify as an official legislation act, but serves only as an expedient measure. These loopholes in the liability context need to be addressed in the future law, taking into account the diversity of space actors and investment, and the relationship between the state and private entities should be settled.

In addition, there is a need to systematically implement the international treaty provisions by domestic law and thereby keep up with the international requirements for transparency improvement. Other spacefaring nations have long been working in this field and have accelerated space legislation implementing international obligations, thereby improving their increasingly transparent practice with regard to space activities. Since the 1990s, for instance, not only space objects but also their re-entries were registered.[45]

The Licensing Measures cannot be qualified as a comprehensive body for the authorization of space activities. Its scope of application is limited to the civil launch projects but does not cover the whole course of civil space activities from the development and production of space vehicles and spacecraft to their re-entry. A legislative vacuum exists concerning the rescue and return of astronauts, the return of other countries' space objects on Chinese territory as well as the compensation for damage caused by space objects.[46] The attribution of non-governmental activities to states is unique in international law and the state parties shall bear international responsibility for national activities carried out in outer space and for ensuring that national activities are carried out in conformity with international law, regardless of the nature and purpose of space activities.[47] China's incomplete domestic legislation does not release it from its international responsibility and liability under the Outer Space Treaty, the Liability Convention and the Rescue Agreement, but might cause neglect and delay of compliance.[48]

As a third point, these documents were drafted by different organs in different forms. Thereby, they are neither systematic nor uniform but often inconsistent with conflicting terms and provisions. This is the result of the multi-departmental decentralized approach of the administration, whereby different ministries and departments promulgate,

---

45 For instance, the Russian Federation and Italy have submitted to the UN a notification on the re-entry of space objects of Mir, Mars 96 and BeppoSAX. Note Verbale from the Permanent Mission of the Russian Federation to the United Nations Secretary-General on the Re-entry of Mars 96, 18 November 1996, A/AC.105/648. Note Verbale from the Permanent Mission of the Russian Federation to the United Nations Secretary-General on the Re-entry of Mir, 23 January 2001 and 28 February 2001, A/AC.105/759 and A/AC.105/759/Add.1. Note Verbale from the Permanent Mission of Italy to the United Nations Secretary-General on the Re-entry of BeppoSAX, 12 December 2002, A/AC.105/803. This is one of the persuasive reasons for China to publish information on its space lab's re-entries.
46 H. Zhao, X. Wu, Reflections on Future Space Legislation in China, Proceedings of the 49th Colloquium on the Law of Outer Space, AIAA, 2007, pp. 440-446.
47 Art. VI of Outer Space Treaty and Liability Convention.
48 A party may not invoke the provisions of its internal law as justification for its failure to perform a treaty. Art. 27 of Vienna Convention on the Law of Treaties, United Nations Treaty Series, Vol. 1155, p. 331.

implement and interpret the rules according to their own needs and understanding. Also, the absence of a basic space law causes a low level of consistency and systematization in the existing regulatory framework.

A considerable number of rules in a collection of various documents interact with each other but these rules are unevenly developed and mostly overgeneralized, and some of them are even unsuitable and difficult to comprehend and execute. Almost all of the military regulatory documents and some of the civil ones are publicly unattainable since they are drafted either in the form of internal management rules or as classified documents.[49] Assessing unsystematic and conflicting rules in this respect is reasonable speculation owing to the unclear line of authority divisions as well as the temporary and awkward coordination, the patch-up approach to regulation in general and the closed-door drafting method.

There are certain signs of systemization among the ministerial regulations and regulatory documents issued by the COSTIND/SASTIND, but the result is far from satisfactory. They are in some ways in concert with each other, but the discrepancy of terminology used in these documents is problematic. For example, the Registration Measures use the term 'space object' with a definition, while the Licensing Measures use the term 'spacecraft' without a definition.

As to the reference to subjects of obligations, the situation is most troublesome owing to inconsistent formulations: in the Registration Measures, reference is made to governmental departments, juridical and natural persons and other organizations that launch or procure the launching of a space object as well as the owners of space objects – in other words, launcher and owners.[50] As to the Interim Measures for the Management of Civil Satellite Projects (Projects Management Measures), promulgated by SASTIND in 2016, owners, users and operators of space objects (who might not be the launchers) are referred to.[51]

As another example, according to the Licensing Measures, the general project contractors for launching civil space objects or the owners of a spacecraft shall be the applicants for licences.[52] But while space debris mitigation is a precondition for obtaining a licence, the enumeration of the responsible actors in this respect does not correspond to the licence applicants. According to the Debris Mitigation Measures, such responsibility is imposed on the units are participating in the development and manufacturing of launch vehicles and spacecraft as well as on the central governmental organs as the

---

49 Sometimes, the formal misplacement is the other way around, suitable in the form of internal rules but represented as a regulatory document. For instance, the Interim Measures for the Management of Civil Satellite Projects are based on the management experience of previous satellites' projects financed by governmental budget, neglecting the diversity of space actors and financial resources in recent years.
50 Arts. 4, 7 and 8 of the Registration Measures.
51 Art. 12 of the Interim Measures for the Management of Civil Satellite Projects.
52 Art. 2 of the Licensing Measures.

clients of the launch services, without mentioning the local governmental organs and other entities, who might be other kinds of actual clients of launch services.[53]

In response to the State Council reformation orders, the COSTIND/SASTIND undertook the examination, updating and revision of all documents of regulatory nature within its competence several times with the aim of improving their consistency, the elimination of unnecessary intervention into market operations and the limitation of individual rights.

At least since 2007, the COSTIND has examined hundreds of administrative regulations, ministerial regulations and regulatory documents whereby some of them were revised or abolished.[54] According to the publicly accessible information, 14 regulatory documents were abolished in 2019, including the ones relating to space activities.[55] There is also a similar reformation effort within the military. But there is no integrated action between the responsible civil and military departments for the space industry. Therefore, this deeply entrenched situation and the absence of a basic law for space activities cannot be improved or remedied through fragmented reformative efforts.

As a fourth point, most documents within the current regulatory framework are at a low or even zero level of binding force with a limited scope of application. The ministerial organs subordinated directly to the State Council may formulate ministerial regulations within the limits of their competence, which are at the second-lowest level in the legislative hierarchy, inferior to that of the Constitution, laws and administrative regulations.[56] The only two systematic regulations on space activities, the Registration Measures and the Licensing Measures, belong to the rules formulated by the State Council's ministries. They furnish a relatively sound space objects registration and launch-licensing regime, but the low hierarchical level and competence of COSTIND/SASTIND limit their scope of application, and there is ignorance about their observance.

The Licensing Measures apply to civilian launch activities on China's territory but also to cases where a spacecraft is owned by a Chinese national and the launch occurs outside the country. Civilian is clarified as 'non-military' and therefore excludes military space launch activities.[57] Occasionally, the Licensing Measures remain unobserved, for instance when small satellites of domestic development are launched by foreign rockets or when payloads are operated by governmental organs of higher hierarchical level than the COSTIND/SASTIND or when civil payload launches are conducted by the PLA.

---

53 Y. Li, L. Shen, An Analysis on the Interim Measures for the Mitigation of Space Debris and Protection of Space Objects, *Space Debris Research (China's Journal in Chinese)*, Vol. 17, 2017, p. 43.
54 The notice on Clearing Out Administrative Regulations and Ministerial Regulations, the State Council General Office, No. 12, 2007, www.gov.cn/zwgk/2007-03/08/content_545924.htm. Last accessed August 2021.
55 The Order on Abolishing Certain Regulatory Documents, the SASTIND, 2019, www.sastind.gov.cn/n4235/c6806821/content.html. Last accessed August 2021.
56 Arts. 2 and 65 of the Law on Legislation.
57 Art. 2 of the Licensing Measures.

In general, the Registration Measures apply to all the space objects launched in Chinese territory as well as to the space objects jointly launched abroad by China and other states.[58] But since these rules are adopted by an organ of the State Council, they can hardly be taken as being obligatory by the military, which is responsible for the launching of most space objects. Therefore, the Registration Measures are unable to guarantee the timely international registration of all space objects launched by China.

The vast majority of regulatory documents are those adopted by the COSTIND/SASTIND and its internal divisions as well as organs of the space programmes. The rules contained in the regulatory documents are not officially recognized as binding rules according to China's Constitution and the Law on Legislation, which substantially affect their scope of application and relevance in practice without the support of higher-level documents.

For example: the regulatory documents on remote sensing data management are formulated by a division of the SASTIND and are applicable only to the national projects on high-resolution Earth observation and government-funded remote sensing satellite projects. The Projects Management Measures are applicable to the satellite projects funded and approved by the State Council and its ministries. The Measures for the Management of Scientific Data of Lunar and Deep Space Exploration Projects address only four units, namely CAS, the space activities division of PLA Strategic Support Force, the CASIC and the CASTC.[59]

As a fifth point, the transparency degree of regulation is low. There is no accessible number as to how many regulatory documents and internal rules and standards have been adopted over the years and how many of them are still applicable. From 1982 to 1992, the former Ministry of Space Industry and its successor, the former Ministry of Aerospace Industry, elaborated around 300 internal regulatory documents concerning various aspects of space programme management such as planning, technology, quality control, security and finance.[60] But most of them were not publicly promulgated and are thereby not generally accessible legal rules in the traditional sense. Since this regulatory and administrative model has remained unchanged, at least to some extent, then given the current size, long-time experience and complexity of China's space programmes, the number of these documents would still grow significantly, albeit with problems of transparency still unsolved.

The low-level transparency of rules renders the compliance process complicated and time-consuming and confers unnecessary discretionary power on entities in charge of the administration. Also, secrecy, together with the fragmented rules and wide discretion,

---

58 Arts. 5, 6, 9, 11 and 12 of the Registration Measures.
59 *See* www.sastind.gov.cn/n4235/c6805195/content.html. Last accessed August 2021.
60 Y. Qi, A Study of Aerospace Legislation of China, *Journal of Space Law*, Vol. 33, 2007, pp. 405-410. H. Zhao, The Status Quo and the Future of Chinese Space Legislation, *Zeitschrift fur Luft und Weltraumrecht*, Vol. 1, 2009, pp. 101-102.

violates the basic requirement imposed by the rule of law for transparency and predictability and is a big hurdle for the participation of 'unconventional' actors, uplifting the threshold for the space industry.

The purpose of the Debris Mitigation Measures, protecting the space environment, determines the necessity of ensuring the widest dissemination of relevant rules to be observed. However, they were first defined as a classified, publicly inaccessible document and were changed into an internal document only after years of arguments and protest, both nationally and internationally.[61]

As for unclassified documents, they are issued through traditional channels, i.e., documents in paper format being delivered to the relevant conventional actors only. There is news with regard to the adoption of some regulatory documents, but their texts cannot be found on the Internet, such as the 2012 Measures for the Implementation and Management Method of National Major Specialized Project of High-Resolution Earth Observation Systems, the 2012 Notice on the Management of Civil Remote Sensing Satellite Data for Scientific Research (annulled in 2019), and the 2014 Interim Provisions of Secrecy Management in Implementing the National Major Specialized Project of High-Resolution Earth Observation Systems. Sometimes, there is a substantial delay in publication. For example, the Measures for the Management of Scientific Data of Lunar and Deep Space Exploration Projects were issued in 2016 but were not published until 2019.[62]

3.3. Why Has No Space Law Been Adopted for Six Decades?

A variety of historical, political, legal and bureaucratic reasons account for the decade-long absence and delay of the space legislation process.

3.3.1. The Starting-Late Development of the Rule of Law

China did not embrace the notion of the rule of law until the late 1990s. Since the foundation of the People's Republic of China, law was marginalized from 1949 to the

---

61 China informed the UN COPUOS of the adoption of the Debris Mitigation Measures and provided some introductory information about its relevant national mechanism without submitting the text. See Z. Gong, CASC Efforts on Dealing with Space Debris toward Space Long Term Sustainability and China Practices on Satellites Post Mission Disposals towards Space Long Term Sustainability, the 50th and 53rd session of the COPUOS Scientific and Technical Subcommittee, 2013 and 2016, www.unoosa.org/pdf/pres/stsc2013/2013lts-03E.pdf and www.unoosa.org/documents/pdf/copuos/stsc/2016/tech-21E.pdf. There is no information on China's national mechanism in the Compendium of Space Debris Mitigation Standards, www.unoosa.org/oosa/en/ourwork/topics/space-debris/compendium.html. Last accessed August 2021.
See http://gaofenplatform.com/contents/153/1019.html. Last accessed August 2021.
62 See www.sastind.gov.cn/n4235/c6807016/content.html. Last accessed August 2021.

late 1970s except briefly in the 1950s. Legal reform began in 1978, when Deng Xiaoping announced his platform to modernize China aiming at economic development, and ever since then China has engaged in perhaps the most rapid development of a legal system in the history of the world.[63] The entire legal system has been rebuilt and fundamentally transformed, driven primarily by the large enterprise of economic reform and benefiting from its participation in the international legal order. The concept of 'socialist market economy' made its way into the Constitution in 1993 with an amendment that stressed the role of economic legislation facilitating the development of a socialist market economy.[64] Thereafter, the legal system has steadily progressed, whereby major historic developments have been achieved by the amendment of the Constitution along the lines of the uppermost maxim of 'ruling the country in accordance with the law and establishing a socialist rule-of-law state' in 1999 and by announcing the finalization of a socialist legal system in 2011 as well as with the focus of the National Party Session on the rule of law in 2014.[65] Since the outset of his mandate, President Xi Jinping has stated that the rule of law is a priority item on his agenda. The Fourth Plenary Session of the 18th Party Congress in 2014 was the first national party session centring on the rule of law with the aim of promoting the governing system and the modernization of governance capabilities as well as the speeding up of the rule-of-law development. This session depicted a blueprint for building the rule of law and proposed new requirements for its comprehensive advancement.[66]

The legislative institutions were overwhelmed by the workload since the 1980s, and they hardly noticed the legal requirements in the outer space domain, which was barely

---

63 A return to law began in 1978 with the introduction of 'socialist legality' in a speech by Deng Xiaoping to the 3rd plenary session of the 11th Central Committee of the Communist Party, explaining the need for a wide-ranging, complete set of authoritative, constantly applied law. M. Delmas-Marty, Present-day China and the Rule of Law: Progress and Resistance, *Chinese Journal of International Law*, Vol. 2, 2003, p. 11. B. L. Liebman, Assessing China's Legal Reforms, *Columbia Journal of Asian Law*, Vol. 23, 2009, p. 18.

64 Constitutional Amendment adopted by the first session of 8th National People's Congress, 29 March 1993, www.npc.gov.cn/wxzl/gongbao/1993-03/29/content_1481290.htm. Last accessed August 2021.

65 Constitutional Amendment adopted by the second session of 9th National People's Congress, 15 March 1999, www.npc.gov.cn/wxzl/wxzl/2000-12/10/content_7075.htm. The construction of a socialist legal system is completely grounded in China's national conditions and reality, consisting of multilevel legal rules, including constitution, law, administrative regulations and local regulation, adaptive to the needs of reformation and opening up and the modernization construction. Speech of Wu Bangguo, the Chairman of NPC Standing Committee, on the completion of constructing a socialist legal system, 26 January 2011, www.gov.cn/ldhd/2011-01/26/content_1793094.htm. The 4th Plenary Session of the 18th Central Committee of the Communist Party adopted the Decision on Major Issues Concerning Comprehensively Advancing the Rule of Law, 23rd November 2014, http://cpc.people.com.cn/n/2014/1029/c64387-25927606.html. Last accessed August 2021.

66 The Decision on Major Issues Concerning Comprehensively Advancing the Rule of Law, 23rd November 2014, *ibid.*

connected to daily life or related to economic development.[67] There were many important matters in need of legal regulation, and many laws need to be updated and amended, which fully occupied the NPC. The first proposal for space legislation emerged at the NPC in the early 1990s, when China's space programmes progressed towards their maturity and began to draw public attention. The space capacity, then, has given China the required capability to enhance its social, economic, industrial and technological development, and space applications have expanded.[68] The phenomenal developments in outer space have become an indispensable part of China's comprehensive national power and have also improved the influential power of the space industry. Some NPC deputies from the space industry were referring to the legal vacuum in space activities and submitting practice-oriented legislation proposals for a law for space activities.[69] At the NPC session in 2007, they jointly submitted the 'Proposal on Speeding up the Legislation of China's Space Activities' for the first time.[70] Initially, it was the NPC deputies from space industry who were advocating for the adoption of a space law with fractional arguments from their own perspectives. In recent years, however, more deputies from within and outside the space industry have come together and submitted convincing proposals during the yearly NPC sessions.[71]

The legal system in China is moving towards greater compliance with the requirements of the rule of law, which has become an important part of state ideology

---

[67] The NPC and its Standing Committee exercise the law-making power in China. *See* Art. 58 of Constitution. China witnessed the massive and rapid enactment and amendments of laws, including constitution, criminal code, and civil law. Between 1976 and 1998, the NPC passed more than 337 laws. Until the end of 2010, there were (then effective) 236 laws, more than 690 administrative regulations and 8600 local regulatory rules. *See* Wu Bangguo Report to the National People's Congress Session of 2011. Until the end of 2020, there are currently effective 275 laws, 609 administrative regulations and 16000 local regulatory rules. *See* the national database of laws and regulations, https://flk.npc.gov.cn/xzfg.html. Last accessed August 2021.

[68] The major space application is in the satellites sphere, including Earth observation satellites, communication and broadcasting satellites, and navigation and positioning satellites. Transformation of other space technology is becoming a business model to provide products and services to relevant industries, such as propelling the development of new materials and intelligent manufacturing. The 2016 White Paper on China's Space Activities, Section 2 (7).

[69] The entire Congress is composed of nearly 3000 deputies, and dozens of deputies compose a small part of it. But the success of space activities and the influence of these deputies guaranteed the attention from the whole Congress and of national society.

[70] Y. Qi, A Study of Aerospace Legislation of China, *Journal of Space Law*, Vol. 33, 2007, p. 407.

[71] For example, Lei Jun, a Chinese business executive who is a co-founder and CEO of electronics maker Xiaomi Corp., submitted a proposal to the NPC on expediting space legislation work to promote the development of commercial space activities, http://tech.china.com.cn/it/20190304/352925.shtml. Last accessed August 2021.

and state legitimacy.[72] Law is beginning to impose meaningful restraints on the ruling power, as demonstrated by the changing concept of administrative law. In the 1980s, administrative law was conceived as a body of law dealing with the restructuring of government organizations and the institutionalization of state administration in order to guarantee the effectiveness and efficiency of administrative functions and powers.[73] There was little discussion about the protection of individuals against the abuse or misuse of government powers until the adoption of 1989 Administrative Litigation Law. This law signified a new concept, with respect to the control of power, which has been gradually translated into legislation and practice.[74] In other words, law is designed to limit the government's power, establish adequate administrative procedures and foster responsible governance. This changing concept of administrative law has been triggered, nourished and pushed forward by many reasons over the last decades. First, the fundamental transformation from the former planned economy into a more market-oriented paradigm makes the new type of governance indispensable. Second, the international obligations, for instance under human rights treaties and the WTO framework, require China's legal environment and law enforcement to be rational and accountable. Third, the increasing legal awareness of ordinary people helps them change their anticipation and perception of the administrative authority, which geared the administrative reform towards the rule of law. Finally, the government has learned a lesson from different incidents and crises and has thereby re-evaluated the importance of power control.[75] However, space programmes have retained a comparatively isolated domain, and space governance needs to be updated in order to catch up with this transformation process.

---

72 The rule of law, as a major political concept, is essentially contested. There is a need to rethink this concept to understand the likely path of China's legal system development and the reasons for differences in its institutions, rules, practices and outcomes. There is considerate direct and indirect evidence that China is in the midst of a transition towards some version of rule of law. R. Peerenboom, *China's Long March towards Rule of Law*, Cambridge: Cambridge University Press, 2002, pp. 5-6. B. L. Liebman, Assessing China's Legal Reforms, *Columbia Journal of Asian Law*, Vol. 23, 2009, p. 17.
73 This initial concept needs to be understood in the historical context of the times. For Deng Xiaoping, the major problems inherent in the party and state leadership and the cadre system were bureaucratization, over-concentration of power and privileges of various kinds. His major concern was the efficiency of government and not government accountability, at least not towards the governed.
74 This law was followed by the 1990 Administrative Reconsideration Regulations, the 1990 Administrative Supervision Regulations, the 1994 State Compensation Law, the 1996 Administrative Penalty Law, the 2003 Administrative Licensing Law, the 2005 Law on Public Servants and their amendments. From 1990 to the end of 2004, there were 1,246,270 administrative cases adjudicated, with the annual caseload increasing by 17% on average. From 2000 to 2019, the number of administrative lawsuits has increased from 85,760 in 2000 to 220,398 in 2015 and to 223,712 in 2019, almost tripled over 10 years. Though considerably less than the number of civil lawsuits during the same period, this is still a big number. For the statistics, *see* the Work Report of the Supreme People's Court of corresponding years and the website of the Ministry of Justice, www.moj.gov.cn/organization/content/2020-09/29/560_3257263.html. Last accessed August 2021.
75 K. Zou, Administrative Reform and Rule of Law in China, *The Copenhagen Journal of Asian Studies*, Vol. 24, 2006, pp. 5-7.

3.3.2. The Initial Lack of Need for Space Legislation Owing to China's Model Development

China's space capabilities have evolved and passed significant milestones since their inception in the mid-1950s with no legal rules in the official form until 2001. The initiation of China's space programmes had its origins in the systematic competition of the superpowers during the Cold War with more or major emphasis on military capacity and national prestige than on social and technological advancement.[76] The policy-administrative-order-oriented approach was rooted in the Cold War era and the planning economy. The Chinese government and its affiliated organs, including state-run or state-owned enterprises and government-funded research organs, have been the dominant players and the sole participants in space activities ever since. Space activities have long been governed by the policy and administrative decree system so that space law at the national level did not appear to be a necessity.[77] There was no need for authorization and supervision until the non-governmental entities began to invest or to participate in space activities.

China as a spacefaring nation that lacks a proper space law for many years is not unique owing to its development model and relative slowness in embracing the commercial potential of space. There was no space law in the USSR after the launch of Sputnik in 1957, and the regulation of space activities was embodied in special resolutions and decisions of governmental and political bodies.[78] The Law on Space Activities, which was the first of its kind in the history of Russia (succeeding the USSR), was passed in 1993, when the nature of space activities in the Russian Federation transformed in that country.[79] The Russian Federation took the major share of Soviet space activities, and this transformation was accompanied by increasing opportunities for private or quasi-private entities to be involved in such activities. The promulgation of the 1993 Space Law was motivated largely by a desire to deal with the private involvement in outer space.[80]

As for France, the third major spacefaring country and the main launching state in Europe, space activities had been regulated by general civil, administrative and criminal

---

76 M. Bourbonniere, National-Security Law in Outer Space: The Interface of Exploration and Security, *Journal of Air Law and Commerce*, Vol. 70, 2005, p. 3.
77 J. Li, Progressing towards New National Space Law: Current Legal Status and Recent Developments in Chinese Space Law and Its Relevant to Pacific Rim Space Law and Activities, *Journal of Space Law*, Vol. 35, 2009, p. 442.
78 S. P. Malkov, C. Doldirina, Regulation of Space Activities in the Russian Federation, in R. S. Jakhu (ed.), *National Regulation of Space Activities*, Dordrecht: Springer, 2010, p. 315.
79 The 1993 Law on Space Activities is comprehensive and covers a wide range of relations with respect to the organization of space activities, the powers of the state administration in space matters, the financing of the space sector, the licensing process and the registration of objects launched into outer space. N. R. Malysheva, *Space Law and Policy in the Post-Soviet States*, The Hague: Eleven, 2018, pp. 51-52.
80 E. Kamenetskaya, V. S. Vereshchetin, E. Zhukova, Legal Regulation of Space Activities in Russia, *Space Policy*, Vol. 9, 1991, pp. 121-123. F. von der Dunk, Two New National Space Laws: Russia and South Africa, *Proceedings of the 48th Colloquium on the Law of Outer Space*, AIAA, 1995, p. 252.

law and by specific laws applicable to telecommunication and broadcasting activities, and this model had, throughout the 1990s, proven inadequate in regulating the emergence of new systems designed and financed exclusively by the private sector.[81] The French Space Operation Act was enacted in 2008 to accompany the momentum of privatization of space activities, and the main motivation for its legislative approach was to allow a smooth and safe privatization of space operations.[82]

Japan was also a 'latecomer' to the field of national space legislation, enacting a basic space law only in 2008, having already had an adequate level of space activities by non-governmental actors until the early 21st century.[83] Through this law, Japan recognized the commercial potential of space and enjoined the Japanese government to enact legislation to promote space development and use in the private sector. This led to the adoption of two major space-related laws in 2016: Space Activities Act and Remote Sensing Act, which reflect Japan's commitment to supporting commercial space activities.[84] Japan has a coordinated centralized administration for space activities as the product of a long process of consolidation. One of the goals for this consolidation is to encourage the private sector to take advantage of the wide-ranging commercial possibilities of space.[85]

In China the idea of adopting space legislation had been barely considered, and its necessity and importance were not acknowledged until the 1990s, when the first proposal for space legislation appeared at the NPC in 1993.[86] This was only the beginning of the recognition of the necessity of space legislation. In 1996, He Qizhi, a distinguished space law expert and legal consultant of the MFA, wrote to the CNSA administrator, suggesting the adoption of national space law for the regulation of space activities carried out by

---

81   P. Achilleas, Regulation of Space Activities in France, in R. S. Jakhu (ed.), *National Regulation of Space Activities*, Dordrecht: Springer, 2010, p. 109. G. Carminati, French National Space Legislation: A Brief "Parcours" of a Long History, *Houston Journal of International Law*, Vol. 36(1), 2014, pp. 1-18.
82   P. Clerc, *Space Law in the European Context: National Architectures, Legislation and Policy in France*, The Hague: Eleven, 2018, p. 97.
83   S. Aoki, Current Status and Recent Development in Japan's National Space Law and Its Relevance to Pacific Rim Space Law and Activities, *Journal of Space Law*, Vol. 35(2), 2009, p. 363, pp. 366-367. A commercial satellite launch did not occur in Japan until 2008.
84   M. Ogasawara, J. Greer, *Japan in Space: National Architecture, Policy and Legislation and Business in the 21st Century*, The Hague: Eleven, 2021, p. 7.
85   *Ibid.*, p. ix.
86   The earliest proposal dates back to 1993 during the eighth NPC. The Shanghai delegation signed unanimously and submitted to the Congress a bill for legislating space law. In the bill it was pointed out that China's space technology developed rapidly and has entered the international market of launching services. The bill suggested that China adopt a space law as soon as possible in order to solve the new problems encountered in developing space technology in the new situation. This bill was prepared by the Ministry of Aerospace Industry through an investigative group. The group did promising preparatory work for the space legislating by consulting the Shanghai NPC standing committee, related organs within the NPC and the State Council for comments and opinions, collecting and translating space laws of the US, Russia, Ukraine and others and proposing an outline for the future space law. Y. Qi, A Study of Aerospace Legislation of China, *Journal of Space Law*, Vol. 33, 2007, pp. 406, 408.

private, 'non-traditional' space actors.[87] The next year, during the 15th National Communist Party Congress, the president of the Space Technology Research Academy proposed a draft space law with the aim of ensuring that the exploration and utilization of outer space should safeguard the national interest, protect the space properties and promote the development of the space industry.[88]

The aim of adopting a comprehensive law has been prevailing as evidenced by the White Paper series on Space Activities and other policy documents. The 2000 White Paper highlights the need for strengthening legislative work and adopting laws and regulations for space activities to ensure orderly development.[89] The 2006 White Paper also reiterates that it is one of the major development measures to strengthen legislation in this regard.[90] The COSTIND's 11th Five-Year Plan for Space Development, released in 2007, expressed the determination to speed up legislation work so that the law should be able to keep up with the development of space activities. This was once optimistically interpreted as the new phase towards the rapid development of space legislation.[91] The 2011 White Paper emphasized the role of strengthening legislative work as development promoting measures.[92] The 2016 White Paper declared that efforts have been made to accelerate the formation of a legal system to regulate space activities in order to create favourable conditions for sustainable development.[93] The 2021 White Paper uses the term 'law-based government' for the first time in this policy series.[94] A positive interpretation would be its implication of a rule-of-law orientation, instead of a rule-by-law orientation, in the formation of a space legal system.

3.3.3. *The Bureaucratic Setbacks and Conundrum About Space Legislation*

China's space-industrial complex extends to government and military organs from different sectors and also involves research and production units from enterprises and universities. These actors have formed a multiline structure and relationship with respect to the formulation of strategy, the adoption of policies, decision-making, attribution of financing as well as the organization of activities – all this without clear external borders

---

87 Ibid., p. 406.
88 Ibid.
89 Section II, China's Space Activities of 2000.
90 China will formulate laws, regulations and policies for guiding and regulating space activities, improving the administration by law and creating a favourable environment for space legislation. Section IV, Development Policies and Measures, the 2006 White Paper on China's Space Activities.
91 H. Zhao, The Status Quo and the Future of Chinese Space Legislation, *Zeitschrift für Luft- und Weltraumrecht (German Journal of Air and Space Law)*, 2009, Vol. 58(1), p. 96.
92 Section 4, Development Policies and Measures, the 2011 White Paper on China's Space Activities.
93 Section 4 (5), Development Policies and Measures, the 2016 White Paper on China's Space Activities.
94 Section 5 (5), Modernizing Space Governance, the 2021 White Paper on China's Space Activities.

and efficient coordination mechanisms, or at the practically expedient level but not established by legislation.

This was the result of several rounds of military, governmental and state-owned enterprises reformation under the programme-oriented development model during the rapid and intense social and economic transformation. The delay in legislation process, particularly after the 1990s, had been caused by such a structure and its constant changes, the lack of a proper space agency as well as the divergent interests – amplified by the lack of an effective coordination mechanism. Space industry and space applications are relevant for more and more State Council and PLA departments. The question of how to reconcile the existing competences among the different players and how to forge a cooperative and coordinated governing network are both the delaying reasons and the conundrums for the legislative work.

The preliminary consideration for legislation focused on the necessity of implementing international legal rules in the obligation of registration was growing increasingly demanding. But the MFA in charge of the submission of information to the UN Office of Space Affairs did not show enough interest in pushing the legislation process forward. So, the COSTIND assumed this responsibility and took the initiative in this respect with great energy. It elaborated substantial legislation after its reformation in 1998 since it financed the most activities of the defence industry and acted as its main administrative body, including civil space activities.[95] It formed two legislative recommendation groups in 1999, one for the registration of space objects and the other for the authorization of launches with regard to civil space objects, which were finalized in two ministerial regulations. Then the COSTIND sponsored a series of seminars and conferences and subsidized several research projects on the legislation structure, the framework of the administrative regime as well as the comparative study of national space legislation adopted by world powers. All this suggested that China should have its own space legal system as a sound foundation for China's national legislation and that legislative process should be promoted. Consequently, the COSTIND initiated the legislative preparatory work for several regulations: a draft Ministerial Regulation on the Compensation for Damages Caused by Space Object was incorporated into the legislation work plan of the State Council, a Ministerial Regulation on the Management of Space Commercialization and Coordination of International Space Cooperation was in

---

95 The establishment of the COSTIND was the result of reforms that separated the builders (the manufacturers) from the buyers (the military) so as to rationalize the procurement system and reduce conflicts of interest and corruption. As a civilian agency, it is in charge of industrial planning and the administrative affairs of the defence industry. Since its formation in 1982, the COSTIND has served more as a military entity that coordinated R&D and procurement relationships between the PLA and the defence-industrial enterprises. The restructured COSTIND functions as the administrative and regulatory agency for major defence enterprises. Its principal responsibilities include drafting the annual plans for R&D, investment and production, formulating laws and regulations relevant to defence-industry operations, organizing international exchange and cooperation and arms sales to other countries and providing export-control administration related to military exports.

the process of being researched and drafted, an Administrative Regulation entitled 'Regulation on Space Activities' was once among its highest priorities, and the consequent legislative proposal and regulation draft were submitted to the Legislative Affairs Office of the State Council in 2007.[96] However, the next year, the COSTIND was integrated into the newly established MIIT as a subordinate agency and was restructured as the State Administration of Science and Technology and Industry for National Defence (SASTIND). This merger cost COSTIND the independent power of formulating administrative regulations, and ten years of legislative efforts were to no avail.

The PLA is a major actor in China's space industry and is naturally influential with regard to legislative initiatives and law formulation work. However, there is no official news with regard to its attitude towards the law on space activities. The Leading Group on Outer Space Law Formulation is composed of 20 units, specifically mentioning the NPC, the State Council Legislative Affair Office, the Ministry of Justice, the MFA and the SASTIND, but not the PLA.[97] This silence is possibly due to the sensitive nature of military participation but inevitably gives rise to the speculation that the PLA has doubts and even resistance towards enacting a space law. This speculation is also based on the PLA's firm belief in the traditional development model without a space law,[98] its delay in space objects registration, and its occasional actions or statements diverging from the positions of others, particularly from the MFA.

3.4. THE EMERGING AND INCREASING INDIGENOUS NEED TO IMPROVE SPACE LEGISLATION

3.4.1. *The Space Activities Have Outgrown the Traditional Regulatory Framework*

The traditional regulatory method relying on policy, regulatory documents and administrative orders has proved inadequate. With the ever-increasing size of space activities and the diversity of investment and actors, there emerges the need to

---

96 W. Yin, China's Space Policy, Proceedings of United Nations/Republic of Korea Workshop on Space Law, United Nations Treaties on Outer Space: Actions at the National Level, ST/SPACE/22, United Nations Office for Outer Space Affairs, 2005, p. 15. Y. Qi, A Study of Aerospace Legislation of China, *Journal of Space Law*, Vol. 33, 2007, pp. 406-408. Y. Zhao, National Space Legislation in Mainland China, *Journal of Space Law*, Vol. 33, 2007, pp. 434-435. H. Zhao, The Status Quo and the Future of Chinese Space Legislation, *Zeitschrift für Luft- und Weltraumrecht (German Journal of Air and Space Law)*, Vol. 58(1), 2009, pp. 102-103. C. Yang, G. Gao, Overview of the Current Situation and Improvement of Chinese Space Legislation, *Annals of Air and Space Law*, 2013, pp. 397-398.
97 www.cnsa.gov.cn/n6758823/n6758838/c6770321/content.html. Last accessed August 2021.
98 During my communication with the military, the most frequently asked question is why it is necessary to have specialized law, considering that China's space programmes have gained great achievements with no space law at all for decades.

transform responsive regulation into preventive regulation and for top-level design establishing basic principles and regimes.

Internally, China's space capacity has surpassed the phase of key-point breakthroughs and reached the phase of comprehensive and systematic building based on social and economic development needs. Previously, certain space capacity was carefully chosen as a breakthrough point, followed by corresponding administrative orders, plans and programmes at the national level in order to integrate all necessary sources. Certain management and organization experience and responses to international norms have developed into a set of random and very basic regulatory rules. But nowadays, the increasing number of space assets, the prolonged length of the operational life of space objects as well as the long-term programmes relating, e.g., to space stations and deep space exploration, need integral, structural and legally binding regulation. The traditional method of pooling resources into major programmes by case-to-case solutions might undermine the implementation effect of space programmes, which would be disproportionate vis-à-vis the high level of political support and funding and could even cause delay, suspension and cancellation by institutional reforms and personnel changes.

Considering that China's space capabilities originated in the planned economy, which still dominates and deeply affects space activities in many ways, it should now be recognized that China's economic system has transformed from a planned economy into a more market-oriented one, and the space industry is catching up with this transformation. This has accentuated the need for upgrading the regulatory method.

Externally, China's emergence as a global power is one of the defining developments of international relations in the 21st century, particularly in the space realm as it has become a pivotal actor. China's actions under international law are under global scrutiny with regard to whether it is a responsible stakeholder in the space community.[99] Meanwhile, China is gradually taking its place on the international scene and is finding its way into the international legal order.[100] There is a conscious decision to be a part of the space norm-creation instead of being faced with the choice of simply accepting or rejecting norms laid down by others. Space legislation is an inseparable part of this dialogue and dynamics between China's legislative powers and international law.

---

99 M. Fullilove, China and the United Nations: The Stakeholder Spectrum, *The Washington Quarterly*, Vol. 34 (3), 2011, pp. 63-85. A. Bowe, China Pursuit of Space Power Status and Implications for the United States, Research Report of U.S.-China Economic and Security Review Commission, 11 April 2019, see www.uscc.gov/sites/default/files/Research/USCC_China%27s%20Space%20Power%20Goals.pdf. Last accessed August 2021.

100 Chatham House Project on China and the Future of the International Legal Order since 2014, www.chathamhouse.org/events/all/research-event/china-and-international-order. Joint Symposium by Harvard International Law Journal and Yale Journal of International Law, 15 October 2020, www.yjil.yale.edu/online-essays/china-symposium. Last accessed August 2021.

3. CHINA'S SPACE LAW

The growth and changes of China's space activities in the context of the domestic rule-of-law construction and China's determination to be a responsible stakeholder are bringing forth and strengthening the indigenous need to improve space legislation by upgrading space governance, better concretizing and implementing international obligations, regulating and promoting the untraditional actors' activities and expanding international cooperation.

3.4.2.   The New Height of Administrative Reforms Requires Upgrading the Space Governance

Under the government transformation from a management type to a service type, law-based governance has become a novel ruling style.[101] But space governance has still maintained the traditional model as it was left out during the administrative reformation and the rule-of-law development process. But modernizing space governance and establishing a proper authorization regime are now the primary tasks of space legislation.

Since the early 1980s, China has launched eight rounds of administrative reforms (1982, 1988, 1993, 1998, 2003, 2008, 2013 and 2018), which means a new initiative emerging roughly every five years, in order to solve the socio-economic problems associated with rapid and all-round development. These reforms are different in focus, scale and result. For instance, the focus of reforms has gradually shifted from structural reconfiguration to functional readjustment.[102] But they are consistent with the same implication that creating a favourable political environment is critical for the success of ongoing and future reform and development endeavours. The administrative reforms are therefore considered as an important part of the overall reform of the political system and of the conditions for setting up a market economy system.[103] They might even be conceived as a link between political and economic reforms, so as to solve the

---

101 Under the framework of governance modernization, Chinese governance has gone through structural changes in the relationships between government and market, between government and society, between central government and local governments in different dimensions, such as functional reformation, reform of public institutions and the building of a law-based government. *See* R. Shen. S. Cao, *Modernization of Government Governance in China*, London: Palgrave Macmillan, 2020.
102 These eight reforms can be divided into four phases: structural reconfiguration that attempted to downsize and streamline the government (1978-1992); strengthening the macro control of the government and loosening the ties between government and enterprises in accordance with the requirement of a market economy (1993-2002); building up a well-functioning administrative system suited to the market economy and in response to the impact of economic globalization (2003-2012); and transforming government function into a service-based one and improving the modernization of state governance (2013-now).
103 Xinhua News Agency, Administrative Reform 'Imperative', 5 March 2008, www.china.org.cn/government/NPC_CPPCC_sessions2008/2008-03/05/content_11593009.htm. Last accessed August 2021.

contradiction between political and economic reality. In other words, the impetus behind administrative reform is the political authority motivated by economic exigency.[104] Consequently, these reforms have become less passive and reactive and more market and law oriented towards problem prevention.[105]

The administrative reforms are getting increasingly into a closer relationship with the rule-of-law construction. Shortly after the 1999 Constitutional amendment, which first endorsed the rule-of-law concept, the State Council issued a decision requesting its subordinated departments and local governments at all levels to tighten administrative law implementation, deepen supervision for administrative law enforcement and enhance administration capacity in accordance with the law.[106] A further document of 2004 ushered in a new era of administrative reform with the pledge to establish a rule-of-law government by 2015.[107] It provides the basic requirements for law-based administration, including lawful administration, reasonable administration, rightful procedure as well as efficiency and convenience provision for the people with power and responsibility combined. The administrative reform of 2008 was intended to build a service-oriented and law-abiding government with one specific aspect of declining excessive administrative interference in the market operation.[108] In order to transform government function into a service-based one, the primary objective of the 2013 and 2018 reform is the improvement and modernization of state governance, particularly restraining excessive bureaucratic behaviour.[109]

The reforming measures for the administrative examinations and approvals are considered as an important aspect of a rule-of-law government. The 2004 Law on Administrative Licensing (LAL) and the subsequent implementing measures were hailed as a boost to China's efforts to build a market economy and to check corruption. The LAL seeks to restrain government interference with market activity and to increase

---

104 Q. Wang, Administrative Reform in China: Past, Present and Future, *Southeast Review of Asian Studies*, Vol. 32, 2010, pp. 111-112.
105 B. Ma, S. An, The Forty-Years of China's Administrative Reformation: The Major Achievement and Future Prospects, *Administrative Reform (Journal in Chinese)*, Vol. 10, 2018, pp. 29-31.
106 The Decision on Comprehensively Pushing Forward Administration in Accordance with the Law, the State Council, No. 23, 1999.
107 The Notice of Implementation Program on Comprehensively Pushing Forward Administration in Accordance with the Law, the State Council, No. 10, 2004, www.gov.cn/gongbao/content/2004/content_70309.htm?gs_ws=tsina_636451536152493584. Last accessed August 2021.
108 The Party Resolution entitled 'Opinions on Deepening Reform of the Administrative System' stated that facing the new situation and new tasks, the existing system of administrative management still has some aspects that are not compliant, including insufficient reorganization of government function, excessive administrative interference in microeconomic operation and relatively weak social management and public services, 3 March 2008, www.gov.cn/gongbao/content/2008/content_946042.htm. Last accessed August 2021.
109 The Report on Institutional Reform and Functional Changes of the State Council to the National People's Congress, 10 March 2013, www.gov.cn/2013lh/content_2350848.htm. The Report on Institutional Reform of the State Council to the National People's Congress, 13 March 2018, www.xinhuanet.com/politics/2018lh/2018-03/14/c_1122533011.htm. Last accessed August 2021.

the transparency of administrative approval procedures by restricting the number of government agencies to issue approvals in the form of licences and by limiting the types of activity that can be so regulated.[110] Accordingly, the administrative licences shall only be laid down by laws and administrative regulations, and the departments within the State Council ceased to have the power to determine whether or not a particular activity requires an administrative permit.[111] A number of steps have been taken to implement this law, which systematically and deeply reform the administrative examination and approval system. First, the State Council swiftly revamped all the approvals and temporarily reserved the ones set down by the legal documents other than laws and administrative regulations. This greatly reduced the amount of administrative licensing, and the number of matters requiring licensing approvals at all levels was nearly halved.[112] A series of notices have been released on the strict control of the allocation of new administrative licences and the cancellation of existing administrative licences.[113] Second, the aims and purposes of reforms have moved beyond deregulation to less regulation and better regulation, corresponding to the similar concepts in other states, such as the United Kingdom, the United States of America, Germany, Canada, Australia, Sweden and the Netherlands.[114] The State Council announced in 2013 that reforming the administrative approval system is a top priority in the reforms to further eliminate non-essential administrative examination and approvals and to construct a more limited and less arbitrary government. The State Council started the process of standardizing the administrative approval system in 2016

---

110 Arts. 1, 4 and 5 of the Law on Administrative Licensing, adopted by the Standing Committee of National People's Congress on 27 August 2003 and entered into force on 1 July 2004.
111 Art. 12 of the Law on Administrative Licensing and Decision on Reservation of Certain Administrative Approvals, State Council, No. 412, 2004.
112 The State Council established a Group Leading Office for the Reform of the Administrative Examination and Approval System for a comprehensive review to reduce the number of items subject to administrative examination and approval. Owing to this rigorous process, between 2002 and 2004, the State Council decided to remove or modify 1795 items on the list, accounting for half of the original amount. See The Notice on Implementing the Law on Law on Administrative Licensing, the State Council, No. 23, 2003, www.gov.cn/zhengce/content/2008-03/28/content_1979.htm. Last accessed August 2021. The Group Leading Office for the Reform of the Administrative Examination and Approval System, Reforming the Administrative Examination and Approval System, Beijing: China Fangzheng Press, 2004.
113 The Notice on the Strict Control of Setting New Administrative Licenses, the State Council, No. 39, 2013, www.gov.cn/zwgk/2013-09/26/content_2495516.htm. The State Council Notices on Abolishing Administrative Licensing Items, No. 16 of 2004, 18 May 2004; No. 33 of 2007, 9 October 2007; No. 52 of 2012, 23 September 2012; No. 18 and 44 of 2013, 15 May and 8 November 2013; No. 5 and 50 of 2014, 28 January and 23 October 2014; No. 11 and 27 of 2015, 24 February and 10 May 2015; No. 10 of 2016, 3 February 2016; No. 46 of 2017, 22 September 2017; No. 28 of 2018, 28 July 2018; No. 6 of 2019, 27 February 2019; No. 13 of 2020, 21 September, 2020, www.gov.cn. Last accessed August 2021.
114 R. Baldwin, M. Cave, M. Lodge (eds.), The Oxford Handbook of Regulation, Oxford: Oxford University Press, 2013, p. 4 and pp. 7-8. C. Hood, The Tools of Government in the Information Age, M. Moran, M. Rein, R. E. Goodin (eds.), The Oxford Handbook of Public Policy, Oxford: Oxford University Press, 2006, pp. 469-481. OECD Report, Alternatives to Traditional Regulation, www.oecd.org/gov/regulatory-policy/42245468.pdf. Last accessed August 2021.

in order to radically eliminate the prevalent problem of non-standard and non-normatized administrative licensing, and thus the administrative licensing regimes preliminarily crossed the threshold of standardization, signalling the change in the reform focus from quantity to quality.[115] The regulatory toolbox has been enlarged, such as the adoption of a recordation system emphasizing not merely prior approval but continuous supervision.[116]

Although the administrative reforms are consistently evolving, there had been no fundamental economic reform in the space industry, and administrative reform has not been extended in this respect: here space governance has still remained basically intact during the last 40-year administrative reform. The establishment of the COSTIND is the result of governmental restructuring in the 1980s, and its function of determining the development policy for the national defence industry was a response to the massive reorganization of the defence industry in the 1990s, which did not bring about fundamental changes to the development and the governance model of space activities. Transparency improvement, in particular, has been a focus of the administrative reforms; however, the nature of the defence industry and the administration by the SASTIND has materially undermined the transparency of space governance.

The space industry has lagged far behind and even runs against the trend of administrative examination, particularly with respect to the approval system. First, the SASTIND is not justifiably entrusted with the power of administering space activities, including the authorization power by any law. This is the major reason for the occasional neglect of applications for a launching licence. Second, there is a pressing need for a proper authorization regime with the involvement of space actors and investment diversification.[117] It is an interesting comparison that there are clear permit requirements for the production and sale of fireworks, while the licensing regime for space activities is inadequate. As for the actors launching civil space objects, they had been subjected to the administrative licences according to ministerial regulations as

---

115 The Notice on Regulating State Council Departments Administrative Approving Action and Improving Administrative Approving Work, the State Council, No 6, 2015, www.gov.cn/zhengce/content/2015-02/04/content_9454.htm. The Guidelines for Administrative Licensing Standardization stipulate the normalized requirements for administrative licensing items, administrative licensing process and administrative licensing service and put forward the specific and operable work guidelines and requirements for promoting administrative licensing standardization. Office of the Administrative Examination and Approval under the State Council, No. 4 [2016], www.gov.cn/xinwen/2016-07/30/content_5096129.htm. Last accessed August 2021.
116 Response Letter to Hebei, Zhejiang and Hubei Provinces on Initiating Administrative Recordation Pilot Reform, the General Office of State Council, No. 68, 2021, www.gov.cn/zhengce/content/2021-07/07/content_5623007.htm. Last accessed August 2021.
117 For instance, the 1995 Civil Aviation Law established the licensing regime, including three types of certificates: the type certificate, the production certificate and the aircraft certificate to cover the whole course of design, production and flight of civil aircraft.

temporarily reserved by the State Council in 2004, and there has been no improvement for more than 15 years.[118]

The major development of administrative licensing was undertaken in the national defence industry within the framework of the reformation of weaponry research and production licences. In 2019 the SASTIND published a new weaponry research and production licence directory to significantly reduce the number of projects requiring licences and replaced them with the recordation system.[119] Yet the procedure for application for a permit for the research and production of carrier rockets remains overly complex and burdensome. Some parts are still 'hidden behind the veil', such as how to apply for and obtain the confidentiality qualification, which is already a precondition for the research and production of launch vehicles.

Therefore, the establishment of a proper authorization regime in the future space law is complicated owing to the administrative reform background of simplifying and reducing the licensing burden. It is facing the challenge of encouraging the space economy by establishing an appropriate threshold for entering space industry so as not to overregulate and interfere unnecessarily with space business.

3.4.3.   *To Better Concretize and Implement the Obligations Assumed by China and Be Considered as a Responsible Space Power*

A useful reference as to the key tone and content of China's future space law is better seen in the implementation of China's international obligations, proving the country a responsible space power but not a rule breaker.

First: National legislation is motivated initially and primarily by the implementation of the Outer Space Treaty and the relevant conventions and agreements subsequently agreed on in the United Nations. The majority of spacefaring nations are observing the treaty obligations as imposed by these instruments preferably by means of national legislation as explicitly and repeatedly recommended by the UN General Assembly as an appropriate tool.[120] Thereby, states tend to conscientiously monitor and control national space activities that are counted among ultra-hazardous activities and that are international in nature, to their national effects.

---

118 The State Council Decisions on Reserving Certain Administrative Licensing Items, No. 412, of 2004, www.gov.cn/zhengce/content/2016-05/30/content_5078063.htm. Last accessed August 2021.
119 Interim Measures for the Recordation Administration of the Scientific Research and Production of Arms and Equipment, State Administration of Science and Technology and Industry for National Defence, 25th July 2019, www.sastind.gov.cn/n112/n117/c6806970/content.html. Last accessed August 2021.
120 The state conducting space activities should consider enacting and implementing national laws in fulfilling their international obligations under the UN treaties on outer space. *See* Resolution on the Application of the Concept of the "Launching State", A/RES/59/115, 10 December 2004. Recommendations on National Legislation relevant to the Peaceful Exploration and Use of Outer Space, A/RES/69/74, 16 December 2013.

Assuming sovereignty in regulating private space activities is necessary to preserve public interest and national security. Therefore, treaty provisions relating to non-governmental activities are also one of the basic contours of national space regulations. Most national space legislation contains an authorization and supervision system, in particular through licensing, as well as provisions with respect to registration as well as to compensation in case of liability for damages caused by space objects. By virtue of these regimes, the government can effectively fulfil its obligations and administer the space activities conducted by various participants.

Second: The existing regulatory framework in China has proved to be inadequate and ineffective in fulfilling international obligations. Take the registration of space objects as an example: Lateness and irregularity are the primary characteristics marking China's actions in fulfilling this obligation. China ratified the Registration Convention in 1988. From 1990 till the end of 2020, it submitted only 25 documents for registration, statistically barely one per year. Among them were three registrations in 1999, 2001 and 2020 and two in 1998 and 2009 but none for the remaining 14 years.[121] During the 10 years from 1990 to 2000, 8 registration documents were submitted referring to 67 space objects launched by China. During the 20 years from 2001 to 2020, 17 documents were submitted containing information about 437 space objects. The registration frequency has been stable during the last 30 years. It has not kept up with the pace of launch activity and the number of space objects launched by China.

As for the establishment of a *national* registry, this is not a prerequisite for fulfilling the international obligation. Among the 66 states that have provided the UN with the information regarding objects launched into outer space in accordance with the Registration Convention or the Registration Resolution, only 42 notifications have been sent to the UN reporting the establishment of a national registry.[122] Nevertheless the national registry, usually established by law, should better guarantee and regularize the implementation of registration obligations. In the case of China, information of its national registry was late in coming. It was in 2001 that China established a national

---

121 Note Verbale from the Permanent Mission of China to the United Nations Secretary-General, ST/SG/SER.E/229, 1990, ST/SG/SER.E/265, 1993, ST/SG/SER.E/312, 1996, ST/SG/SER.E/330, 1998, ST/SG/SER.E/334, 1998, ST/SG/SER.E/356, 1999, ST/SG/SER.E/359, 1999, ST/SG/SER.E/381, 2001, ST/SG/SER.E/386, 2001, ST/SG/SER.E/391, 2001, ST/SG/SER.E/420, 2002, ST/SG/SER.E/427, 2003, ST/SG/SER.E/475, 2005, ST/SG/SER.E/500, 2006, ST/SG/SER.E/549, 2008, ST/SG/SER.E/566, 2009, ST/SG/SER.E/583, 2009, ST/SG/SER.E/602, 2010, ST/SG/SER.E/649, 2012, ST/SG/SER.E/714, 2014, ST/SG/SER.E/741, 2015, ST/SG/SER.E/789, 2017, ST/SG/SER.E/856, 2020, ST/SG/SER.E/898, 2020, ST/SG/SER.E/948, 2020.

122 Art. II of the Registration Convention provides for the obligation of informing the UN with regard to the establishment of a national registry. But Resolution 1721 also serves as a non-binding obligations source for the registration of space objects for nearly 60 years, *see* International Cooperation in the Peaceful Uses of Outer Space, UN General Assembly Resolution 1721, 20 December 1961. For UN register with the index of objects launched into outer space, *see* www.unoosa.org/oosa/en/spaceobjectregister/index.html. Last accessed August 2021.

registry of space objects, and the UN Secretary-General was informed accordingly in 2005, four years later.[123]

In contrast, the US and the Russian Federation have a well-established practice of registering on a two- or four-month basis, although there is no definite time requirement in the Registration Convention in this respect but only the expression of 'as soon as practicable'.[124] China's registration frequency, once every 14 months on average, is significantly lower and unstable. Also, the proportion of its unregistered space objects is much bigger and the contents of the registration documents are comparatively simpler or even arbitrary. They occasionally leave out essential information about orbital parameters, for example. Of course, the mandatory international registration obligation is still 'loose' enough to conceal sensitive information.[125] But it is still proving to be an important standard to be observed for providing timely and reliable information to the international community. China's practice in this respect has generated scepticism or alarmism with respect to its sincerity in honouring its international obligations.

States	Launched Objects	Registered Objects	Unregistered Portion (%)	Times	Frequency (months)
China	623	504	19	25	14
Russia Federation	3593	3554	1	171	2
United States	4329	3849	11	96	4
France	155	155	0	16	12

China's delay in submitting information in the early years could be the result of political hesitation in the historical context of the 1990s and the delay in national registry notification might be owing to the bureaucratic hurdles between COSTIND and MFA since Registration Measures are the product of their first-time cooperation. But the irregularity and delay in complying with registration obligations afterwards indicates the ineffective regulation caused by the lack of proper law. The 2001 Registration Measures apply to all space objects launched from Chinese territory as well as to those

---

123 Information furnished in conformity with the Convention on Registration of Objects Launched into Outer Space, Note Verbale dated 8 June 2005 from the Permanent Mission of China to the United Nations addressed to the Secretary-General, UN Doc. ST/SG/SER.E/INF.17, 21 June 2005.
124 Art. IV of the Registration Convention.
125 The mandatory information in Art. 4 of the Registration Convention is termed as 'general function of the space object', which, in many cases, follows the standard categories of science and application, such as Earth observation, telecommunication or navigation. A military function of a satellite might be described in a general abstract manner. B. Shmidt-Tedd, Article IV of Registration Convention, in S. Hobe, B. Schmidt-Tedd, K. Schrogl (eds.), *Cologne Commentary on Space Law*, Vol. II, Cologne: Heymanns, 2013, p. 301.

jointly launched abroad by China with other states. The required information shall be furnished within 60 days from the entry of space objects into orbit. All governmental departments, juridical and natural persons as well as other organizations that are launching or procuring the launching of a space object are obliged to submit the required information to the COSTIND/SASTIND, which will then transmit such information to the MFA within 60 days for international registration.[126] The defect of this superficially smooth process is that the Registration Measures are a ministerial regulation by nature, so they can hardly prompt effective compliance and change the conservative attitude, especially of other organs, towards the improvement of transparency with respect to space activities. Without the adoption of a space law, there is a lack of authority to collect information on space objects, particularly in the military-related cases that are usually launched and operated by the PLA, although the COSTIND/SASTIND repeatedly issued notices with the aim of strengthening the administration of national registry. The SASTIND seems determined to revise the Registration Measures.[127] But the revision of ministerial regulation cannot substantially improve China's performance in registration obligations, unless it gains the PLA's support.

Third: The future space law could be a chance to admit the existence of military space activities and differentiate militarization and weaponization of outer space. Military use of outer space is not entirely outlawed by international law.[128] The long-lasting silence and denial regarding China's military strategy and purpose in outer space could be the result of a biased interpretation of the term 'peaceful purpose' in the Outer Space Treaty and of the *jus ad bellum* or might even be an intentional choice in order to avoid international attention and pressure in view of a particular historical context as well as a diplomatic show of choosing a higher standard in this respect. Regardless of the reason or motivation in the back of minds, this situation is also clouding China's intention to be a reliable space power and is nurturing international concern of being intensely criticized and discredited as being an obvious weak link in confidence-building measures. A basic law for space activities could present an open window either to admit the status quo and

---

126 *See* Arts. 3, 4 and 9 of the Registration Measures.
127 The 2021 White Paper on China's Space Activities, Section 5 (4).
128 Both militarization and weaponization of outer space aim to gain supremacy over other users in outer space. A starting point for the distinction between militarization and weaponization is that the weaponization of outer space includes the placement of weapons in outer space as well as the development of weapons that will transit outer space or travel from Earth to attack or destroy targets in outer space, while the militarization of space refers to using space-based assets for military operation. In other words, the militarization of space assists armies on the conventional battlefields, whereas via weaponization of outer space, outer space itself emerges as the battleground, sometimes referred to as the 'fourth frontier of war'. A further distinction between militarization and weaponization lies in the nature of space technologies and their utilization and is also due to the provisions in the space treaties, but still there are ambiguities: space technologies are typically dual-use, and the vast majority of satellites in orbit have both military and civilian purposes. The Outer Space Treaty regulates the limits of military operations in outer space but leaves plenty of grey zones by outlawing only the placement of *nuclear* weapons as well as weapons of mass destruction *in Earth orbit* and by permitting the exclusively peaceful uses of *celestial bodies*.

regulate military space activities or to adopt an opening article, providing for a separate regulatory framework.[129]

Fourth: National space law in China could, first of all, address the relationship between China's space legislation and its international obligations since the Chinese Constitution has no express provision on the legal status of international treaties in a domestic context, their relation to municipal law and the procedure of their implementation. The situation was certainly due to inadvertent neglect when the Constitution was being drafted in the early 1980s but could also be an intentional left-open issue in the following amendments.[130] The interaction between Chinese and international law is not a total blank:

First, international norms have played an important role in shaping its domestic legal system and quite a number of them have been transformed into its municipal law through legislation, such as the Agreement on Trade-Related Aspects of Intellectual Property Rights (TRIPS). Many proposals made and measures taken in the reform of criminal law and criminal procedural law have their roots in the standards of international human rights treaties, including the International Covenant on Civil and Political Rights signed by China in 1998 but not yet ratified.[131]

Second, quite some laws, mostly civil and business laws, embrace automatic incorporation, according to which the courts are empowered by specific legislation, rather than a constitutional provision, to give effect to international law in the absence

---

129 A separate regulatory framework has been adopted in the regulation of certain activities, such as patent law and export control. See the Administrative Regulation for National Defence Patents and the Administrative Regulation for Export Control of Military Items and Technologies, www.mod.gov.cn/policy/xzfg.htm. Last accessed August 2021.
130 The relationship between a country's international law and domestic law depends on different views. If this relationship is seen from the perspective of international law, there are views insisting on the supremacy of international law. A state that fails because of the supremacy of its domestic law in the implementation of its obligations has committed an unlawful act. G. Fitzmaurice, General Principles of International Law, Collected Courses of the Hague Academy of International Law, 1957. It is also argued that the supremacy of international law is a concept designed to oversee human rights abuses at the national and the international level. H. Lauterpacht, *International Law and Human Rights*, London: Stevens & Sons Limited, 1950, p. xvi. The perspective of domestic law and constitutionalism will result in the constitution and internal law defining the criteria for acceptance or rejection of the international norms. The relationship between international law and national law and the concept of supremacy of international law are currently very controversial issues. Although the domestic law of many states complies with the ever-increasing demands of international law, it is generally refused to accept the unconditional supremacy of international law on constitutional principles. L. Kodra, The Relationship between International Law and National Law, *Global Journal of Politics and Law Research*, Vol. 6, 2017, pp. 1-11.
131 Art. 6 of the ICCPR emphasizes the right to life but mentions the exception of this right for the reason of 'most serious crimes'. There is no universal definition of most serious crimes, but its interpretation links the components of culpability with violence and loss of life. *See* the General Comment 36 on the Right to Life of the UN Human Rights Committee, CCPR/C/GC/35, 3 September 2019. The latest trend of penal reforms shows China's gradual shift to exclude economic crimes from the list of capital crimes. China abolished the death penalty for 13 and 9 non-violent crimes under the 8th and 9th Amendments to the 1997 Criminal Law in 2011 and 2015, respectively.

of implementing legislation.[132] More than 100 provisions in nearly 80 laws passed between 1978 and 2004 clarified the superior application of treaties to varying extents, except for the reserved provisions.[133] Regrettably, there is no such provision in the Civil Code that replaced the General Principles of Civil Law, Contract Law, Tort Law and other civil laws of 1 January 2021. The deletion of such articles reflects an uncertain position of the NPC owing to the constitutional gap and the growing complexity surrounding the relationship between international obligations and internal law.

Third, the courts have significantly increased their application of international law over the past four decades. China's constitutional silence regarding international law contributes to the flexibility of its domestic judicial application.[134] In civil and commercial cases between private entities, the application of international treaties has become a standard practice when the international treaties are chosen by the parties and determined by the courts as *lex causae*.[135] Moreover, the application of international treaties has expanded to the other fields. From 2013 to 2018, there is reference to international human rights treaties in 57 judicial cases, mostly initiated by the parties. But in seven of these cases, it was the courts on their own initiatives that applied the Convention on the Rights of the Child (CRC), ratified by China in 1992, when there were no similar provisions in domestic laws, or when the court interpreted the similar provisions both in domestic laws and the CRC as a way to strengthen its reasoning, or when the courts interpreted domestic law in conformity with the international obligations under the CRC.[136]

---

132 C. Cai, International Law in Chinese Courts During the Rise of China, *The American Journal of International Law*, Vol. 110(2), 2016, p. 273.

133 Y. Wang, *Fundamental Theory of the Application of Treaties in China*, Beijing: Peking University Press, 2007, p. 146. For instance, Art. 142 of 1986 General Principles of Civil Law, Art. 268 of Maritime Law, Art. 260 of Civil Procedural Law, Art. 44 of Meteorological Law, Art. 184 of Civil Aviation Law and Art. 95 of Negotiable Instruments Law follow the same pattern, providing that if any treaty concluded or acceded to by China contains provisions different from those in this law, the provisions of the international treaty shall apply unless China has made reservations.

134 C. Cai, International Law in Chinese Courts During the Rise of China, *The American Journal of International Law*, Vol. 110(2), 2016, p. 273.

135 Among the 18 typical cases concerning the one belt and one road construction issued by the Supreme People's Court in its case guidance project, 5 of them applied international treaties, to which China is adhering as a member state, including the UN Convention on Contracts for the International Sales of Goods, the Convention for the Unification of Certain Rules for International Carriage by Air, the Convention on the Recognition and Enforcement of Foreign Arbitral Awards, the International Convention on Civil Liability for Oil Pollution Damage, and International Convention for Safety of Life at Sea. *See* the first and second series of typical cases concerning the construction of One Belt and One Road, Supreme People's Court, 2015 and 2017, www.court.gov.cn/zixun-xiangqing-14897.html and www.court.gov.cn/zixun-xiangqing-44722.html. Last accessed August 2021.

136 R. Dai, Judicial Application of International Human Rights Treaties in China: Global Perspective, *Human Rights in China*, 5 May 2020, www.humanrights.cn/html/2020/zxyq_0512/51267.html. Last visited November 2021.

The Chinese version of Lunar Embassy lawsuit is the first and only space-treaty-related case until now.[137] The legitimacy over lunar ownership and sales was at the core of this case. Both Beijing Haidian District Court and Beijing First Intermediate Court cited Outer Space Treaty, ruling out the possibility of lunar ownership and emphasizing that any exploitation of outer space should benefit all human beings.[138]

There is no mention of international treaties in the two ministerial regulations on the registration of space objects and the licensing of launches, although some articles have similar or same elements as in the treaties. There is also a legal vacuum for the domestic application of four space treaties acceded by China. One article in the future space law following the existing pattern of automatic incorporation might be sufficiently convincing evidence for honouring its international obligations.[139] The transformation of international obligations into the domestic context through the enactment of legislation is essential for improving transparency and for building trust and confidence.[140] This could also echo and bolster China's international position and be of help in asserting its space power status on the international stage. In addition, the future practice in applying and interpreting space treaties would be a pilot project for a constitutional amendment, exploring the acceptable principle for the application of international law to our domestic legal system beyond the norms of civil and business law.

---

137 A company, inspired by the Lunar Embassy in the US, sold land on the moon and lost two rounds of lawsuits to recover its business licence that was revoked by Beijing Administration for Industry and Commerce for illegal profit seeking by trading unlawful commodities.

138 The Lunar Embassy of China lost this case against Beijing Administration for Industry and Commerce, October 2006 and March 2007, www.chinacourt.org/article/detail/2006/10/id/221779.shtml and www.chinacourt.org/article/detail/2007/03/id/239435.shtml. "Real estate" agent loses bid to sell land on Moon, *China Daily*, 21 October 2006, www.chinadaily.com.cn/cndy/2006-10/21/content_713474.htm. Last accessed August 2021.

139 There is a general duty to bring internal law into conformity with obligations arising from the treaty obligations. I. Brownlie, *Principles of Public International Law*, Oxford: Oxford University Press, 5th ed., 1998, p. 35. The national law serves as evidence to fulfil a nation's international obligations but cannot be invoked as a justification for its failure. Art. 27 of the Vienna Convention on the Law of Treaties.

140 A. G. Koroma, Foreword, National Regulation of Space Activities, in R. S. Jakhu (ed.), *National Regulations of Space Activities*, Dordrecht: Springer, 2010, p. v.

3.4.4. To Regulate and Encourage Commercial Space Activities and Foster A Sustainable Space Economy

Outer space, no longer a state-monopolized area, has become a field for commercial activities, and the space economy has emerged with great commercial potential.[141] The space economy has been a very active sector for decades, prompting many to call it NewSpace as in the US.[142] This is the primary reason for the trend towards strengthening national space legislation. More importantly, national institutions are adapting to the advancement of space commerce and are thereby becoming a soft power of space nations, influencing international negotiations that are shaping the upcoming dedicated international legal framework governing space activities, such as space mining, for example.

The international rules concerning space activities are of public nature, directed at states and do not address the particularities of non-governmental participation. Therefore, the application and further development of this normative system to commercial space activities depend on its domestic implementation through national legislation. The early enactment and frequent revision of space law was undertaken in the United States, where commercial space activities emerged and developed. [143] A growing number of states have promulgated national space legislation that establishes

---

141 The Organization for Economic Cooperation and Development proposed a broad definition of the term space economy, referring to all public and private actors involved in developing and providing space-enabled products and services. It comprises a long value-added chain, starting with the research and development actors and manufacturers of space hardware and ending with the providers of space-enabled products and services to the final users. *The Space Economy at a Glance*, Paris: OECD, 2007, p. 17. The economic relevance of space, both as a sector of activity by itself and as a huge driver for innovation and knowledge-intensive services, cannot be overlooked. C. Venet, The Economic Dimension of Space Activities, C. Brünner, A. Soucek (eds.), *Outer Space in Society, Politics and Law*, Studies in Space Policy, Vol. 8, Vienna: European Space Policy Institute, 2011, p. 70. The global size of the space economy was conservatively estimated to be hundreds of billion US dollars and rose to US$447 billion in 2020, 55% higher than a decade ago. The share of commercial activities in the global space economy has grown steadily since the 1990s, surpassing the government budgets in recent years. Commercial space grew 6.6% in 2020, as part of a five-year trend of uninterrupted growth. This verified that the global space economy not only weathered but also actually emerged stronger from the worldwide pandemic. See the Space Reports, Colorado Springs: Space Foundation, 2010-2020, www.spacefoundation.org. Last accessed August 2021.

142 X. Wu, "NewSpace" in China in Need of New Laws, Proceedings of the 60th Colloquium on the Law of Outer Space, Eleven, 2018, pp. 501-506.

143 The National Space Policy of the Reagan Administration specified space commerce as one of its most important goals in 1982. E. Walter, The Privatization and Commercialization of Outer Space, in C. Brünner, A. Soucek (eds.), *Outer Space in Society, Politics and Law*, Studies in Space Policy, Vol. 8, Vienna: European Space Policy Institute, 2011, p. 494. Some of the pieces of US space legislation are: the National Aeronautics and Space Act of 1958; the Launch Act of 1984; the Land Remote Sensing Commercialization Act of 1984, replaced by the 1992 Land Remote Sensing Policy Act; the Commercial Space Act of 1998, and the Commercial Space Launch Competitiveness Act of 2015. In 2010, all the space acts were compiled as Title 51 of the U.S. Code, National and Commercial Space Programs.

space regulatory institutions to authorize and supervise the space activities of private actors, for instance, the United Kingdom and the Netherlands.[144]

Furthermore, the commercial space activities have gradually changed the demands for and the emphasis on national law, evolving from a mere instrument for the implementation of international obligations to the creation of a stable and amicable legal environment for ensuring the sustainable growth of the space economy. The increasing involvement of non-governmental entities has strengthened the role of national law as an instrument for ensuring compliance with international law and for the organization of national activities as well as the optimization of the environment for commercial space activities as a key role in space activities. There seems to be an ongoing regulatory competition between states to attract investment into their countries by lowering authorization standards and facilitating authorization procedures as well as for obtaining safety by proving insurance cover.[145] Space legislation in the US, the United Kingdom, Australia and France has streamlined the licensing procedures and fixed maximum levels of compensation to be paid by private entities in case of damage caused by space activities, which are designed to attract commercial investment by significantly reducing cumbersome obstacles to a realistic degree.[146]

In addition, national space regulatory frameworks have adopted some new interpretations of the space treaties in order to accommodate the new forms of space

---

144 British companies started carrying out space activities, and this made the elaboration of an appropriate legal framework necessary, which led to the adoption of the Outer Space Act in 1986. M. S. Aranzamendi, Economic and Policy Aspects of Space Regulations in Europe, Part I: The Case of National Space Legislation – Finding the Way between Common and Coordinated Action, ESPI Report 21, 2009, p. 17. The 2018 Space Industry Act, replacing the 1986 Outer Space Act within the UK territory, and the associated regulations set out a high-level enabling framework for commercial space activities to be carried out from the UK, See Understanding the Space Industry Act, https://assets.publishing.service.gov.uk/government/uploads/system/uploads/attachment_data/file/777686/190208_Understanding_the_SIA_-_Final_For_Publication_-_Legal_Cleared_-_Initial_Publication.pdf. Last accessed August 2021. The legislation in the Netherlands was a response to the general tendency to accept private parties as partners in space endeavours. F. von der Dunk, Regulation of Space Activities in the Netherlands: From Hugo Grotius to the High Ground of Outer Space, in R. S. Jakhu (ed.), *National Regulation of Space Activities*, Dordrecht: Springer, 2010, pp. 229-231. The need for legislation became apparent when Dutch companies started to engage in space activities. F. von der Dunk, Implementing the United Nations Outer Space Treaty – The Case of the Netherlands, in C. Brünner and E. Walter (eds.), *National Space Law – Development in Europe – Challenges for Small Countries*, Vienna: Boehlau Verlag, 2008, p. 92.

145 D. Linden, The Impact of National Space Legislation on Private Space Undertakings: A Regulatory Competition between States?, *Proceedings of the 58th IISL Colloquium on the Law of Outer Space*, Eleven, 2016, pp. 3-21. P. S. Dempsey, National Law Governing Commercial Space Activities: Legislation, Regulation and Enforcement, *Northwestern Journal of International Law and Business*, Vol. 36(1), 2016, pp. 1-44.

146 This method was first adopted by the United States and followed by some other states. For example, the provisions of 1998 Australian Space Activities Act, 2008 French Law concerning Space Operations and the 2018 UK Space Industry Act have similar elements. The 2020 Luxembourg Law on Space Activities, among other provisions, include the tax exemption of insurance contracts covering the space object registered by Luxembourg and an adaptation of the rules regarding the tax credit for investment in order to allow operators of space objects to benefit from tax credit.

activities, especially with regard to the legal status of space resources and the non-appropriation principle. The regulation of new types of commercial activities and the protection of private investment interests are the focal points of some recent regulation enactment, such as in the US and Luxembourg, respectively, in 2015 and 2017 with emphasis on space mining as well as on the relevant property rights.[147] This has reversely initiated international negotiations to fill in the loopholes of space treaties.[148]

The participation of unconventional space actors in China in response to the welcome policy signals and the rapid development of space legislation in other states has magnified the inadequacy of China's current regulatory framework and further built up the pressure and necessity of improving legislation. The importance of national legislation for reducing uncertainty and stimulating commercial activities has been repeatedly underlined and recognized worldwide. A law with the aim of establishing certainty, stability and predictability is essential for commercial investment.[149] The lack of a clear legal framework prevents potentially interested parties from taking advantage of opportunities for economic and technical gains in the field of outer space.[150]

The combination of a limited industrial base as well as turmoil in domestic and foreign policies led to the deferral of space commerce development in China in many cases over many years. But recently, the primary reason for hesitation is the absence of essential regulations pertaining to the participation of non-conventional actors. It is hard to convince them to be seriously involved in space activities instead of mostly just

---

[147] The American Commercial Space Launch Competitiveness Act of 2015 recognized commercial property rights in the resources extracted from extraterrestrial bodies. The Luxembourg Law on the Exploration and Use of Space Resources of 2017 provides that space sources are capable of being owned. M. Sundahl, Regulating Non-Traditional Space Activities in the United States in the Wake of the Commercial Space Launch Competitiveness Act, *Air and Space Law*, Vol. 42(1), 2017, pp. 29-42. V. Blanchette-Séguin, Reaching for the Moon: Mining in Outer Space, *New York University Journal of International Law and Politics*, Vol. 49(3), 2017, pp. 959-970. R. S. Jahku et al. (eds.), *Space Mining and Its Regulation*, New York: Springer, 2017. M. Manoli, Mining Outer Space: Overcoming Legal Barriers to a Well Promising Future, *Proceedings of the 58th IISL Colloquium on the Law of Outer Space*, Eleven, 2016, pp. 937-951.

[148] The Outer Space Treaty does not explicitly address space resources, while the Moon Agreement addresses this issue to some extent but has very limited scope for application, being ratified by 18 countries, mostly non-spacefaring states. Ambiguities in the Outer Space Treaty and the recent space legislation led to calls for action within the COPUOS. The COPUOS Legal Subcommittee agreed to scheduled information consultations on "potential legal models for activities in exploration, exploitation and utilization of space resources" to take place at the 2020 session, but had to be cancelled due to COVID-19. Informal consultations were rescheduled to its 2021 annual session. The proposals submitted by China, the Russian Federation, Austria, Belgium, the Czech Republic, Finland, Germany, Greece, Poland, Portugal, Romania, Slovakia and Spain all supported the creation of a working group tasked with the issue of space resources, but with focus on different proposed areas and perspectives, www.unoosa.org/oosa/en/ourwork/copuos/lsc/space-resources/scheduled-informal-consultations.html. Last accessed August 2021.

[149] T. S. Twibell, Circumnavigating International Space Law, *ILSA Journal of International and Comparative Law*, Vol. 4, 1997, p. 259. F. Kosmo, The Commercialization of Space: A Regulatory Scheme that Promotes Commercial Ventures and International Responsibility, *Southern California Law Review*, Vol. 61, 1988, p. 1058. J. M. Filho, Private, State and International Public Interests in Space Law, *Space Policy*, Vol. 12 (1), 1996, p. 67.

[150] F. Tronchetti, *Fundamentals of Space Law and Policy*, New York: Springer, 2013, p. 138.

3. CHINA'S SPACE LAW

limiting their activities to 'water-test' investment without a long-term or a large-scale perspective.

A recent positive development in this respect is a notice through a regulatory document on the promotion of the orderly development of commercial launch vehicles, issued by the SASTIND and the EDD of the Central Military Commission in 2019.[151] The scope of this notice is rather broad, regulating the production of commercial rockets through all phases, from the research stage to the readiness for launch. It reiterated the requirements for the safety of scientific research and production of rockets, their launching permit and export control as contained in the previous documents but did not add any new regulatory rules. It rather aims at the confirmation of the characteristics and capabilities of entities that are already involved in the research and production of space carrier rockets instead of amending the conditions in order to attract more companies to enter this field.[152] But, at least, it demonstrates the awareness of regulators of the need to improve space legislation and their recognition of the strategic relevance of the commercial space launch industry.

Within the context of the rule-of-law development, however, such regulatory documents are not a proficient choice, considering their overabundant amount and low level of efficiency without connection to legally binding norms. Rather, it would have been imperative to properly address the pressing regulatory challenges in response to the unease of the new entities engaged in the production of space launch rocket technologies and their success in launching tests, such as i-Space's successful launch of a rocket in 2018 and a satellite in 2019.[153] This choice of legislation, filling the gaps by emphasizing national strategies and adapting outdated regulatory rules to the present reality further evidences the lack of original institution design and interpretation of space treaties in comparison with other space powers.

---

151 This Notice contains a preamble and six sections. Its preamble emphasizes the role of this Notice in facilitating the implementation of national strategies of civil-military integration and innovation-driven development relating to the production, testing, launching and technical control of commercial rockets. The first section defines its subject matter and emphasizes its implications from a national security perspective. The second one indicates that the SASTIND is responsible for licence administration. The third one addresses the actual launch of a commercial rocket by referring to the 2002 Licensing Measures. The fourth section reiterates the rules applicable to the operation of launching and testing sites. Section 5 addresses research and production safety of commercial rockets and matters of export control. Section 6 encourages commercial companies to make full use of military facilities, including launching and testing sites. The Notice on Promoting and Regulating Orderly Development of Commercial Carrier Rockets, the SASTIND, No. 647 of 2019, www.sastind.gov.cn/n157/c6806483/content.html. Last accessed August 2021.
152 *See* F. Tronchetti, H. Liu, The 2019 Notice on Promoting the Systematic and Orderly Development of Commercial Carrier Rockets: The First Step towards Regulating Private Space Activities in China, *Space Policy*, Vol. 57, 2021.
153 This is contrary to the conclusion of the 2019 notice, which indicates a preference towards enacting limited and dedicated regulatory instruments rather than comprehensive and detailed national space legislation, at least in the short term. *See* F. Tronchetti, H. Liu, The 2019 Notice on Promoting the Systematic and Orderly Development of Commercial Carrier Rockets: The First Step towards Regulating Private Space Activities in China, *Space Policy*, Vol. 57, 2021.

3.4.5. To Break Down Political Obstacles and Unlock the Potential of Space Cooperation

The political relevance of outer space is substantial, and international cooperation is one concrete expression of the political relevance of space activities.[154] Space-related international interactions are prioritized in China's space policy. Beijing no longer lacks the political willingness and technological and financial resources for international cooperation, and its space capacities and platforms are becoming more and more interesting, such as manned space flights and deep space exploration. Legislative improvement can play an essential role in breaking the long-existing bottleneck through confidence building and smoothing the export control administration.[155] This would make China's space programmes more interconnected with its foreign policies and initiatives, such as Belt and Road Initiative (BRI), and enlarge its joint space undertaking to be proportionate to its space capability and international status.

Building and gaining mutual trust is the vital element for expanding international cooperation, and the improvement of national legislation could contribute to melting down the political obstacles in cooperative engagements.[156] The enactment of space law is also an effective method for decreasing misinterpretation, ill assumptions, doubts and bias of potential partners about China's intentions in space, and it could stimulate communication and strengthen common understanding. The hurdles in China's space cooperation are political in nature. Its cooperation with the Western countries has been modest owing to fears of technological espionage and the anxiety arising from political prejudice and military and ideological concerns, reflected by the strict export control system towards China. The admission of military space activities and separating them from civilian ones in legislation would significantly reduce the misconception of China being a threat to space security, which would be of help in establishing a certain degree of strategic trust and would lead to collaboration in producing tangible benefits.

---

154 C. Venet, The Political Dimension of Space Activities, in C. Brünner, A. Soucek (eds.), *Outer Space in Society, Politics and Law, Studies in Space Policy*, Vol. 8, Vienna: European Space Policy Institute, 2011, p. 73.

155 The principles of national sovereignty and the use of constitutions have been a part of the post-Westphalian political order towards a balance of sovereign nation-states, on the one hand, and voluntary cooperation between them on an interstate level, on the other. D. Held, *Cosmopolitan Democracy in Models of Democracy*, London: Polity Press, 1997, p. x.

156 X. Wu, International Cooperation in China's Space Undertakings: Melting down Political Obstacles through Legal Means, *Proceedings of the 59th IISL Colloquium on the Law of Outer Space*, Eleven, 2017, pp. 589-595.

Cooperation triumphs rivalry, and a ban on cooperation is a lose-lose situation.[157] China and the US must interact with each other and find a way out of the stalemate.[158] The Chinese government should be more proactive to move away from mistrust and towards interdependence. This is not without precedent. The US rationale behind the MOAs in the 1980s and the 1990s was trading with the enemy, i.e., utilizing China's launch capabilities after the Challenger accident and preventing the transfer of satellite technology to China by specifying the security procedures and establishing a price and quota system.[159] One of the reasons that the US excludes China from the ISS and the total ban on space collaboration is that they identify the PLA as the key controlling actor and participatory entity as well as the fact that the COSTIND/SASTIND is not equivalent to the civilian U.S. NASA.[160] Based on the determination to draw a line between civilian and military on a legislative level, China should take the initiative to renew the bilateral agreements with the US in small scientific and commercial projects, demonstrating them as a good way to promote the development of mutual trust and respect and the smooth and effective functioning of the international space market.[161]

Moreover, the existing domestic law, without structural institutional arrangements, was insufficient to provide clear regulations and proved problematic for the critical parts of the cooperation process. There are no specific export control rules for space

---

157 The policy of strict export control has proved unsuccessful in denying technologies to thwart China's development of space and missile capabilities. China has outmanoeuvred the sanctions by developing an indigenous space capability and by forging partnerships with other countries. Cooperation banning is ineffective and counterproductive in nature. It significantly increased the investment of China and has been a loss of market share for the American space industry, undermining its business competitiveness in key technological and defence-industrial sectors.
158 Even during the Cold War, a joint US-Soviet space docking exercise in 1975 achieved an important technical and political breakthrough in many ways.
159 The MOA on Satellite Technology Safeguards of 1988, the MOA on Liability for Satellite Launches of 1988, the MOA regarding International Trade in Commercial Launch Services of 1989, and Memorandum of Agreement Regarding International Trade in Commercial Launches Services between the USA Government and the PRC Government of 1995, see the annex of the agreement on international space cooperation. Y. Zhao, *National Space Law in China: An Overview of the Current Situation and Outlook for the Future*, Leiden: Hotei Publishing, 2015, pp. 48-49. H. Meijer, *Trading with the Enemy: The Making of US Export Control Policy toward the People's Republic of China*, Oxford: Oxford University Press, 2016, pp. 92-95.
160 R. Handberg, China's Space Strategy and Policy Evolution, in E. Sadeh (ed.), *Space Strategy in the 21st Century: Theory and Policy*, New York: Routledge, 2013, p. 249.
161 There is some degree of cooperation between China and the US. A payload delivered to the International Space Station in 2017 was an experiment developed by Deng Yulin, a professor at the Beijing Institute of Technology in China, and selected by an American company, Nanoracks. J. Foust, One Small Step for U.S.-China Space Cooperation, https://spacenews.com/one-small-step-for-u-s-china-space-cooperation. Last accessed August 2021.

products, technologies and services, and they are all subject to the regulations for military assets in practice.[162]

The export licensing procedures are composed of 'three applications, three approvals,' i.e., export project, export contract and export licence. This is time-consuming, unpredictable and unsuitable, taking into account the fast rhythm of the international market. The export licensing decisions are under the authority of the SASTIND, while the Ministry of Defence, Ministry of Commerce and the General Administration of Customs and the MFA shall be consulted to assess the impact of transfers on China's international relations and international legal obligations in "politically sensitive and potentially controversial cases."[163] Worse than the vague expression, there is no formalized inter-agency mechanism and no clear provision of who shall be consulted and when, and the relevant practice is hardly systematic or coherent.

The 2020 Export Control Law (ECL) establishes China's first comprehensive framework for restricting exports of military and dual-use products, technologies and services.[164] The ECL provides for a general framework, and crucial elements will be specified through the drafting of new implementing measures and conforming revisions of existing regulations. It largely preserves the decentralized administrative structure, which is resulting in overlapping licensing regimes and controls lists based on different nomenclature and procedures.[165] The controlled items are defined as dual-use items, military products and nuclear materials without prescribing the format, methodology or scope for various controlled items.

---

162 The relevant regulatory documents include the Regulation on the Administration of Arms Export Control (amended in 2002); the Regulation on Export Control of Missiles and Missile-Related Items and Technologies, and the Measure for Administration on Import and Export License for Dual-Use Items ad Technologies.
163 Art. 3 of the Regulation on the Administration of Arms Export Control.
164 The ECL was passed by the NPC Standing Committee in October 2020 and took effect on 1 December 2020. The previous export control rules were scattered in Foreign Trade Law, the Customs Law and a series of administrative and ministerial regulations. These regulations are the Regulation on Export Control of Nuclear Dual-Use Items and Related Technology, the Regulation on Export Control of Dual-Use Biological Agents and Related Equipment and Technology, the Regulation on the Administration of Controlled Chemicals, the Measures on Export Control of Certain Chemicals and Related Equipment and Technology and the corresponding lists.
165 The ministries under the State Council and departments under the Central Military Commission that are fulfilling the functions of export control are collectively defined as state export control authorities with responsibility for export control activities within their respective jurisdictions. An export control coordination mechanism will be established, and ministries under the State Council (but not the Central Military Commission) shall collaborate and share information. Arts. 4 and 5 of the ECL.

As a negligible fraction, the particularities of the space industry were scarcely considered during the sudden hasty legislative process, which renders the preparation of a separate list under the ECL unfeasible.[166] Primarily aiming at the consolidation of existing mechanisms for safeguarding the national interest in response to foreign trade pressure, the export control administration in the space field has not visibly improved. For instance, the export of military and dual-use items is still subject to three approvals.[167] Therefore, the main content of the existing rules and lists remains, overemphasizing the military nature of space products, technologies and services. This shall be remedied by the future space legislation, establishing a proper export control regime with an individual list, loosening control on some products, technologies and services.

3.5. The Prospects of Space Legislation

3.5.1. The Legislation Path and Major Content of Future Outer Space Law

A basic law is the major step for the vacuum to be filled and the core task to be accomplished for the improvement of space legislation. After years of discussion and preparation, Outer Space Law was incorporated into the NPC's five-year legislation plan in 2013 and 2018.[168] Based on the degree of maturity, the NPC legislation plan is categorized as will be deliberated, could be deliberated, and in need of further study and analysis. Space Law was first listed in the last category and moved up to the second one in 2018.[169] The State Council is usually in charge of the law drafting concerning one sector of the society such as a law for outer space, which was further assigned to the

---

166 It is a long-standing goal to elevate and consolidate the ministry-level export control authorities under one national-level legal framework: the legislation work was accelerated, starting from a June 2017 draft prepared by the Ministry of Commerce, and ended with the promulgation of the final law in October 2020, a year after the US had adopted export controls targeted at Chinese companies such as Huawei. The final part includes several provisions that appear to be aimed at creating a Chinese policy counterweight to the US government's use of export authorities to restrict the transfer of US dual-use technology to China, including provisions for retaliatory action and extraterritorial jurisdiction.
167 Art. 24 of ECL.
168 There were once debates over a space law or an administrative regulation and over the title being outer space law or the law for outer space activities, both of which have been ended by the official incorporation into the NPC legislation plan. The NPC enacts and amends criminal, civil, and state organic laws and other basic laws. The Standing Committee enacts and amends all laws other than those to be enacted by the NPC. Arts. 62 and 67 of Constitution. So, a space law should at least be enacted by the Standing Committee. *See* www.gov.cn/zhengce/content/2016-04/13/content_5063670.htm. Last accessed August 2021.
169 *See* www.npc.gov.cn/zgrdw/npc/xinwen/syxw/2013-10/31/content_1812101.htm and www.npc.gov.cn/npc/c30834/201809/f9bff485a57f498e8d5e22e0b56740f6.shtml. Last accessed August 2021.

SASTIND.[170] Great efforts have been made for its formulation, and the drafts have been circulated to the relevant governmental and military organs seeking advice and suggestions.

The legislation models can be roughly divided in two categories, centralized and decentralized. The Russian Federation, the Netherlands, France, Australia and some other nations have a basic space law, whereas there are component and parallel laws in different space activities fields as in the US. The former prevails in stability but might lack flexibility, while the latter is easy to modify and expand along with the development of space activities but could suffer from the absence of coherence and consistency. As for China, a basic law supplemented by a set of administrative regulations, ministerial regulations and regulatory documents has been determined. This model has proved to be effective in China's rule-of-law construction history. The majority of laws are normally composed of intentionally loosely drafted general principles in consideration of the enormous size of the national territory and population, a vast regional variety and the rapid speed of development.[171] A specialized law will be formulated to provide the fundamental legal directions to space activities, with the content of basic principles and core regimes being regarded as necessary to be encompassed. The primary purpose and function of lower-level regulation documents to be adopted by relevant State Council ministries, PLA departments and the local governments will be the implementation of this law through further specific and precise provisions covering one core regime regulating space activities (such as by updating the already existing Registration Measures and Licensing Measures) or certain types of space activities (such as remote sensing data management), major space programmes (such as the lunar programme) and their application in some areas.[172] After the promulgation of Outer Space Law, the Registration Measures and the Licensing Measures will be revised, and the regulations on liability caused by space objects and international space cooperation will probably be adopted accordingly. Ideally, this multilevel structure will have the advantages of both centralized and decentralized models, satisfying the need for legal regulation while leaving sufficient room for future advancement and maintaining the balance between stability and flexibility that is required by the constant evolution of space activities. It

---

170 A legislative bill can be introduced by the State Council, the Central Military Committee, the Supreme People's Court, the Supreme People's Procuratorate or its subcommittee to the NPC or its Standing Committee. The drafting mission of space law is assigned to the SASTIND, which will submit a space law draft text through the State Council to the NPC. Once a bill is put on the agenda of the NPC or the Standing Committee's session, it shall be deliberated three times before being voted on. The opinions from various methods, such as panel discussions, feasibility study meetings and hearings, shall be heard, and comments from relevant governmental organs, organizations and experts shall be complied with in the course of deliberation. *See* Arts. 7, 14.2, 26 and 29 of the Law on Legislation.
171 More than 200 laws are supported and supplemented by hundreds of administrative regulations, thousands of ministerial regulations and tens of thousands of local regulatory rules.
172 Arts. 65, 73 and 82 of Law on Legislation.

would be a key issue as to how to guarantee comprehensiveness yet avoid ambiguity and a low level of operability in overly generalized principles and regimes.

This 'one plus many and multilevel' method corresponds to the already existing space regulation practice in some areas, such as the remote sensing data management. Similarly, the regulatory documents for certain aspects of lunar exploration are also drafted along with programme performance, which might be transformed into higher-level legislation documents. The ongoing legislative work for the regulation of satellite navigation also adopts this method.

Considering the maturity of the Beidou system, the Administrative Regulation of Satellite Navigation was incorporated into the States Council's legislative work plan in 2016, and the organization of draft work was assigned to the EDD of the Central Military Commission.[173] Meanwhile, the State Council ministerial organs and the local governments, such as Shanghai, Guangdong province and Shandong provinces, have formulated hundreds of standards and rules for Beidou's application within their competence in the fields of city planning, agriculture, transportation and geographic surveying and mapping.[174]

China legal reforms have been successful partly owing to the ability to select and adapt foreign laws to domestic conditions.[175] Legal transplant and comparative preparatory work are a routine practice in China's law making, helping to avoid mistakes by relying on already existing and well-approved patterns.[176] In this regard, a remarkable diversity can also be identified in the existing body of national space legislation as to their scope, extent and approach because states are enacting their legal framework in tune with their specific needs and practical considerations, often closely corresponding to the types of their space activities.[177]

There is thus no reason not to search also overseas for reference examples in space legislation. As for the UN Resolution on space legislation, the guidelines, as elaborated by

---

173 As for the State Council legislation work plan of 2016, see www.gov.cn/zhengce/content/2016-04/13/content_5063670.htm. The aim and purpose of formulating this administrative regulation are to promote the construction, operation and application of Beidou navigation system, to clarify its legal status as a national major space information infrastructure, to promote its industrial and commercial development and international cooperation, and to further consolidate the Beidou system's capacity in providing service at the national, regional and global levels, www.scio.gov.cn/xwfbh/xwbfbh/wqfbh/33978/34658/zy34662/Document/1480514/1480514.htm. There is apparent transparency in its draft work with the stable participation of law professors and other experts and the release of a designated report in 2021. See the Report on the Legal Construction of Beidou Satellite Navigation System, www.beidou.gov.cn/xt/gfxz/202105/P020210527502247416827.pdf. Last accessed August 2021.
See www.beidou.gov.cn/zt/zcfg and the Report on the Legal Construction of Beidou Satellite Navigation System. Last accessed August 2021.
174 *Ibid.*
175 B. L. Liebman, Assessing China's Legal Reforms, *Columbia Journal of Asian Law*, Vol. 23, 2009, p. 30.
176 V. Behr, Development of a New Legal System in the People's Republic of China, *Louisiana Law Review*, Vol. 67, 2007, p. 63.
177 I. Marboe, National Space Law, in F. von der Dunk, F. Tronchetti (eds.), *Handbook of Space Law*, Cheltenham: Edward Elgar Publishing, 2015, pp. 183-184.

the International Law Association, as well as the legislative experience of space nations have been most helpful in the elaboration of the basic regulatory regime for space activities.[178] They will certainly be absorbed in the Chinese context, i.e., into the provisions relating to the scope of application, the major governing authorities and their competence and obligations, the authorization, supervision and licensing of national space activities, the registration of space objects, international responsibility and liability for damage caused by space objects, assistance to and rescue of astronauts and space objects, environmental protection and space debris mitigation. The reason for this is that certain issues, such as the governing authority, the liability regime and the launch permits, must be governed by law according to the Law on Legislation and the Law on Administrative Licenses.[179] In accordance with the routine of other domestic laws, the other indispensable elements might be the purpose of enacting the Outer Space Law, the strategic status of space activities in national development, the fundamental principles for carrying out space activities, such as peaceful and cooperative development and the generic developing direction of space activities and measures for the implementation of the fundamental principles.

3.5.2.   The Core Controversy Over the Space Legislation

The continuous development of space activities brought up more and more issues calling for solutions within institutional regimes and legal rules, which reversely increase the complexity of space legislation and the difficulty of designing regimes and drafting rules. Usually, the controversy in drafting a space law stems from the unique nature of space activities, which are an extremely small field but have far-reaching military, political, technological and economic significance. In China, this demonstrates how to

---

178 Sofia Guidelines for a Model Law on National Space Legislation, ILA Res. No. 6/ 2012; ILA Draft Model Law for National Space Legislation and Explanatory Notes, Final Report of the Sofia Conference, 2012. Recommendations on national legislation relevant to the peaceful exploration and use of outer space, UN Res. 68/74, 16 December 2013. T. C. Brisibe, An Introduction to United Nations COPUOS Recommendations on National Legislation relevant to the Peaceful Exploration and Use of Outer Space, *Zeitschrift für Luft- und Weltraumrecht (German Journal of Air and Space Law)*, Vol. 62(4), 2013, pp. 728-739. S. Hobe, The ILA Model Law for National Space Legislation, *Zeitschrift für Luft- und Weltraumrecht (German Journal of Air and Space Law)*, Vol. 62(1), 2013, pp. 81-95.
179 The following affairs shall only be governed by law: affairs concerning state sovereignty; the formation, organization and the function and powers of the people's congress, governments, courts and procuratorates at all levels, the systems of regional national autonomy, the system of special administrative regions, criminal offences and their punishment, mandatory measures and penalties involving deprivation of citizens' political rights or restriction of their personal freedom, basic taxation regimes, expropriation and requisition of non-state-owned property, *basic civil regimes*, fundamental economic systems and basic fiscal, customs, financial and foreign trade regimes, litigation and arbitration regimes. See Art. 8 of the Law on Legislation. The administrative licences must be established and implemented in accordance with the competence, scope, conditions and procedures prescribed by law. See Art. 4 of the Law on Administrative Licenses.

streamline the governance structure, how to limit the long-lasting and widespread military involvement and how to accommodate the NewSpace into the traditional development model. The problem is that answers to these questions, at least the primary ones, are necessary for completing a space legal system, but the solutions are often more than space law can accomplish. Coherent outer space legislation would therefore be an enabling element of the arduous journey of the systematic overhauling of the space industry, especially by upgrading the development model and adapting it to China's new status in international society. Solving the conundrum in drafting Outer Space Law is thereby also about the question as to how to explore its enabling function at this critical time:

First, the strong interaction between law and politics invests space governance with utmost importance, especially the decision-making process for sensitive and crucial issues. The technological, economic, military and strategic significance of space activities demands a high-level and rule-based governing system. Worldwide, a major purpose of space legislation is the establishment of specialized authorities, and, occasionally, this is the only purpose of a space act or at least the starting point for national legislation.[180] In China, one of the basic principles in a law-making process is that all laws must scientifically and rationally prescribe the powers and responsibilities of a state organ or several state organs.[181] China's space governance should be improved to strengthen the relations among different sectors and actors as well as for the coherence, transparency and efficiency of policy formulation, decision-making, organization and supervision of space activities.[182]

There is already some governance structure for decision-making, allotment of finances and organization of activities after a development of six decades. Naturally, there are two options in this respect: the relatively easy one is to legalize and streamline the current governance mechanism with the addition of specific elements for authorizing and supervising commercial space activities. One feasible method in this respect could be to officially designate the governing power for civil activities to the SASTIND or the CNSA, making the latter's name match the reality. Another solution would be to use

---

180 For instance, the Argentina No. 995/91 National Decree created the National Commission on Space Activities in 1991. The Brazilian Law No. 8.854 established its Space Agency in 1994. The Canadian Space Agency Act was established in 1990 by a space act. Chile No. 338 Decree established a Presidential Advisory Committee known as its Space Agency in 2001. The first space-related law in Japan was the 1969 Law concerning the National Space Development Agency. A Nigerian act established its National Space Research and Development Agency in 2010. A 2018 Philippine act created its Agency. The South African National Space Agency Act was enacted in 2008. A Ukraine presidential decree established its National Space Agency in 1992. The first US space act created NASA in 1958 and has been revised seven times since. See www.unoosa.org/oosa/en/ourwork/spacelaw/nationalspacelaw/index.html. Last accessed August 2021.
181 Art. 6 of the Law on Legislation.
182 H. Zhao, The Status Quo and the Future of Chinese Space Legislation, *Zeitschrift für Luft- und Weltraumrecht (German Journal of Air and Space Law)*, Vol. 58(1), 2009, p. 98.

this chance for reform in terms of establishing and reinforcing transparent and efficient space governance in line with the special features of China's space activities. This could fulfil the purpose of restructuring the state organs, transforming their roles and responsibilities and manifesting the administrative approach evolving from being responsive to becoming preventive. A governing system across sectors and domains is at least composed of a body at the top level and two major governing authorities within the State Council and the PLA. The top body shall be responsible for making the major decisions for space capacity development and the overall coordination of space activities, reconciling, in particular, the differences and discrepancies between the civil and the military. The institutional boundaries of the governmental and military organs and their interaction need clarification in order to simplify the existing governance structure and to avoid wasteful use of national resources.

In particular, the governance system should be improved with special regard to the importance of international communication, well-informed decision-making based on necessary technical and legal knowledge, other expertise as well as narrative skills. The White Papers were criticized because of their bureaucratic language, overgeneralized aspirations and quite bland statements in terms of diplomacy.[183] The drafting of policy documents as well as space diplomacy, in general, needs advancement by giving a deeper and wider comprehension of China's views and intentions instead of repeating standard propaganda, thereby generating misunderstanding and unwarranted suspicions or leading even to expressions of hostility.

Second, it is a difficult task to separate civil and military activities and to reduce military participation. Primary functions in the space programmes have been and still are – even after rounds of reformation – performed and dominated by or within the military, which originated in the historical context under the guiding principle of pooling resources. The PLA is the main operator of space assets, including the launching sites and space tracking and telemetry centres. A relatively clear baseline between the civilian and military and the limitation of the latter's massive involvement, for instance, to the extent of high-level and national security-related research and development, would facilitate the implementation of Civil Military Integration (CMI) strategy, better foster the industrialization of space technologies and significantly improve the transparency of space activities. But the sheer complexity of reformation is already a primary hindrance for establishing regulatory regimes. It requires lowering the long-standing institutional barriers between different departments and sectors and forging a close and smooth cooperative relation for coordinative and integrated development. Of course, such a procedure would imply the irrefutable admission of military space activities and needs careful decision-making and handling.

---

183 B. Harvey, China's Space Program: Emerging Competitor or Potential Partner?, in J. C. Moltz (ed.), *New Challenges in Missile Proliferation, Missile Defense and Space Security*, CNS Occasional Paper No. 12, Monterey: Center for Non-Proliferation Studies, 2003, p. 54.

Third, the legislation is facing a double-edged problem, namely the extent to which to preserve the proven success of the traditional development model and the extent to which to welcome and embrace NewSpace. The former requires legal regulation, and the latter is in need of promotion and encouragement through the combination of law and policy. Although these approaches appear to be contradictory in nature, they are linked in a way that maintains the dynamic development within space industry. A decision in this regard implies clarifying to what extent the space industry shall be adaptive to the market demand and the market forces, how to balance defence and economic resources and activities (taking into account the decade-old frustration about the invigoration of the defence industrial base) and how to define itself in international society. So far some of the debatable topics are the following: the distinctive elements between policy and law and how to define the role of government vis-à-vis the market in fostering the development of space economy; whether and how to follow the example of the US in promoting commercial activities and international legal development; whether the encouragement should be rather vague in tone and expressed in general principles or with supporting institutional arrangements.

An example of this debate is mirrored in the question of whether and how to address the issue of space mining. Officially, China's stance is not clear as it is adopting a wait-and-see attitude. Internally, there is divergence as to whether space mining shall be explicitly regulated. According to some, China's space capacity and its ambitious plans might enable the exploitation and utilization of space-based resources and could be necessary to regulate these kinds of space activities for the sake of legislative stability. Also, the space capacity gap between China and the US is narrowing, and the states' positions could change along with the technological development and the lowering cost. China could use national legislation to influence and actively participate in international negotiation. But there are opposing opinions. The key reason behind the adoption of the US and Luxembourg laws protecting the property rights of space resources was the pressure exercised by private companies supporting their space resource utilization plans. China's capabilities in deep space exploration are confined to the traditional governmental actors, and no private companies have and will have, realistically, the capacity or express the plan to exploit space resources in quite some years. China does not have the need and motivation to enact a similar regulating regime.

3.6. Concluding Remarks

China's space legislation has been lagging behind its space activities and the development towards the rule of law. China's space activities, which are still characterized by the fundamental feature of a planned economy, have reached the historical phase of transformation and upgrading. China's policy-oriented regulatory framework has proved insufficient to bring about major changes to large-scale, state-funded space programmes and activities in the framework of an immature market condition. The consensus on the importance and the endogenous need for legal regulation are no more to be stopped or reversed owing to the dynamic development of the rule of law and the growth of China's space capacity. A common view on the importance of an overall and comprehensive law has been achieved, improving the outdated nature of the existing regulatory framework, ensuring the orderly and sustainable development of space activities and enhancing China's capabilities in outer space affairs. Outer Space Law is rushing to the finishing line of its marathon.

Annexes
Policy Documents, Regulatory Rules and Diplomatic Statements

1. WHITE PAPERS ON SPACE ACTIVITIES[1]

1.1. CHINA'S SPACE ACTIVITIES OF 2000

Information Office of the State Council
November 2000
(Official English Version)

Foreword

The scope of mankind's activities has experienced expansion from land to ocean, from ocean to atmosphere and from atmosphere to outer space. Space technology, which emerged in the 1950s, opened up a new era of man's exploration of outer space.

Having developed rapidly for about half a century, mankind's space activities have scored remarkable achievements, greatly promoted the development of social productivity and progress and produced profound and far-reaching effects. Space technology has turned out to be one field of high technology that exerts the most profound influence on modern society. The continuous development and application of space technology has become an important endeavor in the modernization drive of countries all over the world.

The Chinese nation created a glorious civilization in the early stage of mankind's history. The gunpowder "rocket" invented by ancient Chinese was the embryo of modern space rockets. After the People's Republic of China was founded in 1949, China carried out space activities on its own and succeeded in developing and launching its first man-made satellite in 1970. China has made eye-catching achievements and now ranks among the world's most advanced countries in some important fields of space technology. In the 21st century, China will continue to promote the development of its space industry in the light of its national situation and make due contributions to the peaceful use of outer space, the civilization and progress of mankind.

At the turn of the century, it is of significance to give a brief introduction to the aims and principles, present situation, future development and international cooperation concerning China's space activities.

---

[1] All policy documents of this section are the official English version of White Papers on China's Space Activities, cited from www.china.org.cn and www.scio.gov.cn, last accessed August 2021.

I. Aims and Principles

The Chinese government has all along regarded the space industry as an integral part of the state's comprehensive development strategy and upheld that the exploration and utilization of outer space should be for peaceful purposes and benefit the whole of mankind. As a developing country, China's fundamental tasks are developing its economy and continuously pushing forward its modernization drive. The aims and principles of China's space activities are determined by their important status and function in protecting China's national interests and implementing the state's development strategy.

The aims of China's space activities are: to explore outer space and learn more about the cosmos and the Earth; to utilize outer space for peaceful purposes, promote mankind's civilization and social progress and benefit the whole of mankind; and to meet the growing demands of economic construction, national security, science and technology development and social progress, protect China's national interests and build up the comprehensive national strength.

China carries out its space activities in accordance with the following principles:

- Adhering to the principle of long-term, stable and sustainable development and making the development of space activities cater to and serve the state's comprehensive development strategy. The Chinese government attaches great importance to the significant role of space activities in implementing the strategy of revitalizing the country by reliance on science and education and that of sustainable development, as well as in economic construction, national security, science and technology development and social progress. The development of space activities is encouraged and supported by the government as an integral part of the state's comprehensive development strategy.

- Upholding the principle of independence, self-reliance and self-renovation and actively promoting international exchanges and cooperation. China shall rely on its own strength to tackle key problems and make breakthroughs in space technology. Meanwhile, due attention shall be given to international cooperation and exchanges in the field of space technology and self-renovation in space technology shall be combined organically with technology import on the principles of mutual benefit and reciprocity.

- Selecting a limited number of targets and making breakthroughs in key areas according to the national situation and strength. China carries out its space activities for the purpose of satisfying the fundamental demands of its modernization drive. A limited number of projects that are of vital significance to the national economy and social development are selected so as to concentrate strength to tackle major difficulties and achieve breakthroughs in key fields.

- Enhancing the social and economic returns of space activities and paying attention to the motivation of technological progress. China strives to explore a more economical

and efficient development road for its space activities so as to achieve the integration of technological advance and economic rationality.
- Sticking to integrated planning, combination of long-term development and short-term development, combination of spacecraft and ground equipment and coordinated development. The Chinese government develops space technology, application and science through integrated planning and rational arrangement in the aim of promoting the comprehensive and coordinated development of China's space activities.

II. Present Situation

Since its birth in 1956, China's space program has gone through several important stages of development: arduous pioneering, overall development in all related fields, reform and revitalization and international cooperation. Now it has reached a considerable scale and level. A comprehensive system of research, design, production and testing has been formed. Space centers capable of launching satellites of various types and manned spacecraft as well as a TT&C (Telemetry Tracking and Command) network consisting of ground stations across the country and tracking and telemetry ships are in place. A number of satellite application systems have been established and have yielded remarkable social and economic benefits. A space science research system of a fairly high level has been set up and many innovative achievements have been made. And a contingent of qualified space scientists and technicians has come to the fore.

China's space industry was developed on the basis of weak infrastructure industries and a relatively backward scientific and technological level, under special national and historical conditions. In the process of carrying out space activities independently, China has opened a road of development unique to its national situation and scored a series of important achievements with relatively small input and within a relatively short span of time. Now, China ranks among the most advanced countries in the world in many important technological fields, such as satellite recovery, multi-satellite launch with a single rocket, rockets with cryogenic fuel, strap-on rockets, launch of geo-stationary satellites and TT&C. Significant achievements have also been gained in the development and application of remote-sensing satellites and telecommunications satellites and in manned spacecraft testing and space micro-gravity experiments.

1. Space Technology

(1) Man-Made Satellites: China's first man-made satellite, the "Dongfanghong-I", was successfully developed and launched on April 24, 1970, making China the fifth country in the world with such capability. By October 2000, China had developed and launched 47 satellites of various types, with a flight success rate of over 90%. Altogether, four satellite series have been initially development in China, namely, recoverable remote-sensing satellites, "DFH (Dongfanghong)" telecommunications satellites, "FY (Fengyun)" meteorological satellites and "SJ (Shijian)" scientific research and technological experiment satellites. The "ZY (Ziyuan)" earth resource satellite series will come into being soon. China is the third country in the world to have mastered the technology of satellite recovery, with the success rate reaching the advanced international level and the fifth country capable of developing and launching geo-stationary telecommunications satellites independently. The major technological index of China's meteorological and earth resource satellites have reached the international level of the early 1990s. The six telecommunications, earth resources and meteorological satellites developed and launched by China in the past few years are in stable operation and have generated remarkable social and economic returns.

(2) Launching Vehicles: China has independently developed the "Long-March" rocket group, containing 12 types of launching vehicles capable of launching satellites to near-earth, geo-stationery and sun-synchronous orbits. The largest launching capacity of the "Long-March" rockets has reached 9,200 kg for near-earth orbit and 5,100 kg for geo-stationary transfer orbit, able to basically meet the demands of customers of all kinds. Since 1985, when the Chinese government announced to put the "Long-March" rockets into the international commercial launching market, China has launched 27 foreign-made satellites into space, thus acquiring a share of the international commercial launching market. Up to now, the "Long-March" rockets have accomplished 63 launches and made 21 consecutive successful flights from October 1996 to October 2000.

(3) Launching Sites: China has set up three launching sites – in Jiuquan, Xichang and Taiyuan – which have successfully accomplished various kinds of test flights of launching vehicles and launches of a variety of satellites and experimental space- craft. China's spacecraft launching sites are capable of making both domestic satellite launches and international commercial launches and carrying out international space cooperation in other fields.

(4) TT&C: China has established an integrated TT&C network comprising TT&C ground stations and ships, which has successfully accomplished TT&C missions for near-earth orbit and geo-stationary orbit satellites and experimental spacecraft. This network has acquired the capability of sharing TT&C resources with international network and its technology has reached the international advanced level.

(5) Manned Spaceflight: Initiating its manned spaceflight program in 1992, China has developed a manned spacecraft and high-reliability launching vehicle, carried out engineering studies in aerospace medicine and aerospace life science, selected reserve astronauts and developed equipment for aerospace remote-sensing and aerospace scientific experiments. China's first unmanned experimental spacecraft – "Shenzhou" was successfully launched and recovered November 20-21, 1999, symbolizing a breakthrough in the basic technologies of manned spacecraft and a significant step forward in the field of manned spaceflight.

2. Space Applications

China attaches importance to developing all kinds of application satellites and satellite application technology and has made great progress in satellite remote-sensing, satellite telecommunication and satellite navigation. Remote-sensing and telecommunications satellites account for about 71% of the total number of satellites developed and launched by China. These satellites have been widely utilized in all aspects of economy, science and technology, culture and national defense and yielded remarkable social and economic returns. Related departments of the state have also made active use of foreign application satellites for application technology studies, with satisfactory results.

(1) Satellite Remote-Sensing: China began to use domestic and foreign remote-sensing satellites in the early 1970s and eventually carried out studies, development and promotion of satellite remote-sensing application technology, which has been widely applied in meteorology, mining, surveying, agriculture, forestry, water conservancy, oceanography, seismology and urban planning. To date, China has established the National Remote- Sensing Center, National Satellite Meteorology Center, China Resources Satellite Application Center, Satellite Oceanic Application Center and China Remote-Sensing Satellite Ground Station, as well as satellite remote-sensing application institutes under related ministries of the State Council, some provinces and municipalities and the Chinese Academy of Sciences. These institutions have made use of both domestic and foreign remote- sensing satellites to carry out application studies in weather forecasting, territorial survey, agricultural output assessment, forest survey, natural disaster monitoring, maritime forecasting, urban planning and mapping. The regular operation of the meteorological satellite ground application system, in particular, has greatly improved the accuracy of forecasting disastrous weather and significantly reduced the economic losses of the state and people from such weather.

(2) Satellite Telecommunications: In the mid-1980s, China began to utilize domestic and foreign telecommunications satellites and developed related technology to meet the increasing demands of the development of telecommunications, broad- casting and education. In the field of fixed telecom service, China has built scores of large and medium-sized satellite telecom earth stations, with more than 27,000 international satellite telephone channels connected to more than 180 countries and regions worldwide. The establishment of the domestic satellite public communication network, with more than 70,000 satellite telephone channels, has initially solved the problem of communication in remote areas. The VSAT (Very Small Aperture Terminal) communication service has developed very rapidly in recent years. There are now in the country 30 domestic VSAT communication service providers and 15,000 small-station users, including over 6,300 two-way users. More than 80 specialized communication networks for dozens of departments like finance, meteorology, transportation, oil, water resources, civil aviation, power, public health and the media have been built, with over 10,000 VSAT. A satellite TV broadcasting system covering the whole world and a satellite TV education system covering the whole country have been established. China started to use satellites for TV broadcasting in 1985 and has formed a satellite transmission network with 33 telecommunications satellite transponders responsible for transmitting 47 TV programs and educational TV programs of CCTV (China Central Television) and local TV stations throughout the country, 32 programs of the Central Broadcasting Station domestically and abroad and about 40 local broadcasting programs. Ever since the opening of satellite education TV broadcasting programs over a dozen years ago, more than 30 million people have got college or secondary technical school education and training through it. China has also set up a satellite direct broadcasting experimental platform to transmit CCTV and local satellite TV programs by digital compression to the vast rural areas which wireless TV broad- casting cannot cover. In this way, China's TV broadcasting coverage has been greatly increased. China has about 189,000 satellite TV broadcasting receiving stations. The China broad-band multi-media education satellite transmission network has also been established on the satellite direct broadcasting experimental platform to provide comprehensive remote education and information technology services.

(3) **Satellite Navigation:** In the early 1980s, China began to utilize other countries' navigation satellites and develop the application technology of satellite navigation and positioning, which is now widely used in many fields including land survey, ship navigation, aircraft navigation, earthquake monitoring, geological calamity monitoring, forest fire prevention and control and urban traffic control. After joining the COSPAS-SARSAT in 1992, China established the Chinese Mission Control Center, thus greatly improving the capability of the emergency alarm service for ships, aircraft and vehicles.

3. Space Science
China started to explore the upper atmosphere using rockets and balloons in the early 1960s. In the early 1970s, China began to utilize the scientific exploration and technological testing satellites of the "SJ" group in a series of space explorations and studies and acquired a large amount of valuable data about the space environment. Research on space weather forecasting and related international cooperation have also been carried out in recent years. In the late 1980s, recoverable remote-sensing satellites were employed for various kinds of aerospace scientific experiments and have yielded satisfactory achievements in crystal and protein growth, cell cultivation and crop

breeding. Innovative achievements have been scored in the study of basic theory of space science. The establishment of advanced and open state-level laboratories specializing in space physics, micro- gravity and space life science and the founding of the Space Payload Application Center provide the country with the basic ability to support aerospace scientific experiments. The "SJ" group has been used in recent years to detect charged particles in terrestrial space and their effects. In addition, the first micro- gravity space experiment on double-layer fluid was accomplished, in which remote operation of space experiments was realized.

With the establishment and improvement of China's socialist market economic mechanism, the state guides the development of space activities through macro-control, makes overall plans for the development of space technology, space application and space science, promotes the R&D and system integration of important space technologies and the application of space science and technology in the fields of economy, science and technology, culture and national defense. The state has also carried out reforms in the space science and technology industry to achieve sustainable development of the space industry. The state has strengthened legislation work and policy management, enacted laws and regulations and promulgated industrial policies for the space industry to ensure orderly and standardized development of space activities. Research institutions, industrial enterprises, commercial enterprises and institutions of higher learning are encouraged to make full use of their advantages and participate in space activities under the guidance of the state's space policies. The state supports renovation in space technology and the establishment of a space technological renovation system with Chinese characteristics, with the aim of improving the self-renovation capability and industrialization of space activities. Space activities for public welfare and R&D work with commercial prospects are also supported by the state and the state's supervision over space activities is being continuously strengthened. The China National Space Administration (CNSA) is China's govern- mental organization responsible for the management of satellites for civilian use and inter-governmental space cooperation with other countries.

III. Future Development

The 21st Century will witness vigorous development of space activities across the world. China is drafting a space development strategy and plans oriented to the 21st century according to the actual demands and long-term target of national development to spur the growth of the space industry.

1. Development Targets

The short-term development targets (for the next decade) are:
- To build up an earth observation system for long-term stable operation. The meteorological satellites, resource satellites, oceanic satellites and disaster monitoring satellites can develop into an earth observation system for long-term

stable operation to conduct stereoscopic observation and dynamic monitoring of the land, atmosphere, oceanic environments of the country, the peripheral regions and even the whole globe;
- To set up an independently operated satellite broadcasting and telecommunications system. Positive support will be given to the development of commercial broadcasting and telecommunications satellites such as geo-stationary telecom satellites and TV direct broadcasting satellites with long operating life, high reliability and large capacity, so as to form China's satellite telecom industry;
- To establish an independent satellite navigation and positioning system. This will be achieved by setting up a navigation and positioning satellite group step by step and developing a relevant application system, which will eventually bring into being China's satellite navigation and positioning industry;
- To upgrade the overall level and capacity of China's launching vehicles. This will be achieved by improving the performance and reliability of the "Long-March" group, developing the next generation of launching vehicles with non-toxic, non-polluting, high-performance and low-cost qualities, forming a new group of launching vehicles and strengthening the capability of providing international commercial launching services;
- To realize manned spaceflight and establish an initially complete R&D and testing system for manned space projects;
- To establish a coordinated and complete national satellite remote-sensing application system by building various related ground application systems through overall planning, setting up a remote-sensing data receiving, processing and distributing system covering the whole country for data sharing and forming a fairly complete application system in major application fields of satellite remote-sensing; and
- To develop space science and explore outer space by developing a scientific research and technological experiment satellite group of the next generation, strengthening studies of space micro-gravity, space material science, space life science, space environment and space astronomy and carrying out pre-study for outer space exploration centering on the exploration of the moon.

The long-term development targets (for the next 20 years or more) are as follows:
- To achieve industrialization and marketization of space technology and space applications. The exploration and utilization of space resources shall meet a wide range of demands of economic construction, state security, science and technology development and social progress and contribute to the strengthening of the comprehensive national strength;
- To establish a multi-function and multi-orbit space infrastructure composed of various satellite systems and set up a satellite ground application system that harmonizes spacecraft and ground equipment to form an integrated ground-space

network system in full, constant and long-term operation in accordance with the overall planning of the state;
- To establish China's own manned spaceflight system and carry out manned spaceflight scientific research and technological experiments on a certain scale; and
- To obtain a more important place in the world in the field of space science with more achievements and carry out explorations and studies of outer space.

2. Development Concepts

China develops its space activities with the following approaches:
- Accelerating the industrialization of space technology and its application. Enterprises engaged in space science and technology are guided and encouraged to renovate institutions and technology and establish an operational mechanism geared toward both the domestic and international markets, so as to speed up the industrialization of space technology and its applications step by step, with the stress on telecom satellites and satellite telecom and launching vehicles.
- Deploying space activities rationally. Space science, technology and application shall be developed in a well- coordinated manner through overall planning. The work in these three fields will be given differentiated importance from "preferential arrangement," "active support" and "proper development" to "follow-up studies," so as to ensure the comprehensive and coordinated development of China's space industry.
- Strengthening pre-study and technological infrastructure construction. Efforts will be concentrated on tackling key technological problems to grasp core technology and attain independent intellectual property rights. At the same time, technological infrastructure construction will be strengthened in the three aspects of space activities and international cooperation will be broadened to sustain the development momentum of China's space industry.
- Speeding up the development of talented people in the space industry and forming advantages in this regard. Special policies will be adopted to promote space education and train qualified personnel to foster a contingent of young and highly qualified space scientists and engineers. Efforts will be made to publicize space knowledge and motivate all sectors of society to support the development of the space industry.
- Improving scientific management for better quality and benefits. Since space activities involve huge investments, high risks, sophisticated technology and complicated systems, systems engineering and other modern management tolls shall be applied to promote scientific management, increase system quality, lower system risks and enhance comprehensive benefits.

IV. International Cooperation

China persistently supports activities involving the peaceful use of outer space and maintains that international space cooperation shall be promoted and strengthened on the basis of equality and mutual benefit, mutual complementarity and common development.

1. Guiding Principles

The Chinese government holds that international space cooperation should follow the fundamental principles listed in the "Declaration on International Cooperation on Exploring and Utilizing Outer Space for the Benefits and Interests of All Countries, Especially in Consideration of Developing Countries' Demands," which was approved by the 51st session of the UN General Assembly in 1996. China adheres to the following principles while carrying out international space cooperation:

- The aim of international space cooperation is to peacefully develop and use space resources for the benefit of all mankind.
- International space cooperation should be carried out on the basis of equality and mutual benefit, mutual complementarity and common development and the generally accepted principles of international law.
- The priority aim of international space cooperation is to simultaneously increase the capability of space development of all countries, particularly the developing countries and enable all countries to enjoy the benefits of space technology.
- Necessary measures should be adopted to protect the space environment and space resources in the course of international space cooperation.
- The function of the United Nations Office of Outer Space Affairs (OOSA) should be consolidated and the outer space application programs of the United Nations shall be backed up.

2. Fundamental Policies

The Chinese Government adopts the following policies in developing international space cooperation:

- Persisting in the independence and self-reliance policy, carrying out active and pragmatic international space cooperation to meet the needs of the national modernization drive and the demands of the domestic and international markets for space science and technology.
- Supporting multilateral international cooperation on the peaceful use of outer space within the framework of the United Nations.
- Attaching importance to the Asian-Pacific regional space cooperation and supporting space cooperation in other regions of the world.
- Attaching importance to space cooperation with both developed and developing countries.

– Enhancing and supporting research institutions, industrial enterprises and universities and colleges to develop international space exchanges and cooperation in different forms and at different levels under the guidance of relevant state policies, laws and regulations.

3. Important Events

China's participation in international space cooperation started at the mid-1970s. During the last two decades or more, China has joined bilateral, regional, multi-lateral and international space cooperation in different forms, such as commercial launching service, which have yielded extensive achievements.

(1) Bilateral Cooperation: Since 1985, China has successively signed inter-governmental or inter-agency cooperative agreements, protocols or memorandums and established long-term cooperative relations with a dozen countries, including the United States, Italy, Germany, Britain, France, Japan, Sweden, Argentina, Brazil, Russia, Ukraine and Chile. Bilateral space cooperation is implemented in various forms, from making reciprocal space programs and exchanges of scholars and specialists and sponsoring symposiums, to jointly developing satellites or satellite parts and providing satellite piggyback service and commercial launching service.

In 1993, a Sino-German joint venture – EurasSpace GmbH – was established and a contract on the development and manufacture of Sinosat-1 was signed with DASA and Aerospeciale in 1995. Sinosat-1, which was successfully launched in 1998, was the first cooperative project on satellite development between the Chinese and European aerospace industries.

The collaboration between China and Brazil on the project of an earth resources satellite is making good progress and the first such satellite was successfully launched by China on October 14, 1999. In addition to cooperation on complete satellites, China and Brazil are cooperating in the areas of satellite technology, satellite application and satellite components. The cooperation between China and Brazil in the space sector has set a good example for the developing countries in "South-South Cooperation" in the high-tech field.

(2) Regional Cooperation: China attaches great importance to space cooperation in the Asian-Pacific region. In 1992, China, Thailand, Pakistan and some other countries jointly sponsored the "Asian-Pacific Multilateral Space Technology Cooperation Symposium." Thanks to the impetus of such regional cooperation, the governments of China, Iran, the Republic of Korea, Mongolia, Pakistan and Thailand signed the "Memorandum of Under- standing on Cooperation in Small Multi- Mission Satellite and Related Activities" in Thailand in April, 1998. Besides the signatory countries, other countries in the Asian-Pacific region may also join the cooperative project, which has helped to enhance the progress of space technology and space application in the Asian-Pacific region.

(3) Multilateral Cooperation: In June 1980, China dispatched an observer delegation to the 23rd Meeting of UN COPUOS for the first time and on November 3, 1980, China became a member of COPUOS. Since then, China has participated in all the meetings of UN COPUOS and the annual meetings held by its Scientific and Technological and Legal Sub-committee. In 1983 and 1988, China acceded to the Treaty on Principles Governing the Activities of States in the Exploration and Use of Outer Space, Including the Moon and Other Celestial Bodies, Agreement on the Rescue of Astronauts, the Return of Astronauts and the Return of Objects Launched into Outer Space, Convention on International Liability for Damage Caused by Space Objects, and Convention on Registration of Objects Launched into Outer Space, and has strictly performed its responsibilities and obligations.

China supports and has participated in the UN space application program. Since 1988, China has provided other developing countries every year with scholarships for long-term space technology training. In 1994, together with ESCAP, China hosted in Beijing the first Asian-Pacific regional "Ministerial Conference on Space Applications for Sustainable Development in Asia and the Pacific," and the "Beijing Declaration" issued after the conference has had a far-reaching influence. In September 1999, in collaboration with the UN and ESA, the Chinese government held in Beijing the "Symposium on Promoting Sustainable Agricultural Development with Space Applications." From July to August 2000, together with the OOSA of the UN and ESCAP, relevant departments of the Chinese government opened the Short-term Training Course for Asian-Pacific Multilateral Cooperation in Space Technology and Applications. Trainees from ten developing countries in the Asian-Pacific region attended the course.

The issue of space debris is a big challenge to further expansion of space activities. The relevant governmental departments and units in China pay great attention to the problem and have carried out research on this issue with related countries since the beginning of the 1980s. In June 1995, CNSA acceded to the Inter-Agency Space Debris Coordination Committee. China will continuously make efforts to explore, together with other countries, ways and means to mitigate and reduce space debris and promote international cooperation on this issue.

In addition, China has participated in multilateral cooperative projects, such as Committee on Earth Observation Satellites, World Weather Monitoring, UN Decade of Disaster Mitigation and International Solar Terrestrial Physics.

(4) Commercial Launching Service: Ever since the Chinese government made the declaration in 1985 that China's 'Long March' launching vehicles would serve the

1. White Papers on Space Activities

international market and provide international satellite launching service, up to October 2000, China has successfully launched 27 foreign-made satellites for users in Pakistan, Australia, Sweden, the United States, the Philippines, as well as domestic users. The service of 'Long March' launching vehicles in the international satellite launching market is a beneficial supplement to international commercial satellite launching services and it has provided foreign clients with new options.

4. Priority Cooperation Areas
The Chinese government will continuously render support to international exchanges and cooperation in space technology, space applications and space science, with priority being given to cooperation in the following areas:
- Actively enhancing multilateral cooperation in space technology and applications in the Asian-Pacific region and promoting regional economic growth and environmental and natural calamity monitoring with space technology.
- Supporting Chinese space enterprises to participate in international space commercial launching services in line with the principles of equality, equity and reciprocity.
- Giving support to using China's mature space technology and space application technology to carry out cooperation with other developing countries and provide services to cooperating countries on the basis of mutual benefit.
- Supporting international exchanges and cooperation in earth environment monitoring, space environmental exploration and studies of micro-gravity science, space physics and space astronomy, particularly international exchanges and cooperation in micro-gravity fluid physics, space materials science, space life science and space biology.

(www.china.org.cn)

1.2. CHINA'S SPACE ACTIVITIES OF 2006

Information Office of the State Council
October 2006
(Official English Version)

The State Council Information Office published a white paper entitled China's Space Activities in 2006. The document is composed of five chapters – Aims and Principles of Development; Progress Made in the Past Five Years; Development Targets and Major Tasks for the Next Five Years; Development Policies and Measures; International Exchanges and Cooperation.

Half a century has passed since China embarked on the splendid road to developing its own space industry. For 50 years, China has trail-blazed in this field. Its achievements have been eye-catching and the nation now ranks among the world's most advanced countries in some crucial fields of space technology. China has always followed the road of peaceful development and maintained that outer space should be explored for the common wealth of mankind. While supporting all international efforts that utilize outer space for peaceful purposes, China continues to explore and use the cosmos to make new contributions to the development of humanity's space programs.

China's space industry has made great progress since the Chinese government issued the China's Space Activities white paper in 2000. This is the second white paper that the Chinese government has issued since 2000 concerning China's space activities. The full text of the white paper follows:

Preface

Space activities around the world have been flourishing in the first few years of the 21st century. Leading countries in the area of spaceflight have formulated or readjusted their development strategies, plans and goals in this sphere. The role of space activities in a country's overall development strategy is becoming increasingly salient and their influence on human civilization and social progress is increasing.

It has been 50 splendid years since China embarked on the road to develop its space industry, starting in 1956. For half a century, China has worked independently in this field. It has made eye-catching achievements and ranks among the world's most advanced countries in some important fields of space technology. China is unflinching in taking the road of peaceful development and always maintains that outer space is the common wealth of mankind. While supporting all activities that utilize outer space for peaceful purposes, China actively explores and uses outer space and continuously makes new contributions to the development of man's space programs.

China has set the strategic goal of building itself into a well-off society in an all-round way, ranking it among the countries with the best innovative capabilities in the first 20 years of the 21st century. The development of the space industry in China now faces new opportunities and higher requirements. In the new stage of development, China will adhere to the scientific outlook on development as guidance, center its work on the national strategic goals, strengthen its innovative capabilities and do its best to make the country's space industry develop faster and better.

China's space industry has made great progress since the Chinese government issued the white paper China's Space Activities in 2000. In order to give people around the world a better understanding of the development of China's space industry over the past five years and its plans for the near future, we hereby offer an expanded introduction to some related issues.

I. Aims and Principles of Development

The aims of China's space activities are: to explore outer space and enhance understanding of the Earth and the cosmos; to utilize outer space for peaceful purposes, promote human civilization and social progress and benefit the whole of mankind; to meet the demands of economic construction, scientific and technological development, national security and social progress; and to raise the scientific quality of the Chinese people, protect China's national interests and rights and build up the comprehensive national strength.

When developing the space industry, China will follow the principles guiding the development of the country's scientific and technological programs, namely, making innovations independently, making leapfrogging development in key areas, shoring up the economy and leading future trends. In the new development stage, the principles of development for China's space industry are as follows:

- Maintaining and serving the country's overall development strategy and meeting the needs of the state and reflecting its will. China considers the development of its space industry as a strategic way to enhance its economic, scientific, technological and national defense strength, as well as a cohesive force for the unity of the Chinese people, in order to rejuvenate China. Since the space industry is an important part of the national overall development strategy, China will maintain long- term, stable development in this field.

- Upholding independence and self-reliance policy, making innovations independently and realizing leapfrogging development. China relied completely on itself when it developed its space industry from scratch and has made constant progress through making independent innovations. Therefore, increasing the capability for independent innovation is a strategic basis for developing the space industry. In light of the country's actual situation and needs, China will focus on certain areas while ignoring less-important ones. It will choose some limited targets, concentrate its strength on making key breakthroughs and realize leapfrogging development.

Maintaining comprehensive, coordinated and sustainable development and bringing into full play the functions of space science and technology in promoting and sustaining the country's science and technology sector, as well as economic and social development. China will strengthen strategic planning, making overall plans for the development of space technology, space application and space science. It will encourage progress in space science and technology to promote the development of high technology and industry, as well as the transformation and upgrading of traditional industries. Meanwhile, it will protect the space environment and develop and utilize space resources in a rational manner.

- Adhering to the policy of opening up to the outside world and actively engaging in international space exchanges and cooperation. China supports all activities that utilize outer space for peaceful purposes. It will strengthen exchanges and cooperation in this field with other countries on the basis of the principles of equality, mutual benefit, peaceful utilization of outer space and common development.

II. Progress Made in the Past Five Years

From 2001 to 2005, China's space industry has developed rapidly, making many achievements. A group of research and development and testing bases of the advanced world level has been built and the system of research, design, production and testing has been further improved, markedly enhancing the country's basic capabilities in space science and technology. With breakthroughs in important key technologies, the overall level of China's space technology has been improved remarkably. Having made a historic breakthrough in manned spaceflight, China has embarked on a comprehensive lunar exploration project. Space application systems have taken shape, the range of application has been further expanded, application benefits have been noticeably enhanced and important achievements have been made in space scientific experiments and research in this regard.

1. Space Technology

(1) Man-Made Satellites. Over the past five years, China has independently developed and launched 22 different types of man-made satellites, upgrading its overall level in this field markedly. On the basis of the four satellite series initially developed, China has developed two more satellite series, to bring the total to six – the recoverable remote-sensing satellites, "DFH" (Dongfanghong, or The East is Red) telecommunications and broadcasting satellites, "FY" (Fengyun, or Wind and Cloud) meteorological satellites, "SJ" (Shijian, or Practice) scientific research and technological experiment satellites, "ZY" (Ziyuan, or Resources) Earth resource satellite and "Beidou" (Plough) navigation and positioning satellites. In addition, the oceanic satellite series will come into being soon. China has speeded up the implementation of the plan to establish "a constellation of small satellites for environment and disaster monitoring and forecasting." Research and development of the payload of some new, high-performance satellites have been successful and many application satellites have begun regular operation. The Fengyun I and Fengyun II meteorological satellites have been listed by the World Meteorological Organization in the international satellite series for meteorological services. Important breakthroughs have been made in key technologies related to the common platform for big geostationary orbit satellites. Periodical achievements have been made in the research and development of large-capacity telecommunications and broadcasting satellites. Substantial progress has been made in the research and development and application of small satellites.

(2) **Launching Vehicles.** Over the past five years, "Long March" rockets independently developed by China have made 24 consecutive successful flights and their major technological functions and reliability have been notably upgraded. From October 1996 to the end of 2005, "Long March" rockets made 46 consecutive successful flights. Important breakthroughs have been made in key technologies of the new-generation launching vehicles. Research and development of the 120-ton thrust liquid-oxygen/kerosene engine and the 50-ton thrust hydrogen-oxygen engine are proceeding smoothly.

(3) **Launching Sites.** The construction of three launching sites at Jiuquan, Xichang and Taiyuan, has made new progress and their comprehensive test and launch capabilities have been enhanced. Various launching vehicles, man-made satellites, unmanned experimental spacecraft and manned spacecraft have been successfully launched from the three launching sites many times.

(4) **Telemetry, Tracking and Command (TT&C).** The overall performance of the country's TT&C network has been improved and expanded. It has provided TT&C support to man-made satellites traveling in different orbits and to unmanned experimental spacecraft and manned spacecraft during launch, operation in orbit, return and landing.

(5) **Manned Spaceflight.** On November 20 and 21, 1999, China launched and retrieved the first "Shenzhou" unmanned experimental spacecraft. It then launched three more "Shenzhou" unmanned experimental spacecrafts not long afterwards. On October 15 and 16, 2003, it launched and retrieved the "Shenzhou V" manned spacecraft, China's first of its kind. Having mastered the basic technologies for manned spacecraft, China became the third country in the world to develop manned spaceflight independently. From October 12 to 17, 2005, the "Shenzhou VI" manned spacecraft completed a five-day flight with two astronauts on board. This was the first time for China to have men engage in experiments in space, another major achievement in the sphere of manned spaceflight.

(6) **Deep-space Exploration.** Advance studies and engineering work of the lunar-orbiting project has been conducted, making important progress.

2. Space Application

(1) **Satellite Remote-sensing.** The fields and scale where satellite remote-sensing is used have been constantly expanded. Breakthroughs have been made in a large number of key application technologies; infrastructure facilities have been strengthened; the technological level and operational capabilities of the application system have been

notably improved; and a national satellite remote-sensing application system has taken shape. China has built and improved the National Remote- Sensing Center, National Satellite Meteorology Center, China Resources Satellite Application Center, National Satellite Oceanic Application Center and China Remote-Sensing Satellite Ground Station, as well as satellite remote-sensing application and certification institutes of relevant state departments, provinces and cities. An optical remote-sensing satellite radiation calibration station has also been completed and put into operation. Many remote-sensing products and services are provided by using data resources obtained from observation of the Earth by both Chinese and foreign satellites of multiple wavelengths of wide scope and long duration. Satellite remote-sensing application systems have been put into regular operation in many important fields, particularly in meteorology, mining, surveying, agriculture, forestry, land mapping, water conservancy, oceanography, environmental protection, disaster mitigation, transportation and regional and urban planning. They are playing an important role in the nationwide land resources survey, ecological construction and environmental protection, as well as in major state projects, such as the South-North Water Diversion Project, the Three Gorges Project and the Project to Transmit Natural Gas from West to East.

(2) Satellite Telecommunications and Broadcasting. Satellite telecommunications and broadcasting technologies are developing rapidly, their application is becoming more extensive and an application industry in this field has taken initial shape. By the end of 2005, China had more than 80 international and domestic telecommunications and broadcasting Earth stations and 34 satellite broadcasting and TV link stations. Dozens of departments and some large corporations have established altogether some 100 satellite specialized communication networks and more than 50,000 Very Small Aperture Terminals (VSAT). The development and application of satellite radio and TV broadcasting services has increased the coverage and improved the quality of the programs all over China, particularly in the vast countryside. Satellite telecommunications and broadcasting technologies play an irreplaceable role in the projects "to give every village access to broadcasting and TV" and "to give every village access to telephones." A tele-education broadband satellite network and a telemedicine satellite network have been established. As a member of the International Maritime Satellite Organization, China has established a maritime satellite communication network covering the whole world, ranking it among the advanced countries in the application of international mobile satellite communication.

(3) Satellite Navigation and Positioning. China has implemented several major related projects, one of which is called "industrialization of satellite navigation and positioning applications." By employing domestic and foreign navigation and positioning satellites, China has made great progress in the development, application and services of satellite navigation and positioning technologies. The range and fields where satellite navigation and positioning are applied are being continuously expanded and the size of the national market for satellite navigation and positioning doubles every two years. Satellite navigation and positioning technologies have been widely used in transportation, basic surveying and mapping, project surveys, resources investigation, earthquake monitoring, meteorological exploration, oceanic surveys, etc.

3. Space Science

(1) Sun-Earth Space Exploration. In cooperation with the European Space Agency (ESA), China has carried out the Double Star Satellite Exploration of the Earth's Space Plan. Together with the four space exploration satellites of the ESA, China's satellites completed the world's first joint, synchronous six-point exploration of the Earth's space, obtaining important data. Advance research into exploration of the lunar and the solar systems was also conducted.

(2) Micro-gravity Scientific Experiments and Space Astronomical Observation. China has carried out many items of experimental research in such fields as space life science, space materials science and micro-gravity science by using the "Shenzhou" spacecraft and recoverable satellites. It has also conducted trial tests of mutant crop breeding and high-power astronomical observation in space and scored important achievements.

(3) Space Environment Research. China has conducted research into space environment monitoring and forecasting and made important progress in the observation, reduction and forecasting of space debris. It now has the ability to make forecasts of the space environment on a trial basis.

III. Development Targets and Major Tasks for the Next Five Years

"The Outline of the 11th Five-Year Program for National Economic and Social Development" and "The National Guideline for Medium- and Long-term Plans for Science and Technology Development (2006-2020)" formulated by the Chinese government in 2006 put the space industry in an important position. Based on the above two documents, the Chinese government has drawn up a new development plan for China's space industry, defining development targets and major tasks for the next five years or more. According to this plan, the country will launch and continue key space projects, including manned spaceflight, lunar exploration, high-resolution Earth observation, new-generation carrier rockets and a group of priority projects in key sectors. It will also strengthen basic research, make arrangements ahead of schedule, develop frontier space technology and accelerate progress and innovation in space science and technology.

1. Development Targets

To remarkably improve the country's capabilities and reliability of carrier rockets in space; to build a long-term, stably operated Earth observation system and a coordinated and complete national satellite remote-sensing application system; to set up a relatively complete satellite telecommunications and broadcasting system and remarkably enhance the scale and economic efficiency of the satellite telecommunications and broadcasting industry; to establish a satellite navigation and positioning system step by step to meet the demand and bring into being China's satellite navigation and positioning application industry; and to achieve the initial transformation of applied satellites and satellite application from experimental application type to operational service type.

To enable astronauts to engage in extravehicular activities and achieve spacecraft rendezvous and docking; to realize the lunar-orbiting probe; and make important and original achievements in space science research.

2. Major Tasks

- To develop nontoxic, pollution-free, high-performance, low-cost and powerful thrust carrier rockets of the new generation, eventually increasing the carrying capacity of near-Earth orbiters to 25 tons and that of geostationary orbiters to 14 tons; develop in an overall way the 120-ton thrust liquid- oxygen/kerosene engine and the 50-ton thrust hydrogen-oxygen engine; and increase the reliability and adaptability of the present "Long March" carrier rockets.
- To start and implement a high-resolution Earth observation system; develop and launch new-type sun synchronous orbit and geostationary-orbit meteorological satellites, oceanic satellites, Earth resources satellites, small satellites for environmental protection and disaster mitigation monitoring and forecasting; and to start research into key technologies of new-type remote-sensing satellites, including stereo mapping satellites. To form an all-weather, 24-hour, multi-spectral, differential- resolution Earth observation system for stable operation and achieve stereoscopy and dynamic monitoring of the land, atmosphere and sea.
- To make an overall plan for the development of a satellite remote-sensing ground system and an application system; to integrate and improve the present satellite remote-sensing ground system, establish and improve a national satellite remote-sensing data center and set up and improve supporting facilities for quantitative application, including a remote-sensing satellite radiation calibration station and preliminarily materialize the common sharing of remote-sensing data to serve the public good; to set up a satellite environmental application institute and a satellite disaster- mitigation institute, forming several important application systems; and to make breakthroughs in major satellite remote-sensing application fields.
- To develop and launch geostationary orbit telecommunications satellites and direct TV broadcasting satellites with long operating life, high reliability and large capacity;

and to develop satellite technologies for live broadcast, broadband multi-media, emergency telecommunications and telecommunications and broadcasting for public service. To continuously develop and improve the service functions of satellite telecommunications and broadcasting and increase value-added services in the field of satellite telecommunications and broadcasting. To actively accelerate the commercialization of satellite telecommunications and broadcasting and expand the industrial scale of telecommunications and broadcasting satellites and applications.

- To improve the "Beidou" navigation satellite test system and launch and implement the "Beidou" navigation satellite system project. To develop independently application technologies and products in applying satellite navigation, positioning and timing service and set up a standard positioning service supporting system and popular application terminus related to satellite navigation and positioning, expanding the application fields and market.
- To develop and launch new-technology test satellites, conduct more spaceflight experiments of new technologies, materials, apparatus and equipment, enhance the independent research and development level and increase product quality and reliability.
- To develop and launch the "breeding" satellite and promote integration of space technology and agricultural breeding technology and expand the application of space technology in the field of agricultural science research.
- To develop scientific satellites, including space telescope and new-type recoverable satellites; to conduct basic research in the fields of space astronomy, space physics, micro-gravity science and space life science and make important and original achievements in these fields; and to strengthen the ability to monitor the space environment and space debris and initially set up a space environment monitoring and warning system.
- To enable astronauts to engage in extravehicular operations and conduct experiments on spacecraft rendezvous and docking; and to carry out research on short-term manned and long-term autonomously orbiting space laboratories, which is of certain application scale and carry out follow- up work of manned spaceflight.
- To realize lunar-orbiting probe, make breakthroughs in developing basic technologies for lunar exploration and develop and launch China's first lunar probe satellite "Chang'e I" for lunar science and lunar resources exploration; and to carry out final-period work for the lunar exploration project.
- To increase the comprehensive experimental ability and returns of spacecraft launching sites, optimize the layout and enhance the reliability and automation level of the facilities and equipment of the sites.
- To advance the technology and capability of TT&C network, enlarge the coverage rate of the network and acquire the ability to satisfy the basic demand for deep-space exploration.

IV. Development Policies and Measures

The Chinese government, under the guidance of the scientific outlook on development, has made overall plans in the three fields of space technology, space application and space science to promote independent innovations in space science and technology, make space activities create more economic and social benefits, ensure the orderly, normal and healthy development of space activities and achieve the set goals.

The major policies and measures for China's space industry at present and in the near future are as follows:
- To make overall plans for and deploy rationally space activities. To give priority to the development of applied satellites and satellite applications, develop in a proper way manned spaceflight and deep- space exploration and give active support to space science exploration.
- To muster strength in implementing key space scientific and technological projects, strengthen basic research and make plans for frontier technologies in advance. To muster superior forces to make leapfrogging development in space science and technology by making breakthroughs in core technologies and resources integration. To increase the sustainable innovative ability of space science and technology through strengthening basic research in the space field and developing several frontier technologies in advance.
- To promote space application and accelerate the industrialization of space activities. To strengthen the development of space application technologies, promote resource sharing and expand the scope of application. With emphasis on telecommunications satellites, satellite telecommunications, satellite remote-sensing, satellite navigation and carrier rockets, to vigorously construct a comprehensive chain of space industry covering satellite manufacturing, launching services, ground equipment production and operational services. To strengthen the spread, transformation and secondary development of space technology and transform and upgrade the traditional industries.
- To attach importance to the infrastructure construction of the space science, technology and industry. To strengthen the building of infrastructure facilities for developing, producing and experimenting with spacecraft and carrier rockets. To give support to key laboratories and engineering research centers of space science and technology, strengthen the work on informatization, intellectual property rights and standardization of space activities.
- To promote the building of a space technology innovation system. To guide the reform, restructuring, transformation and updating of the space science, technology and industry and accelerate the building of world-class large space corporations. To actively construct a space technology innovation system integrating production, education and research with space science and technology enterprises and national scientific research institutes at the core.

- To improve the scientific management of space activities. To adapt to the progress of the socialist market economy, actively make innovations in the system and mechanisms of scientific management, improve the sense of quality and profit among personnel, apply system engineering and other modern management tools to promote scientific management, increase system quality, minimize system risks and enhance comprehensive benefits.
- To strengthen legislation work. To formulate laws, regulations and space industrial policies for guiding and regulating space activities, increase the level of administration by law and create a legislative environment favorable for the development of space activities.
- To guarantee input of funds for space activities. The Chinese government will increase input to the space industry and at the same time encourage the establishment of a diverse, multi-channel space funding system, so as to guarantee the sustainable and stable development of the space industry.
- To encourage people of all walks of life to participate in space-related activities, including encouraging industrial enterprises, scientific research institutes, commercial corporations, institutions of higher learning and social organizations, under the guidance of national space policies, to give full play to their advantages, take an active part in space activities and participate in international space- related exchanges and cooperation. To encourage satellite operation enterprises and application units to use Chinese satellites and satellite-application products.
- To strengthen the fostering of talented people for the space industry. To spare no efforts for the education and cultivation of personnel, give attention to whetting their sense of innovation through practice. In particular, it is necessary to pay more attention to fostering a rationally structured contingent of young and highly qualified space scientists and engineers. To make efforts to publicize space knowledge and culture and attract more outstanding personnel into the space industry.

The Chinese government continues to strengthen its administration and macro-guidance concerning space activities. The China National Space Administration (CNSA) is the country's governmental organization responsible for the management of space activities for civilian use and international space cooperation with other countries and responsible for implementing corresponding governmental functions.

V. International Exchanges and Cooperation
The Chinese government holds that outer space is the common wealth of all mankind and each and every country in the world enjoys equal rights to freely explore, develop and utilize outer space and celestial bodies; and that all countries' outer space activities should be beneficial to the economic development, social progress of nations, to security,

subsistence and development of mankind and to friendly cooperation between people of different countries.

International space cooperation should adhere to the fundamental principles stated in the "Declaration on International Cooperation in the Exploration and Use of Outer Space for the Benefit and in the Interest of All States, Taking into Particular Account the Needs of Developing Countries." China maintains that international space exchanges and cooperation should be strengthened on the basis of equality and mutual benefit, peaceful utilization and common development.

1. Fundamental Policies
The Chinese government has adopted the following policies with regard to developing international space exchanges and cooperation:
- Adhering to the principle of independence and taking the initiative in our own hands, carrying out active and practical international cooperation in consideration of the overall, rational utilization of domestic and international markets and resources to meet the needs of the national modernization drive.
- Supporting activities regarding the peaceful use of outer space within the framework of the United Nations. Supporting all inter- governmental activities for promoting the development of space technology, space application and space science as well as those conducted between non- governmental space organizations.
- Attaching importance to space cooperation in the Asia-Pacific region and supporting other regional space cooperation around the world.
- Reinforcing space cooperation with developing countries and valuing space cooperation with developed countries.
- Encouraging and endorsing the efforts of domestic scientific research institutes, industrial enterprises, institutions of higher learning, as well as social organizations to develop international space exchanges and cooperation in different forms and at different levels under the guidance of relevant state policies, laws and regulations.

2. Major Events
Over the past five years, China has developed bilateral space cooperation with a host of countries. It has successively signed 16 international space cooperation agreements and memorandums with 13 countries, space agencies and international organizations and propelled multilateral cooperation in space technology and its application in the Asia-Pacific region and the process of establishing a space cooperation institution for the region. China has joined relevant activities sponsored by the United Nations and other relevant international organizations and supported international space commercial activities. These measures have yielded positive results.

(1) Bilateral Cooperation: Over the past five years, China has signed cooperation agreements on the peaceful use of outer space and space project cooperation agreements with Argentina, Brazil, Canada, France, Malaysia, Pakistan, Russia, Ukraine, the ESA and the European Union Committee and has established space cooperation subcommittee or joint commission mechanisms with Brazil, France, Russia and Ukraine. It has signed space cooperation memorandums with space organizations of India and Britain and has conducted exchanges with space-related bodies of Algeria, Chile, Germany, Italy, Japan, Peru and the United States.

China continues to collaborate with Brazil on the Earth resources satellite program. Following the successful launch of the Sino-Brazil Earth Resources Satellite 02 in October 2003, the Chinese and Brazilian governments signed supplementary protocols on the joint research and manufacturing of satellites 02B, 03 and 04 and on cooperation in a data application system, maintaining the continuity of data of Sino-Brazil Earth resources satellites and expanding the application of such satellites' data regional wide and worldwide.

China and France have developed extensive space exchanges and cooperation. Under the mechanism of the Sino-French Joint Commission on Space Cooperation, the exchanges and cooperation between the two countries have made important progress in space science, Earth science, life science, satellite application and satellite TT&C.

The space cooperation between China and Russia has produced marked results. Within the framework of the Space Cooperation Sub-Committee of the Committee for the Regular Sino-Russian Premiers' Meeting, a long-term cooperation plan has been determined. In addition, exchanges and cooperation in the sphere of manned spaceflight have been carried out, including astronaut training.

China has unfolded space exchanges and cooperation with Ukraine. Under the mechanism of the Sino-Ukrainian Joint Commission on Space Cooperation, the two countries have determined cooperation plans.

China and the ESA have carried out the Sino-ESA Double Star Satellite Exploration of the Earth's Space Plan. China's relevant departments and the ESA have implemented the "Dragon Program," involving cooperation in Earth observation satellites, having so far conducted 16 remote-sensing application projects in the fields of agriculture, forestry, water conservancy, meteorology, oceanography and disasters.

(2) Multilateral Cooperation: In October 2005, the representatives of China, Bangladesh, Indonesia, Iran, Mongolia, Pakistan, Peru and Thailand signed the Asia-Pacific Space Cooperation Organization (APSCO) Convention in Beijing and in June 2006 Turkey signed the Convention as well. APSCO will be headquartered in Beijing. This marks a significant step toward the official establishment of APSCO.

China continues to promote the Asia-Pacific Region Multilateral Cooperation in Small Multi-Mission Satellites Project. Together with Bangladesh, Iran, the Republic of

Korea, Mongolia, Pakistan and Thailand, China has started the joint research, manufacture and application of small multi-mission satellites, to be launched in 2007.

China takes a positive part in activities organized by the United Nations Committee on the Peaceful Uses of Outer Space (UNCOPUOS) and its Scientific and Technical Subcommittee and Legal Subcommittee. China has acceded to the Treaty on Principles Governing the Activities of States in the Exploration and Use of Outer Space, Including the Moon and Other Celestial Bodies, Agreement on the Rescue and Return of Astronauts and on the Return of Objects Launched into Outer Space, Convention on International Liability for Damage Caused by Space Objects and Convention on the Registration of Objects Launched into Outer Space and strictly fulfills its responsibilities and obligations. China actively participates in the relevant activities organized by the UN COPUOS to implement the recommendations made by the Third United Nations Conference on the Exploration and Peaceful Uses of Outer Space (UNISPACE III). In particular, China, alongside Canada and France as co-chairs, has propelled the work of the space-system-based disaster mitigation and disaster management of the Action Team (AT-7) joined by 40 member states of COPUOS and 15 international organizations and has actively taken part in the work of an ad hoc expert group to study the possibility of creating a coordination mechanism for disaster mitigation and management. China has acceded to a disaster mitigation mechanism consisting of space organizations from different countries in the light of the Charter on Cooperation to Achieve the Coordinated Use of Space Facilities in the Event of Natural or Technological Disasters. In cooperation with the UN, China has hosted UN/ESA/China basic space science workshops and a UN/China workshop on tele-health development in Asia and the Pacific. China has also hosted, in collaboration with the Multilateral Cooperation Secretariat of the Asia-Pacific Space Cooperation Organization and the UN Economic and Social Commission for Asia and the Pacific, training courses and symposia on space technology applications and has provided financial support for these activities. China has also taken part in a program promoting the application of space for sustainable development in Asia and the Pacific organized and implemented by the UN Economic and Social Commission for Asia and the Pacific.

China has actively participated in activities organized by the Inter-Agency Space Debris Coordination Committee, started the Space Debris Action Plan and strengthened international exchanges and cooperation in the field of space debris research. It has participated in the relevant activities organized by the Committee on Earth Observation Satellites (CEOS) and hosted the 18th CEOS plenary and 20th anniversary activities in Beijing in November 2004. In May 2005, China officially became a member of the ad hoc inter-governmental Group on Earth Observations (GEO) and an executive committee member as well. In July 2006, China held in Beijing the 36th COSPAR (Committee on Space Research) Scientific Assembly and the 8th International Lunar Exploration Working Group (ILEWG) International Conference on the Exploration and Utilization of the Moon. In addition, China has taken part in the relevant activities of the International Telecommunications Union (ITU), World Meteorological Organization (WMO), International Astronautical Federation (IAF) and Committee on Space Research (COSPAR).

(3) Commercial Activities: China launched a communications satellite APSTAR VI into orbit in April 2005. In December 2004, China signed a commercial contract for a communications satellite with Nigeria, providing in-orbit delivery service to that country. In November 2005, China signed a commercial contract for a communications satellite with Venezuela, providing in-orbit delivery service and associated ground application facilities.

3. Priority Cooperation Areas
The Chinese government continuously renders support to international exchanges and cooperation in space technology, space application and space science, with priority given in the next five years to cooperation in the following areas:
- Scientific research into space astronomy, space physics, micro-gravity science, space life science, lunar exploration and planet exploration;
- Data sharing and services of Earth observation satellites and application and research in the areas of resources investigation, environment monitoring, prevention and mitigation of disasters and global climate change monitoring and forecasting;
- Sharing of space TT&C network resources and mutual provision of space TT&C assistance;
- Design and manufacture of communications satellites and Earth observation satellites;
- Manufacture of ground facilities and key components of satellite communications, remote sensing and navigation and positioning;
- Application of satellite communications and broadcasting in tele-education and tele-medicine and expansion of application scope of satellite broadcasting and TV and related services for satellite navigation and positioning;
- Commercial satellite launching services, export of satellites and their components and parts and construction and services of satellite ground TT&C and application facilities;
- Exchanges and training of personnel in various fields of space activities.

(www.china.org.cn)

1.3. China's Space Activities of 2011

Information Office of the State Council
December 2011
(Official English Version)

Preface

Outer space is the common wealth of mankind. Exploration, development and utilization of outer space are an unremitting pursuit of mankind. Space activities around the world have been flourishing. Leading space-faring countries have formulated or modified their development strategies, plans and goals in this sphere. The position and role of space activities are becoming increasingly salient for each active country's overall development strategy and their influence on human civilization and social progress is increasing.

The Chinese government makes the space industry an important part of the nation's overall development strategy and adheres to exploration and utilization of outer space for peaceful purposes. Over the past few years, China's space industry has developed rapidly and China ranks among the world's leading countries in certain major areas of space technology. Space activities play an increasingly important role in China's economic and social development.

The next five years will be a crucial period for China in building a moderately prosperous society, deepening reform and opening-up and accelerating the transformation of the country's pattern of economic development. This will bring new opportunities to China's space industry. China will center its work on its national strategic goals, strengthen its independent innovative capabilities, further open to the outside world and expand international cooperation. In so doing, China will do its best to make the country's space industry develop better and faster. At the same time, China will work together with the international community to maintain a peaceful and clean outer space and endeavor to make new contributions to the lofty cause of promoting world peace and development.

In order to help people around the world gain a better understanding of the Chinese space industry, we herewith offer a brief introduction to the major achievements China has made since 2006, its main tasks in the next five years and its international exchanges and cooperation in this respect.

I. Purposes and Principles of Development

The purposes of China's space industry are: to explore outer space and to enhance understanding of the Earth and the cosmos; to utilize outer space for peaceful purposes, promote human civilization and social progress and to benefit the whole of mankind; to meet the demands of economic development, scientific and technological development, national security and social progress; and to improve the scientific and cultural knowledge of the Chinese people, protect China's national rights and interests and build up its national comprehensive strength.

China's space industry is subject to and serves the national overall development strategy and adheres to the principles of scientific, independent, peaceful, innovative and open development.

- Scientific development. China respects science and the laws of nature. Keeping the actual situation of its space industry in mind, it works out comprehensive plans and arrangement of its activities regarding space technology, space applications and space science, in order to maintain comprehensive, coordinated and sustainable development of the industry.
- Independent development. Keeping to the path of independence and self-reliance, China relies primarily on its own capabilities to develop its space industry to meet the needs of modernization, based upon its actual conditions and strength.
- Peaceful development. China always adheres to the use of outer space for peaceful purposes and opposes weaponization or any arms race in outer space. The country develops and utilizes space resources in a prudent manner and takes effective measures to protect the space environment, ensuring that its space activities benefit the whole of mankind.
- Innovative development. China's strategy for the development of its space industry is to enhance its capabilities of independent innovation, consolidate its industrial foundation and improve its innovation system. By implementing important space science and technology projects, the country concentrates its strength on making key breakthroughs for leap-frog development in this field.
- Open development. China persists in combining independence and self-reliance with opening to the outside world and international cooperation. It makes active endeavors in international space exchanges and cooperation on the basis of equality and mutual benefit, peaceful utilization and common development, striving to promote progress in mankind's space industry.

II. Progress Made Since 2006

Since 2006, China has made rapid progress in its space industry. Breakthroughs have been made in major space projects, including human spaceflight and lunar exploration; space technology has been generally upgraded remarkably; the economic and social benefits of space applications have been noticeably enhanced; and innovative achievements have been made in space science.

1. Space Transportation System

Since 2006, Long March rockets have accomplished 67 successful launches, sending 79 spacecraft into planned orbits and demonstrating noteworthy improvement in the reliability of China's launch vehicles. The Long March rocket series have been improved and major progress has been made in the development of new-generation launch vehicles.

2. Man-Made Earth Satellites

(1) Earth Observation Satellites

China has developed Fengyun (Wind and Cloud), Haiyang (Ocean), Ziyuan (Resources), Yaogan (Remote-Sensing) and Tianhui (Space Mapping) satellite series, plus a constellation of small satellites for environmental and disaster monitoring and forecasting. Fengyun satellites are now capable of global, three-dimensional and multispectral quantitative observation. The Fengyun-2 geostationary Earth orbit (GEO) meteorological satellite succeeded in double satellite observation and in-orbit backup; while the Fengyun-3 polar orbit meteorological satellite succeeded in networking observation of morning and afternoon satellites. Ocean watercolor satellites have obtained their images of doubled width and their revisiting period reduced. The first Haiyang dynamics environmental satellite launched in August, 2011 is capable of all-weather and full-time microwave observation. The Ziyuan satellite series have seen their spatial resolution and image quality greatly enhanced. The small satellites for environmental and disaster monitoring and forecasting are now capable of disaster monitoring with medium-resolution, wide-coverage and high-revisit rate disaster monitoring. In 2010, China formally initiated the development of an important special project – a high-resolution Earth observation system.

(2) Communications and Broadcasting Satellites

China has won successes in its high-capacity GEO satellite common platform, space-based data relays, tracking, telemetry and command (TT&C) and other key technologies, showing remarkable improvement in the technical performance of China's satellites and in voice, data, radio and television communications. The successful launch and stable operation of the Zhongxing-10 satellite demonstrated a significant increase in the power and capacity of China's communications and broadcasting satellites. Similarly, the successful launch of the Tianlian (Space Chain)-1 data relay satellite demonstrated China's preliminary capability of both space-based data relays and space-based TT&C.

(3) Navigation and Positioning Satellites

In February 2007, China successfully launched the fourth Beidou (Bid Dipper) navigation experiment satellite, further enhancing the performance of the Beidou navigation experiment system. China has comprehensively launched the building of a Beidou regional navigation system, consisting of five GEO satellites, five inclined geosynchronous orbit (IGSO) satellites and four medium-Earth-orbit (MEO) satellites. Since April 2007, China has launched 10 such satellites and has been able to provide trial services for Asia-Pacific users.

(4) Scientific Satellites and Technological Test Satellites

China has developed and launched several Shijian (Practice) satellites and small and micro satellites, providing supporting platforms for space environment exploration, space scientific test and new technology demonstration.

3. Human Spaceflight

From September 25 to 28, 2008, China successfully launched the Shenzhou-7 (Divine Ship-7) manned spaceship. China also became the third country in the world to master the key technology of astronaut space extravehicular activity, completing a space material test outside the spaceship and an experiment on deploying and accompanying flight of a small satellite. In September and November 2011, China successively launched the Tiangong-1 (Space Palace-1) and Shenzhou-8 spaceship and accomplished their first space rendezvous and docking test, laying the foundation for the construction of future space laboratories and space stations.

4. Deep-space Exploration

On October 24, 2007, China successfully launched its first lunar probe, Chang'e-1 and achieved its objectives of "accurate orbital transfer and successful orbiting," also retrieving a great deal of scientific data and a complete map of the moon and successfully implementing a controlled crash onto the lunar surface. The success of Chang'e-1 was another milestone for China's space industry, after man-made satellites and human spaceflight, signifying that China has become one of the countries capable of deep-space exploration.

On October 1, 2010, China successfully launched its second lunar probe, Chang'e-2, created a full higher-resolution map of the moon and a high-definition image of Sinus Iridium and completed several extended tests, including circling the Lagrangian Point L2, which laid the foundation for future deep-space exploration tasks.

5. Space Launch Sites

China has improved its three existing launch sites in Jiuquan, Xichang and Taiyuan, enhancing their comprehensive test capabilities and high-intensity launching capabilities. These sites have successfully launched manned spaceship, lunar probes and a variety of satellites. At present, China is building a new space launch site in Hainan to accommodate the launch of new-generation launch vehicles.

6. Space Telemetry, Tracking and Command (TT&C)

China has improved its TT&C ground stations and ships and has established a very long baseline interferometry (VLBI) network comprising four observation stations and a data processing center, indicating that China has acquired space-based TT&C capabilities; it has also established a multi-functioning TT&C network featuring space and ground integration, complete sets of equipment and ability to complete various tasks. At present, China's TT&C network is expanding from the ground to space and from geospace TT&C to deep-space TT&C. The network is able to not only satisfy satellite TT&C demands, but also support human spaceflight and deep-space exploration.

7. Space Applications

(1) Applications of Earth Observation Satellites

The fields and scope in which Earth observation satellites are used have been constantly expanding; these satellites' capabilities in providing business services have also been growing and an Earth observation satellite application system has initially taken shape. China has built four new satellite data-receiving stations, enhancing its ability to receive data from meteorological, ocean and land observation satellites. China has also established, based on comprehensive planning, the ground data processing system for Earth observation satellites, extending its ability in centralized data processing, data archiving, data distribution and services provision. China has established centers for environmental satellite application, satellite disaster-relief application, satellite mapping application and other application institutes for Earth observation satellites, promoting the spread and utility of Earth observation satellite data. China has improved calibration services of remote-sensing satellite radiation calibration fields, enhancing the quantitative application level of Earth observation satellites.

Today, Earth observation satellite data has been widely used in various fields for economic and social development. Fengyun satellites have effectively monitored typhoons, floods, forest and grassland fires, droughts, sandstorms and other natural disasters; their weather forecasting and climate change monitoring capabilities have also been enhanced remarkably. The ocean satellite series have monitored China's maritime territory and the world's key waters and their forecasting accuracy for sea ice, ocean temperatures and wind fields have increased greatly and their time efficiency in monitoring dangerous sea conditions has also been notably enhanced. The resource satellite series have played an important role in efforts to investigate, monitor and manage the resources of land, minerals, agriculture, forestry and water conservancy, as well as geological disasters and city planning. Remote-sensing and Tianhui satellites have played an important role in scientific experiments, land censuses, mapping and other fields. The small satellites for environmental and disaster monitoring and forecasting have provided critical technical support for surface water quality and atmospheric environmental monitoring, major pollution events addressing and major natural disaster monitoring, assessment and relief.

(2) Applications of Communications and Broadcasting Satellites

China has steadily promoted the applications of communications and broadcasting satellites and has brought into being a market of certain scale. It has improved its satellite radio and TV network: in 2008 China established a satellite service platform to give every village access to direct broadcast and live telecasts. It also implemented satellite broadcasting and transmissions of China National Radio and China Central Television programs and one channel program of provincial radio and TV stations, thus greatly increasing the radio and TV program coverage. China has strengthened development of its satellite tele-education broadband network and tele-medicine network, mitigating to some extent the problem of shortage of education and medical resources in remote and border areas. China has also strengthened its satellite capacity in emergency communications, providing important support for rescue and relief work and for major disaster management.

(3) Applications of Navigation and Positioning Satellites

China's applications of navigation and positioning satellites have embarked on the road of industrialized development and are now developing at a high speed and important progress has been made in developing navigation- and positioning-satellite applications. Through both domestic and foreign navigation and positioning satellites, China has been applying these technologies more broadly; as a result, the market for this industry has expanded rapidly. China strives to promote the application of its Beidou satellite navigation system and the system has been used in transportation, sea fishing, hydrological monitoring, communications and timing service, power dispatching and disaster reduction and relief.

8. Space Science

(1) Sun-Earth Space Exploration

China has implemented the Double Star Program to explore the Earth's magnetosphere in concert with the Cluster Program of the European Space Agency (ESA), obtaining much new data and making important progress in space physics.

(2) Lunar Scientific Research

Through lunar exploration projects, China has studied the morphology, structure, surface matter composition, microwave properties and near-moon space environment, further enhancing its knowledge of the moon.

(3) Experiments on Microgravity Science and Space Life Science
Using the Shijian satellites and Shenzhou spaceship, China has carried out space experiments in life science, materials science, fluid mechanics and other fields under conditions of microgravity and strong radiation. It has also conducted experiments on crop breeding in space.

(4) Space Environment Exploration and Forecasting
Using Shenzhou and other spacecraft, China has explored the space environment's major parameters and effects, worked on space environmental monitoring and forecasting and studied space environmental effects.

9. Space Debris
China has monitored space debris and given early warnings against them, ensuring safe flight of Chang'e-1 and Chang'e-2 lunar probes and Shenzhou-7 manned spaceship. China has steadily pushed forward its work on space debris mitigation, fully inactivating Long March rockets and moving a few aging GEO satellites out of orbit. China has also worked on protecting manned spaceship from space debris.

III. Major Tasks for the Next Five Years
In the next five years, China will strengthen its basic capacities of the space industry, accelerate research on leading-edge technology and continue to implement important space scientific and technological projects, including human spaceflight, lunar exploration, high-resolution Earth observation system, satellite navigation and positioning system, new-generation launch vehicles and other priority projects in key fields. China will develop a comprehensive plan for construction of space infrastructure, promote its satellites and satellite applications industry, further conduct space science research and push forward the comprehensive, coordinated and sustainable development of China's space industry.

1. Space Transportation System
China will build a stronger space transportation system, keep improving its launch vehicle series and enhance their capabilities of entering space.

It will enhance the reliability and adaptability of launch vehicles in service and develop new-generation launch vehicles and their upper stages, implement the first flight of the Long March-5, Long March-6 and Long March-7 launch vehicles. The Long March-5 will use non-toxic and pollution-free propellant and will be capable of placing 25 tons of payload into the near-Earth orbit, or placing 14 tons of payload into the GEO orbit. The Long March-6 will be a new type of high-speed response launch vehicle, which will be capable of placing not less than 1 ton of payload into a sun-synchronous orbit at a height of 700 km. The Long March-7 will be capable of placing 5.5 tons of payload into a sun-synchronous orbit at a height of 700 km.

It will conduct special demonstrations and pre-research on key technologies for heavy-lift launch vehicles.

2. Man-Made Earth Satellites

China will build a space infrastructure frame composed of Earth observation satellites, communications and broadcasting satellites, plus navigation and positioning satellites and will develop a preliminary long-term, sustained and stable service capability. China will develop new types of scientific satellites and technological test satellites.

(1) Earth Observation Satellites

China will improve its present meteorological, oceanic and resource satellite series and its small satellites constellation for environmental and disaster monitoring and forecasting. It aims at developing and launching new-generation GEO meteorological satellites, stereo mapping satellites, radar satellites for environment and disaster monitoring, electromagnetic monitoring test satellites and other new-type Earth observation satellites. It will work to make breakthroughs in key technologies for interferometric synthetic-aperture radar and gravitational field measurement satellites. It will initiate a high-resolution Earth observation system as an important scientific and technological project and establish on the whole a stable all-weather, 24-hour, multi-spectral, various-resolution Earth observation system.

(2) Communications and Broadcasting Satellites

China will improve satellites for fixed communications services, television and radio service satellites and data relay satellites; develop satellites for mobile communication service; and develop a platform of higher capacity and higher power for new-generation GEO communications and broadcasting satellites.

(3) Navigation and Positioning Satellites

Based on "three-step" development plan – from experimental system to regional system and then to global system, China will continue building its Beidou satellite navigation system, implementing a regional Beidou satellite navigation system before 2012, whose navigation and positioning, timing and short-message services will cover the Asia-Pacific region. China aims at completing the global Beidou satellite navigation system by 2020, comprising five GEO satellites and 30 non-GEO satellites.

(4) Scientific Satellites and Technological Test Satellites

China will develop and launch a Hard X-ray Modulation Telescope satellite, Shijian-9 new technology test satellite and returnable satellites. It will begin to implement projects of quantum science test satellite and dark matter probing satellite.

3. Human Spaceflight

China will push forward human spaceflight projects and make new technological breakthroughs, creating a foundation for future human spaceflight.

It will launch the Shenzhou-9 and Shenzhou-10 spaceships and achieve unmanned or manned rendezvous and docking with the in-orbit Tiangong-1 vehicle.

China will launch space laboratories, manned spaceship and space freighters; make breakthroughs in and master space station key technologies, including astronauts' medium-term stay, regenerative life support and propellant refueling; conduct space applications to a certain extent and make technological preparations for the construction of space stations.

China will conduct studies on the preliminary plan for a human lunar landing.

4. Deep-space Exploration

China carries out deep-space exploration in stages, with limited goals.

Based on the idea of "three steps" – orbiting, landing and returning – for continuing lunar probe projects, China will launch orbiters for lunar soft landing, roving and surveying to implement the second stage of lunar exploration. In the third stage, China will start to conduct sampling the moon's surface matters and get those samples back to Earth.

China will conduct special project demonstration in deep-space exploration and push forward its exploration of planets, asteroids and the sun of the solar system.

5. Space Launch Sites

China will enhance the reliability and automation level of launch site facilities and equipment, strengthen the comprehensive capability of launch of spacecraft and satisfy the launch demands. It will also complete the construction of the Hainan space launch site and put it into service.

6. Space TT&C

China will improve its space TT&C network, build deep-space TT&C stations, develop advanced TT&C technologies and enhance its TT&C capabilities in all respects to satisfy the demands for remote TT&C.

7. Space Applications

China will further improve its satellite application and service system, expand satellites application scope and promote the national new strategic industries, to meet demands of national economic and social development.

(1) Applications of Earth Observation Satellites

China will improve its ground facilities for receiving, processing, distributing and applying satellite data and will strengthen the development of calibration fields and other facilities. It will improve the sharing and comprehensive application of data retrieved from Earth observation satellites, make more self-obtained space data and guide social resources to actively develop market-oriented data application services. It will implement application demonstration projects and promote the wide utilization and industrialization of Earth observation satellites.

(2) Applications of Communications and Broadcasting Satellites

China will strengthen the applications of communications and broadcasting satellites in public service and major industries of the national economy. It plans to expand value-added business in the satellite communication field, further commercialize satellite communication and expand the industrial scale of the application of communications and broadcasting satellites.

(3) Applications of Navigation and Positioning Satellites

China will build and improve ground TT&C segments and develop a system for monitoring and assessing performance of the global satellite navigation system, strengthen technological research, product development and standardization system of navigation and positioning satellites, enhance application level, promote position-based services, expand the industrial scope and focus on promoting further use of the Beidou satellite navigation system in various fields of China's national economy.

8. Space Science

China will strengthen the development of its space science research system, upgrade the quality of space science research and enhance popularization of space science knowledge in the whole nation.

By the implementation of lunar exploration projects, China will make in-situ analyses, morphological and structural surveys of the lunar surface in landing and roving areas, conduct environmental surveys of the lunar surface and make moon-based astronomical observations.

By using spacecraft, China will study the properties of black holes and physical laws under extreme conditions, explore properties of dark matter particles and test basic theories of quantum mechanics. It will also conduct scientific experiments on microgravity and space life science, explore and forecast the space environment and study their effects.

9. Space Debris
China will continue to strengthen its work on space debris monitoring and mitigation and its work on spacecraft protection.

China will develop technologies for monitoring space debris and pre-warning of collision and begin monitoring space debris and small near-Earth celestial bodies and collision pre-warning work. It will set up a design and assess system of space debris mitigation and take measures to reduce space debris left by post-task spacecraft and launch vehicles. It will experiment with digital simulation of space debris collisions and build a system to protect spacecraft from space debris.

IV. Development Policies and Measures
To ensure completion of the set goals and tasks, the Chinese government has formulated policies and measures to be taken for the development of China's space industry as follows:

- Making comprehensive plans for and prudently arrange space activities. To give priority to applied satellites and satellite applications, develop human spaceflight and deep-space exploration properly and give active support to space science exploration.
- Strengthening innovation capability in space science and technology. To focus on implementing important space science and technological projects and to realize leapfrog development in space science and technology by way of making new breakthroughs in core technologies and resource integration. To actively build a space technology innovative system featuring integration of the space industry, academia and the research community, with space science and technology enterprises and research institutions as the main participants; to strengthen basic research in the space field and develop multiple advanced frontier technologies to increase sustainable innovative capacity in space science and technology.
- Vigorously promoting development of the satellite application industry. To make comprehensive plans and construct space infrastructure; promote public sharing of satellite application resources; foster enterprise clusters, industrial chains and market for satellite applications.
- Strengthening basic capability in space science, technology and industry. To strengthen construction of infrastructure for development, production and test for spacecraft and launch vehicles. To strengthen construction of key laboratories and engineering research centers for space science and technology. And to strengthen work on informatization, intellectual property rights and standardization of space activities.

- Strengthening legislative work. To actively carry out research on a national space law, gradually formulate and improve related laws, regulations and space industrial policies guiding and regulating space activities and create a legislative environment favorable to the development of space activities.
- Guaranteeing the sustainable and steady financial investment for space activities. To gradually establish a diverse, multi-channel space funding system to ensure the investment sustainable and steady, especially to provide larger amounts for important space scientific and technological projects, applied satellite and satellite applications, frontier technologies and basic researches.
- Encouraging organizations and people in all walks of life to participate in space-related activities. To encourage scientific research institutes, enterprises, institutions of higher learning and social organizations, under the guidance of national space policies, giving full play to their advantages and taking an active part in space activities.
- Strengthening training of professionals for the space industry. To vigorously develop a favorable environment for the development of professional personnel, fostering leading figures in the space industry and forming a well-structured contingent of highly qualified personnel in the course of conducting the important projects and basic researches. To publicize space knowledge and culture and attract more outstanding personnel into the space industry.

V. International Exchanges and Cooperation

The Chinese government holds that each and every country in the world enjoys equal rights to freely explore, develop and utilize outer space and its celestial bodies and that all countries' outer space activities should be beneficial to economic development, the social progress of nations and to the security, survival and development of mankind.

International space cooperation should adhere to the fundamental principles stated in the "Declaration on International Cooperation in the Exploration and Use of Outer Space for the Benefit and in the Interest of All States, Taking into Particular Account the Needs of Developing Countries." China maintains that international exchanges and cooperation should be strengthened to promote inclusive space development on the basis of equality and mutual benefit, peaceful utilization and common development.

1. Fundamental Policies

The Chinese government has adopted the following fundamental policies with regard to developing international space exchanges and cooperation:
- Supporting activities regarding the peaceful use of outer space within the framework of the United Nations. Supporting all inter-governmental and non-governmental space organizations' activities that promote development of the space industry;

- Emphasizing regional space cooperation in the Asia-Pacific area and supporting other regional space cooperation around the world;
- Reinforcing space cooperation with developing countries and valuing space cooperation with developed countries;
- Encouraging and endorsing the efforts of domestic scientific research institutes, industrial enterprises, institutions of higher learning and social organizations to develop international space exchanges and cooperation in diverse forms and at various levels under the guidance of relevant state policies, laws and regulations;
- Appropriately using both domestic and foreign markets and both types of resources and actively participating in practical international space cooperation.

2. Major Events

Since 2006, China has implemented international space exchanges and cooperation in various forms. It has signed a number of cooperation agreements and memoranda on the peaceful utilization of outer space with a host of countries, space agencies and international organizations. China has taken part in relevant activities sponsored by the United Nations and other relevant international organizations and supported international space commercial cooperation. These measures have yielded positive results.

(1) Bilateral Cooperation
- China has established a long-term cooperation plan with Russia through the mechanism of the Space Cooperation Sub-committee under the Prime Ministers' Meeting between Russia and China. The two nations have signed a number of cooperation agreements on space science, deep-space exploration and other areas and their national space administrations have opened representative offices mutually. In the field of human spaceflight, the two nations have also carried out many cooperation projects.
- China has undertaken extensive cooperation with Ukraine under the Space Cooperation Sub-committee mechanism of the Sino-Ukrainian Cooperation Commission and the two sides have signed the "Sino-Ukrainian Space Cooperation Program."
- China and the European Space Agency (ESA) have signed the "Status Quo of China-Europe Space Cooperation and the Cooperation Plan Protocol" under the mechanism of the China-Europe Joint Commission on Space Cooperation. The two sides cooperated closely during the lunar exploration missions of Chang'e-1 and Chang'e-2 and signed the "Agreement on Mutual Support for the TT&C Network and Operation" in September 2011.
- China and Brazil, through the mechanism of the Space Cooperation Sub-committee of the Sino-Brazilian High-level Coordination Commission, have worked out a

comprehensive bilateral space cooperation plan, actively promoted the research and development of the China-Brazil Earth resources satellites, continued to maintain data consistency of their Earth resources satellites and expanded the application of their data into regional and global application.
- China has signed a cooperation framework agreement on space and marine science and technology with France under the mechanism of the Sino-French Joint Commission on Space Cooperation, aiming at developing bilateral cooperation on astronomic satellite, ocean satellite and other satellite programs.
- China and Britain have established a joint laboratory on space science and technology, jointly organized a seminar on space science and technology and conducted exchanges on lunar exploration, Earth observation, space science research and experiment, personnel training and other areas.
- China has signed a framework agreement with Germany on bilateral cooperation in the field of human spaceflight. Under the framework, the two countries have carried out a cooperative experiment project on the Shenzhou-8 concerning space life science.
- The director of the U.S. National Aeronautical and Space Administration (NASA) visited China and the two sides will continue to make dialogue regarding the space field.
- China has signed a memorandum of understanding on technological cooperation in the peaceful utilization and development of outer space with Venezuela and the two nations have established a technology, industry and space sub-committee under the China-Venezuela Senior Mixed Committee. Under this framework, the two nations have promoted bilateral cooperation in communications satellites, remote-sensing satellites, satellite applications and other areas.
- China has signed the "Cooperation Agreement on the Application, Exchange and Distribution of Meteorological Satellite Data" with the European Organization for the Exploitation of Meteorological Satellites (EUMETSAT), to promote the sharing in and application of meteorological satellite data.
- China has actively promoted the extensive applications of Earth observation satellite data with various countries. China has given to many countries free receiving stations for meteorological satellite broadcasting systems and comprehensive systems for meteorological information analysis and processing. With China's help, a data receiving station of the Sino-Brazilian Earth Resources Satellite Program was established in South Africa and another station for receiving environmental and disaster data from Chinese satellites was set up in Thailand. China has provided related earth observation satellite data products to the above-mentioned countries.
- China has implemented international exchanges and cooperation with a number of countries in frequency coordination, compatibility and interoperability, applications

and other international exchanges and cooperation in the area of satellite navigation systems.

(2) Multilateral Cooperation
- China has taken part in activities organized by the United Nations Committee on the Peaceful Uses of Outer Space (UN COPUOS) and its Scientific and Technical Sub-committee and Legal Sub-committee.
- China has signed relevant agreements with the United Nations on disaster management and emergency response based on the space-based information platform. A Beijing office of the program has been established. Through this office, China has provided drought risk-monitoring products to the "Horn of Africa," and contributes to the regional disaster mitigation effort by offering training, capacity building, data service, disaster emergency response, QDGS (Quick Draw Graphics System) and other services.
- China has cooperated with the space institutes of various countries through the mechanism of the "International Charter on Space and Major Disasters." Through this mechanism, satellite data support was provided to the Wenchuan earthquake, the forest fire in Australia and other major disaster relief work.
- In 2008, the Asia-Pacific Space Cooperation Organization (APSCO) was established with the joint effort of Asia-Pacific nations. Under the APSCO frame, the Chinese government actively participates in the cooperation and study of various projects, including the development of a space data-sharing platform, its demonstration and application; an Earth-based optic space target observation network; compatible navigation terminals. China assisted APSCO in the formulation and release of its policy on small satellite data in Asia-Pacific multilateral cooperation and has promoted space cooperation in the Asia-Pacific region.
- China participates in activities organized by the International Committee on Global Navigation Satellite Systems, International Space Exploration Coordination Group, Inter-Agency Space Debris Coordination Committee, Group on Earth Observations, World Meteorological Organization and other inter-governmental international organizations. China has also developed multilateral exchanges and cooperation in satellite navigation, Earth observation and Earth science and research, disaster prevention and mitigation, deep-space exploration, space debris and other areas. China's Beidou satellite navigation system has become one of the world's four core system suppliers accredited by the International Committee on Global Navigation Satellite Systems and will gradually provide regional and global navigation and positioning service as well as strengthened compatibility and interoperability with other satellite navigation systems. China will do its best to host the Seventh Meeting of the International Committee on Global Navigation Satellite Systems in 2012. The nation's independently developed space debris protective design system has also been

incorporated into the protection manual of the Inter-Agency Space Debris Coordination Committee.
- China takes part in activities organized by the International Astronautical Federation, International Committee on Space Research, International Academy of Astronautics and other non-governmental international space organizations and academic institutes. It has also organized a series of international academic conferences, including the Global Lunar Conference and has fostered discussion and exchanges in deep-space exploration, space debris and other issues.

Commercial activities
China actively promotes the participation of Chinese enterprises in international commercial activities in the space field. China has exported whole satellites and made in-orbit delivery of communications satellites to Nigeria, Venezuela and Pakistan; provided commercial launch services for the Palapa-D satellite of Indonesia and the W3C satellite of Eutelsat and signed commercial satellite and ground system export contracts with Bolivia, Laos, Belarus and other countries.

3. Key Cooperation Areas
In the next five years, China's international space exchanges and cooperation will be mainly in the following areas:
- Scientific research on space astronomy, space physics, micro-gravity science, space life science, deep-space exploration, space debris and other areas.
- Applications of Earth observation satellites in environment and disaster monitoring, global climate change monitoring and forecasting, marine monitoring and other areas.
- Applications of communications satellites in broadcasting and television, long-distance education, telemedicine and other areas.
- Applied technological cooperation, research and development of terminal equipment, reinforced facility building, specific industrial services and other areas of satellite navigation systems.
- Technological cooperation on a space lab and a space station in China's human spaceflight program; space science research and experiments and other areas.
- Space TT&C cooperation, support and others.
- Commercial satellite launch service, import and export of whole satellites, satellite parts and components, import and export of ground test equipment and building and service of satellite ground TT&C and satellite application facilities as well as related services, etc.
- Personnel exchanges and training in the field of space.

(www.scio.gov.cn)

1.4. CHINA'S SPACE ACTIVITIES OF 2016

Information Office of the State Council
December 2016
(Official English Version)

Preamble
Space activities make up one of the most challenging hi-tech fields which exert enormous impact on other fields. Space activities have greatly improved man's knowledge of space and provide an important driving force for social progress. Currently, more and more countries, including developing ones, are making the development of space activities an important strategic choice. Thus, space activities around the world are flourishing.

The Chinese government takes the space industry as an important part of the nation's overall development strategy and adheres to the principle of exploration and utilization of outer space for peaceful purposes. Over the past 60 years of remarkable development since its space industry was established in 1956, China has made great achievements in this sphere, including the development of atomic and hydrogen bombs, missiles, man-made satellites, manned spaceflight and lunar probe. It has opened up a path of self-reliance and independent innovation and has created the spirit of China's space industry. To carry forward this spirit and stimulate enthusiasm for innovation, the Chinese government set April 24 as China's Space Day in 2016.

To explore the vast cosmos, develop the space industry and build China into a space power is a dream we pursue unremittingly. In the next five years and beyond China will uphold the concepts of innovative, balanced, green, open and shared development and promote the comprehensive development of space science, space technology and space applications, so as to contribute more to both serving national development and improving the well-being of mankind.

To enable the world community to better understand China's space industry, we are publishing this white paper to offer a brief introduction to the major achievements China has made in this field since 2011, its main tasks in the next five years and its international exchanges and cooperation efforts.

I. Purposes, Vision and Principles of Development

1. Purposes
To explore outer space and enhance understanding of the earth and the cosmos; to utilize outer space for peaceful purposes, promote human civilization and social progress and benefit the whole of mankind; to meet the demands of economic, scientific and technological development, national security and social progress; and to improve the

scientific and cultural levels of the Chinese people, protect China's national rights and interests and build up its overall strength.

2. Vision

To build China into a space power in all respects, with the capabilities to make innovations independently, to make scientific discovery and research at the cutting edge, to promote strong and sustained economic and social development, to effectively and reliably guarantee national security, to exercise sound and efficient governance and to carry out mutually beneficial international exchanges and cooperation; to have an advanced and open space science and technology industry, stable and reliable space infrastructure, pioneering and innovative professionals and a rich and profound space spirit; to provide strong support for the realization of the Chinese Dream of the renewal of the Chinese nation and make positive contributions to human civilization and progress.

3. Principles

China's space industry is subject to and serves the national overall development strategy and adheres to the principles of innovative, coordinated, peaceful and open development.
- Innovative development. China takes independent innovation as the core of the development of its space industry. It implements major space science and technology projects, strengthens scientific exploration and technological innovation, deepens institutional reforms, stimulates innovation and creativity and promotes rapid development of the space industry.
- Coordinated development. China rationally allocates various resources, encourages and guides social forces to take an orderly part in space development. All space activities are coordinated under an overall plan of the state to promote the comprehensive development of space science, space technology and space applications and to improve the quality and efficiency of overall space development.
- Peaceful development. China always adheres to the principle of the use of outer space for peaceful purposes and opposes the weaponization of or an arms race in outer space. The country develops and utilizes space resources in a prudent manner, takes effective measures to protect the space environment to ensure a peaceful and clean outer space and guarantee that its space activities benefit the whole of mankind.
- Open development. China persists in combining independence and self-reliance with opening to the outside world and international cooperation. It actively engages in international exchanges and cooperation on the basis of equality and mutual benefit, peaceful utilization and inclusive development, striving to promote progress of space industry for mankind as a whole and its long-term sustainable development.

II. Major Developments Since 2011

Since 2011 China's space industry has witnessed rapid progress manifested by markedly enhanced capacity in independent innovation and access to outer space, constant improvement in space infrastructure, smooth implementation of major projects such as manned spaceflight, lunar exploration, the Beidou Navigation System and high-resolution earth observation system and substantial achievements in space science, technology and applications.

1. Space Transportation System

From 2011 to November 2016 the Long March carrier rocket series completed 86 launch missions, sending over 100 spacecraft into target orbit with a success rate of 97.67 percent, indication of increasing effectiveness and high-density launching capability of carrier rockets. The Long March 5 (CZ- 5), China's newest generation of carrier rockets with a maximum carrying capacity, made its maiden flight and increased the diameter of liquid fuel rocket from 3.35 m to 5 m, with a maximum payload capacity of about 25 tons to low earth orbit and about 14 tons to geostationary transfer orbit, significantly improving the carrying capacity of the Long March rocket family and becoming a symbol of the upgrading of China's carrier rockets. The development of the 120-ton liquid oxygen and kerosene engine was test fired, which powered Long March 6 and Long March 7 on their maiden flights. The Long March 11, a solid-fuel carrier rocket, also made a successful maiden launch, further enriching the Long March rocket family.

2. Man-Made Satellites

(1) Earth Observation Satellites. The function of the Fengyun (Wind and Cloud), Haiyang (Ocean), Ziyuan (Resources), Gaofen (High Resolution), Yaogan (Remote-Sensing) and Tianhui (Space Mapping) satellite series and constellation of small satellites for environment and disaster monitoring and forecasting has been improved. The Fengyun polar orbit meteorological satellite has succeeded in networking observation by morning and afternoon satellites, while its geostationary earth orbit (GEO) meteorological satellite has formed a business mode of "multi-satellites in orbit, coordinated operation, mutual backup and encryption at the appropriate time." The Haiyang-2 satellite is capable of all-weather, full-time and high- accuracy observation of marine dynamic parameters such as sea height, sea wave and sea surface wind. The Ziyuan-1 02C satellite was launched, the Ziyuan-3 01 and 02 stereo mapping satellites have achieved double star networking and operating. The China High-resolution Earth Observation System program has been fully implemented; the Gaofen-2 is capable of sub-meter optical remote-sensing observation, the Gaofen-3 has a Synthetic Aperture Radar (SAR) imaging instrument that is accurate to one meter and the Gaofen-4 is China's first geosynchronous orbit high-resolution earth observation satellite. Satellite C of the environment and disaster monitoring and forecasting small satellite constellation has been put into use. The successful launching of the Kuaizhou-1 and Kuaizhou-2, which adopted integrated design of the satellite and the launch vehicle, has improved China's emergency response capability in space. The Jilin-1, a high-resolution remote-sensing satellite for commercial use has been launched and put into service.

(2) **Communications and Broadcasting Satellites.** China has comprehensively advanced the construction of fixed, mobile and data relay satellite systems. The successful launch of communications satellites such as Yatai and Zhongxing represented the completion of a fixed communications satellite support system whose communications services cover all of China's territory as well as major areas of the world. The Tiantong-1, China's first mobile communications satellite, has been successfully launched. The first-generation data relay satellite system composed of three Tianlian-1 satellites has been completed and high-speed communication test of satellite-ground laser link has been crowned with success. In addition, the development of the DFH-5 super communications satellite platform is going smoothly.

(3) **Navigation and Positioning Satellites.** The Beidou Navigation Satellite System (Beidou-2) has been completed, with the networking of 14 Beidou navigation satellites, officially offering positioning, velocity measurement, timing, wide area difference and short-message communication service to customers in the Asia-Pacific region. Beidou's global satellite navigation system is undergoing smooth construction.

(4) **New Technological Test Satellites.** China has launched the Shijian-9 satellite series for technological experiments, providing an important way to test new technologies.

3. Manned Spaceflight
In June 2012 and June 2013, the Shenzhou-9 and Shenzhou-10 manned spacecraft were launched to dock with the target spacecraft Tiangong-1. They used manual and automatic operations respectively, symbolizing breakthroughs for China in spacecraft rendezvous and docking technology and full success in its first operation of a manned space transportation system. In September and October 2016, the Tiangong-2 space laboratory and Shenzhou-11 manned spacecraft were launched and formed an assembly that operates steadily, with the mission of carrying out science and technology experiments in space, indicating that China has mastered technologies concerning astronauts' mid-term stay in orbit and long-term ground mission support. Currently, China has mastered major space technologies such as manned space transportation, space extravehicular activity, space docking, operating in assembly and astronauts' mid-term stay in orbit.

4. Deep Space Exploration

In December 2012 the Chang'e-2 lunar probe made a successful observation trip over asteroid 4179 (Toutatis). In December 2013 the Chang'e-3 realized the first soft landing on the surface of an extraterrestrial body by a Chinese spacecraft and completed patrol and exploration on the surface of the moon. In November 2014 China achieved success in the reentry and return flight test of the third-phase lunar exploration engineering, indicating that China has mastered the key technology of spacecraft reentry and return flight in a speed close to second cosmic velocity.

The Lunar Exploration Program helped mankind to acquire a high-resolution map of the moon and a high-definition image of Sinus Iridum and conducted research of lunar surface morphology, lunar structure, elemental composition of the lunar surface, lunar surface environment, lunar space environment and moon-based astronomical observation.

5. Space Launch Sites

In June 2016 the Wenchang Launch Site held its first launch, marking a new-generation launch site designed and built by China. The site is environmentally friendly and made breakthroughs in innovation. Renovations have also been accomplished in the Jiuquan, Taiyuan and Xichang launch sites, forming a launch site network covering both coastal and inland areas, high and low altitudes and various trajectories to satisfy the launch needs of manned spaceships, space laboratory core modules, deep space probes and all kinds of satellites.

6. Space Telemetry, Tracking and Command (TT&C)

The Tianlian-1 data relay satellite series have achieved global networking and operating. The Yuanwang-7, a spacecraft tracking ship has made its maiden voyage. Deep space TT&C stations have been built and put into use. China is constantly improving its space telemetry, tracking and command setups and established a multi-functioning TT&C network featuring space, marine and ground integration with a proper scale. The flight control ability of spacecraft has been gradually improved, completing the TT&C missions of the Shenzhou spacecraft series, Tiangong-1 target spacecraft, Chang'e lunar probe series and earth orbit satellites.

7. Space Applications

(1) Application of Earth Observation Satellites. The ground system and applications of earth observation satellites are improving, the fields and levels in which these satellites are used are expanding and the application benefits are growing. The ground stations receiving data from land, ocean and meteorological observation satellites are operating based on comprehensive planning, a satellite data ground network with the capacity of receiving data from high- and low-orbit satellites and reasonable arrangement at home and abroad. China has also established, based on comprehensive planning, a ground data processing system for earth observation satellites, common application supporting platform and multi-level network data distribution system, greatly increasing its ability in data processing, archiving, distribution, services provision and quantitative applications. Industrial application system building is in full swing, having completed 18 industrial and two regional application demonstration systems and set up 26 provincial-level data and application centers. An integrated information service sharing platform for a high-resolution earth observation system has been built. Earth observation satellite data is now widely used in industrial, regional and public services for economic and social development.

(2) Application of Communications and Broadcasting Satellites. The ground facilities such as TT&C station, gateway station, uplink station and calibration field of communications satellites have been improved. A satellite communications network and satellite radio and TV network of adequate scale to meet the needs of certain services have been built, further improving the communications service ability. These applications play an important role in radio and television services, distance education and telemedicine. The emergency satellite communications system has provided important support for the fight against flood and drought, for rescue and relief work and for handling major emergencies.

(3) Application of Navigation and Positioning Satellites. The Beidou Navigation Satellite System has significantly improved its accuracy and reliability, bringing into play an independent, controllable, complete and mature Beidou industrial chain and the three systems of Beidou industrial guarantee, application promotion and innovation. The Beidou Navigation System is widely used in transportation, maritime fisheries, hydrological monitoring, weather forecasting, surveying and mapping, forest fire prevention, time synchronization of communication, power dispatching, disaster reduction and relief and emergency rescue, influencing all aspects of people's life and production and injecting new vitality into global economic and social development.

(4) Transformation and Application of Space Technology. A new business model featuring the Internet plus satellite applications is coming into being, providing more convenient and high-quality services to the public. Secondary development, transformation and applications of space technology make possible the provision of high-quality products and services to relevant industries and help to support and propel the development of new materials, intelligent manufacturing and electronic information, among others.

8. Space Science

(1) **Space Science Satellites.** China has successfully launched the Dark Matter Particle Explorer, Shijian-10 and Quantum Science Experiment Satellite, offering important means for frontier scientific research.

(2) **Space Environment Scientific Experiments.** China has carried out a series of space science experiments using space science satellites, Chang'e lunar probe, Shenzhou spacecraft series and Tiangong-1 target aircraft, deepening the understanding of the mechanism of biological growth and materials preparation under the conditions of space microgravity and intense radiation and achieving some influential research findings.

(3) **Space Environment Detection and Forecast.** China has identified the space environment's major parameters and effects using space science satellites and the Shenzhou spacecraft series to provide space environmental monitoring and forecasting services for the safe operation of spacecraft.

9. Space Debris

China has improved the monitoring and mitigation of and early warning and protection against space debris. It has also enhanced standards and regulations in this regard. The monitoring of and early warning against space debris have been put into regular operation, ensuring the safe operation of spacecraft in orbit. China has also made breakthroughs in protection design technologies, applying them to the protection projects of spacecraft against space debris. In addition, all Long March carrier rockets have upper stage passivation and discarded spacecraft are moved out of orbit to protect the space environment.

III. Major Tasks for the Next Five Years

In the next five years China plans to expedite the development of its space endeavors by continuing to enhance the basic capacities of its space industry, strengthen research into key and cutting-edge technologies and implement manned spaceflight, lunar exploration, the Beidou Navigation Satellite System, high-resolution earth observation system, new-generation launch vehicles and other important projects. Furthermore, the country is to launch new key scientific and technological programs and major projects, complete, by and large, its space infrastructure system, expand its space applications in breadth and depth and further conduct research into space science, promoting the integrated development of space science, technology and applications.

1. Space Transport System

We will develop and launch medium-lift launch vehicles which are non-toxic and pollution-free, improve the new-generation launch vehicle family and enhance their reliability.

Endeavors will be made to research key technologies and further study the plans for developing heavy-lift launch vehicles. Breakthroughs are expected in key technologies for the overall system, high-thrust liquid oxygen and kerosene engines and oxygen and hydrogen engines of such launch vehicles. Thereafter the heavy-lift launch vehicle project will be activated.

China will conduct research into the technologies for low-cost launch vehicles, new upper stage and the reusable space transportation system between the earth and low-earth orbit.

2. Space Infrastructure

China is to improve its satellite systems and their basic related items, develop the three major satellite systems of remote-sensing, communications and broadcasting and navigation and positioning and build a space-ground integrated information network. In this way, a space infrastructure system capable of providing steady and sustained services will take shape, boosting the satellite and related applications industrial sector.

(1) Satellite Remote-sensing System. In accordance with the policy guideline for developing multi-functional satellites and creating networks of satellites and integrating them, we will focus on three series of satellites for observing the land, ocean and atmosphere, respectively. China is to develop and launch satellites capable of high-resolution multi-mode optical observation, L-band differential interferometric synthetic aperture radar imaging, carbon monitoring of the territorial ecosystem, atmospheric radar detection, ocean salinity detection and new-type ocean color observation. We will take steps to build our capabilities of highly efficient, comprehensive global observation and data acquisition with a rational allocation of low-, medium- and high-spatial resolution technologies and an optimized combination of multiple observation methods. China will make overall construction and improvement on remote-sensing satellite receiving station networks, calibration and validation fields, data centers, data-sharing platforms and common application supporting platforms to provide remote-sensing satellite data receiving services across the world.

(2) Satellite Communications and Broadcasting System. This system is oriented toward industrial and market applications and mainly operates through business models while meeting public welfare needs. China will develop both fixed and mobile communications and broadcasting as well as data relay satellites, build a space-ground integrated information network consisting of space-based systems such as high-earth-orbit broadband satellite systems and low-earth-orbit mobile satellite systems and ground-based systems such as satellite-access stations. TT&C stations, gateway stations, uplink stations, calibration fields and other satellite ground facilities are to be built synchronously. These efforts are expected to bring about a comprehensive system capable of providing broadband communications, fixed communications, direct-broadcast television, mobile communications and mobile multimedia broadcast services. A global satellite communications and broadcasting system integrated with the ground communications network will be established step by step.

(3) Satellite Navigation System. China is to continuously enhance the service capacities of the Beidou-2. With sustained efforts in building the Beidou global system, we plan to start providing basic services to countries along the Silk Road Economic Belt and 21st-century Maritime Silk Road in 2018, form a network consisting of 35 satellites for global services by 2020 and provide all clients with more accurate and more reliable services through advancing the ground-based and satellite-based augmentation systems in an integrated way.

3. Manned Spaceflight

China plans to launch the Tianzhou-1 cargo spacecraft to dock with the earth-orbiting Tiangong-2 space laboratory and research and master key technologies for cargo transport and replenishment to accumulate experience in building and operating a space station.

We aim to complete the main research and development work on the space station modules and start assembly and operation of the space station.

We strive to acquire key technologies and conduct experiments on such technologies to raise our manned spaceflight capacity, laying a foundation for exploring and developing cislunar space.

4. Deep-space Exploration

China will continue its lunar exploration project and strive to attain the automated extraterrestrial sampling and returning technology by space explorers. We plan to fulfill the three strategic steps of "orbiting, landing and returning" for the lunar exploration project by launching the Chang'e-5 lunar probe by the end of 2017 and realizing regional soft landing, sampling and return. We will launch the Chang'e-4 lunar probe around 2018 to achieve mankind's first soft landing on the far side of the moon and conduct in situ and roving detection and relay communications at earth-moon L2 point. Through the lunar exploration project, topographic and geological surveys will be implemented and laboratory research conducted on lunar samples; geological survey and research as well as low-frequency radio astronomy observation and research will be carried out targeting the landing area on the far side of the moon for a better understanding of the formation and evolution of the moon.

China intends to execute its first Mars exploration operation and grasp key technologies for orbiting, landing and roving exploration. It plans to launch the first Mars probe by 2020 to carry out orbiting and roving exploration. It will conduct further studies and key technological research on the bringing back of samples from Mars, asteroid exploration, exploration of the Jupiter system and planet fly-by exploration. When conditions allow, related projects will be implemented to conduct research into major scientific questions such as the origin and evolution of the solar system and search for extraterrestrial life.

5. Experiments on New Space Technologies
China is to perform experiments on new space technologies to provide solid technological support for its space industry.

China will develop and launch technology experiment satellites, including the Shijian-13, Shijian-17 and Shijian-18 and a global carbon dioxide monitoring satellite and conduct experiments on key technologies for new electric propulsion, laser communications and common platforms of new-generation communications satellites. It plans to build in-orbit servicing and maintenance systems for spacecraft and make in-orbit experiments on new theories, technologies and products by tapping various resources.

6. Space Launch Sites
China will improve its existing space launch sites by raising the reliability and IT application level and conducting adaptive improvements to ground facilities and equipment and increasing the complementarity of mission enforcement and backup capacities of space launch sites, equipping them with basic capacities to carry out various launch missions. It will explore and advance the building of space launch sites that are open to cooperation and sharing, form a new space launch system featuring rational division of work, mutual complementarity, smooth coordination, security and reliability. The integrated capacities and functions of space launch sites will be enhanced and exploited to meet various needs.

7. Space Telemetry, Tracking and Command
China will enhance its existing space TT&C systems. It aims to build and operate a second-generation relay satellite system, raise the accuracy of the orbit determination process for spacecraft, improve its TT&C capabilities in managing in-orbit spacecraft and strengthen integrated and efficient utilization of TT&C resources, to build a space-ground integrated TT&C network featuring security, reliability, quick response, flexible access, efficient operation and diverse services. It plans to explore the development of

commercial TT&C systems, seek new service modes and intensify international cooperation and networking in the field of TT&C, forming a new TT&C service pattern marked by openness and sharing.

8. Space Applications
China will improve its space application service system oriented toward industries, regions and the public, expand integrated application of space information and improve the application and marketing of scientific and technological results. Consequently, the scale, operational standards and industrialization level of space applications will be raised to serve national security and national economic and social development.

(1) **Industrial Applications.** In view of the need for global land surveying and geographic information acquisition, resource development and environmental protection, maritime development and management and the protection of related rights and interests, natural disaster prevention and reduction and emergency response, global climate change control, food security, social management and public services, China plans to consolidate the integrated application of space infrastructure and enhance its ability to provide timely, accurate and steady services.

(2) **Regional Applications.** In view of the need for regional urban planning, construction, operation management and social services, China will develop comprehensive satellite applications, such as new urbanization layout and smart towns and smart transport applications, to serve the coordinated development of the eastern, central, western, northeastern parts of the country, collaborated development of Beijing, Tianjin and Hebei, building of the Yangtze River Economic Belt and economic and social development of other regions in China. In addition, China will intensify its services oriented toward the nationally targeted poverty alleviation and eradication and operate space information services targeting old revolutionary base areas, ethnic minorities regions, frontier areas, poverty-stricken areas and islands in the sea.

(3) **Public Services.** Aiming at public information consumption and services, including smart tourism, broadcasting and TV, distance learning, telemedicine and cultural communication, China is determined to develop smart terminals of satellite applications and wearable electronics, improve space information fusion applications and advance the industrialization of space applications, fostering new growth points for the national economy.

9. Space Science

Targeting major frontier areas of space science and technology, China will implement a series of new space science satellite programs, establish a series of space science satellites featuring sustainable development and reinforce basic application research. Major discoveries and breakthroughs are expected in the frontier areas of space science to further mankind's knowledge of the universe.

(1) Space Astronomy and Space Physics. China will seek evidence of the existence of dark matter by using dark matter particle exploration satellites to detect high-energy electrons and high-energy gamma rays in the universe. It plans to launch a hard X-ray modulation telescope to study the matter dynamics and high-energy radiation processes in the strong gravitational field of compact celestial bodies and black holes. Relevant resources will be brought into play for research into large-scale structure and interaction models of solar wind and the magnetosphere and response to magnetospheric substorm change process.

(2) Scientific Experiments in Space. The Shijian-10 recoverable satellite, Chang'e probes, Shenzhou spacecraft, Tiangong-2 space laboratory and Tianzhou-1 cargo spacecraft are to be used to implement scientific experiments and research in biology, life sciences, medicine and materials in the space environment.

(3) Quantum Experiments in Space. Quantum experiment satellites are to be used to conduct experiments and research in the fields of quantum key transmission, quantum entanglement distribution and quantum teleportation.

(4) Basic and Applied Research. China will carry out basic research into sun-earth space environment, space climate and solar activity and its impact on space climate and implement space-related interdisciplinary research as well. Comprehensive techniques will be developed for analyzing data from space observations on the properties of X-rays, the energy spectrum and spatial distribution of high-energy electrons and high-energy gamma rays, space physics, extraterrestrial celestial bodies and the earth's electromagnetic field and ionosphere, to promote the application of space research findings.

10. Space Environment

China will improve the standardization system for space debris, near-earth objects and space climate. It will enhance the space debris basic database and data-sharing model and advance the development of space debris monitoring facilities, the early warning and emergency response platform and the online service system, through reinforcing integrated utilization of resources. The protection systems of spacecraft will be further strengthened. Furthermore, efforts will be made to improve the space environment monitoring system and to build a disaster early warning and prediction platform to raise our preventative capability. It will conduct studies on the building of facilities for monitoring near-earth objects and put the plan into operation to elevate our capability to monitor and catalog such objects.

IV. Policies and Measures for Development

The Chinese government has formulated policies and measures to support the space industry and create favorable conditions for its sustainable, sound and rapid development.

The China National Space Administration is the government agency in charge of China's civil space activities and international space cooperation and performs corresponding functions of administration.

1. Rationally Arrange Space Activities

Priority is given to the construction and application of space infrastructure, alongside support for space exploration and space science research, in China's ongoing efforts to expand its capacity to enter and utilize space and enhance guarantee for space security.

2. Greatly Enhance Space Innovation

A number of major projects and scientific and technological programs have been implemented to promote significant progress of space science and technology and enhance the overall level of China's science and technology.

The roles of various players are clearly defined in the formation of a framework of innovation featuring the coordinated efforts of the government, enterprises, universities, research institutions and consumers and the creation of technical and industrial innovation partnerships, so as to shape a chain of innovation to match the overall industrial chain.

Efforts are being made to build a space research base and plan in advance strategic, fundamental and forward-looking research projects to tackle key technical problems, so as to substantially increase China's capacity for original innovation and create a state-of-art platform in this field.

The customization development of space technologies has been enhanced to put research findings into industrial production and lead national economic development.

3. Transform and Upgrade Space Industry Capacity

Efforts are constantly being made to build an integrated and open system comprising system integrators, specialized contractors, market suppliers and public service providers, based on the national economy and covering all links from scientific research to production.

A project to reinforce space science infrastructure has got off the ground with the goal of removing the basic bottlenecks and obstacles concerning key materials, core spare parts and advanced technology and improving such systems as standards and measurements.

Information technology has been further applied to make space industry capacity more digitalized, Internet- and artificial intelligence-based.

4. Accelerate the Development of Satellite Application Industry

Industrial policies related to satellite application, national standards and quality systems have been improved. Supportive mechanisms for satellite data sharing have been established and improved and platforms for sharing satellite data and resources upgraded to create a satisfactory environment for the satellite application industry and boost the overall performance of satellite application.

Industrial clusters and markets for satellite application are being cultivated to improve the industrial chain. Development for integration application of satellite technologies is encouraged to promote the integrated development of satellite application with the Internet, big data, Internet of Things and other emerging industries, so as to create new products, new technologies, new modes of business and new points of growth and give impetus to the mass entrepreneurship and innovation.

5. Strengthen the Relevant Legislative Work

Efforts have been made to accelerate the formation of a legal system centering on the legislation of a national law to govern the space industry, including studying and formulating regulations on space data and their application management, the management of the export of astronautic products and technologies. The regulations in force on permits for space launch projects, registration of space-related items and permits for scientific and technological research and production have been improved to guide and regulate various space-related activities in accordance with the law, which provides legal guarantee for building China's space industry.

China has undertaken studies of international space law and actively participated in the formulation of international rules regarding outer space.

6. Improve Diverse Funding System

The scope of government investment is being clearly specified, the way in which such investment is arranged is optimized and investment management is regulated and sustainable and steady government financial support for space activities is guaranteed.

The mechanism for market access and withdrawal has been improved. A list of investment projects in the space industry has been introduced for better management in this regard. Non-governmental capital and other social sectors are encouraged to participate in space-related activities, including scientific research and production, space infrastructure, space information products and services and use of satellites to increase the level of commercialization of the space industry.

The government has increased its cooperation with private investors and the mechanism for government procurement of astronautic products and services has been improved.

7. Strengthen the Training of Professionals for Space Industry

The mechanisms related to the training, assessment, flow of and incentives for professional personnel are being improved in an effort to form a well- structured contingent of highly qualified personnel in the course of construction of important projects and major programs, which consists of strategic scientists, leading researchers and technicians, entrepreneurs and high-caliber professionals, as well as experts in international cooperation.

8. Disseminate Knowledge about Space Science

Events have been organized around China Space Day, World Space Week and Science and Technology Week to disseminate knowledge and culture about space, promote the Spirit of the Manned Space Program, inspire the nation, especially its young people, to develop an interest in science, explore the unknown and make innovations and attract more people into China's space industry.

V. International Exchanges and Cooperation

The Chinese government holds that all countries in the world have equal rights to peacefully explore, develop and utilize outer space and its celestial bodies and that all countries' outer space activities should be beneficial to their economic development and social progress and to the peace, security, survival and development of mankind.

International space cooperation should adhere to the fundamental principles stated in the Treaty on Principles Governing the Activities of States in the Exploration and Use of Outer Space, Including the Moon and Other Celestial Bodies and the Declaration on International Cooperation in the Exploration and Use of Outer Space for the Benefit and in the Interests of All States, Taking into Particular Account the Needs of Developing Countries. China maintains that international exchanges and cooperation should be strengthened on the basis of equality and mutual benefit, peaceful utilization and inclusive development.

1. Fundamental Policies

The Chinese government has adopted the following fundamental policies with regard to international space exchanges and cooperation:
- Supporting activities regarding the peaceful use of outer space within the framework of the United Nations;

- Supporting all inter-governmental and non-governmental space organizations' activities that promote development of the space industry;
- Strengthening bilateral and multilateral cooperation which is based on common goals and serves the Belt and Road Initiative;
- Supporting the Asia-Pacific Space Cooperation Organization to play an important role in regional space cooperation and attaching importance to space cooperation under the BRICS cooperation mechanism and within the framework of the Shanghai Cooperation Organization.
- Encouraging and endorsing the efforts of domestic scientific research institutes, industrial enterprises, institutions of higher learning and social organizations to develop international space exchanges and cooperation in diverse forms and at various levels under the guidance of relevant state policies, laws and regulations.

2. Major Events

Since 2011 China has signed 43 space cooperation agreements or memoranda of understanding with 29 countries, space agencies and international organizations. It has taken part in relevant activities sponsored by the United Nations and other relevant international organizations and supported international commercial cooperation in space. These measures have yielded fruitful results.

(1) Bilateral Cooperation
- China and Russia signed the Outline of China-Russia Space Cooperation from 2013 to 2017 through the mechanism of the Space Cooperation Sub-committee during the Prime Ministers' Meeting between Russia and China. The two countries have actively promoted cooperation in deep space exploration, manned spaceflight, earth observation, satellite navigation, space-related electronic parts and components and other areas.
- China and the European Space Agency (ESA) signed the Outline of China-ESA Space Cooperation from 2015 to 2020 within the mechanism of the China-Europe Joint Commission on Space Cooperation. The two sides have declared their determination to cooperate in deep space exploration, space science, earth observation, TT&C services, space debris and space-related education and training and launched the panoramic imaging satellite for solar wind and magnetosphere interaction. The two sides have completed cooperation on the Dragon 3 cooperation program.
- China and Brazil, through the mechanism of the Space Cooperation Sub-committee of the Sino-Brazilian High-level Coordination Commission, have conducted constant cooperation in the China-Brazil Earth Resources Satellite (CBERS) program. They successfully launched CBERS-4, signed the Supplementary Agreement of China and Brazil on the Joint Development of CBERS-04A and Cooperation Agreement of

China and Brazil on Remote-Sensing Satellite Data and Application, maintaining CBERS data consistency. The two countries also updated CBERS data receiving stations in South Africa and Singapore, expanding CBERS data application regionally and globally. They have worked together to set up the China-Brazil Joint Laboratory for Space Weather.
- China and France, within the mechanism of the Sino-French Joint Commission on Space Cooperation, have engaged in bilateral cooperation on astronomic, ocean and other satellite programs. The two countries have signed a letter of intent on space and climate change to promote the application of space technology in global climate change governance.
- China and Italy set up the Sino-Italian Joint Commission on Space Cooperation and have steadily carried forward research and development of the China-Italy Electromagnetic Monitoring Experiment Satellite Program.
- China and Britain have promoted construction of a joint laboratory on space science and technology, upgraded their exchanges in space science and technology personnel and launched cooperative studies on remote-sensing applications.
- China and Germany have promoted dialogue between their space industry enterprises and strengthened cooperation in high-end space manufacturing.
- China and the Netherlands signed a memorandum of understanding on space cooperation, promoting cooperation in remote-sensing applications in agriculture, water resources and atmospheric environment and stating that Chang'e-4 would carry a Dutch payload in its mission.
- China and the United States, within the framework of the China-U.S. Strategic and Economic Dialogue, carried out a civil space dialogue, stating that the two countries would strengthen cooperation in space debris, space weather, response to global climate change and related areas.
- China signed space cooperation agreements and established bilateral space cooperation mechanisms with Algeria, Argentina, Belgium, India, Indonesia, Kazakhstan to strengthen exchanges and cooperation in such areas as space technology, space applications and space science, education and training.

(2) Multilateral Cooperation

- China takes an active part in activities organized by the United Nations Committee on the Peaceful Uses of Outer Space and its Scientific and Technical Sub-committee and Legal Sub-committee and negotiations on international space rules such as the long-term sustainability of outer space activities. It signed the Memorandum of Understanding between the China National Space Administration and the United Nations on Earth Observation Data and Technical Support, actively promoting data sharing and cooperation between China's earth observation satellites on the UN platform.

1. White Papers on Space Activities

- China supports the relevant work of the Beijing office of the United Nations Platform for Space-based Information for Disaster Management and Emergency Response. The UN set up the Regional Center for Space Science and Technology Education in Asia and the Pacific (China) in Beijing to promote personnel training in the international space arena.
- Within the framework of the Asia-Pacific Space Cooperation Organization (APSCO), China actively participated in the APSCO Joint Small Multi-Mission Satellite Constellation Program. It also organized the APSCO Development Strategy Forum with the theme of the Belt and Road Initiative for Facilitating Regional Capacity Building of the Asia-Pacific Countries, at which the Beijing Declaration was adopted.
- China and the space agencies of Brazil, Russia, India and South Africa co-sponsored and actively promoted cooperation in the BRICS remote- sensing satellite constellation.
- China launched the China-ASEAN Satellite Information Maritime Application Center and Lancang-Mekong River Spatial Information Exchange Center.
- China actively participated in activities organized by the Inter-Agency Space Debris Coordination Committee (IADC), International Charter on Space and Major Disasters, Group on Earth Observations and other intergovernmental organizations. It hosted the 31st Council of the International Charter on Space and Major Disasters, the 32nd Meeting of the IADC and other international conferences.
- China actively participated in activities organized by the International Committee on Global Navigation Satellite Systems (ICG) and held the Seventh ICG Conference. It actively improved the compatibility and interoperability of the Beidou system with other satellite navigation systems, popularized satellite navigation technology and cooperated with a number of countries and regions in satellite navigation applications.
- China actively participated in activities organized by the International Astronautical Federation, International Committee on Space Research, International Academy of Astronautics, International Institute of Space Law and other non-governmental international space organizations and academic institutes. It held the 64th International Astronautical Congress, 2014 United Nations / China / APSCO Workshop on Space Law, 36th International Conference on Earth Science and Remote-Sensing and related international conferences. It also held the First Seminar on Manned Spaceflight Technology within the framework of the United Nations Program on Space Applications.
- China actively participated in the international coordination of global disaster prevention and reduction and provided satellite data support and technical services for major international disaster-relief efforts through the United Nations Platform for Space-based Information on Disaster Management and Emergency Response, United

Nations Economic and Social Commission for Asia and the Pacific, International Charter on Space and Major Disasters and related mechanisms.

(3) Commercial Activities
China encourages and supports Chinese enterprises to participate in international commercial activities in the space field. It has exported satellites and made in-orbit delivery of Nigeria's communications satellite, Venezuela's remote-sensing satellite-1, Bolivia's communications satellite, Laos' communications satellite-1 and Belarus' communications satellite-1. In addition, it provided commercial launch service for Turkey's Gokturk-2 earth observation satellite and when launching its own satellites took on small satellites for Ecuador, Argentina, Poland, Luxembourg and other countries. It has also provided business services concerning space information.

3. Key Areas for Future Cooperation
In the next five years, China will, with a more active and open attitude, conduct extensive international exchanges and cooperation concerning space in the following key areas:
- Construction of the Belt and Road Initiative Space Information Corridor, including earth observation, communications and broadcasting, navigation and positioning and other types of satellite-related development; ground and application system construction; and application product development.
- Construction of the BRICS remote-sensing satellite constellation.
- Construction of the APSCO Joint Small Multi-mission Satellite Constellation Program and University Small Satellite Project Development.
- The Moon, Mars and other deep space exploration programs and technical cooperation.
- Inclusion of a space laboratory and a space station in China's manned spaceflight program.
- Research and development of a space science satellite, a remote-sensing satellite, payloads, etc.
- Construction of ground infrastructure such as data receiving stations and communications gateway stations.
- Satellite applications, including earth observation, communications and broadcasting, navigation and positioning.
- Exploration and research on space science.
- Launching and carrying services.
- Space TT&C support.
- Space debris monitoring, early warning, mitigation and protection.
- Space weather cooperation.

1. WHITE PAPERS ON SPACE ACTIVITIES

- Import and export of and technical cooperation in the field of whole satellites, sub-systems, spare parts and electronic components of satellites and launch vehicles, ground facilities and equipment and related items.
- Research on space law, policy and standards.
- Personnel exchanges and training in the space field.

Conclusion

In the present-day world, more and more countries are attaching importance to and taking an active part in developing space activities. Moreover, space technology is being widely applied in all aspects of our daily life, exerting a major and far-reaching influence on social production and lifestyle.

It is mankind's unremitting pursuit to peacefully explore and utilize outer space. Standing at a new historical starting line, China is determined to quicken the pace of developing its space industry and actively carry out international space exchanges and cooperation, so that achievements in space activities will serve and improve the well-being of mankind in a wider scope, at a deeper level and with higher standards. China will promote the lofty cause of peace and development together with other countries.

(www.scio.gov.cn)

1.5. CHINA'S BEIDOU NAVIGATION SATELLITE SYSTEM OF 2016

Information Office of the State Council
December 2016
(Official English Version)

Preface

The Beidou Navigation Satellite System (hereinafter referred to as the BDS) has been independently constructed and operated by China with an eye to the needs of the country's national security and economic and social development. As a space infrastructure of national significance, the BDS provides all-time, all-weather and high-accuracy positioning, navigation and timing services to global users.

In the late 20th century, China started to explore a path to develop a navigation satellite system suitable for its national conditions and gradually formulated a three-step strategy of development: to complete the construction of the BDS-1 and provide services to the whole country by the end of 2000; to complete the construction of the BDS-2 and provide services to the Asia-Pacific region by the end of 2012; and to complete the construction of the BDS and provide services worldwide around 2020.

Along with the development of the BDS project and service ability, related products have been widely applied in communication and transportation, marine fisheries, hydrological monitoring, weather forecasting, surveying, mapping and geographic information, forest fire prevention, time synchronization for communication systems, power dispatching, disaster mitigation and relief, emergency search and rescue and other fields. These products are gradually penetrating every aspect of social production and people's life, injecting new vitality into the global economy and social development.

Navigation satellite systems are public resources shared by the whole globe and multi-system compatibility and interoperability has become a trend. China applies the principle that "The BDS is developed by China and dedicated to the world" to serve the development of the Silk Road Economic Belt and the 21st Century Maritime Silk Road (Belt and Road Initiative for abbreviation) and actively pushes forward international cooperation related to the BDS. As the BDS joins hands with other navigation satellite systems, China will work with all other countries, regions and international organizations to promote global satellite navigation development and make the BDS better serve the world and benefit mankind.

I. Goals and Principles of Development
China lays store by the construction of the BDS, ranking it one of its national key technical projects that supports its innovative development strategy.

1. Goals of Development
Building a world-class navigation satellite system to meet the needs of the country's national security as well as economic and social development and providing continuous, stable and reliable services for global users; developing BDS-related industries to support China's economic and social development, as well as improvement of people's living standards; and enhancing international cooperation to share the fruits of development in the field of satellite navigation, increasing the comprehensive application benefits of Global Navigation Satellite System (GNSS).

2. Principles of Development
China upholds the principles of "independence, openness, compatibility and gradualness" in the BDS construction and development.
- By "independence", it means to uphold independent construction, development and operation of the BDS and acquire the capability to independently provide satellite navigation services to global users.
- By "openness", it means to provide open satellite navigation services free of charge and encourage all-scale, multilevel and high-quality international cooperation and exchange.

- By "compatibility", it means to enhance BDS compatibility and interoperability with other navigation satellite systems and encourage international cooperation and exchanges, so as to provide better services to users.
- By "gradualness", it means to carry out the BDS project step by step, enhance BDS service performance and boost the development of satellite navigation industry in a comprehensive, coordinated and sustainable manner.

II. Development of the BDS

Based on its national conditions, China has independently developed the BDS step by step with constant improvement.

1. Three-Step Strategy of Development

- The first step is to construct the BDS-1 (also known as Beidou Navigation Satellite Demonstration System). The project was started in 1994 and the system was completed and put into operation in 2000 with the launching of two Geostationary Earth Orbit (GEO) satellites. With an active-positioning scheme, the system provided users in China with positioning, timing, wide-area differential and short message communication services. The third GEO satellite was launched in 2003, which further enhanced the system's performance.
- The second step is to construct the BDS-2. The project was started in 2004 and by the end of 2012 a total of 14 satellites – 5 GEO satellites, 5 Inclined Geosynchronous Satellite Orbit (IGSO) satellites and 4 Medium Earth Orbit (MEO) satellites – had been launched to finish the space constellation deployment. Based on a technical scheme which was compatible with the BDS-1, the BDS-2 added the passive-positioning scheme and provided users in the Asia-Pacific region with positioning, velocity measurement, timing, wide-area differential and short message communication services.
- The third step is to construct the BDS. The project was started in 2009 to inherit the technical schemes of both active and passive services. The goal is to provide basic services to the countries along the Belt and Road and in neighboring regions by 2018 and to complete the constellation deployment with the launching of 35 satellites by 2020 to provide services to global users.

2. Main Components of the BDS

The BDS is mainly comprised of three segments: space segment, ground segment and user segment.
- The space segment. The BDS space segment is a hybrid navigation constellation consisting of GEO, IGSO and MEO satellites.

- The ground segment. The BDS ground segment consists of various ground stations, including master control stations, time synchronization/uplink stations and monitoring stations.
- The user segment. The BDS user segment consists of various kinds of BDS basic products, including chips, modules and antennae, as well as terminals, application systems and application services, which are compatible with other systems.

3. Characteristics of the BDS

The BDS development follows a model of developing regional service capacities, then gradually extending the service globally. This practice has enriched the development models for navigation satellite systems worldwide.

The BDS possesses the following characteristics: First, its space segment is a hybrid constellation consisting of satellites in three kinds of orbits. In comparison with other navigation satellite systems, the BDS operates more satellites in high orbits to offer better anti-shielding capabilities, which is particularly observable in terms of performance in the low-latitude areas. Second, the BDS provides navigation signals of multiple frequencies and is able to improve service accuracy by using combined multi-frequency signals. Third, the BDS integrates navigation and communication capabilities for the first time and has five major functions – real-time navigation, rapid positioning, precise timing, location reporting and short message communication services.

4. Improvement of BDS Performance

To meet the increasing user demand, BDS technical research and development in the areas of satellites, atomic clocks and signals will be strengthened and a new generation of navigation, positioning and timing technologies will be explored to improve service performance.
- Providing global services. China will launch new-generation navigation satellites, develop airborne atomic clocks with enhanced performance, further improve the performance and lifetime of satellites and build more stable and reliable inter-satellite links. It will broadcast additional navigation signals and enhance the compatibility and interoperability with other navigation satellite systems, so as to provide better services for global users.
- Strengthening service capabilities. China will establish a grounded test and validation bed to accomplish the full coverage of tests and validation for space and ground equipment; continue to build and improve satellite based and ground-based augmentation systems to substantially enhance BDS service accuracy and reliability; optimize the technical system of location reporting and short message communication to expand user volume and service coverage.
- Maintaining spatio-temporal reference. The BDT is related to the Coordinated Universal Time and the time bias information is broadcast in the navigation

message. China will push forward the clock bias monitoring with other navigation satellite systems and improve their compatibility and interoperability. It will develop a BDS-based worldwide location identification system, increase the interoperability between BDS coordinate frame and that of other navigation satellite systems and constantly refine the reference frame.

III. Reliable and Safe Satellite Navigation Services

China is committed to ensuring the safe and reliable operation of the BDS by taking multiple measures and to providing continuous, stable and reliable open services to users free of charge.

1. Ensuring Safe and Reliable BDS Operations

- Improving the management mechanism on operation. Perfecting a normalized multi-party response mechanism for BDS space segment, ground segment and user segment. Continuously enhancing the capability of assurance to manage the operation of large-scale constellations.
- Establishing a GNSS monitoring and assessment network. Constructing an international GNSS Monitoring and Assessment System, actively implementing international cooperation, extensively exploiting international resources, carrying out monitoring and assessment of the constellation status, signal accuracy, signal quality and service performance of the BDS at every scale and providing references for users' applications.
- Taking a redundant and backup approach. Adopting a satellite backup strategy both in-orbit and on-ground to reduce and avoid the effects of emergent in-orbit satellite fault affecting service performance. Redundant and backup design is adopted to enable ground facilities to eliminate weak links and to enhance BDS reliability.

2. Providing Open Services Free of Charge

Currently, B1I and B2I open service signals are being broadcast by the operating BDS-2 to provide open services to the Asia-Pacific region free of charge. The services cover an area extending 55 degrees North-55 degrees South and 55 degrees East-180 degrees East, with positioning accuracy less than 10 meters, velocity measurement accuracy less than 0.2 meter per second and timing accuracy less than 50 nanoseconds.

3. Disseminating BDS Information in a Timely Manner

- Publishing BDS documents related to open services and signals to provide inputs for global BDS product development efforts. The Interface Control Document of B1I and B2I signals has been published, which defines the interface specifications between the BDS-2 satellites and user terminals. It specifies the signal structures, basic characteristics, ranging codes, NAV messages and other contents. The Open Service

Performance Standard has been published, which defines the service coverage area, accuracy, continuity, availability and other performance indexes of the BDS-2. In the future, related documents will be updated and published in step with BDS construction and development.
- Establishing a multi-channel information dissemination mechanism. China holds news conferences when appropriate to disseminate important information about BDS development and releases the latest news of the system in a timely manner through the official BDS website (www.beidou.gov.cn) from the aspects of system construction, operation, application and international cooperation. It also issues notifications worldwide in advance before carrying out plans which might affect user services.

4. Protecting the Utilization of Radio-Navigation Satellite Frequency Spectrum
- Protecting the radio-navigation satellite frequency spectrum according to law. China protects the utilization of BDS frequency spectrum and ensures the safety of BDS operation and BDS users pursuant to the national laws and regulations regarding the radio frequency spectrum.
- Firmly rejecting harmful interference. China prohibits the production, sale and use of illegal interference devices, investigates and punishes in accordance with the law any hostile interference actions that affect the system operations and services.

IV. BDS Application and Industrial Development

China strives to enhance BDS application development, in an effort to build a BDS industrial chain which comprises the basic products, application terminals, application systems and operational services, keeps strengthening BDS-related industrial supporting, promotion and innovation systems, continuously improves the industrial environment, expands the application scale for integrated development and increases the economic and social benefits of the satellite navigation industry.

1. Establishing an Industrial Supporting System
- Industrial policies. China has formulated development plans for the satellite navigation industry, making overall arrangement for medium- and long-term satellite navigation industrial development and encourages competent departments and local governments to enact relevant policies to support BDS application and industrial development.
- Equitable market environment. China is making efforts to build a development environment for the satellite navigation industry marked by orderly competition and increase the efficiency and effectiveness of resource allocation. It encourages and supports domestic and overseas organizations, including scientific research

institutions, enterprises, colleges, universities and social organizations, to actively develop BDS applications and fully release market vitality.
- Standardization process. In 2014 the National Technical Committee on Beidou Satellite Navigation of Standardization Administration of China was established and the Beidou Satellite Navigation Standard System was set up, which has been constantly improved. China promotes the standards verification and implementation and expedites the formulation and revision of standards, which are fundamental, generally applicable, and in urgent need, so as to enhance the quality and benefits of the procedure-based development of satellite navigation.
- Product quality system. China is working to establish and improve a public service platform for satellite navigation product quality assurance. It also actively promotes third-party quality test, type approval and authentication efforts of BDS basic products used in the security sector and application products in key fields. It is regularizing satellite navigation application services and operations and cultivating the Beidou brand. It aims to gradually establish satellite navigation product test and authentication institutions, strengthen admissibility of third-party certification, promoting the upgrading of the core competitiveness of BDS products on all scales and pushing forward BDS applications in line with international conventions.
- Comprehensive service system of location data. China welcomes commercial operation to be introduced to help build the basic platform of location service based on its BDS augmentation systems, which will have extensive coverage of application fields and interconnections and provide support services to different regions and industries and to public customers.

2. Establishing an Industrial Application Promotion System
- Application in key sectors. Great efforts are being made to promote the application of BDS technologies and products, which are compatible with other systems, in the key sectors related to national security and economy, to provide important assurance for the steady and safe running of the national economy.
- Industrial and regional applications. China is pushing forward close integration between satellite navigation and each industry in the national economy, carrying out demonstrations of BDS industrial applications, formulating comprehensive application solutions for industries and promoting transformation and enhancement in the areas of transportation, national land resources, disaster prevention and reduction, agriculture, forestry and water conservancy, surveying and exploration and emergency response and rescue. It encourages BDS regional application demonstrations to meet the requirements of the state strategies on regional development, such as the "Coordinated Development for the Beijing-Tianjin-Hebei Region", the building of "Yangtze River Economic Zone" and the development of smart cities. It is also promoting commercial and large-scale BDS

applications and enhancing BDS-related industries, as well as regional economic and social development.
- Mass market application. The goal is to produce miniaturized, low power-consuming and highly-integrated BDS- related products, oriented to the mass market in the sectors of smart phones, vehicle-borne terminals and wearable devices. The focus is on pushing forward the adoption of satellite navigation and positioning functions based on the BDS and other compatible systems as a standard configuration in the fields of vehicle-borne and intelligent navigation and promoting diversified applications in social services, transportation, caring for vulnerable groups and smart cities.

3. Establishing an Industrial Innovative System
- Research and development of basic products. To make breakthroughs in key technologies, China is developing chips, modules, antennae and other basic products based on the BDS and other compatible systems and fostering an independent BDS industrial chain.
- Establishment of an innovation system. China encourages and supports the construction and development of key laboratories for satellite navigation application technologies, research centers of engineering (technology), technology centers of enterprises and other innovative bodies, enhances the capacity of engineering experiment platforms and achievement transformation platforms, supports relevant enterprises and makes more efforts to protect intellectual property rights, so as to form a technology innovation system which relies on the enterprise as the main body and combines the efforts of universities, research institutes and application.
- Integrated industrial development. China encourages the integrated development of the BDS and Internet+, big data and cloud computing, supports the integrated positioning and innovative utilization of satellite navigation together with mobile communications, WLAN, pseudo-satellites, ultra-wide band and Ad Hoc Network signals, promotes integrated development of satellite navigation and emerging industries such as the Internet of Things, geographic information, satellite remote sensing and communication and mobile Internet and encourages people to start their own businesses and make innovations, so as to vigorously upgrade the innovation capability of the industry.

V. International Cooperation and Exchanges

China will push forward the international development of the BDS, actively carry out international cooperation and exchanges in this field, so as to serve the Belt and Road Initiative, promote the development of global satellite navigation and enable the BDS to serve the world and benefit mankind better.

1. Strengthening Compatibility and Joint Applications with Other Navigation Satellite Systems

China actively pushes forward the cooperation and exchanges between the BDS and other navigation satellite systems in the fields of system construction and application from all perspectives, strengthening compatibility and interoperability, achieving resource sharing, complementarity and technology advancement, improving the services of navigation satellite systems and providing users with more qualified, diversified, safe and reliable services.

2. Utilizing Frequency and Orbital Slot Resources According to International Rules
As limited and valuable natural resources, frequencies and orbital slots provide a critical foundation for the development of navigation satellite systems. Adhering to the International Telecommunication Union (ITU) rules, China works to facilitate coordination of BDS frequencies and orbital slots through negotiations, actively participates in the research and formulation of ITU rules and other relevant activities and expands radio-navigation frequency resources through cooperation with other nations. Since 2000 China has held effective coordination activities on more than 300 satellite networks with more than 20 countries, regions and international organizations.

3. Promoting the Ratification of the BDS by International Standards
The ratification of the BDS by international standards is a milestone for the integration of the BDS into international systems. China spares no effort to get the BDS ratified by the International Organization for Standardization and other international organizations in the industrial and professional application sectors. Currently, positive efforts are being made to advance the recognition of the BDS in the International Civil Aviation Organization, International Maritime Organization, Third-Generation Mobile Communication Standard Partnership Project and other organizations. China advocates the involvement of enterprises, scientific research, colleges and universities in the formulation of satellite navigation terminals and application standards. In November 2014 the BDS gained recognition from the International Maritime Organization.

4. Participating in Multilateral Activities in the Field of International Satellite Navigation
The BDS is one of the major GNSS providers and China actively participates in international satellite navigation affairs, attends the activities held by the International Committee on Global Navigation Satellite Systems (ICG) and other relevant international organizations, supports academic exchanges and cooperation in this area and promotes satellite navigation applications with the contribution of the BDS. China actively takes part in relevant tasks within the orbit of the United Nations, successfully held the Seventh Meeting of the ICG in 2012, when the proposals for the international GNSS Monitoring and Assessment and the BDS/GNSS Application Demonstration and Experience Campaign were initiated and the Joint Statement of Global Navigation Satellite Systems for serving the whole was issued. The China Satellite Navigation Conference is held

annually and plays a positive role in the development of satellite navigation technologies and applications worldwide.

5. Promoting International Satellite Navigation Applications
- To intensify publicity and popularization in this field, China has implemented the "BDS Tour" series of events, pushed forward the establishment of BDS Centers to enable better understanding of the BDS. BDS Centers have been jointly set up in a number of nations. The Beidou International Exchange and Training Center has been opened and a demonstration platform for education and training in the field of satellite navigation has been set up. In addition, academic education, summer schools, short-term training courses and symposiums and other international education and training activities have been regularly held.
- To advance and implement internationalization projects, China is promoting research and consultancy services regarding the policies, markets, laws and finance related to international satellite navigation applications and improving comprehensive international service capabilities. In line with the Belt and Road Initiative, China will jointly build satellite navigation augmentation systems with relevant nations, provide highly accurate satellite navigation, positioning and timing services, improve the overseas BDS service performances and promote international applications of navigation technologies. China will also carry out application demonstrations in the fields of transportation, tourism, maritime application, disaster reduction and relief and agriculture and boost application on a large scale, through establishing an operation and service platform for highly accurate satellite navigation, positioning and timing services.

Conclusion

Navigation satellite systems are the common wealth of the development of mankind and also a space infrastructure which can provide all-time precise time and space information. They promote the development of emerging industrial clusters that are technology- and knowledge-intensive with huge growth potentials and sound comprehensive benefits, thus becoming critical support for national security, economic and social development and increasingly improve the people's production and living activities.

China will continue its BDS construction, improve the system performance and fulfill its service commitments. It will persist in opening up and cooperation, promote the popularization in this field, strive to advance satellite navigation applications worldwide and make satellite navigation better benefit the wellbeing of the people and the progress of mankind.

(www.scio.gov.cn)

1.6. China's Space Program: A 2021 Perspective

Information Office of the State Council
January 2022
(Official English Version)

Preamble
"To explore the vast cosmos, develop the space industry and build China into a space power is our eternal dream," stated by President Xi Jinping. The space industry is a critical constituent element of the overall national strategy, and China upholds the principle of exploration and utilization of outer space for peaceful purposes.

Since 2016, China's space industry has made rapid and innovative progress, manifested by a steady improvement in space infrastructure, the completion and operation of the Beidou Navigation Satellite System, the completion of the high-resolution earth observation system, the steady improvement of the service ability of satellite communications and broadcasting, the conclusion of the last step of the three-step lunar exploration program ("orbit, land, and return"), the first stages of building the space station, and a smooth interplanetary voyage and landing beyond the earth-moon system by Tianwen-1, followed by the exploration of Mars. These achievements have attracted worldwide attention.

In the next five years, China will integrate space science, technology and applications while pursuing the new development philosophy, building a new development model and meeting the requirements for high-quality development. It will start a new journey towards a space power. The space industry will contribute more to China's growth as a whole, to the construction of a community of share future for mankind, and the promotion of human progress.

We are publishing this white paper to offer a brief introduction to China's major achievements in the space field since 2016 and its main tasks and missions in the next five years, in order to help the international community better understand China's space industry.

I. A New Journey Towards a Strong Space Presence
1. The Purposes of Development
The purposes of China's space program are: to explore outer space to expand humanity's understanding of the earth and the cosmos; to facilitate the construction of a community of shared future for mankind based on global consensus on our shared responsibility in utilizing outer space for peaceful purposes and safeguarding its security for the benefit of all humanity; to meet the demands of economic, scientific and technological development, national security and social progress; and to raise the scientific and

cultural levels of the Chinese people, protect China's national rights and interests, and build up its overall strength.

2. Vision
China aims to strengthen its space presence in an all-round manner: to enhance its capacity to better understand, freely access, efficiently use, and effectively governance of outer space; to defend national security, improve self-reliance and self-improvement capacity and efforts in science and technology, and promote high-quality economic and social development; to advocate sound and efficient governance of outer space, and pioneer human progress; and to make a positive contribution to China's socialist modernization and to peace and progress for all humanity.

3. Principles
China's space industry is subject to and serves the overall national strategy. China adheres to the principles of innovation-driven, coordinated and efficient, and for peaceful progress based on cooperation and sharing to promote the high-quality development of space industry.
Innovation-Driven Development. Innovation is at the core of China's space industry. It aims to boost strategic scientific and technological strength in the space industry by implementing major space programs in science and technology. To strengthen original innovation, the environment for innovation will be optimized to achieve industrial production as early as possible and improve China's independent capacity to build a sustainable space industry.
Coordinated and Efficient Development. China adopts a holistic approach in building its space industry. It mobilizes and guides different sectors to take part in and contribute to this key industry, and coordinates all relevant activities under an overall plan. To ensures that technology plays a greater role in promoting and guiding space science and applications, the growth of new forms and models of business for the industry shall be facilitated. These measures aim to raise the quality and overall performance of China's space industry.
Development for Peaceful Purposes. China has consistently advocated the exploration and utilization of outer space for peaceful purposes, and opposes any attempt to weaponize the outer space, turn outer space into a battlefield or start an arms race in outer space. China develops and utilizes space resources in a prudent manner, takes effective measures to protect the space environment, ensures that space remains peaceful and clean, and guarantees that its space activities benefit the whole of mankind.
Development for Cooperation and Sharing. China always combines independence and self-reliance and opening up to the outside world. It actively engages in high-level international exchanges and cooperation, and expands global public services for space technology and products. It takes an active part in solving major challenges facing

1. WHITE PAPERS ON SPACE ACTIVITIES

humanity, helps to realize the goals of the United Nations 2030 Agenda for Sustainable Development, and facilitates the construction of a community of shared future for mankind with regard to outer space exploration and utilization.

II. Development of Space Technology and Systems

China's space industry serves its major strategic needs, and targets world-leading, cutting-edge technology. Spearheaded by the major space projects, the country has accelerated the research work of core technologies, stepped up their application, and redoubled its efforts to develop space technology and systems. As a result, China's capacity to access and exit outer space, and its ability to engage in space exploration, utilization and governance have grown markedly along a sustainable path.

1. Space Transportation System

From 2016 to December 2021, 207 launch missions were completed, including 183 by the Long March carrier rocket series. The total number of launches exceeded 400.

The Long March carrier rockets are being upgraded towards non-toxic and pollution-free propellant launch, and they are becoming smarter boosted by modular technology. The Long March-5 and Long March-5B carrier rockets have been employed for regular launches; Long March-8 and Long March-7A have made their first flights with increased payload capacity.

China now provides a variety of launch vehicle services. The Long March-11 carrier rocket has achieved commercial launch from the sea; the Smart Dragon-1, Kuaizhou-1A, Hyperbola-1, CERES-1 and other commercial vehicles have been successfully launched; successful demonstration flight tests on reusable launch vehicles have been carried out.

In the next five years, China will continue to improve the capacity and performance of its space transportation system, and move faster to upgrade launch vehicles. It will further expand the launch vehicle family, develop and launch new-generation manned carrier rockets and high-thrust solid-fuel carrier rockets, and speed up the R&D of heavy-lift launch vehicles. It will continue to strengthen the research into key technologies for reusable space transportation systems, and conduct test flights accordingly. In response to the growing need for regular launches, China will develop new rocket engines, combined cycle propulsion, and upper-stage technologies to improve its capacity to access and exit outer space in an efficient and diverse manner.

2. Space Infrastructure
(1) Remote-Sensing Satellite System

The space-based section of the High-resolution Earth Observation System has been largely completed, enabling high-spatial-resolution, high-temporal-resolution and high-spectrum-resolution earth observation. China now provides improved land observation services, having launched the Ziyuan-3 03 earth resources satellite, the Huanjing Jianzai-

2A/2B satellites for environmental disaster management, a high-resolution multi-mode imaging satellite, a hyper-spectral observation satellite, and a number of commercial remote-sensing satellites.

In ocean observation, China is now able to view multiple indexes of contiguous waters around the globe on all scales, with high-resolution images from the Haiyang-1C/1D satellites and the Haiyang-2B/2C/2D satellites.

China's ability to observe the global atmosphere has achieved a significant increase. Its new-generation Fengyun-4A/4B meteorological satellites in the geostationary orbit are able to perform all-weather, precise and uninterrupted atmospheric monitoring and disaster monitoring to boost response capability. The successful launches of Fengyun-3D/3E satellites enable coordinated morning, afternoon and twilight monitoring, and the Fengyun-2H satellite provides monitoring services for countries and regions participating in the Belt and Road Initiative.

With further improvements to the ground system of its remote-sensing satellites, China is now able to provide the service of receiving and processing remote-sensing satellite data across the world.

(2) Communications and Broadcasting Satellite System

China has made steady progress in developing fixed communications and broadcasting satellite network, which now covers more areas with greater capacity. The Zhongxing-6C and Zhongxing-9B satellites ensure the uninterrupted, stable operation of broadcasting and television services. The Zhongxing-16 and APSTAR-6D satellites are respectively each with a 50Gbps capacity. All this signify that satellite communications in China have reached the stage of high-capacity service.

The mobile communications and broadcasting satellite network has expanded with the launch of the Tiantong-1 02/03 satellites, operating in tandem with the Tiantong-1 01 satellite, so as to provide voice, text messages and data services for hand-held terminal users in China, its neighboring areas, and certain parts of the Asia-Pacific region.

The relay satellite system is being upgraded with the launch of the Tianlian-1 05 and Tianlian-2 01 satellites, giving a powerful boost to comprehensive capacity of communication satellite system.

The ground system of communications and broadcasting satellites has been improved to form a space-ground integrated network that provides satellite communications and broadcasting, internet, Internet of Things, and information services around the globe.

(3) Navigation Satellite System

The completion and operation of the 30-satellite Beidou Navigation Satellite System (BDS-3) represents the successful conclusion of the Beidou system's three-step strategy and its capacity to serve the world. Beidou's world-leading services include positioning, navigation, timing, regional and global text message communication, global search and rescue, ground-based and satellite-based augmentation, and precise point positioning.

In the next five years, China will continue to improve its space infrastructure and integrated technological development for remote-sensing, communications, navigation, and positioning satellite systems. It will: upgrade its spatial information services featuring extensive connection, precise timing and positioning, and all dimension sensoring; develop satellites for geostationary microwave monitoring, new-type ocean color observation, carbon monitoring of the territorial ecosystem, and atmospheric environmental monitoring; develop dual-antenna X-band interferometric synthetic aperture radar (InSAR), land water resources and other satellite technology for the aim of efficient, comprehensive earth observation and data acquisition across the globe; build a satellite communications network with high and low orbit coordination, test new communications satellites for commercial application, and build a second-generation data relay satellite system; study and research navigation-communications integration, low-orbit augmentation and other key technologies for the next-generation Beidou Navigation Satellite System, and develop a more extensive, more integrated and smarter national positioning, navigation and timing (PNT) system; continue to improve the ground systems for remote-sensing, communications and navigation satellites.

3. Manned Spaceflight
The Tianzhou-1 cargo spacecraft has docked with the earth-orbiting Tiangong-2 space laboratory. With breakthroughs in key technologies for cargo transport and in-orbit propellant replenishment, China has successfully completed the second phase of its manned spaceflight project.

The launch of the Tianhe core module marks a solid step in building China's space station. The Tianzhou-2 and Tianzhou-3 cargo spacecraft and the Shenzhou-12 and Shenzhou-13 manned spacecraft, together with the Tianhe core module to which they have docked, form an assembly of space station and began to steady operation. Six astronauts have worked in China's space station, performing extravehicular activities, in-orbit maintenance, and scientific experiments.

In the next five years, China will continue to implement its manned spaceflight project. The plans are: launch the Wentian and Mengtian experimental modules, the Xuntian space telescope, the Shenzhou manned spacecraft, and the Tianzhou cargo spacecraft; complete China's space station and its operation, build a space laboratory on board, and have astronauts on long-term assignments performing large-scale scientific experiments and maintenance; continue studies and research on the plan for a human lunar landing, develop new-generation manned spacecraft, and research key technologies to lay a foundation for exploring and developing cislunar space.

4. Deep Space Exploration

(1) Lunar Exploration

Achieving relay communications through the Queqiao satellite, the Chang'e-4 lunar probe performed humanity's first soft landing on the far side of the moon, and conducted roving exploration. The Chang'e-5 lunar probe brought back 1,731 g of samples from the moon, marking China's first success in extraterrestrial sampling and return and the completion of its three-step lunar exploration program of orbiting, landing and return.

(2) Planetary Exploration

The Tianwen-1 Mars probe orbited and landed on Mars; the Zhurong Mars rover explored the planet and left China's first mark there. China has achieved a leap from cislunar to interplanetary exploration.

In the next five years, China will continue its lunar and planetary exploration. The plans are: launch the Chang'e-6 lunar probe to collect and bring back samples from the polar regions of the moon; launch the Chang'e-7 lunar probe to perform a precise landing in the moon's polar regions and a hopping detection in lunar shadowed area; complete R&D on the key technology of Chang'e-8, and work with other countries, international organizations and other partners to build an international research station on the moon; launch asteroid probes to sample near-earth asteroids and probe main-belt comets; complete key technological research, such as on Mars sampling and return, exploration of the Jupiter system; study plans for boundary exploration of the solar system.

5. Space Launch Sites and Telemetry, Tracking and Command (TT&C)

(1) Space Launch Sites

Adaptive improvements have been completed at the Jiuquan, Taiyuan and Xichang launch sites, with a new launch pad installed at Jiuquan for the commercial launch of liquid fuel rockets, and the operational service of Wenchang Launch Site. China has formed a launch site network covering both coastal and inland areas, high and low altitudes, and various trajectories to satisfy the launch needs of manned spaceships, space station modules, deep space probes, and all kinds of satellites. In addition, its first sea launch site has begun operation.

(2) Space TT&C

China's leap from cislunar to interplanetary TT&C communications, with growing space-based TT&C capacity, represents a significant progress. Its space TT&C network has improved to form an integrated space-ground TT&C network providing security, reliability, quick response, flexible access, efficient operation and diverse services. TT&C missions of the Shenzhou and Tianzhou spacecraft series, Tianhe core module,

Chang'e lunar probe series, and Tianwen-1 Mars probe have been completed successfully. TT&C station networks for commercial satellites are growing quickly.

In the next five years, China will strengthen the unified technical standard-setting for its space products, and on this basis will: further adapt the existing launch site system to better serve most launch missions, and make launch sites smarter, more reliable and more cost-effective to support high-intensity and diversified launch missions; build commercial launch pads and launch sites to meet different commercial launch needs; improve the space TT&C network in terms of organization, technology and methodology, grow the capacity to utilize and integrate space- and ground-based TT&C resources, and build a space TT&C network providing ubiquitous coverage and connections; coordinate the operation and management of the national space system for greater efficiency; strengthen the TT&C communications network to support the implementation of the deep-space exploration programme.

6. Experiments on New Technologies

China has launched a number of new technological test satellites, and tested new technologies such as the common platforms of new-generation communications satellites, very high throughput satellites' telecommunication payload, Ka-band communications, satellite-ground high-speed laser communications, and new electric propulsion.

In the next five years, China will focus on engineering application of new technology, conduct in-orbit tests of new space materials, devices and techniques, and test new technologies in these areas: smart self-management of spacecraft; space mission extension vehicle; innovative space propulsion; in-orbit service and maintenance of spacecraft; space debris cleaning.

7. Space Environment Governance

With a growing database, China's space debris monitoring system is becoming more capable of collision warning, and space event awareness and coping, effectively ensuring the safety of in-orbit spacecraft.

In compliance with the Space Debris Mitigation Guidelines and the Guidelines for the Long-term Sustainability of Outer Space Activities, China has applied upper stage passivation to all its carrier rockets, and completed active deorbiting of the Tiangong-2 and other spacecraft in the end of their operation, making a positive contribution to mitigating space debris.

Progress has been made in the search and tracking of near-earth asteroids and data analysis. A basic space climate service system is now in place, capable of providing services in space climate monitoring, early warning, and forecasting, and its broader applications are being explored.

In the next five years, China will continue to expand its space environment governance system. It will: strengthen space traffic control; improve its space debris monitoring system, cataloguing database, and early warning services; conduct in-orbit maintenance of spacecraft, collision avoidance and control, and space debris mitigation, to ensure the safe, stable and orderly operation of the space system; strengthen the protection of its space activities, assets and other interests by boosting capacity in disaster backup and information protection, and increasing invulnerability and survivability; study plans for building a near-earth object defense system, and increase the capacity of near-earth object monitoring, cataloguing, early warning, and response; build an integrated space-ground space climate monitoring system, and continue to improve relevant services to effectively respond to catastrophic space climate events.

III. Developing and Expanding Space Application Industry

To serve the economy and society, China has promoted public and commercial application of its satellites and space technology aiming for greater efficiency of the space industry.

1. Boosting the Public Services of Satellites

The service capacity of satellite applications has been remarkably improved. The significant role of satellites is seen in the protection of resources and the eco-environment, disaster prevention and mitigation, management of emergencies, weather forecasting and climate change response, and also felt in social management and public services, urbanization, coordinated regional development, and poverty eradication. The space industry helps to improve people's lives.

The remote-sensing satellite system has been used by almost all departments at national and provincial levels to conduct emergency monitoring of over 100 major and catastrophic natural disasters around the country. It provides services to tens of thousands of domestic users and foreign users in over 100 countries, having distributed over 100 million scenes of data.

The communications and broadcasting satellite network has made direct services available to over 140 million households in China's rural and remote areas, provided returned data for over 500 mobile phone base stations, and ensured efficient emergency communications during the responses to the forest fire in Liangshan, Sichuan province, to the heavy rainstorm in Zhengzhou, Henan province and to other major disaster relief work.

The Beidou Navigation Satellite System has guaranteed the safety of over seven million operating vehicles, provided positioning and short message communication services to over 40,000 seagoing fishing vessels, and offered precise positioning services for the freighting of supplies and tracking of individual movement for Covid-19 control, and for hospital construction.

In the next five years, under the overarching goal of building a safe, healthy, beautiful and digital China, we will intensify the integration of satellite application with the development of industries and regions, and space information with new-generation information technology such as big data and Internet of Things. We will also extend the integrated application of remote-sensing satellite data on land, ocean and meteorology, advance the construction of infrastructure for integrated application of the Beidou Navigation Satellite System, satellite communications, and the ground communications network, and improve our capacity to tailor and refine professional services. All these efforts will help to achieve the goals of peaking carbon dioxide emissions and carbon neutrality, to revitalize rural areas, and to realize new-type urbanization, coordinated development between regions and eco-environmental progress.

2. Space Application Industry
The commercial use of satellite technology is thriving, which expands the applications market for governments, enterprises and individuals. A group of competitive commercial space enterprises are emerging and realizing industrialized large-scale operation. A variety of products and services, such as high-accuracy maps using remote-sensing data, full dimensional images, data processing, and application software, are improving the service to users in public transportation and e-commerce, the trading of agricultural products, the assessment of disaster losses and insurance claims, and the registration of real estate.

The ability to commercialize satellite communications and broadcasting services has further improved. Four 4K Ultra HD television channels in China were launched and TV viewers now have access to over 100 HD channels. Internet access is also available on-board ocean vessels and passenger aircraft. Tiantong-1, a satellite mobile communication system, is in commercial operation.

The satellite navigation industry has witnessed rapid growth as evidenced by sales of over 100 million chips compatible with the Beidou system. Its industrial applications have been widely introduced into mass consumption, the sharing economy, and the daily life. Achievements in space technology have helped traditional industries transform and upgrade, supported emerging industries such as new energy, new materials and environmental protection, enabled new business models such as smart cities, smart agriculture and unmanned driving to grow, making a great contribution to building China's strengths in science and technology, manufacturing, cyberspace and transport.

In the next five years, China's space industry will seize the opportunities presented by the expanding digital industry and the digital transformation of traditional industries, so as to promote the application and transfer of space technology. Through innovative business models and the deep integration of space application with digital economy, more efforts will be made to expand and extend the application scope of satellite remote-sensing and satellite communications technologies, and to realize the industrialized operation of the Beidou Navigation Satellite System. This will provide more advanced, economical, high-quality products and convenient services for all industries and sectors and for mass consumption. New business models for upscaling the space economy, such as travel, biomedicine, debris removal, and experiment services, will be developed to expand the industry.

IV. Research on Space Science

China's research on space science focuses on the scientific questions, such as the origin and evolution of the universe, and the relationship between the solar system and humanity. It has launched projects to explore space and conduct experiments, advanced research on basic theories, and incubated major research findings.

1. Research on Space Science

(1) Space Astronomy

The Dark Matter Particle Explorer (DAMPE) Satellite obtained the precise measurements of the energy spectrums of cosmic ray electrons, protons and the GCR helium. The Huiyan (Insight) Hard X-ray Modulation Telescope was successfully launched; it has discovered the strongest magnetic field in the universe and obtained a panoramic view of the black hole binary explosion process. The Xihe observation satellite was successfully launched, which obtained the multiple solar spectroscopic images at different wavelengths in the Hα waveband.

(2) Lunar and Planetary Science

Based on its lunar exploration program, China has achieved significant advances in the comprehensive surveying of the moon's geology and subsurface structure, in dating the lunar magmatic activity, and in analyzing its mineralogical features and chemical elements. In planetary exploration, China has built a deeper understanding of the geological evolution of Mars by conducting analysis of its surface structure and soil and the composition of its rocks.

(3) Space Earth Science

Zhangheng-1, also known as the China Seismo-Electromagnetic Satellite, helped to obtain the data on and build models of the global geomagnetic field, and the in-situ data of ionosphere parameters. A high-precision global carbon flux map, developed by using the data from the Chinese Global Carbon Dioxide Monitoring Scientific Experimental Satellite, is shared globally free of any charge.

(4) Space Physics

With the help of Mozi, the world's first quantum communication satellite, China has carried out experiments on satellite-based quantum teleportation and entanglement distribution over thousand kilometers, on gravitational induced decoherence of quantum entanglement, and on entanglement-based secure quantum cryptography over thousand kilometers with no trusted relay. It has also launched the Taiji-1 and Tianqin-1 satellites to support the space gravitational wave detection program.

In the next five years, China will continue with the research and development of programs such as the satellite for space gravitational wave detection, the Einstein Probe, the advanced space-based solar observatory, the panoramic imaging satellite for solar wind and magnetosphere interaction, and the high precision magnetic field measurement satellite, focusing on the subjects of the extreme universe, ripples in time and space, the panoramic view of the sun and the earth, and the search for habitable planets. China will continue to explore frontier areas and research into space astronomy, heliospheric physics, lunar and planetary science, space earth sciences, and space physics, to generate more original scientific findings.

2. Science Experiments in Outer Space

With the help of the Shenzhou spacecraft series, the Tiangong-2 space laboratory, and the Shijian-10 satellite, China has achieved mammalian embryonic development in space and in-orbit verification of the world's first space cold atom clock, expanded the understanding of the mechanisms behind particle segregation in microgravity, pulverized coal combustion, and material preparation, and achieved research findings in space science of international standing.

In the coming five years, China will make use of space experiment platforms, such as the Tiangong space station, the Chang'e lunar probe series, and the Tianwen-1 Mars probe, to conduct experiments and research on biology, life, medicine, and materials, so as to expand humanity's understanding of basic science.

V. Modernizing Space Governance

The Chinese government has been proactive in developing the space industry, through the formulation and implementation of policy measures and well-thought-out plans for space activities. Better alignment between a well-functioning market and an enabling government gives full play to the roles of both, endeavoring to create a favorable environment for the growth of a high-quality space industry.

1. Enhancing the Innovative Capacity of Space Program

In order to create a new configuration in which the upper, middle and lower industrial chains are coordinated, and large, small and medium-sized enterprises advance in an integrated way, China is building a strategic force of space science and technology, encouraging original innovation by research institutes and bringing together enterprises, universities, research institutes and end-users in creating and applying new technologies. A technological innovation alliance is emerging in the key areas of space science.

A number of major space and science projects are in place to promote the leapfrog development of space science and technology, which spearheads overall technical advances.

China is making forward-looking plans for strategic, fundamental and technological breakthroughs in space science, integrating the application of new-generation information technology in the space sector, and accelerating the engineering application of advanced and, especially, revolutionary technologies.

The secondary development of space technologies will be further reinforced to put research findings into industrial production and boost the economy.

2. Strengthening the Basic Industrial Capabilities

The space industry will continue to improve its integrated and open industrial system, comprising of system integrators, specialized contractors, market suppliers, and public service providers, and covering all links from research to production.

To strengthen the industrial and supply chains of its space industry, and transform and upgrade the basic industrial capabilities, China will optimize the industrial structure and upgrade R&D, manufacturing, launch operations, and application services, further integrate industrialization with information technology, and build intelligent production lines, workshops and institutes.

3. Accelerating the Development of Space Application Industry

China will improve the policies for its satellite application industry, including coordinating public interest and market demand, integrating facilities and resources, unifying data and product standards, and streamline the channel for sharing and utilization. It is committed to improving satellite application services with unified standards and customized choices.

China will move faster to grow its satellite application market, where various market entities are encouraged to develop value-added products. By creating new application models, China is fostering a 'space plus' industrial ecosystem and promoting the development of space-related, emerging strategic industries.

4. Encouraging the Development of Commercial Space

China will formulate guidelines on commercial space to promote its development. It will expand the scope of government procurement of space products and services, grant relevant companies the access and sharing rights to major scientific research facilities and equipment, and support these companies in participating in the R&D of major space projects. It will establish a negative list to open the market access to space activities, to ensure the fair competition and the orderly entry and exit of commercial companies.

China will optimize the participation of commercial companies in the space industrial chain, and encourage and guide them to engage in satellite application and the transfer and transformation of space technologies.

5. Promoting the Law-Based Governance

To promote the law-based governance of the space industry, China will accelerate the formulation of a national space law and establish a legal system centering on this law. The future efforts are: studying and formulating regulations on satellite navigation, strengthening the administration of satellite navigation activities, revising space objects registration measures, and improving the regulation of the sharing and use of space data and the licensing regime for civil space launches; studying and formulating the regulations on the administration of satellite frequency and orbit resources, and strengthening the declaration, coordination and registration of these resources to safeguard the country's legitimate rights and interests in this regard. China will strengthen the research on international space law, and actively participate in the formulation of International Telecommunication Union standards and international rules regarding outer space, with the aim of maintaining the international order in outer space based on international space law, and contributing to a fair and reasonable global governance system for outer space.

6. Strengthening the Fostering of Professionals for Space Industry

China will step up its efforts to become a world center for talent and innovation in space science, and create favorable conditions for the development of professionals and the expansion of their ranks. It will improve the personnel training mechanism – fostering a pool of strategic scientists, leading and young scientists, and teams with strong innovation capacity, and cultivating a large number of outstanding engineers, top technicians championing fine craftsmanship, and visionary entrepreneurs with a sense of social responsibility. China will improve its human resources management mechanisms to regulate and guide the rational flow of professionals. It will also upgrade incentives with greater rewards and stronger support, and strengthen specialty disciplines in universities to cultivate a reserve force of aerospace personnel.

7. Promoting the Publicity of Space Knowledge and Space Culture

China will continue to hold events to celebrate its Space Day, to publicize space knowledge and culture during World Space Week and National Science and Technology Week, and through Tiangong Classroom and other platforms, and promote the culture and spirit embodied in the development of the atomic and hydrogen bombs, missiles, man-made satellites, manned spaceflight, lunar probes and the Beidou Navigation Satellite System in the new era. The goal is to inspire the nation, especially the young people, to develop an interest in science, to create and explore the unknown, and to increase scientific knowledge among the general public.

China will protect its major space heritage and build more space museums and experience parks to publicize space science and provide education and training. It will encourage the creation of space-related literary and art works to promote space culture.

VI. International Cooperation

The rights to peaceful exploration, exploitation and utilization of outer space are equally enjoyed by all countries. China calls on all countries to work together to build a community of shared future for mankind and carry out in-depth exchanges and cooperation in outer space on the basis of equality, mutual benefit, peaceful utilization, and inclusive development.

1. Guiding Principles

China's guiding principles for international exchanges and cooperation are as follows:

Safeguarding the central role of the United Nations in managing outer space affairs; abiding by the Treaty on Principles Governing the Activities of States in the Exploration and Use of Outer Space, Including the Moon and Other Celestial Bodies; upholding the guiding role of relevant UN principles, declarations and resolutions; actively participating in the formulation of international rules regarding outer space; and promoting the long-term sustainability of space activities;

Strengthening international exchanges and cooperation on space science, technology and application; working together with the international community to provide public products and services; and contributing to global efforts to address common challenges;

Strengthening international space cooperation that is based on common goals and serves the Belt and Road Initiative, and ensuring that the space industry benefits the Initiative's participating countries, especially the developing countries;

Supporting the Asia-Pacific Space Cooperation Organization (APSCO) to play an important role, and attaching importance to space cooperation under the BRICS and Group 20 mechanisms and within the framework of the Shanghai Cooperation Organization;

Encouraging and endorsing the efforts of domestic research institutions, industrial enterprises, universities and colleges, and social organizations to engage in international space exchanges and cooperation in different forms and at various levels under the guidance of state policies, laws and regulations.

2. Major Achievements

Since 2016, China has signed 46 space cooperation agreements or memoranda of understanding with 19 countries and regions and four international organizations. It has actively promoted global governance of outer space, and carried out international cooperation in space science, technology and application through bilateral and multilateral mechanisms. These measures have yielded fruitful results.

(1) Global Governance of Outer Space

China participates in consultations within in the framework of United Nations on issues, such as the long-term sustainability of outer space activities, the development and utilization of space resources, and the prevention of arms race in outer space. Together with other parties, it has proposed discussions on space exploration and innovation, and advanced the Space2030 Agenda of the UN.

China supports the work of the Beijing office of the United Nations Platform for Space-based Information for Disaster Management and Emergency Response, and has participated in the activities of the International Committee on Global Navigation Satellite Systems in an in-depth manner. It has joined international mechanisms such as the Space Missions Planning Advisory Group and the International Asteroid Warning Network.

China plays its role as the host country of APSCO, and supports the organization's Development Vision 2030.

China has strengthened international exchanges on space debris, long-term sustainability of outer space activities, and other issues through mechanisms such as the Space Debris Work Group of China-Russia Space Cooperation Sub-committee and the Sino-US Expert Workshop on Space Debris and Space Flight Safety.

China supports the activities of international organizations such as the International Telecommunication Union, Group on Earth Observations, Inter-Agency Space Debris Coordination Committee, Consultative Committee for Space Data Systems, International Space Exploration Coordination Group, and the Interagency Operations Advisory Group.

(2) Manned Spaceflight

China has carried out gamma-ray burst polarization monitoring research with the European Space Agency on the Tiangong-2 space laboratory, conducted human body medical research in a micro-gravitational environment with France during the Shenzhou-11 manned spaceflight mission, carried out joint CAVES training and maritime rescue drills with the European Astronaut Centre.

China has completed the selection of the first batch of international space science experiments to be conducted on Chinese space station, and conducted technological cooperation and exchanges with Germany, Italy and Russia on on-board scientific experiments and the development of space station modules.

(3) Beidou Navigation Satellite System

China has promoted the coordinated the development of China's Beidou Navigation Satellite System with United States' Global Positioning System, Russia's GLONASS system, and Europe's Galileo system. It has carried out in-depth cooperation with them in the fields of compatibility, interoperability, monitoring and assessment, and joint application.

China has improved the international standardization of the Beidou system, which has been included in the standard systems of the International Electrotechnical Commission and many other international organizations in the fields of civil aviation, maritime affairs, international search and rescue, and mobile communications.

China has increased the Beidou system's global service capacity by establishing Beidou cooperation forum mechanisms with the League of Arab States and the African Union, completing the first overseas Beidou center in Tunisia, and conducting satellite navigation cooperation with other countries, such as Pakistan, Saudi Arabia, Argentina, South Africa, Algeria, and Thailand.

(4) Deep-Space Exploration
China launched the project for International Lunar Research Station, together with Russia, and initiated the Sino-Russian Joint Data Center for Lunar and Deep-space Exploration. It is working with the Russia Federation to coordinate Chang'e-7's lunar polar exploration mission with Russian LUNA-Resource-1 orbiter mission.

In Chang'e-4 lunar exploration mission, China cooperated with the Russia Federation and the European Space Agency on engineering technology, and with Sweden, Germany, the Netherlands and Saudi Arabia on payloads for scientific missions. It has launched the international cooperation for onboard payloads in Chang'e-6 lunar exploration mission.

In Tianwen-1 mission, its first Mars exploration project, China cooperated with the European Space Agency on engineering technology, and with Austria and France on payloads for scientific missions. It has established an orbit data exchange mechanism for Mars probe with the United States, and launched international cooperation for onboard payload in its asteroid exploration mission.

In the fields of lunar and deep-space exploration, China cooperated on TT&C with the European Space Agency, Argentina, Namibia, and Pakistan.

(5) Space Technology
China has developed and successfully launched the China-France Oceanography Satellite, China-Brazil Earth Resources Satellite 04A, and the Ethiopian Remote-Sensing Satellite. It has launched the Student Small Satellites (SSS) for APSCO. It is jointly developing the MisrSat-2 remote-sensing satellite with Egypt.

China completed the in-orbit delivery of the Pakistan Remote-Sensing Satellite (PRSS-1), Venezuelan Remote-Sensing Satellite (VRSS-2), Sudan Remote-Sensing Satellite (SRSS-1), and the Algerian Communications Satellite (Alcomsat-1).

China has provided satellite payload or launching services for Saudi Arabia, Pakistan, Argentina, Brazil, Canada, and Luxembourg.

China has conducted space product and technology cooperation with Russia, Ukraine, Belarus, Argentina, Pakistan, and Nigeria.

China has helped the developing countries boost their capacity in space science and research. It has built satellite research and development infrastructure with the countries including Egypt, Pakistan and Nigeria. It has implemented with the construction of the Belt and Road Initiative Space Information Corridor, and opened China's space facilities to the developing countries.

(6) Space Applications

China has established an emergency support mechanism for disaster prevention and mitigation for the international users of Fengyun meteorological satellites, and the data from China's meteorological satellites have been widely used in 121 countries and regions.

China has signed the cooperation agreements of BRICS Remote-Sensing Satellite Constellation, cooperated with the European Space Agency on earth observation satellite data exchange, and built the China-ASEAN Satellite Information Offshore Service Platform and the Remote-Sensing Satellite Data-Sharing Service Platform. It has worked with Laos, Thailand, Cambodia, and Myanmar to build the Lancang-Mekong Space Information Exchange Center.

China has built satellite data receiving stations in cooperation with the countries including Bolivia, Indonesia, Namibia, Thailand and South Africa.

China has actively participated in the mechanism of the International Charter on Space and Major Disasters, providing satellite remote-sensing data totaling 800 scenes and adding eight new on-duty satellites (constellations) to the satellite system, thereby improving the international community's capacity for disaster prevention and mitigation.

China has actively provided satellite emergency monitoring services. It has initiated emergency monitoring in response to 17 major disasters in 15 countries. For instance, in response to the severe drought in Afghanistan, the dam collapse in Laos in 2018, and the cyclone that struck Mozambique in 2019, it provided monitoring services for the authorities of affected countries.

China released its GEO Strategic Plan 2016-2025: Implementing GEOSS. It served as the rotating chair of the Group on Earth Observations in 2020, and promoted the construction of a global earth observation system.

China participated in the international Space Climate Observatory platform, promoting China's best practices in space technology to address climate change, and facilitating international cooperation on space climate observation.

(7) Space Science

Using the science satellites including Wukong, Mozi, Shijian-10, and Insight, China has conducted joint scientific research and experiments with the countries, including Switzerland, Italy, Austria, the United Kingdom, and Japan.

China co-developed and successfully launched the China-Italy Electromagnetic Monitoring Experiment Satellite. It has continued the joint development of the Sino-European Panoramic Imaging Satellite for Solar Wind and Magnetosphere Interaction, Sino-French Astronomic Satellite, and China-Italy Electromagnetic Monitoring Experiment Satellite 02. It has joined countries, including Italy and Germany, in developing and calibrating the payloads of satellites such as the advanced space-based solar observatory, Einstein Probe, and enhanced X-ray timing, and polarimetry observatory.

Using the China-Brazil Joint Laboratory for Space Weather, it co-built the space environment monitoring and research platform for South America.

(8) Personnel and Academic Exchanges

China has taken part in the activities organized by the International Astronautical Federation, International Committee on Space Research, International Academy of Astronautics, and International Institute of Space Law. It has hosted the 2017 Global Space Exploration Conference, the 13th Meeting of the International Committee on Global Navigation Satellite Systems, the United Nations/China Forum on Space Solutions: Realizing the Sustainable Development Goals, the Wenchang International Aviation and Aerospace Forum, the Zhuhai Forum, the International Summit on BDS Applications, and the Fengyun Satellite User Conference.

China has helped the developing countries train the professionals for space activities. Through the Regional Centre for Space Science and Technology Education in Asia and the Pacific (China) (Affiliated to the United Nations), it has trained almost 1,000 space-related professionals from more than 60 countries, and established the 'Belt and Road Initiative' Aerospace Innovation Alliance and the Association of Sino-Russian Technical Universities. It has also promoted personnel exchanges in remote-sensing and navigation technology through the international training program for the developing countries and other channels.

China has promoted scientific and technological exchanges in the fields of space science, remote sensing and navigation through the China-Europe Space Science Bilateral Meeting, the China-EU-ESA Dialogue on Space Technology Cooperation, and the Dragon Programme, a joint undertaking between ESA and the Ministry of Science and Technology of China.

3. Key Areas for Future Cooperation

In the next five years, China will be more open and active in expanding the bilateral and multilateral cooperation mechanisms, and will engage in extensive international exchanges and cooperation in the following key areas:

(1) Global Governance of Outer Space

Within the framework of the United Nations, China will actively participate in formulating the international rules regarding outer space, and will work together with other countries to address the common challenges in ensuring the long-term sustainability of outer space activities.

China will actively participate in the discussions on international issues and the establishment of international mechanisms, such as those in the fields of space environment governance, near-earth objects monitoring and response, planet protection, space traffic management, and the exploitation and utilization of space resources.

China will advocate the cooperation in international governance of outer space, so as improve the efficiency of space crisis management and comprehensive governance, conduct dialogue with Russia, the United States and other countries as well as the relevant international organizations on outer space governance, and actively support the construction of APSCO's space science observatory.

(2) Manned Spaceflight

China will employ its space station to conduct space-based astronomical observations, earth science research, and space science experiments under the microgravity condition.

China will promote more extensive international cooperation in astronaut selection and training, joint flights and other fields.

(3) Beidou Navigation Satellite System

China will continue to participate in the activities of the UN's International Committee on Global Navigation Satellite Systems and promote the establishment of a fair and reasonable order for satellite navigation.

China will actively improve compatibility and interoperability of global satellite navigation systems, such as the Beidou Navigation Satellite System and other such systems as well as satellite-based augmentation systems.

China will prioritize the cooperation and exchanges on the application of the Beidou Navigation Satellite System, and share its mature solutions so as to boost the socio-economic development of partner countries.

(4) Deep-Space Exploration

China will advance the cooperation in the project of International Lunar Research Station. It welcomes international partners to participate in the research and construction work of this station at any stage and level in its missions.

It will expand the cooperation in the fields of asteroid and interplanetary exploration.

(5) Space Technology

China will support the cooperation on satellite engineering and technology. It will complete the joint research and development of MisrSat-2, and launch the SVOM (Space-based multiband astronomical Variable Objects Monitor), and the China-Italy Electromagnetic Monitoring Experiment Satellite 02. It will promote the follow-up cooperation in the China-Brazil Earth Resources Satellites program.

China will engage in the cooperation on space TT&C support. It will continue to cooperate with the European Space Agency in the field of TT&C support, and further advance the building of ground station networks.

China will support the international cooperation on commercial spaceflight, including, (a) launching services; (b) technical cooperation on whole satellites, on sub-systems, spare parts, and electronic components of satellites and launch vehicles, on ground facilities and equipment, and on other related items.

It will prioritize the development of communications satellites for Pakistan and the cooperation on the construction of the Pakistan Space Center and Egypt's Space City.

(6) Space Applications

China will promote the global application of data from Chinese meteorological satellites, support the World Meteorological Organization access to data from the China-France Oceanography Satellite, and promote the global sharing and scientific application of data obtained by Zhangheng-1, China's seismo-electromagnetic satellite.

China will continue to accelerate the construction of the Belt and Road Initiative Space Information Corridor, and strengthen the cooperation on the application of remote-sensing, navigation, and communications satellites.

China will promote the construction of the data-sharing service platform of APSCO.

China will advance the construction and application of the BRICS remote-sensing satellite constellation.

China will participate in the construction and use of the Space Climate Observatory.

(7) Space Science

Relying on the deep-space exploration project, including the extraterrestrial samples and exploration data, China will conduct joint research in fields such as the space environment and planetary origin and evolution. Through the United Nations, the scientific data obtained by Chang'e 4 satellite will be made available to the international community.

China will boost the joint R&D work based on space science satellites, focusing on the subjects, such as dark matter particles, solar burst activities and their influence, and spatial gravitational wave.

(8) Personnel and Academic Exchanges

China will continue personnel exchanges and training in the space industry.

China will hold high-level international academic exchange conferences and forums.

Conclusion

In the present-day world, a growing number of countries are attaching importance to space and making more efforts in developing space activities. Space industry around the world has entered a new stage of rapid development and profound transformation, exerting a major and far-reaching impact on human society.

Standing at a new historical starting line towards a modern socialist country, China is determined to quicken the pace of becoming a major space power. Guided by the concept of a community of shared future for mankind, it will work actively with other countries to carry out international space exchanges and cooperation, safeguard outer space security, and strive for long-term sustainability of space activities. By doing so, China will contribute more to protecting the Earth, improving the well-being of mankind, and serving human progress.

(www.scio.gov.cn)

2. OTHER POLICY DOCUMENTS ON SPACE ACTIVITIES

2.1. NOTICE ON PROMOTING THE DEVELOPMENT OF SATELLITE APPLICATION INDUSTRY[1]

National Development and Reform Commission and
State Commission of Science and Technology and Industry for National Defense
2007

(Unofficial English translation by WU Xiaodan, assisted by Ms. WU Tong)

In order to implement the Outline of the Eleventh Five-Year Plan for National Economic and Social Development, the Outline of the National Medium-and Long-Term Science and Technology Development Plan (2006 – 2020), the Eleventh Five-Year Plan for the Development of High-Tech Industries and the Eleventh Five-Year Plan for Aerospace Development, vigorously promote the development of China's satellite application industry, enhance the ability of independent innovation in satellite applications and better serve the national economic and social development, the National Development and Reform Commission and the Commission of Science and Technology and Industry for National Defense have jointly formulated the Notice on Promoting the Development of Satellite Application Industry.

Satellite application industry is a national, strategic and high-tech industry. The development and production of satellite application has been serialized and is changing from experimental application model to business service model. The satellite application industry has become an essential support for economic construction, social development and government decision-making. In accordance with the Outline of the Eleventh Five-Year Plan for National Economic and Social Development and the Outline of the National Medium- and Long-Term Science and Technology Development Plan (2006 – 2020), in order to implement the Eleventh Five-Year Plan for the Development of High-tech Industries and the Eleventh Five-Year Plan for Aerospace Development, accelerate the development of satellite application industry with its cores capacity in communication and broadcasting, navigation and remote sensing, establish a complete industrial chain of satellite operation services, ground equipment and user terminal

---

[1] The original Chinese version of this policy is published on the website of the State Administration of Science and Technology and Industry for National Defense, www.sastind.gov.cn, last accessed August 2021.

manufacturing, system integration and information integrated services and promote the satellite application industry to better serve the economic and social development, the following suggestions are put forward:

I. The Guiding Principles of Accelerating the Development of Satellite Application Industry

To make the satellite application industry an essential means to strengthen and improve the macro-management and scientific decision-making of government, to continuously improve the operational capability of satellite application and to form a new-emerging industry with domestic and international market competitiveness, the guiding principles for the development of satellite application industry are: implementing the scientific outlook on development; adhering to the principles of combining short- and long-term, military and civilian, independent research and development and international cooperation; driving by the major needs of national economic, social development and public security; aiming at the development of business and scale; focusing on strengthening independent innovation capacity and public service capacity building; promoting the sharing of public resources for satellite applications and cultivating satellite application enterprise clusters and industrial chains; approaches being the institutional mechanism innovation and open development; making strengthening and fostering satellite application market as the breakthrough point; enhancing national macro-management and policy guidance for satellite application industry, national overall planning and construction of satellite and its application system and increasing support for satellite application industry.

II. The Major Development Goals of the Satellite Application Industry

By 2020, the transformation of application satellites from experimental application model to business service model will be completed; the localization rate of ground equipment will reach 80 percent; a relatively complete satellite application industry system will be established and the development of satellite application integrated services will be promoted; promote the large-scale development communication and broadcasting satellites and navigation satellites and industrialization of remote sensing satellite operational services; the average annual growth rate of the output value of the satellite application industry will be more than 25 percent, becoming a new growth point for the high-tech industry.

III. Promote the Intensive Development of Communication and Broadcasting Satellites Industry

Make full use of the irreplaceable role of communication and broadcasting satellites as the critical national information infrastructure, actively develop integrated communication and broadcasting satellite services and support the development of

2. OTHER POLICY DOCUMENTS ON SPACE ACTIVITIES

public welfare satellite communication undertakings such as disaster emergency communication, long-distance education and real-time telemedicine system.

1. Further improve the administering and managing policies, mechanisms and institution of communication and broadcasting satellites, reasonably and effectively integrate and optimize the domestic satellite communication enterprises and promote the development of integrated services to comprehensively combine satellite communication and broadcasting and applications in other related industries.

2. Further improve the performance of domestic communication and broadcasting satellites in terms of capacity, life, accuracy, security and reliability and actively develop new types of operational satellites such as mobile communication, broadband access, mobile multimedia broadcasting and direct satellite broadcasting, etc.

3. Continuously improve the development, production and manufacturing level for the core technologies of satellite communication broadcasting terminals, ground systems and equipment in line with the national information security management regulations, vigorously support the industrialization of innovative achievements with self-reliant intellectual property rights and improve the proportion of localization and application proportion of ground equipment.

4. Guided by policy promotion and market demand, actively promote the industrial development of communication and broadcasting satellites manufacturing and improve the industrial scale and competitiveness in the international market of communication and broadcasting satellite manufacturing and service enterprises.

IV. Promote the Rapid and Large-Scale Development of the Satellite Navigation Industry.

Accelerate the establishment of self-reliant satellite positioning and navigation systems, improve the basic support capabilities for satellite navigation applications, vigorously promote the industrialization of satellite navigation terminal equipment and promote the development of related industries for satellite navigation operation.

1. Accelerate the formation of a civil navigation industry system with the Beidou Satellite Navigation System as the core. Establish an overall coordination mechanism; study and formulate the policy for civil application of Beidou Satellite Navigation System and promote the industrial application of Beidou Satellite Navigation System. The important industrial fields involving national economy and public security shall gradually utilize the service system of Beidou Satellite Navigation compatible with other satellite navigation systems and encourage other industries and fields to adopt the service system of Beidou Satellite Navigation compatible with other satellite navigation systems.

2. Strengthen the construction of basic support system for satellite navigation applications. Accelerate the construction of Beidou Satellite Navigation System; plan the development of national high-precision satellite navigation enhancement system as a whole; improve the accuracy and integrity of navigation and positioning plus its service ability; establish and improve the satellite navigation terminal products detection platform and credibility evaluation mechanism and continuously improve the quality of navigation terminal products.

3. Promote the development of satellite navigation operating enterprises and the industrialization of satellite navigation terminal equipment. Vigorously promote the large-scale and standardized development of satellite navigation operation industry; and encourage the standardization and industrialization of products including satellite navigation receiving chips, key components, electronic maps and user terminals with self-reliant intellectual property rights.

V. Make Efforts to Establish an Operational and Integrated Application and Service System of Self-Reliant Remote Sensing Satellites.
Take the establishment of a national high-resolution earth observation system as an historic opportunity to improve the capacity and level of remote sensing satellite applications and services, push forward the public sharing and effective utilization of remote sensing satellite data resources and promote the formation of remote sensing satellite application industry.

1. Promote the development, utilization, opening and public sharing of remote sensing satellite data in China. Strengthen the construction of remote sensing satellite services and application systems, accelerate the optimization of resources and gradually build a unified national remote sensing data receiving and processing ground system from earth observation, meteorological and marine satellites. To promote the public welfare services, commercial services and international market services based on China's remote sensing satellite data, construct the national remote sensing satellite data platform, together with the national database of natural resources and geospatial fundamental information; formulate unified standards and policies for earth observation remote sensing data and form a mechanism for the opening and sharing of remote sensing satellite data on the premise of ensuring national security.

2. Strengthen the utilization of remote sensing satellite data in the development of essential industries and regions. Accelerate the research and development of application technologies and the construction of application systems; promote the utilization of remote sensing data in the fields of land resources, agriculture, forestry, water conservancy, meteorology, ocean, environment, disaster reduction, surveying and mapping, transportation, education, regional development, urban and rural management and major projects; carry out application demonstration projects, cultivate remote sensing service enterprises and expand the industrial chain of remote sensing satellite application services.

2. OTHER POLICY DOCUMENTS ON SPACE ACTIVITIES

3. Comprehensively improve the self-reliant support ability of remote sensing satellite data sources in China. Improve the level of development, operation and management of remote sensing satellites in China; accelerate the construction of the national high-resolution earth observation system and the operational remote sensing satellite system; form a continuous, stable, timely and high-quality operational data service capability; improve the technical support system for the application and industrialization of remote sensing satellite data, such as remote sensing calibration test sites; and promote the development and implementation of remote sensing satellite data products and public application platforms.

VI. Strengthen the National Overall Planning and Macro-Management of Satellite Applications.
Establish a coordination mechanism among government sectors and departments; study and formulate relevant policies; make overall plans for the development of satellite, satellite applications and related infrastructure and coordinate the construction of major projects involving the utilization of space resources and key infrastructure. While actively implementing the relevant national overall plan, the local governments and relevant departments at all levels should, in the light of reality, actively promote the comprehensive utilization and typical demonstration of satellite applications in regions and industries.

VII. Strengthen the Promotion and Utilization of Satellite Data, Products and Systems with Self-Reliant Intellectual Property Rights.
The satellite application fields involving national security and national economy lifelines and the government investment projects shall give priority to the utilization and procurement of satellite data, products and systems with self-reliant intellectual property rights; when valuating government investment projects involving satellite applications in various fields, the relevant evaluation organs should add the feasibility assessment of utilization of domestic satellite data and products. The competent governments departments at all levels should accelerate their research on policies relating to the intellectual property rights of satellite data, incorporate intellectual property rights into the evaluation and management activities of satellite application projects and incorporate intellectual property protection as the essential part of their administrative work.

VIII. Strengthen the Construction of Satellite Application Standardization System in China.
Accelerate the top-level design of satellite application standards and research and formulation of important basic standards; strengthen the formulation and dissemination of key technical standards combining various industries with satellite

application fields and actively participate in international cooperation for the standardization of satellite applications.

IX. Increase the Support for the Infrastructure Construction of Satellite Application Industry.

Increase government investment in the major infrastructure construction of satellite application business system; promote basic capacity building of satellite application industry; strengthen planning and coordination of orbit, frequency and other resources utilization and accelerate the formation of basic conditions for the development of satellite application industry.

X. Strengthen the Support for and Investment in the Research and Development of Science and Technology Related to Satellite Applications and Their Industrialization.

Strengthen the capacity building of satellite application innovation; establish several national satellite application engineering centers, engineering laboratories and key laboratories; exploit the advantages to the full of scientific research institutions and institutions of higher learning and form an enterprise-oriented innovation system of satellite application technology combining production, education and research; increase the support for common character of satellite applications, the development of key technologies, the integration of engineering systems and the construction of major application projects.

XI. Encourage the Non-government Capital and Enterprises to Participate in the Satellite Application Industry.

The central and local governments at all levels shall grant investment subsidies or loan discounts to major satellite application projects with industrialization prospects that are included in the national development plan and mainly invested by non-governmental capital. Through the construction of the policy environment, actively guide non-government investment to develop satellite application industry and promote the diversification of investors.

XII. Accelerate the Transformation of Research Results and Promote the Industrialization of Satellite Applications.

Encourage the competent governmental departments and scientific research institutes to publish the technological achievements of satellite applications in a timely manner and promote the transformation, popularization and application of the latest research results in satellite applications. To provide services for promoting the application of satellite application technologies and products, efforts should be made to organize and implement the special projects for the industrialization of satellite applications, the application demonstration projects and the industrial development bases; popularize the application of research results and experiences; actively cultivate and develop intermediary institutions and gradually establish evaluation and certification mechanisms for satellite application system products.

XIII. Expand the Opening-up and International Cooperation in Satellite Application Industry.

Actively carry out international cooperation to improve the overall technical level of applications; support the efforts to develop overseas markets and promote the export of satellite application products and services.

XIV. Strengthen the Relevant Training and Education and Information Dissemination.

Strengthen the construction of education and training system combining technologies and their application, accelerate the training of satellite application human resources, actively carry out multi-level, on-the-job training of satellite application technologies and vigorously publicize and popularize satellite application knowledge.

2.2. Medium and Long-Term Development Plan for China's Satellite Navigation Industry[2]

The General Office of State Council
2013
(Unofficial English translation by WU Xiaodan, assisted by Ms. WU Tong)

The satellite navigation industry is an emerging high-tech industry consisting of the satellite positioning, navigation and timing system, the manufacturing industry of user terminal system, the operation and maintenance of satellite positioning system and the navigation information services. The development of the satellite navigation industry has important practical significance and long-term strategic significance for promoting industrial restructuring, improving social production efficiency, improving the people's quality of life and enhancing the core competitiveness of our country. In order to promote the rapid and healthy development of China's satellite navigation industry and promote the large-scale application of the Beidou Satellite Navigation System, the plan has been formulated in accordance with the Twelfth Five-Year Plan for National Economic and Social Development, the Twelfth Five-Year National Strategic Emerging Industry Development Plan and the implementation of major special projects of the second-generation satellite navigation system.

---

2   The original Chinese version of this policy is published on the website of the State Administration of Science and Technology and Industry for National Defense, www.sastind.gov.cn, last accessed August 2021.

I. The Status Quo and Development Trend

1. The international satellite navigation industry is developing rapidly with a profound impact on economic and social development.

The international satellite navigation industry has formed a relatively complete industrial system. The performance of navigation services has been continuously improved with the continuous and rapid expansion of application scope and market size. The application of satellite navigation technologies has become an indispensable and important means for economic and social development of developed countries. It also has a profound impact on the scientific development of resource utilization, environmental protection and public services.

2. The countries around the world are competing to build satellite navigation systems and the development and integration of navigation is accelerating.

While the Beidou Satellite Navigation System is building in China, the United States has further strengthened and improved the Global Positioning System (GPS) and the satellite navigation systems independently developed by Russia, the European Union, Japan and India are developing in a competitive manner. Moreover, the development trend of the global satellite navigation industry are threefold: the transformation from single GPS application to multi-system compatible application; the transformation from mainly for navigation applications to integrated applications of navigation, mobile communications and Internet connection; the transformation from mainly for application terminal equipment to equal emphasis on products and services. The co-existence of competition and cooperation at the international level and the trend of industrial integration and development will certainly promote the deep development of the application of satellite navigation technologies in a wider range of fields, as well as promote the comprehensive development of satellite navigation and related industries.

3. The construction of Beidou Satellite Navigation System has made breakthroughs and the satellite navigation industry in China has achieved considerate progress.

The theoretical research and technology development of satellite navigation application is developing rapidly in China, leading up to major breakthroughs in the key technologies and their productization including navigation chip and antenna. The Beidou Satellite Navigation System has regional service capability, playing an important role in transportation, marine fishery and many other fields and the construction of its global system is steadily going forward. With the integration and development of satellite navigation and transportation, intelligent terminals and mobile Internet, the navigation application technologies have been improved significantly and the manufacturing and service capabilities of products have been improved rapidly. Consequently, China has become a major exporter of vehicle navigation terminal products.

4. China's satellite navigation industry is bound to have a vast market space, though facing multiple pressures, i.e., system construction lagging behind industrial

development needs and core technologies subject to constraints of optimizing the consumers' needs and industry development environment.

With the rapid development of the modern information society, the public demands for innovative and comprehensive spatio-temporal information services are intensively growing. In the future, the application of Beidou Satellite Navigation System, with its advantages of short message communication, will be greatly expanded in key economic areas, industries and public services. Its location service application integrating mobile communication and Internet technology will effectively promote the upgrading of satellite navigation industrial structure and release a broader market space. However, considering the global context, i.e., the competition and rapid industrial development of several satellite navigation systems, China's satellite navigation industry faces outstanding challenges. First, the construction of China's satellite navigation system lags behind the industrial development needs and its applications mainly rely on foreign systems. Second, there is a lack of coordinative planning, resulting in the insufficient capacity and the redundant construction of the ground application infrastructure. Third, independent innovation capability is insufficient. In the absence of the core technologies, the integration capability is weak and the relevant products and solutions are far left behind their counterpart of the international advanced level. As a result, the market space of Beidou Satellite Navigation System has been seriously squeezed. Fourth, the industrial development environment needs be optimized and promoted urgently through the improvement of the relevant policies, regulations and standards and the concentration of whole industry with leading enterprises. Therefore, to facilitate the healthy and sustainable development of China's satellite navigation industry, there is need to accelerate the construction of China's global satellite navigation system and promote the development of Beidou's civilian application system.

II. The Guiding Thoughts, Basic Principles and Development Goals

1. The Guiding Thoughts

Thoroughly implement the scientific concept of development. Firmly grasp and take full advantage of the strategic opportunities for the development of the satellite navigation industry, oriented on the major needs of the future economic and social industrialization, informationization, urbanization and agricultural modernization. Make the enterprise as the main body; grasp the core and key technologies; cultivate new service forms; expand the marketization and application of technologies; enhance international competitiveness; construct complete industrial system; consolidate the industrial base; improve the policy environment and innovate the development models so as to promote the rapid development of China's satellite navigation industry and provide the support for the sustainable economic and social development.

2. The Basic Principles

(1) Overall Planning and Coordinated Development

Strengthen the planning of industrial development and clarify industrial development priorities and key links as well as the direction and focus of development. Strengthen the coordination and cooperation among departments and sectors; promote the integration development of military and civilian; optimize the regional layout with connection to the major national science and technology projects and plans. Moreover, guide the formation of a good pattern of coordinated development of satellite navigation industry and avoid blind development and duplicated construction.

(2) Market Orientation with Policy Support

Market-oriented develop, giving full play to the basic role of market allocation of resources and mobilizing the enthusiasm of enterprises. Improve the policies for application service and strive to create a good market environment. Strengthen the guiding roles of policy, fulfill international obligations, safeguard national security and promote the application of Beidou Satellite Navigation System in the key areas of national security, economic construction and social development.

(3) Consolidate the Foundation and Strengthen the Innovative Development

Strengthen the construction of major infrastructure facilities, the construction of measurement standards, the protection and utilization of intellectual property rights and the training of personnel to lay down a solid foundation for industrial development. Furthermore, strengthen the innovation of technology and application, business mode and industrial organization and promote the formation of a new mode of integration and development.

(4) Be Open and Inclusive to Promote Cooperation and Advance

Implement a more proactive and opener strategy, a long-term stable, open and inclusive policy for international service. With the continuous improvement of global application service capability of Beidou Satellite Navigation System, foster international cooperation and competitive advantages and actively utilize resources and markets both at the domestic and international level, so as to achieve the coordinated development of internationalization and industrialization.

3. The Development Goals

By 2020, the innovative development pattern of China's satellite navigation industry will be basically formed, the scale of industrial application and the level of internationalization will be greatly improved and the size of industry will exceed 400 billion yuan. The Beidou Satellite Navigation System and its compatible products will be widely used in important industries and key fields of the national economy, will be gradually become a popular choice in the mass consumer market. The Beidou Satellite Navigation System will contribute 60% of the domestic satellite navigation application market, among which more than 80% in the important application fields and will have a strong international competitiveness in the global market.

(1) Optimize and Upgrade the Industrial Satellite Navigation System.

The national satellite navigation industry infrastructure construction will be further improved to become an industrial system with complete categories, reasonable layout and optimized structure. Form a competitive industry chain composed of navigation, location and time service and a number of satellite navigation industry gathering areas. Cultivate a number of industry backbone enterprises and innovative medium- and small sized enterprises. Build a number of public service platforms with broad coverage and strong support.

(2) The Ability to Innovate Will Be Increased Significantly.

On the basis of overall planning and considering the layout of scientific research, fully integrate and utilize existing scientific and technological resources, promote the construction of innovative platforms such as key laboratories of satellite navigation application technologies and enterprise technology innovation centers, so as to enhance the sustainable capability to innovate. Break through a number of key core technologies in chips, embedded software and other fields and form a series of patents and technical standards with intellectual property rights to support the industry's technological progress and application model innovation.

(3) The Scale and Level of Application Will Be Significantly Improved.

The satellite navigation technology will be widely applied in various fields of economy and society to meet the basic needs of economic and social development. The Beidou Satellite Navigation System will be fully applied in energy (electricity), finance, communications and other important fields and largely applied in the fields of key industries, consumer markets and public services.

(4) The Beidou Satellite Navigation System Will Have Open and Compatible Global Service Capability.

The service performance of Beidou Satellite Navigation System will be further improved, including the compatibility and interoperability with other satellite navigation systems. The international competitiveness of Beidou application will be significantly improved with more intensive application range.

III. The Key Development Directions and Main Tasks

Consolidate the foundation of industrial development driven by the market demands, focusing on the key areas and weak links of industrial development and the research and development of key technology and enhancing the overall level of industrial development and international competitiveness.

1. Improve Navigation Infrastructure.

Accelerate the construction of a unified, coordinated, complete and open satellite navigation infrastructure, emphasizing on the national strategic needs and application needs in key areas and aiming at improving the performance of satellite navigation services. Focus on the construction of major ground infrastructure such as multi-mode continuous operation of reference stations network, promote data sharing, improve the efficiency of resource utilization, innovative service model, consolidate the foundation of industrial development, as well as enhance the ability of industrial sustainable development.

Table 1 – Navigation and Positioning Infrastructure Construction

Time	2020
Goals	The global coverage of Beidou Satellite Navigation System with the ability to provide navigation and positioning services for global users; strengthen the construction of ground infrastructure to provide real-time decimeter-level and post-centimeter-level positioning services for industrial and mass applications in China and most of its surrounding areas; provide basic support for indoor and outdoor seamless location service coverage for key areas and specific locations.
Main tasks	**The Construction of Beidou Satellite Navigation System:** a global satellite navigation system consisting of more than 30 satellites and ground operation control system with global service capability; a satellite navigation signal monitoring and evaluation system and a navigation signal interference detection and weakening system to ensure the safe and reliable operation of the Beidou system. **The Construction of Multi-mode Continuous Operation Reference Station Network:** the unified national multi-mode continuous operation reference station network to provide support for various types of user navigation enhancement services and data sharing for signal monitoring and evaluation and scientific research. **The Construction of Location Data Integrated Service System:** a complete and interconnected location service platform based on multi-mode continuous operation reference station network and providing support services for the regional, industrial and public share applications. **The Construction of Integrated Navigation System:** integrating a variety of technologies to solve the key areas and specific places of navigation, positioning and time service coverage issues, enhancing seamless navigation service capabilities in the cities, canyons and indoor and outdoor. **Major Projects:** foundation projects enhancing satellite navigation performance
Major policy	Formulate relevant provisions to protect satellite navigation services from harmful interference and establish mechanisms to combat illegal production, sale and use of satellite navigation jammers, illegal interference with satellite navigation services and damaging service infrastructure. Establish the information sharing mechanism of multi-mode continuous operation reference station network and location data integrated service system.

2. Make Breakthrough in the Key Technologies.

Further promote the technological level of satellite navigation chip, compatibility of Beidou Satellite Navigation System with other satellite navigation systems, make breakthrough achievement in the integration of satellite navigation and mobile communications, the Internet, remote sensing and other fields of application technology. Promote the upgrading of core basic products and the scale production of cost-effective products such as navigation, timing, precision measurement, attitude determination and orientation. Support the innovation capacity building of key enterprises and research institutes, strengthen the capacity building of engineering experiment platform and achievement transformation platform and form a technological innovation system combining production, study and research.

Table 2 – The Innovation of Key Technologies and Industrialization of General Purposed Product

Time	2020
Goals	A group of technological innovation achievements with intellectual property rights and core competitiveness, the design and manufacturing technology of the core devices of satellite navigation up to the international advanced level and a number of general-purpose products with high performance price ratio, intellectual property rights and international competitiveness.
Main tasks	**Core Technologies:** breaking through the bottleneck of the developing core chips, software and high-end products; focusing on improving the design level and manufacturing process for chips; improving chip integration and reduce energy consumption; supporting the innovation of satellite navigation application technology, breaking through high-precision positioning technology, indoor and outdoor seamless positioning technology, satellite navigation vulnerability monitoring and mitigation technology, intelligent service technology and key technologies based on multi-mode integrated navigation. **Core Components:** vigorously innovating the development of navigation, communications and other multi-mode fusion chips and antennas, as well as core components for integrating navigation and sensing. **General Purposed Products:** R&D of navigation, timing, precision measurement, attitude and orientation and other industrial applications, as well as integrated positioning and navigation functions of smart phones, tablet computers, vehicle navigation and other terminal electronic products; comprehensive improving product cost-effectiveness and maturity, achieving product standardization and integrating with the international market, as well as promoting industrial development and enter the international market. **The Construction of Innovation Capacity:** supporting a number of key laboratories oriented to basic research and a number of engineering (technology) research centers oriented to industries, fields and regions. Forming a number of technological innovation and application innovation bases. **Major Projects:** innovation projects enhancing core technology capability.
Major policy	Improving the relevant policies to encourage the promotion and exportation of the Beidou Satellite Navigation System and its compatible products. Formulating policies to encourage enterprises to develop the key technologies of satellite navigation system.

3. Advance the Protection of Time and Frequency of Navigation Satellite Application.
Trace the Beidou time to the national time frequency measurement benchmark to provide time frequency guarantee for the important areas of national security and national economy. Promulgate national standards and relevant policies and measures, strengthen financial support, combine with the upgrading of infrastructure in key areas of national security and promote the in-depth application of Beidou Satellite Navigation System and its compatible navigation timing technologies and products in energy (electricity), communications, finance, public security and other important areas of national economic and security to ensure the stable and safe operation of national economy.

Table 3 – Application of Important Products

Time	2020
Goals	The application of Beidou timing equipment in important industries and areas related to national security and national economic development.
Main tasks	**Advancing Satellite Navigation Application in Important Areas:** promoting the application of Beidou Satellite Navigation System and its compatible navigation and timing technologies and products in energy (electricity), communications, finance, public security and other industries, as well as encouraging the application of Beidou Satellite Navigation System and its compatible products in other areas. **Major Projects:** safety projects advancing the application of Beidou system in important fields.
Major policy	Formulating standards and policies conforming to national security needs and the characteristics and development stages of satellite navigation industry.

4. Promote Industrial Innovation and Application.
To meet the application needs of key industries and fields; make full use of the special advantages of Beidou Satellite Navigation System, such as short message communication and combine the development of new generation of information technology; innovate application service modes; strengthen the deep integration of satellite navigation with important industries of national economic and social development; vigorously promote the large-scale application of satellite navigation products and services in public security, transportation, disaster prevention and mitigation, agriculture, forestry and water conservancy, meteorology, land and resources, environmental protection, public security and police affairs, surveying and mapping exploration, emergency rescue and other important industries and fields. Promote the wide integration and linkage of satellite navigation with the Internet of Things, mobile interconnection and triple play and actively encourage the development of new applications. Promote the formation of industry comprehensive application solutions, improve the efficiency of industry operation and promote the transformation and upgrading of related industries.

2. OTHER POLICY DOCUMENTS ON SPACE ACTIVITIES

Table 4 – The Key Industries and Areas of Applications

Time	2020
Goals	Satellite navigation products and services will be widely used in public security, transportation, disaster prevention and mitigation, agriculture, forestry and water conservancy, meteorology, land and resources, environmental protection, public security and police, surveying and mapping exploration, emergency rescue and other important industries and fields.
Main tasks	**Industry Integrated Application Solutions:** relying on the national satellite navigation infrastructure, innovating application service model and building a comprehensive application service platform for industry and domain application needs, as well as forming a systematic solution for comprehensive application of the satellite navigation industry. **Large Scale Application of the Satellite Navigation Industry:** combining with the industry development planning, solving the industry application of key common technologies, developing a series of special equipment, promoting navigation and industry integration development and promoting the transformation and upgrading of related industries.
Major policy	Formulating application guidance policies conforming to the characteristics of the satellite navigation industry to continuously deepen its application.

5. Expand the Scale of Mass Application.

Innovate the business and service models with an emphasis on location services and build a comprehensive information system for location information so as to adapt to the mass-market demand for satellite navigation in vehicles and personal applications. Focus on promoting satellite navigation function to become the standard configuration of car navigation and smart phone terminals and promote its diversified applications in social services, tourism, vulnerable groups and smart cities, etc.

Table 5 – The Mass Application

Time	2020
Goals	Forming a variety of location service products and mature business and service models and creating a number of large-scale, influential enterprises so as to produce application benefits.
Main tasks	**Vehicle Information Services:** promoting the development and improvement of vehicle location service system and the scale application of vehicle monitoring, navigation and integrated information services. **Personal Location Services:** promoting the development of personal location service system and its scale applications in social services, tourism, vulnerable groups, smart cities and other fields. Major projects: mass application projects promoting the scale development of satellite navigation industry.

Table 5 – The Mass Application

Time	2020
Major policy	Formulating user location reporting administrative mechanism and personal privacy protection policy.

6. Promote the Development of Overseas Market.

Strengthen the strategic research for international cooperation, actively participate in various forms of international cooperation in the field of satellite navigation, jointly carry out international standard research and formulation and accelerate the internationalization of Beidou Satellite Navigation System and its application industry. Strengthen intellectual and technical cooperation to improve the service capability and industrial application level of Beidou Satellite Navigation System; actively implement the " go global " strategy, increase the promotion of Beidou Satellite Navigation System overseas applications, encourage qualified enterprises to establish research and development centers and marketing service networks abroad, vigorously expand international market, as well as encourage foreign enterprises to utilize Beidou Satellite Navigation System. Establish and improve the support system for industrial internationalization development and enhance the service support ability for globalization.

Table 6 – The Development of Internationalization

Time	2020
Goals	Building a number of overseas application demonstration projects, establishing and promoting the Beidou Satellite Navigation System brand in the surrounding areas, forming a complete marketing and operation service network and building an international support and security system.
Main tasks	**The Construction of Overseas Demonstration Projects:** meeting the application requirements of international users for emergency rescue, comprehensive disaster reduction, ship/vehicle monitoring and command and construct several overseas application demonstration projects to promote the internationalization of the satellite navigation industry. **The Construction of Global Marketing and Service Network:** strengthening the overseas market layout; establishing overseas development and promotion center; building international marketing network and establishing a global operating service system. **The Construction of Internationalization Service System:** providing research and advisory services in policy, market, law and finance to related governmental organs and enterprises for international satellite navigation applications; comprehensively enhancing the service ability to support and guarantee global and regional market development and carrying out related intellectual and technical cooperation. **Major Projects:** internationalization projects developing the global application market.

2. OTHER POLICY DOCUMENTS ON SPACE ACTIVITIES

Table 6 – The Development of Internationalization

Time	2020
Major policy	Implementing and improving the fiscal, taxation and financial services policies to encourage enterprises to "go out".

IV. Major Projects

A number of major projects will be organized and implemented focusing on the overall objectives and main tasks of satellite navigation industrial development, so as to accelerate the cultivation and development of satellite navigation industry and promote the upgrading of basic industrial capacity, technological innovation in key areas, large-scale application and international development.

1. The Foundation Projects Enhancing Satellite Navigation Performance

Formulate the construction plan of the national multi-mode continuous operation reference station network, unify the national standards and integrate the resources of the domestic continuous operation reference station network. Form the unified management reference station network through optimizing, transforming, upgrading and supplementing to enhance the navigation performance and improve the precision of the satellite navigation system. Establish a national integrated service system for location data by integrating map and geographic information, remote sensing data information, traffic information, meteorological information and environmental information. Accelerate the construction of auxiliary positioning system and promote indoor and outdoor seamless positioning technology in key areas and specific places. Through the implementation of these projects, a complete supporting system for integrated application of satellite navigation will be formed with the capability of real-time decimeter and centimeter application service, effectively enhancing the performance and service capability of the satellite navigation system and laying down a foundation for expanding the application scale. In five years or so, the basic integration of resources will be realized and the initial application foundation support system will be constructed.

2. The Innovation Projects Enhancing Core Technology Capability

In response to the bottleneck restriction – the "no chips" situation – and aiming at building China's satellite navigation industry technology innovation system, efforts will be made to strengthen the R&D and application of Beidou chips and terminal products; accelarate product maturity and improve core competitiveness; adapt to the application requirements with a focus on making breakthrough achievement in a series of basic frontiers and common key technologies integrating chip, integrated navigation, application integration and outdoor and indoor seamless positioning; develop a number of high-performance low-cost navigation devices and products and vigorously enhance innovation capabilities; integrate existing scientific and technological resources and promote key the construction and development of laboratories, engineering (technical) research centers and enterprise technology centers for satellite navigation application technologies.

3. The Safety Projects Advancing the Application of Beidou System in Important Fields

Promote the improvement of related standards, legal rule and improve the level of satellite navigation application technology and product quality. The advancement of the Beidou Satellite Navigation System and its compatible products will be implemented in phases in the fields of energy (electricity), communications, finance and public security. Strengthen policy guidance to promote the large-scale application of Beidou satellite navigation system in the fields of public safety, transportation, disaster prevention and mitigation, agriculture, forestry and water conservancy, meteorology, land resources, environmental protection, public security police, surveying and mapping and emergency rescue so as to promote the transformation and upgrading of related industries.

4. The Mass Application Projects Promoting the Scale Development of Satellite Navigation Industry

Oriented with the needs of the mass market, integrate the dynamic time and space information for transportation, meteorology and geography based on the development of new generation information technology. Take advantage of the rapid development of automobile manufacturing industry and mobile communication industry as an opportunity, promote Beidou compatible satellite navigation function to become the standard configuration of car navigation and smart phones based on the demand for public travel information services. Promote the diversified applications of satellite navigation system in social services, tourism, vulnerable groups and smart cities. Innovate the business and service model, promote the industrialization of Beidou Satellite Navigation System products and form the scale application benefits of the terminal product.

5. The Internationalization Projects Developing the Global Application Market

In consideration of the application needs of international users for emergency rescue, comprehensive disaster reduction, ship/vehicle monitoring and command and dispatch, increase the application and promotion of Beidou Satellite Navigation System. Build several overseas application demonstration projects to develop the international market. Incorporate the Beidou Satellite Navigation System into International Civil Aviation Organization and the International Maritime Organization to promote its applications in civil aviation and ocean vessels. Construct an enhanced satellite navigation system covering the Asia-Pacific region and a unified space-time benchmark system, as well as a basic project and a comprehensive service project for the internationalization of the satellite navigation industry. Carry out research and advisory services in the fields of policy, market, law and finance for the international application of satellite navigation to enhance the ability to provide international integrated services.

V. Safeguarding Measures
In order to implement the plan in an all-round way, implement the key tasks earnestly and create a favorable environment for industrial development, it is necessary to strengthen organization and coordination and take strong safeguard measures.

1. Strengthen Overall Coordination and Form Joint Development Efforts.
Accelerate the establishment and improvement of a coordinated mechanism for the development of national satellite navigation industry. Strengthen communication and coordination between the military and civilians and departments and sectors and pool central, local and other social resources together. Overall plan for the construction and application of the satellite navigation infrastructure. Study and formulate industrialization promotion policies, as well as guide the optimization of industrial layout. Improve market supervision and management mechanism, strengthen market information monitoring and early warning and implement dynamic adjustment according to the development situation. Make full use of the role of industry guidance, coordination and service of professional organizations such as industry associations. Strengthen the industry and enterprise self-discipline system and build a benign competitive environment for the development of satellite navigation industry.

2. Promulgate National Policies to Promote Application Services.
The White Paper on Beidou Satellite Navigation System will be issued regularly, introducing its development purpose, principles, policies and relevant agreement standards, how it provides free, open, safe and reliable civil services, the progress of its construction and operation services and guiding the social application of Beidou Satellite Navigation System. Make full use of the initiative of market participants and vigorously carry out market cultivation and application demonstration. Encourage application services and business model innovation, intensify the implementation of major projects and promote the large-scale application of Beidou Satellite Navigation System.

3. Improve the Related Policies and Regulations and Optimize the Development Environment.
Formulate policies to promote the use of Beidou Satellite Navigation System in important areas involving national security and national economy. Promote the application of Beidou Satellite Navigation System and their compatible products in the fields of

energy (electricity), communications and finance. Study and formulate management systems related to market access and location security and establish and improve satellite navigation product quality testing and certification systems and quality supervision mechanisms. Integrate existing resources, promote the construction of satellite navigation product quality testing centers, standardize the satellite navigation application services and operations and enhance the participation enthusiasm of backbone enterprises and innovative enterprises. Promote the protection of intellectual property rights and support the qualified enterprises to apply for foreign patents. Improve financial policies that encourage technological innovation in the satellite navigation industry and guide investment and consumption.

4. Strengthen the Construction of Standards and Improve the Level of Development.
Accelerate the establishment and improvement of a standard system to support the healthy development of the satellite navigation industry. Encourage all parties involved in production, education and research to jointly develop technical standards. Promote the universalization and resource sharing of satellite navigation and civilian standards and promote the integration and development of satellite navigation and Internet of Things and mobile communications. Encourage key enterprises and R&D institutions to participate in the formulation of relevant international standards. Promote the compatible development of Beidou and other satellite navigation systems. Increase the standard publicity, improve the standard information service, certification, testing system and the supervision of standards implementation and promote the development of conformity assessment, product certification services and international cooperation to promote the global application of Beidou Satellite Navigation System.

5. Expand Investments and Encourage Industrial Innovation.
Expand investment utilizing the existing policies and financial funds channels and attract diversified capital investment in the organization and implementation of major projects to accelerate the development of the satellite navigation industry. Expand investment in key infrastructure construction, key technology research and development and typical demonstration applications to enhance the innovation and development capabilities of core technologies and core products. Strengthen the cultivation of specialized human resources; improve the ability to create, utilize and protect intellectual property; help the advanced enterprises to become stronger and bigger and encourage industrial concentration and competitiveness through the establishment of industrial alliances and the mergers and acquisitions.

2. OTHER POLICY DOCUMENTS ON SPACE ACTIVITIES

2.3. MEDIUM AND LONG-TERM DEVELOPMENT PLAN FOR NATIONAL CIVIL SPACE INFRASTRUCTURE (2015-2025)[3]

National Development and Reform Commission
Ministry of Finance
State Administration of Science and Technology and Industry for National Defense
2015
(Unofficial English translation by WU Xiaodan, assisted by Ms. WU Tong)

Civil space infrastructure refers to the space-ground engineering facilities that utilize space resources to provide remote sensing, communication and broadcasting, navigation and positioning and other products and services, composed of space systems, ground systems and their related systems being coordinated in function and stable in operation. Civil space infrastructure is of strategic significance in modernization and making the society information-oriented and intelligence-oriented, an essential bolster for national security and a vital method to push forward scientific development, transform economic development mode and realize an innovation-driven society. It is of great strategic meaning for China's modernization construction to accelerate establishing a self-reliant, open, safe, stable, reliable and long-term operating civil space infrastructure.

In order to push forward the healthy and rapid development of China's civil space infrastructure, this plan is formulated according to major requirements and general guidelines for the national economy and social development, including the Outline of the 12th Five-Year Plan for National Economic and Social Development of the People's Republic of China and the 12th Five-Year Plan for National Strategic Emerging Industries.

I. The Current Situation and Development Trend

1. The Upgrading and Updating of Space Infrastructure Is Accelerating Worldwide.
At present, the space infrastructure has entered a new era of systematic development with the ability of providing global service. With the development of remote sensing satellite to worldwide observation and multi-satellite network observation, the global comprehensive observation has been gradually formed with three-dimensional or multi-dimensional ability and the integration of high, middle and low-resolution; all kinds of business models of satellite communications and broadcasting services tend to converge and develop towards broadband multimedia and the next generation of mobile

---

3   The original Chinese version of this policy is published on the website of the National Development and Reformation Commission, www.ndrc.gov.cn, last accessed August 2021.

communication satellite constellations is accelerating in deployment; satellite navigation is stepping from the era of US-led single GPS (Global Positioning System) into the new era, in which there is competition among the four global systems of the United States, Russia, China and Europe and two regional systems of Japan and India. The global satellite and its application industries have increased rapidly, whose annual growth rate has maintained over 10% in the twenty-first century. The development and improvement of an independent space infrastructure have become a strategic choice for the developed countries and regions to pursue a leading position in the space field, seize the commanding point of economic science and technology competition, develop new industries and safeguard the security interests.

2. The Development of China's Space Infrastructure Is Amid a Critical Period of Transition.

After more than 50 years of construction, the development of China's space infrastructure has formed a complete set of space industrial system. The capabilities of developing, producing and launching satellites is among the world's advanced ranks; the remote sensing satellites for natural resources, oceans, meteorology and environmental disaster reduction have certain capabilities to provide business services; the basic system for satellite communications such as fixed communication and broadcasting has been completed; as well as the Beidou satellite navigation system has provided regional services. Satellite application has become an indispensable means for innovative administration, protection of resources and environment, upgrading of disaster reduction capabilities, providing universal information services and cultivating new industries. Meanwhile, China's space infrastructure is in a critical transitional period of development. The technological capability is transforming from catching up with the world-advanced technologies to independent innovation; the service mode is converting from the application experiment oriented-model to business service oriented-model; the industrial applications are transiting from mainly relying on external data to mainly relying on independent data; the development mechanism is changing from governmental investment to a diversified and commercialized investment. Grasping the opportunity of transition and accelerating the construction of civil space infrastructure is the primary strategic measure to adapt to the needs of development, promote the transformation and upgrade and cultivate the high-end industries.

3. There Are Urgent Needs in Developing Civil Space Infrastructure for Economic and Social Development.

With the rapid economic and social development and the continuous progress of space technologies, various fields, departments and sectors have put forward more extensive and more urgent needs for the construction of an independent and open civil space infrastructure. Some of them are diversified, refined and high timeliness observation from remote sensing satellite applications in the areas of national territory, ocean, surveying and mapping, environmental protection, civil affairs, meteorology, agriculture, forestry, water conservancy, earthquake, traffic, statistics, public security, energy and urban and rural construction. Some of them are the telecommunications and broadcasting satellite applications with the characteristics of broad coverage, large capacity and high security in the fields of broadcasting, education, culture, health care, communication, transportation, diplomacy, emergency response and disaster relief. Some of them are innovative, more precise and more integrated services from satellite navigation applications in the areas of public safety, transportation, disaster prevention and disaster reduction, agriculture, forestry, water conservancy, meteorology, land and resources, environmental protection, public security police, surveying and mapping and emergency rescue.

(4) The Overall and Coordinated Construction of China's Civil Space Infrastructure Admits of No Delay.

A various aspects of China's development are highly dependent on the continuous development and stable operation of the space infrastructure. It could safeguard major national interests in supporting energy resource development, food security, maritime rights and interests maintenance and climate change. Its wide-area and refined applications in the critical areas of national economy are critical in land and resources management, disaster prevention and mitigation, environmental protection, agriculture, forestry and water conservancy and transportation. It would meet the urgent needs for high quality universal information services in the fields of culture, education, medical care and other areas of people's livelihood. With the rapid growth of new industrialization, informatization, urbanization and agricultural modernization in China, it is increasingly urgent to accelerate the construction of civil space infrastructure, meet the major needs of the national economy and social development, as well as enhance the new competitive advantage of China's space industry.

II. The Guiding Thoughts and Development Principles

1. The Guiding Thoughts

Fully implement the spirits of the 18th National Congress of the CPC and its Second, Third and Fourth Plenary Sessions, the decisions of the Party Central Committee and the State Council. Meet the enormous demands of national economy and social development. Seize the opportunities of the world's new scientific and technological revolutions and industrial revolutions. Avoid duplication of planning and construction, guide by the overall advanced plan, support by technological innovations and drive by institutional reforms. The fundamental goal is to meet demands, enhance application efficiency and promote industrial development. The main line is to coordinate intensive construction, systematic development and efficient service. Inheritance and development should be attached to equal importance and public welfare and business services must develop simultaneously. Formulate and improve relevant policies and regulations, innovate the development modes, as well as consolidate the industrial foundation. Accelerate the construction of a national civil space infrastructure system up to an advanced international level so as to provide strong support for the construction of modernization and the sustainable development of the economy and society of our country.

2. The Development Principles
(1) Application-Orientated and Coordinated Development
Adhere to service users and coordinate needs and capabilities, construction and application, technology and industry, current and long-term development. Establish the related mechanisms for multi-use of one satellite, multi-star networking, multi-network collaboration and data integration services. Make full use of domestic and foreign resources, give priority to meet the strategic and common needs, as well as reasonably meet the pilot and special needs. Consolidate the backbone of the satellite business system, develop new business systems on demand, as well as vigorously promote business applications.

(2) Innovation-Driven and Self-Reliance Development
Adhere to independent innovation, strive to make breakthrough development in core key technologies, as well as focus on develop new technologies, new systems and new application models. Realize the supporting and leading role of science and technology and achieve the effective link between technical research and development and business application. Promote the construction and upgrading of civil space infrastructure in an orderly manner to continuously meet new demands and grasp self-reliant development ability.

(3) Outer Space and Earth Coordinated and Synchronous Development
Adhere to the integrated development in the outer space and on the earth. The space systems and ground systems shall be synchronously planned, developed, constructed and used. Optimize the payloads configuration and the constellation network; rationally distribute the ground system station networks and the data centers; strengthen the support service ability and the business application ability and improve their overall efficiency.

4. Government-Guided and Open Development
Adhere to the national top-level planning and overall management. Formulate and perfect the relevant policies and regulations for improving satellite manufacturing and the national standards of satellites application, satellite data sharing and the policies of market access. The development mechanisms of civil space infrastructure construction, operation, sharing and industrialization should be established and improved. The market

should play a decisive role in the resources allocation. Form a diversified and open development pattern based on the government guidance, department coordination, social participation and international cooperation, so as to promote the development of commercialization and internationalization.

III. The Development Goals

The national civil space infrastructure, composed of three major systems, i.e., remote sensing satellite, satellite communication broadcasting and satellite navigation and positioning, is gradually built in phases, with the characteristics of advanced technologies, independence, rational layout and global coverage. The national civil space infrastructure will be capable of meeting the primary application needs of the industry and the region and supporting the development requirements of China's modernization, national security and improvement of the people's livelihood.

During the period of "12th Five-Year Plan" or later, the backbone framework of the national civil space infrastructure will be basically formed, the business satellite development model and service mechanism will be established and the policy of data sharing will be formulated.

During the period of 13th Five-Year Plan, the core systems of national civil space infrastructure system will be constructed and provide continuous and stable business services, composed of three systems, i.e., remote sensing satellites, communication and broadcasting satellites and navigation and positioning satellites. The data sharing service mechanism will be completed with matching standards and specifications system and the commercial development mode will be formed with the ability to provide international service.

During the period of 14th Five-Year Plan, the construction of a national civil space infrastructure system will be finished with advanced technologies, global coverage and efficient operation. Its commercialization, marketization and industrialization have reached the advanced international level. The sustainable development mechanism will be constantly improved based on innovation drive, demand pushing and market resources allocation, so as to effectively support economic and social development and participate in international development.

IV. Construct the Systems of Remote Sensing Satellites, Communication and Broadcasting satellites and Navigation and Positioning Satellites

Through the combined application of different series and constellation of satellites and coordinated and cooperative data service from different centers, the comprehensive space information service of multi-type, high quality, stable and reliable and large-scale will be provided to support the different application needs in various industries.

1. The Remote Sensing Satellites System

According to the development approaches of multi-use of one satellite, multi-star networking and multi-network cooperation, based on the technical characteristics of observation tasks and the characteristics of users' needs, the development focus is three series satellites for land observation, ocean observation and atmospheric observation. A remote sensing satellites system consisting of seven constellations and three special thematic satellites with balanced combination of various observation techniques will be constructed to gradually possess the comprehensive and efficient global observation ability and data acquisition capability at high, medium and low spatial resolution. The overall construction of remote sensing satellites receiving station network, data centers and the common application support platform will be developed with the capabilities of global reception of remote sensing data and providing global services.

(1) The Construction of Space System

The space system will mainly include the land observation satellite series, the marine observation satellite series and the atmospheric observation satellite series.

i. The Land Observation Satellite Series

Based on the needs for medium and high resolution remote sensing data in different industries and sectors, such as land and resources, environmental protection, disaster prevention and mitigation, water conservancy, agriculture, forestry, statistics, seismology, surveying and mapping, transportation, housing, urban and rural construction, health and other industries, taking into account the needs for oceanographic and atmospheric observations, make full use of the technological bases in national major projects of resource satellites, small satellite constellations for reducing environmental disasters and high-resolution earth observation system, further develop and improve the methods for optical observation, microwave observation and geophysical field detection, construct the three observational constellations of high-resolution optics, medium resolution optics and synthetic aperture radar (SAR) and develop the geophysical field detection satellites to constantly increase the quantitative application level of land observation satellites.

High-resolution Optical Observation Constellations. To satisfy the needs for high precision and high revisit observation in different industries and sectors and areas, including necessary geographic information, land utilization, vegetation coverage, mineral exploitation, fine agriculture, urban construction, transportation, water conservancy facilities, ecological construction, environmental protection, soil and water conservation, disaster assessment and hot spot emergency, the polar orbit high resolution optical constellation will be developed with the ability to acquire global refined data.

Medium Resolution Optical Observation Constellations. To meet the demands for wide, rapid coverage and comprehensive observations in resources survey, environmental monitoring, disaster prevention and reduction, carbon source carbon sink survey, geological survey, water resource management and agricultural monitoring, the medium resolution optical constellation will be constructed with reasonable allocation in high and low orbit to realize rapid dynamic daily observation at the global scale and hourly observation at the national range.

Synthetic Aperture Radar (SAR) Observation Constellation. To satisfy the needs for the all-weather, all-day, multi-scale observations with high precision deformation observation requirements in different industries and sectors, including natural disaster monitoring, resource monitoring, environmental monitoring, agricultural monitoring, bridge and tunnel deformation monitoring, ground subsidence, necessary geographic information and global change information acquisition, make full use of the observation superiority of SAR satellites under complex meteorological conditions, coordinate with optical observation methods and construct the satellite constellations equipped with a reasonable allocation of high and low orbit and multiple observation bands and the ability of multi-frequency range and multi-mode comprehensive observation.

The Geophysical Field Detection Satellite. The meet the demands of monitoring the geophysical environment changes by earthquake, disaster prevention and mitigation, surveying and mapping, develop technologies of electromagnetic monitoring and gravity gradiometer and establish the global geodetic datum framework with geophysical field detection capabilities and earthquake warning services.

ii. The Marine Observation Satellites Series

To meet the major needs of implementing China's marine power strategy in the marine resources exploitation, marine environmental protection, oceanic disaster prevention and mitigation, marine rights and interests protection, the utilization and management of sea areas, island and coastal zone investigation and polar ocean inspection, taking both land and atmospheric observation needs into account, develop a variety of optical and microwave observation technologies, construct the ocean water color and ocean dynamics satellite constellation and ocean surveillance and monitoring satellites and improve the comprehensive observation capabilities of ocean observation satellites continuously.

The Ocean Watercolor Satellite Constellation. To meet the application needs for marine resources exploitation and observation on oceanic environmental, pollution prevention and control and large-amplitude variations, particularly wide and rapid global coverage observation on the environmental elements of ocean watercolor such as seawater Chlorophyll, suspended sediment, dissolved organic matter, red tide and green tide, develop high noise-signal ratio of visible light, infrared multispectral and hyperspectral observation technologies, construct the ocean watercolor satellite constellation and improve the timeliness of observation.

The Ocean Dynamics Satellite Constellation. To meet the application needs for the marine disaster prevention and mitigation, marine resource exploitation, environmental protection, marine fisheries and marine transportation and the high precision requirements for ocean dynamic environment elements such as sea surface height, sea surface wind field, ocean wave, sea water temperature and sea salinity, develop microwave radiometer, scatterometer, altimeter and other observation technologies and construct the marine dynamics satellite constellation.

The Marine Environment Surveillance and Monitoring Satellites. Focus on the all-day, all-weather and near-real-time monitoring needs for marine environmental monitoring, sea area utilization and management, marine rights and interests protection, disaster prevention and mitigation. Develop high orbit gaze optics and high orbit SAR technologies, combine the ability of the low orbit SAR satellite constellation and realize joint high and low orbit optical and SAR observation.

iii. The Atmospheric Observation Satellites Series

Based on the atmospheric observation requirements for meteorological forecast, atmospheric environment monitoring, meteorological disaster monitoring, global climate observation and global climate change, taking into account the needs of ocean and land observation, improve the ability to detect large scale active and passive optical and passive microwave, construct the two satellite constellations of weather observation and climate observation, establish the atmospheric composition detection satellite which will share and integrate with the related satellite data of the World Meteorological Organization (WMO) and form a complete atmospheric observation capability.

The Weather Observation Satellite Constellation. Focus on the needs for accurate weather forecast and meteorological disaster prediction, develop high orbit, high resolution observation ability and achieve the minute observation ability of national land and surrounding areas through optical and microwave satellite networking.

The Climate Observation Satellite Constellation. Focus on the standard monitoring needs for climate change, meteorological disasters, numerical weather prediction, develop comprehensive observation capabilities with global coverage through multi means and construct the constellation composed of morning satellite, afternoon satellites and morning twilight satellites.

The Atmospheric Composition Detection Satellite. Focus on the observation and detection needs for atmospheric particulate matter, pollution gases and greenhouse gas and develop hyper spectral, laser, polarization and other observation technologies.

(2) The Construction of Ground System

The ground system is mainly composed of remote sensing satellite reception station network, data centers, common application support platform and data shared network platform. In accordance with the requirements of efficient networking, collaborative operation and integrated services, utilize the already-having ground system to achieve the overall construction of ground facilities, actively expand overseas construction stations, realize the multi-station cooperative operation, coordinate land, sea and weather satellite data center services so as to eventually comprehensively meet the business needs of various fields.

i. The Reception Station Networks

Promote the coordinated reception of land, ocean and atmospheric observation satellites. Make full use of the current station network and construct the static and polar orbiting receiving antennas at homeland, in polar and other regions and the mobile receiving facilities at sea so as to realize global, multi-station data coordination and integrated reception.

ii. The Data Centers

Make full use of the existing foundation, build the infrastructure of remote sensing satellite mission management and data processing, storage and distribution services, have the land, ocean and meteorological satellite data centers mutually support, complement and backup and promote the efficient use and sharing of satellites, data and computing resources.

iii. The Common Application Support Platform

Common application support platform consists of the calibration and authenticity test field network and the public support platform for research and development of common technologies. The calibration and authenticity test field network aims at coordinating various needs for satellite and data products services to realize the public sharing and utilization of resources and data. Through the combination of on-board calibration, digital calibration, cross-calibration and other means, the calibration field network will meet various requirements for payload performance calibration. The authenticity test network will be tightly integrated with the observation systems in multiple industries, relying on observation stations and test sites with high accuracy and long-term data stability. The public support platform for research and development of common technologies will focus on the common technologies such as standard specification, data processing, sharing service, inspection evaluation, simulation verification and basic database and construct the technology research and development support capability and generic technology test system of open architecture, information integration and sharing so as to effectively promote common technical services and sharing.

iv. The Data Sharing Network Platform

Build a shared network platform effectively connecting the three large data centers and various levels of application systems, timely publish the satellite operation status and user observation requirements and efficiently utilize various kinds of computing and data resources so as to widely provide applications and services for users.

2. The Communication and Broadcasting Satellites System

Based on the application needs in various industries, sectors and areas, mainly relying on the commercialization model and ensure the development of public welfare, the development focus are communication broadcasting satellites and mobile communication broadcasting satellites and simultaneously construct TT & C stations, gateway stations, uplink stations and calibration sites. Gradually form the service capabilities of broadband communication, fixed communication, live broadcast, mobile communication and mobile multimedia broadcasting and construct the satellite communication and broadcasting system that covers the significant areas of the world and integrate with the ground communication network so as to serve the strategies of broadband China and globalization and promote the construction of international communication capacity.

(1) The Construction of Space System

Develop the satellites series of fixed telecommunications broadcasting and mobile radio broadcasting.

i. A Series of Fixed Communication Broadcasting Satellites

Construct three types of satellites including fixed communications, live television and broadband communications and provide fixed communication and broadcasting services for land, surrounding areas and critical regions in the world.

The Fixed Communication Satellites. To meet the needs for telecommunications, radio and television in ocean, oil and other industries, based on existing on-orbit satellites, accelerate the development of a fixed communication satellite system and continuously improve the capacity of fixed communication.

The Television Living Broadcast Satellites. To achieve live broadcast and live broadcast, steadily develop the television direct broadcast satellite system based on the existing satellites.

The Broadband Communication Satellites. To realize the two-way communication services capability in distant education, telemedicine, disaster prevention and reduction information, rural and agricultural informationization, develop the broadband communication satellite system with the abilities of satellite broadcasting, film and television and digital distribution service.

ii. A Series of Mobile Communication Broadcasting Satellites

Construct the mobile communications and mobile multimedia broadcasting satellites so as to achieve the global coverage of mobile communication services and the national coverage of mobile multimedia broadcasting services.

The Mobile Communication Satellites. The mobile communication satellite system should be constructed according to the regional-first and global-later arrangements. The regional mobile communication satellite system will carry out voice and information services for industries and individuals and then construct the mobile communication satellite system with global coverage.

The Mobile Multimedia Broadcasting Satellites. To realize mobile multimedia broadcasting such as telecommunications, radio and television in transportation, emergency disaster reduction and other industries, the mobile multimedia broadcasting satellite system will be developed.

In addition, the data acquisition satellite (DCSS) technology verification system will be developed.

(2) The Construction of Ground System
Based on the needs for developing the space system and relying on the existing network resources, carry out the necessary renewal and transformation of the existing ground facilities and construct the ground facilities such as the TT&C station, the gateway station, the uplink station, the calibration field facilities so as to make full use of the space systems.

3. The Navigation and Positioning Satellites System
The construction of satellite navigation space system and ground system has incorporated into major projects for the overall planning and implementation of China's second-generation satellite navigation system. By 2020, Beidou Global Satellite Navigation System consisting of 35 satellites will be constructed and will be able to provide global users with ten meter-level positioning service and 20 nanosecond-level timing service.

According to the objectives and tasks set by the Medium and Long Term Development Plan for China's Satellite Navigation Industry, in line with major projects of China's second-generation satellite navigation system, proactively elevate the ground application service ability of Beidou system. Overall plan the Beidou Satellite Navigation foundation reinforcement system, integrate the existing resources of reference station networks that allow multiple modules to operate continuously and construct a national reference station network so as to uplift service performance of the system with the ability to provide meter/decimeter-level accuracy in real time, centimeter-level accuracy for professional use and millimeter-level accuracy after post-processing in China and neighboring areas. Comprehensively integrate basic information including geographical information, remote sensing data, architecture, traffic, disaster relief and reduction, water conservancy, meteorology, environment and regional borders and establish a comprehensive service system with national high-accuracy positioning data. Construct an auxiliary positioning system to achieve seamless indoor and outdoor location in key areas and specific locations.

V. The Pre-Arrangement of Scientific Research Tasks
Face the future, target at the global frontier technology, focus on the key bottlenecks restricting development and advance the deployment of scientific research tasks. Effectively link up with the relevant national scientific and technological plans, develop new technologies and innovate new systems and construct new systems with the major technical indicators reaching the advanced international level and continuously improve the ability of independent innovation so as to support the upgrading of national civil space infrastructure and cultivate new needs.

1. The Scientific Research Tasks for Remote Sensing Satellites

To satisfy the application demands and give priority to the research and verification test of remote sensing satellite data processing and application technologies, advance the basic and advanced algorithm for remote sensing satellite data processing and grasp the technologies for satellite platform with long life, high stability, high positioning accuracy, large carrying capacity and strong agility ability, make breakthrough in payload technologies such as high resolution, high accuracy, high reliability and comprehensive detection to improve satellite performance and quantitative application level. Innovate the observation system and fill the technical gaps in high track microwave observation, laser measurement, gravity measurement, interference measurement, ocean salinity detection and high precision atmospheric composition detection.

2. The Scientific Research Tasks for Communication and Broadcasting Satellites

Focus on the needs for new businesses in fixed communication broadcasting, mobile communication and broadcasting and the demands for satellite performance enhancement, develop high power, large capacity and long-life advanced satellite platform technologies and advanced payloads with high power, large antenna, multi-beam and frequency reusable ability. Enhance the performance of satellites and fill the technical gaps in broadband communications and mobile multimedia broadcasting and promote the upgrading of broadband communications and mobile communications technologies. Carry out the research and verification of advanced technologies such as laser communication, quantum communication, satellite information security and anti-jamming.

3. The Development of Space-Ground Integration Technologies

Carry out the development of space-ground integrated technologies, critical techniques in constructing ground system and common application technologies, strengthen the design, simulation and evaluation of the space-ground integrated system and realize the synchronous and coordinated development of the space-ground integrated system so as to improve the application efficiency of the space infrastructure.

VI. Proactively Push Forwards the Major Applications.

The users in various industries and sectors are encouraged to use different constellations, different series of satellites and data resources according to their own business needs and specific application targets, as well as to build a comprehensive application system of satellite applications in their own field to achieve the continuous acquisition and complete application of multi-source information. Actively carry out multi-level, comprehensive application demonstration of remote sensing, communication and navigation in different industries, regions to promote the industrialization, internationalization and scientific and technological development of these satellites system. Strengthen the ability of resource sharing and comprehensive information service in cross-fields, accelerate the integration of Internet of things, cloud computing, massive data and other new technologies and applications so as to promote the sustainable development of satellite application industry and develop and upgrade the application level of new information technology.

1. The Comprehensive Applications for Resources, Environment and Ecological Protection

Target at the major needs for resource exploitation, food security, environmental safety, ecological protection, climate change in implementing China's the marine and global strategies and carry out comprehensive application demonstration in the fields of land, surveying, energy, transportation, marine, environmental protection, meteorology, agriculture, disaster reduction, statistics, water conservancy and forestry, provide timely, accurate and stable space information services for the dynamic monitoring, early warning, evaluation and management of resources and environment so as to support macro decision-making and ensure the strategic security of resources, energy, grain, sea and ecology.

2. The Comprehensive Applications for Disaster Prevention and Mitigation and Emergency Responses

Focus on the needs for disaster prevention and mitigation and emergency response and the major tasks such as monitoring, early warning, emergency response, comprehensive assessment and post-disaster reconstruction of heavy natural disasters, combine the needs in civil affairs, earthquake, meteorology, ocean, energy, transportation, urban infrastructure, water conservancy, agriculture, statistics, land, forestry and environmental protection and carry out the comprehensive applications and demonstrations of typical disaster areas, such as the frequent earthquake disaster area, the geological calamity of the mountainous and cloudy and rainy mountainous areas in Southwest China, the drought and cold tide in North and North China, the disaster of forest and grassland, the frequent area of flood and waterlogging, the urban disaster, the typhoon rainstorm, the red tide, the vast wave in the southeast coast. Promote the establishment of space information service platform for urban and rural regional natural disaster monitoring and evaluation, emergency command information and communication service and comprehensive disaster prevention and reduction. Provide information service of rapid disaster response, business coordination and emergency management based on space-time information and location services.

3. The Comprehensive Applications for Social Administration, Public Services and Production Safety

Focus on the essential demands for safe production and stable operation in the economy and society and the delicacy of social administration, especially the safe operation of municipal public, transportation, energy, communications, agriculture, forestry and water conservancy and the response of public health emergencies, carry out comprehensive application and demonstration and expand the application of space infrastructure in the dynamic monitoring, early warning and fine management of critical targets so as to support the effective promotion of social administration.

4. The Comprehensive Applications for New-Type of Urbanization and Regional Sustainable Development

Target at the administration and social service requirements in urban and rural construction, energy, transportation, civil affairs and environmental protection, carry out the comprehensive application of the new urbanization layout, "smart city", "smart energy", "smart transportation" and "digital disaster reduction". Focus on the sustainable development and universal service needs in the western region and carry out the integrated application of regional satellite. Satisfy the needs of regional ecological environment protection, urbanization, development and utilization of renewable resources, education and medical resources sharing in areas such as Beijing-Tianjin-Hebei region, the Yangtze River Delta and the Pearl River Delta and carry out comprehensive application in different regions and fields.

5. The Comprehensive Applications for Public Information Consumption and Industrialization

In order to promote the mass service, consumption, industrialization and commercialization of space information in China, focus on the multilevel demand of the public to space information, make full use of the technologies and resources of remote sensing, communication and broadcasting and navigation satellites, innovate the business models and excavate, cultivate and develop information consumption application services for mass tourism, location service, communication, culture, health care, education, disaster reduction and statistics. Expand the satellite communication and broadcasting services in the areas with weak ground systems such as the central and western regions and carry out space information applications service in the benefit of local people.

6. The Comprehensive Applications for Global Observation and Earth System Science

To meet the needs of global development and strengthen international cooperation, make full use of relevant international cooperation platforms, as well as promote the application of the virtual satellite constellations and the global exploration plan. Carry out the pilot research, monitoring and application in the areas of climate change, disaster prevention and disaster reduction, human and nature, geophysics, space environment and the carbon cycle. Enhance our independent innovation capability and international influence and contribute to the sustainable development of humanity.

7. The Global Services and Applications

To serve China's "Going out" strategies and "One Belt One Road" strategy, establish the globally integrated information service platform combining the remote sensing satellite, satellite communication and broadcasting, satellite navigation and geographic information capabilities and provide services for global mapping, global ocean observation, global asset management, food security and production monitoring of major agricultural products, environmental monitoring, forestry and mineral resources monitoring, water resources monitoring, logistics management and safety and emergency responses. Through extensive international cooperation, construct the enhancement system of Beidou global wide area, improve Beidou system service performance and enhance Beidou's international competitiveness. Focus on the international applications such as comprehensive disaster reduction, emergency rescue, resource management and intelligent transportation, joint develop space infrastructure application products and services and vigorously expand the international market so as to support the worldwide sharing and service of remote sensing data in the framework of the Earth Observation Organization.

VII. Policy and Measures

1. Improve the Relevant Policy Framework.

Research and formulate the policy for promote the construction, administration, operation and applications of national civil space infrastructure, the policy for national remote sensing data, the policy for the establishment and improvement of the government procurement to purchase commercial remote sensing satellite data and services. Gradually open the civilian remote sensing satellite data with spatial resolution better than 0.5 meters and promote the open sharing and efficient utilization of satellite data. Promote the industrialization policy of live satellite TV. Formulate the policy and standards for Beidou satellite navigation system and its compatible technologies and products. Establish the application mechanisms for civil satellite frequency and orbit resources.

2. Promote The Diversified Investment and Industrialization Application.

The private capital investment is welcome to participate in satellite development and system construction so as to enhance the vitality of development. Support all kinds of enterprises to carry out value-added product development, operation service and industrialization application and popularization of civil space infrastructure and form a benign development pattern of basic public service, diversified professional service and mass consumption service.

3. Increase Financial and Taxation Support.
Integrate the existing policy and make full use of existing funding channels, establish a sustainable and stable financial input mechanism to support the construction of satellite systems, the development and production of scientific research satellite, the research and development of common key technologies, as well as the construction of major common application support platforms so as to support and guide major demonstrations applications of various industries and regions. Encourage financial institutions to innovate financial means and increase credit support for the construction and application of space infrastructure and improve and implement tax support policies to promote innovation.

4. Strengthen the Innovation-Driven Model.
Accelerate the establishment and improvement of technological innovation systems and strengthen the construction of innovative platforms, such as national key laboratories and engineering centers. Improve the original innovation, integration and innovation and the ability to introduce and absorb innovation. To strengthen the innovation of satellite technology and application model for space-ground integration, promote the innovative development of the key components, payloads, application technologies and other key areas and critical links through the national scientific and technological plans. Encourage open competition and enhance self-reliance development capability and promote the rapid application of advanced technologies and products and the deep integration of satellite and business applications to improve the services level. Accelerate the establishment and improvement of the relevant technical standards system in the field of satellite development, terminal equipment, data products and information services.

5. Encourage International Development.
Study and formulate the specific measures for international development and make use of the domestic and foreign resources and markets. Strengthen international coordination and actively participate in the formulation of important rules and standers in relevant international organizations. Actively expand the channels for international cooperation and strengthen international cooperation in technological R & D, satellite development, system construction and data application. Encourage and support the construction of an integrated platform for international cooperation and vigorously promote the exportation of satellites, data and application services so as to enhance the international service capabilities and application benefits.

VIII. Organization and Implementation

1. Clarify Tasks, Duties and Responsibilities.
The Development and Reform Commission, the Ministry of Finance and the State Administration of Science and Technology and Industry for National Defense will work together with the relevant departments and units to study the various tasks and duties in implementing this plan on civil space infrastructure and establish the tasks, duties and responsibilities mechanism in various departments. Organize and coordinate the major elements in the plan implementation, strengthen the binding role of the plan, as well as prevent repetitive planning, investment and construction. The development and Reform Commission and the Ministry of Finance are responsible for the funding channels for satellites and ensuring the implementation of satellite series development. The Ministry of Finance and the State Administration of Science and Technology and Industry for National Defense will organize and optimize the input mechanism of scientific research satellites to ensure the implementation of scientific research tasks. For the remote sensing satellite mainly based on state investment, the Development Reform Commission and the State Administration of Science and Technology and Industry for National Defense will work together with the relevant departments and units to establish the user management committee mainly composed of user representatives to promote the efficient utilization of satellite application by fully absorbing the needs of the relevant users and having them participating in the system demonstration, construction, operation management and efficiency evaluation. The related governmental departments in satellite application are responsible for incorporating the construction and operation of application system into its business development plan with appropriately in-advance deployment.

2. Fix the Investment Entities and Origin.
The Development and Reform Commission, the Ministry of Finance and the State Administration of Science and Technology and Industry for National Defense will work with relevant departments and units to study and implement the corresponding investment entities according to the nature of planning tasks. The investment for construction and operation of scientific research, public welfare satellite and ground system are mainly state fund; the investment for the public welfare and commercial projects will be a combination of state fund and social capital; and the main investment for commercial projects will be social capital. Accelerate the main responsible entities and the legal person for this plan implementation, encourage and support the qualified enterprises to invest and construct the planned satellites and actively promote the enterprise operation of public welfare satellite services.

3. Accelerate the Construction of Projects.

The State Administration of Science and Technology and Industry, in conjunction with the relevant departments, will ensure the effective connection of this plan with the national science and technology major projects in other related plans, expedite project approval for the research and development of the scientific research satellites, strengthen the effectiveness evaluation, as well as carry out the business application in a timely manner. The Development and Reform Commission, in conjunction with the relevant departments, will push forward the task of constructing business-based satellites in the period of "12th Five-Year" and "13th Five-Year", ensure the continuous operation of the backbone business system and give priority to the deployment of application satellites with high operational requirements, mature application technologies. The Development and Reform Commission, in conjunction with the relevant departments, will accelerate coordination of space-ground integration and promote the typical applications and demonstrations of ground systems construction to ensure the coordinated development of business-based satellites and their applications. The Development and Reform Commission and the State Administration of Science and Technology and Industry, in conjunction with the relevant departments, will expedite the completion of the China land observation satellite data center and promote the coordinated operation and data sharing of the land, ocean and meteorological satellite data centers. The Development and Reform Commission, in conjunction with relevant departments, will expedite the overall establishment of common application support platforms and actively promote the construction and development of application systems in various industries.

4. Strengthen Supervision and Evaluation.

The development and Reform Commission, the Ministry of Finance and The State Administration of Science and Technology and Industry will lead the research and establishment of supervision and evaluation mechanism and effectiveness evaluation mechanism for the national civil space infrastructure. They should carry out tracking analysis, supervision, inspection on a regular basis and the third-party assessment of planning implementation and application benefits in due time, as well as study and solve the new situation and new problems in the implementation of this plan, reporting major problems to the State Council in time. In the medium period of this plan implementation, the Development and Reform Commission, the Ministry of Finance and The State Administration of Science and Technology and Industry will deepen the research for the follow-up tasks and further optimize this plan for the following tasks and adjust the construction tasks according to the technical progress, the development needs and the space situation in combination with the evaluation of this plan implementation.

2. OTHER POLICY DOCUMENTS ON SPACE ACTIVITIES

2.4. THE GUIDING OPINIONS ON ACCELERATING THE CONSTRUCTION AND APPLICATION OF THE "ONE BELT ONE ROAD" SPACE INFORMATION CORRIDOR[4]

The State Administration of Science and Technology and Industry for National Defense
National Development and Reform Commission
2016
(Unofficial English translation by WU Xiaodan, assisted by Ms. PENG Xuhan)

To further exploit the advantages of China's space technologies and platforms, promote the marketization and internationalization of the space information industry and effectively promote the "One Belt One Road" initiative, according to the relevant requirements of to promote the "One Belt One Road" construction and the "medium and long-term development plan for national civil space infrastructure (2015-2025)", after deliberation and approval by the leading group of the "One Belt, One Road" construction work, the guiding opinions are put forward as following:

I. The Important Significance

After 60 years of independent development, China has established a relatively complete system of space science, technologies and industry and certain space technologies are among the advanced world ranks. China has initially finished the construction of a complete satellite application system mainly composed of communication, navigation and earth observation satellites. China have signed agreements on space cooperation with more than 30 countries and established a good governmental and business cooperation mechanism with the "One Belt One Road" countries, which has laid a good foundation for promoting the application of space information technologies. However, China's satellite application technologies need to be further improved. It is urgent to make full use of the existing satellites, cultivate leading enterprises of space information services with international market competitiveness, strengthen the ability of Chinese enterprises to 'going out' and enhance the industrialization, marketization and internationalization of space information technology applications.

The "One Belt One Road" space information corridor is mainly based on the communication satellites, navigation satellites and remote sensing satellite resources in orbit, in construction or in planning, appropriately supplemented by the space-based resources and ground information sharing network. The "One Belt One Road" space information corridor will form a four-in-one space information service system of "sense, transmission, knowledge and use", so as to provide space information service

---

4 The original Chinese version of this policy is published on the website of the State Administration of Science and Technology and Industry for National Defense, www.sastind.gov.cn, last accessed August 2021.

capabilities for all countries and regions along the routes of "One Belt One Road" and to achieve information interconnection. Promoting the construction and application of "One Belt One Road" space information corridor is an important task to promote the establishment of the "One Belt One Road" construction work as a powerful starting point for the "One Belt One Road" construction work. The implementation of this corridor is conducive to promote the cooperation between China and the "One Belt One Road" countries in the field of high and new technology, improve the level and quality of industrial cooperation with these countries; promote international cooperation among these countries in disaster prevention and reduction, ecological environmental monitoring and scientific research and provide public products for the "One Belt One Road" construction so as to enhance popular feelings and cultural exchanges and create the image of China being a responsible big country; enhance the international competitiveness of Chinese enterprises in "going out" ; improve the efficiency and technology level of China's space infrastructure utilization, enhancing the internationalization level of the space information industry and the global development of space information technologies, products and services.

II. The General Requirements

1. The Guiding Thoughts
Fully implement the spirits of the 18th National Congress of the CPC and its Second, Third, Fourth and Fifth Plenary Sessions, guide by the spirit of important speeches by President Xi Jinping, promote "One Belt One Road" construction work and the deep military and civil integration, utilize China's space information resources and construct reliable, high-quality and wide space information corridor so as to actively serve the all-round and mutually beneficial cooperation between China and other "One Belt One Road" countries, motivate the "One Belt One Road" construction and promote the marketization and internationalization of China's space information industry.

2. The Basic Principles
(1) Overall Planning with Emphasis
Coordinate the development both at home and abroad and the relationship between construction and application and between technologies and industries. Make full use of the enthusiasm of governmental sectors and local governments, as well as promote the solid cooperation with key countries in priority areas and key projects to form a demonstration-driven effect.

(2) Government Guidance and Market Operation
Make use of the government's role in macro planning, policy support and service guidance. Improve the construction, operation, service and industrialization of space information corridor. Make full use of the decisive role of market in resources

allocation, highlight the dominant position of enterprises, innovate business models and actively promote the development of marketization and internationalization.

(3) Joint Construction and Sharing; Mutual Benefit and Win-Win Result
With an open and inclusive spirit, strengthen the communication and consultation with the "One Belt One Road", ensure linking-up with and results sharing with the relevant national science and technology projects and promote deep cooperation in the construction, operation and application of space information corridor so as to provide space information service support for the economic and social development of the countries along the routes of "One Belt One Road".

(4) Resources Intensivism and Emphasis on Applications
To meet the needs of space information service at home and abroad, make full of the existing and planned space infrastructure and improve the space information systems. Vigorously promote the application of space technologies, strengthen the integration and transformation of technological achievements and enhance the ability to provide space information services.

3. The Overall Goals

Build the "One Belt One Road" space information corridor with complete facilities and efficient services within 10 years, focusing on the Southeast Asia, South Asia, West Asia, Central Asia and North Africa and spanning to Oceania, Central and Eastern Europe and Africa. The space information corridor will become a new highlight of the "One Belt One Road" through construction work between China and all other countries and benefit the economic and social development of the "One Belt One Road" countries. This process will help the marketization and internationalization of China's space information industry to reach the world's advanced level and lay a solid foundation for going out to the whole world.

III. The Main Tasks

1. Upgrading the Space Information Coverage Capability in the "One Belt One Road" Countries.

(1) Accelerate the Construction of China's National Satellite Systems.
Based on China's existing in-orbit satellite resources, accelerate the implementation of major projects regarding the high-resolution earth observation satellite system and the second generation of satellite navigation system, promote the development, launching and application of the national civil space infrastructure satellites, initiate the major projects constructing the ground-space integrated information network, enhance the service support capability of China's autonomous satellite system and laydown the foundation framework of the "One Belt One Road" space information corridor.

(2) Strengthen International Cooperation in the Field of Satellite Systems.

Through the means such as sharing space resources, integration development, data exchange and joint observation, establish a cooperative mechanism of "One Belt One Road" broadband communication satellite network, navigation satellite augmentation system, meteorological satellite and high-resolution satellite joint observation system. Several virtual constellations will be jointly constructed at the platforms of the Asia-Pacific Space Cooperation Organization, the BRICS and other international cooperative organizations, as well as through intergovernmental and inter-enterprise cooperation. Construct an integrated Earth observation system and jointly develop new satellite systems such as mobile, broadband and multi-functional communication satellites and data acquisition satellite constellations so as to form a satellite service system with uniform goal and standards.

(3) Actively Promote the Development of Satellite Systems for Commercial Ends.
Actively promote the procurement of space data and services by the "One Belt One Road" countries' governments and continuously explore new market-driven mechanisms under government guidance. Encourage the commercialized companies to provide market-oriented services to the governments and the public. Support the enterprise-based, market-oriented new development model for commercial space activities, as well as encourage social and international business investment to go into the commercial satellites and test satellites through various cooperation mechanism between government and social capital, such as Public-Private Partnership, so as to improve the space information corridor.

(4) Improve the Ground System and Application Service of Space Information.
Based on the needs for open service and integrated application of space information in the "One belt, one road" countries, further improve the national data centers and application service platforms. Establish a linkage mechanism based on the needs and requirement for space information, ground receiving and application service in the "One Belt One Road" countries and regularly release service guidance on space information. Encourage the use of national public application platforms to serve the "One Belt One Road" countries and jointly construct necessary service facilities. Jointly construct a number of distributed satellite application centers and space information service platforms with "One Belt One Road" countries, so as to improve the operation and service capabilities of space information corridor.

(5) Construct a Sharing Service Network for Space Information.
Encourage the enterprises to participate in the construction and cooperative operation of Beidou satellite navigation augmentation systems, communication satellite telecom ports, remote sensing satellite receiving station networks, distribution service network and regional cloud data centers. Construct multi-level online platforms for space information sharing, exchange and collaboration and provide online image maps and positioning information services with the ability to expand space information services to the public and enterprises.

2. Support and Help China's Enterprises to "Go Out".[5]

(1) Boost the Infrastructure Construction Enterprises to "Go Out".

Focus on the key infrastructure such as railways, water conservancy and hydropower, ports, information and communication, support the major national projects on "One Belt One Road" to carry out development and research on space information applications. Target at the needs for engineering design, construction supervision and operation management and provide space information services such as remote sensing satellite monitoring and evaluation, location information collection and time base and satellite broadband information transmission. Provide timely remote sensing satellite images and real-time navigation information services for the design and construction of highway and railway and the operation management enterprises and support vehicle dispatching and safe operation to improve traffic efficiency. Provide remote sensing satellite information support for the site selection, construction supervision and operation management of water conservancy and hydropower. Based on the pilot application of domestic coastal ports, strengthen cooperation with port construction and operation enterprises along the "One Belt One Road" to enhance the information acquisition, precise positioning and communication transmission capacity of ports and shipment.

(2) Promote the Enterprises and Major Equipment in the Field of Natural Resources to "Go Out".

Support the construction projects of oil, gas and mineral resources and provide space information support and natural resources and ecological environment impact monitoring services for the whole process of resource exploration, mining, transportation and supervision. Support the combination of high-end equipment development and intelligent manufacturing enterprises with satellite communication, navigation and remote sensing technologies and data services. Provide space information services such as remote monitoring, remote diagnosis and product maintenance for the after-sales service of major equipment.

(3) Support the Modern Service Industry to "Go Out".

Provide safe and controllable communication guarantee and unified space-time reference service for the "going out" of financial and insurance enterprises. Make use of the advantages of satellite communication coverage and accurate positioning and large-scale observation, as well as support traditional telecommunications enterprises and Internet enterprises to explore service areas. Encourage the cooperation between strong enterprises with the ability of contracting major infrastructure projects and providing

---

5   The "going out" strategy was first introduced in 2001. This demonstrates the decision of shifting China's focus from welcoming foreign investment into China to diversifying Chinese investment abroad. This is part of its overall more activist foreign policy and is driven by its domestic economic development. The "One Belt One Road" initiative is consistent with the "going out" strategy since they are both focused on overseas outward investment and construction contracts on infrastructure.

space information service enterprises to construct and operate major infrastructure and space information service facilities simultaneously so as to promote joint efforts in exploring the international market.

3. Provide Public Services and Products.
(1) Establish Emergency Service Platforms.
In alliance with the space information corridor, establish a transnational cooperative space information emergency response mechanism and service network, jointly construct with the "One Belt One Road" countries the satellite-ground integrated facilities for the rapid acquisition, analysis and interpretation of space information to provide space information protection for remote sensing image acquisition, emergency communication and navigation and positioning services for regional natural disaster monitoring and various emergency response, as well as promote space information services for public emergencies including international humanitarian relief, disaster early warning, security cooperation and counter-terrorism.
(2) Improve Maritime Space Information Guarantee.
Accelerate the construction of China-ASEAN Satellite Application Information Center depending on the marine environmental monitoring satellites, high-resolution satellites, wind and cloud meteorological satellites, navigation satellites and search and rescue satellite systems. Further expand its service areas and establish a three-dimensional maritime space information service system covering the maritime Silk Road and enhance the capacity of space information services in maritime law enforcement, sea route safety, maritime search and rescue, marine resources exploitation, marine disaster prevention and mitigation and coastal environmental monitoring, etc.
(3) Support the Development of Cooperation along the Cross-Border Rivers.
Promote the implementation of projects such as the Lancang-Mekong River Space Information Exchange and Cooperation Center, promote the use of space information services deriving from the high-resolution satellites, satellite positioning and navigation systems and satellite data acquisition systems. Promote the resources exploitation and informatization management cooperation of cross-border rivers and boundary river with the "One Belt One Road" countries, so as to promote the interconnection of information and the economic, social and ecological cooperation and development.
(4) Support the Enterprises to Carry Out Cooperative Operations in Public Services.
Support the enterprises to cooperate with the "One Belt One Road" countries to provide products and services emergency telecommunications, positioning, resource surveys, environmental ecological monitoring, disaster monitoring and evaluation and space information integrated service platforms and strengthen the production and standardization of public service products so as to improve the public service capacity and social administration level of the "One Belt One Road" countries.

2. OTHER POLICY DOCUMENTS ON SPACE ACTIVITIES

4. Promote the Exportation of Space Information Equipment and Services.
(1) Promote the Exportation of Satellites.
Implement the satellite export program of developing and launching Laos No. 1 communication satellite, Belarusian communication satellite and Pakistan remote sensing satellite. Encourage the enterprises to expand the international market of broadband communication, mobile communication and high-resolution satellites and services and commercial cooperation projects for the construction of microsatellites and constellation to meet the needs of the "One Belt One Road" countries.
(2) Promote the Exportation of Satellite-related Products and Standards.
Support the cooperation with the "One Belt One Road" countries in joint design, collaborative development and operation management of satellite systems and promote the exportation of satellite technological standards, satellite assembly test equipment, key products and components of satellites so as to build up the brand of Chinese satellites.
(3) Encourage the Exportation of Operational Services and Application Systems.
Encourage the enterprises to invest in, construct and operate satellite telecommunication port and satellite receiving and communication processing station network along the "One Belt One Road" route and the exportation of space information products and services including meteorological satellite data broadcasting, marine satellite information service and satellite mapping and geographic information. Strengthen the commercialized services based on the positioning, navigation and timing capability of the Beidou system and support the exportation of mobile communication terminal products for the Beidou system so as to make full use of China's space information technologies for the economic development of the "One Belt One Road" countries.

5. Strengthen the Cooperation in Regional Space Information Industry.
(1) Strengthen the Cooperation in Space Information Industry with the Central Asia, West Asia and North Africa Countries.
Accelerate the construction of high-resolution Earth observation system application demonstration zone, the Beidou navigation application demonstration project and anti-terrorism space information comprehensive service system in Xinjiang Uygur Autonomous Region and further construct a space information service research and development foundation so as to strengthen the cooperation with Central Asian countries. Support the Ningxia Hui Autonomous Region to make full use of the China-Arab cooperation platform and construct a "One Belt One Road" regional data center and cloud-computing platform relying on the Zhongguancun Western Cloud Base so as to promote the cooperation with the Arab countries in space information industry. Strive to construct international space information ports and expand the local space information consumption market and drive the output of China's space information production capacity. Establish a set of unified standards for space information service

system so as to promote the regional co-construction, utilization, opening and public sharing of space information facilities.

(2) Strengthen the Cooperation in Space Information Industry along the 21st Century Maritime Silk Road.

In combination with the local development needs in Fujian Province, strive to establish a marine satellite application research and development base to carry out the research and development of application products for marine ecological environment protection, marine resources development and coastal economic development so as to expand the space information service market of ASEAN and South Asian countries. Promote the construction of and cooperation in China-Malaysia Qinzhou Satellite Application Industrial Park, Pakistan Telecom Port and China-ASEAN Information Port. Support the enterprises to cooperate in the construction of Beidou ground augmentation system and Beidou-based indoor and outdoor positioning service system in ASEAN countries, including Thailand, Laos, Indonesia and Cambodia so as to promote the application of Beidou satellite navigation system in the ASEAN region.

(3) Promote the Space Information Demonstration Services for Aviation Logistics.

Promote the construction of Zhengzhou aviation logistics space information port and the application of satellite navigation, ADS-B and other technologies in aviation logistics. Explore the space information service system for aviation logistics and promote the interconnection and integration of regional aviation logistics services.

(4) Strengthen the Construction of "Space Information +" Industrial Ecosystem.

Combine with the construction of six major economic corridors along the "One Belt One Road" and actively carry out multi-level, comprehensive cooperation in space information industry with the countries along the route. Support the joint construction of demonstration zones for the development and application of space information industry in Southeast Asia, South Asia, Central Asia, West Asia and North Africa, promote the integration of space information with Big Data, the Internet of Things, mobile communications, digital television and cloud computing, construct the "space information +" industrial development ecosystem and expand the smart services of space, for instance, smart cities, smart water conservancy, smart ports, smart logistics and smart power grid.

6. Significantly Improve the Level of Marketization and Internationalization.
(1) Help Making the Big Enterprises for Satellite Operation and Services.
Encourage the social capital to participate in the construction and operation services of space infrastructure with market value, for instance, high-resolution Earth observation satellites, mobile communication satellite constellations and data acquisition satellite constellations. Support the jointly formation of industry alliances between the Chinese satellite operator enterprises and the enterprises of the "One Belt One Road" countries and conduct cooperation in the fields including satellite communications, remote sensing

satellite and satellite navigation so as to help them grow into internationally competitive satellite operation service enterprises.

(2) Help the Space Information Service Enterprises Become Stronger.
Encourage social capital to participate in the construction and operation of space information-based industries and regional cloud data centers, as well as enhance the "one-stop" service capability of space information and expand the development of "space information +" value-added service industry. Help the growth of a group of space information service enterprises to gain strong independent development capabilities and international influence.

(3) Strengthen the Sharing Services of Space Information Products.
Implement the space information application and promotion programs in the ASEAN, South Asia, West Asia and North Africa regions. Expand the depth, breadth and the degree of marketization of the space information services applications in the areas of positioning, communication, culture, medical care, education, food safety, water security and public safety in the "One Belt One Road" countries.

7. Promote the International Cooperation and Exchange in Space Information Technologies.

(1) Jointly Support the Cutting-Edge Research of Space Information.
Establish the open laboratories for space technologies and applications to carry out research on the cutting-edge space information technologies and services. Joint support with the "One Belt One Road" countries to carry out research on major scientific issues relevant to the long-term stable and sustainable development, such as carbon source and carbon sink, land degradation, soil erosion and microscopic characteristics of aerosols. Actively promote the research cooperation on the basis of space information regarding the major issues involving global change, such as El Niño, La Nina, water cycle, ecological change and climate evolution.

(2) Jointly Conduct Scientific and Technological Research in the Field of Comprehensive Earth Observation.
Meet the needs for geo-space information and technologies in the "One Belt One Road" countries, make full use of multilateral and bilateral cooperation mechanisms and jointly conduct comprehensive Earth observation and scientific and technological research on the issues such as ecological environment, water resources, meteorology, transportation, urbanization, mineral resources and energy, geological disasters, protection and utilization of world heritage, satellite mapping and numerical prediction so as to address the challenges in sustainable development, global change and major disasters.

(3) Strengthen the Multi-level Communication and Exchange.
Encourage the relevant societies, industry associations and industry alliances to regularly organize training and technical exchange activities on space information technologies and applications to connect supply and demand. Encourage the communication and

cooperation in various forms to promote human resources exchanges in satellite applications and related fields.

IV. Organization and Safeguarding Measures

1. Strengthen the Organization and Coordination.
All regions, relevant departments and enterprises should regard the promotion of cooperation and popularization in space information technologies and applications as an important task in promoting the construction of "One Belt One Road" and emphasize on the implementation of responsibilities division according to their functions. The State Administration of Science and Technology and Industry for National Defense and the National Space Agency, in conjunction with relevant departments, will formulate the implementation plans for the construction and application of "One Belt One Road" space information corridor and organize their implementation. The Development and Reform Commission and the State Administration of Science and Technology and Industry for National Defense will strengthen their coordination in guidance, supervision and inspection, summarize the work progress at the end of each year and put forward the next year's work plan, which will be submitted to the leading group for construction work of the "One Belt One Road" for approval.

2. Improve the Publicity and Promotion Abroad.
Pay more attention to the cooperation, application and promotion of space information technologies in the exchange activities such as diplomacy, economy and trade, humanities and climate change with an emphasis on the new development achievements of Chinese space information technologies. In accordance with China's unified foreign aid policy and the urgent needs of relevant countries, support foreign aid through the utilization of China's space technologies, products and the provision of access to space information. Promote the implementation of relevant projects through bilateral and multilateral space cooperation mechanisms. Make full use of the constructive role of the existing foreign exchange platforms and fully demonstrate China's space information technologies and products through international forums and exhibitions. Mobilize the enthusiasm of relevant associations, societies, chambers of commerce and industry alliances and carry out the all-round, multi-level publicity and promotion work.

3. Improve Policies and Other Measures.
The construction and application of space information corridor construction shall be incorporated into the construction plans of the "One Belt One Road" formulated by different departments, such as for cooperation with certain country and in the

2. OTHER POLICY DOCUMENTS ON SPACE ACTIVITIES

establishment of economic corridors, economic and trade cooperation zones. Actively assist the aid recipient countries in improving their space information infrastructure and promoting the implementation of foreign aid projects using China's space information technologies and products. Strengthen the planning, coordination and guidance in the utilization of satellite frequency and orbit spots. Study on how to lower the industrial threshold and export restrictions for satellite systems, ground systems and related equipment and services (production, operation services, etc.). Study and explore the feasibility of establishing civilian satellite launch sites and encourage social capital to participate in the construction and operation of the "One Belt One Road" space information corridor. Accelerate the implementation of the medium and long-term development plan of the national civil space infrastructure and the construction of China's second-generation satellite navigation system and high-resolution Earth observation system to ensure the space infrastructure support for the construction of the "One Belt One Road" space information corridor. Accelerate the introduction of national policies on civil remote sensing satellite data to encourage and increase procurement of remote sensing data.

4. Increase Financial Support.
Encourage and guide social capital to participate in the construction and application of the "One Belt One Road" space information corridor. The special funds related to the central and local governments shall, in accordance with the relevant policies and regulations, support the construction of the "One Belt One Road" space information corridor construction project that meets the requirements. The Silk Road Fund, China-ASEAN Maritime Cooperation Fund, China-Central and Eastern Europe Investment Cooperation Fund, China-Eurasia Economic Cooperation Fund and other financial platforms must study and participate in the investment space information corridor construction application project within the scope of the prescribed business. Development, policy and commercial financial institutions such as the China Development Bank, China Exim Bank and Export Credit Insurance Corporation should actively provide financial services to relevant construction and application enterprises under the conditions of compliance with regulations and risks. The study encourages social capital to adopt a market-oriented approach to lead the establishment of the "One Belt One Road" space information corridor construction application fund.

5. Strengthen Human Resources Training and Education.
Encourage relevant departments to use the national foreign aid training program and apply for relevant subject training. Moreover, support relevant departments and units to use their own funds to carry out training activities independently and cultivate national space information application and service talents in countries along the "One Belt One Road". Through the United Nations-affiliated Asia-Pacific Regional Center for

Space Science and Technology Education and the Asia-Pacific Space Cooperation Organization (APSCO) Education and Training Center, provide the online and offline space information technology and application training. Focus on cultivating China's compound talents with international vision, knowledge of space information technology and familiar with national conditions along the routes.

3. Policy Documents Applicable to Space Activities

Some policy documents are partially concerning programs and policies for space activities. The relevant parts are as follows:

3.1. White Paper on China's National Defense[1]

Information Office of State Council
2010

[...]
Section X. Arms Controls and Disarmament
China attaches importance to and takes an active part in international efforts in the field of arms control, disarmament and non-proliferation. It adheres to the complete fulfillment of its role in this regard within the UN framework and that of other related international organizations and multilateral mechanisms. The existing multilateral arms control, disarmament and non-proliferation systems should be consolidated and strengthened and the legitimate and reasonable security concerns of all countries should be respected and accommodated so as to maintain the global strategic balance and stability.
[...].
(4) Prevention of an Arms Race in Outer Space
The Chinese government has consistently advocated the peaceful use of outer space, and opposes weaponization of and an arms race in outer space. China believes that the best approach for the international community to prevent weaponization of and an arms race in outer space is to negotiate and conclude an international legally-binding instrument. In February 2008, China and Russia jointly submitted to the Conference on Disarmament (CD) a draft Treaty on the Prevention of the Placement of Weapons in Outer Space and the Threat or Use of Force against Outer Space Objects (PPWT). In August 2009, China and Russia jointly submitted their working paper responding to the questions and comments raised by the CD members regarding the draft treaty. China is looking forward to starting negotiations on this draft treaty at the earliest possible date, hopefully to conclude a new outer space treaty.
[...]

---

1 The English version of this policy is published on the website of Information Office, State Council, www.scio.gov.cn, last accessed August 2021.

3.2. White Paper on China's Military Strategy[2]

Information Office of State Council
2015
[…].
Section IV. The Building and Development of China's Armed Forces
[…]
(2) The Arm Force Development in Critical Security Domains
[…]
Outer space has become a commanding height in international strategic competition. Some countries are developing their space forces and instruments and the first sighs of weaponization of outer space have appeared. China has all along advocated the peaceful use of outer space, opposed the weaponization of and arms race in outer space and taken an active part in international cooperation. China will keep abreast of the dynamics of outer space, deal with security threats and challenges in that domain, secure its space assets to serve its national economic and social development and maintain outer space security.
[…]

3.3. Made in China 2025[3]

State Council
2015
(Unofficial English translation by WU Xiaodan)

Preamble
[…]
China's manufacturing sector is large but not strong and there is obvious gaps in innovation capacity, efficiency of resource utilization, quality of industrial infrastructure and degree of digitalization. The task of upgrading and accelerating technological development is urgent.
[…]

Section III. The Strategic Missions and Emphases
[…]

---

2   The English version of this policy is published on the website of the Information Office, State Council, www.scio.gov.cn, last accessed August 2021.
3   The Chinese version of this policy is published on the website of the State Council, www.gov.cn, last accessed August 2021.

(6) Promoting the Breakthrough Development in the Key Fields
[...]
iii. The Equipment for Aviation and Space Activities
[...]
Develop new generation, heavy-lift launch vehicles to improve space access capacity. Accelerate the construction of space infrastructure for civil purposes and develop space platforms and payloads to obtain space information service capability with stable, sustainable remote sensing, communication and navigation satellites. Carry out the projects of manned flights, lunar exploration and deep space exploration. Promote the transformation and application of space technologies.
[...]

3.4. National 13th Five-Year Plan for the Scientific and Technological Innovation[4]

State Council
2016
(Unofficial English translation by WU Xiaodan)

This plan is formulate to clarify the general principle, development goals, major tasks and safeguarding measures and is the guidance for the overall planning of national major projects in scientific and technological innovation and for our national advancement towards a innovative country.
[...]

Chapter IV. The National Major Specialized Projects of Science and Technologies That Affect the Overall and Long-Term Development

The national major specialized projects are the important grasp to reflect national strategic goals, integrate science and technology resource and achieve leapfrog development in key fields and areas. During the period of 13th Five-Year Plan, another series of national major specialized projects of science and technologies will be funded to reflect national strategic intention, explore the new nationwide mechanism for scientific and technological innovation under the condition of socialist market economy, improve the organizational model for national major specialized projects, seize the commanding heights of future competition in strategic fields, open up new directions for industrial development, cultivate new economic growth point, promote the leapfrog development

---
[4] The Chinese version of this policy is published on the website of the State Council, www.gov.cn, last accessed August 2021.

of productivity and provide powerful support to enhance comprehensive competitiveness and safeguard national security.

I. Thoroughly Implement the Current National Major Specialized Projects.
Among the 14 listed national major specialized projects in various fields and areas, such as software products, manufacturing equipment for large-scale integrated circuit, exploration and development of large oil and gas fields, water pollution control and treatment, breeding new varieties through transgenic methods, AIDS, hepatitis and other major infectious disease control and prevention, two of them are in the space activities arena:

1. High-Resolution Earth Observation System: complete the construction of space- and airspace based Earth observation system, ground system, application system and the construction of land, atmospheric and oceanic observation system.

2. Manned Flights and Lunar Exploration: launch new-type heavy-lift carriers, spacelab of Tiangong II and test core module of space station, manned spacecraft and cargo spacecraft; grasp the technologies for cargo transportation and middle- and long-term stay of astronauts to lay down the foundation for the completion of low-Earth orbit space station. Make breakthrough development in the key technologies of moon arrival, high-rate of data communication, high precision of navigation and positioning and exploitation of lunar resources. Break through the technologies for automatic return of extraterrestrial bodies and develop the technologies for lunar sample return to achieve soft landing in certain lunar area and sample return.

II. Initiative New National Major Specialized Projects.
Among the 15 listed national major specialized projects in various fields and areas, such as aircraft engine, deep ocean station, quantum communication and quantum computers, brain science, national security in Internet space, high efficient and clean utilization of coal resource, big data and artificial intelligence, two of them are space-related:

1. Deep Space Exploration and in-orbit Service and Maintenance System for Spacecraft. Make breakthrough development of in-orbit service and maintenance technologies and improve the utilization efficiency of space assets to ensure safe and reliable operation of spacecraft.

2. Space-Earth Integrated Information Network. Promote the comprehensive integration of space-based information network, Future Internet and mobile

communication network to form globe covering, space-Earth integrated information network.
[…]

Chapter VII. Develop the Technology System to Safeguard National Security and Strategic Interest

Strengthen the breakthrough development of key technologies in exploring and utilizing the oceans, outer space and polar region and improve the exploration and utilization capability for strategic space to provide technological support for promoting the utilization of common humankind resources and safeguarding national security.

II. Develop Outer Space Exploration and Utilization Technologies.

Develop new generation technologies to explore and utilize outer space, improve satellite and payload capacity and strengthen the comprehensive servicing and support role of outer space technologies for national security and defense, social and economic development and the layout of global strategic power. Strengthen the research on new space science and technologies for outer space exploration activities. Comprehensively promote technological capacity for outer space transportation and research on new-generation outer space transportation technologies.

1. A Series of Space Science Satellites

Carry out research on the frontiers of basis science based on the series of space science satellites and make major scientific discoveries and breakthroughs in dark matter, the completion of quantum mechanics, space physics, black holes, microgravity science and space life science based on the already launched satellites of dark mater particle explorers. Develop and launch around 2020 the satellites of solar wind magnetospheric interaction panoramic image, Einstein probe, global water cycling observation and advance space-based solar observatory to provide foundation for original innovation results and to guide and lead cutting-edge technological development in the fields of Earth space coupling law, gravitational wave electromagnetic counterpart detection, global change and water cycling and the relationship between the solar magnetosphere and explosive activity.

2. Deep Space Exploration

Focus on the major scientific issues such as the origin and evolution of the solar system and earth-moon system, the impact of asteroids and solar activities on the earth and search for extraterrestrial life information, aim at improving China's deep space exploration and scientific research capabilities and strive to obtain original scientific achievement. Launch Chang'e 4 in 2018 and land rover on the far side of the Moon for the first time in world history. Complete the thorough demonstration of and acquire key technologies for deep space exploration projects for asteroids, Jovian system and follow-up Lunar Exploration around 2020.

3. First Mission of Mars Exploration

Focus on the scientific issues such as research on Mars environment and geology and exploring life information, adopt the development approach of first step orbiting, landing and roving and second step being sample return, launch first Mars probe in 2020, make breakthrough development in Mars orbiting, landing and roving technologies, carry out international and comprehensive scientific exploration mission, complete first Mars mission with high starting point and achieve breakthrough capabilities in moon-beyond deep space exploration.

4. Earth Observation and Navigation

Make breakthroughs in key technologies such as the acquisition of accurate and refine information, the application of quantitative remote sensing and the generic technologies of complex system integration, carry out research on forward-looking technologies and theories in earth observation and navigation and research on generic key technologies and application demonstration so as to lay down the foundation for constructing a comprehensive, accurate, self-reliant and controllable technology system of earth observation and navigation information application.

5. New Types of Spacecraft

Make breakthroughs in key technologies such as distributed reconfigurable elastic space system and technology system, distributed reconfigurable spacecraft collaborative measurement and control and energy transfer, strengthen the research and development of technologies such as super performance spacecraft platform, repairable and reusable satellite and space robots and focus on the construction of new generation space system and promote intelligent, high-quality satellite platforms. Promote the strategic transformation of China's space systems and the development of new space exploration mechanism, frontier theories of space technologies and self-reliant key technologies.

6. Heavy-lift Carrier Rockets

Focus on the large-scale space programs and mission such as deep space exploration and manned lunar landing and develop low-Earth orbit, heavy-lift carrier rockets with capacity of 100 ton. Make breakthrough in key technologies such as rocket structure with large diameter being 10 meters and heavy-lift rocket engines.

[...]

3.5. National 13ᵀᴴ Five-Year Plan for the Development of Strategic Emerging Industries

State Council
2016
(Unofficial English translation by WU Xiaodan)

Preamble
The aim and purpose of this national plan is directing and supporting the development of strategic emerging industries during the 13th five-year period (2016-2020), including space industry, further optimizing national industrial structures and increase the industrial added value of strategic emerging industries from 8 percent in 2015 to 15 percent by 2020 of China's GDP. The supporting measures to ensure policies implementation are improving management mechanisms, building industrial creative systems, strengthening protection and use of the intellectual property and increasing financial tax policies support.
[…]

Section VII. The Layout of Strategic Industries and Cultivating Their New Advantages for Future Development

(1) The Aviation, Outer Space and Ocean Industry
Significantly enhance the capability for access and exit of outer space. Make breakthrough development in the key technologies of high thrust engine and design, manufacturing and operation of large diameter launch vehicles. Develop heavy-lift launch vehicles to guarantee the implementation of major space missions. Develop fast-ready, cheap and re-useable earth orbit transportation system for small payloads.
Accelerate the development of new-type space vehicles. Strengthen the development of key technologies in ultrahigh resolution; ultrahigh precision spatiotemporal reference; ultrahigh speed secure communication; high performance on-board processing; high power supply; new type materials. Develop new type of satellites. Establish advanced outer space scientific experiment platform with life support system. Develop lightweight and miniaturization technologies and materials for spacecraft and promote the standard and orderly development of microsatellites, nano-satellites and pico-satellites. Develop and launch new type of experiment satellites. Accelerate the development of new type of spacecraft including near-space craft and reusable spacecraft.
[…]

---

5   The Chinese version of this policy is published on the website of the State Council, www.gov.cn, last accessed August 2021.

3.6. National 13ᵗʰ Five-Year Plan for Satellite Surveying and Mapping[6]

National Administration of Surveying, Mapping and Geographic Information, Ministry of Natural Resources
2016
(Unofficial English translation by WU Xiaodan, assisted by Ms. WU Tong)

Preamble
Satellite surveying and mapping is important means of obtaining geographic information and providing geographic information services based on various surveying and mapping satellites. The capability and application level of satellite surveying and mapping is a direct reflection of a country's ability to observe the earth. Strengthening the capacity building of satellite surveying and mapping and improving the application level of satellite surveying and mapping are of great significance to seize the commanding height of earth observation and meet the urgent demand of economic and social development for geographic information technology and application. At present, there is rapid development of satellite surveying and mapping around the world, the continuous improvement of satellite performance, the qualitative leap in positioning of space time and spectral resolution, the constant upgrading and innovation of application level and business model and the obvious trend of deep integration with technologies such as big data and cloud computing. In recent years, China's satellite surveying and mapping has made great progress, i.e., significant improvement of satellite performance and remarkable result of satellite application, and the gap with the international advance level has been narrowing. However, there are problems in satellite surveying and mapping, such as insufficient overall application system capability, imperfect system standards, limited in the depth and scope of application and slow industrialization and internationalization process.
[…]
I. Overall Plan
[…]
3. Development Goals
Focus on the domestic high-resolution remote-sensing satellite for surveying and mapping and the Beidou satellite system, promote the development of relevant commercial remote-sensing satellites and vigorously strengthen satellite surveying and mapping capabilities. Construct a self-reliant surveying and mapping and Earth observation system with multi-type and multi-model satellites of 1:50,000 and 1:10,000 measuring scale, form a three-dimensional mapping capability with a resolution of 0.7

---

[6] The Chinese version of this policy is published at the website of the Ministry of Natural Resources, www.mnr.gov.cn, last accessed August 2021.

meter to 2 meter and uplift the self-sufficient rate of high-resolution remote sensing images to 80%. Establish satellite mapping and surveying system of technologies, product and standards integrating the overall design, simulation and verification, the data processing service and quality control of surveying and mapping satellites. Promote the development of commercial remote-sensing satellites and satellite surveying and mapping capability and develop the capability for production and application of geographic information products with multiple resolutions and scales so as to support the development of the geographic information industry.

II. Main Tasks

Based on the actual needs of developing surveying, mapping and geographic information, push forward in an all-around way, guarantee key points and make a reasonable industrial layout. Focus on the series of optical, radar, laser, gravitational and navigational surveying and mapping satellites and carry out top-level design and overall planning for the construction and application of technology innovation and application promotion system. Establish the policy and standard system of satellite surveying and mapping and the technology, product and service system of Earth observation.

1. Improve the Policy and Standard System of Satellite Surveying and Mapping.

(1) Strengthen the Policy Formulation for Satellite Surveying and Mapping Application.

According to the types and application scope of satellite surveying and mapping data, establish a service mechanism for the use and distribution of satellite surveying and mapping data and study and adopt the measures for protection and administration of intellectual property rights of satellite surveying and mapping data. In conjunction with relevant government departments, establish a mechanism for the secure application and classification evaluation of satellite surveying and mapping data suitable for the public and overseas users and improve market supervision and administration capabilities. Further optimize the policy environment for the business model, commercial service and internationalization of China's civil remote sensing satellite surveying and mapping data.

(2) Improve Civil-Military Integration Development Mechanism for Satellite Surveying and Mapping.

Thoroughly implement the Guidelines on the Integrated Development of Economic Development and National Defense promulgated by the State Council and Central Military Commission, form a civil-military integration development mechanism of satellite surveying and mapping and gradually establish a civil-military integration and coordination framework of satellite surveying and mapping that is compatible in peacetime and wartime with due consideration to the mutual benefit of military and civil needs. Strengthen the source sharing and coordinated scientific and technological innovation of satellite surveying and mapping. Establish a coordination mechanism to ensure satellite surveying and mapping support for emergency, a coordination mechanism for national major specialized projects with regard to satellite surveying and mapping and a sharing mechanism for transformation and sharing of dual-use scientific and technological innovation results.

(3) Strengthen the Establishment of a Standard System for Satellite Surveying and Mapping Application.

Gradually establish and improve a series of standards and specifications for the data processing of various remote sensing satellites, the supervision and inspection of production quality, product distribution services and formulate technical standards for value-added product, such as theme-specific application, information acquisition and change detection. Formulate standardized procedure and specifications for data acquisition and technical service of surveying and mapping and remote sensing satellites. Incorporate the establishment of the Beidou application standards system into the standardization plan for satellite surveying and mapping, study and establish the standards system framework of Beidou application and promote the formulation and revision of generic and basic standards in the urgent need of operation.

2. Construct Satellite Surveying and Mapping and Earth Observation System.

(1) Construct Surveying and Mapping Satellite Constellation with a Resolution of 0.7 Meter to 2 Meter.

Based on the needs of geographic information industry, accelerate the development of 1:50,000 and 1:10,000 optical stereoscopic surveying and mapping satellites and realize their long-term, stable operation in orbit. Accelerate the implementation of Gaofen-7 satellite project so as to achieve a global topographic surveying and mapping capability of 1:10,000. Actively promote the project approval of the operational satellites of Ziyuan 3 and Gaofen 7 so to provide stable satellite data sources for 1:50,000 and 1:10,000 surveying and mapping in China.

(2) Develop Interferometry Radar Satellites.

In accordance with the relevant national plans for space infrastructure, accelerate the application research of L-band differential interferometric SAR (L-SAR) satellite surveying and mapping so as to realize the interferometry of the image acquisition from domestic satellites for cloudy and rainy areas and support global 1:50,000 digital elevation model date acquisition and regional surface deformation monitoring.

(3) Construct Other Types of Surveying and Mapping Satellites.

Accelerate the construction of surveying and mapping satellites, such as ultra-high-resolution optical satellites, laser altimetry satellites and gravity gradiometry survey satellite to improve the accuracy of satellite altimetry and global gravity field model. Actively promote the construction of a commercial remote sensing satellite system composed of self-reliant high-resolution optical satellites and high-end optical satellites.

Accelerate the construction of satellite surveying and mapping system for Earth observation with a full range of functions and complementary scales and gradually develop a comprehensive and efficient global observation date acquisition capability with a reasonable combination of various observation technologies including optics, radar, laser and gravity.
[...]

3.7. Guidelines on Deepening Civil-Military Integration in Science and Technology and Industry for National Defense[7]

General Office of State Council
2017
(Unofficial English translation by WU Xiaodan)

Preamble

The science and technology and industry for national defense are a key area and an important component part of implementing the national strategy of civil-military integration, which is of great significance to promote the level of advanced science and technology and industry for national defense with Chinese characteristics, support the construction of national defense forces, promote scientific and technological progress and serve economic and social development. The current and future period is a period of strategic opportunity for civil-military integration, also a critical period for the transition from initial integration to deep integration and realizing leapfrog development. There is huge potential for civil-military integration in science and technology and industry for national defense. With the approval of the State Council, the guidelines are as following to promote the deep development of civil-military integration in science and technology and industry for national defense:
[...]

V. Safeguard Development in Key Areas

19. Strengthen Overall Planning in Space Activities.

Accelerate the overall construction of space infrastructure in response to military and civilian needs. Accelerate the demonstration and implementation of a number of major projects and programs for civil-military integration, including heavy-lift carrier rockets, nuclear power source and equipment for space activities, deep space exploration and in-orbit servicing and maintenance system for space vehicles. Take remote sensing satellite as a breakthrough and formulate national policy on remote sensing data to promote

---

[7] The Chinese version of this policy is published on the website of the State Council, www.gov.cn, last accessed August 2021.

satellite resources and satellite data sharing between the military and civil. Explore and study the construction of open and shared space launching sites and track and control system for space activities.
[...]
VI. Promote Military Industry Serving the National Economic Development
[...]
26. Expand Military Trade and International Cooperation.
Make full use of the role of the National Space Administration as a platform for international cooperation and deepen cooperation in the field of space activities.
[...]
VIII. Improve the Legal and Policy System.

29. Reinforce Law and Regulation.
Strengthen laws and regulations on science and technology and industry for national defense, accelerate the adoption of the Law on Atomic Energy and actively promote the space legislation. Improve the relevant regelation, policies and rules, constantly improve the regulatory mechanism for civil-military integration and further guide and standardize the development of civil-military integration in science and technology and industry for national defense.
[...]

3.8. WHITE PAPERS ON CHINA'S NATIONAL DEFENSE[8]

Information Office of State Council
2019

[...]
Section III. Fulfilling the Missions and Tasks of China's Armed Forces
[...]
(4) Safeguarding National Interests in Major Security Fields
[...]
Outer space is a critical domain in international strategic competition. Outer space security provides strategic assurance for national and social development. In the interest of the peaceful use of outer space, China actively participates in international space cooperation, develops relevant technologies and capabilities, advances holistic management of space information resources, strengthens space situation awareness,

---

8   The English version of this policy is published on the website of the Information Office, State Council, www.scio.gov.cn, last accessed August 2021.

safeguards space assets and enhances the capacity to safely enter, exit and use of outer space.
[...]

3.9. White Paper on China's International Development Cooperation in the New Era[9]

Information Office of State Council
2021

Preface
[...]
China entered a new era after the 18th National Congress of the Communist Party of China (CPC) in 2012. President Xi Jinping has considered China's responsibilities from a global perspective, and proposed the vision of a global community of shared future and the Belt and Road Initiative. China is committed to pursuing the greater good and shared interests, and upholding the principles of sincerity, real results, affinity, and good faith for developing relations with other developing countries and the principles of amity, sincerity, mutual benefit, and inclusiveness for expanding relations with neighboring countries. To this end, President Xi has taken advantage of many major international occasions to announce a broad range of cooperation measures. This presents China's approach, offer its vision, and contribute its strength to resolving global development issues and implementing the United Nations 2030 Agenda for Sustainable Development. In response to the call of the times, China has been upgrading its foreign assistance to a model of international development cooperation, taking on new initiatives and achieving greater results in this new era.

I. International Development Cooperation in the New Era and a Global Community of Shared Future
[...]
2. China's Approaches to Development Cooperation
Based on its experience in international development cooperation since the 18th CPC National Congress, China has formed distinctive approaches in keeping with the new era while maintaining its fine traditions, as elaborated below.
- Promoting a global community of shared future is the mission of China's international development cooperation. Humanity shares a common stake in development, and world stability and prosperity cannot be achieved unless

---
9 The English version of this policy is published on the website of the Information Office, State Council, www.scio.gov.cn, last accessed August 2021.

developing countries can progress. By helping other developing countries reduce poverty and improve their people's lives, China works together with them to narrow the North-South gap, eliminate the deficit in development, establish a new model of international relations based on mutual respect, equity, justice and win-win cooperation, and build an open, inclusive, clean and beautiful world that enjoys lasting peace, universal security and common prosperity.

- Pursuing the greater good and shared interests, with higher priority given to the former, is the underlying guideline. This represents one of China's cultural traditions and embodies its belief in internationalism. Under this guideline, China strives to make the cake of prosperity bigger, and hopes developing countries will advance faster to share the opportunities and benefits offered by open development. Observing the principle of mutual benefit for win-win outcomes, it offers as much assistance as it can while taking into consideration of the interests and needs of other developing countries.
- South-South cooperation is the focus. In spite of China's tremendous achievements, two realities have not changed: China is in the primary stage of socialism and will remain so for a long time to come, and China is still the world's largest developing economy. China's development cooperation is a form of mutual assistance between developing countries. It falls into the category of South-South cooperation and therefore is essentially different from North-South cooperation. China is a staunch supporter, active participant and key contributor of South-South cooperation. It will continue to shoulder the international responsibilities commensurate with its development level and capacity, and further expand South-South cooperation, so as to promote joint efforts for common development.
- Belt and Road cooperation is a major platform. The Silk Road Economic Belt and the 21st Century Maritime Silk Road are significant public goods China offers to the whole world and a major platform for international development cooperation. China has joined hands with other countries to promote policy, infrastructure, trade, financial and people-to-people connectivity, to build the Belt and Road into a path towards peace, prosperity, opening up, innovation, green development, cultural exchanges, and clean government.
- Helping other developing countries to pursue the UN 2030 Agenda for Sustainable Development is a key goal. The 2030 Agenda is a guiding blueprint for development cooperation around the world and has a lot in common with the Belt and Road Initiative. The international community has made initial progress in achieving the agenda's goals in recent years, but global development remains unbalanced and inadequate. The Covid-19 pandemic has posed a serious threat to the 2030 Agenda, making it a tough task to achieve its goals in all countries and for all people as scheduled. Through international cooperation on improving development capacity and optimizing development partnerships, China has helped other developing

countries mitigate the impact of the pandemic, so as to accelerate action for the 2030 Agenda and achieve common prosperity.
[...]

VI. Supporting the Endogenous Growth of Developing Countries.

Guided by the conviction that "it is more helpful to teach people how to fish than to just give them fish", China aims to help developing countries to enhance their capacity for independent development. It has increased targeted assistance for this purpose through human resources development and technical cooperation, in new forms and with new measures, to share its experience and approach with other developing countries, help them improve their capacity for governance, planning, and economic development, and train technical professionals and capable personnel in governance.
[...]

2. Promoting Technological Progress.

Science and technology are the primary productive forces. China has strengthened technology transfer and application to help other developing countries improve their capacity for technological innovation and their workers' industrial and vocational skills.
- Sharing technological achievements. China has shared its achievements in science and technology with other developing countries, and opened training programs on space and satellite applications, 3D printing technology, metering technology, and marine biotechnology.

4. REGULATORY RULES ON SPACE ACTIVITIES

4.1. LAW ON NATIONAL SECURITY[1]

Standing Committee of the National People's Congress

1st July 2015
(Unofficial Translation by WU Xiaodan)

Article 2
National security means a status in which the regime, sovereignty, unity, territorial integrity, welfare of people, sustainable and healthy development of economy and society and other major interest are relatively secure, free from internal and external threats and the capacity to maintain a sustained security status.

[…]

Article 32
The State shall adhere to the peaceful exploration and utilization of outer space, international seabed areas and polar regions, enhance the capability for safe access and exit, scientific investigation, development and exploitation, strengthen international cooperation and maintain the security of activities, assets and other interests in outer space, international seabed areas and polar regions.

4.2. LAW ON NATIONAL DEFENSE[2]

National People's Congress
Adopted on 14th March 1997 and Revised on 26th December 2020
(Unofficial Translation by WU Xiaodan)

Article 2
This law shall apply to military activities conducted by the State to prepare against and resist aggression, prevent armed subversion and secession, safeguard the sovereignty,

---

1 The Chinese version of this law is published on the website of the National People's Congress, www.npc.gov.cn, last accessed August 2021.
2 The Chinese version of this law is published on the website of the National People's Congress, www.npc.gov.cn, last accessed August 2021.

unity, territorial integrity, security and development interest of the state, as well as military-related activities in political, economic, diplomatic, scientific, technological, educational and other fields.

[…]

Article 30

The territorial land, territorial waters and territorial airspace of the People's Republic of China are sacred and inviolable. The State shall build fortified and stable modern border defense, maritime defense and air defense, and take effective defense and administration measures to defend the security of the territorial land, territorial waters and territorial airspace and safeguard the maritime rights and interests of the State.

The State shall take necessary measures to maintain the security of activities, assets and other interest in other major security fields, including outer space, electromagnetic space and cyberspace.

4.3. MEASURES FOR THE ADMINISTRATION OF REGISTRATION OF OBJECTS LAUNCHED INTO OUTER SPACE[3]

Commission of Science and Technology and Industry for National Defense
Ministry of Foreign Affairs
8th February 2001
(Unofficial Translation)

Article 1

These Measures are formulated for the purpose of strengthening the administration of outer space activities, establishing national registry of space objects, protecting the legitimate interests of China as a launching State of space objects and effectively fulfilling the obligations of a contracting State of the Convention on Registration of Objects Launched into Outer Space.

Article 2

For the purpose of these Measures, the term "space object" refers to an artificial satellite, crewed spacecraft, space probe, space station, launch vehicle and parts of thereof and other human-made objects launched into outer space. The sounding rocket and ballistic missile that temporarily crosses outer space shall not be regarded as a "space object."

---

[3] The Chinese version of this regulatory document is published on the website of the State Administration of Science and Technology and Industry for National Defense, www.sastind.gov.cn, last accessed August 2021. This is the unofficial translation version provided by the Faculty of International Law, China University of Political Science and Law, Journal of Space Law, Vol. 33(2), 2007, pp. 437-440.

Article 3
These Measures shall apply to all the space objects launched in the territory of China and the space objects jointly launched abroad by China and other States. The term "launching State" means a State that launches or procures the launching of a space object and a State from whose territory or facility a space object is launched.

Article 4
China carries out the system of registering space objects. All government departments, juridical persons, other organizations and natural persons which launch or procure the launching of a space object shall have the obligation to register the space object in accordance with these Measures.

Article 5
The Commission of Science Technology and Industry for National Defense (Hereinafter referred to as the COSTIND) shall take charge of the administration of national registration of space objects and the Department of International Cooperation shall be responsible for the routine work. For the national registration involving other joint launching States, the COSTIND, if necessary, after consultation with the Ministry of Foreign Affairs, determines which one of them shall register the space object.

Article 6
China establishes and maintains a National Register. The information in the National Register shall mainly include: registration number, registrant, owner of the space object, an appropriate designator of the space object, basic characters of the space object, launching enterprise of the space object, name of the launch vehicle, date and territory or location of launch, basic orbital parameters of the space object and the status of the launching and orbiting of the space object. See Annex: Form of National Registration of Space Objects.

Article 7
Subject to the provisions of Article VIII of these Measures, the owner of a space object shall register the space object in the national register. Where there are more than one owners of a space object, the main owner shall register the space object on behalf of all the owners.

The launching enterprise of a space object shall provide necessary assistance in the national registration of such a space object.

Article 8
Where a space object launched from the territory of China is owned by the government, juridical persons, organizations or natural persons of a State other than China, the corporation that provides the international launching service of the space object shall register it at national registry.

Article 9
The registrant of a space object referred in Article 7 and Article 8 shall furnish registration information to the COSTIND and complete the registration formalities within sixty days in accordance with Article 6 after the space object has entered the space orbit. When major changes (e.g. change of orbit, break up, cease working or reentry into atmosphere) of the conditions of the space object registered in accordance with these Measures occur, the registrant of the space object shall amend the information of the registration within sixty days after the conditions of the space object have changed.

Article 10
The National Register specifically includes sections for Hong Kong and Macau. The specific measures for the registration of space objects that owned or launched by Hong Kong Special Administrative Region and Macau Special Administrative Region shall be instituted separately.

Article 11
The COSTIND shall maintain the National Register. With the permission of the COSTIND, the relevant government departments and juridical persons, other organizations and natural persons under the authorization of the competent governmental departments may apply to the keeper of the National Register for access to the information in this Register.

Article 12
A space object shall be registered internationally in accordance with the Registration Convention by the COSTIND, via the Ministry of Foreign Affairs within sixty days after the national registration of the space object, at the Secretariat of the United Nations.

Article 13
According to Article IV(1) of the Registration Convention, the following information concerning each space object carried on its registry: name of launching State or States, an appropriate designator of the space object or its registration number, date and territory or location of launch, basic orbital parameters and general function of the space object, shall be included in international registration.

Article 14
For the international registration of a space object jointly launched by China and other States, the State of Registry shall be determined by the Ministry of Foreign Affairs after consultation with concerned States in accordance with the Registration Convention.

Article 15
The provisions of these Measures related to national registry shall be interpreted by the COSTIND; the provisions related to the Registration Convention and international registry shall be interpreted by the Ministry of Foreign Affairs.

Article 16
These Measures shall enter into force upon the date of promulgation.

4.4. INTERIM MEASURES ON THE ADMINISTRATION OF LICENSING THE PROJECTS OF LAUNCHING CIVIL SPACE OBJECTS[4]

Commission of Science and Technology and Industry for National Defense
21st November 2002
(Unofficial Translation)

Chapter I. General Provisions

Article 1
These Measures are formulated with a view to regulating the administration of the project of launching civil space objects, promoting the sound development of the civil space industry, maintaining national security and the public interests and fulfilling the obligations of China as a contracting State to international outer space treaties.

Article 2
For the purpose of these Measures, the term "project of launching civil space objects" (hereinafter referred to as "project") means the launch of a spacecraft such as a satellite from the territory of China into outer space for non-military purpose and the launch of such a spacecraft into outer space from outside of the territory of China while the spacecraft is owned by, or the ownership of the spacecraft has been transferred on-orbit to, the persons, natural or juridical or the organizations of the People's Republic of China.

---

[4] The Chinese version of this regulatory document is published on the website of the State Administration of Science and Technology and Industry for National Defense, www.sastind.gov.cn, last accessed August 2021. This is the unofficial translation version provided by the Faculty of International Law, China University of Political Science and Law, Journal of Space Law, Vol. 33(2), 2007, pp. 442-448.

Article 3
The administration regime of licensing shall apply to the projects. Any persons, natural or juridical, or organizations undertaking such a launch project shall, in accordance with these Measures, apply for examination and approval and shall not carry out the project until he/it is found to be qualified upon examination and has obtained a license for the project.

Article 4
The Commission of Science and Technology and Industry for National Defense (hereinafter referred to as "the COSTIND") shall plan and administrate the projects and shall be responsible for examining, approving and supervising the projects.

Chapter II. Application, Evaluation and Authorization Procedures

Article 5
The general project contractor shall be the applicant for a license. Where there is no domestic general project contractor, the final owner of the satellite or other spacecraft shall be the applicant for the license. The applicant for a license is required:
(a) To abide by the laws and regulations of China and maintain the national secrets;
(b) Not to endanger the national security; endanger the national interests; or violate the national diplomatic policies or the international conventions to which China is a State Party by the project under application;
(c) Not to cause irremediable danger to public health, safety or properties by the project under application due to major negligence or intentional acts;
(d) To have the relevant approved documents issued by the competent state departments for carrying out the project under application;
(e) To have technical staff, financial means and technology information needed for carrying out the project under application;
(f) To meet other requirements provided by laws, regulations or rules.

Article 6
The applicant shall, nine months prior to the scheduled launch of the project, submit the following documents (in triplicate) to the COSTIND:
(a) An application form for a project license and documents on the qualifications of the applicant for evaluation;
(b) The relevant documents proving that the project conforms to national laws and regulations on environmental protection;
(c) For a project being executed in a domestic launching site, the following information shall be provided: the scheduled time for launch, the technical requirements for the

satellite, the launching vehicle and the communication system for launch, observation and control, the detailed orbital parameters of the launching vehicle; the survey report on the landing area or recovering place and the documents on detailed orbital parameters of the satellite and the use of frequency resources; for a project being executed at a foreign launching site, copies of the legal documents on orbital parameters, of the launching vehicle and the satellite, copies of the documents permitting the use of the relevant frequency resources shall be provided and a Chinese satellite launch enterprise shall provide a copy of the "Radio Station License of the People's Republic of China" issued by the Ministry of Information Industry for the radio station in outer space;

(d) The safety design report relating to the project and documents relating to public security; supplementary documents concerning the reliability of key safety system, the affects of the launching vehicle, either in normal condition or malfunction during the launch, to the property and personal safety near the launching site and within the range of the launch track, the prevention from pollution and space debris and other relevant safety; for a foreign-involved project, the documents concerning policy evaluation, confidentiality and security evaluation must also be submitted.

Article 7

The COSTIND shall, within thirty days as of receipt of the application documents, examine the project under application and issue a license where the requirements are met. Otherwise, no license shall be issued. The applicant and the relevant departments shall be so notified in writing.

Article 8

Where the applicant challenges the conclusion from evaluation, it may apply to the COSTIND for re-evaluation or administrative review in accordance with the law.

Article 9

The relevant evaluation of a foreign-involved project must be carried out by a foreign trade company designated by the Chinese government and the contract on such a project shall not enter into force until it is authorized by the COSTIND.

Chapter III. Supervision and Administration

Article 10
A license shall mainly contain:
(a) The applicant and its legal representative;
(b) The registered address (the applicant's domicile);
(c) Main contents of the project;
(d) The scheduled time for launch;
(e) The expiration date of the license;
(f) The organ issuing the license and the time of issuance.

Article 11
The license shall be limited to an authorized project and shall be automatically terminated after the completion of the project.

Article 12
A license shall not be altered or transferred.

Article 13
Where any content in a license needs to be modified, the licensee shall, ninety days prior to the expiry of the license, file an application to the COSTIND for modification. The license shall not be modified until the modification has been approved upon examination.

Article 14
With respect to a project under planned cancellation, the licensee shall, ninety days prior to the expiry of the license, apply to the COSTIND for cancellation and the license shall be nullified upon approval.

Article 15
With respect to a project that is impossible to be accomplished due to inappropriate management of the licensee, the COSTIND shall nullify the project license.

Article 16
The COSTIND shall order the licensee to rectify within a time limit, or withdraw the license in a severe case if the licensee:
(a) Violates the relevant national laws or regulations or the agreement between China and other states on maintaining confidentiality during execution of the project;

(b) Conducts any actions, during execution of the project, endangering national security; endangering national interests; or violating national diplomatic policies or international conventions to which China is a State Party;
(c) Carries out the launch activities beyond the limit approved by the license;
(d) Conducts other actions in violation of these Measures.

Article 17
With respect to a project for which the license is withdrawn, the applicant for the project shall not, within two years as of the withdrawal, file a second application for a license regarding the same project.

Article 18
Where, due to a licensee's actions, any content of the project is changed, or the project is delayed or cancelled, thus resulting in expenses in relevant aspects, the corresponding liability and the expenses to be borne shall be clarified in the contract by the licensee and the concerned parties.

Article 19
A licensee must comply with the relevant national regulations to insure himself against liability incurred in respect to damage or loss suffered by third parties and against other liability incurred by launching a space object.

Article 20
For a project being executed in a domestic launching site, the licensee shall, six months prior to the scheduled launch, report the launching plan of the project to the COSTIND. The licensee shall, before commencing the working phase in a launching site, file an application to the COSTIND for approval to release the project from the factory and provide:
(a) Documents on technical conditions of the launching vehicle, quality control, flight test outline, security and confidentiality and other required documents;
(b) Copies of the effective insurance policy of third-party liability for the project, copies of the relevant documents (in triplicate) and copies of the relevant effective insurance policies (in triplicate). In exceptional circumstances, written documents shall be provided to the COSTIND and shall be dealt with specifically. The working phase in a launching site of the project shall not commence until it has been approved.

Article 21
For a project being executed in a foreign launching site, the licensee shall, sixty days prior to the scheduled date for launch, file an application to the COSTIND for approval to

release the project from the factory and attach copies of the final documents (in triplicate) legally binding in respect of the liability insurance for third parties, the relevant insurances, security, confidentiality and shall not continue carrying out the project until it has been approved.

Article 22

A licensee must, within one month after the completion of a launch project, report to the COSTIND in writing on the accomplishment of the project.

Article 23

The COSTIND shall supervise and irregularly inspect the carrying out of the approved projects and the authorized officials shall have the right to be present and inspect the relevant activities during the carrying out of the project.

Chapter IV. Legal Responsibility

Article 24

A licensee shall have administrative penalties imposed in accordance with the law if he conceals the truth, practices frauds or damages the national interests during application or carrying out of the project. A licensee shall be held criminally responsible in accordance with the law if he commits a crime.

Article 25

If any person, natural or juridical, or any organization undertakes an unauthorized project without a license, the COSTIND shall order the cessation of the illegal activities. Persons or organizations so involved shall have administrative penalties imposed in accordance with the law, or, if they commit a crime, shall be held criminally responsible in accordance with the law.

Article 26

An organ or an official, which examines the applications for licenses and neglects its/his/her duties or abuses its/his/her powers during the examination and approval of applications, thus causing loss to the People's Republic of China, shall have administrative sanctions imposed, or shall be held criminally responsible in accordance with the law if it/he/she commits a crime.

Chapter V. Supplementary Articles

Article 27
The competent authorities to interpret the present Measures shall remain with the COSTIND.

Article 28
The present Measures shall enter into force on December 21, 2002.

4.5. REGULATION ON THE LICENSING ADMINISTRATION OF THE SCIENTIFIC RESEARCH AND PRODUCTION OF ARMS AND EQUIPMENT[5]

Commission of Science and Technology and Industry for National Defense
Central Military Commission
6th March 2008
(Unofficial Translation by WU Xiaodan, assisted by Ms. PENG Xuhan)

Chapter I. General Provisions

Article 1
This Regulation is formulated for the purpose of maintaining the order of scientific research and production of arms and equipment, intensifying the confidentiality and safety administration in the scientific research and production of arms and equipment, ensuring the stability and quality of arms and equipment and satisfying the needs of national defense.

Article 2
The activities of scientific research and production of arms and equipment in the licensing list of scientific research and production of arms and equipment (hereinafter refers to the licensing list) shall be subject to licensing administration. However, the scientific research of specialized arms and equipment shall be excluded.
The licensing list shall be joint formulated by the administrative department of science and technology and industry for national defense within the State Council, the General Armament Department of the People's Liberation Army of China (hereinafter referred to as the GAD) and the administrative department of military electronic industry and shall

---

[5] The Chinese version of this regulatory document is published on the website of the State Administration of Science and Technology and Industry for National Defense, www.sastind.gov.cn, last accessed August 2021.

be adjusted in a timely manner. The relevant departments of the State Council and PLA shall be consulted when formulating and adjusting the licensing list.

The licensing of the scientific research and production of arms and equipment shall be subject to classification administration within the scope as determined in the licensing list.

Article 3

No scientific research and production activities of arms and equipment in the licensing list can be engaged without a license for the scientific research and production of arms and equipment. However, those approved by the State Council and the Central Military Commission are excluded.

Article 4

The licensing administration of the scientific research and production of arms and equipment shall follow the principles of overall planning, rational distribution, encouraging competition and ensuring safety and confidentiality.

Article 5

The administrative department of science and technology and industry for national defense within the State Council shall supervise and administrate the licensing for the scientific research and production of arms and equipment throughout the country in accordance with this Regulation.

The GAD shall be consulted and coordinate with the administrative department of science and technology and industry for national defense within the State Council to supervise and administer the licensing for the scientific research and production of arms and equipment throughout the country.

The administrative department of science and technology and industry for national defense within the government of a province, autonomous region or municipality shall supervise and administer the licensing for the scientific research and production of arms and equipment within its administrative area in accordance with this Regulation.

Article 6

An entity that has obtained the license for the scientific research and production of arms and equipment shall carry out the scientific research and production of arms and equipment within the licensed scope and shall provide qualified scientific results, arms and equipment under the government requirements or the contractual terms.

Chapter II. Licensing Procedure

Article 7
To apply for a license for the scientific research and production of arms and equipment, an entity is required:
1. Having a legal person status;
2. Having professional technicians who are qualified for the scientific research and production of arms and equipment;
3. Having scientific research and production conditions and inspection, testing and experiment means required for the scientific research and production of arms and equipment;
4. Having technologies and techniques required for the scientific research and production of arms and equipment;(5) Having a qualified quality management system that has passed evaluation;(6) Having safe production capabilities required for the scientific research and production of arms and equipment; and(7) Having the confidentiality qualifications required for the scientific research and production of arms and equipment.

Article 8
The application for a license for the scientific research and production of arms and equipment shall be filed to the administrative department of science and technology and industry for national defense within the government of a province, autonomous region or municipality.

Where the licensing list requires an license application for the scientific research and production of arms and equipment being filed to the administrative department of science and technology and industry for national defense within the State Council, the applicant shall directly file the application to the administrative department of science and technology and industry for national defense within the State Council and shall simultaneously submit the application documents to the GAD.

Article 9
After the administrative department of science and technology and industry for national defense within the State Council or the administrative department of science and technology and industry for national defense within the government of a province, autonomous region or municipality receives an application, they shall process it in accordance with the Administrative Licensing Law of the People's Republic of China.

Article 10
The administrative department of science and technology and industry for national defense within the government of a province, autonomous region or municipality

organize the review on the applicant entity, consult the Military Representative Institution dispatched by the People's Liberation Army (hereinafter referred to as the MRI), finish the review within 30 days from the day when it receives the application and submit the review opinions and all the application documents to the administrative department of science and technology and industry for national defense within the State Council and simultaneously to the GAD.

Article 11
After the administrative department of science and technology and industry for national defense within the State Council receives an application, it shall review it and make a decision within 60 days from the day when it receives the application or within 30 days from the day when it receives the review opinions and the complete application documents submitted by the administrative department of science and technology and industry for national defense within the government of a province, autonomous region or municipality. If it decides of approval, it shall, within ten days as of the date of decision, issue to the applicant a license for the scientific research and production of arms and equipment. If it decides of disapproval, it shall give the applicant a written notice specifying reasons.
Before the administrative department of science and technology and industry for national defense within the State Council makes a decision, it shall consult in writing the GAD and the GAD shall reply within 10 days.

Article 12
The administrative department of science and technology and industry for national defense within the State Council may, according to the national requirements for capacity distribution of the scientific research and production of arms and equipment and the actual needs of the scientific research and production of arms and equipment, restrict the license numbers for the scientific research and production of arms and equipment with special requirements after it consults the GAD.

Article 13
A license for the scientific research and production of arms and equipment shall specify the entity's name and its legal representative, the licensing specialty or product name, the certificate sequence number and certificate issuance date, the valid period and other relevant contents.
The format of licenses for the scientific research and production of arms and equipment shall be provided by the administrative department of science and technology and industry for national defense within the State Council.

Article 14
An entity, which has obtained the license for the scientific research and production of arms and equipment, shall properly and confidentially preserve the aforesaid license and shall not divulge the relevant information indicated in the aforesaid license.

Article 15
An entity, which has obtained the license for the scientific research and production of arms and equipment, shall indicate the sequence number of its license for the scientific research and production of arms and equipment in its arms and equipment scientific research and production contracts and its product ex-factory certificates.

Article 16
No entity or individual may forge or alter the license for the scientific research and production of arms and equipment. No entity, which has obtained the license for the scientific research and production of arms and equipment, may lease, lend or transfer its license through other means.

Article 17
The administrative department of science and technology and industry for national defense within the State Council and the administrative department of science and technology and industry for national defense within the government of a province, autonomous region or municipality shall file all the documents applying for the license of the scientific research and production of arms and equipment in a timely manner and properly and confidentially preserve them.

Article 18
An entity, which has obtained the license for the scientific research and production of arms and equipment and untaken the tasks of the scientific research and production of arms and equipment shall accept the supervision of the representative military institution.

Chapter III. Confidentiality Administration

Article 19
An entity, which has obtained the license for the scientific research and production of arms and equipment, shall abide by the relevant laws, regulations and other rules on secrecy, establish a proper confidentiality administration system and, in accordance with the principle of active prevention, definite priority, strict criterions and clear responsibilities, regularly or irregularly inspect the implementation of confidentiality

administration system so as to timely study and solve the problems arising in the confidentiality work.

Article 20
An entity, which has obtained the license for the scientific research and production of arms and equipment, shall establish a leader responsibility system for the confidentiality administration and its major person-in-charge shall intensify the organization and administration of the confidentiality work of this entity to fulfill its confidentiality duties and obligations.

Article 21
An entity, which has obtained the license for the scientific research and production of arms and equipment, shall establish a confidentiality work unit and equip it with confidentiality administrators.
A confidentiality administrator shall be familiar with the laws, regulations and other relevant rules on secrecy, be qualified to do the confidentiality administration work, have grasped the basic knowledge of confidentiality technologies and have received necessary training and examination.

Article 22
An entity, which has obtained the license for the scientific research and production of arms and equipment, shall sign a position-related confidentiality responsibility contract with the personnel who participate in the scientific research and production task of arms and equipment and have the access to state secrets, so as to clarify their position-related confidentiality responsibilities and offer them confidentiality education and training on a frequent basis.
Personnel who have access to state secrets shall be familiar with the laws, regulations and other relevant rules on secrecy and shall strictly fulfill their confidentiality obligations in accordance with their position-related confidentiality responsibility contracts.

Article 23
An entity, which has obtained the license for the scientific research and production of arms and equipment, shall formulate, receive, distribute, transmit, use, copy, preserve and destroy the carriers with state secrets and strictly control the range of persons who have access to the carriers with state secrets in accordance with the laws, regulations and relevant rules on secrecy.

Article 24

An entity, which has obtained the license for the scientific research and production of arms and equipment, shall take measures to install safe and reliable confidentiality facilities in its key departments and locations involving state secrets.

Article 25

An entity, which has obtained the license for the scientific research and production of arms and equipment, shall take safety and confidentiality measures for the computers and information systems involving state secrets in accordance with the laws, regulations and relevant rules on secrecy and shall not use any equipment without safety and confidentiality measures to process, transmit or store the state secret information.

Article 26

Where an entity, which has obtained the license for the scientific research and production of arms and equipment, hosts a conference or event involving state secrets, it shall formulate a special confidentiality work plan and arrange particular personnel to take charge of the confidentially work. The conference involving state secrets shall be hosted at a place with safety and confidentiality measures and the range of attendees shall be strictly controlled.

Article 27

An entity, which has obtained the license for scientific research and production of arms and equipment, shall keep the state secrets confidential during international exchange, cooperation and negotiation. The provision of relevant documents, materials and physical samples to the overseas parties shall be subject to a prior approval under the prescribed procedures.

Article 28

An entity, which has obtained the license for the scientific research and production of arms and equipment, shall establish a secrecy archives system, recording the information about personnel administration who have access to state secrets and the investigation and punishment of state secrets divulgence and filing them into archives in a timely manner, so as to effectively administrate the archives involving state secrets in accordance with the laws, regulations and relevant rules on secrecy.

Chapter IV. Legal Responsibility

Article 29
Where an entity without the authorization under this Regulation engages in the scientific research and production of arms and equipment in the scope of licensing list, it shall be ordered to stop the illegal engagement, have its illegally manufactured products confiscated and be fined no less than 1 time but no more than 3 times the value of the products. If there are any illegal gains, the illegal gains shall be confiscated.

Article 30
Where an entity, which has obtained the license for the scientific research and production of arms and equipment, leases, lends or transfers its license through other means, it shall be fined 100,000 yuan and its license shall be revoked under serious circumstance. If an entity illegally accepts and uses the license for the scientific research and production of arms and equipment of other entities', it shall be ordered to stop the scientific research and production activities of arms and equipment, have its illegally manufactured products confiscated and be fined no less than 1 time but no more than 3 times the value of the illegal products. If there are any illegal gains, the illegal gains shall be confiscated.

Article 31
Any entity that forges or alters a license for the scientific research and production of arms and equipment shall be ordered to stop its violation and be fined 100,000 yuan. If there are any illegal gains, the illegal gains shall be confiscated.

Article 32
When an entity has obtained the license for the scientific research and production of arms and equipment by fraudulence or bribery or other illegitimate means, it shall be fined no less than 50,000 yuan but no more than 200,000 yuan and shall be punished in accordance with the Administrative License Law of the People's Republic of China.

Article 33
Where the administrative department of science and technology and industry for national defense within the State Council or the administrative department of science and technology and industry for national defense within the government of a province, autonomous region or municipality or any of its functionaries violates this Regulation, if it (he) is under any following circumstances, it (he) shall be ordered to rectify by the supervision organ at the same level; if the circumstance is serious, the person-in-charge and other directly liable persons shall be punished in accordance with the relevant law

and disciplinary rules: (1) Failing to accept the application that satisfies the conditions as prescribed in this Regulation; or (2) Failing to specify reasons regarding the disapproval of a license.

Article 34
Where the administrative department of science and technology and industry for national defense within the State Council or the administrative department of science and technology and industry for national defense within the government of a province, autonomous region or municipality is under any following circumstances, it shall be ordered to rectify by the supervision organ at the same level and the person-in-charge and other directly liable persons shall be punished in accordance with the relevant law and disciplinary rules: (1) Approving the license to any applicant who has not met the requirements as prescribed in this Regulation or making a license approval decision by exceeding its statutory power; (2) Disapproving the license to any applicant who has met the requirements as prescribed in this Regulation or failing to make a license approval decision to such an application within the statutory time limit; or (3) Finding any illegal activities of the scientific research and production of arms and equipment in the licensing list without a license under this Regulation but failing to investigate and punish such activities in a timely manner.

Article 35
Where an entity, which has obtained the license for the scientific research and production of arms and equipment, violates Article 19, 20, 21, 22 or 28, it shall be ordered to rectify within a prescribed time limit. If it fails to rectify within the time limit, it shall be fined no less than 50,000 yuan but no more than 200, 000 yuan. The person-in-charge and other directly liable persons shall be punished in accordance with the relevant law and disciplinary rules.

Article 36
Where an entity, which has obtained the license for the scientific research and production of arms and equipment, violates Article 23, 24, 25, 26 or 27, it shall be ordered to rectify and be fined no less than 50,000 yuan but no more than 200,000 yuan. The person-in-charge and other directly liable persons shall be punished in accordance with the relevant law and disciplinary rules. Under serious circumstances, it shall be ordered to suspend operation for rectification and have its license for the scientific research and production of arms and equipment revoked.

Article 37
Where an entity, which has obtained the license for the scientific research and production of arms and equipment, violates this Regulation and has its license for the scientific

research and production of arms and equipment being revoked, it shall not apply for a new one within three years.

Article 38
The administrative punishments as prescribed in this Regulation shall be imposed by the administrative department of science and technology and industry for national defense within the State Council.

Article 39
If anyone who violates this Regulation and commits a crime, he/she shall be held criminally responsible in accordance with the law.

Chapter V. Supplementary Articles

Article 40
No fee may be charged for the licensing of the scientific research and production of arms and equipment under this Regulation.

Article 41
An entity, which has already been engaging in the scientific research and production of arms and equipment before this Regulation enters into force, shall, from the day when this Regulation enters into force, apply for a license for the scientific research and production of arms and equipment under this Regulation within the time period as prescribed by the administrative department of science and technology and industry for national defense within the State Council.

Article 42
The licensing administration of the scientific research and production in the military electronic industry shall be exercised by the relevant administrative department in analogy to this Regulation.

Article 43
This Regulation shall enter into force on April 1, 2008.

4. REGULATORY RULES ON SPACE ACTIVITIES

4.6. MEASURES FOR THE IMPLEMENTATION OF SCIENTIFIC RESEARCH AND PRODUCTION LICENSING OF ARMS AND EQUIPMENT[6]

State Administration of Science and Technology and Industry for National Defense
31st March 2010
(Unofficial Translation by WU Xiaodan, assisted by Ms. PENG Xuhan)

The *Measures for the Implementation of the Scientific Research and Production Licensing of Arms and Equipment*, as deliberated and adopted at the 7th executive meeting of the Ministry of Industry and Information Technology of the People's Republic of China on November 12, 2009 and deliberated and adopted by the General Armament Department of the People's Liberation Army, are hereby promulgated and shall enter into force on May 10, 2010.

Chapter I. General Provisions

Article 1
These Measures are formulated for the purpose of regulating the licensing administration of the scientific research and production of arms and equipment in accordance with the *Regulation on Licensing Administration of the Scientific Research and Production of Weapons and Equipment*.

Article 2
Any scientific research and production of arms and equipment as listed in the licensing list of scientific research and production of arms and equipment (hereinafter referred to as the "licensing list") shall apply for a license in accordance with these Measures; the scientific research and production of arms and equipment shall not be conducted without a license for the scientific research and production of arms and equipment. The activities approved by the State Council and the Central Military Commission as well as specialized scientific research activities of arms and equipment shall be excluded.
The term "the scientific research and production of arms and equipment" as mentioned in these Measures refers to the scientific research and production activities on the complete sets, systems and special matching products of the arms and equipment.
The term "the scientific research of specialized arms and equipment" as mentioned in these Measures refers to the activities of theoretical and fundamental scientific research in the field of arms and equipment.

---

[6] The Chinese version of this regulatory document is published on the website of the State Administration of Science and Technology and Industry for National Defense, www.sastind.gov.cn, last accessed August 2021.

Article 3
The licensing administration of the scientific research and production of arms and equipment shall be based on the demands of national defense construction and the development of arms and equipment and follow the principle of overall planning, rational distribution, encouraging competition, being safe and confidential, strict administration and ensuring fairness and impartiality.

Article 4
The license of the scientific research and production of arms and equipment shall be classified into Class A and Class B according to the importance degree of the arms and equipment and their special matching products. The classification of the license shall be prescribed in the licensing list. The licensing list shall be joint formulated and promulgated by the State Administration of Science and Technology and Industry for National Defense (hereinafter referred to as the "SASTIND") with the General Armament Department of the People's Liberation Army (hereinafter referred to as the "GAD") and shall be adjusted in due time.

Article 5
The SASTIND shall be responsible for the licensing administration of the scientific research and production of arms and equipment throughout the country and perform the following duties:
(1) Formulating the policies and rules on the licensing administration of scientific research and production of arms and equipment;
(2) Jointly formulating the licensing list with the GAD;
(3) Accepting and examining the applications for Class A license, approving, issuing, canceling and withdrawing the licenses for the scientific research and production of arms and equipment and modification and extending and revoking of the licenses for the scientific research and production of arms and equipment;
(4) Organizing and carrying out the supervision and inspection over the licensing implementation of the scientific research and production of arms and equipment.
The office for the licensing administration of the scientific research and production of arms and equipment under the SASTIND shall be responsible for the above-mentioned work.

Article 6
The GAD shall be responsible for the joint administration of the licensing of the scientific research and production of arms and equipment throughout the country. The department for the joint administration of the licensing of the scientific research and production of arms and equipment under the GAD (hereinafter referred to as the

"department for the joint licensing administration under the GAD") shall perform the following duties:

(1) Participating in the formulation of policies and provisions on the licensing administration of the scientific research and production of arms and equipment;
(2) Jointly formulating the licensing list;
(3) Jointly examining the licensing applications, the issuing, modification, extension, withdrawal and revocation of the licenses for the scientific research and production of arms and equipment and providing opinions on the administrative penalties;
(4) Organizing the military representative offices dispatched by the People's Liberation Army to relevant entities or regions (hereinafter referred to as the "dispatched military representative offices") to participate in the on-site examination on the licensing of the scientific research and production of arms and equipment; and
(5) Jointly carrying out the supervision and inspection over the licensing implementation of the scientific research and production of arms and equipment.

Article 7
The administrative departments of science and technology and industry for national defense within the governments of provinces, autonomous regions and municipalities (hereinafter referred to as the "local administrative departments of science and technology and industry for national defense") shall perform the following duties:
(1) Accepting and examining the applications for Class B license within their respective administrative regions and providing examination opinions;
(2) Being responsible for the supervision and administration of the entities of scientific research and production of arms and equipment obtaining Class B license within their respective administrative regions; investigating and verifying the entities and activities engaging in illegal scientific research and production of arms and equipment and providing suggestions to the SASTIND;
(3) Assisting the SASTIND in the on-site examination on the entities that apply for Class A license within their respective administrative regions; and
(4) Assisting the SASTIND in the supervision and administration of the entities obtaining Class A licenses for the scientific research and production of arms and equipment within their respective administrative regions.

Article 8
The dispatched military representative offices shall, according to the internal division of responsibilities of the army, carry out the examination, supervise and administer the licenses of the scientific research and production of arms and equipment within their dispatched regions jointly with the local administrative departments of science and technology and industry for national defense.

Article 9

The SASTIND shall, according to the national distribution requirements of scientific research and production capabilities of arms and equipment and the actual needs of scientific research and production of arms and equipment, impose quantitative restrictions on Class A licenses after consulting the GAD. The specific specialties or products subject to the quantitative restriction and the restricted number shall be prescribed separately.

Chapter II. Application and Acceptance

Article 10

To apply for a license for the scientific research and production of arms and equipment, an entity shall conform to the requirements as prescribed in Article 7 of the *Regulation on Licensing Administration of the Scientific Research and Production of Arms and Equipment*. Among them, an entity that applies for the licensing of the scientific research and production of complete sets and systems of arms and equipment shall have the corresponding engineering organization and coordination abilities.

Article 11

An entity that applies for a license for the scientific research and production of arms and equipment shall submit an application form for *Licenses for the Scientific Research and Production of Arms and Equipment* and the following documents and materials (in photocopies):
(1) The business license of an enterprise legal person or the legal person certificate of a public institution;
(2) The corresponding authentication certificate of quality management systems;
(3) The certification document of reaching the production safety standards (the production safety license or an appraisal report on the production safety shall be submitted for an application for the production of dangerous hazardous articles);
(4) The confidentiality qualification certificate;
(5) The documents of verification or reaching the standards of environmental protection and fire control as prescribed by laws and administrative regulations; and
(6) The other documents and materials that the applicants deem that may prove its abilities and qualifications.

Article 12

An entity that applies for a license for the scientific research and production of arms and equipment shall file an application in accordance with the following:

(1) An application for Class A license or an application for both Class A license and Class B license shall be filed to the SASTIND and the application materials shall be submitted in triplicate (including an electronic text in a compact disc).

(2) An application for Class B license shall be filed to the administrative department of science and technology and industry for national defense within the governments of provinces, autonomous regions and municipalities and the application materials shall be submitted in triplicate (including an electronic text in a compact disc).

One copy of the application materials (including an electronic text in a compact disc) of Class A license and Class B license shall be submitted to the department for the joint licensing administration under the GAD simultaneously.

Article 13

The SASTIND and the local administrative departments of science and technology and industry for national defense shall examine the application in accordance with Article 32 of the *Administrative License Law of the People's Republic of China*, make an acceptance decision within 5 days for those that conforming to the acceptance conditions. They may notify the applicant of all necessary supplements and corrections to its application on the spot or within 5 days if the application materials are incomplete or not in the statutory form, or notify the applicant of refusal within reasons in writing if a non-acceptance decision is made.

Article 14

The department for joint licensing administration under the GAD shall, within 4 days after receiving the application materials, provide its examination opinions on the licensing application materials back to the SASTIND or the local administrative departments of science and technology and industry for national defense.

Chapter III. Examination and Approval

Article 15

The SASTIND and the local administrative departments of science and technology and industry for national defense shall, after accepting the applications, organize the experts to conduct an on-site examination on the license applications for the scientific research and production of arms and equipment and the department for joint licensing administration under the GAD shall designate the dispatched military representative offices to participate in such examination. Where it is unsuitable to conduct an on-site examination for involving any core state secrecy, a written examination may be conducted in light of the actual situation. The time needed by the experts to conduct the on-site examination shall not be included in the time limit for licensing as prescribed in this Chapter.

The specific measures for the on-site examination on the licensing of the scientific research and production of arms and equipment and experts administration shall be separately formulated by the SASTIND and the GAD.

Article 16
Where the local administrative departments of science and technology and industry for national defense are responsible for organizing the examination on the applicant entities, they shall complete the examination and consulting the dispatched military representative offices within 30 days after accepting the applications and submit the examination opinions and all application materials to the SASTIND and the department for the joint licensing administration under the GAD simultaneously.

Article 17
The SASTIND shall decide whether grant the license or not within 30 days after receiving the examination opinions and all application materials from the local administrative departments of science and technology and industry for national defense.
Where the SASTIND directly accepts an application and organizes the examination, it shall decide whether grant the license or not within 60 days after accepting the application.
The SASTIND shall, before deciding whether grant the license or not, consult the GAD in writing. The GAD shall provide its opinions back within 10 days.
When making a decision of approval, the license for the scientific research and production of arms and equipment shall be issued within 10 days as of the date of decision. When making a decision of disapproval, the applicant shall be so notified in writing with specific reasons.

Article 18
A license for the scientific research and production of arms and equipment shall contain:
(1) The name of the applicant;
(2) The applicant's legal representative;
(3) The registered address (the applicant's domicile);
(4) The address of the scientific research and production place;
(5) The names of the licensed specialties or products;
(6) The serial number of the license;
(7) The organ issuing the license;
(8) The date of issuance (re-issuance); and
(9) The validity period of the license.

Article 19
The validity period of a license for the scientific research and production of arms and equipment is 5 years. The licenses shall be uniformly printed by the SASTIND.

Chapter IV. Modification and Extension

Article 20
Where the name of the legal person, the legal representative or the registered address changes within the validity period of the license for the scientific research and production of arms and equipment, the licensee shall, within 60 days as of the date of change, file an application to the SASTIND for modification, whose photocopy shall be simultaneously submitted to the department for the joint licensing administration under the GAD and the department that examined the original license.

Article 21
Where an licensee applies for the modification of the name of the legal person or the registered address, it shall submit the approval document from its superior organ or the relevant organs, as well as the correspondingly changed documents of business license of an enterprise legal person or the legal person certificate of a public institution and the confidentiality qualification certificate.

Where an licensee applies for the modification of its legal representative, it shall submit the appointment document from its superior organ or other certification document from relevant state organs, as well as the correspondingly changed business license of enterprise legal person or the legal person certificate of a public institution and the confidentiality qualification certificate.

Among them, if the change of the name of the legal person, registered address or legal representative is caused by asset restructuring or any other asset changes, the licensee shall submit a written explanation as well as supporting documents such as its articles of association.

Article 22
The SASTIND shall, after receiving an application for modification, examine in accordance with relevant laws and regulations and organize expert on-site inspection when necessary. If it conforms to the requirement for modification, the SASTIND shall modify the license within 30 days after accepting the application. The time needed for expert on-site inspection shall not be included in the time limit as prescribed in this Article.

Article 23
Where a licensee applies for license of the scientific research and production of additional or special areas of products of arms and equipment within the validity period of the license, it shall file a new application in accordance with these Measures.

Article 24
Where a licensee intends to apply for extending the license validity period, it shall file an application for the license extension in accordance with Article 12 of these Measures 6 months before the expiration of license validity period.
The SASTIND and the local administrative departments of science and technology and industry for national defense shall, before the expiration of validity period, examine the application for license extension in accordance with the requirements and procedures as prescribed by these Measures and the SASTIND shall, in accordance with Article 17 of these Measures, decide whether approve the extension or not. If it makes a decision of approval, it shall reissue a license for the scientific research and production of arms and equipment; if it makes a decision of disapproval, it shall so notify the applicant in writing with specific reasons.

Article 25
Where a licensee does not intend to extend the validity period of its license for the scientific research and production of arms and equipment, it shall, 6 months before the expiration of the validity period, file a written report to the SASTIND. Before the SASTIND makes appropriate arrangements in consultation with the GAD, no entity may cease the scientific research and production of arms and equipment without approval.

Chapter V. Supervision and Administration

Article 26
The SASTIND shall supervise the entities engaged in the activities of scientific research and production of arms and equipment listed in the licensing list throughout the country, establish a supervision and inspection system, organize the supervision and inspection activities and conduct supervision and inspection on the lawfulness of duty performance in the licensing administration of the scientific research and production of arms and equipment by the local administrative departments of science and technology and industry for national defense.
The GAD shall jointly supervise the entities engaged in the activities of scientific research and production of arms and equipment as listed in the licensing list throughout the country and supervise the duty performance of joint licensing administration of the

scientific research and production of arms and equipment by the dispatched military representative offices.

The local administrative departments of science and technology and industry for national defense shall, in accordance with Article 7 of these Measures, supervise the entities engaged in the activities of scientific research and production of arms and equipment as listed in the licensing list within their respective administrative regions.

The dispatched military representative offices shall supervise licensee's sustained requirements satisfaction and task performance of the licenses of the scientific research and production of arms and equipment. Any problem found shall be timely reported to its superior organs level by level. The SASTIND or the local administrative department of science and technology and industry for national defense shall be notified thereof.

The specific measures for the supervision and inspection of the licensees of scientific research and production of arms and equipment shall be separately formulated by the SASTIND and the GAD.

Article 27
An entity that has obtained the license for the scientific research and production of arms and equipment shall perform the following obligations:
(1) Abiding by the laws, administrative regulations and these Measures;
(2) Properly preserving the license for the scientific research and production of arms and equipment and strictly obeying the confidentiality requirements without divulging the contents indicated in the aforesaid license;
(3) Engaging in the scientific research and production activities of arms and equipment within the licensed scope;
(4) Maintaining its scientific research and production capacity corresponding to the licensed activities of scientific research and production of arms and equipment;
(5) Undertaking the task of scientific research and production of arms and equipment as required by the State, accepting the orders of scientific research and production of arms and equipment of the State and providing qualified scientific research achievements, arms and equipment or matching products in accordance with the contract terms;
(6) Labeling the serial numbers of licenses on the contracts and product ex-factory certificates of scientific research and production of arms and equipment;
(7) Establishing an annual self-inspection system and submitting the annual self-inspection report as required; and
(8) Accepting the supervision and inspection of the SASTIND, the local administrative department of science and technology and industry for national defense as well as the GAD and the dispatched military representative office.

Article 28

An entity that has obtained the license for the scientific research and production of arms and equipment shall establish a system for reporting major issues. Where the major changes, such as public listing on the stock exchange, bankruptcy, business suspension, restructuring, reorganization, relocation of scientific research and production and lack of key equipment and facilities for scientific research and production, occur within the validity period of the license, the information of such changes shall be reported to the SASTIND in writing within 30 days as of the date of changes, whose copies shall be simultaneously sent to the department for the joint licensing administration under the GAD and the local administrative department of science and technology and industry for national defense. The SASTIND shall organize examination and make a decision in consultation with the GAD and notify the relevant entities in writing.

Where an entity that has obtained the license for the scientific research and production of arms and equipment intends to receive feign investment in asset restructuring or public listing on the overseas stock exchange, it shall file a written report to the SASTIND in advance. These activities may be carried out only after they are approved by the SASTIND in consultation with the GAD.

Article 29

An entity that has obtained the license for the scientific research and production of arms and equipment shall abide by the relevant laws, regulations and other rules on secrecy, establish a proper confidentiality administration system in accordance with Chapter III of the *Regulation on Licensing Administration of the Scientific Research and Production of Arms and Equipment*, establish a confidentiality administration leaders responsibility system, designate confidentiality organs and personnel, clarify their confidentiality responsibility, conduct confidentiality training, strictly administer the confidentiality-related personnel, install security facilities in the key confidential departments and locations and guarantee the security of confidentiality-related carriers and state secrets.

Article 30

No entity or individual may forge or alter any license for the scientific research and production of arms and equipment. No entity that has obtained the license for the scientific research and production of arms and equipment may resell, lease, lend or transfer its license by other means. Where a license for the scientific research and production of arms and equipment is lost or damaged, this shall be timely reported to the SASTIND and an application shall be filed for re-issuance.

Article 31

Under any of the following circumstances, the SASTIND may, after consulting with the GAD, make a decision to revoke a license for the scientific research and production of arms and equipment according to law:

(1) Any functionary of the SASTIND or the local administrative department of science and technology and industry for national defense abuses his authorities or neglects his duties in making the decision to grant a license;
(2) Exceeding the statutory authorities in making the decision to grant a license;
(3) Violating the statutory procedures in making the decision to grant a license;
(4) Granting the license to an unqualified applicant entity or an entity that does not meet the statutory requirements; or
(5) Any other circumstance under which the license may be legally revoked.

Article 32

The SASTIND shall, after consulting the GAD, process the licenses termination and notify the relevant entities, if any entity that has obtained the license for the scientific research and production of arms and equipment is under any of the following circumstances:

(1) The validity period of the license has expired and the extension renewal is not approved;
(2) The license has been legally revoked;
(3) The license has been legally withdrawn;
(4) The legal person is legally terminated or bankrupt; or
(5) Any other circumstance under which the license shall be terminated.

Article 33

The SASTIND shall establish an archives administration system for the licenses of the scientific research and production of arms and equipment and a database of such licenses, share the relevant information with the GAD, formulate and issue oriented a Directory of Licenses for the Scientific Research and Production of Arms and Equipment and timely inform the relevant entities of the issuance, alteration, extension, withdrawal, revocation and cancellation of licenses as well as the administrative punishment on the illegal entities and other information.

Article 34

The SASTIND and the local administrative departments of science and technology and industry for national defense shall timely file the relevant materials in processing the licensing of the scientific research and production of arms and equipment into archives, properly preserve them and strictly keep them confidential.

Chapter VI. Legal Responsibility

Article 35

Where an entity that fails to obtain a license for the scientific research and production of arms and equipment in accordance with these Measures and engages in the activities of scientific research and production of arms and equipment listed in the licensing list without approval, it shall be ordered to rectify, have its illegally manufactured products confiscated and be fined no less than 1 time but no more than 3 times the value of the products; if there is any illegal gains, the illegal gains shall be confiscated.

Where an entity is engaged in the activities of the scientific research and production of arms and equipment without authorization that may seriously endanger the public social safety, such as the scientific research and production of complete sets of arms and equipment, guns, ammunitions, radioactive nuclear materials and hazardous chemicals for military use, it shall be fined 3 times the value of the products. If there are any illegal gains, the illegal gains shall be confiscated.

Article 36

Where any entity, which has obtained the license for the scientific research and production of arms and equipment, fails to continuously meet the capacity and requirements corresponding to the activities of the scientific research and production of arms and equipment it is engaged in within the validity period of its license, it shall be ordered to recover such capacity and requirements within a prescribed time limit; if it fails to do so within the time limit, it shall be given a warning or imposed a fine of 10,000 yuan up to 30,000 yuan according to the seriousness of its impact on the scientific research and production of arms and equipment task.

Article 37

Where any entity that has obtained the license for the scientific research and production of arms and equipment illegal ceases the scientific research and production of arms and equipment or refuses to undertake the corresponding tasks of scientific research and production of arms and equipment, it shall be ordered to rectify and be given a warning; if it refuses to rectify, it shall be imposed a fine of 10,000 yuan up to 30,000 yuan.

Article 38

Where any entity that has obtained the license for the scientific research and production of arms and equipment fails to report any major change as listed in Article 28 of these Measures within the prescribed time limit, it shall be given a warning and ordered to submit a supplementary explanatory report regarding the major changes in 10 days; if it is found, upon examination, not to meet the requirements for licensing any more, the SASTIND shall make a decision in consultation with the GAD.

Article 39
Where any entity that has obtained the license for the scientific research and production of arms and equipment resells, leases, lends or transfers its license by any other means, it shall be imposed a fine of 100,000 yuan; if the circumstance is serious, its license shall be revoked. If it illegally accepts and uses the license for scientific research and production of arms and equipment provided by someone else, it shall be ordered to cease the activities of the production of arms and equipment, have its illegally manufactured products confiscated and be fined no less than 1 time but no more than 3 times the value of the illegal products. If there are any illegal gains, the illegal gains shall be confiscated.

Article 40
Where any entity that has obtained a license for the scientific research and production of arms and equipment conceals the relevant information, provides any false documents or refuses to accept the supervision and inspection as prescribed in Article 27 of these Measures or fails to submit the annual inspection report in accordance with relevant provisions, it shall be given a warning; if the circumstance is serious, it shall be imposed a fine of 10,000 yuan up to 30,000 yuan.

Article 41
Where any entity that has obtained the license for the scientific research and production of arms and equipment violates Article 3 of *the Regulation on Licensing Administration of the Scientific Research and Production of Arms and Equipment*, it shall be punished in accordance with the relevant provisions of this Regulation; any other act of divulging any state secret shall be imposed a fine of 10,000 yuan up to 30,000 yuan.

Article 42
Any entity that forges or alters a license for the scientific research and production of arms and equipment shall be ordered to cease the illegal act and be imposed a fine of 100,000 yuan. If there are any illegal gains, the illegal gains shall be confiscated.
Any entity that loses a license for the scientific research and production of arms and equipment and causes divulging of state secret shall be punished in accordance with *the Law of the People's Republic of China on State Secrecy*.

Article 43
Any entity, which has obtained the license for the scientific research and production of arms and equipment by fraudulence or bribery or other unjustifiable means, shall be

imposed a fine of 50,000 yuan up to 200,000 yuan and shall be punished in accordance with *the Administrative License Law of the People's Republic of China.*

Article 44
Where any functionary of the SASTIND or the local administrative department of science and technology and industry for national defense violates these Measures, he shall be ordered to rectify by the supervisory organ at the same level under any of the following circumstances; if the circumstance is serious, the person-in-charge and other directly liable persons shall be punished according to the laws:
(1) Failing to accept the application that meets the requirements as prescribed in these Measures;
(2) Failing to notify the applicant all the necessary supplements and corrections once if the application materials are incomplete or not in the statutory form; or
(3) Failing to give the disapproval reasons for a license application according to the laws.

Article 45
Where the SASTIND or the local administrative department of science and technology and industry for national defense is under any of the following circumstances, it shall be ordered to rectify by the supervisory organ at the same level and the person-in-charge and other directly liable persons shall be punished according to law:
(1) Approving a license application to any applicant entity that does not meet the requirements as prescribed in these Measures or making a license approval decision by exceeding its statutory power;
(2) Disapproving a license application to any applicant entity that meets the requirements as prescribed in these Measures or failing to reach a license approval decision within the statutory time limit; or
(3) Finding any illegal activities of scientific research and production of arms and equipment as listed in the licensing list without a license but failing to timely investigate and punish according to the laws.

Article 46
Where any functionary of the joint licensing administration department under the GAD or the dispatched military representative office who participates in the licensing administration violates these Measures, the GAD shall process it jointly with the relevant department of the army according to the laws.

Article 47

Where an entity that obtained the license for the scientific research and production of arms and equipment is found in violation of these Measures and has its license being revoked, it shall not file for a new application within 3 years.

Article 48

Where an entity applying for a license of the scientific research and production of arms and equipment conceals relevant information or provides any false materials and causes the termination of on-site licensing examination, it shall be given a warning. This applicant entity shall not file for another application within 1 year.

Article 49

The administrative penalty prescribed by these Measures shall be executed by the SASTIND.

Chapter VII. Supplementary Articles

Article 50

The license for the scientific research and production of military electronic equipment obtained before the entry into force of these Measures shall continue to be valid within its term of validity and the follow-up administration shall be governed by these Measures.

Article 51

The measures for the licensing administration of the activities of scientific research and production of arms and equipment of the units subordinated to the People's Liberation Army shall be separately formulated.

Article 52

These Measures shall enter into force on May 10, 2010. *The Measures for the Administration of Licenses for the Scientific Research and Production of Military Electronic Equipment* promulgated on December 14, 2004 (Order No.32 of the Ministry of Information Industry of the People's Republic of China) and *the Measures for the Implementation of the Scientific Research and Production Licensing of Weapons and Equipment* promulgated on May 26, 2005 (Order No.15 of the Commission of Science and Technology and Industry for National Defense of the People's Republic of China) shall be repealed simultaneously.

4.7. **Interim Measures for the Recordation Administration of the Scientific Research and Production of Arms and Equipment**[7]

State Administration of Science and Technology and Industry for National Defense
25th July 2019
(Unofficial Translation by WU Xiaodan, assisted by Ms. PENG Xuhan)

Article 1
These Measures are formulated in accordance with the relevant provisions of laws and administrative regulations with a view to implement the reform requirements of the State Council of "simplifying procedures, decentralizing powers, combining decentralization with appropriate control and optimizing services", to simplify the ex-ante authorization as well as regulate and strengthen the during and ex-post administration of the scientific research and production of arms and equipment without authorization requirements.

Article 2
The State Administration of Science and Technology and Industry for National Defense (hereinafter referred to as the "SASTIND") shall carry out the recordation administration over scientific research and production activities of the arms and equipment as listed in the Recordation Catalogue of the Scientific Research and Production of Specialized Areas (Products) Arms and Equipment (hereinafter referred to as "the Recordation Catalogue").

The combination of Licensing List of the Scientific Research and Production of Equipment and Recordation Catalogue compose the comprehensive administration system for the scientific research and production of arms and equipment. The licensing and recordation administration is utilized to obtain information relevant to the capacity maintenance of enterprises and institutions engaged in the activities of scientific research and production of arms and equipment and effectively monitor and control over the completeness, advancement and safety of scientific research and production system of arms and equipment. The Recordation Catalogue shall be formulated, adjusted and promulgated in due time by the SASTIND.

Article 3
Any enterprise and public institution engaged in the scientific research and production activities of arms and equipment as listed in the Recordation Catalogue shall apply for the recordation of the scientific research and production of arms and equipment within 3 months after signing a supply contract or undertaking a research and production task.

---

7   The Chinese version of this regulatory document is published on the website of the State Administration of Science and Technology and Industry for National Defense, www.sastind.gov.cn, last accessed August 2021.

Article 4

The SASTIND shall be responsible for the recordation administration of the scientific research and production of arms and equipment throughout the country, formulate the policies and rules on the recordation administration, formulate and promulgate the list of recordation entities, organize to carry out the supervision and inspection over the recordation of the scientific research and production of arms and equipment, instruct the administrative departments of science and technology and industry for national defense within the governments of provinces, autonomous regions and municipalities (hereinafter referred to as the "local administrative departments of science and technology and industry for national defense") to administer, supervise and inspect the recordation of the scientific research and production of arms and equipment within their respective administrative regions and deal with the misconduct of enterprises and public institutions that has obtained the recordation of the scientific research and production of arms and equipment (hereinafter referred to as "the recordation entities"). The licensing administration office for the scientific research and production of arms and equipment under the SASTIND shall be responsible for the routine work.

The local administrative departments of science and technology and industry for national defense shall be responsible for the recordation administration, supervision and inspection of the scientific research and production of arms and equipment within their respective administrative regions, formulate the local policies on the recordation administration of the scientific research and production of arms and equipment, organize and carry out inspection and verification of the recordation entities within their respective administrative regions, deal with the misconduct of recordation entities, assist the SASTIND in supervision and inspection and provide safety measures and relevant services to the recordation entities in the scientific research and production of arms and equipment.

Any department in charge of the system and subsystems of arms and equipment, such as military industry corporation and the China Academy of Engineering Physics, shall assist the SASTIND and local administrative departments of science and technology and industry for national defense in organizing and carrying out the supervision and inspection of recordation entities and report to or notify the SASTIND in a timely manner any major problem found in the recordation entities when they evaluate their suppliers' system and subsystem integration units of arms and equipment.

Any department in charge of the recordation entities shall obtain the relevant recordation information in a timely manner.

Article 5

An entity that applies for the recordation of the scientific research and production of arms and equipment shall file an application to the local administrative departments of science and technology and industry for national defense (hereinafter referred to as "the recordation department"). The following documents and materials shall be submitted (in photocopies) with an electronic text in a compact disc:

(1) An Application Form for the Recordation of the Scientific Research and Production of Arms and Equipment (Annex 1) which has been filled out and the legal representatives shall promise on the authenticity of its contents and other materials to be submitted;

(2) The business license of an enterprise legal person or the legal person certificate of a public institution;

(3) The documents that can prove tasks undertaken including the supply contracts and research assignment letters or contracts corresponding to the recorded specialized areas (products); and if there are too many documents, the list of products indicating the serial number of contracts and sources of tasks can be submitted instead;

(4) The confidentiality qualification certificate or the letter of responsibility for confidentiality signed with the user entities;

(5) The qualified certificate of quality management system or other national standard quality system certificates and documents that the applicant entities believes that may prove that its quality management system may meet the supplication requirement; and

(6) The other documents and materials that the applicant enterprise deems believes that may prove its abilities and qualifications.

Any enterprise that has obtained the license for the scientific research and production of arms and equipment intends to engage in the activities of the scientific research and production of arms and equipment as listed in the Recordation Catalogue may only submit the documents materials as required by paragraph 1 and 3 and the recordation specialized area (products) shall be excluded from its license.

Any enterprise that could have the requirements for the license for the scientific research and production of arms and equipment, may simultaneously apply for a recordation to the local administrative departments of science and technology and industry for national defense when it applies for the license of the scientific research and production of arms and equipment.

Article 6

The local administrative departments of science and technology and industry for national defense shall examine whether the application materials submitted by the applicant enterprise are complete and process the applications within 7 working days:

(1) Inform the applicant entity if the recorded specialized areas (products) are not in the recordation catalogue or not subject to recordation;

(2) Inform the applicant entity that it shall apply for a license for the scientific research and production of arms and equipment if the specialize areas (products) are in the Licensing List of the Scientific Research and Production of Weapons and Equipment;

(3) Notify the applicant entity of all the necessary supplements and corrections once in writing if the application documents and materials are incomplete or inconsistent with the specialized areas (products) the applicant entity applies for recordation;

(4) Make an acceptance decision on the recordation application if the application materials are complete and consistent with the specialized areas (products) the applicant entity applies for recordation.

When accepting or rejecting an application for recordation, the local administrative departments of science and technology and industry for national defense shall issue a written confirmation with the special seal of the administrative organ and a clear indication of specific date.

Article 7

The local administrative departments of science and technology and industry for national defense shall, after accepting the applications, complete the printing of recordation certificates for the scientific research and production of arms and equipment (hereinafter referred to as the "recordation certificate") within 20 working days as of the date of acceptance, which will be preserved by the recordation entity. A unified format for recordation certificates shall be formulated by the SASTIND (see Annex 2 for the format).

The format of the recordation number shall be: (the first two digits of the administrative division code of the province, autonomous region or municipality) -WQZB- (four-digit sequential number). The sequential number shall be edited by the local administrative departments of science and technology and industry for national defense on its own.

The validity term of recordation of the scientific research and production of arms and equipment is 5 years.

Article 8

A recordation entity shall obey and perform the following obligations:

(1) Good faith and guaranteeing the authenticity and validity of the recordation application documents and materials;

(2) Undertaking the task of scientific research and production of arms and equipment and providing the qualified scientific research results, arms and equipment or matching products in accordance with the state plan and contract terms;

(3) Having the quality, production safety and confidentiality administration system corresponding to the products that it will provide and obtaining the corresponding required qualifications and signing contracts with the users; and

(4) Accepting the supervision and inspection of the SASTIND and the local administrative department of science and technology and industry for national defense and the supervision of the user entities.

Article 9

The SASTIND and the local administrative departments of science and technology and industry for national defense shall provide the recordation entities with relevant policy support and services, incorporate the recordation into the coordinated administration of major matters, such as government green channels, offer demand information, promote the connection between supply and demand and coordinate and provide support in implementing the national preferential policies.

The local administrative departments of science and technology and industry for national defense may formulate the preferential policies for recordation entities within their respective administrative regions based on local circumstances.

Article 10

The arms and equipment system and subsystem integration entities shall prioritize in evaluating, selecting and incorporating the recordation entities into their supplier lists.

Article 11

Where the name of the legal person or its registered address changes within the recordation validity term of the scientific research and production of arms and equipment, the recordation entities shall, within 2 months as of the date of change, report and follow the change formalities, i.e., filling out the Application Form for the Recordation Alteration of the Scientific Research and Production of Arms and Equipment (Annex 3) and submitting the local administrative departments of science and technology and industry for national defense a change explanation (with its official seal) with the relevant information and materials, including the changed business license of an enterprise legal person or the changed legal person certificate of a public institution.

Article 12

The local administrative departments of science and technology and industry for national defense shall examine the application materials of alteration submitted by the recordation entity, notify the recordation entity of all necessary supplements and corrections once in writing within 7 working days if the application materials are incomplete and make an acceptance decision if the documents and materials are complete and replace recordation certificates (record numbers and terms of validity unchanged) within 20 working days after receiving the alteration application.

Article 13

Where any recordation entity applies for adding or changing the recorded specialized areas or products within the recordation validity term, it shall file a new application and be granted the recordation certificate (record number unchanged). The validity term shall commerce from the day when the new recordation is issued.

A recordation entity is not required to undergo recordation change formalities unless the added suppliers or products categories are not included in the recorded specialized areas (products).

Any recordation entity, if loses the scientific research production capacity corresponding to its arms and equipment scientific research and production activities, shall report to the original local recordation department and apply for recordation termination within 2 months as of the date of change.

Article 14
Any recordation entity that intends to continuously undertake the task of scientific research and production of arms and equipment, shall, 3 months before the expiration of the validity term, file a new recordation application in accordance with Article 5 of the Measures and be issued another recordation certificate (recordation number unchanged). The validity term shall commerce from the day when the new recordation is issued.

Article 15
The local administrative departments of science and technology and industry for national defense shall establish an recordation database, collect and update the information on recordation entities in a timely manner, obtain the recordation application, alteration and cancellation information of recordation entities, fill out the Information Form for the Recordation Administration of Scientific Research and Production Recordation of Arms and Equipment (Annex 4) (including a written copy and an electronic text in a compact disc) collecting and updating the information on all the local recordation entities and submit to the SASTIND together with the Application Recordation Forms for the Scientific Research and Production of Arms and Equipment (including an electronic text in a compact disc) annually before December 31 of each year.

Article 16
The SASTIND shall be responsible for the establishment of a national recordation database of the scientific research and production of arms and equipment, collect and update the information on recordation entities in a timely manner, incorporate these information into the list of recordation entities and circulate among the relevant departments within the State Council, the local administrative departments of science and technology and industry for national defense, the military industry corporations and the military armament departments on a regular basis.

Article 17
Any recordation entity shall fill out an Annual Self-inspection Report on the Recordation of the Scientific Research and Production of Arms and Equipment (Annex 5) as required by the end of each year and submit to the recordation departments before the end of

March of the following year. The recordation departments shall submit the Annual Self-inspection Reports on the Recordation of the Scientific Research and Production of Arms and Equipment (an electronic text in a compact disc) to the SASTIND before the end of June of the following year.

Article 18
The SASTIND shall organize and carry out the supervision and inspection, randomly select recordation entities every year to verify the authenticity of their application documents materials and inspect their scientific research and production capacity and their performance and management in undertaking the task or fulfilling a contract in the scientific research and production of arms and equipment. The local administrative departments of science and technology and industry for national defense shall randomly select a certain proportion of the recordation entities to be supervised and inspected based on their local circumstances and assist the SASTIND in the supervision and inspection. The materials that shall be submitted by the recordation entities for inspection see Annex 6.

Any recordation entity that has been on-site examined or inspected for the licensing of the scientific research and production of arms and equipment may be exempted from the supervision and inspection over the recordation for a year.

Article 19
After receiving complaints or reports on the recordation entities' violation of the provisions related to the scientific research and production of arms and equipment from user departments (entities) or from other enterprises or individuals, the SASTIND shall investigate and verify the relevant situation and organize on-site investigation or authorize the local administrative departments of science and technology and industry for national defense to organize experts investigation and verification as needed.

Article 20
Under any of the following circumstances, a recordation entity shall be ordered to rectify according the requirements of relevant authorities and report to the recordation departments thereafter:
(1) Looseness in quality management causing adverse consequences;
(2) A production safety accident causing serious injuries or deaths;
(3) Causing severe environmental pollution;
(4) Looseness in confidentiality administration causing serious secret divulge; and
(5) Deficiency in the scientific research and production capacity and failing to fulfill its tasks or contracts on schedule overdue for a long period of time or for many times.

Article 21

The local administrative departments of science and technology and industry for national defense shall withdraw or revoke its recordation of scientific research and production of arms and equipment, if a recordation entity is under any of the following:

(1) Fails to be file a new application for recordation when the validity term has expired;
(2) The legal person is legally terminated or bankrupt;
(3) Disable to carry out the scientific research and production of arms and equipment;
(4) Provides false materials, or reneges on promises, or its scientific research and production capacity and management situation is seriously contrary to the actual status, or frauds in research and production, or delivers fake and inferior products;
(5) Ineffective rectification action or refuse to rectify in accordance with Article 20 of the Measures.

If the local administrative department of science and technology and industry for national defense intends to withdraw or revoke a recordation, it shall notify the recordation entity before making such a decision.

Article 22

Where a recordation entity refuses to rectify in accordance with Article 20 of the Measures or is under the circumstances of paragraph 4 of Article 21 of the Measures and the local administrative department of science and technology and industry for national defense decides to revoke the recordation after organizing and carrying out investigation and verification, such decision shall be reported to the SASTIND. The SASTIND shall circulate this decision to the relevant departments within the State Council, the local administrative departments of science and technology and industry for national defense, the military industry corporations and the military armament departments.

Any recordation entity committing fraud in research and production or delivering fake and inferior products shall be included in the blacklist of dishonest enterprises established and issued by the SASTIND.

Article 23

The recordation administration of the scientific research and production of arms and equipment under the Measures shall not charge the recordation entities any fee.

Article 24

The Measures shall be subject to the interpretation by the SASTIND.

Article 25

The Measures shall come into force on the date of promulgation.

4.8. Regulation on the Export Control of Military Items[8]

State Council and Central Military Commission
Promulgated on 22nd November 1997 and Amended on 15th October 2002
(Unofficial Translation by WU Xiaodan, assisted by Ms. WU Tong)

Chapter 1. General Provisions

Article 1
The Regulation is formulated to strengthen the unified administration of military exports and maintain the regular military exportation order.

Article 2
The military exports in the present Regulation refer to the trading exports of military-purpose equipment, specialized production facilities and other materials, technologies and related services.

The military exports referred to in the preceding paragraph shall be included in the military exports list, which shall be formulated, adjusted and promulgated by the national military export control authorities.

Article 3
Under the leadership of the State Council and the Central Military Commission, the national military export control authorities shall be responsible for the administration and supervision of military export activities nationwide.

Article 4
There shall be a national, unified military export administration mechanism to prohibit any military export activities that damage the national interests and security and legally maintain the military export order.

Article 5
All military exports shall be consistent with the following principles: (1) Assisting the recipient country in its legitimate self-defense capabilities;
(2) Not jeopardizing peace, security and stability in relevant regions and around the world; (3) Not interfering in the internal affairs of the recipient country.

---

[8] The Chinese version of this regulatory document is published on the website of the State Administration of Science and Technology and Industry for National Defense, www.sastind.gov.cn, last accessed August 2021.

Article 6
The provisions of the international treaties that the People's Republic of China has concluded or accepted shall prevail in case they are different from the present regulations except for the provisions that the People's Republic of China has made reservation statements.

Chapter 2. Military Trading Companies

Article 7
The military trading companies in the present Regulation refer to the corporate legal persons that have legally obtained military export trading authorization to engage in military export activities within the approved business scope.

Article 8
The military export trading authorization is examined and granted by the national military export control authorities and the specific measures will be formulated by the national military export control authorities.

Article 9
The military trading companies shall operate legally and independently and be responsible for their own profits and losses.

Article 10
The military trading companies shall abide by their contracts, guarantee their product quality and improve their after-sales services.

Article 11
The military trading companies, as required by the regulations of the national military export control authorities, shall accurately and truthfully submit the documents and materials related to their military export activities. The national military export control authorities shall preserve the trade secrets and safeguard the legitimate rights and interests of military trading companies.

Article 12
The military trading companies may entrust the export transportation and other related businesses to the authorized military export transportation corporations. The national military export control authorities shall formulate the specific measures.

Chapter 3. Military Exportation Administration

Article 13
The administration system of licensing shall apply to the military exports.
The military exports projects and contracts shall be filed for review and approval in accordance with the present Regulation. The military exports shall be carried out after obtaining a military export license.

Article 14
The Military exports projects shall be reviewed and approved by the national military export control authorities or in conjunction with the relevant departments within the State Council and the Central Military Commission.

Article 15
After the military export project is approved, the military trading company may sign the military export contract with the overseas buyers. The signed military export contract shall be submitted to the national military export control authorities for review and approval and the national military export control authorities shall decide within 20 days upon receipt of the application. The military export contract may only take effect upon such approval.
The military trading companies shall incorporate the valid certification documents from the recipient countries into the military export contract approval application submitting to the national military export control authorities.

Article 16
The major military exports projects and contracts shall be reviewed by the national military export control authorities in conjunction with the relevant department of the State Council and the Central Military Commission and be submitted to the State Council and the Central Military Commission for approval.

Article 17
The military trading companies shall, after obtaining the approval documents for the export contracts and prior to the military exports, apply to the national military export control authorities for the military export license. The national military export control authorities shall issue the military export licenses within 10 days upon receipt of the application if it conforms to the military export contract terms.
The Customs shall accept the customs declarations in accordance with the military exports license and examine and allow passage of the items in accordance with the relevant regulations.

Article 18

The national military export control authorities shall formulate the measures for reviewing and approving military exports projects and contracts and for issuing military export licenses.

Article 19

The military export notifications shall be issued jointly by the national military export control authorities in conjunction with other relevant departments. Upon receipt of the notifications, the relevant departments and local people's governments shall seriously and legally fulfill their duties to ensure the safety, promptness and accuracy of military exports.

Chapter 4. Military Exports Order

Article 20

No units or organizations shall engage in the military export activities without obtaining export authorization in advance.
Individuals are prohibited from conducting the military exports activities.

Article 21

The military trading companies shall abide by the laws and administrative regulations in their military export activities to ensure the regular order of military exports.

Article 22

The military trading companies may not conduct any of the following in their military export activities: (1) Endangering national security or social and public interests; (2) Excluding competitors through unfair competitive means; (3) Infringing upon the intellectual rights protected by the laws of the People's Republic of China;
(4) Forging, altering, fraudulently obtaining or transferring the military export approval documents, contract approval documents, licenses, valid certificates from recipient countries and other documents; (5) Exceeding the defined and approved scope of activities; (6) Other activities that violate laws and administrative regulations.

Article 23

The national military export control authorities, on its own initiative or upon the requests from other military trading companies, may deal with the conducts that interfere with the normal military export order.

Chapter 5. Legal Responsibility

Article 24

The national military export control authorities will warn the military trading companies and order to rectify within a time limit if they violate Article 11 of the present Regulation. If no rectification is made within the prescribed period of time, a fine of more than 20,000 yuan but less than 100,000 yuan will be imposed and the military export authorizations will be suspended or revoked.

Article 25

The military trading companies that violate paragraph 4 and 5 of Article 22 of the present Regulation and shall be held criminally responsible in accordance with the law if they commit the crimes of illegal business operations; forging, altering or trading official documents, credentials or seals of the state organs or other crimes. If the circumstances are not serious enough to impose criminal punishment, the national military export control authorities will give a warning, confiscate the illegal gains and impose a fine of more than 1 time but less than 3 times of the illegal gains. If there is illegal gains less than 100,000 yuan, a fine of more than 100,000 yuan but less than 300,000 yuan will be imposed and the military export authorizations granted to this offending company will be suspended or revoked.

The military trading companies that violate paragraph 1, 2 and 3 of Article 22 of the present Regulation or other laws and administrative regulations will be penalized and punished by the relevant state authorities in accordance with the relevant laws and administrative regulations and the national military export control authorities may suspend or revoke the military export authorizations. The military trading companies shall be held criminally responsible in accordance with the law if they commit a crime.

Article 26

Those that violate Article 20 of the present Regulation will have their illegal activities closed down by the national military export control authorities. Those shall be held criminally responsible in accordance with the law if they commit the crimes of illegal business operations or other crimes. If the circumstances are not serious enough for criminal punishment, the national military export control authorities will give a warning, confiscate the illegal gains and impose a fine of more than 1 time but less than 5 times of the illegal gains; and if the illegal gains are less than 100,000 yuan, a fine of more than 100,000 yuan but less than 500,000 yuan will be imposed.

Article 27

The military trading companies that refuse to accept the specific administrative actions conducted by the national military export control authorities shall first apply for administrative reconsideration pursuant to the law; those that still refuse to accept the administrative reconsideration decision may bring administrative case to the people's court.

Article 28

The functionaries in the national military export administration posts who abuse their powers, neglect their duties or accept and demand bribes shall be held criminally responsible if they commit the crime of abusing the powers, the crime of neglecting the duties, the crime of accepting bribes or other crime and disciplinary penalties will be imposed to those whose conducts are not serious for criminal punishment.

Chapter 6. Supplementary Articles

Article 29

The present Regulations shall apply to the exports of police-use equipment.

Article 30

The present Regulations shall enter into force on 15th November 2002.

4.9. Regulation on the Export Control of Missiles and Related Items and Technologies[9]

State Council
22nd August 2002
(Unofficial Translation by WU Xiaodan, assisted by Ms. WU Tong)

Article 1

The present Regulation is formulated for the purpose of strengthening the export control over the missiles and related items and technologies and safeguarding the security of the state as well as the public social good.

Article 2

The term "export of missiles and related items and technologies" in the present Regulation refers to the trading export of the missiles and related equipment, materials and technologies as mentioned in the List of Related Items Subject to Export Control (hereafter "the List of Export Control") as well as technological transfer through the

---

9   The Chinese version of this regulatory document is published on the website of the State Administration of Science and Technology and Industry for National Defense, www.sastind.gov.cn, last accessed August 2021.

means of foreign donations, exhibitions, scientific and technological cooperation, providing aid and services, etc.

Article 3
The state administers rigid control over the export of missiles and related items and technologies to prevent the proliferation of missiles and other carrier systems as mentioned in the List of Export Control that can be employed to carry massive destructive weapons.

Article 4
The administration system of licensing shall apply to the export of missiles and related items and technologies. No entity or individual may, without approval, export any missile or related items or technology.

Article 5
The items and technologies as mentioned in Part II of the List of Export Control shall be exported according to the Regulation of the People's Republic of China on Export Control of Military Items and other relevant regulations.
The items and technologies as mentioned in Part II of the List of Export Control (hereafter referred to as missile-related items and technologies) shall be subject to the examination and approval as provided from Articles 7 to 13 of the present Regulation. However, the export of missile-related items and technologies for military purposes shall be subject to the preceding paragraph.

Article 6
The recipient party of the export of missile-related items and technologies shall promise not to employ the missile-related items and technologies provided by China to any purposes other than the declared ultimate purposes, not to transfer any of the missile-related items and technologies provided by China to any third parties other than the declared end-users unless it has obtained the approval of the Chinese government.

Article 7
Any business actor that is engaged in the export of missile-related items and technologies shall be subject to registration at the administrative department of foreign economic relations and trade within the State Council. Without registration, no entity or individual may be engaged in the export of missile-related items and technologies. The specific measures for registration shall be formulated by the administrative department of foreign economic relations and trade within the State Council.

Article 8

To export missile-related items and technologies, an application shall be filed to the administrative department of foreign economic relations and trade within the State Council, filling in a Form of Application for Exporting Missile-Related Items and Technologies (hereafter "Application Form") and submitting the following documents:

(1) The identification paper of the legal representative, major management personnel and dealers of the applicant;
(2) A copy of the contracts or agreements;
(3) The technical specifications of missile-related items and technologies;
(4) The certification of ultimate-users and certification of ultimate utilization purpose;
(5) The promise as provided in Article 6 of the present Regulation;
(6) The other documents as required by the administrative department of foreign economic relations and trade within the State Council.

Article 9

The applicant shall truthfully fill in the Application Form.

The Application Forms shall be uniformly formulated and printed by the administrative department of foreign economic relations and trade within the State Council.

Article 10

The administrative department of foreign economic relations and trade within the State Council shall examine the application when it receives the Application Forms as well as the documents as provided in Article 8 of the present Regulation, or consult the relevant departments of the State Council and the relevant departments of the Central Military Committee and make the decision of approval or disapproval within 45 workdays.

Article 11

If the export of missile-related items and technologies has significant impact on national security or public interests, the administrative department of foreign trade and economic cooperation shall consult the relevant departments and report to the State Council and the Central Military Committee for approval.

When the export of missile-related items and technologies is subject to the approval of the State Council and the Central Military Committee, the time limits as provided in Article 10 of the present Regulation does not apply.

Article 12

Where application for the export of missile-related items and technologies is approved, the administrative department of foreign economic relations and trade within the State

Council shall issue a license for the export of missile-related items and technologies (hereafter "export license") and inform the customs offices.

Article 13
Where the license holder needs to change the export of the missile-related items and technologies, it shall return the original export license and file the applications to obtain a new export license according to the relevant provisions of the present Regulation.

Article 14
When exporting missile-related items and technologies, the exporter shall present to the customs offices its export license, go through the customs process according to the relevant provisions of the Customs Law and accept the supervision of the customs offices.

Article 15
Where the recipient party violates its promise in Article 6 of the present Regulation or there arises the proliferation risks of the missiles and other carrier systems that can be employed to carry massive destructive weapons as listed in the List of Export Control, the administrative department of foreign economic relations and trade within the State Council shall suspend or revoke the export licenses that it has issued and inform the customs offices in written form.

Article 16
Where the exporter knows or should have known that the missile-related items and technologies to be exported will be directly used by the recipient party in the development programs of missiles and other carrier systems that can be employed to carry the massive destructive weapons as mentioned in the List of Export Control, the present Regulation shall be applicable even though the item or technology is not mentioned in the List of Export Control.

Article 17
The administrative department of foreign economic relations and trade within the State Council may, upon the approval of the State Council and the Central Military Committee, consult the relevant departments and decide to control the export of specific items and technologies that are not mentioned in the List of Export Control according to the present Regulation.

Article 18
Those who export missile-related items and technologies without approval or exports missile-related items and technologies beyond the license permission shall be held criminally responsible according to the laws if they commit the crimes of smuggling, illegal business operation, divulging state secrets or other crimes. If the circumstances are not serious enough to impose criminal punishment, they shall be punished according to the relevant provisions of the Customs Law based on the specific situations and the administrative department of foreign economic relations and trade within the State Council may give a warning, confiscating its illegal gains, impose a fine of not less than 1 time but not more than 5 times the amount of the illegal gains and suspend or revoke its international trading authorization.

Article 19
Those who forge, alter, sell or purchase the licenses for export of missile-related items and technologies shall be held criminally responsible according to the laws if they commit the crime of illegal business operation, forging, altering or trading the official documents of the state organs, certificates or seals and other crimes. If the circumstances are not serious enough impose criminal punishment, they shall be punished according to the relevant provisions of the Customs Law and The administrative department of foreign economic relations and trade within the State Council may revoke their international trading authorization.

Article 20
For those who obtain their license for the export of missile-related items and technologies by fraudulent or other unjustifiable means, the administrative department of foreign economic relations and trade within the State Council shall withdraw the licenses, confiscate the illegal gains thereof, impose the fine of an amount that is smaller than the illegal gains, suspend and revoke their international trade authorization.

Article 21
For those who violate the provisions of Article 7 of the present Regulation by exporting missile-related items and technologies without registration, their illegal activities shall be closed down by the administrative department of foreign economic relation and trade within the State Council and they shall be punished by the relevant administrative departments according to relevant laws and administrative regulations.

Article 22
Where any employee of the state organs that exert control over the export of missile-related items and technologies abuses his powers, neglects his duties, or accept brides by taking advantage of his position, they shall be held criminally responsible according to

the laws, if they commit the crimes of abusing power, neglecting duties, accepting bribes or other crimes. If the circumstances are not serious enough to impose criminal punishment, they shall be administratively punished according to law.

Article 23
The administrative department of foreign economic relation and trade within the State Council may, in collaboration with relevant departments, adjust the List of Export Control according to the practical situations, which shall be implemented after obtaining the approval of the State Council and the Central Military Committee.

Article 24
The present regulation shall enter into force on the day of promulgation.

4.10. INTERIM MEASURES FOR THE MANAGEMENT OF CIVIL SATELLITE PROJECTS[10]

State Administration of Science and Technology and Industry for National Defense
29th November 2016
(Unofficial Translation by WU Xiaodan, assisted by Ms. WU Tong)

Chapter I. General Provision

Article 1
These Measures are formulated to standardize the management of civil satellite projects, strengthen the supervision of space industry, implement the requirements of the Medium and Long Term Development Plan of National Civil Space Infrastructure (2015-2025) by the State Council and make full use of the investment and application benefits of the satellite projects.

Article 2
These Measures shall apply to the science satellite projects, operational satellite projects and other civil satellite projects that are fully or partially funded by the central government funds and approved by the State Council or other governmental departments.

---

10 The Chinese version of this regulatory document is published on the website of the State Administration of Science and Technology and Industry for National Defense, www.sastind.gov.cn, last accessed August 2021.

Article 3
The basic principles for the management of civil satellite projects are science and justice, standardization and efficiency, clear rights, power and responsibility and being pragmatic. Strengthen the process control and milestone assessment, unify the development and construction process and establish the standard and normative system for quality supervision and management so as to realize the healthy and coordinated development of space and ground resources.

Article 4
The civil satellite project is generally composed of six systems: satellite system, carrier rocket system, launch site system, measurement and control system, ground system and application system. The development and construction process of civil satellite project can be generally divided into phases of project demonstration, scheme and draft, prototype sample, model sample, on-orbit test deliver and summary evaluation. The development and construction process can be simplified for the satellite engineering with high technical maturity.

Article 5
The management of civil satellite project refers to the management of activities related to the whole process from demonstration to satellite decommissioning, which is mainly composed of comprehensive demonstration, project establishment, overall design, system coordination, development and production, launch measurement and control, on-orbit test, delivery operation, summary evaluation and off-orbit disposal.

Chapter II. The Organization and Management of Civil Satellite Projects

Article 6
The State Administration of Science and Technology and Industry for National Defense (hereinafter referred to the SASTIND) will establish a trans-departmental and trans-unit coordination mechanism for the management of civil satellite projects, consulting the administrative, research, construction, launch, measurement and control and users departments and units of satellites projects.

The SASTIND is responsible for the organization, management and overall coordination of civil satellite projects, clarifying the overall support units of the project and undertaking the cross-departmental and cross-system organization and coordination tasks, such as the optimization of implementation plan and the organization of project development and construction.

Article 7

The user units are responsible for the application requirements demonstration of satellite projects, the construction and operation of application system and the organization and management of satellite application. The ground construction units are responsible for the construction and management of the ground system. The launch measurement and control units are responsible for the organization and implementation of satellite launch, measurement and control and in-orbit long-term management. The satellites and rockets development units are responsible for the organization and implementation of the tasks they undertake.

Article 8

In accordance with the Regulations on the Leaders Management of Model Development of the SASTIND, a "two general" system of civil satellite projects shall be established, a chief engineer for a civil satellites project and a chief commander for a national major project if necessary. The chief engineer is responsible for the overall design of civil satellite project, the interfaces of different systems, the integration of space and earth and the decision-making of major technical issues. The main systems of the project will establish corresponding "two general" of the models, who are responsible for the organization and implementation of their work.

Article 9

The National Committee for Civil Satellite Users will be established, forming a coordination mechanism for the integration of satellite application needs and trans-department coordination, evaluating the on-orbit satellite applications and benefits, strengthening the overall planning of users' needs for the on-orbit satellites so as to improve the utilization efficiency.

Article 10

The civil satellite projects shall apply radio frequency and orbit slots to the International Telecommunication Union through the Ministry of Industry and Information Technology in accordance with the Radio Regulations of the International Telecommunication Union and the relevant domestic regulations.
During the project demonstration phase, the availability demonstration of satellite radio frequency and orbit slots shall be carried out synchronously, analyzing their feasibility, evaluating the potential risk and putting forward the risk control scheme. The radio frequency and orbit slot applicants are responsible for the application, coordination, operation and maintenance of radio frequency and orbit slots and shall apply to the Ministry of Industry and Information Technology and obtain a radio frequency license before applying for launch license.

Article 11

The civil space launches shall be subject to the licensing administration system. The final owner of the satellite or the general project contractor shall, in accordance with *the Law on Licensing and the Interim Measures for Administration of Licensing the Projects of Launching Civil Space Objects*, submit an application for the launch license to the SASTIND 9 months before the scheduled launch month and obtain a license for launching civil space objects. Launch license are also required for the spacecraft with civil and commercial payloads.

Article 12

The State carries out the system of registering space objects. All space objects launched in the territory of China, as well as space objects jointly launched abroad by China and other States, shall be registered domestically by the final owner, user and operator of the space object in accordance with *the Measures for the Administration of Registration of Objects Launched into Outer Space*.

Article 13

The SASTIND shall supervise and administer the space debris mitigation and safety protection of civil spacecraft and launch vehicles, organize and formulate relevant administration measures and standards. In the course of project development, launch and in-orbit operation, the relevant departments units shall fulfill their space debris mitigation responsibilities in accordance with the requirements of *the Measures for Space Debris Mitigation and Protection*.

Article 14

The SASTIND shall, after consultation with relevant departments, formulate policies and regulations on satellite remote sensing date and other satellite data, so as to strengthen satellite data sharing and improve the utilization efficiency of satellites.

Article 15

The SASTIND, after consultation with relevant departments, shall promote the construction of the standardization system and formulate and promulgate the relevant standards and norms, so as to strengthen the formulation of standards on the ground systems, application system and satellite data and promote the connection between national and international standards. The development and construction departments and units shall strictly conform to the standards and norms in the development, construction and operation phase of the project.

Article 16
The satellite projects can be managed based on contracts if feasible. Competitive selection is encouraged in satellite projects management with proper supervision.

Article 17
The SASTIND (China National Space Administration) is responsible for foreign exchanges and international cooperation in satellite projects, the negotiation and implementation of international conventions and agreements, the signature of intergovernmental and inter-departmental cooperation agreements on behalf of the Chinese Government and organizing to carry out international cooperation in different forms, such as technology research and development, projects development and implementation, system operation and application promotion.

Article 18
The confidentiality of civil satellite projects shall be subject to their respective responsibilities in accordance with the division of projects tasks and the implementation and management of the project organization shall strictly abide by *the Law on State Secrecy* and relevant regulations and rules. The news release shall be subject to the centralized administration of the SASTIND and the news involving key indicators and sensitive matters of the civil satellites projects shall be submitted to the SASTIND for examination in advance.

Chapter III. The Implementation of Civil Satellites Projects

Article 19
In accordance with the Five-Year Plans for Space Industry Development and the Medium and Long-term Development Plan for National Civil Space Infrastructure, the main users shall consult the competent departments and units of development and construction, draft and submit the needs and tasks of science satellite projects and coordinate the other users in drafting and reporting the user requirements of satellites.

Article 20
The SASTIND shall organize and carry out the efficiency optimization design of the civil satellite projects, initiate the comprehensive demonstration of the project approval and the guarantee conditions for the development and scientific research of projects, organize and draft the overall plan of the projects and the coordination plan so as to form a comprehensive foundation of the projects for their examination and approval.

Article 21

The development and construction departments and units shall jointly, after consulting the main user departments and units, draft and submit the satellite project proposal and the project implementation outline. The science and operational satellite projects as the national civil space infrastructure shall be examined and approved by the SASTIND, the National Development and Reform Commission and the Ministry of Finance. The other civil satellite projects shall be examined and approved in accordance with relevant regulations and rules.

Article 22

The feasibility study report of science satellite project shall be led by the research and construction departments and units. The feasibility study report and preliminary design of the operational satellite project shall be led by the main user departments and units, after consultation with the relevant departments and units of the 6 main projects systems, and submit for approval.

Article 23

The project shall be organized to carry out the overall coordination of interfaces and major matters among the 6 systems, strengthen the control and management of the technical state and inspect on the research and development progress. Based on the research and construction plan of the 6 system, the general technical documents shall be drafted, such as the general requirements for project development and construction, training outlines for satellites and launch vehicles, launch flight (test) outlines, on-orbit test outlines, engineering and technical manuals and be examined by the "two general" of the project and the SASTIND before being issued and implemented.

Article 24

The project shall be organized to overall coordinate the technical interfaces, product standards, planning progress and data interfaces between the ground systems, application systems and other systems. The main user departments, if possible, shall participate in the coordination work. The ground system and application system are submitted and approved through different channels, synchronously or moderately in advance with the development and construction of the project so as to realize it coordinated development and operation and the integration of space and earth.

Article 25

According to the approval and the overall requirements of the project, the research and construction departments and units shall organize and carry out the research and construction work at all stages of the project, be responsible for the technology, quality, progress and funds of the tasks undertaken, ensure that the requirements of the tasks are met, organize transition stage reviews with the user departments and units and submit the current state work summary and the work plan for the next stage to the SASTIND for recordation. The development transition stage of the major projects shall be organized by the SASTIND.

Article 26
The excessive carrying capacity of the carrier rocket shall be used to carry out the satellite payload launch. For a project with excessive carrying capacity, the applicant shall put forward satellite payload proposal and incorporate it into the project demonstration during feasibility study report stage.

Article 27
In accordance with the provisions on quality and reliability management, the research and construction departments and units shall organize and implement the project, establish a quality management system and maintain its effective operation, fulfill their responsibilities step by step, formulate a product (quality) assurance outline, strengthen the recheck and review, enhance the quality control of key parts, important elements and outsourcing products and be responsible for the tasks undertaken and the product quality. For the essential, high-risk parts, products and technologies with impact on the success or failure of the project, the third party should be organized to carry out independent evaluation or design review.

Article 28
The main systems of the project shall be organized to carry out the development and construction of the project according to the schedule requirements, strengthen the risk identification and management control of the technical progress in the whole task cycle and formulate corresponding measures and evaluate regularly. The delay of the project shall be dealt with in accordance with the approval requirements and the contract terms; if the delay exceeds six months, the research and construction departments and units shall submit a written notification report with adjustment measures suggestions based on the actual situation.

Article 29
The research and construction departments and unites of the satellite and launch vehicle, together with the main user departments and units, shall submit application for the satellite and launch vehicles to exit the factory one month in advance. In accordance with *the Verification and Test Procedures for the Satellites and Launch Vehicles to Exit the Factory*, the SASTIND, together with relevant departments and unites, will organize the examination and approval of satellites and launch vehicles.

Article 30
The launch, measurement and control departments and units are responsible for the organization and implementation of the mission preparation, satellite launching and measurement and control of satellites.

Article 31
The research and construction and the user departments and units shall strictly conform to the reporting system for major quality problems and accidents. The major quality problems and emergencies in project development, launch and in-orbit operation of satellite shall be properly handled by the relevant departments and shall be reported to the SASTIND within 12 hours.

Article 32
The research and construction departments and units shall strictly conform to standards and requirements for the closed loop control of space products with quality problems and complete the closed loop of quality problems in a timely manner. At the key points such as transition stage and before exiting the factory, the implementation of loop closing measures and the to-do items shall be checked one by one to ensure the effectiveness of the closed-loop control.

Article 33
The project research and construction, operation and application, use of funds, project adjustment and other works shall be strictly carried out accordance with the relevant regulations and rules. The project adjustments that have an impact on the objectives, quality, progress and funds of the project shall be implemented only after the overall review of the project "two general" and the consent of the project examination and approval departments. The SASTIND, in conjunction with the relevant departments, shall supervise and inspect the implementation of the project, report the results of the inspection and handle the units and individuals violations in accordance with the laws.

Chapter IV. The Summary and Evaluation of Civil Satellite Projects

Article 34
After the satellite is launched into orbit, the project general and the main user departments and units shall, in conjunction with the relevant departments and units, organize the on-orbit test. After the satellite passes the on-orbit test, the SASTIND, in conjunction with the relevant departments, shall organize the satellite to be put into operation.

Article 35
To improve the efficiency of satellite application and ground system operation, the user departments and units shall organize and carry out the evaluation with regard to project index satisfaction, typical satellite application and ground system operation service after the satellite is put into operation and report it.

Article 36
After completing all the research and construction tasks, the project will organize the overall summary on the project development and construction, examine and appraise the satellite technical status and maturity and carry out the evaluation of the project efficiency, quality and reliability.

Article 37
After the satellite is delivered for operation, being flied into the archives and finally audited, the application for acceptance will be submitted by the research and construction departments and units. The SASTIND, the National Development and Reform Commission and the Ministry of Finance will organize the acceptance of the satellite project.

Article 38
The satellite, ground, application and measurement and control systems shall coordinate and cooperate, strengthen the technical support for the whole life period of in-orbit satellite, monitor the satellite status and provide emergency safeguarding such as preventing and early warning on space objects collision so as to guarantee the achievement of satellite functions and tasks.

Article 39
The operation management of remote sensing satellites is organized in accordance with relevant management methods and data policies. In principle, the communications satellites and commercial satellites shall be operated on a commercial basis. In case of emergencies and other critical situations, the SASTIND, in conjunction with the relevant departments, shall organize and coordinate the emergency disposal and management of in-orbit satellites.

Article 40
The satellite project is evaluated according to the project evaluation criteria. Establish and improve the project evaluation mechanism based on the credit history of project participation, reward the satellite project that has been identified as excellent projects with good quality, high technical level, longer time-span than designed life with

effectively functional performance. For the satellites projects that fail to reach their designed life in advance, the responsible departments and units causing the problems shall be notified and be dealt with the relevant rules.

Article 41

Before the satellite loses its main operational function or active deorbiting capability, the main user departments and units shall apply for satellite decommissioning to the SASTIND. The SASTIND, in conjunction with relevant departments, shall examine, approve and make overall arrangements for the satellite application expansion and off-orbit disposal.

Chapter V. Supplementary Articles

Article 42

The commercial satellites and international cooperative satellite projects shall be implemented in principle with reference to the present Measures.

Article 43

The SASTIND and China National Space Administration shall be responsible for the interpretation of the present Measures.

Article 44

These Measures shall enter into force on the date of promulgation. *The Interim Measures for the Development and Management of Civil Satellite Projects* issued by the SASTIND on 11 January 2008 shall be repealed on the same date.

4.11. INTERIM MEASURES FOR THE MANAGEMENT OF REMOTE SENSING SATELLITES DATA IN THE NATIONAL MAJOR SPECIALIZED PROJECT OF HIGH-RESOLUTION EARTH OBSERVATION SYSTEM[11]

The High-Resolution Observation Project Office,
State Administration of Science and Technology and Industry for National Defense
20th August 2015
(Unofficial Translation by WU Xiaodan, assisted by Ms. PENG Xuhan)

---

11 The Chinese version of this regulatory document is published on the website of the State Administration of Science and Technology and Industry for National Defense, www.sastind.gov.cn, last accessed August 2021.

Chapter I. General Provisions

Article 1

The Interim Measures are formulated to strengthen and standardize the management of remote sensing satellite data (hereinafter referred to as the high-resolution data) from the national major specialized project of high-resolution earth observation systems (hereinafter referred to as the High-Resolution Major Specialized Project) organized and implemented by the State Administration of Science and Technology and Industry for National Defense (hereinafter referred to the SASTIND), to vigorously promote the extensive application of high-resolution data in various fields and make full use of the supporting and serving role of high-resolution data in national security and economic and social development, in accordance with *"The Implementation Plan of the National Major Specialized Project of High-Resolution Earth Observation Systems"* approved by the State Council in 2011, *"The Measures for the Implementation and Management Method of National Major Specialized Project of High-Resolution Earth Observation Systems"* approved by SASTIND in 2012 and *"The Interim Provisions of Secrecy Management in Implementing the National Major Specialized Project of High-Resolution Earth Observation Systems"* approved by SASTIND in 2014, as well as other relevant laws, regulations and documents.

Article 2

The Interim Measures shall apply to all kinds of organizations and individuals in the whole process of receiving, processing, archiving, distribution and application of high-resolution data.

Article 3

The management of high-resolution data shall follow the principles of safeguarding national security and promoting public service; ensuring data openness and strengthening data sharing; innovating business models and promoting the application of high-resolution data; regulating market behavior and creating innovation space; strengthening overall coordination and improving service quality.

Article 4

The high-resolution data includes raw data received from remote sensing satellites and the processed products of different levels and categories, all of which are owned by the State. The processors and users of data information and its products have the right to use the data according to law and use the high-resolution data as required by these Interim Measures.

4. REGULATORY RULES ON SPACE ACTIVITIES

Article 5
The application of high-resolution data shall prioritize in meeting the needs of national emergency and the requirements of national security. The high-resolution data shall ensure the application and demonstration need of the high-resolution major project, the need of application technology research and development and public welfare services. The high-resolution data shall explore commercial application according to the market mechanism.

The companies registered in China, public institutions, social organizations, universities and colleges, governmental departments and Chinese citizens (hereinafter referred to as the users) can apply for the use of high-resolution data and use the high-resolution data according to law.

Chapter II. Main Responsibility

Article 6
The SASTIND Major Specialized Project Center (including the SASTIND High Resolution Observation Project Office and Earth Observation and Data Center of China National Space Administration, hereinafter referred to as the Major Specialized Project Center) is responsible for coordinating the needs of users and the overall management of high-resolution data; organizing and formulating the mission plan for high-resolution satellite observation; organizing and formulating the regulatory documents for the high-resolution data such as policies, standards and management methods; promoting and implementing the application, industrialization and international cooperation of high-resolution data; the establishment of a integrated information sharing and service platform of high-resolution data and related meta-databases and expanding the access channels of high-resolution data product.

Article 7
Under the coordination of Major Specialized Project Center, the government departments in charge of certain industry administration are responsible for organizing the relevant units to carry out the application of high-resolution data. Their responsibilities are formulating the policies for the application and promotion of high-resolution data in different industry; putting forward the use need for high-resolution data; carrying out the application evaluation of high-resolution data; constructing the production, distribution, application and sharing service system of high-resolution data product; formulating the relevant lists of data products, technical achievements and software and hardware products and the corresponding standards and norms; strengthening the application technology training and application promotion of high-resolution data in different industry; and promoting the operational application of high-resolution data in different industry. In addition, as the user representative of each

industry, they are responsible for participating in the coordination of satellite observation mission planning; regularly summarizing the applications situation to the Major Specialized Project Center so as to update the relevant content of the integrated information sharing and service platform of high-resolution data.

Article 8
The local administrative departments of science and technology and industry for national defense, which has established provincial data and application centers of high-resolution earth observation system, are responsible for organizing the distribution and application of high-resolution data in their respective regions, the unified deployment of the local high-resolution earth observation system at the provincial data and application centers and the operation of the relevant high-resolution data and application systems, participating in the coordination of satellite observation mission programming and planning as regional user representatives and organizing and drafting the annual reports on high-resolution data application in their region and submit to the Major Specialized Project Center.

Article 9
Under the coordination of Major Specialized Project Center, China Center for Resources Satellite Data and Application is responsible for accepting satellite observation requirements, preparing observation mission programs and plans, generating observation mission instructions and reception plans and conducting the processing, calibration, distribution and archive management of data product. The Institute of Remote Sensing and Digital Earth of the Chinese Academy of Sciences is responsible for receiving high-resolution data according to the mission programs and plans, in cooperation with the National Satellite Meteorological Center of the China Meteorological Administration and the National Satellite Ocean Application Center of the State Oceanic Administration.

Article 10
To promote the establishment of technical systems and industrial systems of high-resolution data applications, it is encouraged to establish application promotion and support organs and cultivate the leading enterprises. Among them, the technical system is composed of the application technology center and the geometric correction center of High-Resolution Major Specialized Project and other entities; the industrial system is composed of industrial promotion center, authorized the high-resolution data distribution entities, public service entities and other entities.

Chapter III. The Classification and Grade of Data

Article 11
The high-resolution data is divided into the raw data received by the satellite ground stations and all levels of processed products. Among them, level 0 products are raw data; level 1-2 products are primary products; level 3 and above level products are advanced products.

Article 12
The primary products of high-resolution data can be divided into public open and classified.
The public open data is the data that can be used directly by the public. The spatial resolution of the public open high-resolution optical data primary product is no more than (greater than or equal to) 0.5 m; the spatial resolution of the disclosed high-resolution microwave data primary product is no more than (greater than or equal to) 1 m.
The spatial resolution of the classified high-resolution optical data primary product is more than 0.5 m; the spatial resolution of the classified high-resolution microwave data primary product is more than 1 m. According to laws and regulations on state secrecy, the high-resolution data primary products involving secret information, sensitive areas and sensitive time periods are managed in accordance with classified situations.

Article 13
The advanced products of high-resolution data shall be devided as public open and classified according to relevant classification regulations with publicly accessible lists of products, lists of services and corresponding lists of standard specifications.

Chapter IV. Data Use Application and Distribution

Article 14
The high-resolution data primary product are distributed through four types of organs: the China Resources Satellite Application Center, authorized data distribution entities in different fields and industries, authorized the high-resolution Earth observation system data and application entities in provinces (including autonomous regions, municipalities) and other authorized entities. China Resources Satellite Application Center can distribute level 0-2 products and all the other entities can distribute level 1-2 products in respective authorized fields.

Article 15
According to their needs, the users can submit data use applications, which are to be registered and recorded, to the four types abovementioned distribution entities in their own fields. After the application being examined and approved, the users must sign relevant data management agreements with the high-resolution data distribution entities. The high-resolution data distribution entities should summarize the users information semi-annually and submit to the Major Specialized Project Center.

Article 16
Based on the data requirements and priority criteria proposed by the users, the Major Specialized Project Center should organize the user representatives of different industry and regions and the ground system operation units of High-Resolution Major Specialized Project to coordinate and formulate the annual satellite observation plan. The China Resources Satellite Application Center is responsible for formulating the monthly plan and weekly plan and collecting user needs and requirement feedbacks in a timely manner. In drafting annual plan, monthly plan and weekly plan, if there is conflict between the users needs and the proposed plan, the observation tasks proposed by the main satellite users and satisfying multi-user needs are prioritized.

When there are considerable differences in the formulation of weekly observation plans, emergency tasks and plans adjustment, they should be submitted to the Major Specialized Project Center for overall coordination.

Article 17
In principle, the level 0 products of high-resolution data are not distributed to users; if necessary, the distribution shall be coordinated by the Major Specialized Project Center.

Chapter V. Data Dissemination and Application and Achievement Management

Article 18
The High-Resolution Major Specialized Project is encouraged to support high-resolution data application technology research, application development, value-added services and industrial applications to strengthen the establishment of market-oriented mechanisms and commercialized service models and promote the wide and deep utilization of high-resolution data resources.

Article 19
The level 1-2 products of high-resolution data for the application demonstration tasks of High-Resolution Major Specialized Project are distributed based on authorization during the task period; for public welfare purpose are distributed free of charge; for non-public

welfare purposed are distributed with charges. The specific price is determined by the distribution entities of high-resolution data primary product with reference to the costs of similar products at home and abroad.

Article 20
The Major Specialized Project Center shall organize the collection and integration of high-resolution data products, draft the related services and standard specifications and form them into corresponding lists. They will be uniformly released through the high-resolution comprehensive information service and sharing platform of the National Space Administration, be used and shared freely within the high-resolution major project, but not for profit purposes.
The products and services and other achievement provided by High-Resolution Major Specialized Project are encouraged to transform outside the major specialized project to create a market-oriented operational environment and to accelerate the industrialization process.

Article 21
The High-Resolution Major Specialized Project is encouraged to develop industrial applications, regional applications and education and research applications based on high-resolution data. The data distribution entities in different industries can distribute high-resolution data to their local counterparts for public welfare purposes.
The local department of science and technology and industry for national defense shall provide relevant guarantees and management for the high-resolution data applications and promotion within their regions.
Various associations, societies and other social groups are supported to organize high-resolution data quality evaluation, application evaluation and data and results promotion, etc.

Article 22
The high-resolution data products and related applications are managed in accordance with relevant laws and regulations on intellectual property rights. The users are obliged to report data utilization and related applications. The application units and other users of different industries, regions and industrialization demonstration shall summarize the reception and application of high-resolution data semi-annually and submit reports to the Major Specialized Project Center with the lists of related products, services and standard specifications.
The China Resources Satellite Application Center, the data distribution entities of different industries and provinces (including autonomous regions and municipalities) shall summarize the distribution and application of high-resolution data semi-annually

and submit to the Major Specialized Project Center with the lists of related products, services and standard specifications.

The users should consciously protect the intellectual property rights of high-resolution data and are obliged to label the high-resolution data used in their applications. The users who receive the high-resolution data for free shall not transfer high-resolution data to a third party without consent or approval.

Article 23
In accordance with the relevant tasks requirements for the industrialization demonstration of high-resolution major project, the Major Specialized Project Center actively supports the development of leading enterprises in the field of domestic space information application and actively promotes the formation of a commercial operational environment including through the means of government procurement.

Chapter VI. International Cooperation and Services

Article 24
International cooperation and services in high-resolution data and related ground systems, application systems, application services and satellite operations will follow the principle of equality and friendship, sincere cooperation, business-oriented model and mutual benefit and reciprocity.

Article 25
The international cooperation and service of high-resolution data is administered by the States Administration of Science and Technology and Industry for National Defense (National Space Administration). The relevant domestic departments, units or entities are encouraged to undertake international obligations, such as disaster mitigation, climate change and ecological environment monitoring in accordance with international agreements.

Article 26
It is encouraged to use the high-resolution data to carry out scientific research, education and technical exchanges and cooperation. The distribution entities of high-resolution data primary product are encouraged to provide a small amount of data free of charge to domestic and foreign users for public welfare exchanges and cooperation purposes such as research and education.

Article 27
According to the relevant international cooperation agreements signed by Chinese government, relevant departments and the National Space Administration, under the premise of ensuring national information security and with the authorization from the States Administration of Science and Technology and Industry for National Defense (CNSA), domestic enterprises and united are encouraged to sell the high-resolution data, related ground systems and application systems and provide commercial services, such as data applications and satellite operations, to domestic international trading companies and foreign users.

Article 28
The high-resolution data of China's territory shall not be provided to any foreigner organization or individual without approval. The reception or use of overseas data shall be based on a country-specific policy with the necessary restrictions on data sales and commercial services involving sensitive areas and sensitive time periods. The overseas distribution is carried out on a region-specific basis and the foreign governmental agencies, enterprises and individuals can only distribute data of their own countries.

Chapter VII. Security Confidentiality and Legal Responsibilities

Article 29
The users applying for classified high-resolution data should have appropriate credentials or meet the relevant confidentiality requirements.

Article 30
The users who use the classified high-resolution data should strictly conform to *the Law on State Secrets, the Interim Provisions on Secrecy Management of National Major Specialized Project of High-resolution Earth Observation System* and the related regulations. The users shall conduct confidentiality management of the classified data.

Article 31
In the case of the following circumstances, the Major Specialized Project Center will issue a notice of criticism to the relevant departments and units. If the circumstances are severe, the data service may be terminated unilaterally. If there is violation of laws and relevant regulations, responsibility will be imposed.
- Application for the data utilization in the name of public welfare but used for non-public welfare purposes;
- Application for the data utilization for other purposes in the name of specific tasks of national major project;

- Concealing, falsely reporting for data application purposes and malicious filing of data applications;
- The primary product of the high-resolution data is distributed to a third party without obtaining the written approval from the Major Specialized Project Center;
- The distribution of high-resolution domestic data to foreign countries or transmission to foreign countries through domestic entities without approval;
- The violations of data confidentiality management and other data distribution management rules.

Chapter VIII. Supplementary Articles

Article 32
The high-resolution data management of other civilian remote sensing satellites, including the ones converted from military satellites, can be implemented in accordance with these Interim Measures.

Article 33
These Measures are interpreted by the High-Resolution Observation Project Office, State Administration of Science and Technology and Industry for National Defense.

Article 34
These Measures shall enter into force on the date of promulgation. Where the previous relevant provisions on the High-Resolution Major Specialized Project are inconsistent with these Measures, the present Measures shall prevail.

4.12. INTERIM MEASURES FOR THE MANAGEMENT OF REMOTE SENSING SATELLITES DATA FROM CHINA'S CIVILIAN SATELLITES[12]

State Administration of Science and Technology and Industry for National Defense
National Development and Reform Commission
Ministry of Finance
28th December 2018
(Unofficial Translation by WU Xiaodan, assisted by Ms. PENG Xuhan)

---

12 The Chinese version of this regulatory document is published on the website of the State Administration of Science and Technology and Industry for National Defense, www.sastind.gov.cn, last accessed August 2021.

Chapter I. General Provisions

Article 1

In order to implement the national strategies of civil-military integration, innovation-driven development and others, standardize the management of remote sensing data from China's civilian satellites (hereinafter referred to as remote sensing data), promote the remote sensing data opening and sharing as well as application and the relevant industrialization development, and maximize the important role of remote sensing data in economic and social development and national security, these Measures are formulated, in accordance with, among others, the Interim Measures for the Management of the Opening and Sharing of Remote Sensing Satellite Data and the National Medium and Long-Term Development Plan for Civil Space Infrastructure (2015-2025).

Article 2

These Measures shall apply to the management of remote sensing data financed by central fiscal funds in whole or in part. The management of remote sensing data from commercial satellites operated independently in China shall be governed by these Measures, mutatis mutandis.

Article 3

The following principles shall be followed in the management of remote sensing data: strengthening policy guidance, guaranteeing data security and promoting opening and sharing; strengthening overall coordination, breaking down inter-industry and cross-departmental barriers and improving application benefits; and promoting the development of the satellite remote sensing industry and enhancing international competitiveness based on market operation.

Chapter II. Division of Function and Duties

Article 4

The SASTIND, in conjunction with NDRC and MOF, shall organize and coordinate the major issues, including the operation and maintenance, interconnection and interworking, sharing and common use of the national civil satellite remote sensing system, and be responsible for the overall planning and coordination work of remote sensing data for their civil military integration and major emergency response, among others.

Given their functions as the satellite data centers, the China Earth Observation Satellite Data Center, the National Satellite Meteorological Center and the National Satellite

Ocean Application Service are respectively responsible for the acquisition, processing, archiving and distribution of relevant remote sensing data. The CNSA Earth Observation System and Data Center shall effectively make satellites missions planning and carry out remote sensing data management, particularly the data from national major specialized project of high-resolution earth observation satellite system.

The processing, archiving and distribution of remote sensing data partly financed by central fiscal funds shall be implemented in accordance with the duties of all parties as prescribed in the project approvals, investment approvals or Public and Private Partnership (PPP) contracts, etc.

Article 5

The users of remote sensing satellites financed by central fiscal funds shall include the main users and the other users. The main users are the ministries and commission with the State Council and their affiliating organs specified by the SASTIND (CNSA), NDRC and MOF.

Chapter III. Data Classification and Grading

Article 6

According to the observation means and the main characteristics of observation objects, remote sensing data are divided into three categories, namely, optical data, microwave data and geophysical field data. According to the public accessibility and technical indicators, remote sensing data are categorized into public data and confidential data. According to the degree of processing, remote sensing data are divided into raw data, level 0 products, primary products and advanced products.

Raw data means the data or signals received directly from satellites and demodulated.

Level 0 products mean the data products generated by decompressing the raw data and organized based on the data unit of orbit or scene.

Primary optical and microwave data products refer to the level 1 and level 2 data products acquired from level 0 products through processing steps such as basic radiometric correction and systematic geometric correction. The primary product of primary geophysical field data is defined by relevant codes of conduct.

Advanced products refer to the data products of level 3 or higher levels obtained from the primary products through geographic element matching or inversion.

Chapter IV. Acquisition, Sharing and Application Promotion

Article 7
The satellite data centers shall coordinate and formulate the overall plans for satellite observation based on the users' needs, satellite observation capabilities and other factors. The satellite observation plans shall be formulated to primarily meet the following needs:
(1) Needs of major emergencies, major emergency response and national security, etc.
(2) Needs of main users.
(3) Needs of national major projects.
(4) Needs of public scientific research and education application, etc.
(5) Needs for fulfilling international obligations and conducting international cooperation, etc.
The satellite data centers shall respond to the users' needs in a timely manner and regularly provide feedback to the users on the observation plan implementation. When a major natural disaster or any other emergency occurs, the satellite data centers shall respond immediately.

Article 8
The satellite data centers shall provide remote sensing data to the main users through the agreed methods.
When the satellite data centers provide remote sensing data to other users, there should be procedural requirements, including user authentication, request review and data use agreement. The satellite data centers shall reply within 5 working days upon receiving other users' data acquisition request.

Article 9
The satellite data centers and other units are encouraged to utilize the remote sensing satellites financed by central fiscal funds so as to expand the remote sensing data resources through different ways, including cooperative observation and data exchange with foreign remote sensing satellites.

Article 10
The satellite data centers shall organize the calibration work of national civilian remote sensing satellites, be responsible for examining and improving the remote sensing data quality and offer qualified and stable remote sensing data. When the quality of remote sensing data changes, it shall be announced in a timely manner.

Article 11

The spatial resolution of publicly accessible primary products of optical remote sensing data shall be no better than 0.5m and the spatial resolution of publicly accessible primary products of synthetic aperture radar remote sensing data shall be no better than 1 m. When necessary, the SASTIND shall, in conjunction with relevant military and governmental departments, adjust the public accessible standards of remote sensing data in accordance with relevant procedures.

Article 12

In principle, the satellite data centers shall only provide primary remote sensing data products to the users.

The primary remote sensing data products shall be provided free of charge to meet the needs of main users, the scientific research and education, intergovernmental international cooperation, and others public needs. The quality and efficiency of remote sending data application shall be evaluated by an independent third-party institution designated by the SASTIND (CNSA), NDRC and MOF, considering the data needs of users.

The primary remote sensing data products used for commercial purposes shall be subject to compensated distribution. Reasonable charging standards shall be formulated in accordance with the relevant rules and non-profitable principles, which shall be publicized and subject to supervision. The resulting revenues shall be turned over to the central treasury in full amount in accordance with the relevant rules on government non-tax income and centralized state treasury administration and be filed in the category of paid use of other state-owned resources (assets) (10307990) under the Classification of Items of Government Revenues and Expenditure.

Article 13

The existing national-owned satellite remote sensing ground infrastructure shall be fully utilized for its application in remote sensing data industry, education and scientific research. The development and commercial application of advanced remote sensing data products shall be encouraged and promoted. The social organization, such as industry and trade associations and academic societies, shall be encouraged to promote the remote sensing data application and service.

Article 14

Domestically produced satellite remote sensing data and services shall be prioritized in government procurement and utilization. State-owned enterprises and public institutions, scientific research institutions, colleges and universities and social organizations, among others, shall be encouraged to purchase domestic satellite remote sensing data and services.

Article 15
The national civil military integration development strategy shall be implemented to advance the opening and sharing of remote sensing data from China's civilian satellites and to serve the economic and social development and the national security construction.

Chapter V. International Exchange and Cooperation in Remote Sensing Data

Article 16
The SASTIND (CNSA) shall be responsible for the overall planning and coordination of international exchange and cooperation in remote sensing data and signing remote sensing data cooperation agreements between intergovernmental organs.

All competent entities shall be encouraged to conduct international exchange and cooperation activities related to remote sensing data applications and services and shall be supported in conducting international exchange and cooperation activities with other countries in respect of remote sensing data education, scientific research, disaster prevention and mitigation, and applications demonstration to serve the construction of the Belt and Road Initiative.

On the premise of complying with relevant national policies and international rules, all departments, regions, enterprises and institutions shall be encouraged to strengthen the export of domestic satellite remote sensing data applications and services.

Article 17
The relevant units can apply for central fiscal funds to construct, remold and upgrade satellite ground stations and ground systems abroad to receive remote sensing data from China's civilian satellites, and they shall submit the applications for approval according to relevant rules and procedures.

All entities can construct, remold, upgrade and rent satellite ground stations and ground systems abroad with their own funds to receive remote sensing data from China's civilian and commercial satellites and they shall comply with the relevant rules regarding national investment and project approval, etc.

Article 18
The satellite data centers shall, on the basis of the observation needs of overseas users, coordinate and formulate an overall overseas satellite observation plan in accordance with the following principles:
(1) Supporting the signing and implementation of relevant intergovernmental agreements and fulfilling international obligations;
(2) Jointly carrying out remote sensing data evaluation and application promotion of remote sensing date;

(3) Initiating and participating in the research on global and regional hot issues;
(4) Developing the international market of remote sensing data.

Chapter VI. Confidentiality and Safety

Article 19
Without authorization, the remote sensing data of China shall not be provided to overseas organizations or individuals. The remote sensing data involving sensitive areas and sensitive periods shall be subject to authorized distribution.
The safety management of remote sensing data from the commercial satellites operated independently in China shall be subject to this article.

Article 20
The users applying for the use of confidential data shall have the corresponding confidentiality qualifications or meet the relevant confidentiality requirements and shall manage and use the data in accordance with the confidentiality rules.

Article 21
The satellite data centers and other entities shall be responsible for constructing safe, stable and reliable data backup and disaster recovery systems so as to effectively prevent emergencies and guarantee the safety of remote sensing data.

Chapter VII. The Users' Rights and Obligations

Article 22
The users may appraise and put forward improvement opinions on the quality of remote sensing data in the process of remote sensing data research and applications.

Article 23
The remote sensing data financed by central fiscal funds in whole shall be owned by the state and those financed by central fiscal funds in part shall enjoy the related rights as agreed. The primary remote sensing data products obtained by the users from the satellite data centers free of charge shall not be transferred to the third parties without consent. The users shall, when using the aforementioned remote sensing data, indicate and explain the data sources in their application results.

Article 24

When applying and promoting the remote sensing data financed by central fiscal funds, the users shall feedback to the satellite data centers in order to support the formulating and release of national remote sensing application reports.

Article 25

The satellite data centers shall provide the main users lists and data service information on a regular basis. The SASTIND (CNSA) shall, in conjunction with the NDRC and the MOF, designate an independent third-party institution to evaluate the remote sensing data quality, the satellite data centers services and the remote sensing data utilization by the main users.

Article 26

The users shall, when using remote sensing data, comply with the relevant laws, regulations and ministerial rules and shall not engage in activities that endanger national security, public interests and the others' legitimate rights and interests.

Chapter VIII. Supplementary Articles

Article 27

These Measures shall apply, mutatis mutandis, to the management of remote sensing data from foreign satellites acquired through commercial channels and intergovernmental space cooperation.

Article 28

The satellite data centers and other entities shall formulate relevant detailed implementation and service rules according to these Measures.

Article 29

These Measures shall be subject to the interpretation by the SASTIND (CNSA), NDRC and MOF.

Article 30

These Measures shall enter into force on the date of promulgation. In case of any discrepancy between the previously promulgated provisions of the management measures of remote sensing data from China's civilian satellites and these Measures, these Measures shall prevail.

4.13. MEASURES FOR THE MANAGEMENT OF SCIENTIFIC DATA OF LUNAR AND DEEP SPACE EXPLORATION PROJECT[13]

State Administration of Science and Technology and Industry for National Defense
China National Space Agency
12 September 2016
(Unofficial Translation by WU Xiaodan, assisted by Ms. PENG Xuhan)

Chapter I. General Provisions

Article 1 Aims and Purposes
In order to standardize the management of scientific data of Lunar and Deep Space Exploration Project (hereinafter as scientific data), effectively promote data research and application and maximize scientific output, these Measures are formulated.

Article 2 Definition of Data
The scientific data means scientific and application information acquired from lunar and deep space exploration activities, such as remote sensing of celestial bodies, in situ exploration and sensing and outer space observation.

Article 3 Scope of Application
These Measures shall apply to processing, storage, archiving, application, distribution, application research and achievements management of the scientific data and relevant international cooperation and exchange. The scientific data acquired from international cooperation on lunar and deep space exploration shall be governed mutatis mutandis by these Measures, unless it is otherwise agreed in inter-governmental cooperation.

Article 4 Management Mode
The management of scientific data is modeled on decentralized administration and level-to-level responsibility.

Chapter II. Organization Structures and Their Functions

Article 5 Organization Structure
The SASTIND shall be responsible for the centralized administration of scientific data, authorizing the Lunar Exploration Project and Activities Center (hereinafter as the Project Center) to conduct administration over scientific data. The National

---

[13] The Chinese version of this regulatory document is published on the website of the State Administration of Science and Technology and Industry for National Defense, www.sastind.gov.cn, last accessed August 2021.

Astronomical Observatories of the Chinese Academy of Sciences shall be the supporting entity of the Project Center.

Article 6 Functions of the Project Center
The main functions of the Project Center are:
(1) Formulating the regulatory regimes and rules on the management of scientific data;
(2) Constructing and maintaining the scientific data platform on www.clep.org.cn and issuing scientific data information monthly;
(3) Conducting technical review on the request applications for scientific data;
(4) Determining the category of scientific data that shall be to publicly accessible;
(5) Forming and publishing the lists of scientific achievements;
(6) Conducting international cooperation and exchange of scientific data;
(7) Coordinating the submission and organization of scientific data from project participatory units;
(8) Monitoring and inspecting the publication and application of scientific data;
(9) Coordinating and coping with the problems and requirements derived from research and application of scientific data;

Article 7 Functions of the National Astronomical Observatories
The main functions of the National Astronomical Observatories are:
(1) Formulating code of conduct for the reception, process, interpretation and formats of scientific data;
(2) Processing and interpreting the raw scientific data delivered from spacecraft and storing data products arising therefrom;
(3) Formulating the lists of data products and the corresponding application instruction;
(4) Making preparation and issuance of scientific data in accordance with the technical review results of the Project Center;
(5) Producing scientific data information monthly.

Article 8 Functions of Other Units
The lunar exploration participatory project units except the National Astronomical Observatories shall summarize and submit scientific data derived thereby to the Project Center.

Article 9 Duties of Users
The scientific data users (hereinafter referred to as "the users") shall, when applying and exchanging the scientific data, comply with these Measures and relevant laws and regulations. In case of violation, their user qualification shall be cancelled and in cases of serious violation, they shall be punished by law.

Chapter III. Scientific Data Products Classification and Application Authority

Article 10 Scientific Data Classification
The data from the spacecrafts and preprocessed shall be classified into Level 0, Level 1 and Level 2.
Level 0 data: Level 0A is the source package data of the detectors generated from the process such as ground demodulation, frame synchronization, descrambling, channel decoding and frame decoding. Level 0B is the acquired data of the detectors generated from combining the data from various ground stations (if applicable), sorting out the repetitive data, eliminating package structures and decompressing the Level 0A.
Level 1 data: generated from the numeric conversions of instrument parameters including temperatures, voltages and currents of Level 0B and reorganizing in accordance with the detection periods.
Level 2 data: generated from revising the Level 1 in accordance with calibration results and providing geometric information.
The format of Level 0's is binary, whereas the format of Level 1 and Level 2 is usually the PDS standard.

Article 11 Data Processing
When receiving the raw data, the National Astronomical Observatories shall generate the first batch of scientific data after five- or six-months processing. Thereafter, the data derived from the operational detectors shall be processed continuously and the information shall be updated monthly.

Article 12 Application Authority
After generating the first batch of scientific data, all project participatory units providing payload can use scientific data of all levels from that particular payload in accordance the result of technical review. The other users are permitted to utilize level 1 or level 2 scientific data in accordance the result of technical review and shall indicate if follow-up data are needed.

Article 13 Data Publication
The Project Center shall determine the category of scientific data that are publicly accessible 12 months after the first batch of data generation based on the processing and research work of scientific data.

Chapter IV. Issuance Authorization Procedure of Scientific Data

Article 14 Qualifications
The domestic users shall have the corresponding scientific research qualifications with explicit data research plans and objectives.

Article 15 Applications for Scientific Data
After registering on the data information platform, the users shall fill in and submit the application form for the scientific data of lunar and deep space exploration project.

Article 16 Data Request Review
The Project Center shall conduct the technical review of the application form for scientific data of lunar and deep space exploration project within 10 working days and inform the National Astronomical Observatories of the opinions on the issuance of scientific data.
The National Astronomical Observatories shall make preparation for the issuance of scientific data within 10 working days, notifying the users the download link by email with a copy sent to the Project Center. The availability of download links shall not be less than 1 month.

Article 17 Download of Publicly Accessible Data
The publicly accessible scientific data are available on the data information platform.

Chapter V. International Cooperation and Exchange

Article 18 Intergovernmental Agreements
Providing scientific data to foreign partners under the intergovernmental cooperation agreements or cooperation agreement between China and international organizations shall be implemented after the Project Center applies to and obtains approvals from the CNSA.

Article 19 Foreign Payload Data
The access method and authorization of the scientific data generated from the foreign payloads onboard China's spacecraft are subject to intergovernmental agreements or others.

Article 20 Domestic Payload Data
The scientific data generated from Chinese payloads onboard foreign spacecraft shall be summarized and submitted to the data information platform unless violating the corresponding intergovernmental agreements.

Chapter VII. Application Promotion and Achievements Management

Article 21 Encouragement Principle
The domestic departments, scientific institutions and universities are encouraged to actively carry out scientific data research, achievements transformation, and application promotion. The public is supported to participate in the related scientific research and application development.

Article 22 Data Source Indication and Achievements Recording
"Scientific data supplied by the SASTIND" and "Scientific data supplied by the CNSA" shall be indicated in the users' domestic and international publication or academic exchange activities. It shall be recorded on the data information platform within 3 months after the publication.

Article 23 Achievements Management
The academic achievement and products arising from the scientific data shall be managed in accordance with the related laws and regulations on intellectual property, which is summarized by the Project Center and published on the data information platform.

Chapter VII. Supplementary Articles

Article 24 Interpretation
These Measures shall be subject to the interpretation by the SASTIND.

Article 25 Effective Date
These Measures shall come into force on the date of issuance. The Measures for the Management of Release of Scientific Data of Lunar Exploration Project issued in January of 2010 shall be simultaneously annulled.

4.14. Measures for the Management of Lunar Samples[14]

China National Space Administration
17th December 2020
(Official English Version)

Chapter 1. General Provisions

Article 1
These Measures are formulated for the proper storage, management and utilization of lunar samples for scientific research and social benefits.

Article 2
The lunar samples refer to the materials collected on and below the surface of the Moon through China's lunar exploration program and the lunar materials obtained by China National Space Administration (CNSA) through other channels.

Article 3
These Measures shall be applicable to the whole process covering unsealing, classification, preparation, documentation, storage, request application, distribution, transportation, utilization, return, disposition, information management, and achievement management.

Chapter 2. Functions

Article 4
China National Space Administration is in charge of the management of lunar samples and the main functions are:
(1) Formulating policies and regulations for the management of lunar samples;
(2) Supervising application and commercialization of lunar sample scientific research achievements; and
(3) International cooperation on lunar samples.

Article 5
Lunar Exploration and Space Engineering Center (hereinafter referred to as LESEC) of the CNSA has authorized by the CNSA to carry out the management of lunar samples, and its functions are:

---

[14] This is the official English version from the website of Chinese National Space Agency, the first one of its kind. http://www.cnsa.gov.cn/n6758823/n6758838/c6811123/content.html, last accessed August 2021.

(1) Reviewing the standards and code of conduct formulated by the relevant storage units;

(2) Establishing an expert committee on lunar samples;

(3) Reviewing the applications for requesting and borrowing lunar samples;

(4) Supervising and coordinating the process of unsealing, classification, preparation, documentation, storage, request application, distribution, transportation, utilization, return, disposition, information management and achievement management;

(5) Publishing the information of lunar samples on a regular basis through data information platform; and

(6) Monitoring scientific achievement and manage their applications, and preparing and publishing the list of publications and achievements.

Article 6

The lunar samples are stored at the CNSA and its designated storage units. The main storage unit is the National Astronomical Observatories of the Chinese Academy of Sciences, and there are other storage units.

The storage units, under the macro supervision of CNSA and specific guidance of LESEC, shall provide information of lunar samples to the LESEC in a timely manner, and report the storage and distribution information of lunar samples on a regular basis. When emergency occurs, such as lunar sample contamination and damages, it shall be reported to the LESEC immediately.

When the storage units borrow the lunar samples, they shall obey the application procedure and utilization requirement in these Measures.

Article 7

The functions of the main storage unit are:

(1) Formulating standards and code of conduct for lunar samples;

(2) Implementing the unsealing, classification, preparation, documentation, and storage of lunar samples;

(3) Implementing the distribution, return and disposition of lunar samples in accordance with the procedure requirements;

(4) Building and maintaining the lunar sample storage facilities with the capability to carry out the necessary work; and

(5) Establishing a lunar sample storage catalog so as to secure their safety.

Article 8

The functions of other storage units are:

(1) Participating in the formulation of the standards and code of conduct for lunar samples;

(2) Building and maintaining storage facilities; and
(3) Establishing a lunar sample storage catalog so as to secure their safety.

Article 9
The request for lunar samples borrow shall be made by a legal person (hereinafter referred to as the requesting subject), and the main duties of the requesting subject are:
(1) Conducting scientific research or socially beneficial activities in accordance with the relevant approvals and borrow agreements;
(2) Ensuring the safety of the lunar samples and be responsible for their damages, contamination, or loss caused by operational and storage negligence;
(3) A dedicated person shall be appointed to be responsible for the lunar sample safety as indicated in the borrow request;
(4) Reporting the scientific achievement of lunar samples research to the LESEC.

Chapter 3. Classification, Disposition and Information Release

Article 10
According to the fundamental uses, lunar samples are categorized as: permanently stored samples, permanently stored backup samples, research samples, and samples for public benefit. The permanently stored samples and permanently stored backup samples are sealed and maintained in a pristine state as the original samples; the research samples are used for scientific research, and the samples for public benefit are used for activities such as exhibition, dissemination of science, and education.

Article 11
The main storage unit, after reception, shall conduct preliminary sample processing and form the relevant information according to the basic uses within a period of no more than six months.

Article 12
After the preliminary processing, the LESEC will publicize the lunar sample information through the data information platform and regularly update the sample information according to the sample borrowing circumstances.

Chapter 4. Borrow Request and Distribution

Article 13
Borrow request refers to applying for lunar samples borrow for the use of scientific research (including non-destructive and destructive experiments) and public benefit

activities (including education and exhibition) and the return of samples at an agreed time after the completion of such activities.

Article 14
The requesting subject shall have the qualified conditions for the sample's storage and safety. The requesting subject applying for research purpose shall have the corresponding research qualification.

Article 15
The requesting subject shall submit a borrow application form for lunar samples through the data information platform.

Article 16
The LESEC reviews the request applications at the end of each quarter and respond to the requesting subjects in a timely manner. Once the request is approved, the LESEC will sign a Lunar Sample Loan Agreement with the requesting subject and the main storage unit will distribute the sample.

Article 17
The borrow term of lunar sample for research purpose shall, in principle, be no more than one year. In case of absolute necessity, the request can be renewed once for a period of no more than six months. The requesting subject shall submit an application for renewal to the LESEC thirty days before the expiration of borrow term.

Article 18
Considering the precious nature of lunar samples, the borrowed lunar samples for research purpose shall be used economically. The destructive experiments on lunar samples shall be reduced to the minimum and there shall be detailed destruction demonstration and explanation in the research plan.

Article 19
The borrow term of lunar sample for public benefit shall, in principle, be no more than two months. In case of absolute necessity, the request can be renewed once for a period of no more than one month. The requesting subject shall submit an application for renewal to the LESEC fifteen days before the expiration of borrow term.

Article 20
The main storage unit shall complete the preparation and distribution of the corresponding sample within thirty days in accordance with the written notice of

LESEC, the approved request application form and the signed Lunar Sample Loan Agreement, providing feedback to the LESEC.

Chapter 5. Utilization and Return

Article 21
The requesting subject shall record the entire use of lunar sample in writing and the destructive experiments must be recorded in video, so as to ensure the traceability of the lunar sample utilization and facilitate the supervision, return and redistribution of the lunar sample.

Article 22
The requesting subject is subject to the inspection by LESEC on the utilization of lunar samples.

Article 23
The requesting subject is not entitled to sublet the lunar sample to a third party. If the experiments, testing and other work is conducted by a third party, there shall be explanation in the request application form of the requesting subject, which must be approved by the LESEC.

Article 24
If the requesting subject violates the loan agreement, LESEC will terminate the agreement and request the requesting subject to return the lunar sample immediately.

Article 25
Within five working days after the borrow term expiration, the requesting subject shall submit a return application form to the main storage unit in a timely manner, with the lunar sample, loan agreement and necessary documents attached. The sample use record in the return application form shall be clear and complete, and the video record of destructive experiments (including complete destruction without any remaining material) shall be provided. The borrowed sample shall be returned in full, and for any sample that cannot be returned completely due to destructive experiments, the remaining part shall be returned.

Article 26
The main storage unit shall verify the integrity of the items returned after receiving the return application form. In case of any missing items, the requesting subject shall make supplementary submission within the specified period. The main storage unit will inspect

the returned lunar sample, form an inspection opinion, and report to the LESEC. When necessary, the LESEC will organize a review by the committee of experts and draw a conclusion. If the returned sample meets the requirements, the main storage unit is responsible for the registration, storage, and other related work. If the returned sample does not meet the requirements, the main storage unit is responsible for the follow-up processing in accordance with the relevant provisions of Lunar Sample Loan Agreement.

Chapter 6. Management of Scientific Achievement

Article 27
Publication, academic exchanges and other activities that are based on the research work of lunar sample shall clearly identify the serial number of lunar sample and indicate that "Lunar Sample Provided by CNSA".

Article 28
Publication and application for intellectual property derived from the utilization of lunar samples shall be reported through the data information platform within three months, which will be published by LESEC to promote the scientific research sharing of lunar samples.

Article 29
The LESEC is in charge of organizing a committee of experts to evaluate the scientific achievements of lunar sample on a regular basis and to promote the transformation and application of scientific achievements.

Article 30
The requesting subjects' commercial activities of the lunar samples or the relevant scientific achievements and products shall be subject to the written approval by the LESEC in accordance with the Lunar Sample Loan Agreement.

Chapter 7. Safety Management

Article 31
The requesting subject shall possess the corresponding safety facility and management conditions to ensure that the lunar sample is safe and free from contamination.

Article 32
If a lunar sample is lost, the requesting subject shall report to the local police immediately and report to the LESEC. In case of contamination and other damages, the requesting

subject shall submit a written explanation within 24 hours. In serious circumstances, the LESEC will request the CNSA and other relevant authorities to investigate and press legal charges in accordance with the law.

Chapter 8. International Cooperation

Article 33
The management and utilization of lunar samples shall comply with the relevant international treaties that the People's Republic of China has ratified and acceded to.

Article 34
The CNSA encourages joint international research of lunar sample and promote the international sharing of scientific achievement.

Article 35
The LESEC shall organize joint research, exchanges, exhibition, and goodwill gifts of lunar samples in accordance with the relevant agreements and approvals of the CNSA.

Chapter 9. Supplementary Articles

Article 36
If there is violation of these Measures, responsibility will be imposed based on the investigation of the CNSA and relevant authorities.

Article 37
These Measures shall enter into force on the date of promulgation and subject to the interpretation of the CNSA.

5. CHINA'S SPACE-RELATED STATEMENTS AND PROPOSALS IN THE UN[1]

5.1. CHINA'S STATEMENTS, PROPOSALS AND OTHER INFORMATION SUBMITTED TO UNCOPUOS

5.1.1. China's Activities on International Cooperation in the Peaceful Uses of Outer Space

A/AC.105/679/Add.1
1998

China's space policy includes the substantial development of applied satellites, accelerating their development process and putting them to widespread use. This conforms to the needs of national economic construction and sustainable social development, creates an environment responsive to the needs of the country and contributes to positive growth. At the same time, it also aims at keeping abreast of international technological advances, facilitating space exploration and research and applying space technology in other technical fields, as well as promoting international cooperation.

I. Satellite Applications

1. Remote Sensing Technology and Its Application
China's commitment in the field of remote sensing is designed to satisfy the needs of national economic construction. After strenuous efforts during the past two decades, China has increased its application capabilities to serve the needs of national economic construction. A dynamic information service system on resources and environment, with an emphasis on agro-resources, is being developed, using remote sensing data to conduct a nationwide investigation of land resources in an effort to profile China's land resources on a macro scale. In the area of combating natural disasters, a remote sensing system for monitoring and assessing major natural disasters, focusing on flood and drought control has been set up. An aerial remote sensing real-time transmission system has been developed, thus making it possible to transmit real-time images of disaster-stricken

---

[1] All the documents of this section are cited from www.unoosa.org, www.unog.ch and www.chinesemission-vienna.at, unless otherwise indicated. Last accessed August 2021.

areas. During the period 1996-2000, further improvements will be made to the system, which will then be put into service in the relevant departments.

On 10 June 1997, China successfully launched its Fengyun-2 meteorological satellite from the Xichang satellite-launching center, using the Long March-3 launch vehicles. On 17 June, under the control of the land-based monitoring and control station, the satellite was successfully positioned at 105 degrees east longitude over the equator. With an operational life of three years, it provides 100 domestic and 33 international channels for data transmission. This geostationary satellite is able to capture visible light images of clouds, 24-hour infrared images of clouds and pictures of vapour distribution, in addition to being capable of broadcasting climate pictures. The satellite is now operating normally. Its data can be received free of charge in China and by neighbouring countries.

Since 1995, the Chinese Government has organized a number of major research and development projects in response to the urgent needs in the field of resources and environment management. They include:

(1) Remote sensing, Geographic Information System (GIS) and Global Positioning System (GPS) technologies and their comprehensive utilization, featuring dynamic monitoring of land resources and environment, monitoring and assessment of accidental natural disasters, evolving into a practical and operational macro information service system to provide the country with constant macro information on resources and environment and information in support of analysis and decision-making. In the meantime, an operational monitoring and assessment system on major natural disasters has been set up which is able to carry out real-time monitoring on an instant basis in case of major natural disasters of floods, contributing to disaster mitigation and relief and minimization of damages by providing relevant data on disasters. At present, work on information collection, test area selection and system construction is well under way;

(2) Aerial remote sensing real-time transmission systems, designed for the monitoring and assessment of accidental natural disasters such as floods, forest fires and earthquakes. The construction of the systems has been completed and trial operation has begun;

(3) Crop yield estimation by way of remote sensing technology. In terms of yield estimation for staple crops, fields of winter wheat, maize and paddy rice, comprising 85 per cent of total grain output, have been chosen for the work, covering 10 provinces and municipalities. Using the county as the statistical unit, yield estimates at the provincial (or regional) level have been forecasted. The yield estimation accuracy (area and total output) for wheat is above 95 per cent; for maize, above 90 per cent; and for paddy rice, above 85 per cent. Output forecast can be provided 1-2 weeks in advance of harvest. Experiments of yield estimation for wheat and maize in northern China and paddy rice in southern China have been completed. Work on a more extensive application of the technology is in full swing;

(4) Application of remote sensing technology in farmland investigation. Four provinces or autonomous regions – Heilongjiang, Gansu, Nei Mongol and Xinjiang – and a group of agricultural counties have been chosen as test areas for investigation of typological and acreage changes in land;

(5) Development of China's GIS software. Domestic institutions have been called upon in its joint development and evaluation, so as to come up with, and put into widespread use, a package of GIS software under China's own patent;

(6) Remote sensing monitoring of spontaneous ignition in coalfields. Remote sensing and GIS technologies are being used to conduct fundamental surveys of 56 spontaneous ignition spots in coalfields in northern China, including the impact and extent of conflagration etc., with a view to providing a scientific basis for coal fire control and extinction;

(7) Remote sensing monitoring of the marine environment. An all-dimensional marine monitoring system receiving data from satellites, aircraft and land is being developed to monitor environmental elements such as sea temperature, water colour, sea waves, mud and sand suspending in sea water and superficial oil pollution.

At the same time, considerable progress has also been made in remote sensing archaeology, radar application and basic theoretic research.

2. Satellite Communications and Application

On 12 May 1997, China succeeded in launching its Dongfanghong-3 broadcasting and communication satellite, which was developed exclusively by its own efforts. The satellite, with 24 transponders on board and an operational life of eight years, was positioned on 21 May at 125 degrees east longitude over the sky in the geosynchronous Earth orbit. This satellite, together with the satellite channels currently rented, constitute China's national network of broadcasting, television, telephone and satellite communication, ushering the country's telecommunication industry and its application into a period of modern construction. In the meantime, the setting up of a satellite television network for education has brought remarkable changes to the backward status quo in education and literacy in remote regions. In addition to public networks, rapid advances have also been made in the construction of specialized satellite networks.

In recent years, China has made considerable progress in applying satellite communication technologies in the areas of banking, civil aviation, tele-education via satellite television, petroleum, transportation, water conservancy and power supply. The use of very small aperture terminals (VSAT) has also increased extensively. There are now more than 500 two-way VSAT stations and over 1,000 one-way stations in the country, and the number is growing rapidly. In China, VSAT systems are being used in voice and data transmission, e-mail, faxes, video-conferencing and dedicated lines of communication. Meanwhile, mobile communication in recent years has found extensive application and received increasing attention, becoming one of the fastest developing fields. China has successfully used VSAT technology in pager relocation and regional networking of mobile communication. The advanced technology has also been used extensively in telephone, live TV broadcasting and emergency communication.

II. Applied Satellites

Research and manufacturing of applied satellites is currently one of the fastest developing high-technology fields in China. Intensified efforts are being made to develop the China-Brazil Earth Resources Satellite, a small satellite for observing the colour of ocean water, and the Fengyun-1 polar orbiting satellite. The development of these satellites will substantially enhance China's capabilities in satellite data collection. Meanwhile, ground stations of remote sensing satellites that have already been set up in the country have provided the relevant departments and local governments with a large amount of data for remote sensing applications. Basic research in space applications has also been further enhanced. For example, efforts are being intensified to develop a new generation of high- resolution on-board radar sensors and scientific experimental satellites. The construction of ground systems and preliminary studies are also under way.

In the coming years, China will try to develop small satellites, with an emphasis on small-scale Earth observation satellites.

III. Space Research Activities

On 20 October 1996, using the LM-2D launch vehicle, China successfully launched the seventeenth recoverable satellite for scientific exploration and technological experiments. Following its successful entry into the intended orbit, all the equipment on board the satellite functioned normally. The satellite was then successfully recovered after 15 days of orbiting in space. Apart from obtaining remote sensing data, experiments in biological development, crop seeds and crystal composition under microgravity and biological tests were carried out using on-board scientific devices.

The agencies concerned continued to carry out space research. In 1997, the Chinese Academy of Sciences completed tests related to the release of balloons in high altitudes and the improvement of monitoring and control equipment. It also continued high-altitude balloon tests, such as atmosphere aerosol tests, solar ultraviolet spectrum tests and hard X-ray astronomic observations. Experiments will be conducted at the Beijing Observatory using its solar magnetic field telescope with high-altitude (above 30 km) balloons.

Scientific research in microgravity with recoverable satellites is also continuing.

IV. Launch Vehicles

Since April 1970, China has developed and launched over 40 satellites of various categories, successfully launched 10 satellites for foreign clients, undertaken many scientific space explorations and conducted more than 300 on-board experiments in

5. CHINA'S SPACE-RELATED STATEMENTS AND PROPOSALS IN THE UN

space. A number of important results have been achieved. China's LM-3A launch vehicle is an improvement over the LM-3, with many advanced technologies and its carrying capabilities at geosynchronous Earth orbit having been raised to 2,600 kg. China's more recent development – the LMB-3B – is a tethered three-stage liquid-powered launch vehicle, capable of delivering a 5,000 kg payload of mass into geosynchronous Earth orbit. It represents, for the present time, China's most powerful rocket for launching satellites into geosynchronous transfer orbit. The following are some recent examples of successful launches:

(1) On 3 July 1996, China's LM-3 launch vehicle successfully sent the AP-1A communication satellite into space. Manufactured by the Hughes Company, United States of America, the satellite weighed 1.4 tons, with 24 C- band transponders on board and a designed operational life of 10 years. After finally being positioned at 134 degrees east longitude over the equator, it is providing communication services to the Asian and Pacific region;

(2) On 12 May 1997, a DFH-3 communication satellite developed in China was successfully launched from the Xichang satellite launching centre, using a new type of launch vehicle – the LM-3A;

(3) On 10 June 1997, the LM-3 launch vehicle successfully launched the Fengyun-2 meteorological satellite into orbit from the Xichang satellite launching centre. In the morning of 17 June, the satellite was successfully positioned at 105 degrees east longitude over the equator.

(4) On 20 August 1997, the new launch vehicle, the LM-3B, a product of China's own efforts and the most powerful rocket currently in China, successfully delivered into the intended orbit the Mabuhay satellite, which was manufactured by United States Space Systems/Loral for the Philippines, an indication of the fact that rockets of the LM series are capable of delivering a 5,000 kg payload into high orbit.

V. Space Debris

Since becoming a member of the Inter-Agency Coordination Committee on Space Debris in 1995, China's National Space Agency has conducted extensive research on the reduction of space debris, including, inter alia, minimizing the generation of space debris through eliminating the potential risks of in-orbit disintegration of the upper stage of the LM-4 launch vehicle and the completion of a three-dimensional vulnerability model structure of spacecraft and an analysis of the extent of risks for the environment of space debris. At the same time, research in the field of space debris monitoring and control is also under way at the relevant institutions.

VI. International Cooperation

In October 1996, the forty-seventh session of the International Astronautical Federation (IAF) was held in Beijing. It was attended by over 2,000 experts and officials from 54 countries, regions and related international organizations. Events such as major exhibitions and study tours were also arranged during the meeting. China acted as the host and offered conference services. As a practical contribution of China to the programme of peaceful uses of outer space, China covered all the in-session expenses of 29 representatives from developing countries at the United Nations/IAF seminar.

In August 1997, the International Symposium on Geo-information Science and the International Symposium on Geographic Information Systems were held in Beijing. The symposia, which were attended by over 500 representatives from 18 countries, covered geo-information science, scientific forecasting, regional sustainable development, research on global changes and access to geo-information. In addition to academic exchanges and exploring possibilities of cooperative research, demonstrations of GIS technology and presentations on new achievements were held. The symposia contributed to the development of GIS technology and its application.

Since 1995, China has provided 5-7 scholarships each year on remote sensing applications for countries in the Asian and Pacific region, making a valuable contribution to human resources development for developing countries. This initiative will continue in the future.

The Asian Pacific Multilateral Cooperation Initiative on Space Technology and Application, sponsored mainly by China, Pakistan, the Republic of Korea and Thailand, has already made substantive progress. The countries concerned have reached consensus on an intergovernmental memorandum of understanding on the cooperation project of small multi-task satellites, and intends to initial the instrument at the Fourth Multilateral Cooperation Conference on Space Technology and Application in Asia and the Pacific, to be held in Bahrain in December 1997.

In the field of space technology and application, China has signed a number of bilateral cooperation agreements with other countries, for example, the cooperation agreement between China and Chile; the agreement between China and Brazil on scientific and technological cooperation in peaceful uses of outer space; and the agreement between China and France on cooperation in research and peaceful uses of outer space. At the same time, China has also carried out extensive cooperation in space and remote sensing application with Australia, Italy, Japan, the United States of America, the European Community and the Association of South-East Asian Nations.

5. China's Space-Related Statements and Proposals in the UN

5.1.2. China's Submissions Regarding the UNCOPUOS Discussion on the Safety of Space Nuclear Power Sources

A/AC.105/C.1/2012/CRP.5
2012

I. Introduction

Since the successful launch of the Chang-e 1 lunar probe in October 2007, China has continued to accelerate its exploration of outer space and has made additional progress in terms of the format of explorations and the distances involved. A lunar probe, scheduled to be launched in 2013, will carry landing gear and a surveying device to enable it to land on the moon and study the moon's surface. As space technology continues to progress, China will progressively explore deeper space providing that conditions are suitable in order to increase man's understanding of outer space.

The main issue to be considered in outer space exploration is which power source a spacecraft should use. The increased distance involved in the exploration of planets located at great distances from Earth leads to a marked decrease in the solar constants. Solar-powered technology therefore has virtually no capacity to support a mission of that kind. Nuclear power sources (NPS) are consequently a logical alternative given present technological conditions. Currently, isotope batteries and reactors are the main NPS used in space. The nuclides used are Pu-238 and Pu-235. The former is radioactive in its own right while the latter's reactive yields are radioactive. It is vital to study the safety of those nuclides in order to protect people and the environment.

The international community has been engaged in space exploration and the use of nuclear power for over forty years. NPS have been used both in near-Earth orbits and in outer space. Space NPS are essential in outer space exploration as they enable the exploration of cosmic bodies located in areas of the solar system beyond Jupiter. It is also paramount to minimize the safety risks associated with such power sources both on Earth and in space.

In view of those considerations, the United Nations Office of Outer Space Affairs (OOSA) and the International Atomic Energy Agency (IAEA) jointly published the Safety Framework for Nuclear Power Source Applications in Outer Space in 2009. The document contains guidance for the safe use of NPS in outer space by the international community and provides administrative and technical suggestions on how countries can develop space NPS in a safe manner.

II. The Use of Nuclear Power Sources in Space

In the soft landing missions of the lunar exploration project currently being carried out by China, both the landing gear and the surveying device use Pu-238-based isotope power sources to enable the landing gear and the surveying device to function in nighttime temperatures on the moon.

III. Analysis of the Potential for Using Nuclear Power Sources in Outer Space

Currently, the main power sources that can be used in spacecraft are chemical, solar and nuclear energies. The main types of nuclear energy used to generate electricity are radioisotope and reactor NPS. The size of the opening mechanism and the configuration of a solar or nuclear power device have a direct impact on the size and dynamic characteristics of the space vehicle system. The selection of a suitable power source helps reduce the overall size of the spacecraft and the complexity of the design of the attitude and temperature controls and structural configuration.

Early recoverable Earth observation satellites tended to use chemical power sources, but such satellites would not spend more than a month in orbit.

Solar energy, in the form of solar battery panels, is currently the most commonly used power source in space. The use of solar power systems with moderate conversion efficiency in relation to output efficiency is highly developed. Their mass-power ratio and area-power ratio have both reached relatively advanced technological levels.

As power requirements increase, so do the requirements for the standard solar wings used in solar power systems. The technical complexity of the system to lock in place the opening mechanism is also increasing. The structure also needs to be reinforced to ensure that it is sufficiently rigid. Structural reinforcement tends to cause a significant increase in the total mass of the power source system. Once the power requirements for a spacecraft reach a certain level, the total mass and size of the solar power system required pose serious technical challenges for the systematic design and manufacture of the flight mission and spacecraft. It thus becomes necessary to find a new power source to increase the efficiency of the whole system.

As a spacecraft increases its distance from the sun, the advantage of using a space nuclear power source over a solar power source becomes increasingly clear. Analysis has shown that solar battery units, once they have reached a distance of five astronomical units from the sun, will decrease in efficiency to a level that is no longer acceptable (and, theoretically, the solar constant at that distance will also decrease to 1/25 of the reference value close to the Earth). That phenomenon makes it a priority to use space NPS when sending spacecraft to Jupiter and other more distant planets in the solar system.

The above-mentioned factors demonstrate that space NPS are the logical choice for the exploration of planets located at greater distances from Earth than Jupiter. The exploration of space, and outer space in particular, needs to opt for space NPS in view of the fact that solar power is not available owing to the effects of natural conditions such as moon-lit nights and the fact that chemical power sources are insufficient to meet requirements.

IV. Understanding the Safety of Space Nuclear Power Sources

The presence of radioactive materials or nuclear fuels in space NPS and any accidents caused by them pose a danger to people and the environment in the Earth's biosphere. The public at large are therefore concerned about the safety implications of space NPS.

A number of nuclear accidents have taken place across the world in previous years. Accidents at nuclear power plants include the Three Mile Island nuclear accident in 1979, the Chernobyl nuclear accident in 1986 and the accident at Fukushima in 2011. Accidents involving space nuclear reactors re-entering the Earth's atmosphere include the crash of the RORSAT NPS into the Pacific Ocean to the north of Japan following its failed launch in 1973, the re-entry of a COSMOS satellite into the atmosphere over north-west Canada in 1978, which scattered radioactive debris over an area covering one hundred thousand square kilometers, and the crash of a COSMOS satellite into the Atlantic Ocean upon re-entry in 1983. All the accidents became subjects of public concern and debate and led to widespread concern about nuclear safety.

NPS have been used in space for over 40 years and have been powering a range of spacecraft, from ocean observation satellites on lower-Earth orbits to those designed to explore the planets on the outer edges of the solar system. The majority of the spacecraft completed their missions successfully and met the design requirements and thus did not release radioactive pollution into the environment in which they had been operating. The safety measures adopted for those spacecraft were therefore feasible and effective and can serve as reference points for the use of space NPS in the future.

For the foreseeable future, NPS will become the essential technological solution for powering spacecraft designed to explore outer space. However, more attention must be paid to space nuclear safety so that safety considerations are fully taken into account in the design and use of space NPS. Safety issues must be considered at all stages, with regard to the space NPS, spacecraft, launch system, design of the flight mission and flight control. Studies must be conducted on the control and technology aspects of nuclear protection and accident policies in order to increase safety capacity, identify measures to deal with problems and find appropriate solutions as part of efforts to reduce safety risks and potential accidents in the use of NPS.

V. Reflection on the Safe Use of Space Nuclear Power Sources

Space NPS are essential technological components for supporting missions to explore outer space and have a role to play in enhancing man's understanding and exploration of the universe. As space NPS are brought into use, it is also vital to take measures to limit injury and damage to people and their living environment to levels that are acceptable even in the worst-case scenario.

In order to further develop space nuclear technology, it is useful to draw on the successful experience of those countries that have launched NPS into space and to learn from past accidents so as to ensure space nuclear safety and radiation protection. As far as policy measures and administrative checks are concerned, a regime for the design, construction and operation of space NPS should be established at national level to regulate nuclear activities in space, develop technologies to ensure the safety of NPS and radiation protection, analyse the possible consequences of a failure of a space NPS, conduct thorough risk assessments and develop policies for dealing with accidents to reduce risks to an acceptable level.

1. Safety Assessment and Control
The safety of a space NPS is assessed throughout a project, beginning with the decision on the project and then during the programme design, research and development, construction and launch stages. A safeguards and emergency plan report for the nuclear power unit forms part of the assessment of the safety of the flight mission. The report, which is a requirement for evaluating whether a project can go ahead is submitted to a review group. Once adopted by the group, it is presented to the competent State administrative agency for approval. The project may only proceed to the development stage on the basis of agreement and approval.

The standards and regulations for safety assessments refer to and draw on the work of the State in relevant areas. The safety standards for space NPS are divided into a number of sections and cover all areas relating to space nuclear safety. They mainly include radiation safety and occupational health certificates and requirements relating to staff qualifications, transport, storage, protection, retirement and emergency measures.

2. Safety Control of Space Nuclear Power Sources
Safety control of space NPS is divided into four parts, namely the start-up of the NPS, operation control, disposal at the end-of-service phase and safeguards.

In China, responsibility for the safety of a space NPS lies mainly with the manufacturer. The developer of the NPS, the developer of the space vehicle and the authority that manages the launch site also have their own respective responsibilities in relation to safety control.

(1) Start-up of the Nuclear Power Source
The start-up and operation of the space reactor will only commence after the spacecraft enters the safety orbit. The reactor remains shut down until entry into orbit. An outer space probe fitted with a nuclear device is also present in the safety orbit. The flight path will not include a return to Earth, nor will the spacecraft re- enter the Earth's orbit during the leveraging flight.

(2) Flight Control
When the space NPS is in normal operation mode the amount of radiation released from the power source into the spacecraft must not exceed the levels set by the State and must not have any marked impact on the space environment in which the spacecraft is operating, beyond a specified period of time.

The design of the flight path of a spacecraft fitted with an NPS must not include a return to Earth. Payload stability should be maximized in order to help minimize the probability of the spacecraft's accidental re-entry. If an accidental re-entry occurs, the NPS must be designed in such a way that it remains undamaged.

(3) Disposal at the End-of-Service Phase

Once a spacecraft with an NPS on a lower-Earth orbit reaches the end-of-service phase it will be sent into a special orbit for disused spacecraft. Nuclear-powered spacecraft operating in outer space must also follow a clear plan for safe disposal.

(4) Safeguards

The design of space NPS incorporates safety specifications. As far as the NPS on the spacecraft is concerned, the container used for the power source on Earth is specially designed to help identification and specially designed signs are used on the power sources to help ensure safety and facilitate identification. Strict measures are also adopted to control the nuclear devices and materials and to protect them from theft, removal, loss or damage.

3. Technology and Relevant Work to Safeguard Space Nuclear Power Sources

The reliability of NPS should be increased to prevent critical safety accidents. Important measures to protect the NPS should also be adopted to ensure the safety of the environment and the spacecraft.

At the programme design stage, relevant nuclear safety requirements will be added to the functions and performance requirements and the resulting design will be reviewed and evaluated.

At the prototype stage, special tests will be carried out to assess the safety of the space NPS in addition to the routine environmental tests. They should include assessments of a power source's response to heavy vibration and resistance to heat, burning, pressure, impact and corrosion. Once the tests have been completed, the results will be reviewed and evaluated.

At the stage when the product is finalized, and in addition to the tests and experiments conducted on the spacecraft as a whole, tests will also be carried out to assess the safety of the NPS. The results will be reviewed and evaluated.

Conclusion

As regards the safety of space NPS, China takes a similar view to that contained in the Safety Framework.

5.1.3. China's Activities in the Field of International Cooperation in the Peaceful Uses of Outer Space

A/AC.105/C.1/2013/CRP.8
2013

Outer space is the common wealth of mankind and exploration of outer space are an unremitting pursuit of mankind. China always adheres to the peaceful exploration and use of outer space, and works together with the international community to maintain a peaceful and clean outer space and endeavour to make new contributions to the lofty cause of promoting world peace and development. In 2012, based on the independent development, China positively conducted international exchanges and cooperation in diversified ways and has made rapid progress in the three areas including space technology, space applications and space science.

I. Space Technology
In 2012, China has made 19 space launches, sending 28 spacecraft including manned spaceship, communications satellites, navigation satellites, remote sensing satellites and scientific and technological test satellites.

1. Manned Spaceship
On June 16, the Shenzhou 9 spaceship was launched successfully, sending first Chinese female astronaut into space. The Shenzhou 9 conducted automatic and manual rendezvous and docking with the target vehicle Tiangong 1 in space respectively on June 18 and June 24. On June 29, the Shenzhou 9 returned to the Earth safely.

2. Navigation Satellites
Six Beidou navigation satellites were launched successfully on February 25, April 30, September 19 and October 25 respectively. Up to now, China has launched 16 Beidou navigation satellites successfully and the Beidou Regional Satellite Navigation System has been established formally. According to the planning, the Beidou Satellite Navigation System will formally provide free passive positioning, navigation and timing services for the most part of the Asia-Pacific Region from early 2013.

3. Communications Satellites
On March 31, the French Thales Alenia Space built APSTAR 7 communications satellite was sent into space successfully. The satellite was formally put into operation on May 15 to provide television transmission and satellite communications services for Asia, Middle East, Africa, Australia and Europe.

5. China's Space-Related Statements and Proposals in the UN

On May 26, the ChinaSat-2A was launched successfully. The satellite can provide broadcast, TV and broadband multimedia transmission services for radio and television stations, radio transmitting stations and cable television networks.

On July 25, China's third GEO data relay satellite Tianlian 1-03 was launched successfully. The Tianlian 1 satellites have realized a global networking operation, indicating that China's first generation of data relay satellite system has been established formally.

On November 27, the ChinaSat 12 developed by the French Thales Alenia Space was sent into space successfully. The satellite can provide commercial communications services for Asian, African and European countries.

4. Remote Sensing Satellites

On January 9, China's ZY-3 satellite, together with the Luxembourgian Vesselsat-2 microsatellite, was sent into space successfully. The ZY-3 is mainly used for geographic mapping and geographic information acquisition.

On January 13, the FY-2F satellite was successfully launched and formally put into operation. The satellite is mainly used for weather analysis, forecast and early warning such as typhoon, rainstorm and dense fog, monitoring disasters such as sandstorm, drought and forest fire and environment as well as meteorological support for space activities.

On May 6, the Tianhui 1B mapping satellite was sent into space successfully. The satellite is mainly used for scientific experiments in such areas as scientific research, land resources survey and mapping.

On November 19, the SAR Earth observation satellite HJ-1C, a small satellite for environment and disaster monitoring and forecast, was successfully launched, marking the formal establishment of China's Small Satellite Constellation for Environment and Disaster Monitoring and Forecast. The constellation is capable of conducting all-time, all-weather and large-scale dynamic monitoring for disasters, and providing stable and reliable remote sensing data support.

At present China is building its new-generation Earth observation system with emphasis on the development of the Earth observation platforms based on high-resolution satellites, stratospheric airships and airborne remote sensing, establishment of the data centres and ground operation systems, thus forming the capabilities of all-weather and all-time Earth observation data acquisition and applications. The system will provide spatial data and information services in such socio-economic development areas as disaster prevention and reduction, environment protection and climate change, and participate in the global environment protection and joint efforts to tackle serious natural disasters.

5. Scientific Satellites and Technological Test Satellites

The Yaogan 14, 15 and 16 satellites were successfully launched on May 10, May 29 and November 25 respectively. These satellites are mainly used for scientific experiments, land resources survey, crop yield estimation and disaster prevention and reduction.

On October 14, SJ-9 A/B satellites were sent into space successfully. The two satellites are mainly used for experiments such as long lifetime and high reliability, high accuracy and high performance, indigenous core components as well as satellite formation and inter-satellite experiments.

II. Space Applications

In 2012, China has widely applied space technology in such areas as meteorology, ocean, disaster prevention and reduction, environment monitoring and navigation, which has made great contributions to economic construction, social development and scientific progress.

1. Meteorological Observation

China has both polar-orbiting and geostationary orbit meteorological satellites with 7 in-orbit meteorological satellites. China has also formed a meteorological satellite ground receiving and processing system including 5 stations and 1 centre. Up to now, the FY meteorological satellite data has over 2500 users in more than 70 countries and regions all over the world and has played an important role in the early warning for typhoon, waterlogging, forest and grasslands fire, drought and sand storm as well as the weather forecast and climate change monitoring.

2. Ocean Observation

At present, the HY satellites can monitor China's entire sea area including the Huangyan Island, the Diaoyu Islands and the Paracel Islands. Recently, China actively promotes the applications and services of the HY satellite data in the fields such as oil spill, sea ice, green tide, sea surface temperature, ocean colour, sea surface wind field and marine fisheries, and has produced the sea surface temperature data products for the China seas and their vicinity and the global sea areas to realize the real-time monitoring report and timely distribution of the sea ice situation; produced the ocean colour information including the chlorophyll concentration distribution of China's seas and their surrounding areas; irregularly produced the ocean colour environment information products of some regions; and made remote sensing survey of the sea surface wind field and waves in the area around the South Pole.

3. Environment Monitoring

China makes macro, rapid and dynamic ecological environment monitoring and evaluation and tracks the occurrence and development of the sudden environment pollution events such as oil spill and water blooms by use of the Small Satellite Constellation for Environment and Disaster Monitoring and Forecast. At present China has made the environment air remote sensing monitoring in the whole country and the key city groups and analyzed the distribution and change patterns of the main pollutants such as aerosol grains and Sulfur dioxide; made remote sensing monitoring for the water environment in the Taihu Lake, Chaohu Lake, Dianchi Lake and the offshore area to provide important information on China's water environment quality; made remote sensing monitoring for the natural protection zones, ecological function zones and biodiversity protection zones; and made remote sensing monitoring applications for the environmental and ecological issues in the cross-border area, cities and typical river valleys.

4. Disaster Prevention and Reduction

The ground disaster reduction applications system for the environment and disaster reduction satellites has been put into operation and successfully integrated into the operational system of the National Disaster Reduction Center of China, and has played a positive role in the daily disaster management. Now China has made disaster risk monitoring for flood, drought and snow within the whole country, conducted training on remote sensing technology applications for disaster reduction, and provided the relevant data products and services.

III. Space Science

In 2012, China continued to strengthen the construction of the space science research system to greatly improve its research level with emphasis on such areas as deep space exploration, space debris and space weather.

1. Deep Space Exploration

China released the full moon map with a resolution of 7 meters acquired by the Chang'e 2 lunar probe. It also made a total of 746 7-meter-resolution full moon framing image products, 50-meter-resolution standard framing image products and full moon data mosaic image products.

After finishing a series of extended tests beyond its lifetime, Chang'e 2 made further extended tests. Chang'e 2 flew away from the Lagrangian Point L2 orbit on June 1. And after flying for 196 days, it rendezvoused with the Asteroid Toutatis, about 7 million kilometers away from the Earth, realizing pass-by exploration of an asteroid for the first time.

2. Space Debris

China has conducted research on detection technology and accurate early- warning technology for space debris and provided early-warning services for launch and in-orbit operation of the important spacecraft. China has also finished the falling prediction of the body residue of the LM-4B launch vehicle, inactivated the final stages of the Long March rockets, and moved a few aging satellites out of orbit.

China has conducted comprehensive protection design for the manned spaceships and improved their in-orbit operation safety, and made material performance testing and protection structural tests for the advanced protection structure. Moreover, China has also made research on domestic protection database construction and hypervelocity ground test technology.

3. Space Weather

China's ground-based space weather monitoring network has been preliminarily established and put into operation, initially resulting in a seamless exploration covering ground meteorology, middle atmosphere, upper atmosphere and ionosphere, which has provided an important data source for the space weather monitoring and early warning together with the FY series satellites.

China has also established its national space weather forecast operation and service platform, which accurately forecasted the whole space weather situation and key weather process for supporting the manned rendezvous and docking between Tiangong 1 and Shenzhou 9, especially the occurrence and development of the magnetic storm and its effect on the spacecraft orbit.

IV. International Exchanges and Cooperation

In 2012, China positively conducted space exchanges and cooperation with many countries, space agencies and international organizations; participated in the related activities organized by the United Nations Committee on the Peaceful Uses of Outer Space (UNCOPUOS) and other relevant international organizations; actively provided resources to help mitigate the effects of disasters on human life and property as a member of the International Charter on Space and Major Disasters (CHARTER); supported international commercial space activities, which has yielded positive results.

1. China participated in all the activities organized by the UNCOPUOS and its Scientific and Technical Subcommittee and Legal Subcommittee. The Chinese Government continued to support the operation of United Nations Platform for Space-based Information for Disaster Management and Emergency Response (UN-SPIDER) Beijing Office, and co-organized in Beijing together with the UN-SPIDER Beijing Office.

2. China positively participated in the relevant activities organized by the International Committee on Global Navigation Satellite Systems (ICG), and hosted the Seventh Meeting of the ICG (ICG-7) from November 5 to 9, 2012 in Beijing. Nearly 20 topics relating to the construction and development of satellite navigation system were discussed during the meeting and a Joint Declaration on Global Satellite Navigation System (GNSS) (Beijing Declaration) was issued.

5. CHINA'S SPACE-RELATED STATEMENTS AND PROPOSALS IN THE UN

3. China has fulfilled the work relating to CHARTER in 2012. Altogether, China performed its duty as an Emergency on-Call Officer for 42 days in 6 periods, i.e. 1008 hours. While serving on duty, China received and responded to 4 help requests from all over the world and arranged timely satellite imaging plan for the disaster-stricken areas. China activated the CHARTER for the catastrophic flood in Min County, Gansu Province and the earthquake in Yiliang County, Yunnan Province, and made the disaster scope evaluation as well as the monitoring and evaluation for the destroyed houses, the damaged roads, the affected crops and the damaged infrastructure.

4. China positively participated in the joint observation for the falling of the hazardous targets organized by the Inter-Agency Space Debris Coordination Committee (IADC). According to the requirements of the UN Space Debris Mitigation Guideline, China continued to promote and implement its management measures on space debris mitigation, conducted demonstration on space debris mitigation design and evaluation system, and carried out research on space debris mitigation technology.

5. China actively participated in all the activities organized by the World Meteorological Organization (WMO), and hosted WMO training courses and the workshop on applications of meteorological satellites in the fields of disaster prevention and reduction and environment. The FY-2 satellites have been listed into the operational satellites for global observation by the WMO and become an important part of the global integrated observing system.

6. China positively participates in all the activities organized by the International Astronautical Federation (IAF) and is preparing the 64th International Astronautical Congress (IAC), which will be held in Beijing in September 2013. The theme of the congress is "Promoting Space Development for the Benefits of Mankind".

7. China positively promotes the international commercial space activities of its enterprises. On September 29, China successfully sent the Venezuelan Remote Sensing Satellite 1 (VRSS-1) into the preset orbit. The VRSS-1 is China's first remote sensing satellite exported in an in-orbit delivery way and mainly used for land resource survey, environment protection, disaster monitoring and management, crop yield estimation and urban planning in Venezuela. On December 19, China successfully sent the Turkish GK-2 Earth observation satellite into the preset orbit with a LM-2D launch vehicle. GK-2 is mainly used for environmental protection, land and mineral resources survey, urban planning and disaster monitoring and management in Turkey. Moreover, the cooperative communications satellite projects between China and Bolivia, Belarus and Laos are proceeding smoothly.

5.1.4. Statement by Ma Xinmin

At the 58th COPUOS Session on the Future Role of UNCOPUOS 2015

Mr. President,

The Committee on the Peaceful Uses of Outer Space (COPUOS) serves as a major UN platform for the deliberation of peaceful use of outer space, it is also a facilitator of the rule of law in outer space, a coordinator of outer space affairs and a leader in outer space capacity building. With flourishing outer space technologies and their applications nowadays, the actors and types of outer space activities have become increasingly diversified, which brings about many challenges to COPUOS. The Chinese delegation supports COPUOS to fully play its role in comprehensively promoting mankind's peaceful use of outer space.

The Chinese delegation believes that strengthening the rule of law in outer space, capacity building in outer space and international cooperation in outer space are important pillars of COPUOS that safeguard the sustainable development of outer space activities. Looking forward, COPUOS should conform to new development trend, improve efficiency and effectiveness of its work with new working methods, so as to make progress in the above mentioned areas.

First and foremost, COPUOS should further strengthen the rule of law in outer space. COPUOS is the most important platform for legislation in outer space that enjoys a unique status in the development, interpretation, revision and application of outer space rules. China believes that, COPUOS should focus its work on the following areas: firstly, to promote the practical application of existing outer space treaties and their fundamental principles in accordance with new development of outer space activities. Secondly, to coordinate the setting of agenda items of COPUOS and its two subcommittees based on consensus of all parties, so as to promote joint efforts in the rule of law in outer space, and to facilitate the regulation and promotion of well-organized new outer space activities. Thirdly, to strengthen coordination with relevant international organizations in outer space legal affairs to ensure that the legal system of outer space is unified and fragmentation is avoided.

Secondly, COPUOS should improve capacity building in outer space. Currently, the Office for Outer Space Affairs (UNOOSA) has adopted various measures in space basic science study, space technology application, research and teaching of outer space law and domestic legislation under the guidance of COPUOS, which have effectively improve countries' capacity in outer space. China proposes that COPUOS should fully utilize platforms such as Basic research in space science, The Human Space Technology Initiative (HSTI), seminars on space law, so as to strengthen technical exchange and data sharing, improve developing countries' capacity with targeted measures, eliminate technology embargo and technological barriers so that all countries can equally explore and use outer space. COPUOS should also continue to focus its support on regional centers and to strengthen cooperation and exchange of different regional centers.

Thirdly, COPUOS should deepen international cooperation in outer space. International cooperation serves both as a key principle of existing outer space treaties and an important purpose of COPUOS. China always actively supports the deliberation of the agenda item international mechanisms for cooperation in the peaceful exploration and use of outer space by Legal Subcommittee. China supports countries to exchange experience in cooperation, to find out legal mechanism for cooperation and to discuss concrete model for cooperation so as to regulate and facilitate international cooperation in outer space. At the same time, China believes that COPUOS should focus more on developing countries' needs, and to promote action oriented, project-based, equal and mutually beneficial international cooperation so as to enable outer space development.

The number and complexity of outer space affairs is growing together with the development of mankind's outer space activities. International mechanisms and rules related to outer space increase in number and interconnectivity. The Chinese delegation is of the view that, COPUOS should play a better coordinative and leading role among different mechanisms and processes within and outside of the UN framework so as to form synergy and avoid duplication and waste of resource. COPUOS may focus its attention on the following areas of work in the immediate term: First, strength communication with Conference on Disarmament, taking into account of the Joint meeting of the First and Fourth Committees. Secondly, to actively consider the ongoing discussion on all soft law processes in a coordinative manner. Thirdly, to harmonize the relationship between space technology and global sustainable development in view of the UN post 2015 development agenda. Fourthly, to develop and coordinate COPUOS's way forward based on UNISPCE+50 activity.

China stands ready to work with all parties to facilitate COPUOS to make greater contribution to the promotion of peaceful exploration and use of outer space.

Thank you, Mr. President.

5.1.5.   Keynote Speech of Shi Zhongjun

At the 10th UN Workshop on Space Law
2016

September 5, Ambassador SHI Zhongjun attended the opening ceremony of the 10th United Nations Workshop on Space Law, and made a keynote speech on China's perspective on the promotion of security and sustainability of outer space in round table section.

Ambassador SHI said, Outer space is the common heritage of mankind. Exploration and use of outer space for peaceful purposes is the common cause and in the common interests of all countries. With the rapid development of outer space activities, challenges to the security and sustainability of outer space have also increased and become an important issue concerning the interests of all countries. On this issue China has the following views and positions.

1. Demilitarization is the Fundamental Guarantee to Maintain Security and Sustainability of Outer Space.

The security and sustainability of outer space is facing multiple threats, such as a deterioration of the space environment, space congestion and space debris. However, the most fundamental threat is the weaponization of and an arms race in outer space. Outer space should be the new frontier of human wellbeing instead of a new killing field. If we cannot ensure that outer space is used exclusively for peaceful purposes, the security and sustainability of outer space will be out of the question.

China firmly supports the arms control process for outer space. In 2008, China and Russian jointly submitted to the Conference on Disarmament a Draft Treaty on the Prevention of the Placement of Weapons in Outer Space and of the Threat or Use of Force against Outer Space Objects (PPWT), and updated it based on feedback from other parties in 2014. The draft PPWT has received support from many countries. China hopes that other parties will show the political will to start negotiations based on the draft PPWT, and achieve an international treaty to prevent the weaponization of and an arms race in outer space as early as possible.

In 2014, the draft resolution jointly sponsored by China, Russia and other countries entitled "No first placement of arms in outer space" (A/RES/69/32) was adopted with overwhelming support. This fully reflects the common aspiration of the international community to prevent the weaponization of outer space.

China believes that appropriate and feasible Transparency and Confidence Building Measures (TCBMs) in outer space activities will help enhance mutual trust and reduce miscalculations. In this regard, the report of the Group of Governmental Experts on TCBMs in 2013 represents important progress and provides an important reference for all countries. China welcomes this achievement, and believes that while TCBMs can serve as a useful supplement to the prevention of the weaponization of and an arms race in outer space, they should not substitute negotiations on an outer space arms control treaty.

2. The Rule of Law Is an Important Foundation for Maintaining the Security and Sustainability of Outer Space.

To maintain the security and sustainability of outer space, the international community needs to define through uniform rules what can or cannot be done. All states should earnestly comply with international rules and judge right and wrong, resolve differences and promote cooperation in accordance with rules.

First, the outer space activities of States should be conducted in line with the UN Charter and the relevant treaties on outer space. All countries should act in accordance with the rules, fully fulfill their international obligations, exercise their rights in good faith, and be the practitioners and defenders of international rules governing outer space.

Second, we must advance with the times and constantly improve the system of outer space law and rules. Since 1979, the international community hasn't concluded any new outer space treaty. Outer space law has lagged behind the development of space activities. New issues such as space debris, space traffic management, and the commercial exploitation of outer space need to be properly regulated. States should actively support and participate in discussions under the UN auspices, in particular work of the Legal Subcommittee of Committee on the Peaceful Uses of Outer Space (COPUOS) to discuss and handle the new legal challenges.

Third, steadily develop "soft laws" on outer space, and give full play to its role. Declarations, principles and guidelines on outer space adopted by United Nations should be the guidance to the space activities of all states. The "Guidelines on the long-term sustainability of outer space activities (LTS) ", developed under the auspices of COPUOS is comprehensive and covering many new issues, and will be a groundbreaking soft law with great value in regulating outer space activities and promoting their sustainability. China welcomes the significant progress made in the negotiations on the LTS guidelines and will continue participating actively in the way forward.

3. The United Nations is the Authoritative Platform for Promoting the Security and Sustainability of Outer Space.

In the nearly 60 years of human space activities, the United Nations has played an important, irreplaceable role in establishing and improving the system of space governance, and provided a basic institutional framework for the security and sustainability of outer space. Under the new circumstances, the United Nations, as the most authoritative and universal international organization, should continue to play a central role in this area.

China supports COPUOS and the Conference on Disarmament, the First and Fourth Committees of the General Assembly, as well as other institutions to play their respective roles and appropriately enhance coordination in a joint effort to promote outer space governance. The year of 2018 will mark the Fiftieth Anniversary of the First United Nations Conference on the Exploration and Peaceful Uses of Outer Space. The international community should take this opportunity to summarize achievements, identify challenges, and plan for the future in order to increase the influence and improve the implementation capacity of the United Nations in the field of outer space, so that it may better lead the international community in promoting security and sustainability in outer space.

4. International Cooperation Is the Essential Way to Promote Outer Space Security and Sustainability.
The security and sustainability of outer space concern the common interests of all countries, and no country has the ability to address and deal with it alone. All states should bear in mind that we are in a community of interests in outer space, and we need to deliberate and govern together, and jointly meet challenges.

Space governance should be open and inclusive. Space governance cannot be monopolized by a few countries, introducing their own rules as international rules. More countries, in particular developing countries, should be encouraged to participate in and fully express their views on outer space rule-making. The making of any rules should take into account the needs of countries at different development stages, and should not hinder the participation of developing countries in outer space activities.

We should adhere to multilateralism within the UN framework. Only arrangements reached by consensus through equal and democratic multilateral discussions can have vitality and authority, and are capable of practical and effectively implementation.

International cooperation in space technology development, application and capacity-building should be further strengthened. Cooperation is vital to promote and spread the benefits of space technology among all countries, as well as enhance mutual understanding and trust. In this regard, developed space-faring nations should help developing countries enhance their space capabilities and share with them the space exploration "dividend".

In conclusion, Ambassador SHI pointed out that, China is a staunch supporter of security and sustainability of outer space. The peaceful use of outer space and opposition to the militarization of outer space has been enshrined in Chinese law. China has introduced Administrative Measures on Space Debris Mitigation, and conducted active debris removal experiments. China actively helps developing countries enjoy the benefits of outer space in such fields as communication, navigation, disaster

5. CHINA'S SPACE-RELATED STATEMENTS AND PROPOSALS IN THE UN

reduction, and space education. China also actively carries out international cooperation and exchanges to enhance transparency. In March this year, China and the United Nations Office of Outer Space Affairs signed Framework Agreement concerning Cooperation on the Utilization of China's Space Station. In May this year, China and the United States held the first outer space security dialogue. China is willing to work together with the international community to make greater contributions to promoting the security and sustainability of outer space.

5.1.6. Safety Practice of Space Nuclear Power Sources in China

A/AC.105/C.1/2016/CRP.12
2016

Summary

The Chinese government attaches great importance to the safety of space nuclear power sources. China has been actively engaging in all kinds of tasks sponsored by Nuclear Power Sources Working Group (NPS WG), Scientific and Technical Subcommittee (STSC), Committee on the Peaceful Uses of Outer Space (COPUOS), United Nations (UN). During the practices of space nuclear power sources, *Principles Relevant to the Use of Nuclear Power Sources in Outer Space* adopted by the General Assembly in 1992 were closely referred to, in the meantime, guidance contained in *Safety Framework for Nuclear Power Source Applications in Outer Space* which was jointly published by STSC, COPUOS, UN and IAEA was applied widely.

Safety practices of space nuclear power sources were successfully carried out in Chang'E-3 (CE-3) mission. As for management aspects, regulations of space nuclear safety management were issued, a special coordination panel was formed, personnel safety measures were taken, an emergence response organization and the whole emergency response system were established, all kinds of levels of safety training and safety rehearsals were performed. As for technical aspects, safety design of space nuclear power sources was done, special safety experiments and tests were carried out, and radiation doses were measured. In the following missions, the Chinese government will make constant effort on improving the level of safety work of space nuclear power sources.

I. Introduction

1. The Chinese government attaches great importance to the safety of space nuclear power sources. China has actively been engaged in all kinds of tasks sponsored by Nuclear Power Sources Working Group (NPS WG), Scientific and Technical Subcommittee (STSC), Committee on the Peaceful Uses of Outer Space (COPUOS),

United Nations (UN). During the practices of space nuclear power sources, *Principles Relevant to the Use of Nuclear Power Sources in Outer Space* adopted by the General Assembly in 1992 were closely referred to, in the meantime, guidance contained in *Safety Framework for Nuclear Power Source Applications in Outer Space* which was jointly published by STSC, COPUOS, UN and IAEA was applied.

2. In order to endure the long moon night, Radioisotope Heater Units (RHUs) were used in the lander and rover of CE-3 mission, which were launched in 2013. Extensive work has been done to ensure the safety of the nuclear power sources during the mission, which has proved a great success.

II. Management Practices

3. China has a complete set of regulations, which comprise national laws, ordinance, standards and policies regarding the safety management of radioisotope products. Radiation safety licensing, occupational sanitation licensing, import and transfer, transportation, storage, protection, occupational health, personnel, retirement, emergency preparedness and response and others are covered by the regulations. Corresponding government bodies in charge are made clearly. Qualification and licensing processes, responsibilities and duties are also clearly stated in the regulations.

4. A special coordination panel was established, which acted on behalf of the national government to deal with all the high-level management issues, such as safety reviews and compliance check-ups. Experts on nuclear safety and space technologies are part of the panel. The panel works under the guidance – Ensure people and facilities safe, Make influence minimum. A series of actions has been taken to make sure that technical issues are all clear and full-mission-life management are effective.

5. Safety working items and responsibilities of corresponding action entities were clearly defined. With spacecraft, launch vehicle and launch site systems participating, a full-mission-life working flow of nuclear related products was made in consultation with prestigious experts of related fields. In the flow, working items, objects, emergency response, working sites and responsible entities were defined.

6. Personnel Safety Management:

(1) Transportation safety measures. Transportation undertakers should be qualified. Corresponding procedures should be strictly performed in accordance with national standards. Participating drivers and operators should have been trained and qualified. During transportation, protective containers should be used and radiation doses should be limited to an acceptable level. Participating vehicles should meet the safety requirements defined by corresponding standards and they should also be equipped with radiation monitoring and measuring devices.

(2) Safety measures for storage, tests and experiments. Those who would enter the storage, tests and experiments sites should receive safety training first and then get qualification certificates. The storage, tests and experiments sites of RHUs were

constructed according to national standards and also qualified to store and deal with radioactive materials. Those who enter and get out of the sites would have to be booked in detail. Operations should be done according to signed documents. Security measures should meet the requirements of national standards. Radiation protection and doses measurement devices were necessary for these sites.

(3) Safety measures for equipment mounting. All workers should receive safety training first and then get qualification certificates. During assembly, integration and testing (AIT), RHUs are replaced by electric heating simulators. The checking-up of real RHU nuclear power sources were done in separate rooms with radiation protection conditions. Real RHU nuclear power sources were not mounted until the spacecraft had been loaded onto the launching tower so as to reduce radiation exposure of workers. Shielding, time and distance protection methods were used to reduce radiation doses of personnel. Workers were working in a duty-shifting manner so that per person dose would be minimized. Long-distance operations were also effective measures to reduce doses. Besides, all the operations were carried out under the guidance of nuclear safety experts. Radiation dose monitoring devices were used in the working sites. Simulations and on-the-site rehearsals were carried out before mounting real nuclear powers sources. The working sites were qualified. Those who enter and get out of the sites would have to be booked in detail. Operations should be done according to signed documents. Different alarming and monitoring measures were taken according to different levels of radiation danger.

7. Emergency preparedness and response:

(1) National Command for Special Nuclear Emergency Tasks was established under the leadership of The National Office for Nuclear Emergencies, with Luna Exploration and Space Engineer Center (a subsidiary of SASTIND) and other mission related entities participating. The Command was responsible for nuclear emergency rehearsals, emergency forces deployment and notification of launching.

(2) A special nuclear emergency plan for CE-3 mission in launching phase was made and authorized by National Committee on Nuclear Emergencies. Emergency tasks were carried out according to possible radioisotope accident scenarios. According to different scenarios, different emergency response working flows were made, equipment, responsibilities and working procedures of every working group were detailed in the plan.

(3) Nuclear emergency response teams (front-line and back-line ones respectively) were formed. Each team consisted of radiation detection, prediction and evaluation, protection and medicine, pollution removal, communication and logistics groups. The teams were responsible for radiation monitoring, radiation prediction and evaluation, protection and medical care, pollution removal, experiments, analysis and technical guidance.

(4) A special comprehensive nuclear emergency drilling was conducted in 2013. The drilling was based on presumed radioisotope accident scenarios and the whole emergency

response flow was examined. Through the drilling, the applicability of the special nuclear emergency plan for CE-3 mission and in-the-field capabilities of related emergency rescue forces were evaluated.

(5) Emergency equipment used solely for nuclear emergency was allocated. Fixed-line telephones, interphones, mobile phones, satellite phones and navigators comprised of communication equipment. Different kinds of radiation analysis devices, radiation source detection devices, detection devices used at night and nuclear material recycling devices comprised of radiation processing equipment.

(6) Before launching, the public who might be influenced according to careful analysis were evacuated and hidden in safe areas.

8. Training:

(1) Special radiation safety handbooks were compiled and then used as preliminary training materials for all related personnel.

(2) For the radiation safety training of the management and designers, related effective regulations were compiled while some new ones were specially issued for the mission.

(3) Special operation procedures were made. Workers, who were responsible for nuclear products related operations, would not be allowed to change their posts unless there were no other choices, in order to make sure that they were proficient in the operations. Mock-up operations were specially designed to train the workers.

(4) For those engaged in emergency response, training courses were carried out, which included fundamentals of radiation safety, radioisotope accident scenarios, emergency response working flow, performance and operations of emergency response equipment.

III. Technical Practices

9. Safety design. The types of rays and their characteristics were analyzed. Radiation safety analysis and protection designs were made. Safety analysis and protection designs were also carried out for accident conditions.

10. Safety verification. 9 special safety experiments and tests were carried out, which were free falling, mechanical impact, high temperature tolerance, thermal shock, external overpressure, aerodynamic overheating, high temperature ablation, mechanical impact in high temperature and seawater erosion. The RHUs of CE-3 have past all the experiments and tests.

11. Monitoring and analysis of radiation doses. To ensure the safety of workers on the launching tower, radiation doses of CE-3 nuclear power sources were quantitatively predicted using numerical models. The results were used to design safety protection measures on the launching tower. Statistics of doses were also made for workers based on possible working time and working places. It was found that for mounting workers the worst-case radiation dose was 2.16mSv, while the natural annual effective radiation dose for Chinese residents in 2010 was 3.1mSv. Results of the above analysis showed that the

safety measures of CE-3, which were taken before launching, were effective, and radiation doses were controlled to an acceptable level and met the requirements of radiation protection standards of China.

IV. Conclusion

12. RHUs were used for CE-3 mission. Related guidance in *Safety Framework for Nuclear Power Source Applications in Outer Space* was implemented accordingly. China has gained successful experiences in management and technical practices of space nuclear power sources.

5.1.7. Position Paper on the Issue of Long-Term Sustainability of Outer Space Activities

A/AC.105/C.1/2016/CRP.13
2016

1. Since the first artificial satellite was launched into outer space in 1957, the peaceful exploration and use of outer space by States have brought great benefits to the economic and social development of humankind, and have made significant contributions to the improvement of human welfare, the support of global sustainable development and the achievement of the Millennium Development Goals. Outer space and space activities have become part and parcel of modern human life. At the same time, with the in-depth development of space activities and space applications, challenges to outer space security and development have increased as well and turned into a strategic issue affecting the long-term sustainability of outer space activities and relating to the survival and development of humankind.

2. China believes that the United Nations treaties on outer space activities, adopted during the 1960s-1970s, have established basic legal norms for the international community to govern space activities. However, those United Nations treaties need further implementation and refinement in the operational aspects, and meanwhile also need to respond in a timely fashion to new changes on the part of States in their space activities as well as the latest demand for development in the protection of space environment and the maintenance of space security, in order to effectively promote the long-term sustainability of terrestrial environment while ensuring the long-term sustainable development of outer space activities.

3. China is a proactive advocator for the establishment of the agenda item on Long-term Sustainability of Outer Space Activities (LTS) within the framework of the United Nations Committee on the Peaceful Uses of Outer Space. China appreciates the work of the Scientific and Technical Subcommittee of the Committee on the Peaceful Uses of

Outer Space in putting LTS onto its agenda items as of the 47th Scientific and Technical Subcommittee session in 2010 and establishing the LTS Working Group for focused studies. China believes that such an agenda item has set up a consultative forum for enhancing mutual trust and cooperation among States in space governance, facilitating States, according to their national conditions, to jointly adopt "Transparency and Confidence-building Measures" (TCBMs) in the peaceful exploration and use of outer space, and promoting the peaceful and perpetual use of outer space for our current and future generations by the international community. Experts appointed by China have comprehensively participated in the research work of the four Expert Groups under the LTS Working Group, proactively provided comments and suggestions on the drafting of the Working Group Report and relevant Guidelines, and reached broad consensus on many issues through extensive and in-depth communications with delegations and experts of various States.

4. China highly appreciates the effective work carried out by the LTS Working Group under the leadership of Mr. Peter Martinez, and appreciates the significant contributions made by all experts from the four Expert Groups in drafting the Working Group Report and relevant Guidelines. China highly appreciates the various convenience provided to the Working Group by the Committee on the Peaceful Uses of Outer Space and the Office for Outer Space Affairs, and appreciates the constructive comments made by States and relevant international organizations on the Working Group Report and relevant Guidelines. China hopes that States will sufficiently exchange views on the final text of the Working Group Report and relevant Guidelines and jointly promote the long-term sustainability of outer space activities.

5. As one of the critical issues faced by the international community in the arena of outer space, the "Long-term Sustainability of Outer Space Activities" is devoted to coping with the issue of long-term sustainable development of space activities. With the continuous increase of space objects, diversification of participants in space activities and the constant expansion of space exploratory frontiers, the humankind is faced with unprecedented opportunities and challenges in space activities. The Committee on the Peaceful Uses of Outer Space is playing a significant role in regulating space activities, maintaining space order, protecting space environment, and promoting space cooperation. China is of the view that the "Long-term Sustainability of Outer Space Activities" is a monumental consensus reached by the international community in the peaceful exploration and use of outer space, showing the generalization and application of the ideology of human sustainable development in outer space.

6. China is aware that, space environmental problems such as orbital congestion and the proliferation of space debris have become ever prominent, while the probability of in-orbit collisions, harmful interference and the threat of space weather events have been on the increase. At the same time, with the strategic position of outer space becoming increasingly prominent, the risk of weaponization of outer space and military

5. CHINA'S SPACE-RELATED STATEMENTS AND PROPOSALS IN THE UN

confrontations in outer space is on the increase with it, posing a potential major threat to peace and security in outer space. These are the toughest challenges to space security, with no single State alone in a position to solve them. China is of the view that the issue of space governance, as a result of its close relevance to space activities of humankind from the very beginning, is an issue on the development aspects, and States share common interests and pursuit in it. The international community, more than ever, needs to establish a common vision and take common actions.

7. China has proactively participated in the multilateral initiatives as set up by the Conference on Disarmament in Geneva and other forums. China is of the view that a fundamental approach to preventing the weaponization of outer space and maintain the peaceful uses and long-term sustainability of outer space is to negotiate and adopt as early as possible an international legal instrument on the prevention of weaponization of outer space, based on the Draft Treaty on the Prevention of the Placement of Weapons in Outer Space and of the Threat or Use of Force against Outer Space Objects (PPWT) jointly submitted by China and Russia to the Conference on Disarmament in Geneva.

8. China appreciates the efforts made by the international community to promote the peaceful and long-term sustainable use of outer space. China always attaches great importance to Transparency and Confidence-building Measures (TCBMs) in outer space. China is among the main States that have sponsored the resolutions on TCBMs in outer space in the General Assembly of the United Nations, has been an active participant in the work of the Group of Governmental Experts (GGE) on TCBMs in outer space, and has made many constructive proposals regarding the possible measures to be taken by States. China maintains that both TCBMs in outer space and LTS of outer space activities are beneficial attempts made by the international community to solve salient problems in outer space from different perspectives within the United Nations framework. Despite the overlaps in some common issues between these two initiatives, experience can be drawn upon from each other so as to jointly promote the modernization of and the rule of law in outer space governance. China believes that appropriate and feasible TCBMs in outer space will help enhance mutual trust, reduce miscalculations, and regulate space activities, in an effort to maintain security in outer space and serve as a useful supplement to the prevention of weaponization of and an arms race in outer space, though they cannot replace initiatives for concluding legal instruments on arms control in outer space.

9. China is of the view that space industry is still on its developing stage, and the long-term sustainability of outer space activities is an issue that has occurred during the development of space industry, and issues in the development process should be resolved by means of development. The international community should be more concerned about how to solve problems during the development process and how to better share the fruits of space activities of humankind, devoted to the resolution of LTS issues such as space debris mitigation and space weather hazards through

development. From a historical perspective, space debris has been produced as a cumulative result from space activities carried out by humankind in the past six decades. It has not been formed overnight and thus is not possible to be settled once for all and forever. Space weather hazards are the common threats facing States in space activities. The international community needs to further achieve consensus, attain synergetic development and build common capabilities in the monitoring and forecasting of space weather as well the prevention of space weather hazards.

10. China believes that international cooperation is not only a significant principle to be enshrined in the connotation of the LTS of outer space activities, but also a crucial means to promote the LTS of outer space activities. The LTS of outer space activities cannot be achieved without international cooperation on the basis of equality, mutual benefit, openness, inclusiveness and non-discrimination, or without the joint efforts of all space-faring and space-using nations. The international community needs to attach greater importance to the advance of LTS of outer space activities through helping developing countries with their capacity building. China is ready to develop practical collaborations with States in space activities and advocates enhancing mutual trust and understanding through practical collaborations. China would like to provide opportunities for more States, especially developing countries, to participate in China's space programs and to share with them the opportunities and benefits of China's space industry development. China advocates that developed countries need to provide necessary technical and financial assistance to developing countries during their implementation of the LTS Guidelines so as to achieve common development of all nations on the basis of equality and mutual benefit. China is against any words or deeds of national discrimination in pragmatic space cooperation, and against any action based on various excuses to prevent other States from carrying out pragmatic space cooperation. China hopes that during the subsequent discussions on the LTS Working Group Report and relevant Guidelines, conditions should be proactively facilitated to attract more developing countries to participate in the discussions and have their concerns and pursuit expressed.

11. China is of the view that the formulation of the LTS Working Group Report and relevant Guidelines shall be carried out in strict accordance with the "Terms of Reference and Methods of Work of the Working Group on the Long-term Sustainability of Outer Space Activities of the Scientific and Technical Subcommittee" (A/66/20, Annex II), "taking into account the concerns and interests of all states, in particular those of developing countries" (A/66/20, Annex II, Paragraph 8). The outer space including the Moon and other celestial bodies does not exclusively belong to any State according to the international law, and each State has its own right to free access to and peaceful exploration and use of outer space. Given that space industry has the characteristics of high investment, high technology and high risks, all States especially the developing countries need to be encouraged to develop their space industries, participate in

international cooperation, promote space applications, and share the benefits and interests brought by outer space. The LTS Working Group Report and relevant Guidelines should be dedicated to the promotion of this purpose and principle. The concept and practice of the "Long-term Sustainability of Outer Space Activities" should be constructive. The LTS Working Group Report and relevant Guidelines should facilitate such purposes and principles with constructive ideology as well as practice. The LTS Working Group Report and relevant Guidelines should "ensure that all countries are able to have equitable access to outer space and the resources and benefits associated with it" (A/66/20, Annex II, Paragraph 12). China is of the view that the adoption of any draft guidelines should be based on the reality of the development of space technologies and space activities, taking into full consideration the concerns of all parties without placing any restriction on developing countries from participating in space activities and developing their own space industries, and in accordance with relevant United Nations Security Council resolutions.

12. China believes that the adoption of any advisory LTS guideline should be in strict compliance with current legal regimes on outer space, without constituting any effective modification or authoritative interpretation to any international principles and norms. Any cutting-edge legal issues and issues concerning interpretations to United Nations treaties on outer space arising during the drafting of the LTS Working Group Report and relevant Guidelines may be submitted to the Legal Subcommittee of the Committee on the Peaceful Uses of Outer Space for focused studies.

13. China is of the view that the Guidelines drafted by the LTS Working Group should "be applied on a voluntary basis by States, either individually or collectively, international organizations, national non-governmental organizations and private sector entities" (A/66/20, Annex II, Paragraph 12), and they "should be voluntary and not be legally binding" (A/66/20, Annex II, Paragraph 13). Upon the precondition of being consistent with international principles and norms, States may decide on their own how to implement the relevant LTS Guidelines in accordance with their domestic legal regimes, stages of development, technology capabilities and regulatory proficiency. States should be allowed to adopt measures to carry out the requirements of the LTS Guidelines stage by stage within their national legal framework and in accordance with their national conditions and capabilities. Insufficient regulation and unnecessary excessive regulation on the space industry should both be avoided, and consideration should be given to "acceptable and reasonable financial and other connotations while taking into account the needs and interests of developing countries" (A/66/20, Annex II, Paragraph 13).

14. China hopes that States will promote the conclusion of a final consensus text on the LTS Working Group Report and Guidelines by following the principle of mutual understanding and seeking common ground while putting aside differences. The LTS Guidelines to be voluntarily implemented by States, international organizations and all other space actors should focus on those "practical and prudent measures that could be

implemented in a timely manner to enhance the long-term sustainability of outer space activities" (A/66/20, Annex II, Paragraph 4). In order to enhance mutual trust and understanding among States, some critical concepts in the LTS Working Group Report and Guidelines with ambiguity among the six official United Nations languages should be expressed clearly and precisely, so as to avoid any logical mess or misinterpretations which may affect the role they are intended to play.

15. The United Nations is the bedrock to maintain international order after World War II, and China has been a firm advocator and proactive founder of the post-War international order and the rule of law in international context. The Charter of the United Nations has established the international order of multilateralism centering on the United Nations, formed the basic principles of international law and code of conduct governing international relationships, and also serves as the basic norms regulating space activities of humankind. In the past six decades of space activities by humankind, the United Nations has played an irreplaceable and significant role in formulating a series of treaties on outer space and establishing an international legal regime on outer space, and is now the best widely-acknowledged forum for negotiating and promulgating norms and rules for outer space governance. States and international organizations should maintain the international order and system in consistence with the purpose and principles of the United Nations Charter and consciously maintain the authority of the United Nations and the United Nations Charter. China supports the United Nations to play an even more significant role in outer space governance.

16. China has been a proactive practitioner and firm advocator for the United Nations legal regime on outer space. As a responsible space-faring nation, China always follows the purposes and principles as enshrined in the United Nations treaties on outer space, always earnestly fulfills obligations arising from the treaties, always actively participates in the multilateral initiatives for outer space governance led by the United Nations, and always conducts its space activities in an open, transparent and responsible manner. The National Security Law of the People's Republic of China promulgated in 2015 makes it clear for the first time ever from the legal aspect that China shall insist on the peaceful exploration and use of outer space. China attaches great importance to its national space legislation and actively promotes the implementation of United Nations treaties on outer space to which it has acceded. China has promulgated a series of regulations, such as the Interim Measures on the Administration of Permits for Civil Space Launch Projects, the Administrative Measures for the Registration of Space Objects, and the Administrative Measures for Space Debris Mitigation and Spacecraft Protection. At present, space legislation has been included in China's national legislation plan and is being carried out as a priority issue. Promoting the rule of law in space activities has become an essential part of the program for promoting the rule of law across China.

17. As a responsible space-faring nation, China will as always strengthen multilateral, regional and bilateral dialogues in a constructive fashion, study and exchange experience

5. CHINA'S SPACE-RELATED STATEMENTS AND PROPOSALS IN THE UN

with States to enhance the long-term sustainability of outer space activities, and proactively facilitate the modernization of and the rule of law in outer space governance within the United Nations framework. China appeals that States should place great importance to the promotion of pragmatic cooperation and communications to enhance the long-term sustainability of outer space activities, facilitate the common development of space activities of humankind by means of even more open and inclusive cooperation, achieve the goal of long-term mutual benefit and win-win outcome in outer space through fair, balanced, rational and feasible space governance measures, and jointly promote the long-term sustainability of outer space activities. China firmly believes that, with all States working together, the international community has sufficient wisdom and courage to resolve the common challenges facing humankind in outer space, ensure the peaceful and sustainable development of space activities, and establish a regulatory framework with both efficiency and equity. On the basis of equality and mutual benefit, China will strengthen communications, mutual learning and cooperation with all States and related international organizations, promote the common security and development in outer space, join hands with all States to establish a community of common destiny, a community of common interests, a community of common development and a community of common responsibility, make space science and technology better serve the long-term global development, and make even greater contributions to building harmonious outer space and to promoting the progress of human civilization.

5.1.8.   *China's Activities in the Field of International Cooperation in the Peaceful Uses of Outer Space*

A/AC.105/1154
2017

In 2017, China made progress in space launches, satellite applications and international cooperation, as described below.

1. Space Launches
Since the beginning of the year, China has conducted a total of 10 space launches, sending 21 space vehicles into space.

In the area of human space flight, China has made important progress. In April, the Tianzhou-1 cargo spacecraft was successfully launched, which proceeded to complete its orbital flight around the Tiangong-2 space lab, as well as a test of automated rapid rendezvous and docking with it. As a result, tasks for the second phase of the country's human space flight programme have been fully accomplished.

Regarding communications satellites, the first high flux volume telecommunications satellite of China, Practice-13, was launched successfully on 12 April. It is the first time that such a high-orbit satellite project has been undertaken with electric propulsion systems autonomously developed in China. Its communication capacity amounts to 20 Gb/s in total, exceeding the combined total of all telecommunication satellites previously developed and launched into space by China.

Regarding remote sensing satellites, the task of launching the Venezuelan remote sensing satellite VRSS-2 came to a successful conclusion on 10 October. Its applications are mainly intended for surveying land resources, environmental protection, disaster monitoring and management, crop estimation and urban planning.

In terms of technological experimentation satellites, a new experimental satellite, Tiankun-1, was launched on 3 March and entered smoothly into its pre-set orbit. Its main purpose is to carry out remote sensing, telecommunications and validation tests of small satellite platforms. On 15 June, China successfully launched its first X-ray astronomical satellite, which significantly enhanced its national programme to develop large scientific satellites and filled the gap in its provision of X-ray satellites for space exploration.

Unfortunately, launch vehicle LM-5/YZ-2 ended in failure during its lift-off on 2 July 2017. Backtracking investigations and thorough examinations for a renewed start are under way. The planned launch of the Chang'e-5 mission has thus been postponed.

2. Satellite Applications

In 2017, the Government of China accelerated the construction and operationalization of a space-based information corridor for its Belt and Road Initiative, applying space technology extensively to various fields such as meteorology, environmental monitoring, disaster mitigation and relief, and space science in order to provide additional impetus to economic development, improvement of livelihoods and scientific and technological advances in countries and regions along the "Belt and Road" routes.

In the area of remote sensing applications, the country's meteorological satellite Fengyun-4 captured its first images and data on 27 February, which represented a successful upgrade to a new generation of geostationary meteorological satellites. In March, Chinese scientists generated the first satellite interference synthetic-aperture radar images in China by using the Gaofen-3 high-resolution radar imaging satellite, marking a breakthrough from nil in the country's capacity in satellite synthetic-aperture radar imaging interferometry.

In the area of space science, the world's first quantum scientific experimentation satellite, Micius, was officially delivered to its intended client on 18 January. It lays the scientific and technological foundation for the development of quantum communication technology and for cutting-edge research and testing, on the outer space scale, involving fundamental issues in quantum physics. It represents a solid step towards the future realization of global coverage by a quantum-based confidential communications network.

3. Major International Conferences

On 24 April 2017, China celebrated its second Space Day of China. A major event dedicated to the theme "Space for a better life" was successfully held in Xi'an, China. Simonetta Di Pippo, Director of the Office for Outer Space Affairs of the Secretariat, attended the event and, together with representatives of several States members of the Committee, observed the lift-off of China's Tianzhou-1 cargo spacecraft, witnessing an important moment in the history of Chinese astronautic development.

On 14 May, the first Belt and Road Forum for International Cooperation was successfully convened in Beijing. The Government of China is enhancing its efforts to promote the construction and utilization of a space-based information corridor for the Belt and Road Initiative, providing support for space-derived information for the economic development and improvement of livelihoods in countries and regions along the "Belt and Road" routes.

On 6 June, the Global Space Exploration Conference 2017 was held in Beijing, bringing together approximately 1,000 guests and representatives from 51 countries and territories around the world to explore opportunities for global activities in deep space exploration.

From 3 to 5 September, leaders from Brazil, the Russian Federation, India, China and South Africa (the BRICS countries) gathered in Xiamen, China, for a successful summit meeting, during which space was identified repeatedly as an important area of cooperation. At the meeting, the importance of the remote sensing satellite constellation to the economic and social development of the BRICS countries was highlighted.

On 23 and 24 November 2017, China and the International Academy of Astronautics (IAA) will jointly hold the Seventh International Conference on Advanced Space Technology, in Shanghai, China, with the aims of building a useful platform for space scientists and researchers and expanding, both in depth and breadth, international academic exchanges and cooperation in space.

4. International Cooperation

As of October 2017, China had signed a total of nine intergovernmental agency agreements.

Regarding deep space exploration, China signed a series of memorandums of understanding on cooperation in respect of the Chang'e-4 mission with Germany, Saudi Arabia and Sweden, giving strong impetus to the cooperation efforts of China in deep space exploration.

Regarding remote sensing satellites, China signed memorandums of understanding on cooperation with the European Organization for the Exploitation of Meteorological Satellites (EUMETSAT), the French Space Agency (CNES) and the Egyptian National Authority for Remote Sensing and Space Sciences that initiated and enhanced cooperation in the field of remote sensing satellites.

With respect to mechanisms for space cooperation, China organized subcommittee meetings on space cooperation with ESA, CNES and the Russian State Corporation for Space Activities (Roscosmos), which further enhanced bilateral cooperation in space.

5.1.9. China's Replies on Transparency and Confidence-Building Measures in Outer Space Activities

A/72/65
2017

China attaches great importance to this issue.

China believes that the adoption by all countries of an appropriate level of transparency and confidence-building measures with respect to their outer space activities will help to increase mutual trust, reduce misunderstandings, promote cooperation in the peaceful use of outer space, and to a certain extent help to prevent the weaponization of outer space and assist in the verification of an outer space arms control treaty in the future. Indeed, the most important transparency and confidence-building measure in that regard would be for all countries to commit to refrain from deploying weapons in outer space and to prevent the weaponization of outer space and a space arms race. However, outer space transparency and confidence-building measures are not legally binding and thus cannot fill the gaps in existing international legal instruments on outer space. Those measures can serve as a useful supplement in the negotiation and conclusion of international legal instruments to prevent the weaponization of outer space and a space arms race, but cannot replace or have the status of legal instruments.

China is confident that the negotiation and conclusion of new international legal instruments is the best way to prevent the weaponization of outer space and a space arms race. China hopes that the Conference on Disarmament will begin substantive work as soon as possible and launch formal negotiations on the draft treaty on outer space submitted by the Russian Federation and China.

China has proactively adopted a series of transparency and confidence- building measures aimed at maintaining peace, security and long-term sustainability in outer space. Those measures include:

5. CHINA'S SPACE-RELATED STATEMENTS AND PROPOSALS IN THE UN

1. Maintaining transparency in its outer space policies. In the latest version of its white paper on outer space, published in December 2016, China reiterated its unwavering stance on the peaceful use of outer space, its opposition to the weaponization of outer space and a space arms race, and explained in detail its aims and principles with respect to outer space activities and the primary tasks in their development over the next five years;

2. Diligently fulfilling its obligations with respect to the Convention on Registration of Objects Launched into Outer Space. China has made public through the media many of its major space launch activities. It has communicated and coordinated with concerned States and international organizations;

3. Using relevant United Nations principles and frameworks as a basis for conducting practice activities related to nuclear power source safety;

4. Engaging in regular bilateral exchanges with concerned States on space debris and satellite collision warnings;

(5) Actively participating in the Committee on the Peaceful Uses of Outer Space, the Inter-Agency Space Debris Coordination Committee and in the formulation of international space debris mitigation guidelines under multilateral mechanisms. China is making unremitting efforts to strengthen its capacity and mechanisms;

6. Signing over 100 cooperation agreements and memorandums of understanding with over 30 States and actively engaging in space cooperation within the framework of the United Nations the BRICS countries (Brazil, the Russian Federation, India, China and South Africa) and the Asia-Pacific Space Cooperation Organization;

7. Hosting, on numerous occasions and on a voluntary basis, visits by government officials and aerospace experts from various States to space launch sites in China.

5.1.10.   *China's Views on Transparency and Confidence-Building Measures in Outer Space Activities*

A/AC.105/1145
2017

China attaches great importance to the role of the United Nations in maintaining peace, security and sustainability in outer space.

Since the start of human space exploration and the use of outer space, the United Nations has adopted the Treaty on Principles Governing the Activities of States in the Exploration and Use of Outer Space, including the Moon and Other Celestial Bodies, the Agreement on the Rescue of Astronauts, the Return of Astronauts and the Return of Objects Launched into Outer Space, the Convention on International Liability for Damage Caused by Space Objects, the Convention on Registration of Objects Launched into Outer Space, the Agreement Governing the Activities of States on the Moon and Other Celestial Bodies, and the General Assembly has adopted a number of resolutions on the matter. Laying the groundwork for the existing international legal system for space exploration and use, the above-mentioned instruments have played an important role in regulating space activities, promoting the peaceful use of outer space and ensuring the exploration of space for the benefit of all human beings, and have paved the way for the further regulation of space activities.

Over the years, the relevant United Nations agencies have conducted a great deal of work on transparency and confidence-building measures in space activities. The Secretary-General has established the Group of Governmental Experts on Transparency and Confidence-Building Measures in Outer Space Activities, which in 2012 and 2013 prepared a report (A/68/189) in which it made recommendations on voluntary transparency and confidence-building measures in space activities. The report has gained extensive international support and has helped to enhance international consensus and promote peace and security in outer space.

China attaches great importance to the role of the United Nations in promoting transparency and confidence-building measures in space activities, and has been an active participant in relevant United Nations work:

1. China has co-sponsored the General Assembly resolutions on transparency and confidence-building measures in space activities. As a member of the Group of Governmental Experts on Transparency and Confidence-building Measures in Outer Space Activities, from 2012 to 2013, China made positive contributions to the conclusion of the final report of the Group. As requested by the General Assembly in its resolution 70/53, entitled "Transparency and confidence-building measures in outer space activities", China has submitted its views on transparency and confidence-building measures in space activities, which will be annexed to the report of the Secretary-General to the General Assembly at its 72nd session;

2. For many years, China and the Russian Federation, along with many other countries, have worked vigorously to promote the negotiation of a treaty on preventing the weaponization of outer space at the Conference on Disarmament and proposed two draft versions. China is of the view that the commitment of countries to refraining from placing weapons in outer space and preventing the weaponization of and an arms race in outer space would be one of the most important transparency and confidence-building measures in outer space activities. In 2006, China and the Russian Federation jointly submitted to the Conference on Disarmament working paper CD/1778, providing detailed ideas on transparency and confidence-building measures in outer space activities;

3. In 2016, China, the Russian Federation and the United States of America made a joint proposal to the United Nations Disarmament Commission on the inclusion of an

5. CHINA'S SPACE-RELATED STATEMENTS AND PROPOSALS IN THE UN

agenda item on space with a view to enabling the Disarmament Commission to make substantive progress and play its role in safeguarding space security;

4. China has been a constructive participant in the work of the Committee on the Peaceful Uses of Outer Space and its Subcommittees, and has actively participated in activities within the United Nations system relating to space law capacity-building and outreach. China has actively participated in the discussion on the guidelines for the long-term sustainability of outer space activities within the Committee on the Peaceful Uses of Outer Space with a view to promoting peace, security and long-term sustainability in outer space. In November 2014, China, the United Nations and the Asia-Pacific Space Cooperation Organization co-hosted a workshop on space law in Beijing;

5. China is of the view that the Committee on the Peaceful Uses of Outer Space is one of the important platforms supporting Member States in the implementation of transparency and confidence-building measures in outer space activities. The Committee and its Subcommittees have established mechanisms enabling member States to exchange views on progress made in space utilization and discuss relevant technical and legal issues, including the long-term sustainability of space activities, space debris, space weather and near-Earth space objects. The Committee will continue to play a positive role in promoting the implementation of transparency and confidence-building measures in outer space activities, as the peaceful use and exploration of outer space will proceed further;

6. China supports the joint session of the First and Fourth Committees of the General Assembly, the aim of which is to promote communication and coordination among the relevant outer space working mechanisms within the United Nations framework, deepen understanding of space-related issues among the international community and facilitate joint efforts by all countries to maintain security and long-term sustainability in outer space;

7. China actively supports international discussions on space security. China has jointly sponsored the annual space security conference organized by the United Nations Institute for Disarmament Research, which provides participating countries with a platform to explore ways to address space security challenges.

In 2015, China, together with the Lao People's Democratic Republic, the Russian Federation and the United States, held the third Association of Southeast Asian Nations Regional Forum Workshop on Space Security with a view to raising awareness of and promoting regional cooperation on the peaceful use of outer space among the countries of the Asia-Pacific region.

China is of the view that appropriate transparency and confidence-building measures in outer space activities are conducive to enhancing mutual trust, reducing miscalculation and promoting cooperation in the peaceful use of outer space, and is to some extent conducive to preventing the weaponization of outer space and the verification of compliance with a future international legal instrument in that regard. However, transparency and confidence-building measures are not legally binding and are inadequate for plugging the loopholes in existing international legal instruments. Those measures can be a useful complement to a negotiated international legal instrument on preventing the weaponization of and an arms race in outer space, but cannot replace such an instrument.

China maintains that the best way to prevent the weaponization of and an arms race in outer space is to conclude a new international legal instrument through negotiation. China and the Russian Federation jointly submitted to the Conference on Disarmament a draft for a treaty on the prevention of the placement of weapons in outer space and the threat or use of force against outer space objects (CD/1839) in February 2008, and an updated version of that draft (CD/1985) in June 2014. In September 2015, in response to certain comments on the draft, China and the Russian Federation jointly submitted another working paper (CD/2042). The draft treaty reflects the call of the international community for the prevention of an arms race in outer space, and the international aspiration to address the most pressing threat to space security. It is the most mature space security initiative taken, and is based on an extensive international consensus. It is hoped that the Conference on Disarmament could conduct substantive work based on the draft and start negotiations at an early date.

As a nation actively engaged in space utilization activities, China has implemented a series of transparency and confidence-building measures to maintain peace, security and long-term sustainability in outer space:

1. China has actively exchanged information on its space policy. It has issued four white papers, in 2000, 2006, 2011 and 2016, each entitled "China's space activities". In the latest of those, which was published in December 2016, China reiterated its position on the peaceful use of outer space, and its opposition to the weaponization of and an arms race in outer space, and elaborated in detail on the purposes and principles of its space activities and major tasks in the following five years, testifying to the transparency in its space policy, programmes and activities;

2. China acceded to the Convention on Registration of Objects Launched into Outer Space in December 1988. It has faithfully implemented the obligations of that Convention and registered the information regarding objects launched into space accordingly. In 2001, China issued legislation entitled "Provisions and procedures for the registration of space objects" to regulate its international and domestic registration of space objects. In 2002, China issued interim measures on the administration of permits for civil space launch projects. Moreover, China usually publicizes major launches in the media or coordinates such launches with relevant countries or international organizations;

3. China attaches great importance to the safety of nuclear power sources in outer space. China has applied strict safety measures to the use of radioactive isotopes in the

operation of Chang'e-3, and given a presentation on the subject at a meeting of the Scientific and Technical Subcommittee of the Committee on the Peaceful Uses of Outer Space. As part of the ongoing preparations for the Chang'e-4 mission, China also provides for the use of radioactive isotopes in outer space, as announced by the delegation of China at the 59th session of the Committee on the Peaceful Uses of Outer Space. China will carry on the safety work in connection with nuclear power sources in outer space in accordance with the relevant United Nations principles and frameworks;

4. China is highly concerned by the risks caused to space assets and activities in recent years by space debris and orbital congestion, and has held regular bilateral exchanges on space debris, the avoidance of satellite collisions and other issues;

5. China attaches great importance to space debris mitigation and spacecraft protection. As an active participant in the work of the Committee on the Peaceful Uses of Outer Space and the Inter-Agency Space Debris Coordination Committee, China has played a positive role in the formulation of relevant international norms. In the meantime, China has made due contributions to international efforts by improving its own debris mitigation capacity and mechanism, and has set national technical standards by issuing legislation entitled "Administrative measures for space debris mitigation and spacecraft protection" and "National standards for the requirements for space debris mitigation";

6. China holds the view that all countries have an equal right to explore, develop and utilize outer space peacefully, and stands for the strengthening of international space exchanges and cooperation on the basis of equality and mutual benefit, the peaceful utilization of outer space and inclusive development. China has concluded over 100 bilateral space cooperation agreements or memorandums of understanding with over 30 countries and has launched satellites for over 10 countries. Currently China is actively promoting international cooperation in relation to the Beidou Navigation System and remote-sensing satellite constellation among Brazil, the Russian Federation, India, China and South Africa (the BRICS countries). China is also dedicated to promoting space cooperation within the framework of transparency and confidence-building measures of the United Nations and the Asia-Pacific Space Cooperation Organization with a view to sharing among all countries the dividends brought by the advancement of space technology and promoting the common development and long-term sustainability of space utilization by all humankind;

7. China has actively and voluntarily invited other countries to carry out launch site visits on its territory. It has invited officials and experts from around the world to its space launch sites to observe space launches on many occasions.

China stands ready to work with all countries to promote the prevention of the weaponization of and an arms race in outer space and explore practical and feasible transparency and confidence-building measures so as to continuously contribute to peace, security and long-term sustainability in outer space.

5.1.11. Note Verbale on the Re-entry of Tiangong-1

A/AC.105/1150
4 May 2017

The Permanent Mission of China to the United Nations (Vienna) has the honour to provide the following notification with respect to the re-entry of the space laboratory Tiangong-1.

Tiangong-1 was launched into outer space on 29 September 2011. It conducted six successive rendezvous and dockings with spacecraft Shenzhou-8, Shenzhou-9 and Shenzhou-10 and completed all assigned missions, making important contributions to China's manned space exploration activities. On 16 March 2016, the Tiangong-1 Target Manned Space Vehicle ceased functioning. It had fully fulfilled its historic mission. To date, Tiangong-1 has maintained its structural integrity. Its operational orbit is under constant and close surveillance by China. Its current average altitude is 349 kilometres and it is decaying at a daily rate of approximately 160 metres. Its re-entry is expected between October 2017 and April 2018. According to the calculations and analysis that have been carried out, most of the structural components of Tiangong-1 will be destroyed through burning during the course of its re-entry. The probability of endangering and causing damage to aviation and ground activities is very low.

China attaches great importance to the re-entry of Tiangong-1 and will take the following measures in terms of monitoring and public information. First, it will further enhance monitoring and forecasting. China will make strict arrangements to track and closely monitor Tiangong-1 in its orbital development and will publish a timely forecast of its re-entry. China will make use of the international joint monitoring information under the framework of the Inter-Agency Space Debris Coordination Committee in order to be better informed about the descent of Tiangong-1. Second, it will improve the information reporting mechanism. Dynamic orbital status and other information relating to Tiangong-1 will be posted on the website of the China Manned Space Agency (www.cmse.gov.cn) in both Chinese and English. In addition, timely information about important milestones and events during the orbital decay phases will be released through the news media. As to the final forecast of the time and region of re-entry, China will issue the relevant information and early warning in a timely manner and bring it to the attention of the United Nations Office for Outer Space Affairs and the Secretary-General of the United Nations by means of note verbale through diplomatic channels.

5. CHINA'S SPACE-RELATED STATEMENTS AND PROPOSALS IN THE UN

5.1.12.   *Note Verbale on the Re-entry of Tiangong-1*

A/AC.105/1150/Add.1
8 December 2017

The Permanent Mission of China to the United Nations (Vienna), with reference to its note verbale of 4 May 2017 (A/AC.105/1150), has the honour to provide the following notification with respect to the re-entry into the atmosphere of the space laboratory Tiangong-1.

China attaches great importance to the re-entry of Tiangong-1. For this purpose, China has set up a special working group, made relevant emergency preparedness plans and been working closely with its follow-up tracking, monitoring, forecasting and relevant analysing. Until 26 November, Tiangong-1 had been orbiting at an average altitude of 296.0 km (perigee: 281.7 km; apogee: 310.2 km; inclination: 42.65°). Currently, it has maintained its structural integrity with stabilized attitude control. According to the latest forecast, its re-entry is expected between the first 10 days of February and the last 10 days of March 2018. Tiangong-1 weighed 8.5 tons at launch, 10.5 metres long, with a maximum diameter of 3.35 metres. Tiangong-1 uses methylhydrazine and dinitrogen tetroxide as its engine fuel. Based on analysis, the remaining small amount of fuel will be burned and destroyed along with its structural components during the course of re-entry and will therefore not cause any damage on the ground.

China will continue to closely track and monitor the operation of Tiangong-1 and will regularly publish relevant information through the website of the China Manned Space Engineering Programme (www.cmse.gov.cn) as well as other relevant media.

5.1.13.   *Note Verbale on the Re-entry of Tiangong-1*

A/AC.105/1150/Add.2
26 March 2018

The Permanent Mission of China to the United Nations (Vienna), with reference to its notes verbales of 4 May 2017 (A/AC.105/1150) and 8 December 2017 (A/AC.105/1150/Add.1), has the honour to provide the following notification with respect to the re-entry into the atmosphere of the space laboratory Tiangong-1.

As at 23 March 2018, Tiangong-1 was at an altitude of approximately 222.4 km in an orbit with a perigee of 215.1 km, an apogee of 229.6 km and at 42.64 degrees inclination. According to the latest prediction, the date of re-entry will be 2 April 2018, with a ±3-day window. The re-entry area will be located between 43 degrees North latitude and 43 degrees South latitude. On the basis of further calculation and review, most structural parts of Tiangong-1 will burn up on re-entry. The probability of damage to aviation activities and human life and facilities on Earth is extremely low. China will continue to closely monitor the status of Tiangong-1 and provide information on its orbit and time of re-entry through the official website of the China Manned Space Engineering Programme (www.cmse.gov.cn).

5.1.14.   Note Verbale on the Re-entry of Tiangong-1

A/AC.105/1150/Add.3
11 April 2018

The Permanent Mission of China to the United Nations (Vienna), with reference to its notes verbales of 4 May 2017 (A/AC.105/1150), 8 December 2017 (A/AC.105/1150/Add.1) and 26 March 2018 (A/AC.105/1150/Add.2), has the honour to provide the following notification with respect to the re-entry into the atmosphere of the space laboratory Tiangong-1.

According to the monitoring and analysis carried out, Tiangong-1 re-entered the atmosphere at around 0815 hours (UTC+8) on 2 April 2018, with the re-entry point located in the central region of the South Pacific Ocean, and most parts of Tiangong-1 burned up in the course of its re-entry into the atmosphere. Before the re-entry of Tiangong-1 into the atmosphere, China issued timely and frequent forecasts for the re-entry time and re-entry area through the official website of the China Manned Space Engineering Programme (www.cmse.gov.cn). After the completion of the re-entry was confirmed, China immediately released information in that regard through the Xinhua News Agency and the official website of the China Manned Space Engineering Programme.

5.1.15.   Note Verbale on the Planned Re-entry of Tiangong-2

A/AC.105/1201
16 July 2019

The Permanent Mission of China to the United Nations (Vienna) has the honour to provide the Secretary-General with the following notification concerning the controlled re-entry into the atmosphere of the Tiangong-2 space laboratory of China.

In accordance with the plan, the Tiangong-2 space laboratory has completed all the expansion tests, and it is scheduled to leave orbit and undergo controlled re-entry into the atmosphere on 19 July (Beijing time). A small amount of debris is expected to fall into the safe area in the southern Pacific Ocean (160–90 degrees West longitude and 30–45 degrees South latitude).

Tiangong-2, which was developed on the basis of the Tiangong-1 backup target vehicle, comprises an experiment module and a resource module. The space laboratory has a total length of 10.4 metres, a maximum diameter of 3.35 metres and a take-off weight of 8.6 tons; its wingspan is about 18.4 metres when the solar panels are deployed. Its functions have been rendezvous and docking with the Shenzou crewed spaceship and the Tianzhou cargo spaceship, in-orbit propellant refueling and conducting a series of scientific and technological experiments.

Tiangong-2 was launched into orbit on 15 September 2016 with an intended two-year orbital lifespan. Thus far, the space laboratory has operated in orbit over 1,000 days. The platform and the payloads are functioning well and are in good condition. Preparations for the controlled re-entry into the atmosphere are proceeding smoothly and to plan. China will report information about the spacecraft in due course once it has re-entered the atmosphere.

5.2. China's Statements and Proposals Submitted to the Conference on Disarmament

5.2.1. Position on and Suggestions for Ways to Address the Issue of Prevention of An Arms Race in Outer Space

CD/1606
2000

Outer space belongs to all mankind. All countries have equal rights in the exploration and use of outer space for peaceful purposes although their levels of economic and scientific development may differ. It is the shared desire of all mankind to forestall the spread of weapons and an arms race in outer space.

Some people believe that since currently there is no arms race in outer space, the CD has no need to discuss its prevention or negotiate the conclusion of international legal instruments in this regard. However, history and reality have both shown not only that there are indeed attempts, programmes and moves unilaterally to seek military and strategic superiority in or control over outer space but that there have been new developments in this respect. Such development, if unchecked, may lead to the weaponization of outer space in the near future or even to a multilateral arms race in outer space. Therefore, it is a present and pressing necessity for the international community to take effective measures to stop such negative developments.

I. Our Views on How to Address the Issue of PAROS at the Conference on Disarmament

As the single multilateral disarmament-negotiating forum, the Conference on Disarmament (Conference) should concentrate on the most pressing and prominent issues in international arms control and disarmament, the ones that have the greatest bearing on global peace and security in the twenty-first century. PAROS is one such important issue, and should therefore be a top priority at the Conference. The Conference should play a primary role in the negotiations to prevent any form of arms race in outer space.

At its fifty-fourth session the United Nations General Assembly once again adopted, by an overwhelming majority, a resolution on PAROS. It was reaffirmed that negotiating an international agreement or agreements to prevent an arms race in outer space remains a priority task of the CD's Ad Hoc Committee. The fact that the resolution was adopted without opposition reflects the common aspiration and insistent demand of the international community to prevent an arms race in outer space.

The General Assembly also adopted at its fifty-fourth session, and also by an overwhelming majority, a resolution on preservation of and compliance with the Anti-Ballistic Missile Treaty, an issue that is related to the prevention of an arms race in outer space. In the resolution the General Assembly recognizes the historical role of the 1972 Treaty as a cornerstone for maintaining global peace and security and strategic stability, reaffirms its continued validity and relevance in the current international situation and supports further efforts by the international community in the light of emerging developments with the goal of safeguarding the inviolability and integrity of the ABM Treaty in which the international community bears strong interest.

Since PAROS was put on the CD agenda in 1982, the Conference has, through the establishment of the Ad Hoc Committee and other means, held discussions on definitions, principles, existing treaties and confidence-building measures, and accumulated experience in this field, preparing the ground for future work in this area. With the accelerated development of outer space weapons, anti-ballistic missiles and other weapon systems, individual countries have stepped up efforts to secure military superiority in outer space and have mapped out and are pursuing plans to secure military superiority on the ground from space. In these circumstances, preventing outer space from becoming a new venue for an arms race without prejudice to its peaceful uses has obviously become the most important and pressing task of the Conference.

To accomplish this, the Conference must first re-establish the Ad Hoc Committee under agenda item 3 to negotiate and conclude an international legal instrument prohibiting the testing, deployment and use of weapons, weapon systems and components in outer space so as to prevent the weaponization of, and an arms race in, outer space.

5. China's Space-Related Statements and Proposals in the UN

In carrying out its mandate, the Ad Hoc Committee must take into account all relevant developments and specific proposals, present and future. As a preliminary step towards the negotiation of an international legal instrument, it might discuss and review all pertinent issues, including current military activities in outer space and related developments, their influence on the prevention of an arms race in outer space; shortcomings in the existing international instruments; and the basic elements of the future international legal instrument.

The Chinese delegation has taken note of the various ideas and suggestions on PAROS put forward in the CD. China believes that the re-established Ad Hoc Committee should be an open-ended, all-embracing mechanism where all participants may air and discuss different views. It should set as its ultimate goal and clear mandate the negotiation and conclusion of one or several international legal instruments to prevent the weaponization of and an arms race in outer space.

II. Our Views on the Existing International Legal Instruments Concerning PAROS

A number of international legal instruments on the peaceful uses of outer space and the prevention of an arms race in outer space have been concluded.

The 1963 Treaty Banning Nuclear Weapon Tests in the Atmosphere, in Outer Space and Under Water prohibits any nuclear weapon test explosion in outer space. The 1996 Comprehensive Nuclear Test Ban Treaty prohibits any nuclear weapon test explosion in any circumstances.

According to the 1967 Treaty on Principles Governing the Activities of States in the Exploration and Use of Outer Space, including the Moon and other Celestial Bodies, outer space, including the moon and other celestial bodies, is not subject to national appropriation by claim of sovereignty, by means of use or occupation, or by any other means. States Parties to the Treaty undertake not to place in orbit around the Earth any objects carrying nuclear weapons or any other kinds of weapons of mass destruction, install such weapons on celestial bodies, or station such weapons in outer space in any other manner. The establishment of military bases, installations and fortifications, the testing of any type of weapons and the conduct of military manoeuvres on celestial bodies is forbidden.

The 1972 Treaty between the United States and the Union of Soviet Socialist Republics on the Limitation of Anti-Ballistic Missile Systems prohibits the development, testing and deployment of space-based ABM systems or components.

Besides these, the 1972 Convention on International Liability for Damage Caused by Space Objects, the 1975 Convention on Registration of Objects Launched into Outer Space and the 1979 Agreement Governing the Activities of States on the Moon and other Celestial Bodies all contain provisions on outer space activities which have helped to constrain some aspects of military activities in outer space to some extent.

However, these instruments have been ineffective in preventing the weaponization of and an arms race in outer space. Some have imposed limited prohibitions and contained many loopholes and ambiguities. Some have not been fully complied with or are in danger of being violated, amended or even abrogated. Most crucially, as they have failed to reflect the latest developments in aerospace technology they cannot prevent the potential weaponization of outer space or an arms race in outer space in the twenty-first century.

The Chinese delegation believes that the most direct and effective way to prevent the weaponization of and an arms race in outer space is to negotiate and conclude new international legal instruments while strictly observing the existing bilateral and multilateral agreements.

III. China's Basic Position on PAROS

China has always opposed arms races, in outer space and elsewhere. It maintains that the exploration and use of outer space should only serve to promote countries' economic, scientific and cultural development and benefit all mankind.

With the use of military satellites, outer space has already been militarized to some extent. Military satellites involve rather complex issues and their role should not be all together negated. Therefore, the primary goal at present in our efforts to prevent the weaponization of and an arms race in outer space is to ban the testing, deployment and use of weapons, weapon systems and components in outer space.

What should be particularly emphasized is that the Powers with the greatest space capabilities bear a special responsibility for preventing the weaponization of and an arms race in outer space and ensuring the use of space for peaceful purposes. Pending the conclusion of a new multilateral legal instrument on the prevention of an arms race in outer space, all countries concerned should undertake not to test, deploy or use any weapons, weapon systems or components in outer space.

IV. Tentative Ideas on New International Legal Instruments

The Chinese delegation tentatively suggests that the new international legal instruments to prevent the weaponization of and an arms race in outer space, in whatever form or by whatever name, might contain the following basic elements:

1. Purposes: to prevent the weaponization of and an arms race in outer space, and to use outer space for peaceful purposes.

2. Basic obligations: not to test, deploy or use weapons, weapon systems or components. Consideration could also be given to an article on "permissible activities" thus helping to distinguish between activities that are prohibited and those that are not, and thereby safeguarding States Parties' lawful right to utilize outer space for peaceful purposes.

3. An article on definitions, providing clear definitions of the concepts mentioned, e.g. "outer space", "space weapons", "weapon systems" and "components of weapon systems".

4. Provision for appropriate national implementation measures and the designation or establishment of organizations to ensure that States Parties implement the instruments consistently and effectively.

5. An article on international cooperation in the peaceful use of outer space promoting international exchanges, technical assistance and cooperation for peaceful purposes so that all countries can share in the economic and technological benefits of scientific advances in outer space, and outer space truly serves all mankind.

6. Verification: we must first consider fully how technically feasible it is, and on that basis determine whether to use inspections or alternative means to prevent treaty violations.

7. Establishment of an appropriate mechanism for consultations, clarifications and resolution of possible disputes in order to appropriately address such suspicions and disputes as might arise among States Parties.

8. Appropriate, rational and workable confidence-building measures to enhance mutual trust among States Parties and forestall unnecessary suspicion about particular activities.

9. The procedural articles commonly found in international legal instruments dealing with amendment, length of validity, signature, ratification, entry into force, depository and authentic texts. These may of course also have to resolve some sensitive and key issues.

The Chinese delegation wishes to emphasize that these are only tentative ideas that need to be developed. Our aim in putting them forward is to give all participants food for thought, pool our collective wisdom and encourage a fuller, more detailed examination of the relevant issues at the Conference. We will participate in such discussions and negotiations with an open mind, listening to and accepting good ideas and proposals from all parties and striving unremittingly to prevent the weaponization of and an arms race in outer space and to ensure the continued peaceful use of outer space for the benefit of all mankind.

5.2.2. Working Paper on Possible Elements of the Future International Legal Instrument on the Prevention of the Weaponization of Outer Space

CD/1645
2001

China is dedicated to promoting the international community to negotiate and conclude an international legal instrument on the prevention of the weaponization of and an arms race in outer space. In February 2000, the Chinese delegation submitted to the Conference on Disarmament a working paper (CD/1606, 9 February 2000) entitled "China's Position on and Suggestions for Ways to Address the Issue of Prevention of an Arms Race in Outer Space at the Conference on Disarmament", which outlined China's tentative ideas on the above mentioned international legal instrument. China has further substantiated and developed these ideas. In our view, the future legal instrument may include, *inter alia*, the following elements:

I. Possible Name of the Instrument
Treaty on the Prevention of the Weaponization of Outer Space.

II. Preamble
Outer space is the common heritage of mankind. It is the common aspiration of mankind to use outer space for peaceful purposes.

Outer space is playing an ever-increasing role in future development of mankind.

There is a potential danger of armament development and combatant activities being extended to outer space.

Prevention of the weaponization of and an arms race in outer space becomes a realistic and pressing task facing the international community.

The United Nations General Assembly has adopted a series of resolutions on peaceful uses of outer space and prevention of an arms race in outer space, which have provided a prerequisite for and a basis of the prevention of the weaponization of and an arms race in outer space.

The existing arms limitation and disarmament agreements relevant to outer prevent the weaponization of and an arms race in outer space.

For the benefits of mankind, outer space shall always be used for peaceful purposes, and shall never be allowed to become a battlefield.

Only strict prevention of the weaponization of outer space can eliminate the emerging danger of an arms race in outer space and fully safeguard the security of outer space properties of all countries, which is indispensable for maintaining global strategic balance, world peace and security of all countries.

III. Basic Obligations

Not to test, deploy or use in outer space any weapons, weapon systems or their components.

Not to test, deploy or use on land, in sea or atmosphere any weapons, weapon systems or their components that can be used for war fighting in outer space.

Not to use any objects launched into orbit to directly participate in combatant activities.

Not to assist or encourage other countries, regions, international organizations or entities to participate in activities prohibited by this legal instrument.

IV. Definitions

Outer space is the space above the earth's atmosphere, i.e. space 100km above the sea level of the earth.

Weapons are devices or facilities that strike, destroy or disrupt directly the normal functions of a target by various destructive ways.

Weapon systems are the collective of weapons and their indispensably linked parts that jointly accomplish battle missions.

Components of weapon systems are subsystems that directly and indispensably involved in accomplishing battle missions.

V. National Measures for Implementation

Each country shall, in accordance with its constitutional process, take any necessary measures to prohibit or prevent any activities in violation of this legal instrument on its territory or in any other place under its jurisdiction or control.

VI. Peaceful Use of Outer Space

This legal instrument shall not be construed as impeding scientific exploration in outer space by all its States Parties or other military uses not prohibited by this legal instrument.

Each country shall abide by general principles of international laws in conducting outer space activities, and shall not undermine the sovereignty, security and interests of the other countries.

VII. Confidence Building Measures

To enhance mutual trust, each State Party shall promulgate its space programme, declare the locations and scopes of its space launch sites, the property and parameters of objects to be launched into outer space, and notify the launching activities.

VIII. Verification Measures
(Needs further consideration and development)

IX. Settlement of Disputes
If a State Party suspects treaty violation by another State Party, States Parties concerned shall undertake to consult and cooperate to resolve the issue. Each State Party shall have the right to request clarification from the suspected State Party. The suspected State Party is obliged to provide relevant information to clarify the matter.

If consultation and clarification fail to produce satisfactory results for the States Parties concerned, the suspecting State Party can file charges to the executive organization of this legal instrument. The charges shall include the supporting evidence as well as the request for the organization to review the matter.

Each State Party undertakes to cooperate in the investigation by the executive organization of this legal instrument in accordance with the request it has received.

X. Executive Organization of this Legal Instrument
In order to achieve the purposes and objectives of this legal instrument, and ensure compliance with the obligations of this instrument, the States Parties hereby establish an executive organization of this legal instrument, whose duties are, inter alia, as follows:

To receive charges of non-compliance by States Parties;

To investigate whether there are non-compliant activities;

To organize consultations on non-compliance concerns between States Parties concerned;

To urge States Parties that have violated this legal instrument to take measures to stop non-compliant activities and make up for the consequences arising therefrom.

XI. Amendments
Any State Party may propose amendments to this legal instrument. The text of any proposed amendment shall be submitted to the deposition who shall circulate it to all the State Parties. Thereupon, if requested to do so by one-third or more of the States Parties, the depositary shall convene a conference, to which he shall invite all the States Parties, to consider such an amendment.

Any amendment to this legal instrument must be approved by a majority of vote of all its States Parties. The amendment shall enter into force for all the States Parties upon the deposit of such instruments of ratification by a majority of all the States Parties.

XII. Duration and Withdrawal
This legal instrument shall be of unlimited duration.

Each State Party to this legal instrument shall, in exercising its national sovereignty, have the right to withdraw from this legal instrument if it decides that extraordinary events, related to the subject matter of this legal instrument, have jeopardized the supreme interests of its country. It shall give notice of such withdrawal to the depositary of this legal instrument six months in advance. Such notice shall include a statement of the extraordinary events it regards as having jeopardized its supreme interests.

XIII. Signature and Ratification
This legal instrument shall be open for signature by all States at United Nations headquarters in New York. Any State which does not sign this legal instrument before its entry into force may accede to it at any time.

This legal instrument shall be subject to ratification by the signatory states. Instrument of ratification or accession shall be deposited with the Secretary-General of the United Nations.

XIV. Entry into Force
This legal instrument shall enter into force upon the deposit of instruments of ratification by XX States including the Permanent Member States of the United Nations Security Council.

For those States whose instruments of ratification or accession are deposited after the entry into force of this legal instrument, it shall enter into force on the date of the deposit of their instruments of ratification or accession.

XI. Authentic Texts
This legal instrument, of which the Arabic, Chinese, English, French, Russian and Spanish texts are equally authentic, shall be deposited with the Secretary-General of the United Nations, who shall send certified copies thereof to all signatory and acceding States.

The Chinese delegation would like to reiterate that the above-mentioned elements are still very tentative. Further revision, amendment, improvement and perfection are needed. We are ready, in an open attitude, to work with other delegations, to conclude at an early date a legal instrument aimed at preventing the weaponization of and an arms race in outer space, through hard work and serious negotiations.

5.2.3. *Working Paper on Possible Elements of a Future International Legal Agreement on the Prevention of the Deployment of Weapons in Outer Space, the Threat or Use of Force against Outer Space Objects*

CD/1679
2002

I. Possible Name of Such Agreement
Treaty on the Prevention of the Deployment of Weapons in Outer Space, the threat or Use of Force Against Outer Space Objects

II. Preamble
Outer space is the common heritage of mankind and plays an ever-increasing role in its future development.

There exists a potential danger of an armed confrontation and combatant activities being extended to outer space.

The prevention of the deployment of weapons and an arms race in outer space becomes a pressing task facing the international community.

The United Nations General Assembly has adopted a series of resolutions on peaceful use of outer space and prevention of an arms race in outer space, which have provided a prerequisite and basis for the prevention of the deployment of weapons and an arms race in outer space.

The existing agreements on arms control and disarmament relevant to outer space, including those bilateral ones, and the existing legal regimes concerning outer space have played a positive role in the peaceful use of outer space and in regulating outer space activities. These agreements and legal regimes should be strictly complied with. However, they are unable to effectively prevent the deployment of weapons and an arms race in outer space.

For the benefit of mankind, outer space shall be used for peaceful purposes, and it shall never be allowed to become a sphere of military confrontation.

Only a treaty-based prohibition of the deployment of weapons in outer space and the prevention of the threat or use of force against outer space objects can eliminate the emerging threat of an arms race in outer space and ensure the security for outer space assets of all countries which is an essential condition for the maintenance of world peace.

III. Basic Obligations
Not to place in orbit around the Earth any objects carrying any kinds of weapons, not to install such weapons on celestial bodies, or not to station such weapons in outer space in any other manner.

Not to resort to the threat or use of force against outer space objects.

Not to assist or encourage other States, groups of States, international organizations to participate in activities prohibited by this Treaty.

IV. National Measures for the Implementation of the Treaty

Each State Party to the Treaty shall, in accordance with its constitutional process, take any measures necessary to prevent or prohibit any activity contrary to this Treaty on its territory, or in any other place under its jurisdiction or control.

V. The Use of Outer Space for Peaceful and Other Military Purposes

This Treaty shall not be construed as impeding the research and use of outer space for peaceful purposes or other military uses not prohibited by this Treaty.

Each State Party to the Treaty shall carry out activities in outer space in accordance with the general principles of international law and shall not violate the sovereignty and security of other States.

VI. Confidence Building Measures

To enhance mutual trust, each State Party to the Treaty shall promulgate its space programme, declare the locations and scopes of its space launch sites, the property and parameters of objects being launched into outer space, and notify the launching activities.

VII. Settlement of Disputes

If a suspicion arises against any State Party to the Treaty that it is violating the Treaty, the suspecting State Party, or a group of the suspecting State Parties to this Treaty shall conduct consultations and cooperate with the suspected State Party to this Treaty in order to settle down the aroused suspicion. Each suspecting State Party to this Treaty shall have the right to request clarification from the suspected State Party to this Treaty, whereas the suspected State Party to this Treaty shall undertake to provide requested clarifications.

If consultations or clarification fail to settle down the dispute, the suspicion that has aroused shall be referred to the executive organization of the Treaty for consideration together with relevant arguments.

Each State Party to this Treaty shall undertake to cooperate in the settlement of the suspicion that has aroused by the executive organization of the Treaty.

VIII. The Executive Organization of the Treaty

To promote the objectives and implementation of the provisions of this Treaty, the States Parties to the Treaty shall hereby establish the executive organization of the Treaty, which shall:

(a) Receive for consideration inquires by any State Party or a group of States Parties to the Treaty related to the suspicion, which has aroused by the violation of this Treaty by any State Party to the Treaty;

(b) Consider matters concerning the compliance with the obligations taken by the States Parties to this Treaty;

(c) Organize and conduct consultations with the States Parties to the Treaty with a view to settling down the suspicion that has aroused against any State Party to the Treaty concerning its violation of this Treaty;

(d) Take necessary measures to end violation of this Treaty by any State Party to the Treaty.

IX. Amendments to the Treaty

Any State Party to this Treaty may propose amendments to the Treaty. The text of any proposed amendment to this Treaty shall be submitted to the Depositary Governments who shall promptly circulate it to all the States Parties to the Treaty. Upon the request of at least one third of the States Parties to the Treaty, the Depositary Governments shall convene a conference to which all the States Parties shall be invited to consider the proposed amendment.

Any amendment to this Treaty must be approved by a majority of the votes of all the States Parties to the Treaty. The amendment shall enter into force for all the States Parties to the Treaty in accordance with the procedures governing the entry into force of this Treaty.

X. Duration of the Treaty and Withdrawal from the Treaty

The Treaty shall be of unlimited duration.

Each State Party to the Treaty shall, in exercising its state sovereignty, have the right to withdraw from this Treaty if it decides that extraordinary events, related to the subject matter of this Treaty, have jeopardized its supreme interests. It shall give notice to the Depository Governments of the decision adopted six months in advance of the withdrawal from the Treaty. Such a notification shall include a statement of the extraordinary events, which the notifying State Party to the Treaty regards as having jeopardized its supreme interests.

XI. Signature and Ratification of the Treaty

This Treaty shall be open for signature by all States at United Nations Headquarters in New York. Any State, which does not sign this Treaty before its entry into force, may accede to it at any time.

The Treaty shall be subject to ratification by signatory States in accordance with their constitutional process. Instruments of ratification or accession shall be deposited with the Depositary Governments.

This Treaty shall be registered by the Depositary Governments pursuant to Article 102 of the Charter of the United Nations.

XII. Entry into Force of the Treaty

This Treaty shall enter into force upon the deposit of instruments of ratification by twenty States, including all Permanent Member States of the United Nations Security Council.

For States whose instruments of ratification or accession are deposited after the entry into force of this Treaty, it shall enter into force on the date of the deposit of their instruments of ratification or accession.

XIII. Authentic texts of the Treaty

This Treaty, of which the Arabic, Chinese, English, French, Russian and Spanish texts are equally authentic, shall be deposited in the archives of the Depositary Governments, who shall send duly certified copies thereof to all the signatory and acceding States.

5.2.4. *Draft Treaty on Prevention of the Placement of Weapons in Outer Space and of the Threat of Use of Force against Outer Space Objects (PPWT)*

CD/1839
2008

The States Parties to this Treaty,

Reaffirming that outer space is playing an ever-increasing role in the future development of mankind,

Emphasizing the right to explore and use outer space freely for peaceful purposes,

Interested in preventing outer space from becoming an arena for military confrontation and ensuring security in outer space and the undisturbed functioning of space objects,

Recognizing that prevention of the placement of weapons in outer space and of an arms race in outer space would avert a grave danger for international peace and security,

Desiring to keep outer space as a sphere where no weapon of any kind is placed,

Noting that the existing agreements on arms control and disarmament relevant to outer space, including bilateral agreements, and the existing legal regimes concerning the use of outer space play a positive role in exploration of outer space and in regulating outer space activities, and should be strictly complied with, although they are unable to effectively prevent the placement of weapons in outer space and an arms race in outer space,

Recalling the United Nations General Assembly resolution on "Prevention of an arms race in outer space", in which, inter alia, the Assembly expressed conviction that further measures should be examined in the search for effective and verifiable bilateral and multilateral agreements in order to prevent an arms race in outer space,

Have agreed on the following:

Article I
For the purposes of this Treaty:

(a) The term "outer space" means the space above the Earth in excess of 100 km above sea level;

(b) The term "outer space object" means any device designed to function in outer space which is launched into an orbit around any celestial body, or located in orbit around any celestial body, or on any celestial body, except the Earth, or leaving orbit around any celestial body towards this celestial body, or moving from any celestial body towards another celestial body, or placed in outer space by any other means;

(c) The term "weapon in outer space" means any device placed in outer space, based on any physical principle, which has been specially produced or converted to destroy, damage or disrupt the normal functioning of objects in outer space, on the Earth or in the Earth's atmosphere, or to eliminate a population or components of the biosphere which are important to human existence or inflict damage on them;

(d) A weapon shall be considered to have been "placed" in outer space if it orbits the Earth at least once, or follows a section of such an orbit before leaving this orbit, or is permanently located somewhere in outer space;

(e) The "use of force" or the "threat of force" mean any hostile actions against outer space objects including, inter alia, actions aimed at destroying them, damaging them, temporarily or permanently disrupting their normal functioning or deliberately changing their orbit parameters, or the threat of such actions.

Article II
The States Parties undertake not to place in orbit around the Earth any objects carrying any kinds of weapons, not to install such weapons on celestial bodies and not to place such weapons in outer space in any other manner; not to resort to the threat or use of force against outer space objects; and not to assist or induce other States, groups of States or international organizations to participate in activities prohibited by this Treaty.

Article III
Each State Party shall take all necessary measures to prevent any activity prohibited by this Treaty on its territory or in any other place under its jurisdiction or control.

Article IV

Nothing in this Treaty may be interpreted as impeding the exercise by the States Parties of their right to explore and use outer space for peaceful purposes in accordance with international law, including the Charter of the United Nations and the Outer Space Treaty.

Article V

Nothing in this Treaty may be interpreted as impeding the exercise by the States Parties of their right of self-defence in accordance with Article 51 of the Charter of the United Nations.

Article VI

With a view to promoting confidence in compliance with the provisions of the Treaty and ensuring transparency and confidence-building in outer space activities, the States Parties shall implement agreed confidence-building measures on a voluntary basis, unless agreed otherwise.

Measures to verify compliance with the Treaty may form the subject of an additional protocol.

Article VII

If a dispute arises between States Parties concerning the application or the interpretation of the provisions of this Treaty, the parties concerned shall first consult together with a view to settling the dispute by negotiation and cooperation.

If the parties concerned do not reach agreement after consultation, an interested State Party may refer the situation at issue to the executive organization of the Treaty, providing the relevant argumentation.

Each State Party shall undertake to cooperate in the settlement of the situation at issue with the executive organization of the Treaty.

Article VIII

To promote the implementation of the objectives and provisions of this Treaty, the States Parties shall establish the executive organization of the Treaty, which shall:

(a) Accept for consideration communications from any State Party or group of States Parties relating to cases where there is reason to believe that a violation of this Treaty by any State Party is taking place;

(b) Consider matters concerning compliance with the obligations entered into by States Parties;

(c) Organize and conduct consultations with the States Parties with a view to resolving any situation that has arisen in connection with the violation of this Treaty by a State Party;

(d) Take steps to put an end to the violation of this Treaty by any State Party.

The title, status, specific functions and forms of work of the executive organization of the Treaty shall be the subject of an additional protocol to this Treaty.

Article IX

International intergovernmental organizations may take part in the Treaty. Provisions setting out different options for, and the procedure for, their participation in the Treaty shall be the subject of an additional protocol to this Treaty.

Article X

Any State Party may propose amendments to this Treaty. The text of any proposed amendment shall be submitted to the Depositary, who shall promptly circulate it to all States Parties. Upon the request of at least a third of the States Parties, the Depositary shall convene a conference to which all States Parties shall be invited to consider the proposed amendment.

Any amendment to this Treaty shall be approved by a majority of the votes of the States Parties. The amendment shall enter into force for all the States Parties in accordance with the procedures governing the entry into force of this Treaty.

Article XI

The Treaty shall be of unlimited duration.

Each State Party shall, in the context of the exercise of its national sovereignty, have the right to withdraw from the Treaty if it decides that extraordinary events related to the subject matter of this Treaty have jeopardized the supreme interests of its country. It shall notify the Depositary of the decision in writing six months in advance of its withdrawal from the Treaty.

Article XII

This Treaty shall be opened for signature by all States at United Nations Headquarters in New York. Any State which has not signed this Treaty before its entry into force may accede to it at any time.

This Treaty shall be subject to ratification by signatory States in accordance with their constitutional norms. Instruments of ratification or accession shall be deposited with the Secretary-General of the United Nations, who is hereby designated the Depositary of this Treaty.

Article XIII

This Treaty shall enter into force upon the deposit of instruments of ratification by twenty States, including all the permanent members of the United Nations Security Council.

For States whose instruments of ratification or accession are deposited after the entry into force of the Treaty, it shall enter into force on the date of the deposit of their instruments of ratification or accession.

Article XIV

This Treaty, of which the Arabic, Chinese, English, French, Russian and Spanish texts are equally authentic, shall be deposited with the Secretary-General of the United Nations, who shall send duly certified copies thereof to all signatory and acceding States.

5.2.5. Answers to the Principal Questions and Comments on the Draft PPWT

CD/1872
2009

This document sets out the principal questions and comments put forward by the delegations to the Conference on Disarmament during consideration of the draft Treaty on Prevention of the Placement of Weapons in Outer Space and of the Threat or Use of Force against Outer Space Objects (document CD/1839) (hereinafter "PPWT") in 2008. They include statements made during formal plenary meetings of the Conference on Disarmament, in the informal thematic debates held on 7 and 21 February and 5 August 2008, and at the open-ended meeting organized jointly on 6 August 2008 by China and the Russian Federation with the participation of the United Nations Institute for Disarmament Research. The document also contains the key proposals and recommendations put forward in non-papers by the delegations of Austria, Belarus, Canada, France, Germany, the Netherlands, New Zealand, South Africa, Sweden, Switzerland, Ukraine, the United Kingdom and the United States of America.

Question 1: *The prohibition of the threat or use of force in outer space is meaningless because it cannot be reliably verified.*
Answer: The draft PPWT prohibits the use or threat of force "against outer space objects"; it does not prohibit the use or threat of force "in outer space".

As for the idea that such a ban cannot be "reliably verified", it should be noted that, from a legal standpoint, the term "threat" means an intent to cause physical, material or other harm that is expressed orally, in writing, through actions or by any other means. In order for the country or countries at which they are directed to perceive them, such threats must be clearly expressed. Thus, the question of the "reliable verification" of the prohibition of the "threat of the use of force" does not arise.

Similarly, the destruction, damaging or taking of any other hostile action against a space object can be detected. Given the current level of development of space surveillance systems, it is quite feasible to identify the source of such hostile acts.

If one accepts the statement in question No. 1, one must abolish one of the fundamental principles of international relations, which is refraining from the use or threat of force. This principle has long been established as a fundamental norm of international law and is clearly stipulated in Article 2, paragraph 4, of the Charter of the United Nations.

This principle is also to be found in General Assembly resolution 3314 (XXIX) of 15 December 1974, on the definition of aggression, in the 1975 Helsinki Final Act of the Conference on Security and Cooperation in Europe and in the 1987 Declaration on the Enhancement of the Effectiveness of the Principle of Refraining from the Threat or Use of Force in International Relations (General Assembly resolution 42/22).

In the field of outer space, article III of the 1967 Treaty on Principles Governing the Activities of States in the Exploration and Use of Outer Space, including the Moon and Other Celestial Bodies (known as the Outer Space Treaty for short), stipulates that all outer space activities shall be carried out in accordance with international law, including the Charter of the United Nations. This provision automatically implies respect for the principle of refraining from the use or threat of force.

Also implicit in this principle is the notion that all States have an obligation to use only peaceful means to settle their disputes.

Many leading international space law experts hold that this principle means that any unauthorized hostile interference with the spacecraft of another State, including destroying or damaging the spacecraft, deliberately impeding its functioning, seizing it or modifying its orbit, is impermissible.

This principle is not, however, explicitly established in the 1967 Outer Space Treaty.

The most important task at present is to reach consensus in the form of a legal commitment and a legal instrument on the prevention of the placement of weapons in outer space and the threat or use of force against outer space objects. In order to facilitate an early consensus, then, it would seem appropriate to set aside the question of verification and other contentious issues for the time being. In the future, as science and technology progress and when the conditions are right, the addition of a verification protocol to PPWT may be considered. The question of verification could also be considered from another standpoint. Although the 1967 Outer Space Treaty does not have a verification mechanism, it is still an important and effective instrument. While it would be ideal if the new treaty had a reliable and effective verification mechanism, it can still, like the Outer Space Treaty, serve its purpose even without verification provisions.

5. CHINA'S SPACE-RELATED STATEMENTS AND PROPOSALS IN THE UN

Question 2: Isn't there a loophole in the provisions of the draft PPWT concerning the right to self-defense (art. V) where the use of anti-satellite weapons is concerned?
Answer: The draft PPWT does not modify the provisions of international law that relate to the right to self-defence, which is an important sovereign right of every State. Article 51 of the Charter of the United Nations does not make this right conditional on certain forms or means of armed attack. Likewise, it does not limit the measures that a State may take in exercise of the right to self-defence, nor does it restrict their application in terms of space.

At present, a State may use in self-defence any weapon that is not prohibited by international law. The draft PPWT does not ban anti-satellite weapons as a weapons class, but limits the proliferation of such weapons by imposing a comprehensive ban on the placement of any kind of weapon (including anti-satellite weapons) in outer space and prohibiting the use for hostile purposes of anti-satellite weapons based anywhere. Thus the draft PPWT does not seek to expand or restrict the relevant provisions of Article 51 of the Charter, nor does it create any loopholes that would permit the use of anti-satellite weapons.

It is understood that the obligations set out above are applicable to the States parties to PPWT. States parties retain their right to self-defence in the event of hostile acts by States that are not parties, and this right is confirmed in article V of the draft PPWT.

Question 3:
Is it true that the draft PPWT does not prohibit:
(1) Ground-based, sea-based and air-based ABM systems or ballistic missiles and their re-entry vehicles;
(2) Ground-based, sea-based and air-based anti-satellite weapon systems or the development or testing thereof;
(3) The testing of artificial satellites intended for use against other space objects for hostile purposes?
If so, why not?
Answer:

(1) PPWT does not prohibit interceptors of ground-based, sea-based or air-based ABM systems or ballistic missiles and their re-entry vehicles. This is because such weapons are not placed in space (they are not sent into orbit or installed on celestial bodies, nor are they placed in space by any other means).

(2) PPWT does not prohibit the development of ground-based, water-based or air-based anti-satellite weapons systems because there is no way that such activity can be effectively verified. Nor does it prohibit the testing of such weapons by a State (including testing on its own targets in space) because such testing (on the Earth's surface, in the atmosphere or aimed at other targets in space) is very difficult to detect and locate accurately. Article II of PPWT does prohibit the use of such systems against

space objects for hostile purposes, which means, in accordance with the definition of "use of force" contained in article I, subparagraph (e), "actions aimed at destroying them, damaging them, temporarily or permanently disrupting their normal functioning or deliberately changing their orbit parameters, or the threat of such actions". This prohibition does not cover situations involving the right to self-defence (cf. the answer to question 2).

(3) If "artificial satellites" are considered to constitute "weapons in space" (used for "destroying [outer space objects], damaging them ... or disrupting their normal functioning"), then PPWT prohibits their placement and testing in outer space.

Question 4: Under the draft PPWT, it remains possible for a State to destroy its own satellite (or another State's satellite at the request of that State), thereby creating space debris. Please comment on this.

Answer: This possibility certainly exists; for example, under exceptional circumstances (such as a satellite going out of control and endangering objects on the Earth's surface, etc.) it may be necessary for a State to destroy an out-of-control space object (or to destroy another State's space object at the request of that State) in order to minimize or eliminate the threat posed to other space objects or to activities on the Earth's surface or in the atmosphere. However, PPWT is not the only instrument governing outer space activities. There are many treaties that contain prohibitions on the accumulation of space debris, including the 1967 Treaty on Principles Governing the Activities of States in the Exploration and Use of Outer Space, including the Moon and Other Celestial Bodies, the 1972 Convention on International Liability for Damage Control by Space Objects, and the Space Debris Mitigation Guidelines of the United Nations Committee on the Peaceful Uses of Outer Space. States should be guided by these instruments when they decide to destroy one of their space objects.

Question 5: Does the phrase "follows a section of such an orbit before leaving this orbit" (art. I, subpara. (d)) mean that the use of partially orbital combat systems, such as ballistic missiles, is prohibited? If this is not the case, please explain why.

Answer: Article I defines the terms and concepts used in the draft PPWT; it does not contain any prohibition clauses. Subparagraph (d) defines weapons that "have been 'placed' in outer space". The phrase "follows a section of such an orbit before leaving this orbit" means that a "weapon" that has orbited halfway around the Earth can either "return" to Earth or "drift" into space.

With regard to "partially orbital combat systems", if they are used in order to "destroy, damage or disrupt the normal functioning" (art. I, subpara. (c)), then the prohibition in article II shall apply.

5. China's Space-Related Statements and Proposals in the UN

Question 6: Does the draft PPWT prohibit the use of laser systems on the ground aimed at "blinding" espionage satellites or ground- or air-based electromagnetic suppression systems? If this is not the case, please explain why.

Answer: The draft PPWT does not prohibit the development or testing of ground-based laser or electromagnetic suppression systems, including their testing against a State's own space targets, because it is difficult to detect or locate such tests (on the Earth's surface, in the atmosphere or against a space target). However, the obligations imposed under article II prohibit the use of laser and electromagnetic suppression systems to take hostile actions against outer space objects, as defined in article I, subparagraph (e). This prohibition does not apply to situations involving the right to self-defence (see answer to question 2).

PPWT does not prohibit the development or the testing elsewhere than in outer space of space-based electromagnetic suppression systems. As electromagnetic suppression systems fall into the category of "weapons in outer space", PPWT prohibits their placement in outer space.

Question 7: The phrase "in any other place under its jurisdiction or control" (art. III) calls for clarification. Does it refer to the maritime exclusive economic zone or to objects such as the International Space Station?

Answer: The phrase "in any other place under [the] jurisdiction or control [of a State]" has the following meaning: in the context of general international law, it refers to territories (occupied, annexed or trust territories) that are controlled and administered by a foreign State as well as to objects situated in the territory of one State but under the jurisdiction of another State; in the context of international maritime law, it refers to the exclusive economic zone, continental shelf and artificial islands and installations of a State and to vessels flying the flag of that State; in the context of international air law, it refers to civilian and military aircraft registered in that State; and in the context of international space law, it refers to space objects registered in that State.

Question 8:
The definition of the term "outer space" in terms of altitude is inadequate and can give rise to legal disputes with regard to objects in outer space and in the atmosphere, objects that only pass through space (ballistic missiles, partially orbital combat systems, including their re-entry vehicles) and aerospace objects that can function in both the atmosphere and outer space. Article I, subparagraph (c), of PPWT refers to both "outer space" (starting at 100 km above sea level) and "the atmosphere" (within 40 km of sea level); what do the 60 km that lie between these two constitute?

Answer: International space law has not determined the limits of outer space or the atmosphere. The United Nations Committee on the Peaceful Use of Outer Space (COPUOS) and its Legal and Technical Subcommittees are currently considering the question of the delimitation of outer space. The definition of outer space in the draft PPWT ("the space above the Earth in excess of 100 km above sea level") was proposed solely for the purposes of the Treaty. This limit is set at the minimum altitude of the perigees of artificial satellite orbits, i.e. 100 km above sea level.

Thus, the prohibition of the placement of weapons in outer space is applicable to any altitude higher than 100 km above sea level; it does not cover space below an altitude of 100 km. Accordingly, the division of space into segments (from sea level to 40 km above and from 40 km to 100 km above sea level) has no legal significance for PPWT.

The term "outer space" in article I, subparagraph (c), refers to targets which weapons placed in outer space could strike. It should be noted that the upper limit of the atmosphere has not been defined in international air law.

Pursuant to article I, subparagraph (c), aerospace objects carrying weapons while in orbit or partial orbit are subject to the obligations set out in PPWT.

Question 9: What is the likelihood that the international community can reach a consensus on the term "weapons in outer space" (art. I, subpara. (c))?

Answer: Article I, subparagraph (c), clearly stipulates that any device considered to be a "weapon in outer space" must be specially produced or converted to perform the tasks enumerated in that subparagraph. Such devices must possess specific features. Other devices that are referred to in discussions as "possible weapons" (including spacecraft used for peaceful purposes) cannot be considered to be weapons because they have not been specially produced or converted for the aforementioned purposes. However, while such spacecraft cannot by virtue of their features be considered to constitute weapons, PPWT nevertheless prohibits their use as a means of exercising force – e.g. by deliberately causing them to collide with another satellite in order to destroy it.

Question 10: Concerning article VII on the settlement of dispute, What are the specific procedures of this dispute settlement mechanism? How will it reach decisions? Will such decisions be binding? If so, what mechanism will exist for their enforcement?

Answer: The dispute settlement mechanism should be established on the basis of the authority and working mechanisms of the executive organization and may become the subject of an additional protocol to PPWT.

Question 11: Concerning the PPWT executive organization provided for in article VIII (1) What will be the composition, functions and dispute-settlement mandate of the executive organization? PPWT should contain specific provisions regarding the establishment, on the basis of objective criteria and solid facts, of a mechanism to deal with violations of the provisions of PPWT.

Answer: We remain open to discussion on this point. The provisions in question might be contained in an additional protocol additional to PPWT.

(2) The draft PPWT does not clearly stipulate what authority the executive organization will have to address violations of the Treaty by member States.
Answer: The draft PPWT is not intended to confer any supranational authority on the executive organization, such as empowering it to take coercive measures to address sovereign States' non-compliance with the Treaty. The reference to steps to put an end to a violation of the Treaty by a State party is understood to mean coordinated efforts aimed at averting a crisis, chiefly by settling disputes relating to alleged instances of non-compliance.

Question 12: Is it advisable to introduce a verification mechanism to monitor compliance with the third fundamental obligation under the draft PPWT ("not to assist or induce other States ... to participate in activities prohibited by [the] Treaty", art. II)? How can transfers of dual-use space technologies be restricted or controlled?
Answer: PPWT does not cover the transfer, control or proliferation of dual-use space technologies. Regardless of the existence of the draft PPWT, the challenges posed by proliferation will remain. This issue should be considered separately.

5.2.6. *The Updated Draft Treaty on Prevention of the Placement of Weapons in Outer Space and of the Threat of Use of Force against Outer Space Objects (PPWT)*

CD/1985
2014

The States Parties to this Treaty,
   Reaffirming that the further exploration and use of outer space is playing an ever-increasing role in the development of humankind,
   Desiring to prevent outer space turning into a new area of weapons placement or an arena for military confrontation and thereby to avert a grave danger to international peace and security,
   Reaffirming the importance of strict compliance with the existing multilateral agreements related to outer space activities and recognizing that observance of the principles and rules of international space law in outer space activities contributes to building confidence in the peaceful intentions of States,
   Noting that the Treaty on Principles Governing the Activities of States in the Exploration and Use of Outer Space, Including the Moon and Other Celestial Bodies, of 27 January 1967 (hereinafter referred to as the 1967 Outer Space Treaty), obliges the States Parties not to place in orbit around the Earth any objects carrying nuclear

weapons or any other kinds of weapons of mass destruction, and not to install such weapons on celestial bodies or station them in outer space in any other manner,

Recognizing that, while the existing international agreements related to outer space and the legal regime provided for therein play a positive role in regulating outer space activities, they are unable to fully prevent the placement of weapons in outer space,

Recalling the United Nations General Assembly resolutions on prevention of an arms race in outer space, which emphasize, inter alia, the need to examine further measures in the search for effective and verifiable bilateral and multilateral agreements in order to prevent an arms race in outer space,

Have agreed as follows:

Article I

For the purpose of this Treaty:

(a) The term "outer space object" means any device placed in outer space and designed for operating therein;

(b) The term "weapon in outer space" means any outer space object or component thereof which has been produced or converted to destroy, damage or disrupt the normal functioning of objects in outer space, on the Earth's surface or in its atmosphere, or to eliminate human beings or components of the biosphere which are important to human existence, or to inflict damage on them by using any principles of physics;

(c) A device is considered to have been "placed in outer space" if it orbits the Earth at least once, or follows a section of such an orbit before leaving that orbit, or is permanently located in outer space or on any celestial bodies other than the Earth;

(d) The term "use of force" means any action intended to inflict damage on an outer space object under the jurisdiction and/or control of other States, and the term "threat of force" means the clear expression in written, oral or any other form of the intention to commit such an action. Actions undertaken in accordance with special agreements with States that provide for actions on the request of such States to stop uncontrolled flight by outer space objects under the jurisdiction and/or control of the requesting States shall not be regarded as the use or threat of force.

Article II

The States Parties to this Treaty undertake:

(a) Not to place any weapons in outer space;

(b) Not to resort to the threat or use of force against outer space objects of States Parties to the Treaty;

(c) Not to engage, as part of international cooperation, in outer space activities that are inconsistent with the object and purpose of this Treaty;

(d) Not to assist or induce other States, groups of States, international, intergovernmental or non-governmental organizations, including non-governmental legal entities established, registered or located in territory under their jurisdiction and/or their control, to participate in activities inconsistent with the object and purpose of this Treaty.

Article III
Nothing in this Treaty may be interpreted as preventing the States Parties from exploring and using outer space for peaceful purposes in accordance with international law, including the Charter of the United Nations and the 1967 Outer Space Treaty.

Article IV
Nothing in the present Treaty shall impair the States Parties' inherent right to individual or collective self-defence, as recognized in Article 51 of the Charter of the United Nations.

Article V
The States Parties recognize the need for measures to verify compliance with the Treaty, which may form the subject of an additional protocol. With a view to promoting confidence in compliance with the provisions of the Treaty, States Parties may implement agreed transparency and confidence-building measures, on a voluntary basis, unless agreed otherwise.

Article VI
To promote the implementation of the objectives and provisions of the Treaty, the States Parties shall establish the executive organization of the Treaty, which shall:
  (a) Consider matters concerning the operation and implementation of the Treaty;
  (b) Accept for consideration communications from any State Party or group of States Parties relating to cases where there is reason to believe that a violation of the Treaty is taking place;
  (c) Organize and conduct consultations with the States Parties with a view to resolving any situation that has arisen in connection with an alleged violation of the Treaty;
  (d) Refer the dispute to the United Nations General Assembly or the United Nations Security Council if a situation that has arisen in connection with an alleged violation of the Treaty remains unresolved;
  (e) Organize and conduct meetings to discuss and adopt proposed amendments to the Treaty;
  (f) Develop procedures for collective data sharing and information analysis;
  (g) Collect and disseminate information provided as part of transparency and confidence-building measures;
  (h) Accept notifications of the accession of new States to the Treaty and submit them to the Secretary-General of the United Nations;

(i) Consider, upon agreement with the States Parties, other procedural and substantive issues.

The procedure for the formation and the composition of the working bodies, as well as the rules and regulations and the arrangement of the work of the executive organization of the Treaty shall form the subject of an additional protocol.

The States Parties shall cooperate with the executive organization of the Treaty to support it in the discharge of its functions.

Article VII
A State Party which has reason to believe that another State Party is failing to fulfill the obligations incumbent upon it pursuant to the Treaty may request that State Party to provide clarification of the situation. The requested State Party shall provide clarification as soon as possible.

If the requesting State Party deems the clarification insufficient to resolve its concerns, it may request consultations with the requested State Party. The requested State Party shall immediately enter into such consultations. The executive organization of the Treaty shall be informed of the results of the consultations and shall transmit the information received to all States Parties concerned.

If the consultations do not lead to a mutually acceptable settlement which has due regard to the interests of all States Parties, any State Party or group of States Parties shall seek the assistance of the executive organization of the Treaty, submitting relevant evidence for the further consideration of the dispute. The executive organization may convene a meeting of States Parties to examine the dispute, make a decision establishing a violation of the Treaty and prepare recommendations based on States Parties' proposals to settle the dispute and remedy the violation. If it is not able to settle the dispute or remedy the violation, the executive organization may bring the issue, including the relevant information and conclusions, to the attention of the United Nations General Assembly or the United Nations Security Council.

In cases subject to the Convention on International Liability for Damage Caused by Space Objects of 1972, the relevant provisions of the Convention shall be used.

Article VIII
References to States in the Treaty, except those in articles IX–XIII, shall also cover any international intergovernmental organization that carries out activities in outer space, if the organization declares that it assumes the obligations provided for under the Treaty and if the majority of its member States are States Parties to the Treaty. Member States of such an organization that are Parties to the Treaty shall take all necessary measures to ensure that the organization makes such a declaration in accordance with the provisions of this article.

Article IX

This Treaty shall be opened for signature by all States at the United Nations Headquarters in New York. Any State which has not signed the Treaty before its entry into force may accede to it at any time.

This Treaty shall be subject to ratification by signatory States in accordance with their internal procedures.

Instruments of ratification or accession shall be deposited with the Secretary- General of the United Nations, who is hereby designated the Depositor of this Treaty.

Article X

This Treaty shall enter into force upon the deposit of instruments of ratification by 20 States, including all the permanent members of the United Nations Security Council.

For States whose instruments of ratification or accession are deposited after the entry into force of the Treaty, it shall enter into force on the date of the deposit of their instruments of ratification or accession.

The Secretary-General of the United Nations shall inform all signatory or acceding States of the date of each signature, the date of deposit of each instrument of ratification or of accession, the date of entry into force of this Treaty, any proposals for amendments to the Treaty, any disputes that arise and their settlement, as well as other notifications, as necessary.

Article XI

Any State Party may propose amendments to the Treaty. The text of any proposed amendment shall be submitted to the Secretary-General of the United Nations for circulation to all States Parties. A conference shall be convened to consider such an amendment, if at least one third of the States Parties so agree.

Amendments shall enter into force upon their acceptance by consensus.

Article XII

This Treaty shall be of unlimited duration.

Each State Party shall, in exercising its national sovereignty, have the right to withdraw from the Treaty if it decides that extraordinary events, related to the subject matter of the Treaty, have jeopardized its supreme interests. It shall notify the Secretary-General of the United Nations of the decision in writing six months in advance of its ithdrawal from the Treaty. Such notice shall include a statement of the extraordinary events that the notifying State Party regards as having jeopardized its supreme interests.

Article XIII

This Treaty, of which the Arabic, Chinese, English, French, Russian and Spanish texts are equally authentic, shall be deposited with the Secretary-General of the United Nations, who shall send duly certified copies thereof to all signatory and acceding States.

5.2.7.   *Comments Regarding the USA Analysis of the 2014 Updated Draft PPWT*

CD/2042
2015

The Russian Federation and the People's Republic of China express their appreciation for the active involvement of the United States of America in the discussion of the updated Russian-Chinese draft treaty on the prevention of the placement of weapons in outer space and of the threat or use of force against outer space objects (PPWT) and, in particular, the comments and proposals contained in document CD/1998, issued on 2 September 2014 at the Conference on Disarmament (CD).

We would like to point out the following in connection with the questions raised by the United States of America about the draft PPWT.

I. Scope

The draft PPWT was not intended to be an instrument aimed at prohibiting a specific type of weapon capable of striking space objects and ground, sea or air targets alike. The Russian Federation and the People's Republic of China consider that issues of arms control in outer space should be addressed gradually. The draft PPWT focuses on banning the placement of weapons in outer space and the use of force against space objects. This is currently the most effective and feasible way of preventing armed conflict in outer space.

The purpose of the future PPWT may seem to some to be rather "broad" and to others, on the contrary, rather "narrow", but in any case, it is very specific: a ban on the placement of weapons of any kind in outer space and on the use of force or threat of the use of force against outer space objects.

The Russian-Chinese draft PPWT is fully in keeping with the fundamental law on outer space – the Treaty on Principles Governing the Activities of States in the Exploration and Use of Outer Space, including the Moon and Other Celestial Bodies of 27 January 1967 (1967 Outer Space Treaty) – which provides for the prohibition of the placement of weapons of mass destruction in outer space (art. IV) but does not address the issue of imposing a complete ban on these types of weapons. PPWT is preventive in nature. It aims at prohibiting certain actions and not weapons per se.

5. CHINA'S SPACE-RELATED STATEMENTS AND PROPOSALS IN THE UN

The Russian Federation and the People's Republic of China maintain that the prohibition against the possession, testing, production and stockpiling of space-based weapons does not contradict the purposes of PPWT. Furthermore, one of the principles that guided us in defining the scope of the treaty consisted in setting limitations that could be monitored. (Such monitoring capability is dealt with, for example, in document CD/1785 submitted by Canada in 2006.) Effective monitoring of "research, development, production, and terrestrial storage of space-based weapons" – on which there is no prohibition, as is pointed out in the United States document – is not feasible in practical terms for objective reasons.

The United States believes that such an approach leaves open the possibility that a party "could build and have in its inventory a readily deployable space-based ASAT or BMD capability". We are convinced that our proposed ban on the placement or use of weapons in outer space and on the use of capabilities for the purpose of inflicting damage on an outer space object of other States would make the very costly development and production of such weapons pointless. In addition, under such circumstances, any effort to test ground-based, sea-based or air-based weapons against space objects would make no sense. Of course, under a ban on the deployment of weapons and the resulting absence of them in outer space, there would be no grounds that would justify space-based weapons testing.

We clearly cannot agree with the assertion by the United States of America that "Article 2 (4) of the United Nations Charter already prohibits the use of force or the threat of force against another State's outer space objects". It is true that Article 2, paragraph 4, of the Charter of the United Nations deals in particular with the obligation to refrain from the threat or use of force "in any other manner inconsistent with the purposes of the United Nations" (i.e., the threat or use of force not related to the infringement of the "territorial integrity or political independence of any State"). However, further criteria must be established, in our view, if this abstract statement is to lend itself to an interpretation which can be agreed upon and form the basis for characterizing a given action as the threat or use of force. Such a level of detail is particularly appropriate when it comes to outer space, where the space system may be affected in a variety of ways given the development of special malware.

It is in this spirit that the Russian Federation took up the issue of reaching a common understanding of the right to self-defence under the Charter as regards outer space in the United Nations Committee on the Peaceful Uses of Outer Space (COPUOS).

Furthermore, it is worth noting that the Charter was drafted before the space age had begun and, consequently, in our view, the unqualified and direct application of the provisions of the Charter to such a sensitive area of international relations as outer space development requires further elaboration and clarification through negotiation between States.

The many attempts to address these questions during the drafting of international agreements (such as article 3, paragraph 2, of the Agreement Governing the Activities of States on the Moon and other Celestial Bodies of 1979) point to the need for clarification of the issue of the use of force in outer space on the grounds provided for under the Charter.

The extent to which an action is "intended" to inflict damage on a space object is put forward as one of the criteria for establishing the "use of force" or "threat of force" under the draft PPWT. Otherwise, almost any action that inflicted damage on a space object would be considered as a violation of PPWT and would give the State affected grounds to take countermeasures without interference. Such a criterion is particularly important in the light of the fact that some national doctrines have a discernible conceptual framework for immediate countermeasures and even preventive action in the event of any provocation or even alleged hostile activities by other States, which in itself is contrary to international law (for example, according to United States Joint Publication 3-14: Space Operations, preventing an adversary's access to space capabilities "can include diplomatic, informational, military, and economic measures"; in paragraph 4 c. (4) of the Department of Defense directive on space policy, No. 3100.10 of 18 October 2012, (space directive) it is stated that "in order to deter attacks on U.S. or allied space systems, DoD will: Possess capabilities, not limited to space, to respond to an attack on U.S. or allied space systems in an asymmetric manner by using any or all elements of national power").

We would also like to point out that, in paragraph 11 of CD/1998, the United States of America acknowledges that the use of force or threat of force is "not explicitly defined under existing international law". That said, in paragraph 12, by referring nevertheless to international law, the United States of America rejects "intention" as a criterion for defining the notion of "use of force" or "threat of force".

However, from a legal point of view, the term "threat" means the expression by any means of the "intention" to cause any harm. Moreover, in paragraph 4 b. of the space directive of 2012, purposeful interference with space systems is considered to be an infringement of United States rights.

The Russian Federation and China believe that an incoherent or overly broad interpretation of elements of international law, including the provisions of the Charter, applied to such a sensitive area as outer space is unacceptable. We are therefore convinced that clarification of the existing rules of international law concerning outer space, in particular the notion of "use of force" or "threat of force", is a key aspect of ensuring security in outer space. Our draft of a legally binding PPWT could make a particularly significant contribution to resolving this problem.

As regards the ban under the draft PPWT on the use of force or threat of force against States parties to the treaty, it should be noted that we view a legally binding PPWT as an important element of international law which is meant only to fill gaps and clarify extremely sensitive provisions that are open to more than one interpretation. In no way does it contradict those provisions, however. This is backed up by the reference to existing international law in article III of the draft.

The same applies to the use of force and sanctions of the Security Council of the United Nations. Reference is made in article IV of the draft PPWT to Article 51 of the Charter which provides for the right of States to self-defence. We regard this article in particular as a reference to the entire Chapter VII of the Charter, which is precisely what is dealt with in the United States document.

We thank the United States of America for the question – which we had anticipated – regarding the fact that actions that cause temporary or reversible effects are no longer included in the updated draft. The amendment was made by us in order to make the text easier to grasp and in the light of the firm belief by the majority of States interested in PPWT that such a level of detail for the purpose of this treaty would be unnecessary. Furthermore, we do not question the notion that the "use of force" or "threat of force" in the context of this draft covers, among other things, temporary or reversible effects on the normal functioning of space objects, however only those that are caused by intentional actions carried out in order to achieve such results.

In the absence of arrangements on how to treat various situations involving the infliction of damage to the spacecraft of a State as a result of the space activities of another State, there is a need to continue the established practice of permitting such situations while not allowing for a unilateral assessment of them, especially one that is liable to lead to an unjustified armed response.

II. Verification

The updated draft PPWT, like the first version of 2008, does not include a ready legally binding verification mechanism.

We drew on past experience with establishing and implementing international space law. The ban on the placement of weapons of any kind in space proposed in PPWT is similar to the provision of the Outer Space Treaty of 1967, which establishes a ban on placing in orbit around the Earth or stationing in outer space in any other manner nuclear weapons and all other weapons of mass destruction. The Outer Space Treaty does not provide for any mechanism for verifying the fulfillment of this obligation and during the half a century that it has been in force no questions about verification have been raised.

Another example of an instrument without a verification mechanism is the Convention on the Prohibition of the Development, Production and Stockpiling of Bacteriological (Biological) and Toxic Weapons and on Their Destruction (BTWC) of 1972. BTWC was originally meant to include provisions on verification. However, owing to the complexity of verification mechanisms, the Convention itself was adopted first. In considering the issue of verification with respect to PPWT, we also had in mind such an option. We note that the United States of America stated it "could not support an approach in which verification provisions were determined only through subsequent negotiations of an additional protocol", although it took part in negotiations over a verification protocol to BTWC. Moreover, it is the United States of America which continues to consider that measures taken at the national level on the implementation of BTWC are sufficient to ensure the prohibition regime established by the Convention.

We would also like to draw attention to the important provisions in the updated version of PPWT that have a direct bearing on verification. For example, article VII provides for a mechanism for consultations, which may be used if a breach of the treaty is suspected. Certain measures of verification may be carried out in a preventive manner through a system of data exchange between States and analysis of the situation in outer space. In order to ensure transparency in ongoing activities, States parties to PPWT could make a yearly statement about their outer space policy and strategy and take appropriate confidence-building measures for that purpose.

However, we continue to believe that the development of a verification mechanism would be desirable for the subsequent full implementation of PPWT. Therefore, article V of the updated draft provides for the possibility of drafting an appropriate additional protocol.

The United States of America considers that such an approach would not allow for the establishment of an "effective" verification regime for the implementation of the treaty. We believe that it is precisely following the entry into force of the PPWT, on the basis of the experience gained in implementing it, that joint efforts could be made to begin to develop a truly effective verification mechanism. An interim measure might be mutually agreed transparency and confidence-building measures (TCBMs). Moreover, we would like to stress we have never regarded TCBMs as an alternative to a possible verification mechanism within the framework of PPWT. We fully agree with the position of the United States of America that TCBMs "can complement, but not substitute for, an effective legally binding verification regime".

Individual TCBMs, once tested in practice at the international level, could be an integral part of the verification mechanism of the treaty. Moreover, the reverse effect must also be taken into consideration: the achievement of some intrusive TCBMs is possible only under legally binding agreements. The establishment of a verification mechanism can thus help to expand the range of confidence-building measures for outer space activities carried out by States.

The Russian Federation and China trust that the United States of America, as a leading spacefaring nation, will be actively involved in international efforts to develop a verification mechanism and agreed TCBMs.

We also believe that, pending a verification mechanism, the fulfillment of obligations under PPWT will be guaranteed, a principle that for half a century has ensured the effectiveness of the 1967 Outer Space Treaty, namely: the perceived benefit from violating or withdrawing from the prohibition regime established under a treaty, as well as the adverse political consequences of such actions, would be outweighed by the dividends from fully complying with such a regime. If the United States of America calls into question the effectiveness of this principle regarding PPWT, then it is calling into question, albeit implicitly, the very credibility of the Outer Space Treaty of 1967. Such a position by the United States of America would be counterproductive.

As regards the issue of verification of compliance with obligations, the working paper entitled "Verification aspects of PAROS" (CD/1781), submitted by the Russian Federation and the People's Republic of China in 2006 at the Conference on Disarmament, provides an analysis of the political technical and financial difficulties involved in verification. The most important task now is to reach consensus on a legal obligation and a legally binding instrument with respect to the prevention of the weaponization of space and an arms race in outer space. It would be useful at this moment to put aside the question of verification and other points of contention in order to reach consensus as soon as possible. The possibility of adding a verification protocol to the proposed draft treaty could be considered at a later date.

III. Terrestrially-based Anti-satellite Weapons

We have taken into account the concerns of the United States of America about the lack of a ban on terrestrially-based anti-satellite weapons in the updated draft PPWT and the previous versions.

It is true that neither terrestrially-based nor, for that matter, sea- or air-based anti-satellite weapons are directly prohibited under the draft PPWT. As we have explained in document CD/1872, while anti-satellite weapons as a class of weapons are not prohibited under the draft PPWT, the proliferation of such weapons is restricted through a comprehensive ban on the placement in outer space of weapons of any kind, including anti-satellite weapons. A ban on ground-based anti-satellite (ASAT) weapon systems has been introduced into PPWT through the ban on the use of force, regardless of its source, against space objects. The draft treaty is thus effective in addressing the ASAT issue. Moreover, a State that conducts repeated testing of its missile defences will also be using the same technology that applies to anti-satellite weapons.

Furthermore, we would like to emphasize that in acceding to PPWT, under which the placement of weapons of any kind in outer space and the use or threat of force are prohibited, all spacefaring nations would have virtually no grounds for developing or using anti-satellite capabilities against objects of other countries. It would be pointless to spend significant resources on the development of anti-satellite weapons and therefore there would be no incentive to possess such weapons. All the concerns of the United States of America on this matter could be dispelled as a result of its active involvement in the elaboration and implementation of the draft PPWT.

In general, the Russian Federation and the People's Republic of China take a positive view of the involvement of the United States of America in the discussion of the contents of the updated draft PPWT. We believe that any arrangements in the field of arms control entail very sensitive mutual compromises on the part of all States parties.

In this regard, we call upon the United States of America and its allies to take a constructive approach, join the efforts of the international community on PAROS and begin collaboration with other relevant States on the draft of PPWT in the common interest of ensuring the safety of space activities and strengthening international security as a whole.

We are disappointed that, instead of constructive proposals on the contents of the draft PPWT, we once again see the appalling attempts of the United States of America to impose on the international community its politicized assessment of the space programmes of certain States. We believe that such an approach on the part of a State that is avoiding having to shoulder any additional international legal obligations as far as outer space is concerned, including in order to ensure that outer space remains free of weapons of any kind, in no way facilitates progress towards a mutually acceptable resolution of issues involving the security of space activities.

That said, the lack of comments by the United States of America directly relating to the text confirms our belief that the updated draft treaty presented on 10 June 2014 at the Conference is a good starting point for full-scale negotiations.

We trust that the United States of America will take a conscientious approach to further international work on such an important topic as the prevention of the placement of weapons in outer space and of the threat or use of force against outer space objects.

5.2.8.   *Joint Statement from XI Jinping, President of China, and Vladimir V. Putin, President of the Russian Federation, to the Conference on Disarmament on Strengthening Contemporary Global Strategic Stability*

CD/2161
2019

The People's Republic of China and the Russian Federation, basing their action on a relationship of comprehensive and equal partnership of trust and strategic interaction between the two States, conscious of their responsibility to ensure international security, and mindful of the importance of maintaining global and regional strategic stability, hereby issue the following statement.

5. CHINA'S SPACE-RELATED STATEMENTS AND PROPOSALS IN THE UN

The Parties recognize that serious challenges to international security have now arisen, and in this connection, they intend to strengthen mutual trust and cooperation in the strategic area and to resolutely defend global and regional strategic stability.

The Parties intend to further work together in the spirit of the Joint Statement of the President of the People's Republic of China and the President of the Russian Federation signed on 25 June 2016 in Beijing to strengthen global strategic stability, and they confirm the importance of the principles that it set forth.

Russia and China note with alarm the extremely dangerous actions of certain States, which, acting in their own geopolitical and even commercial interests, are destroying or altering the existing architecture for arms control and for the non-proliferation of weapons of mass destruction (WMD) to suit their needs. In pursuing strategic superiority in the military field with the intention of ensuring "absolute security", and with the aim of obtaining unlimited opportunities to bring military and political pressure to bear on their opponents, such States are unceremoniously destroying the mechanisms that work to maintain stability.

[…]

The Parties consider that arms control is an important tool for strengthening international security and stability. The central role in the arms control process belongs to the United Nations and its multilateral disarmament mechanism. The Parties are for increasing collective efforts in support of multilateralism and consider that it is essential to renew comprehensive multilateral work on the pressing issues on the arms control agenda and to depoliticize such activities.

[…]

The real prospect of an arms race in outer space and of the transformation of outer space into a scene of military confrontation, which undermines strategic stability, is of serious concern. A ban on the placement of weapons of any type in outer space could prevent the emergence of a serious threat to international peace and security. All countries must first and foremost scrupulously observe international law, which provides for the use of outer space for peaceful purposes, including maintaining international peace and security, promoting international cooperation and expanding mutual understanding among States. The international community must work together to improve the relevant legal system.

China and Russia welcome the work of the United Nations Group of Governmental Experts that was established to consider and develop recommendations for substantive elements of a legally binding international instrument for the prevention of an arms race in outer space, specifically including the prevention of the placement of weapons in outer space, and regret that the United States blocked the adoption of the report in the Group.

The Parties support the negotiation by the international community of a legally binding multilateral document that would provide reliable guarantees for the prevention of an arms race in outer space and the placement of weapons there, on the basis of the Chinese-Russian draft Treaty on the Prevention of the Placement of Weapons in Outer Space and of the Threat or Use of Force against Outer Space Objects. The Conference on Disarmament – the only forum for multilateral disarmament negotiations – plays a key role in negotiating international agreements for the prevention of an arms race in outer space, in all its aspects. Transparency and confidence-building measures help to prevent the placement of weapons in outer space. China and Russia believe that the international community must make active efforts to advance international initiatives and political commitments to refrain from being the first to place weapons in outer space.

5.3. Xi's Speeches Regarding a Community of Shared Future for Mankind

5.3.1. Working Together to Create a New Mutually Beneficial Partnership and Community of Shared Future for Mankind[2]

President Xi Jingping's Speech at the General Debate of the 70th Session of the UN General Assembly
2015

Mr. President, Dear Colleagues,

Seventy years ago, an earlier generation fought heroically and secured victory in the World Anti-Fascist War, closing a dark page in the annals of human history. That victory was hard won.

Seventy years ago, that generation, with vision and foresight, established the United Nations. This universal and most representative and authoritative international organization has carried mankind's hope for a new future and ushered in a new era of cooperation. This was a pioneering initiative never before undertaken.

Seventy years ago, that generation pooled together their wisdom and adopted the Charter of the United Nations, laying the cornerstones of contemporary international order, and establishing the fundamental principles of contemporary international relations. This was an achievement of profound impact.

Mr. President, Dear Colleagues,

On the third of September, the people of China, together with the rest of humanity, solemnly commemorated the 70th anniversary of victory in the Chinese People's War of Resistance Against Japanese Aggression and the World Anti-Fascist War. As the main theater in the East, China made a national sacrifice of over 35 million casualties in its

---

2   At http://www.china.org.cn/chinese/2015-11/06/content_36999256.htm, last accessed August 2021.

5. China's Space-Related Statements and Proposals in the UN

fight against the main forces of Japanese militarism. It not only saved itself and its people from subjugation, but also gave strong support to the forces combatting aggression in the European and Pacific theaters, thus making a historic contribution to ultimate victory.

History is a mirror. Only by drawing lessons from history can the world avoid repeating past calamity. We should view history with awe and through the prism of human conscience. The past cannot be changed, but the future can be shaped. To bear history in mind is not to perpetuate hatred. Rather, its purpose is to ensure that mankind does not forget its lessons. Remembering history does not mean being obsessed with the past. Rather, in doing so, we aim to create a better future and pass the torch of peace from generation to generation.

Mr. President, Dear Colleagues,

Over the past seven decades the United Nations has gone through the tests of time. It has witnessed efforts made by all countries to uphold peace, build their own countries, and pursue cooperation. Having reached a new historical starting point, the United Nations needs to address the central issue of how to better promote world peace and development in the 21st century.

The world is going through a historical process of accelerated evolution. The light of peace, development and progress will be powerful enough to dispel the clouds of war, poverty and backwardness. The movement toward a multi-polar world and the rise of emerging markets and developing countries has become an irresistible trend of history. Economic globalization and the advent of an information age have unleashed and boosted vast new social productive forces. They have created unprecedented development opportunities while giving rise to new threats and challenges which we must face squarely.

As an ancient Chinese adage goes, "The greatest ideal is to create a world truly shared by all." Peace, development, equality, justice, democracy and freedom are common values of all mankind and the lofty goals of the United Nations. Yet these goals are far from being achieved; therefore, we must continue our endeavors. In today's world, all countries are interdependent and share a common future. We should renew our commitment to the purposes and principles of the Charter of the United Nations, build a new model of international relations featuring mutually beneficial cooperation, and create a community of shared future for mankind. To achieve this goal, we need to direct our efforts as follows:

We should build partnerships in which countries treat each other as equals, engage in mutual consultation and show mutual understanding. The principle of sovereign equality underpins the Charter of the United Nations. The future of the world must be shaped by all countries. All countries are equals. The large, the strong and the rich should not bully the small, the weak and the poor. The principle of sovereignty is not just limited to the idea that the sovereignty and territorial integrity of all countries is inviolable, and that their internal affairs are not to be subject to interference. It also means that all countries have a right to make their own choice of social systems and development paths, that this right should be upheld, and that all countries' endeavors to promote economic and social development and improve their people's lives should be respected.

We should be committed to multilateralism and reject unilateralism. We should adopt a new vision of seeking positive outcomes for all, and reject the outdated mindset that one side's gain means the other side's loss, or that the winner takes all. Consultation is an important form of democracy, and it should also become an important means of exercising international governance. We should resolve disputes and differences through dialogue and consultation. We should forge a global partnership at both international and regional levels, and embrace a new approach to state-to-state relations, one that features dialogue rather than confrontation, and seeks partnership rather than alliance. Major countries should follow the principles of no conflict, no confrontation, mutual respect and mutually beneficial cooperation in handling their relations. Major powers should treat small countries as equals, and take an ethical approach to justice and their own interests by putting justice before their own interests.

We should create a security environment featuring fairness, justice, joint participation and shared benefits. In the age of economic globalization, the security of all countries is interlinked and every one impacts on every other. No country can maintain absolute security by its own efforts, and no country can achieve stability by destabilizing other countries. The law of the jungle leaves the weak at the mercy of the strong; it is not the way for countries to conduct their relations. Those who adopt the self-serving approach of using force will find that they are only lifting a rock to drop on their own feet.

We should abandon the Cold War mentality in all its manifestations, and foster a new vision of common, comprehensive, cooperative and sustainable security. We should give full play to the central role of the United Nations and its Security Council in ending conflict and keeping peace, and adopt the dual approach of seeking peaceful solutions to disputes and taking mandatory actions, so as to turn hostility into amity. We should advance international cooperation in both economic and social fields and take a holistic approach to addressing traditional and non-traditional security threats, so as to prevent conflicts from breaking out in the first place.

We should promote open, innovative and inclusive development that benefits all. The 2008 international financial crisis has taught us that allowing capital to blindly pursue profit will result in chaos, and that global prosperity cannot be built on the shaky foundations of a market without moral constraints. The growing gap between rich and poor is both unfair and unsustainable. It is important for us to use both the invisible hand and the visible hand to form synergy between market forces and government functions, and strive to achieve both efficiency and fairness.

Development is meaningful only when it is inclusive and sustainable. To achieve such development requires openness, mutual assistance and cooperation. In the world today, close to 800 million people still live in extreme poverty, nearly 6 million children die before the age of five each year, and nearly 60 million children are unable to go to school. The just-concluded UN Sustainable Development Summit adopted the Post-2015 Development Agenda. We must translate our commitments into actions and work together to ensure that everyone is free from want, has access to development, and lives with dignity.

We should increase inter-civilization exchanges to promote harmony, inclusiveness and respect for differences. The world is more colorful as a result of its cultural diversity. Diversity breeds exchanges, exchanges create integration, and integration makes progress possible.

In their interactions, civilizations must accept their differences. Only through mutual respect, mutual learning, and harmonious coexistence can the world maintain its diversity and thrive. Each social model represents the unique vision and contribution of its people, and no model is superior to others. Different civilizations should engage in dialogue and exchanges instead of trying to exclude or replace each other. The history of mankind is a process of active exchanges, interactions, and integration among different civilizations. We should respect all civilizations and treat each other as equals. We should draw inspiration from each other to boost the creative development of human civilization.

We should build an ecosystem that puts Mother Nature and green development first. Mankind may utilize nature and even try to transform it. But we are ultimately a part of nature. We should care for nature and not place ourselves above it. We should reconcile industrial development with nature and pursue harmony between man and nature to achieve sustainable development throughout the world and the all-round development of humanity.

To build a sound ecology is vital for mankind's future. All members of the international community should work together to build a sound global eco-environment. We should respect nature, follow nature's ways, and protect nature. We should firmly pursue green, low-carbon, circular, and sustainable development. China will shoulder its share of responsibility and continue to play its part in this common endeavor. We also urge developed countries to fulfill their historical responsibilities, honor their emission reduction commitments, and help developing countries mitigate and adapt to climate change.

Mr. President, Dear Colleagues,

More than 1.3 billion Chinese people are endeavoring to realize the Chinese Dream of great national renewal. The dream of the Chinese people is closely connected with the dreams of other peoples of the world. We cannot realize the Chinese Dream without a peaceful international environment, a stable international order, and the understanding, support and help of the rest of the world. The realization of the Chinese Dream will bring greater opportunities to other countries and contribute to global peace and development.

China will continue to participate in building world peace. We are committed to peaceful development. No matter how the international landscape may evolve and how strong we may become, China will never pursue hegemony or expansion, or seek to create spheres of influence.

China will continue to contribute to global development. We will continue to pursue common progress and the mutually beneficial strategy of opening up. We are ready to share our experience and opportunities with other countries and welcome them to join us on our voyage and sail together with us towards common development.

China will continue to uphold the international order. We will remain committed to the path of development through cooperation. China was the first country to put its signature on the Charter of the United Nations. We will continue to uphold the international order and system underpinned by the purposes and principles of the Charter of the United Nations. China will continue to stand together with other developing countries. We firmly support greater representation and say for developing countries, especially African countries, in international governance. China's vote in the United Nations will always belong to the developing countries.

I wish to take this opportunity to announce China's decision to establish a 10-year, US $1 billion China-UN peace and development fund to support the United Nations' work, advance multilateral cooperation, and make a greater contribution to world peace and development. I wish to announce that China will join the new UN Peacekeeping Capability Readiness System, and has thus decided to take the lead in setting up a permanent peacekeeping police squad and building a peacekeeping standby force of 8,000 troops. I also wish to announce that China will provide a total of US$100 million of free military aid to the African Union in the next five years to support the establishment of the African Standby Force and the African Capacity for Immediate Response to Crisis.

Mr. President, Dear Colleagues,

As the United Nations enters a new decade, let us unite ever more closely to create a new mutually beneficial partnership and community of shared future for mankind. Let the vision of a world free of war and enjoying lasting peace take root in our hearts. Let the aspirations of development, prosperity, fairness and justice spread across the world!

Thank you.

5. China's Space-Related Statements and Proposals in the UN

5.3.2. Working Together to Build a Community of Shared Future for Mankind[3]

President Xi Jinping's Speech at the UN Office at Geneva
2017

Your Excellency Mr. Peter Thomson, President of the 71st Session of the UN General Assembly,
Your Excellency Mr. António Guterres, UN Secretary-General,
Your Excellency Mr. Michael Møller, Director-General of the UN Office at Geneva,
Ladies and Gentlemen,
Friends,

As a new year begins, everything takes on a new look, and it gives me great pleasure to visit the United Nations Office at Geneva and discuss with you the building of a community of shared future for mankind, which is the call of our time.

I just attended the World Economic Forum Annual Meeting. In Davos, many speakers pointed out in their speeches that today's world is full of uncertainties and that people long for a bright future but are bewildered about what will come. What has happened to the world and how should we respond? The whole world is reflecting on this question, and it is also very much on my mind.

I believe that to answer this question, we need to get clear about a fundamental issue: Where did we come from? Where are we now? And where are we going?

Over the past century and more, mankind has gone through bloody hot wars and the chilling Cold War, but also achieved remarkable development and huge progress. In the first half of last century, mankind suffered the scourges of two world wars, and the people yearned for the end of war and the advent of peace. In the 1950s and 1960s, people in colonies awakened and fought to shake off shackles and achieve independence. Since the end of the Cold War, people have pursued a shared aspiration, namely, to expand cooperation and promote common development.

Peace and development: this has been the aspiration held dear by mankind over the past century. However, the goal to achieve peace and development is far from being met. We need to respond to the people's call, take up the baton of history and forge ahead on the marathon track toward peace and development.

Mankind is in an era of major development as well as profound transformation and change. The trend toward multi-polarity and economic globalization is surging. IT application in social development and cultural diversity are making continued progress. A new round of scientific and industrial revolution is in the making. Interconnection and interdependence between countries are crucial for human survival. The forces for peace

---

3 At http://www.china.org.cn/chinese/2017-01/25/content_40175608.htm, last accessed August 2021.

far outweigh factors causing war, and the trend of our times toward peace, development, cooperation and win-win outcomes has gained stronger momentum.

On the other hand, mankind is also in an era of numerous challenges and increasing risks. Global growth is sluggish, the impact of the financial crisis lingers on and the development gap is widening. Armed conflicts occur from time to time, Cold War mentality and power politics still exist and non-conventional security threats, particularly terrorism, refugee crisis, major communicable diseases and climate change, are spreading.

There is only one Earth in the universe and we mankind have only one homeland. Stephen Hawking has raised the proposition about "parallel universe", hoping to find another place in the universe where mankind could live. We do not know when his wish will come true. Until today, Earth is still the only home to mankind, so to care for and cherish it is the only option for us mankind. There is a Latin motto inscribed in the dome of the Federal Palace of Switzerland which says *"Unus pro omnibus, omnes pro uno"* (One for all, and all for one). We should not only think about our own generation, but also take responsibility for future ones.

Ladies and Gentlemen, Friends,

Pass on the torch of peace from generation to generation, sustain development and make civilization flourish: this is what people of all countries long for; it is also the responsibility statesmen of our generation ought to shoulder. And China's proposition is: build a community of shared future for mankind and achieve shared and win-win development.

Vision guides action and direction determines the future. As modern history shows, to establish a fair and equitable international order is the goal mankind has always striven for. From the principles of equality and sovereignty established in the Peace of Westphalia over 360 years ago to international humanitarianism affirmed in the Geneva Convention 150-plus years ago; from the four purposes and seven principles enshrined in the UN Charter more than 70 years ago to the Five Principles of Peaceful Coexistence championed by the Bandung Conference over 60 years ago, many principles have emerged in the evolution of international relations and become widely accepted. These principles should guide us in building a community of shared future for mankind.

Sovereign equality is the most important norm governing state-to-state relations over the past centuries and the cardinal principle observed by the United Nations and all other international organizations. The essence of sovereign equality is that the sovereignty and dignity of all countries, whether big or small, strong or weak, rich or poor, must be respected, their internal affairs allow no interference and they have the right to independently choose their social system and development path. In organizations such as the United Nations, World Trade Organization, World Health Organization, World Intellectual Property Organization, World Meteorological Organization, International

5. CHINA'S SPACE-RELATED STATEMENTS AND PROPOSALS IN THE UN

Telecommunication Union, Universal Postal Union, International Organization for Migration and International Labor Organization, countries have an equal voice in decision-making, constituting an important force for improving global governance. In a new era, we should uphold sovereign equality and work for equality in right, opportunity and rules for all countries.

Geneva witnessed the adoption of the Final Declaration on the Problem of Restoring Peace in Indo-China, the first summit meeting for reconciliation between the two blocs during the Cold War and the dialogue and negotiations on hotspot issues like the Iranian nuclear issue and the Syrian issue. What we can learn from both past and present is that dialogue and consultation is an effective way to bridge differences and political negotiation is the fundamental solution to end conflicts. When we have sincere wish, goodwill and political wisdom, no conflict is too big to settle and no ice is too thick to break.

An ancient Chinese philosopher said, "Law is the very foundation of governance." Here in Geneva, countries, on the basis of the UN Charter, concluded a number of international conventions and legal documents on political security, trade, development, social issues, human rights, science and technology, health, labor, intellectual property, culture and sports. The relevance of law lies in its enforcement. It is thus incumbent on all countries to uphold the authority of the international rule of law, exercise their rights in accordance with law and fulfill their obligations in good faith. The relevance of law also lies in fairness and justice. All countries and international judicial institutions should ensure equal and uniform application of international law and reject double standards and the practice of applying international law in a selective way, thus ensuring genuine equality and justice in the world.

"The ocean is vast because it admits all rivers." Openness and inclusiveness have made Geneva a center of multilateral diplomacy. We should advance democracy in international relations and reject dominance by just one or several countries. All countries should jointly shape the future of the world, write international rules, manage global affairs and ensure that development outcomes are shared by all.

In 1862, in his book *Un Souvenir de Solférino*, Henry Dunant pondered the question of whether it is possible to set up humanitarian organizations and conclude humanitarian conventions. The answer came one year later with the founding of the International Committee of the Red Cross. Over the past 150-plus years, the Red Cross has become a symbol and a banner. In the face of frequent humanitarian crises, we should champion the spirit of humanity, compassion and dedication and give love and hope to the innocent people caught in dire situations. We should uphold the basic principles of neutrality, impartiality and independence, refrain from politicizing humanitarian issues and ensure non-militarization of humanitarian assistance.

Ladies and Gentlemen, Friends,

Great visions can be realized only through actions. Actions hold the key to building a community of shared future for mankind. To achieve this goal, the international community should promote partnership, security, growth, inter-civilization exchanges and the building of a sound ecosystem.

– We should stay committed to building a world of lasting peace through dialogue and consultation. When countries enjoy peace, so will the world; when countries fight, the world suffers. From the Peloponnesian War in the fifth century BC to the two world wars and the Cold War that lasted more than four decades, we have drawn painful and profound lessons. "History, if not forgotten, can serve as a guide for the future." By establishing the United Nations, those before us won more than 70 years of relative peace for the world. What we need to do is to improve the mechanisms and means to more effectively resolve disputes, reduce tension and put an end to wars and conflicts.

The Swiss writer and Nobel laureate Hermann Hesse stressed the importance of serving "not war and destruction but peace and reconciliation". Countries should foster partnerships based on dialogue, non-confrontation and non-alliance. Major powers should respect each other's core interests and major concerns, keep their differences under control and build a new model of relations featuring non-conflict, non-confrontation, mutual respect and win-win cooperation. As long as we maintain communication and treat each other with sincerity, the "Thucydides trap" can be avoided. Big countries should treat smaller ones as equals instead of acting as a hegemon imposing their will on others. No country should open the Pandora's box by willfully waging wars or undermining the international rule of law. Nuclear weapons, the Sword of Damocles that hangs over mankind, should be completely prohibited and thoroughly destroyed over time to make the world free of nuclear weapons. Guided by the principle of peace, sovereignty, inclusiveness and shared governance, we should turn the deep sea, the polar regions, the outer space and the Internet into new frontiers for cooperation rather than a wrestling ground for competition.

– We should build a world of common security for all through joint efforts. No country in the world can enjoy absolute security. A country cannot have security while others are in turmoil, as threats facing other countries may haunt itself also. When neighbors are in trouble, instead of tightening his own fences, one should extend a helping hand to them. As a saying goes, "United we stand, divided we fall." All countries should pursue common, comprehensive, cooperative and sustainable security.

Terrorist attacks that have occurred in Europe, North Africa and the Middle East in recent years once again demonstrate that terrorism is the common enemy of mankind. Fighting terrorism is the shared responsibility of all countries. In fighting terror, we should not just treat the symptoms, but remove its root causes. We should enhance coordination and build a global united front against terrorism so as to create an umbrella of security for people around the world. The number of refugees has hit a record high since the end of the Second World War. While tackling the crisis, we should also get to its roots. Why would anyone want to be displaced if they have a home to return to? UNHCR and the International Organization for Migration should act as the coordinator to mobilize the whole world to respond effectively to the refugee crisis. China has decided to provide an additional 200 million yuan of humanitarian assistance for refugees and the displaced of Syria. As terrorism and refugee crises are closely linked to geopolitical conflicts, resolving conflicts provides the fundamental solution to such problems. Parties directly involved should return to the negotiating table, and other parties should work to facilitate talks for peace, and we should all respect the role the UN plays as the main channel for mediation. Pandemic diseases such as bird flu, Ebola and Zika have sounded the alarm for international health security. The WHO should play a leadership role in strengthening epidemic monitoring and sharing of information, practices and technologies. The international community should step up support and assistance for public health in African countries and other developing countries.

– We should build a world of common prosperity through win-win cooperation. Development is the top priority for all countries. Instead of beggaring thy neighbor, countries should stick together like passengers in the same boat. All countries, the main economies in particular, should strengthen macro policy coordination, pursue both current and long-term interests and focus on resolving deep-seated problems. We should seize the historic opportunity presented by the new round of scientific and technological revolution and industrial transformation, shift growth models, drive growth through innovation and further unleash social productivity and social creativity. We should uphold WTO rules, support an open, transparent, inclusive and nondiscriminatory multilateral trading regime and build an open world economy. Trade protectionism and self-isolation will benefit no one.

Economic globalization, a surging historical trend, has greatly facilitated trade, investment, flow of people and technological advances. Since the turn of the century, under the auspices of the UN and riding on the waves of economic globalization, the international community has set the Millennium Development Goals and the 2030 Agenda for Sustainable Development. Thanks to these initiatives, 1.1 billion people have been lifted out of poverty, 1.9 billion people now have access to safe drinking water, 3.5 billion people have gained access to the Internet, and the goal has been set to eradicate extreme poverty by 2030. All this demonstrates that economic globalization is moving in the right direction. Of course, challenges such as development disparity, governance dilemma, digital divide and equity deficit still exist. But they are growing pains. We should face these problems and tackle them, instead of taking no action, as we Chinese like to say, one should not stop eating for fear of getting choked.

We should draw inspiration from history. Historians told us long ago that rapid economic development makes social reform necessary; but people tend to support the former while rejecting the latter. Instead of watching in hesitation, we should move forward against all odds. Answers can also be found in reality. The 2008 international financial crisis teaches us that we should strengthen coordination and improve governance so as to ensure sound growth of economic globalization and make it open, inclusive, balanced and beneficial to all. We should both make the cake bigger and share it fairly to ensure justice and equity.

Last September, the G20 Summit in Hangzhou focused on global economic governance and other major issues, adopted the Blueprint on Innovative Growth, put development for the first time in global macro policy framework, and formulated an action plan.

– We should build an open and inclusive world through exchanges and mutual learning. Delicious soup is made by combining different ingredients. Diversity of human civilizations not only defines our world, but also drives progress of mankind. There are more than 200 countries and regions, over 2,500 ethnic groups and multiple religions in our world. Different histories, national conditions, ethnic groups and customs give birth to different civilizations and make the world a colorful one. There is no such thing as a superior or inferior civilization, and civilizations are different only in identity and location. Diversity of civilizations should not be a source of global conflict; rather, it should be an engine driving the advance of human civilizations.

Every civilization, with its own appeal and root, is a human treasure. Diverse civilizations should draw on each other to achieve common progress. We should make exchanges among civilizations a source of inspiration for advancing human society and a bond that keeps the world in peace.

– We should make our world clean and beautiful by pursuing green and low-carbon development. Man coexists with nature, which means that any harm to nature will eventually come back to haunt man. We hardly notice natural resources such as air, water, soil and blue sky when we have them. But we won't be able to survive without them. Industrialization has created material wealth never seen before, but it has also inflicted irreparable damage to the environment. We must not exhaust all the resources passed on to us by previous generations and leave nothing to our children or pursue development in a destructive way. Clear waters and green mountains are as good as mountains of gold and silver. We must maintain harmony between man and nature and pursue sustainable development.

We should pursue green, low-carbon, circular and sustainable way of life and production, advance the 2030 Agenda for Sustainable Development in a balanced manner and explore a model of sound development that ensures growth, better lives and a good environment. The Paris Agreement is a milestone in the history of climate governance. We must ensure this endeavor is not derailed. All parties should work together to implement the Paris Agreement. China will continue to take steps to tackle climate change and fully honor its obligations.

5. CHINA'S SPACE-RELATED STATEMENTS AND PROPOSALS IN THE UN

Swiss army knife embodies Swiss craftsmanship. When I first got one, I was amazed that it has so many functions. I cannot help thinking how wonderful it would be if an exquisite Swiss army knife could be made for our world. When there is a problem, we can use one of the tools on the knife to fix it. I believe that with unremitting efforts of the international community, such a knife can be made.

Ladies and Gentlemen, Friends,

For us Chinese, China will do well only when the world does well, and vice versa. Many people are quite interested in what policies China will pursue, and we have heard various views. Here, I wish to give you an explicit answer.

First, China remains unchanged in its commitment to uphold world peace. Amity with neighbors, harmony without uniformity and peace are values cherished in the Chinese culture. The Art of War, a Chinese classic, begins with this observation, "The art of war is of vital importance to the State. It is a matter of life and death, a road to either survival or ruin. Hence it demands careful study." What it means is that every effort should be made to prevent a war and great caution must be exercised when it comes to fighting a war. For several millennia, peace has been in the blood of us Chinese and a part of our DNA.

Several centuries ago, China was strong and its GDP accounted for 30% of the global total. Even then, China was never engaged in aggression or expansion. In over 100 years after the 1840 Opium War, China suffered immensely from aggression, wars and chaos. Confucius said, "Do not do to others what you do not want others to do to you." We Chinese firmly believe that peace and stability is the only way to development and prosperity.

China has grown from a poor and weak country to the world's second largest economy not by committing military expansion or colonial plunder, but through the hard work of its people and our efforts to uphold peace. China will never waver in its pursuit of peaceful development. No matter how strong its economy grows, China will never seek hegemony, expansion or sphere of influence. History has borne this out and will continue to do so.

Second, China remains unchanged in its commitment to pursue common development. An old Chinese saying goes, when you reap fruits, you should remember the tree; when you drink water, you should remember its source. China's development has been possible because of the world, and China has contributed to the world's development. We will continue to pursue a win-win strategy of opening-up, share our development opportunities with other countries and welcome them aboard the fast train of China's development.

Between 1950 and 2016, China provided foreign countries with over 400 billion yuan of aid, and we will continue to increase assistance to others as its ability permits. Since the outbreak of the international financial crisis, China has contributed to over 30% of global growth each year on average. In the coming five years, China will import eight trillion US dollars of goods, attract 600 billion US dollars of foreign investment, make 750 billion US dollars of outbound investment, and Chinese tourists will make 700 million outbound visits. All this will bring more development opportunities to other countries.

China pursues a path of development in keeping with its national conditions. We always put people's rights and interests above everything else and have worked hard to advance and uphold human rights. China has met the basic living needs of its 1.3 billion-plus people and lifted over 700 million people out of poverty, which is a significant contribution to the global cause of human rights. The Belt and Road initiative I put forward aims to achieve win-win and shared development. Over 100 countries and international organizations have supported the initiative, and a large number of early harvest projects have been launched. China supports the successful operation of the Asian Infrastructure Investment Bank and other new multilateral financial institutions in order to provide more public goods to the international community.

Third, China remains unchanged in its commitment to foster partnerships. China pursues an independent foreign policy of peace, and is ready to enhance friendship and cooperation with all other countries on the basis of the Five Principles of Peaceful Coexistence. China is the first country to make partnership-building a principle guiding state-to-state relations. It has formed partnerships of various forms with over 90 countries and regional organizations, and will build a circle of friends across the world.

China will endeavor to put in place a framework of relations with major powers featuring general stability and balanced growth. We will strive to build a new model of major country relations with the United States, a comprehensive strategic partnership of coordination with Russia, partnership for peace, growth, reform and among different civilizations with Europe, and a partnership of unity and cooperation with BRICS countries. China will continue to uphold justice and friendship and pursue shared interests, and boost pragmatic cooperation with other developing countries to achieve common development. We will further enhance mutually beneficial cooperation with our neighbors under the principle of amity, sincerity, mutual benefit and inclusiveness. We will pursue common development with African countries in a spirit of sincerity, being result oriented, affinity and good faith. And we will elevate our comprehensive cooperative partnership with Latin America to a higher level.

Fourth, China remains unchanged in its commitment to multilateralism. Multilateralism is an effective way to preserve peace and promote development. For decades, the United Nations and other international institutions have made a universally recognized contribution to maintaining global peace and sustaining development.

China is a founding member of the United Nations and the first country to put its signature on the UN Charter. China will firmly uphold the international system with the UN as its core, the basic norms governing international relations embodied in the purposes and principles of the UN Charter, the authority and stature of the UN, and its core role in international affairs.

The China-UN Peace and Development Fund has been officially inaugurated. We will make funds available to peace and development-oriented programs proposed by the UN and its agencies in Geneva on a priority basis. China's support for multilateralism will increase as the country continues to develop itself.

Ladies and Gentlemen, Friends,

Geneva invokes a special memory to us. In 1954, Premier Zhou Enlai led a Chinese delegation to the Geneva Conference, and worked with the Soviet Union, the United States, the United Kingdom and France to seek political settlement of the Korean issue and a ceasefire in Indo-China. This demonstrated China's desire for peace and contributed Chinese wisdom to world peace. Since 1971 when China regained its lawful seat in the UN and began to return to international agencies in Geneva, China has gradually involved itself in disarmament, trade, development, human rights and social issues, putting forth Chinese proposals for the resolution of major issues and the making of important rules. In recent years, China has taken an active part in dialogues and negotiations on the Iranian nuclear issue, the Syrian issue and other hotspot issues, giving Chinese input to their political settlement. China applied to the International Olympic Committee to host both the summer and winter Olympic and Paralympic Games, and we have won the bids. In addition, we have gained endorsement from the International Union for Conservation of Nature for over a dozen applications for world natural heritage sites as well as world cultural and natural heritage sites. All this has presented Chinese splendor to the world.

Ladies and Gentlemen, Friends,

The ancient Chinese believed that "one should be good at finding the laws of things and solving problems". Building a community of shared future is an exciting goal, and it requires efforts from generation after generation. China is ready to work with all the other UN member states as well as international organizations and agencies to advance the great cause of building a community of shared future for mankind.

On 28 January, we Chinese will celebrate the Chinese New Year, the Year of the Rooster. The rooster symbolizes bright prospects and auspiciousness. As a Chinese saying goes, the crow of the golden rooster heralds a great day for all. With that, I wish you all the very best and a very happy Chinese New Year!

Thank you.

6. AGREEMENTS ON INTERNATIONAL SPACE COOPERATION

6.1. MEMORANDUM ON AGREEMENT ON LIABILITY FOR SATELLITE LAUNCHES BETWEEN CHINA AND THE UNITED STATES[1]

1988

Noting the intention of the People's Republic of China to proceed promptly to become a party to the Convention on International Liability for Damage Caused by Space Objects, which entered into force on September 1, 1972 (hereinafter the "Liability Convention"),
 Have agreed as follows:

Article I
This Memorandum of Agreement applies to the AUSSAT satellites and the ASIASAT satellite and their launch by the People's Republic of China.

Article II
Subject to Article 4 below, the Parties agree that, as between them, the Government of the People's Republic of China assumes and shall compensate the Government of the United States of America for any and all amounts for which the Government of the United States of America may be liable under the Liability Convention; the Treaty on Principles Governing the Activities of States in the Exploration and Use of Outer Space, including the Moon and Other Celestial Bodies (/oosa/en/ourwork/spacelaw/treaties/outerspacetreaty.html), which entered into force on October 10, 1967; or any other applicable international law.

Article III
In the event that a claim for compensation for damage within the scope of Article 2 above is brought against the Government of the United States of America, the Government of the United States of America, as soon as practicable after receiving notice of such claim, shall notify the Government of the People's Republic of China thereof.

---

[1] The MOA on Liability for Satellite Launches and the MOA on Satellite Technology Safeguard were signed on 17 December 1988, while the MOA Regarding International Trade in Commercial Launch Service was signed 26 January 1989. But all these three agreements entered into force on March 16, 1989. The MOA on Liability for Satellite Launches is cited from https://www.unoosa.org/oosa/en/ourwork/spacelaw/national spacelaw/bi-multi-lateral-agreements/china_usa_001.html, last accessed August 2021.

Article IV
1. The Government of the United States of America shall not make any settlement with any such claimant without full consultation with the Government of the People's Republic of China.

In the event that the Government of the People's Republic of China objects to the terms of a proposed settlement between the Government of the United States of America and any such claimant, the Government of the People's Republic of China shall not be obligated to compensate the Government of the United States of America with respect to such claim unless the Government of the United States of America first submits the claim to a claims commission as provided for in the Liability Convention, or, if the claim brought against the Government of the United States of America is not based on the Liability Convention, to a claims commission whose procedures accord with the procedures in Articles XIV through XX thereof. In this event, the Government of the People's Republic of China shall compensate the Government of the United States of America for any settlement of such claim up to the amount recommended by the claims commission. Subejct to Articles XV, XVI, and XVII of the Liability Convention with respect to failure to select a commission member, selection of members by the Government of the United States of America shall require prior consultation with, and the approval of, the Government of the People's Republic of China.

Article V
The Government of the People's Republic of China shall provide to the Government of the United States of America, at the latter's request, all information and cooperation necessary for the defense of any such claim against the Government of the United States of America.

Article VI
Disputes relating to the interpretation or application of this Memorandum of Agreement shall be resolved through consultations between the Parties, or through any other means agreed by the Parties.

Article VII
This Memorandum of Agreement shall enter into force upon notification by the Government of the United States of America to the Government of the People's Republic of China that a license for the export of the ASIASAT or AUSSAT satellites to the People's Republic of China for launch therein has been approved.

IN WITNESS WHEREOF, the undersigned, being duly authorized by their respective governments, have signed this Memorandum of Agreement.

DONE at Washington in duplicate, in the English and Chinese languages, both texts being equally authentic, this 17 day of December, 1988.

6. AGREEMENTS ON INTERNATIONAL SPACE COOPERATION

6.2. MEMORANDUM OF AGREEMENT ON SATELLITE TECHNOLOGY SAFEGUARD[2]

Between the USA Government and the PRC Government
1988

Article I Purpose

This Agreement is entered into between the Government of the United States of America and the Government of the People's Republic of China for the purpose of precluding the unauthorized transfer of sensitive technology associated with the possible launching of the U.S.-manufactured Asiasat and Aussat satellites from the People's Republic of China. It is understood that, except as described in Section II or otherwise authorized by the export licenses issued by the Government of the United States of America, at no time will any of the equipment and technical data described below be transferred. The Government of the People's Republic of China has no intention to obtain any unauthorized proprietary, technical know-how through performing launch services for these satellites.

This Agreement specifies the security procedures to be followed for launch of the Aussat and Asiasat satellites from the territory of the People's Republic of China. This Agreement controls access to the U.S.-manufactured spacecraft (satellite and kickmotors), support equipment, ancillary items, components and spare parts thereof (hereinafter "equipment"), and all related technical data[3] (hereinafter "technical data"). This Agreement applies to all phases of launch activities, including activities at all facilities of Hughes Aircraft Company (hereinafter "consignee") in El Segundo, California or other locations, transportation of the spacecraft between the United States of America and the People's Republic of China, and in the People's Republic of China.

The security procedures specified in this Agreement supplement the procedures detailed in the technology control plans in the contracts regarding the launch of the Aussat and Asiasat satellites between the consignee and China Great Wall Industry Corporation (CGWIC) (hereinafter the "Hughes-CGWIC Plan"). Compliance with both this government-to-government Agreement and the Hughes-CGWIC Plan is required. Any conflict between the provisions of this Agreement and the provisions of the Hughes-CGWIC Plan will be resolved in favor of this Agreement. If the Government of the United States of America determines that there is clear evidence that any provisions of either this Agreement or the technology control plain between Hughes

---

2   This MOA is cited from *International Legal Materials*, Vol. 28(3), 1989, pp. 604-609.
3   "Technical Data" means for the purposes of this Agreement: (a) Classified information relating to the equipment; (b) information covered by an invention secrecy order; and (c) information which is directly related to the design, engineering, development, production, processing, manufacture, use, operation, overhaul, repair, maintenance, modification, or reconstruction of the equipment. This includes, for example, information in the form of blueprints, drawings, photographs, plans, instructions, computer software, and documentation.

and CGWIC have been violated, it may suspend or revoke the export License(s). Furthermore, nothing in this Agreement should be construed to mean that the Government of the United States of America will be constrained from taking any action on the license(s) consistent with United States laws and regulations. Nevertheless, the Government of the United States of America will do its utmost to assure continuity of the license(s) and completion of the transaction covered by the license(s). In the event the license(s) are revoked, the Government of the People's Republic of China agrees to cooperate in the return of any equipment and technical data that was transferred prior to revocation.

Article II Authorized Technical Data
Disclosure of technical data by the consignee will be limited to public domain information, information essential to the fulfillment of contractually designated tasks, and will be limited, additionally, to the interface information specified below.

Disclosure of technical data controlled by the Government of the United States of America will be limited only to the interface information specified below. No additional controlled technical data or other information will be disclosed without the prior written approval of the Government of the United States of America. Only the following interface form, fit, and function data that describe mechanical and electrical mating requirements for attaching the spacecraft to the launch vehicle is authorized for release: orbit requirements; launch window; weight; center of gravity; envelope; dynamic loading; power usage/conditioning; interface adaptor requirements; environmental requirements; propellant requirements; frequency plans, including telemetry, tracking & control (TT&C); safety plans; test flows; separation characteristics; ground handling/test equipment; and test/flight event sequences.

The Government of the People's Republic of China agrees not to transfer any technical data in any form (including assigning personnel to assist third countries or parties) concerning the satellite or interface systems to any third party or country without the prior written approval of the Government of the United States of America.

Article III Unauthorized Technical Data and Assistance
Disclosure of technical data not specifically authorized is prohibited. The People's Republic of China will not seek, and consignee will not provide, any assistance, other than that described in Section II, to the People's Republic of China relating to the design, development, operation, maintenance, modification, or repair of the equipment (as defined in Section I) and the launch vehicle. Any such provision or acquisition of data will constitute a violation of this Agreement.

Article IV Access Controls

1. United States Government Oversight

The Government of the United States of America retains the right to oversee and monitor implementation of the Hughes-CGWIC Plan.

Access to all equipment and technical data will be controlled on a 24-hour basis by U.S. persons[4] who have received training in security procedure from the Government of the United States of America. Such persons will control access throughout launch preparations, satellite transportation, mating/demating, test and checkout, satellite launch, and return of equipment to the United States of America.

The Government of the People's Republic of China agrees that the Government of the United States of America has the right to inspect the equipment and technical data which is provided by the consignee to the People's Republic of China and/or located at the consignee's facilities in El Segundo, California, without prior notice to the Government of the People's Republic of China or the consignee. Furthermore, the Government of the People's Republic of China agrees that the Government of the United States of America has the right to electronically inspect and monitor, including through a closed-circuit television system and electronic devices compatible with launch operations and launch safety, all areas where the consignee's equipment and technical data are located, including the spacecraft clean operation area after the mating of the spacecraft to the launch vehicle. The Government of the United States of America does not intend that these actions interfere with the launch preparation and/or harm launch safety.

2. Badge Access Controls

All persons, including employees of the consignee. Government of the United States of America personnel, and non-U.S. persons, are required to display prominently identification badges while performing duties associated with the launch. In the case of U.S. persons, the badges will be issued by the Government of the United States of America, or a private United States firm designated by the Government of the United States of America, and will identify the individual bearer by name, photo, access authorization, and facility access.

In the case of non-U.S. persons performing launch-associated duties at the consignee's facilities in California, a temporary identification badge will be issued, distinctive in color which will be marked "visitor." Issuance of these badges will be controlled by the consignee.

---

4   "U.S. person(s)" means, for the purposes of this Agreement: a natural person who is a citizen or national of the United States of America, or has been lawfully admitted to the United States of America for permanent residence under the Immigration and Nationality Act of the United States of America and maintains such a residence.

Article V Satellite Processing
1. Spacecraft to Launch Vehicle Integration
Access to the facilities housing the equipment and technical data or facilities where the spacecraft and/or motors are assembled, tested, or stored will only be permitted as specified by the badge and will be limited, to the greatest extent possible, to U.S. persons. Non-U.S. persons will be escorted at all times by U.S, persons who have received training in security procedures from the Government of the United States of America. Access by non-U.S. persons or People's Republic of China representatives at the consignee's facilities in California will be controlled as provided in Section IV of this document. In the case of testing the equipment, non-U.S. persons would be permitted access only as needed for test validation of the adaptors designed by Beijing Wan Yuan Industry Corporation (BWYIC) to tie the spacecraft to the launch vehicle. Testing of the adaptors will be performed at a location separate from the facilities housing the spacecraft. Non-U.S. persons will not be permitted to observe testing of equipment other than the adaptors.

2. Transportation of the Spacecraft
The spacecraft, and other equipment, will be transported to the People's Republic of China aboard a U.S.-registered aircraft operated by U.S. persons. Non-U.S. persons may join the aircraft at the point-of-entry designated by the Government of the People's Republic of China to perform navigational duties from point-of-entry to the launch site. Non-U.S. persons will not be permitted into the cargo area of the aircraft during flight.

The Government of the People's Republic of China agrees that the aircraft carrying the spacecraft, equipment, and technical data can pass through Customs in the People's Republic of China without inspection, and will not be subject to inspection while in the People's Republic of China. However, the flight manifest will be made available to People's Republic of China Customs officials. Issuance of an export license to Hughes by the Government of the United States of America will be conditioned expressly on Hughes4 s commitment not to carry aboard the aircraft transporting the spacecraft (and related equipment and technical data) any contraband goods unrelated to the launch activities. A further condition of the export license will be Hughes's commitment that the aircraft is in compliance with relevant Customs regulations of the People's Republic of China.

In the event of accident or crash in the territory of People's Republic of China of the aircraft, transporting the spacecraft, recovery terms of Section IV will apply.

3. Preparations at Launch Site
Non-U.S. persons may unload the aircraft and deliver the sealed crates to the satellite preparation area at the launch site under supervision of U.S. persons. Unless specifically permitted by persons authorized by the Government of the United States of America, non-U.S. persons will not be allowed into satellite preparation area for any purpose

while the satellite, including the kick motors or any related equipment, is being tested and/or prepared for integration.

4. Launch Pad Operations

U.S. persons will assemble the spacecrafts, add propellant to the spacecraft, and place the spacecraft in the fairing. The transport vehicle carrying the sealed container may be driven by a national of the People's Republic of China, under supervision of U.S. persons. Launch preparation and satellite testing at the launch pad will be conducted by U.S. persons. U.S. persons will monitor access to the spacecraft clean operation area once the spacecraft and the launch vehicle are integrated.

Article VI Launch Failure, Delay, or Cancellation

U.S. persons will control or supervise removal of the fairing or accessing to the payload bay or any U.S.-supplied equipment in the event of a launch delay requiring such procedures. U.S. persons must be present if the satellite is exposed or removed from the launch vehicle after the satellite is mated to the launch vehicle. The satellite will be under U.S. control from the launch pad to the satellite preparation area, where it will be repaired for remating or dismantled for return to the United States of America. U.S. persons will control the satellite upon return to the launch pad and will remate the satellite. The satellite, equipment, and technical data will be loaded under the control of U.S. persons on a U.S.-registered aircraft for return to the United States of America in the event the launch is cancelled.

In the event of a launch failure after liftoff, the Government of the People's Republic of China agrees to permit U.S. persons to assist in the search for and to recover any and all parts/debris from the spacecraft resulting from the accident. A U.S.-controlled "satellite debris recovery site" will be located near the launch facility. Access to this location will be controlled as provided in Section IV of this Agreement. The Government of the People's Republic of China also agrees to return all items associated with the spacecraft recovered by its nationals immediately to the United States of America without having examined or photographed them in any manner. The People's Republic of China further agrees to permit Government of the United States of America satellite accident search and recovery personnel to have access to the accident site.

Article VII Post-Launch Procedures

All equipment and technical data associated with the launch, brought into the People's Republic of China, including equipment to test the satellites and "failed units," will be dismantled by U.S. persons and such equipment and data will be returned to the United States of America aboard a U.S.-registered aircraft.

Procedures described in Section V (B-D) will be followed, including exemption from Customs inspection.

Article VIII Conduct of U.S. Persons While in the PRC

U.S. persons, while in the People's Republic of China supporting these launch activities, shall observe the published laws and regulations of the country. These persons will not engage in business or commercial activities beyond or in conflict with the provisions of this Agreement. U.S. persons shall not engage in activities that will harm launch safety or would lead to the transfer of Chinese launch vehicle and launch operations technology.

Article IX Settlement of Disputes

Disputes between the parties, regarding the application and interpretation of this Memorandum of Agreement, shall be resolved by consultation through diplomatic channels.

Article X Entry into Force

This Agreement shall enter into force upon notification by the Government of the United States of America to the Government of the People's Republic of China that a license for the export of the Asiasat or Aussat satellite(s) to the People's Republic of China for launch therein has been approved.

IN WITNESS WHEREOF, the undersigned, being duly authorized by their respective Governments, have signed this Agreement.

DONE at Washington in duplicate, in the English and Chinese languages, both texts being equally authentic, this 17 day of December 1988.

6.3. MEMORANDUM OF AGREEMENT REGARDING INTERNATIONAL TRADE IN COMMERCIAL LAUNCH SERVICES[5]

Between the USA Government and the PRC Government
1989

Article I Purpose

The Government of the United States of America (U.S.) and the Government of the People's Republic of China (PRC) have entered into this Memorandum of Agreement (Agreement), of which the attached Annex is an integral part, to address certain issues regarding international trade in commercial launch services including entry in an appropriate manner of the PRC into the international market for commercial launch services.

---

5   This MOA is cited from *International Legal Materials*, Vol. 28(3), 1989, pp. 595-603.

6. AGREEMENTS ON INTERNATIONAL SPACE COOPERATION

Article II Trade Issues and Market Entry

The Delegation of the People's Republic of China and the Delegation of the United States of America held two rounds of negotiations in Beijing and Washington, D.C. As a result of these discussions, the parties agreed that certain measures are appropriate to address certain issues regarding international trade in commercial launch services, including entry in an appropriate manner of PRC providers of commercial launch into the international market for commercial launch services. Accordingly, the U.S. and the PRC have agreed as follows:

1. The U.S. and the PRC support the application of market principles to international competition among providers of commercial launch services, including the avoidance of below-cost pricing, government inducements, and unfair trade practices.

2. To bring about entry in an appropriate manner, the PRC shall take steps to ensure that providers of commercial launch services controlled by or operating within the territory of the PRC do not materially impair the smooth and effective functioning of the international market for commercial launch services.

(1) Among these steps, the PRC shall ensure that any direct or indirect government support extended to its providers of commercial launch services is in accord with practices prevailing in the international market.

(2) The PRC shall require that its providers of commercial launch services offer and conclude any contracts to provide commercial launch services to international customers at prices, terms, and conditions which are on a par with those prices, terms, and conditions prevailing in the international market for comparable commercial launch services.

(3) The PRC agrees that it will prevent its providers of commercial launch services from offering introductory or promotional prices for launch services except for the first or, in extraordinary circumstances, second successful commercial launch of a new launch vehicle. In this regard, promotional prices will not be offered for launches on the Long March IIE or III under any contract other than the contract for the successful launch of the Aussat B-1 and B-2 satellites.

(4) The PRC agrees to require its launch service or insurance providers to offer international customers any insurance or reflight guarantees on a par with prevailing rates and practices in international markets for comparable risk.

3. In view of the concerns about the launch services market expressed by several countries, the PRC expressed its understanding. The PRC explained that: China has a limited capability of manufacturing launch vehicles. In addition to meeting the needs of domestic Chinese satellite launches, its providers of commercial launch services are only able to offer a limited number of communications satellites launch each year for international customers. Chinese launch services, therefore, are only a supplement to the world market, providing international customers with a new option.

After mutual and friendly consultations, the U.S. and the PRC agreed:

(1) PRC providers of commercial launch services shall not launch more than 9 communications satellites for international customers (including the two AUSSAT and one ASIASAT satellites) during the period of this Agreement, and

(2) The PRC shall require that any commitments to provide commercial launch services to international customers by PRC launch service providers ore proportionately distributed over the period of the Agreement. To this end, the PRC shall prevent a disproportionate concentration of such commitments during any two-year period of the Agreement. The PRC may make commitments in any 3-year period of the Agreement consistent with subparagraph i above.

(3) The PRC shall also require that PRC launch service providers shall not commit at any time to launch in any calendar year covered by the Agreement more than twice the average annual number of launches permitted under subparagraph i above. The PRC shall seek to ensure that PRC launches of communications satellites for international customers are performed as scheduled in the original launch commitment.

4. The U.S. stated that the U.S. does not provide government inducements of any kind in connection with the provision of commercial launch services to international customers which would create discrimination against launch service providers of other nations and has no intention of providing such inducements in the future. Accordingly, the PRC stated it agreed not to offer inducements of any kind in connection with the provision of commercial launch services to international customers which would create discrimination against launch service providers of other nations.

Article III Non-Discrimination

1. The U.S. stated that U.S. providers of commercial launch services do not discriminate unfairly against any international customers or suppliers and that it is not U.S. Government policy to encourage any such unfair discrimination by U.S. providers of commercial launch services.

2. Accordingly, in implementing its commitments under this Agreement, the PRC shall require that its providers of commercial launch services not discriminate unfairly against any international customers or suppliers.

Article IV Consultations

1. The PRC and U.S. will consult annually with respect to the obligations in this Agreement and related matters, including the nature and extent of direct and indirect government support provided to commercial launch services providers and developments in the international market for commercial launch services.

2. In addition, each party undertakes to enter into consultations within thirty (30) days of a request by the other party to discuss matters of particular concern.

3. During annual consultations, the limitation on the total number of communications satellites that may be launched by PRC providers of commercial launch services may reconsidered upon request of the PRC in light of unforeseen developments in the commercial launch services market. A U.S. decision on such a request shall be made within thirty (30) days after the completion of the annual consultations.

4. The U.S, and the PRC agree to work *toward* a common understanding of the application of market principles to prices, terms, and conditions of commercial launch services for international customers.

5. To facilitate the annual consultations, the U.S. and the PRC agree to exchange information as follows:

(1) The U.S. shall each year in advance of such consultations provide to the PRC such publicly releasable information as it possesses with respect to price, terms and conditions prevailing in the international market for commercial launch services.

(2) The PRC shall each year in advance of such consultations provide comprehensive information to the U.S. regarding prices, terms, and conditions offered by PRC providers of commercial launch services for the launch of satellites licensed by the U.S. The PRC may also provide other information that it believes may have a material effect on pricing practices of PRC providers of commercial launch services.

(3) The PRC may request that the U.S. provide additional publicly releasable information with respect to international prices, terms and conditions, and may in addition request U.S. views regarding prevailing international market conditions and likely future developments, as well as government supports or inducements. The U.S. shall respond to such requests within thirty (30) days. If such information cannot be provided directly because of business confidentiality, the U.S. shall provide such information in summary form.

(4) The U.S. may request additional information with respect to the prices, terms, and conditions offered by PRC providers of commercial launch services and any PRC government supports or inducements. The PRC shall respond to such requests within thirty (30) days. If such information cannot be provided directly because of business confidentiality, the PRC shall provide such information in summary form.

(5) The U.S. and the PRC shall keep all information received from each other under this paragraph strictly confidential and shall not provide it to any other government or any private person without the written consent of the other.

i. The U.S. and the PRC shall also provide each year in advance of annual consultations information on a consolidated basis concerning the commitments their launch service providers have undertaken to provide commercial launch services for international customers. This information may be made publicly available.

ii. If a launch of a communications satellite for an international customer will not be performed as scheduled, the PRC shall notify the U.S. regarding the reasons for the delay and the new date for the launch as soon as possible.

iii. It is understood that the U.S. and the PRC will review the information contained in this Article during annual consultation; in the context of developments in the international market for commercial launch services.

Article V Clarification of Rights and Obligations

1. If, after friendly consultations with the PRC, the U.S. determines that there is clear evidence that the provisions of this Agreement have been violated, the U.S. reserves its right to take any action permitted under U.S. laws and regulations. The U.S. shall seek to avoid actions inconsistent with this Agreement.

2. With regard to export licenses, any application for a U.S. export license will be reviewed on a case-by-case basis consistent with U.S. laws and regulations. Nothing in this Agreement shall be construed to mean that the U.S. is constrained from taking any appropriate action with respect to any U.S. export licenses consistent with U.S. laws and regulations. Nevertheless, the U.S will do its utmost to assure consistent with U.S. laws and regulations, continuity of issued license(s) and the completion of the transactions covered in such license(s).

Article VI Discussions on International Rules

The U.S. and the PRC are prepared to enter into discussions with other interested parties on comprehensive international rules with respect to government involvement in, and other matters relating to, the international market for commercial launch services. It is understood, however, that nothing in this Agreement shall prejudice any position on any issue that either the U.S. or the PRC may take in those discussions.

Article VII Comprehensive Review

The U.S. and the PRC shall engage in a comprehensive review of the terms and operation of this Agreement beginning in September 1991.

Article VIII Entry into Force

This Agreement shall enter into force upon notification by the Government of the United States of America to the Government of the People's Republic of China that a U.S. license for the export of the ASIASAT or AUSSAT satellite(s) or other satellite, to the People's Republic of China for launch therein, has been approved. Unless extended by agreement of the PRC and the U.S., this Agreement shall terminate on December 31, 1994. It may be terminated at any time by mutual agreement if superseded by an international agreement on government involvement in, and other matters relating to, the international market for commercial launch services or under such other circumstances as may be mutually agreed.

IN WITNESS WHEREOF, the undersigned, being duly authorized by their respective Governments, have signed this Agreement.

DONE at Washington, D.C., in duplicate, in the English and Chinese languages, both texts being equally authentic this twenty-sixth day of January, 1989.

ANNEX

The following Agreed definitions constitute an integral part of the Memorandum of Agreement Between the Government of the United States of America and the Government of the Republic of China Regarding International Trade in Commercial Launch Services of January 26, 1989.

1. The term "commercial launch services" refers to any commercially provided launch of any satellite, including communications satellites, for an international customer.

2. The term "communications satellite" refers to any satellite which is a primary payload of a launch; and which provides telecommunications services. It refers primarily to, but is not limited to, communications satellites in geostationary orbit.

3. The term "international customer" refers to the following:

(1) any institution or business entity, other than those institutions or entities located within the territory of the PRC and owned or controlled by PRC nationals; or

(2) any government other than that of the PRC; or

(3) any international organization or quasi-governmental consortium; which is the ultimate owner or operator of a satellite or which will deliver the satellite to such ultimate owner or operator.

4. The term "practices prevailing in the international market" in Article II (b) (i) refers to practices by governments of market economics.

5. The term "prices, terms, and conditions prevailing in the international market for comparable launch services in Article II (b)(ii) includes but is not limited to prices, financing terms and conditions and the schedule for progress payment offered to international customers by commercial launch service providers in market economies.

6. Government "inducements" with respect to particular launch services transactions include, but are not limited to, unreasonable political pressure, the provision of any resources of commercial value unrelated to the launch service competition and offers of favorable treatment under or access to: defense and national security policies and programs, development assistance policies and programs, and general economic policies and programs. (e.g., trade, investment, debt, and foreign exchange policies).

7. The terms "commitment" means any agreement by an international customer with PRC providers of commercial launch services to launch a communication satellite, which effectively removed the launch from international commercial competition. The terms "commitment" does not include reservation agreement.

6.4. Memorandum of Agreement on Satellite Technology Safeguards[6]

Between the USA Government and the PRC Government
1993

Article I Purpose

This Agreement is entered into between the Government of the United States of America and the Government of the People's Republic of China for the purpose of precluding the unauthorized transfer of sensitive technology associated with the possible launching of U.S.-manufactured satellites from the People's Republic of China. It is understood that, except as described in Section II or otherwise authorized by the export licenses issued by the Government of the United States of America, at no time will there be unmonitored or unescorted access to any of the equipment and technical data described below, nor will such equipment and technical data be transferred by any means, including observation. The Government of the People's Republic of China has no intention to obtain any unauthorized proprietary, technical know-how through performing launch services for these satellites.

This Agreement specifies the security procedures to be followed for launch of U.S.-manufactured satellites from the territory of the People's Republic of China. This Agreement controls access to the U.S. - manufactured spacecraft (satellite and kick motors), support equipment, ancillary items, components and spare parts thereof (hereinafter "equipment", and all related technical data[7] (hereinafter "technical data").

This Agreement applies to all phases of launch activities, including activities at all facilities of the satellite supplier (hereinafter "consignee"), transportation of the spacecraft: between the United States of America and the People's Republic of China, and in the People's Republic of China.

The security procedures specified in this Agreement take precedence over the procedures detailed in the technology control plans in the contracts regarding the launch of U.S.-manufactured satellites between the consignee and the Chinese launch provider (hereinafter the "Technology Control Plan"). Compliance with both this government-to-government agreement and the Technology Control Plan is required. Any conflict between the provisions of this Agreement and the provisions of the Technology Control Plan will be resolved in favor of this Agreement. If the

---

[6] At https://aerospace.org/sites/default/files/policy_archives/Tech%20Safeguards%20Agreement%20-%20China%20Feb93.pdf, last accessed August 2021.

[7] "Technical data" means, for the purposes of this Agreement:(a) classified information relating to the equipment; (b) information covered by an invention secrecy order; and (c) information which is directly related to the design, engineering, development, production, processing, manufacture, use, operation, overhaul, repair, maintenance, modification, or reconstruction of the equipment. This includes, for example, information in the form of blueprints, drawings, photographs, plans, instructions, computer software, and documentation.

Government of the United States of America determines that there is clear evidence that any provisions of either this Agreement or the Technology Control Plan between the consignee and the Chinese launch provider have been violated, it may suspend or revoke the export license(s). Furthermore, nothing in this Agreement should be construed to mean that the Government of the United States of America will be constrained from taking any action on the license(s) consistent with United States laws and regulations. Nevertheless, the Government of the United States of America will do its utmost to assure continuity of the license(s) and completion of the transaction covered by the license(s). In the event the license(s) are revoked, the Government of the People's Republic of China agrees to cooperate in the return of any equipment and technical data that was transferred prior to revocation.

Article II Authorized Technical Data
Disclosure of technical data by the consignee will be limited to public domain information and information essential to the fulfillment of contractually designated tasks, and will be limited, additionally, to the interface information specified below.

Disclosure of technical data controlled by the Government of the United States of America will be limited only to the interface information specified below. No additional controlled technical data or other information will be disclosed without the prior written approval of the Government of the United States of America. Only the following interface form, fit, and function data that describe mechanical and electrical mating requirements for attaching the spacecraft to the launch vehicle are authorized for release: orbit requirements; launch window; weight; center of gravity; envelope; dynamic loading; power usage/conditioning; interface adaptor requirements; environmental requirements; propellant requirements; frequency plans, including telemetry, tracking & control (TT&C); safety plans; test flows; separation characteristics; ground handling/test equipment; and test/flight event sequences.

The Government of the People's Republic of China agrees not to transfer by any means (including observation or the assigning of personnel to assist third countries or parties) any technical data in any form concerning the satellite or interface systems to any third party or country without the prior written approval of the Government of the United States of America.

Article III Unauthorized Technical Data and Assistance
Disclosure of technical data not specifically authorized is prohibited. The People's Republic of China will not seek, and the consignee will not provide, any assistance, other than that described in Section II, to the People's Republic of China relating to the design, development, operation, maintenance, modification, or repair of the equipment (as defined in Section I), launch facility, or launch vehicle. Any such provision or acquisition of data will constitute a violation of this Agreement.

Article IV Access Controls
1. United States Government Oversight
The Government of the United States of America shall oversee and monitor implementation of the Technology Control Plan, and the Government of the People's Republic of China shall permit and facilitate that monitoring.

Access to all equipment and technical data will be controlled on a 24-hour basis by U.S. persons[8] who have received training in security procedures from the Government of the United States of America.

Such persons shall control access throughout launch preparations, satellite transportation, mating/demating, test and checkout, satellite launch, and return of equipment to the United States of America.

The Government of the People's Republic of China agrees that the Government of the United States of America has the right to inspect the equipment and technical data which is provided by the consignee to the People's Republic of China and/or is located at the consignee's facilities, without prior notice to the Government of the People's Republic of China or the consignee. Furthermore, the Government of the People's Republic of China agrees that the Government of the United States of America has the right to inspect and monitor, including electronically through a closed-circuit television system and other electronic devices compatible with launch operations and launch safety, all areas where the consignee's equipment and technical data are located, including the spacecraft clean operation area after the mating of the spacecraft to the launch vehicle. The Government of the United States of America does not intend that these actions interfere with the launch preparation and/or harm launch safety.

One side shall give timely notice to the other side of any operations that may create a conflict between access control and monitoring requirements of the two sides so that suitable arrangements can be agreed on to safeguard the controlled equipment, information and technical data of both sides. Under no circumstances shall the United States consignee's control of access and monitoring of all equipment and technical data pertaining to the U.S.-manufactured satellite be denied or interrupted.

2. Badge Access Controls
All persons, including employees of the consignee, Government of the United States of America personnel, and non-U.S. persons, are required to display prominently identification badges while performing duties associated with the launch. In the case of U.S. persons, the badges will be issued by the Government of the United States of America, or a private United States firm designated by the Government of the United

---

8   "U.S. person(s)" means, for the purposes of this Agreement: A natural person who is a citizen or national of the United States of America, or has been lawfully admitted to the United States of America for permanent residence under the Immigration and Nationality Act of the United States of America, as amended, and maintains such a residence.

States of America, and will identify the individual bearer by name, photo, access authorization, and facility access.

In the case of non-U.S. persons performing launch-associated duties at the consignee's facilities, a temporary identification badge will be issued, distinctive in color, which will be marked "visitor." Issuance of these badges will be controlled by the consignee.

Access to the facilities housing the equipment and technical data of facilities where the spacecraft and/or motors are located, assembled, tested, or stored will only be permitted as specified by the badge and will be limited, to the greatest extent possible, to U.S. persons. Non-U.S. persons will be escorted at all times in these areas by U.S. persons who have received training in security procedures from the Government of the United States of America.

Article V Satellite Processing

1. Spacecraft to Launch Vehicle Integration

Access by non-U.S. persons or People's Republic of China representatives at the consignee's facilities will be controlled as provided in Section IV of this document. In the case of testing the equipment, non-U.S. persons shall be permitted access only as needed for test validation of the adaptors designed to tie the spacecraft to the launch vehicle. Testing of the adaptors shall be performed at a location separate from the facilities housing the spacecraft. Non-U.S. persons shall not be permitted to observe testing of equipment other than the adaptors.

2. Transportation of the Spacecraft

The spacecraft, and other equipment, will be transported to the People's Republic of China aboard a U.S.-registered aircraft operated by U.S. persons. Non-U.S. persons may join the aircraft at the point-of-entry designated by the Government of the People's Republic of China to perform navigational duties from the point-of-entry to the launch site. Non-U.S. persons shall not be permitted in the cargo area of the aircraft during flight.

The Government of the People's Republic of China agrees that the aircraft carrying the spacecraft, equipment, and technical data, as well as its cargo, can pass through Customs in the People's Republic of China without inspection, and will not be subject to inspection while in the People's Republic of China. However, the flight manifest will be made available to People's Republic of China Customs officials. Issuance of an export license to the consignee by the Government of the United States of America will be conditioned expressly on the consignee's commitment not to carry aboard the aircraft transporting the spacecraft (and related equipment and technical data) any contraband goods unrelated to the launch activities. A further proviso on the export license will be the consignee's commitment that the aircraft as well as its cargo is in compliance with relevant Customs regulations of the People's Republic of China.

In the event of accident or crash in the territory of the People's Republic of China of the aircraft transporting the spacecraft, recovery terms of Section VI shall apply.

3. Preparations at Launch Site

Non-U.S. persons may unload the aircraft and deliver the sealed crates to the satellite preparation area at the launch site under supervision of U.S. persons. Unless specifically permitted by persons authorized by the Government of the United States of America, non-U.S. persons will not be allowed into the satellite preparation area for any purpose while the satellite or any related equipment, including the kick motors, is being tested and/or prepared for integration. If non-U.S. persons are allowed into the satellite preparation area, they must be escorted at all times by U.S. persons.

4. Launch Pad Operations

U.S. persons shall assemble the spacecraft, add propellant to the spacecraft, and place the spacecraft in the fairing. The transport vehicle carrying the sealed container may be driven by a national of the People's Republic of China, under supervision of U.S. persons. Satellite preparation and testing at the launch pad will be conducted by U.S. persons. U.S. persons shall monitor access to the spacecraft clean operation area once the spacecraft and the launch vehicle are integrated.

At the commencement of joint operations[9], each side shall insure that an official from its appropriate government office, who has comprehensive knowledge and understanding of the requirements of this Agreement, is at the launch site. These officials shall have the necessary authority and seniority to require all personnel of their respective sides, including launch facility, launch vehicle, and satellite personnel, to implement the provisions of this Agreement.

Article VI Launch Failure, Delay, or Cancellation

U.S. persons shall control or supervise removal of the fairing or access to the payload bay or any U.S.-supplied equipment in the event of a launch delay requiring such procedures. U.S. persons must be present if the satellite is exposed or removed from the launch vehicle after the satellite is mated to the launch vehicle. The satellite shall be under U.S. control from the launch pad to the satellite preparation area, where it shall be repaired for remating or dismantled for return to the United States of America. U.S. persons shall control the satellite upon return to the launch pad and shall remate the satellite. In the event the launch is cancelled, the satellite, equipment, and technical data shall be loaded under the control of U.S. persons onto a U.S.-registered aircraft for return to the United States of America under the same procedures pursuant to which the satellite and related

---

9   "joint operations" means for the purposes of this Agreement: operations where nationals of both sides require direct physical and visual access to the satellite, launch vehicle or associated equipment in order to perform integration and testing. Typically, this begins with activities associated with integration of the satellite lo the launch vehicle adaptor.

equipment and technical data initially entered the territory of the People's Republic of China, including the provisions of Section V(B) of this agreement.

In the event of a launch failure after liftoff, the Government of the People's Republic of China agrees to permit U.S. persons to assist in the search for and recovery of any and all parts/debris from the spacecraft resulting from the accident. A U.S.-controlled "satellite debris recovery site" shall be located near the launch facility. Access to this location shall be controlled as provided in Section IV of this agreement.

The Government of the People's Republic of China shall return all items associated with the spacecraft recovered by its nationals immediately to the United States of America without having examined or photographed them in any manner. The People's Republic of China shall permit Government of the United States of America satellite accident search and recovery personnel to have access to the accident site.

Article VII Post-Launch Procedures

All equipment and technical data associated with the launch brought into the People's Republic of China, including equipment to test the satellites and "failed units," shall be dismantled by U.S. persons, and such equipment and data shall be returned to the United States of America aboard a U.S.-registered aircraft. Procedures described in Section V(B-D) will be followed, including exemption from customs inspection.

Article VIII Conduct of U.S. Persons While in the PRC

U.S. persons, while in the People's Republic of China supporting these launch activities, shall observe the published laws and regulations of the country. These persons shall not engage in business or commercial activities beyond or in conflict with the provisions of this Agreement. U.S. persons shall not engage in activities that will harm launch safety or would lead to the transfer of Chinese launch vehicle and launch operations technology.

Article IX Settlement of Disputes

Disputes between the parties, regarding the application and interpretation of this Memorandum of Agreement, shall be resolved by consultation through diplomatic channels.

Article X Entry into Force

The Agreement shall enter into force upon signature by the Government of the United States of America and the Government of the People's Republic of China. Upon entry into force, this Agreement shall supersede the Memorandum of Agreement on Satellite Technology Safeguards between the Governments of the United States of America and the People's Republic of China, done at Washington, December 17, 1988.

In witness whereof, the undersigned, being duly authorized by their respective governments, have signed this Agreement.

Done at Beijing in duplicate, in the English and Chinese languages, both texts being equally authentic, this 11th day of February, 1993.

6.5. Memorandum of Agreement Regarding International Trade in Commercial Launches Services[10]

Between the USA Government and the PRC Government
1995

Article I Purpose

The Government of the United States of America (U.S.) and the Government of the People's Republic of China (PRC) (hereinafter the "Parties") have entered into this Memorandum of Agreement (Agreement), of which the attached Annexes are an integral part, to address certain issues regarding international trade in commercial launch services including continued PRC participation in the international market for commercial launch services. Nothing in this Agreement applies to launches of payloads for military purposes or for use in the non-commercial, civilian space programs of either Party including programs using spacecraft or satellites made by or for the use of the Government of the PRC.

Article II Trade Issues and Market Participation

The Delegation of the People's Republic of China and the Delegation of the United States of America held 5 rounds of negotiations in Beijing and Washington, D.C. As a result of these discussions, the parties believe that the entry of PRC commercial launch services into the international market has facilitated cooperation between the PRC and the U.S. in the space area, and agree that certain measures are appropriate to address certain issues regarding international trade in commercial launch services, including continued PRC participation in the international market for commercial launch services. Accordingly, after mutual and friendly consultations, the U.S. and the PRC have agreed as follows:

A. The U.S. and the PRC support the application of market principles to international competition among providers of commercial launch services, including the avoidance of below-cost pricing, government inducements, and unfair business practices.

B. The PRC shall continue to take steps to ensure that providers of commercial launch services controlled by or operating within the territory of the PRC do not materially impair the smooth and effective functioning of the international market for commercial launch services.

---

10 At https://aerospace.org/sites/default/files/policy_archives/MoA%20on%20Launch%20Services%20Trade%20-%20China%20Mar95.pdf, or https://www.jaxa.jp/library/space_law/chapter_4/4-2-2-13/index_e.html, last accessed August 2021.

6. AGREEMENTS ON INTERNATIONAL SPACE COOPERATION

(i) Among these steps, the PRC shall ensure that any direct or indirect government support extended to its providers of commercial launch services is in accord with practices prevailing in the international market.

(ii) The PRC providers of commercial launch services shall not launch more than 11 principal payloads to geosynchronous earth orbit or geosynchronous transfer orbit for international customers during the period of this Agreement, excluding Apstar II, AsiaSat II, Intelsat 708 and Echostar I, which were reviewed and determined to be covered by the provisions of the 1989 Memorandum of Agreement. Any satellite launched by PRC providers that is entirely leased on orbit to international customers (pursuant to a commitment between the PRC and such customers) represents a launch of a principal payload for purposes of this Agreement. If not entirely leased on orbit to international customers, such a satellite may represent a launch of a principal payload if the satellite's capacity is primarily leased to international customers, depending upon the circumstances and facts of a particular case.

(iii) (a) The United States and the PRC take note of the potential emergence of the market for launches to low-earth-orbit (LEO) since 1989 as a separately identifiable commercial market with its own particular characteristics. It is still under development and is closely related to the rapid evolution of the satellite market and telecommunications market. The two parties further note that participation of its providers of commercial launch services in an appropriate manner in this market segment will contribute to, rather than detract from, the development of this market segment.

(b) Taking into account the current predictions for the growth in, and structure of, the LEO market, the United States recognizes that the participation of PRC launch services providers in that market segment could be substantial, so long as that participation is consistent with the provisions of this Agreement. The PRC states that its participation in the LEO market shall be consistent with the provisions of the agreement and with significant U.S. participation in the development of the LEO market and agrees to take steps to ensure that such participation will be proportionate and non-disruptive.

(c) If either party believes that the other party is participating, or may participate in this market in a manner inconsistent with its commitments under the agreement, the parties shall meet pursuant to the consultations provided for under Article IV (2) to ascertain the facts of the situation and take appropriate corrective action. In assessing the effect, or potential effect of PRC participation in the LEO market relative to its commitments in this Agreement, the United States Government will be guided, inter alia, by the following factors:

1) The extent and growth of overall PRC and U.S. participation in the LEO market;

2) With respect to proposals to deploy LEO communications satellite constellations, the extent of participation by U.S., PRC, and third country launch service providers-in particular, whether the overall level of participation by launch service providers in

countries with whom the U.S. has concluded a bilateral launch services agreement (measured according to distribution of payloads) in the deployment of any single LEO communications satellite constellation is greater than the participation of market economy launch service providers. The following factors should, inter alia, also be taken into account: the extent of PRC and U.S. participation in the deployment; launch scheduling requirements and the need to optimize launch vehicle selection to meet deployment or operational requirements; the availability of competitively-priced market economy launches to meet these requirements; opportunities made available to the parties for participation in the replacement market; reasonable considerations by the proposed system operator regarding commercial risk sharing; customers' requirements.

(iv) The PRC agrees that its providers of commercial launch services shall offer and conclude any contracts to provide commercial launch services to international customers (including sole source or directed procurements) at prices, terms, and conditions which are on a par with those prices, terms and conditions prevailing in the international market for comparable commercial launch services offered by commercial launch services providers from market economy countries, including the United States.

(a) When the differential between a bid, offer or contract by a PRC launch services provider and the bid, offer or contract by a commercial space launch services provider from a market economy country, including the U.S., to provide the commercial space launch services described in subparagraph (ii) above is less than 15 percent, it shall be assumed, unless information is provided to the contrary, that such bid, offer, or contract is consistent with subparagraph (iv) and that no special consultations are needed. When the differential between a bid, offer or contract by a Chinese launch service provider and the bid, offer or contract by a commercial space launch services provider from a market economy country, including the U.S., is greater than 15 percent and after taking into consideration the comparability factors described in Annex II, the U.S. believes that China's launch service prices are not consistent with subparagraph (iv), the parties shall have special consultations under Article IV of this agreement.

(b) With respect to the commercial launch services described in subparagraph (iii) above, the Parties agree to undertake a detailed examination on a per payload basis, of the factors affecting the comparability of bids, offers or contracts for such services with a view towards completing this examination by the end of 1995.

(v) If, after consultations, both parties agree, the PRC may offer an introductory price on only the first test flight of a new type of launch vehicle.

(vi) The PRC agrees that any commitments to provide commercial launch services to international customers by PRC launch service providers shall be proportionally distributed over the period of the Agreement. To this end, the PRC shall make its best efforts to prevent a disproportionate concentration of such commitments during any two-year period of the Agreement. The PRC may make commitments in any three-year period of the Agreement consistent with subparagraph II (B) (ii) above. The PRC shall seek to ensure that PRC launches of principal payloads for international customers are performed as scheduled in the original launch commitment.

(vii) The PRC agrees to require its launch service or insurance providers to offer international customers any insurance or reflight guarantees on a par with prevailing rates and practices in international markets for comparable risk.

(c) The U.S. stated that the U.S. does not provide government inducements of any kind in connection with the provision of commercial launch services to international customers which would create discrimination against launch service providers of other nations and has no intention of providing such inducements in the future. Accordingly, the PRC stated it agreed not to offer inducements of any kind in connection with the provision of commercial launch services to international customers which would create discrimination against launch service providers of other nations.

Article III Non-Discrimination
The U.S. stated that U.S. providers of commercial launch services do not discriminate unfairly against any international customers or suppliers and that it is not U.S. Government policy to encourage any such unfair discrimination by U.S. providers of commercial launch services. Accordingly, in implementing its commitments under this Agreement, the PRC shall require that its providers of commercial launch services not discriminate unfairly against any international customers or suppliers.

Article IV Consultations
1. The PRC and U.S. will consult annually with respect to the obligations in this agreement-in particular, the implementation of Article II (B) (ii), (iii), and (iv), including the nature and extent of direct and indirect government support provided to commercial launch services providers and developments – in particular, those described in Paragraph 3 below – in the international market for commercial launch services.

2. In addition, each party undertakes to enter into special consultations within thirty (30) days of a request by the other party to discuss matters of particular concern.

In particular, special consultations will be held to review the situation in which there is an absence of Western launch availability due to full manifests or launch failures during the required launch period (generally within three (3) months before and after the preferred launch date), if the PRC has reached the limitation set out in Article II (B) (ii), or if the bunching provisions established in Article II (B) (vi) would apply to prevent the launch of a satellite. If information is provided which verifies, to the satisfaction of the U.S., that the situation described above exists, the U.S. may increase the quantity restriction of available launches established under Article II (B) (ii) or relax the bunching provision set out in Article II (B) (vi) to permit the satellite to be placed on the PRC launch vehicle manifest for launch.

3. Semiannually, the limitation on the total number of satellites for international customers that may be launched by PRC providers of commercial launch services will be reviewed by both parties and, if appropriate, adjusted to reflect changes in the demand for launch services (including changes arising from a projected absence of Western launch availability over an extended period) upon request of the PRC in light of developments in the commercial launch services market.

Among the developments which would justify favorable reconsideration and cause the U.S. and the PRC to raise the quantity restriction established under Article II (B) (ii) and/or relax the bunching provision under Article II (B) (vi) are:

a. development of the market for commercial space launch services to GEO that is significantly greater than the estimated average over the life of the agreement of 12-15 commercial launches per year upon which the limitation set out in Article II (B) (ii) is based, taking into account PRC compliance with its commitments under the agreement; or

b. the development of a commercially viable project for satellite services that fundamentally changes demand for launch services.

If the parties agree that either of the above conditions exist, the U.S. may increase the quantity restriction established under Article II (B) (ii) and/or relax the bunching provision set forth in Article II (B) (vi) to satisfy the change in demand for launch vehicles for GEO satellites.

4. With respect to Article II (B) (ii), if the average annual number of commercial launches subject to the provisions of Article II (B) (ii) (including launch failures) is 20 or more over the first three years of the agreement, or if the two governments, by mutual agreement, conclude that commitments (as defined in Annex I) for such launches indicate that average annual launches of 20 or more will occur during that three year period, then the quantitative limit contained in Article II (B) (ii) shall be increased to 13.

If the average annual number of commercial launches subject to the provisions of Article II (B) (ii) (including launch failures) is 20 or more over the first four years of the agreement or, if the two governments, by mutual agreement, conclude that commitments for such launches indicate that average annual launches of 20 or more will occur during the first four years of the agreement, then the quantitative limit contained in Article II (B) (ii) shall be increased to 16.

5. If the U.S. independently determines that any of the conditions listed in paragraphs 2 or 3 of this Article have been met, the U.S. may unilaterally raise the quantity restriction set out in Article II (B) (ii) or relax the bunching provision described in Article II (B) (vi). Before such action, the U.S. shall notify the PRC of its intent to act unilaterally, and the PRC shall have thirty (30) days in which to respond to the proposed U.S. action. If the PRC does not object within thirty (30) days, the U.S. may take unilateral action to increase the quantity restriction or relax the bunching provision.

6. AGREEMENTS ON INTERNATIONAL SPACE COOPERATION

6. The U.S. and the PRC agree to work toward a common understanding of the application of market principles to prices, terms, and conditions of commercial launch services for international customers.

7. To facilitate the annual consultations, the U.S. and the PRC agree to exchange information as follows:

a. The U.S. shall each year in advance of such consultations provide to the PRC such publicly releasable information as it possesses with respect to prices, terms and conditions prevailing in the international market for commercial launch services.

b. The PRC shall each year in advance of such consultations provide comprehensive information to the U.S. regarding prices, terms, and conditions offered by PRC providers of commercial launch services for the launch of satellites. The PRC may also provide other information that it believes may have a material effect on pricing practices of PRC providers of commercial launch services.

c. The PRC may request that the U.S. provide additional publicly releasable information with respect to international prices, terms, and conditions, and may in addition request U.S. views regarding prevailing international market conditions and likely future developments, as well as government supports or inducements. The U.S. shall respond to such requests within thirty (30) days. If such information cannot be provided directly because of business confidentiality, the U.S. shall provide such information in summary form.

d. The U.S. may request additional information with respect to the prices, terms, and conditions offered by PRC providers of commercial launch services and any PRC government supports or inducements. The PRC shall respond to such request within thirty (30) days. If such information cannot be provided directly because of business confidentiality, the PRC shall provide such information in summary form.

e. The U.S. and the PRC shall keep all information received from each other under this paragraph strictly confidential and shall not provide it to any other government or any private person without the written consent of the other.

8. The U.S. and the PRC shall also provide each year, in advance of the annual consultations, information on a connoneated basis concerning the commitments their launch service providers have undertaken to provide commercial launch services for international customers. This information may be made publicly available.

9. If a launch of a satellite for an international customer will not be performed as scheduled, the PRC shall notify the U.S. regarding the reasons for the delay and the new date for the launch as soon as possible.

10. It is understood that the U.S. and the PRC will review the information contained in this Article during annual consultations in the context of developments in the international market for commercial launch services.

Article V Clarification of Rights and Obligations

1. If, after friendly consultations with the PRC, the U.S. determines that there is clear evidence that the provisions of this Agreement have been violated, the U.S. reserves its right to take any action permitted under U.S. laws and regulations, taking into account the harm caused to U.S. interests under the agreement. The U.S. shall seek to avoid actions inconsistent with this Agreement.

2. With regard to export licenses, any applications for a U.S. export license will be reviewed on a case-by-case basis consistent with U.S. laws and regulations. Nothing in this Agreement shall be construed to mean that the U.S. is constrained from taking any appropriate action with respect to any U.S. export license, consistent with U.S. laws and regulations. Nevertheless, the U.S. will do its utmost to assure, consistent with U.S. laws and regulations, continuity of issued license(s) and the completion of the transactions covered in such license(s).

Article VI Discussions on International Rules

The U.S. and the PRC are prepared to enter into discussions with other interested parties on comprehensive international rules with respect to government involvement in and other matters relating to the international market for commercial launch services. It is understood, however, that nothing in this Agreement shall prejudice any position on any issue that either the U.S. or the PRC may take in those discussions.

Article VII Comprehensive Review

The U.S. and the PRC shall complete a comprehensive review of the terms and operation of this Agreement by mid-1998.

Article VIII Entry into Force

This Agreement shall enter into force on January 1, 1995 and shall remain in force until December 31, 2001. It may be terminated at any time by mutual agreement if superseded by an international agreement on government involvement in, and other matters relating to, the international market for commercial launch services or under such other circumstances as may be mutually agreed.

IN WITNESS WHEREOF, the undersigned, being duly authorized by their respective Governments, have signed this Agreement.

DONE at Beijing in duplicate, in the English and Chinese languages, both texts being equally authentic, this 13th day of March, 1995.

6.6. Agreement on Cooperation in the Exploration and Use of Outer Space for Peaceful Purposes[11]

National Space Administration of China
And National Aerospace Research and Development Commission of Peru
2015

China National Space Administration of the People's Republic of China (CNSA) and National Aerospace Research and Development Commission of the Republic of Peru (CONIDA), hereinafter referred to as "the Parties",

CONSIDERING the significant impact of space technology on social progress and economic development;

CONFIRMING the Parties' mutual desire for establishing bilateral cooperation in the field of exploration and use of outer space for peaceful purposes;

NOTING the expired Memorandum of Understanding between China National Space Administration and National Commission on Aerospace Research and Development of Peru on Cooperation in the Exploration and Use of Outer Space for Peaceful Purposes signed on May 27th, 2002;

EMPHASIZING the importance of the efforts made by the Parties in adhering to the exploration and use of outer space for peaceful purposes;

DESIRING to promote the effective practical application of space technologies in the interests of economic and social development of both countries;

The Parties hereby agree as follows:

Article I Objective

The objective of this Agreement is to further enhance and promote the economic and technological cooperation between both Parties in the field of exploration and use of outer space for peaceful purposes.

Complying with the laws and regulations in force in each country as well as the widely accepted international laws and rules, the Parties shall, on the basis of equality and mutual benefit, promote exchanges and cooperation in the field of space technology and its applications.

Article II Nature and Scope

This inter-institutional agreements and activities arising from the agreement will be developed in the field of functional competitions of the respective parties, complying

---

11 See the website of Ministry of Foreign Affairs, http://treaty.mfa.gov.cn/tykfiles/20180718/1531877062254.pdf, last accessed August 2021.

with the applicable laws and regulations in each countries and will not generate the international responsibility of each countries.

Article III Area of Cooperation
The Parties hereby agree to cooperate in the following areas:
   (1) Scientific test satellites, remote sensing satellites and communications satellites as well as related facilities and equipment;
   (2) Space science;
   (3) Launch services of satellites;
   (4) Ground application of space technology;
   (5) Data from remote sensing satellites;
   (6) Other areas in the peaceful application of space technology on which both Parties agree upon consultation.

Article IV Forms of Cooperation
The bilateral cooperation will be accomplished through the following forms:
   (1) Joint scientific research programs;
   (2) Consultation and mutual assistance in the research and use of outer space;
   (3) Exchange of experts, technicians, and specialists for the purposes of training, scientific and technological exchanges, and joint research and consultation;
   (4) Mutual assistance and exchange of scientific and technological information between the Parties;
   (5) Symposia and academic and technological conferences jointly held by the Parties;
   (6) Other cooperation forms agreed to by the Parties.

Article V Point of Contact
The Parties shall nominate respectively the specific point of contact who is responsible for the coordination under the framework of this Agreement.

Article VI Confidentiality
The Parties undertake to protect the information exchanged by virtue of the Agreement in accordance with the national laws and regulations of each country, to a level similar to the one provided by the other party.
   Neither Party shall use the information for any purpose without the authorization by the Party who provided it. Information produced jointly by the Parties shall not be used for any purpose without the authorization of both Parties.
   Neither Party shall disclose any information to any third party without the prior written consent of the party who provided it. Information produced jointly by both Parties shall not be disclosed to any third party without the approval of both Parties.

Article VII Protection of Intellectual Property

The Parties shall sign respective agreements on the protection of intellectual property for the projects arising from the implementation of this agreement.

Article VIII Facilitation of Mutual Change

Subject to their respective laws and regulations, the Parties shall facilitate the implementation of the cooperation projects under the framework of this Agreement.

Article IX Working Language

The language of communication between the Parties under this Agreement shall be English. All information, data, reports and publications shall be exchanged in English. Where such information, data, reports and publications are available in other languages, the Party sending them shall be responsible for the translation of such materials into English.

Article X Amendments

This Agreement may be amended by written agreement between the Parties.

Article XI Settlement of Dispute

Disputes concerning the interpretation or application of this Agreement shall be settled through friendly consultations between the Parties.

Article XII Renewal/Termination

This Agreement shall enter into force on the date of signature and shall remain in force for a period of five (5) years. Unless either of the Parties notifies the other party in writing, no less than six (6) months in advance, of its intention to terminate it, this Agreement shall be automatically extended for a successive period of five (5) years, and shall thereafter be automatically renewable for equal periods.

Unless otherwise agreed between the Parties, the termination of this Agreement shall not affect the on-going implementation of the specific programs, projects and working protocols signed on its basis until the completion of all activities covered by these arrangements.

DONE in Lima on May 22nd, 2015, in duplicate, each in the Chinese, Spanish and English languages, all texts being equally authentic. In the event of any divergence of interpretation, the English text shall prevail.

7. THE JUDICIAL CASES APPLYING AND INTERPRETING THE OUTER SPACE TREATIES

7.1. THE CEO OF MOON VILLAGE OF CHINA LOST HIS CASE AGAINST BEIJING ADMINISTRATION FOR INDUSTRY AND COMMERCE[1]

2006

The Moon Village CEO Li Jie sued Beijing Administration for Industry and Commerce, demanding that the Administration of Industry and Commerce return his Moon Village land ownership certificate and other items. On October 20, 2016, the People's Court of Haidian District, Beijing concluded the case and rejected the plaintiff's claims in accordance with the law.

On October 14, 2005, the Chaoyang Branch of the Beijing Administration for Industry and Commerce (hereinafter referred to as the Chaoyang Branch for Industry and Commerce) discovered during a routine inspection that the Moon Village Company was engaged in lunar land sales activities. On the same day, the Municipal Administration for Industry and Commerce issued a letter of entrusted investigation, entrusting Chaoyang Branch for Industry and Commerce to investigate and handle the case of the Moon Village Company selling lunar land. Chaoyang Branch of Industry and Commerce opened an investigation on the same day. On October 14 and October 28, 2005, the Chaoyang Industrial and Commercial Bureau conducted an on-site inspection of the Moon Village Company. On October 14, 2005, the first inquiry notice was delivered to the Moon Village Company, informing the rights of the Moon Village Company. On October 14 and October 24 of 2015, the entrusted agent of the Moon Village Company Li Huimin was investigated and questioned, and Li Huimin's statement and defense were heard.

The Beijing Municipal Administration for Industry and Commerce confirmed through the investigation of Chaoyang Branch Bureau: from October 14th to 28th, 2005, the Moon Village Company sold 48 acres of Moon Land to 33 people including Mr. Lei at a price of RMB 298 per acre. The total sales amount was RMB 14,304. During the trial, the agent of the Moon Village Company also recognized the above facts ascertained by the Municipal Administration for Industry and Commerce in court.

The Beijing Municipal Administration for Industry and Commerce believes that the sale of lunar land by the Moon Village Company is suspected of engagement in

---

[1] See https://www.chinacourt.org/article/detail/2006/10/id/221779.shtml, last accessed August 2021.

speculation. After approval, it issued a notice on the detention (sealing) of property under Jinggongchaokouzi (2005) No. 245763 on October 28, 2005, and the relevant property of the company shall be detained (sealed up), including the company seal. On the same day, the Municipal Bureau of Industry and Commerce delivered the Notice of Detention (Sealing) of Property in Beijing Industry and Commerce Chaozi (2005) No. 245763 to the Moon Village Company. The Moon Village Company refused to accept the above notice of detained (sealed) property issued by the Municipal Administration for Industry and Commerce, and filed an administrative lawsuit in the court on November 14, 2005.

In addition, on December 26, 2005, the Municipal Administration for Industry and Commerce issued a notice of cancellation of administrative compulsory measures by Jinggongchaojingjiezi (2005) No. 245764, which lifted the administrative compulsory measures that were sued and returned the property to the Moon Village Company except for the lunar land ownership certificate.

After trial, the court held that the defendant Municipal Administration for Industry and Commerce, as the administrative agency for industry and commerce, could impose administrative coercive measures on specific objects in order to maintain the normal market economic order. The defendant Municipal Administration for Industry and Commerce has the statutory authority to detain (seal) the property of the administrative counterpart. The plaintiff did not have legal ownership of the lunar land sold, and the lunar land did not have the characteristics of commodities. Moreover, the Moon Village Company made high profits due to its sales activities. Therefore, the Municipal Administration for Industry and Commerce properly determined that the Moon Village Company selling lunar land was suspected of engagement in speculation In addition, the Municipal Administration for Industry and Commerce has performed administrative procedures such as filing, investigating, informing, listening to the opinions of administrative counterparts, reporting to the director for approval, and serving in the process of making the sued detention (sealing) financial notice to the plaintiff, the Moon Village Company, which conforms to the provisions in relevant laws. In view of this, the court ruled to dismiss the plaintiff's claim, Beijing Moon Village Aerospace Technology Co., Ltd.

After the verdict was pronounced in the first instance, the plaintiff expressed the intention to appeal.

7.2. The Moon Village Sued Beijing Administration for Industry and Commerce and Lost the Final Trial[2]

According to the Beijing News, the Moon Village took the Beijing Municipal Administration for Industry and Commerce Bureau to court because its business

---

2 https://www.chinacourt.org/article/detail/2007/03/id/239435.shtml, last accessed August 2021.

license was revoked for the sale of "Moon Land". On March 16, 2007, the final judgment of Beijing No. 1 Intermediate People's Court rejected the Moon Village appeal request.

The Moon Village CEO Li Jie stated that he saw the news of an American selling lunar land from the Internet, and he was inspired to register and set up a lunar village company to purchase lunar land from that American.

In October 2005, the Moon Village Company sold 48 acres of lunar land to 33 consumers for a total of more than RMB 14,000.

In December 2005, the Beijing Municipal Administration for Industry and Commerce issued an administrative decision that the Moon Village violated the Interim Regulations on Administrative Penalties for the Engagement in Speculation, which imposed the fine of RMB 50,000, revoked its business license and ordered a refund of the money for the sale of lunar land.

The First Intermediate People's Court held that China acceded to the Outer Space Treaty on December 30, 1983. According to the Outer space Treaty, the exploration and use of outer space (including the moon and other celestial bodies) shall be carried out for the benefit and serve in the interests of all countries and the member states are not allowed to claim outer space (including the moon and other celestial bodies) as their own by means of sovereignty claims, use or occupation, or any other means.

Based on this treaty, no country can claim ownership over the moon. The citizens and organizations within a country, consequently, have no right to claim ownership of the moon. Therefore, the Beijing Municipal Administration for Industry and Commerce determined that the Moon Village Company's sale of lunar land was speculative.

Based on this, the First Intermediate People's Court rejected Li Jie's claim.

Bibliography

Books and Chapters

Achilleas, P., Regulation of Space Activities in France, in: R.S. Jakhu (ed.), *National Regulation of Space Activities*, Dordrecht: Springer, 2010,

Aliberti, M., *When China Goes to the Moon*, New York: Springer, 2015.

Baldwin, R., M. Cave & M. Lodge (eds.), *The Oxford Handbook of Regulation*, Oxford: Oxford University Press, 2013.

Brownlie, I., *Principles of Public International Law*, Oxford: Oxford University Press, 5th ed., 1998.

Chen, L., B. Carey & T. Pirard, Welcome to Beijing for Space, Report from the 64h International Astronautical Congress, in: L. Chen, J. Myrrhe (Eds.). *Go Taikonauts: All About China's Space Program*, Issue 10, 2013.

Clerc, P., *Space Law in the European Context: National Architectures, Legislation and Policy in France*, The Hague: Eleven, 2018.

Cliff, R., *Ready for Takeoff: China's Advancing Aerospace Industry*, Santa Monica, CA: Rand Corporation, 2011.

DeLisle, J., China's Approach to International Law: A Historical Perspective, in *Annual Proceedings of American Meeting of American Society of International Law, Vol. 94*, Cambridge: Cambridge University Press 2000.

Doyle, S.E., Nandarisi Jasentuliyana Keynote Address on Space Law, A Concise History of Space Law, *Proceedings of the 55th Colloquium on the Law of Outer Space* (2010), AIAA, 2011.

Dunk, F. von der, Current and Future Development of National Space Law and Policy, Proceedings of UN/Brazil Workshop on Space Law, Disseminating and Developing International and National Space Law: The Latin American and Caribbean Perspective, 2005.

Dunk, F. von der, Implementing the United Nations Outer Space Treaty – The Case of the Netherlands, in: C. Brünner, E. Walter (eds.), *National Space Law – Development in Europe – Challenges for Small Countries*, Vienna: Boehlau Verlag, 2008.

Dunk, F. von der, Regulation of Space Activities in the Netherlands: From Hugo Grotius to the High Ground of Outer Space, in: R.S. Jakhu (ed.), *National Regulation of Space Activities*, Dordrecht: Springer, 2010, pp. 229-231.

Dunk, F. von der, Two New National Space Laws: Russia and South Africa, *Proceedings of the 48th Colloquium on the Law of Outer Space*, AIAA, 1995.

Guo, H. & J. Wu (eds.), *Space Science and Technology in China: A Roadmap to 2050*, Beijing: Science Press and New York: Springer, 2010.

Handberg, R. & Z. Li, *Chinese Space Policy: A Study in Domestic and International Politics*, New York: Routledge, 2007.

Handberg, R., China's Space Strategy and Policy Evolution, in: E. Sadeh (ed.), *Space Strategy in the 21st Century: Theory and Policy*, New York: Routledge, 2013.

Harvey, B., *China in Space: The Great Leap Forward*, New York: Springer, 2013.

Harvey, B., China's Space Program: Emerging Competitor or Potential Partner?, in: J.C. Moltz (ed.), *New Challenges in Missile Proliferation, Missile Defense and Space Security*, CNS Occasional Paper No. 12, Monterey: Center for Non-Proliferation Studies, 2003.

Held, D., *Cosmopolitan Democracy in Models of Democracy*, London: Polity Press, 1997.

Hobe, S., B. Schmidt-Tedd & K. Schrogl (eds.), *Cologne Commentary on Space Law, Vol. I*, Cologne: Carl Heymanns Verlag, 2009.

Hobe, S., B. Schmidt-Tedd & K. Schrogl (eds.), *Cologne Commentary on Space Law, Vol. II*, Cologne: Heymanns, 2013.

Hobe, S., B. Schmidt-Tedd & K. Schrogl (eds.), *Cologne Commentary on Space Law, Vol. III*, Cologne: Carl Heymanns, 2015.

Hood, C., The Tools of Government in the Information Age, in: M. Moran, M. Rein & R.E. Goodin (eds.), *The Oxford Handbook of Public Policy*, Oxford: Oxford University Press, 2006.

Jahku, R.S. et al. (eds.), *Space Mining and Its Regulation*, New York: Springer, 2017.

Julienne, M., *China's Ambitions in Space: The Sky is the Limit*, Paris: French Institute of International Relations, 2021.

Kopal, V., Origins of Space Law and the Role of United Nations, in: C. Brünner, A. Soucek (eds.), *Outer Space in Society, Politics and Law, Studies in Space Policy*, Vol. 8, Vienna: European Space Policy Institute, 2011.

Koroma, A.G., Foreword, National Regulation of Space Activities, in: R.S. Jakhu (ed.), *National Regulations of Space Activities*, Dordrecht: Springer, 2010.

Linden, D,. The Impact of National Space Legislation on Private Space Undertakings: A Regulatory Competition between States? *Proceedings of the 58th IISL Colloquium on the Law of Outer Space*, Eleven, 2016.

Malkov, S.P. & C. Doldirina, Regulation of Space Activities in the Russian Federation, in: R.S. Jakhu (ed.), *National Regulation of Space Activities*, Dordrecht: Springer, 2010.

Malysheva, N.R., *Space Law and Policy in the Post-Soviet States*, The Hague: Eleven, 2018.

Manoli, M., Mining Outer Space: Overcoming Legal Barriers to a Well Promising Future, *Proceedings of the 58th IISL Colloquium on the Law of Outer Space*, The Hague: Eleven, 2016.

Marboe, I., National Space Law, in: F. von der Dunk, F. Tronchetti (eds.), *Handbook of Space Law*, Cheltenham: Edward Elgar Publishing, 2015, pp. 183-184.

Marboe, I., National Space Legislation, in: C. Brünner, A. Soucek (eds.), *Outer Space in Society, Politics and Law, Studies in Space Policy, Vol. 8*, Vienna: European Space Policy Institute, 2011.

McCurdy, H.E., *Space and the American Imagination*, Washington, DC: Smithsonian Institution Press, 1997.

Meijer, H., *Trading with the Enemy: The Making of US Export Control Policy toward the People's Republic of China*, Oxford: Oxford University Press, 2016.

Moltz J.C. (ed.), *New Challenges in Missile Proliferation, Missile Defense and Space Security, Special Joint Series on Missile/Space Issues*, Monterey, CA: Monterey Institute of International Studies, 2003.

Morgan, F.E., *Deterrence and First-Strike Stability in Space: A Preliminary Assessment*, Santa Monica: Rand Corporation, 2010.

Ogasawara, M., & J. Greer, *Japan in Space: National Architecture, Policy, Legislation and Business in the 21st Century*, The Hague: Eleven, 2021.

Peerenboom, R., *China's Long March towards Rule of Law*, Cambridge: Cambridge University Press, 2002, pp. 5-6.

Rathgeber, W., *China's Posture in Space: Implications for Europe*, Vienna: European Space Policy Institute, 2007.

Saul, B., China, National Resources, Sovereignty and International Law, Asian Studies Review, Vol. 37(2), 2013.

Shen, R. & S. Cao, *Modernization of Government Governance in China*, London: Palgrave Macmillan, 2020.

The Group Leading Office for the Reform of the Administrative Examination and Approval System, *Reforming the Administrative Examination and Approval System*, Beijing: China Fangzheng Press, 2004.

Tronchetti, F., *Fundamentals of Space Law and Policy*, New York: Springer, 2013.

Venet, C., The Economic Dimension of Space Activities, in: C. Brünner, A. Soucek (eds.), *Outer Space in Society, Politics and Law, Studies in Space Policy, Vol. 8*, Vienna: European Space Policy Institute, 2011.

Vereshchetin, V.S., The Law of Outer Space in the General Legal Field (Commonality and Particularities), *Proceedings of the 52nd Colloquium on the Law of Outer Space* (2009), AIAA, 2010, p. 11.

Walter, E., The Privatization and Commercialization of Outer Space, in: C. Brünner, A. Soucek (eds.), *Outer Space in Society, Politics and Law, Studies in Space Policy, Vol. 8*, Vienna: European Space Policy Institute, 2011.

Wang, Y., *Fundamental Theory of the Application of Treaties in China*, Beijing: Peking University Press, 2007.

Wei, L., *China's One Belt One Road Initiative*, London: Imperial College Press, 2016.

Wortzel, L.M., *The Chinese People's Liberation Army and Space Warfare: Emerging United States – China Military Competition*, Washington, DC: American Enterprise Institute, 2007.

Wu, X., "NewSpace" in China in Need of New Laws, *Proceedings of the 60th Colloquium on the Law of Outer Space*, The Hague: Eleven, 2018.

Wu, X., China and Space Environment Protection: An Evaluation from an International Perspective, *Proceedings of the 56th IISL Colloquium on the Law of Outer Space*, The Hague: Eleven, 2014.

Wu, X., International Cooperation in China's Space Undertakings: Melting down Political Obstacles through Legal Means, *Proceedings of the 59th IISL Colloquium on the Law of Outer Space*, The Hague: Eleven, 2017.

Yu, H., *Studies on National Space Legislation for the Purpose of Drafting China's Space Law*, (diss.), Leuphana University Lueneburg, 2019.

Zhang, J., *Contemporary China: Establishment of Space Cause*, Beijing: Present Day China Press, 2009.

Zhao, H., & X. Wu, Legal Aspects of International Cooperation in China's Manned Space Flights, *Proceedings of the 53rd (2010) IISL Colloquium on Law of Outer Space*, AIAA, 2012, pp. 454-465.

Zhao, H., & X. Wu, Reflections on Future Space Legislation in China, *Proceedings of the 49th Colloquium on the Law of Outer Space*, AIAA, 2007.

Zhao, Y., Emerging Approaches in Development Efforts: Chinese Perspective on Space and Sustainable Development, in: C. Al-Ekabi, S. Berretti, *Yearbook on Space Policy 2016*, Dordrecht: Springer, 2018.

Zhao, Y., *National Space Law in China: An Overview of the Current Situation and Outlook for the Future*, Leiden: Brill Nijhoff, 2014.

Zhao, Y., *National Space Law in China: An Overview of the Current Situation and Outlook for the Future*, Leiden: Hotei Publishing, 2015.

Articles

Aoki, S., Current Status and Recent Development in Japan's National Space Law and Its Relevance to Pacific Rim Space Law and Activities, *Journal of Space Law*, Vol. 35(2), 2009.

Behr, V., Development of a New Legal System in the People's Republic of China, *Louisiana Law Review*, Vol. 67, 2007.

Blanchette-Séguin, V., Reaching for the Moon: Mining in Outer Space, *New York University Journal of International Law and Politics*, Vol. 49(3), 2017.

Bourbonniere, M., National-Security Law in Outer Space: The Interface of Exploration and Security, *Journal of Air Law and Commerce*, Vol. 70, 2005.

Brisibe, T.C., An Introduction to United Nations COPUOS Recommendations on National Legislation relevant to the Peaceful Exploration and Use of Outer Space, *Zeitschrift für Luft- und Weltraumrecht* (German Journal of Air and Space Law), Vol. 62(4), 2013.

Cai, C., International Law in Chinese Courts During the Rise of China, *The American Journal of International Law*, Vol. 110(2), 2016.

Carminati, G., French National Space Legislation: A Brief "Parcours" of a Long History, *Houston Journal of International Law*, Vol. 36(1), 2014.

Dai, R., Judicial Application of International Human Rights Treaties in China: Global Perspective, *Human Rights in China*, 5 May 2020, www.humanrights.cn/html/2020/zxyq_0512/51267.html.

Delmas-Marty, M., Present-day China and the Rule of Law: Progress and Resistance, *Chinese Journal of International Law*, Vol. 2, 2003.

Dempsey, P.S., National Law Governing Commercial Space Activities: Legislation, Regulation and Enforcement, *Northwestern Journal of International Law and Business*, Vol. 36(1), 2016.

Filho, J.M. & A. F. dos Santos, Chinese-Brazilian Protocol on Distribution of CBERS Products, *Journal of Space Law*, Vol. 31, 2005.

Filho, J.M., Private, State and International Public Interests in Space Law, *Space Policy*, Vol. 12(1), 1996.

Fullilove, M., China and the United Nations: The Stakeholder Spectrum, *The Washington Quarterly*, Vol. 34(3), 2011.

Gorove, S., Freedom of Exploration and Uses in the Outer Space Treaty: A Textual Analysis and Interpretation, *Denver International Journal of Law and Policy*, Vol. 1, 1971.

Hagt, E., China's ASAT Test: Strategic Response, *China Security*, Vol. 3, 2007.

Hitchens, T., U.S.-Sino Relations in Space: From "War of Words" to Cold War in Space?, *China Security*, Vol. 3, 2007.

Hobe, S., The ILA Model Law for National Space Legislation, *Zeitschrift für Luft- und Weltraumrecht* (German Journal of Air and Space Law), Vol. 62(1), 2013.

Hosenball, S.N., The United Nations Committee on the Peaceful Uses of Outer Space: Past Accomplishments and Future Challenges, *Journal of Space Law*, Vol. 7, 1979.

Kamenetskaya, E., V.S. Vereshchetin & E. Zhukova, Legal Regulation of Space Activities in Russia, *Space Policy*, Vol. 9, 1991.

Klinger, J.M., A Brief History of Outer Space Cooperation between Latin America and China, *Journal of Latin American Geography*, Vol. 17(2), 2018.

Koplow, D.A., The Fault Is Not in Our Stars: Avoiding an Arms Race in Outer Space, *Harvard International Law Journal*, Vol. 59, 2018.

Kosmo, F., The Commercialization of Space: A Regulatory Scheme that Promotes Commercial Ventures and International Responsibility, *Southern California Law Review*, Vol. 61, 1988.

Krepon, M., China's Military Space Strategy: An Exchange, *Survival*, Vol. 50(1), 2008.

Li, S., The Role of International Law in Chinese Space Law and Its Relevance to Pacific Rim Space Law and Activities, *Journal of Space Law*, Vol. 35, 2009.

Li, X., K. Yang & X. Xiao, Scientific Advice in China: The Changing Role of the Chinese Academy of Sciences, *Palgrave Communications*, Vol. 2, 2016.

Li, Y. & L. Shen, An Analysis on the Interim Measures for the Mitigation of Space Debris and Protection of Space Objects, *Space Debris Research* (China's Journal in Chinese), Vol. 17, 2017.

Liebman, B.L., Assessing China's Legal Reforms, *Columbia Journal of Asian Law*, Vol. 23, 2009.

Ma, B. & S. An, The Forty-Years of China's Administrative Reformation: The Major Achievement and Future Prospects, *Administrative Reform* (Journal in Chinese), Vol. 10, 2018.

Moltz J.C., The Changing Dynamics of Twenty-First-Century Space Power, *Journal of Strategic Security*, Vol. 12(1), 2019.

O'Brien, K., China and the International Space Station: China's Distance from this Project, *The Newsletter of International Institute for Asian Studies*, Vol. 63, 2013.

Qi, Y., A Study of Aerospace Legislation of China, *Journal of Space Law*, Vol. 33, 2007.

Ronci, R. et al., Communicating Value: Investigating Terminology Challenges in "New Space" and "Commercial Space", *New Space*, Vol. 8(3), 2020.

Sundahl, M., Regulating Non-Traditional Space Activities in the United States in the Wake of the Commercial Space Launch Competitiveness Act, *Air and Space Law*, Vol. 42(1), 2017.

Tronchetti, F. & H. Liu, The 2019 Notice on Promoting the Systematic and Orderly Development of Commercial Carrier Rockets: The First Step towards Regulating Private Space Activities in China, *Space Policy*, Vol. 57, 2021.

Twibell, T.S., Circumnavigating International Space Law, *ILSA Journal of International and Comparative Law*, Vol. 4, 1997, p. 259.

Wang, Q., Administrative Reform in China: Past, Present and Future, *Southeast Review of Asian Studies*, Vol. 32, 2010.

Wu, X., China and Space Security: How to Bridge the Gap between Its Stated and Perceived Intentions, *Space Policy*, Vol. 33, 2015.

Yang, C. & G. Gao, Overview of the Current Situation and Improvement of Chinese Space Legislation, *Annals of Air and Space Law*, Vol. XXXVIII, 2013.

Zhao, H., The Status Quo and the Future of Chinese Space Legislation, *Zeitschrift für Luft- und Weltraumrecht* (German Journal of Air and Space Law), Vol. 58(1), 2009.

Zhao, Y., National Space Legislation in Mainland China, *Journal of Space Law*, Vol. 33, 2007.

Zhao, Y., The 2002 Space Cooperation Protocol between China and Brazil: An Excellent Example of South-South Cooperation, *Space Policy*, Vol. 21, 2005.

Zheng, B., The Commercial Development of Space: The Need for New Treaties, *Journal of Space Law*, Vol. 19(1), 1991.

Zou, K., Administrative Reform and Rule of Law in China, *The Copenhagen Journal of Asian Studies*, Vol. 24, 2006.

Documents, Evaluations and Reports

Aranzamendi, M.S., Economic and Policy Aspects of Space Regulations in Europe, Part I: The Case of National Space Legislation – Finding the Way between Common and Coordinated Action, *ESPI Report 21*, 2009.

Beischl, C., APSCO after Its First Decade: A Critical Assessment of Its Current Political and Legal Cooperative Potential and Related Impediments, *29th Symposium on Space Policy, Regulations and Economics, International Academy of Astronautics*, 2016, IAC-16-E3.1.8.

Bowe, A., China Pursuit of Space Power Status and Implications for the United States, *Research Report of U.S.-China Economic and Security Review Commission*, 11 April 2019, www.uscc.gov/sites/default/files/Research/USCC_China%27s%20Space%20Power%20Goals.pdf.

Gerhard, M. & Kai-Uwe Schrogl, Report of the "Project 2001" Working Group on National Space Legislation – Legal Framework for the Commercial Use of Outer Space, Cologne: Carl Heymanns, 2002.

Houpt, D.M., Does China Have a Comprehensive, Coordinated, and Consistent Space Policy? Implications for U.S. Policymakers, UMI Number: 1491425, Washington, DC, 2011.

Kulacki, G., Strategic Options for Chinese Space Science and Technology: A Translation and Analysis of the 2013 Report from Chinese Academy of Sciences, 2013, www.ucsusa.org/assets/documents/nwgs/strategic-options-for-chinese-space-science-and-technology-11-13.pdf.

Liu, I. et al., Evaluation of China's Commercial Space Sector, Institute for Defence Analysis, Science and Technology Policy Institute, September 2019.

Liu, W., An Introduction to China's Belt and Road Initiative, Oxford International Infrastructure Consortium, Global Infrastructure Conference 2016, www.oxiic.org/wp-content/uploads/2016/09/Session-1_Weidong-Liu_Oxford_Belt-and-Road-Initiative.pdf.

Liu, X. & X. Wang, The First Administrative Regulation on Space Activities in China, in: Proceedings of United Nations/International Institute of Air and Space Law Workshop on Capacity Building in Space Law, ST/SPACE/14, United Nations Office for Outer Space Affairs, 2003.

OECD Report, Alternatives to Traditional Regulation, www.oecd.org/gov/regulatory-policy/42245468.pdf.

The Space Economy at a Glance, Organization for Economic Cooperation and Development, the first, second and third edition, Paris: OECD, 2007, 2011, 2014.

The Space Reports, Space Foundation, Colorado Springs: Space Foundation, 2010-2020, www.spacefoundation.org.

U.S. Congress, Office of Technology Assessment, Assessing the Potential for Civil-Military Integration: Technologies, Process and Practice, 1991.

Yin, W., China's Space Policy, Proceedings of United Nations/Republic of Korea Workshop on Space Law, United Nations Treaties on Outer Space: Actions at the National Level, ST/SPACE/22, United Nations OOSA, 2005, p. 15.

News Articles and Websites

China Inaugurates PLA Rocket Force as Military Reform Deepens, *Xinhua News*, 1 January 2016, www.xinhuanet.com/politics/2016-01/01/c_1117646667.htm.

China's Military in 2015, Towards Historic Reformation, 23 December 2015, www.gov.cn/xinwen/2015-12/23/content_5027047.htm.

David, L., China's First Round-Trip Moon Shot Sets Stage for Bigger Lunar Feats, www.space.com/27661-china-moon-mission-sample-return.html. Last accessed August 2021.

Fergusson, I.F. & K.M. Sutter, U.S. Export Control Reforms and China: Issues for Congress, IF11627, 15 January 2021, https://crsreports.congress.gov.

Gong, Z., CASC Efforts on Dealing with Space Debris toward Space Long Term Sustainability and China Practices on Satellites Post Mission Disposals towards Space Long Term Sustainability, the 50th session of the COPUOS Scientific and Technical Subcommittee, 2013, www.unoosa.org/pdf/pres/stsc2013/2013lts-03E.pdf.

Gong, Z., China Practices on Satellites Post Mission Disposals towards Space Long Term Sustainability, the 53rd session of the COPUOS Scientific and Technical Subcommittee, 2016, www.unoosa.org/documents/pdf/copuos/stsc/2016/tech-21E.pdf.

Kuhn, R.L., The Five Major Development Concepts, *China Daily*, 23 September, 2016, www.chinadaily.com.cn/opinion/2016-09/23/content_26872399.htm.

Listner, M., & R. P. Rajagopalan, The 2014 PPWT: A New Draft with the Same and Different Problems, 11 August 2014, www.thespacereview.com/article/2575/1.

Ren, T., Comprehensive Deepening Reform: The Road of Building a Strong Army with Chinese Characteristics (全面深化改革：中国特色强军之路), *Guangming Daily*, 23 December 2015.

Rose, F.A., Continuing Progress on Ensuring the Long-Term Sustainability and Security of the Space Environment Conference on Disarmament Plenary, 10 June 2014, https://2009-2017.state.gov/t/avc/rls/2014/227370.htm.

Sutter, K.M., "Made in China 2025" Industrial Policies: Issues for Congress, IF10964, 11 August 2020, https://crsreports.congress.gov.

The Background of the Establishment of Chinas Manned Flights Program: the Four-Decade Debate and the Decision-Making Process (中国载人工程立项的背后：40年的争论与决策), *China Youth Daily*, 16 October 2003.

Three New Military Branches Created in Key PLA Reform, *China Daily*, 2 February 2016, www.chinadaily.com.cn/kindle/2016-01/02/content_22904989.htm.

Voronina, A., The How's and Why's of International Cooperation in Outer Space: International Legal Norms of Cooperation of States in Exploration and Uses of Outer Space, 2016, pp. 35-53, https://digitalcommons.unl.edu/spacelawthesis/1.

What Kind of Military Force is the PLA Strategic Support Force? (我军战略支援部队是一支什么样的军事力量?), 24 January 2016, www.gov.cn/xinwen/2016-01/24/content_5035622.htm.

Zhao, L., Civil-Military Integration Will Deepen, *China Daily*, 3 March 2018, www.chinadaily.com.cn/a/201803/03/WS5a99d67ca3106e7dcc13f437.html.

CHINA'S LAW AND REGULATORY RULES

Interim Measures on the Administration of Licensing the Projects of Launching Civil Space Objects, the COSTIND, 2002

Interim Measures for the Management of Civil Satellite Projects, the SASTIND, 2016

Interim Measures for the Management of Remote Sensing Data from China's Civilian Satellites, the SASTIND, the NDRC and the MOF, 2018

Interim Measures for the Management of Remote Sensing Satellite Data in the National Major Specialized Project of High-Resolution Earth Observation System, the High-Resolution Observation Project Office of the SASTIND, 2015

Interim Measures for the Recordation Administration of the Scientific Research and Production of Arms and Equipment, the SASTIND, 2019

Law on Administrative Licensing, the Standing Committee of the NPC, 2003

Law on Export Control, the Standing Committee of the NPC, 2020

Law on Legislation, the NPC, 2000

Law on National Security, the Standing Committee of the NPC, 2015

Law on National Defense, the NPC, 1997

Law on the Procedures of Treaty Conclusion, the Standing Committee of the NPC, 1990

Measures for the Administration of Registration of Objects Launched into Outer Space, the COSTIND and the MFA, 2001

Measures for the Implementation of Scientific Research and Production Licensing of Arms and Equipment, the SASTIND, 2010

Measures for the Management of Lunar Samples, the CNSA, 2020

Measures for the Management of Scientific Data of Lunar and Deep Space Exploration Projects, the SASTIND and the CNSA, 2016

Regulation on the Export Control of Military Items, the State Council and The Central Military Commission, 1997

Regulation on the Export Control of Missiles and Related Items and Technologies, the State Council, 2002

Regulation on the Licensing Administration of Scientific Research and Production of Arms and Equipment, the COSTIND and the Central Military Commission, 2008

China's Policy Documents

Action Plan for Cooperation between China and ASEAN, the MFA, 2012

Action Plan to Implement the Joint Declaration on ASEAN-China Strategic Partnership for Peace and Prosperity (2016-2020), the MFA, 2016

Beijing Action Plan (2019-2021) of Form on China-Africa Cooperation, the MFA, 2018

China-Italy Action Plan on Strengthening Economic, Trade, Cultural and Scientific and Technological Cooperation (2017-2020), the MFA, 2017

China's Participation in Greater Mekong Sub-Regional Cooperation, the MFA, 2008

Decision on Accelerating the Development of Strategic Emerging Industries, the State Council, No. 32, 2010

First Five-Year Plan for Strategic Emerging Industries, the State Council, No. 28, 2012

Guiding Opinions on Accelerating the Construction and Application of the "One Belt One Road" Space Information Corridor, the SASTIND and the NDRC, 2016

Guidelines on Deepening Civil-Military Integration in Science and Technology and Industry for National Defense, the General Office of the State Council, No. 91, 2017

Made in China 2025, the State Council, No. 28, 2015

Guidance on Encouraging Social Investment in the Key Innovation Domains, the State Council, No. 60, 2014

Medium and Long-Term Development Plan of National Navigation Industry, the State Council, No. 97, 2013

Medium and Long-Term Development Plan for National Civil Space Infrastructure (2015-2025), the NDRC, the MOF and the SASTIND, 2015

Notice on Promoting the Development of Satellite Application Industry, the NDRC and the COSTIND, 2007

National 11th Five-Year Guidelines for Economic and Social Development, the National People's Congress, 2006

National 12th Five-Year Plans for Strategic Emerging Industries, the State Council, No. 28, 2012

National 13th Five-Year Plan for Economic and Social Development, the National People's Congress, 2016

National 13th Five-Year Plans for Strategic Emerging Industries, the State Council, No. 67, 2016

National 13th Five-Year Plan for Satellite Surveying and Mapping, the National Administration of Surveying, Mapping and Geographic Information, the Ministry of Natural Resources, 2016

National 13th Five-Year Plan for the Development of Strategic Emerging Industries, the State Council, No. 67, 2016

National 13th Five-Year Plan for the Scientific and Technological Innovation, the State Council, 2016

National 14th Five-Year Plan for Economic and Social Development and Vision Goals Outline for 2035, the State Council, 2021

National Innovation-Driven Development Strategy Outline, the State Council, 2016

National Outlines of Medium and Long-Term Plans for Science and Technology (2006-2020), the State Council, 2006

Policy Paper on Africa, the MFA, 2015

Policy Paper on Arab Countries, the MFA, 2016

Policy Paper on European Union, the MFA, 2003 and 2018

Policy Paper on Latin America and the Caribbean, the MFA, 2008 and 2016

Roadmap for the Development of the Space Transportation System (2017-2045), released by the China Aerospace Science and Technology Corporation on 17 November 2017, China Space News, 17 November 2017

Vision and Actions on Jointly Building Silk Road Economic Belt and 21st Century Maritime Silk Road (推动共建丝绸之路经济带和21世纪海上丝绸之路的愿景与行动), the NRDC, the MFA and the MOC, 2015

Vision for Maritime Cooperation under the Belt and Road Initiative, the NDRC and the State Oceanic Administration, 19 June 2017

White Paper on China's Beidou Navigation Satellite System, the Information Office of the State Council, 2016

White Paper on China's International Development Cooperation in the New Era, the Information Office of the State Council, 2021

White Paper on China's Military Strategy, the Information Office of the State Council, 2015

White Paper on China's National Defense, the Information Office of the State Council, 2010

White Paper on China's National Defense, the Information Office of the State Council, 2019

White Paper on China's Space Activities, the Information Office of the State Council, 2000

White Paper on China's Space Activities, the Information Office of the State Council, 2006

White Paper on China's Space Activities, the Information Office of the State Council, 2011

White Paper on China's Space Activities, the Information Office of the State Council, 2016

White Paper on China's Space Program, the Information Office of the State Council, 2021

China's Diplomatic Statements

Answers to the Principal Questions and Comments on the Draft PPWT, CD/1872, 2009

China's Activities on International Cooperation in the Peaceful Uses of Outer Space, UNCOPUOS, 1998

China's Activities in the field of International Cooperation in the Peaceful Uses of Outer Space, UNCOPUOS, 2013

China's Activities in the field of International Cooperation in the Peaceful Uses of Outer Space, UNCOPUOS, 2017

China's Replies on Transparency and Confidence-Building Measures in Outer Space Activities, UNCOPUOS, 2017

China's Submissions regarding the UNCOPUOS Discussion on the Safety of Space Nuclear Power Sources, UNCOPUOS, 2012

China's Views on Transparency and Confidence-Building Measures in Outer Space Activities, UNCOPUOS, 2017

Comments regarding the USA Analysis of the 2014 Updated Draft PPWT, CD/2042, 2015

Draft Treaty on Prevention of the Placement of Weapons in Outer Space and of the Threat of Use of Force against Outer Space Objects (PPWT), CD/1839, 2008

Human Space Technology Initiative (HSTI) Activities in 2011-2013 and Plans for 2014 and Beyond, A/AC.105/2013/CRP.16, 5 June 2013

Joint Statement from XI Jinping, President of China, and Vladimir V. Putin to the Conference on Disarmament on Strengthening Contemporary Global Strategic Stability, 2019

Keynote Speech of Shi Zhongjun at the 10th UN Workshop on Space Law, 2016

Note Verbale from the Permanent Mission of China to the United Nations Secretary-General on the Re-entry of Tiangong-1, UNCOPUOS, 4 May 2017

Note Verbale from the Permanent Mission of China to the United Nations Secretary-General on the Re-entry of Tiangong-1, UNCOPUOS, 8 December 2017

Note Verbale from the Permanent Mission of China to the United Nations Secretary-General on the Re-entry of Tiangong-1, UNCOPUOS, 26 March 2018

Note Verbale from the Permanent Mission of China to the United Nations Secretary-General on the Re-entry of Tiangong-1, UNCOPUOS, 11 April 2018

Note Verbale from the Permanent Mission of China to the United Nations Secretary-General on the Planned Re-entry of Tiangong-2 Space Lab, UNCOPUOS, 16 July 2019

Position Paper on the Issue of Long-Term Sustainability of Outer Space Activities, UNCOPUOS, 2016

Position on and Suggestions for Ways to Address the Issue of Prevention of An Arms Race in Outer Space, CD/1606, 2000

Safety Practice of Space Nuclear Power Sources in China, UNCOPUOS, 2016

Statement by Ma Xinmin on the Future Role of UNCOPUOS, UNCOPUOS, 2015

The Updated Draft PPWT, CD/1985, 2014

Working Paper on Possible Elements of the Future International Legal Instrument on the Prevention of the Weaponization of Outer Space, CD/1645, 2001

Working Paper on Possible Elements of the Future International Legal Agreement on the Prevention of the Deployment of Weapons in Outer Space, the Threat or Use of Force against Outer Space Objects, CD/1679, 2002

Xi Jinping's speech at the General Debate of the 70th Session of the UN General Assembly, New York, 2015

Xi Jinping's speech at the UN Office at Geneva, 2017

China's Space Cooperation Agreements and Other Documents

Agreement on Cooperation in the Exploration and Use of Outer Space for Peaceful Purposes between National Space Administration of China and National Aerospace Research and Development Commission of Peru, 2015

Convention of the Asia-Pacific Space Cooperation Organization, 2006

Memorandum on Agreement on Liability for Satellite Launches between China and the United States, 1988

Memorandum of Agreement on Satellite Technology Safeguard between the USA Government and the PRC Government, 1988

Memorandum of Agreement on Satellite Technology Safeguards between the USA Government and the PRC Government, 1993

Memorandum of Agreement Regarding International Trade in Commercial Launch Services between the USA Government and the PRC Government, 1989

Memorandum of Agreement Regarding International Trade in Commercial Launches Services between the USA Government and the PRC Government, 1995

The CEO of Moon Village of China lost his case against Beijing Administration for Industry and Commerce, https://www.chinacourt.org/article/detail/2006/10/id/221779.shtml, last accessed August 2021

The Moon Village sued Beijing Administration for Industry and Commerce and lost the final trial, www.chinacourt.org/article/detail/2007/03/id/239435.shtml, last accessed August 2021

The Resolutions of No First Placement of Weapons in Outer Space, UNGA Res. 72/28, 2 November 2017; UNGA Res. 73/31, 11 December 2018; UNGA Res. 74/22, 18 December 2019; UNGA Res. 75/37, 16 December 2020

The Resolutions of Further Practical Measures for the Prevention of an Arms Race in Outer Space. UNGA Res. 72/250, 24 December 2017; UNGA Res. 74/34, 18 December 2019

The Resolution on National Legislation Relevant to the Peaceful Exploration and Use of Outer Space, UN. Doc. A/AC.105/932, 2 February 2009

About the Author

Dr Xiaodan WU is an associate professor at the Law Faculty of China Central University of Finance and Economics in Bejing. She is involved in the space legislation work of her country and provides consultation services to governmental and military organs as well as to other space actors in China.
She is holding a PhD degree in Law from the State University of Milan (Italy) and is the author of many papers and articles about topical issues in space law and policy.

Acknowledgements

The author is most grateful to Dr Marietta Benkö for her enthusiasm and encouragement of this project, as well as for her review of earlier drafts and editorial advice. Dr Wu is also very appreciative of the patience and assistance of Ms Selma Soetenhorst-Hoedt and her dedicated team at Eleven.

Essential Air and Space Law (Series Editor: Marietta Benkö)

Volume 1: Natalino Ronzitti & Gabriella Venturini (eds.), The Law of Air Warfare – Contemporary Issues, ISBN 978-90-77596-14-2

Volume 2: Marietta Benkö & Kai-Uwe Schrogl (eds.), Space Law: Current Problems and Perspectives for Future Regulations, ISBN 978-90-77596-11-1

Volume 3: Tare Brisibe, Aeronautical Public Correspondence by Satellite, ISBN 978-90-77596-10-4

Volume 4: Michael Milde, International Air Law and ICAO, ISBN 978-90-77596-54-8

Volume 5: Markus Geisler & Marius Boewe, The German Civil Aviation Act, ISBN 978-90-77596-72-2

Volume 6: Ulrich Steppler & Angela Klingmüller, EU Emissions Trading Scheme and Aviation, ISBN 978-90-77596-79-1

Volume 7: Heiko van Schyndel (ed.), Aviation Code of the Russian Federation, ISBN 978-90-77596-80-7

Volume 8: Zang Hongliang & Meng Qingfen, Civil Aviation Law in the People's Republic of China, ISBN 978-90-77596-91-3

Volume 9: Ronald M. Schnitker & Dick van het Kaar, Aviation Accident and Incident Investigation. Concurrence of Technical, ISBN 978-94-90947-01-9

Volume 10: Michael Milde, International Air Law and ICAO, second edition, ISBN 978-90-90947-35-4

Volume 11: Ronald Schnitker & Dick van het Kaar, Safety Assessment of Foreign Aircraft Programme. A European Approach to Enhance Global Aviation Safety, ISBN 978-94-9094-793-4

Volume 12: Marietta Benkö & Engelbert Plescher, Space Law: Reconsidering the Definition/Delimitation Question and the Passage of Spacecraft through Foreign Airspace, ISBN 978-94-6236-076-1

Volume 13: Heiko van Schyndel (ed.), Aviation Code of the Russian Federation, second edition, ISBN 978-94-6236-433-2

Volume 14: Alejandro Piera Valdés, Greenhouse Gas Emissions from International Aviation: Legal and Policy Challenges, ISBN 978-94-6236-467-7

Volume 15: Peter Paul Fitzgerald, A Level Playing Field for "Open Skies": The Need for Consistent Aviation Regulation, ISBN 978-94-6236-625-1

Volume 16: Jae Woon Lee, Regional Liberalization in International Air Transport: Towards Northeast Asian Open Skies, ISBN 978-94-6236-688-6

Volume 17: Tanveer Ahmad, Climate Change Governance in International Civil Aviation: Toward Regulating Emissions Relevant to Climate Change and Global Warming, ISBN 978-94-6236-692-3

Volume 18: Michael Milde, International Air Law and ICAO, third edition, ISBN 978-94-6236-619-0

Volume 19: Nataliia Malysheva, Space Law and Policy in the Post-Soviet States, ISBN 978-94-6236-847-7

Volume 20: Philippe Clerc, Space Law in the European Context, ISBN 978-94-6236-797-5

Volume 21: Benjamyn Scott, Aviation Cybersecurity: Regulatory Approach in the European Union, ISBN 978-94-6236-961-0

Volume 22: Dick van het Kaar, International Civil Aviation: Treaties, Institutions and Programmes, ISBN 978-94-6236-972-6

Volume 23: Lasantha Hettiarachchi, International Air Transport Association (IATA): Structure and Legitimacy of its Quasi-International Regulatory Power, ISBN 978-94-9094-758-3

Volume 24: Masataka Ogasawara & Joel Greer, Japan in Space, ISBN 978-94-6236-203-1

Volume 25: Ronald Schnitker & Dick van het Kaar, Drone Law and Policy, ISBN 978-94-6236-198-0

Volume 26: Marietta Benkö & Kai-Uwe Schrogl (eds.), Outer Space, Future for Humankind, ISBN 978-94-6236-225-3

Volume 27: Xiaodan Wu, China's Ambition in Space, ISBN 978-94-6236-277-2